Confrontation Analysis
Theory and Practice

Abraham I. Cohen, Ph.D.

Adjunct Associate Professor of Psychology in
Psychiatry, Cornell University Medical College;
Adjunct Associate Professor of Psychology,
Teachers College, Columbia University, New
York, New York; Faculty, Institute of Advanced
Psychological Studies, Adelphi University, Garden
City, New York

Grune & Stratton
A Subsidiary of Harcourt Brace Jovanovich, Publishers
New York   London
Paris   San Diego   San Francisco   São Paolo
Sydney   Tokyo   Toronto

Grune & Stratton, Inc.
111 Fifth Avenue
New York, New York 10003

Distributed in the United Kingdom by
Academic Press Inc. (London) Ltd.
24/28 Oval Road, London NW 1

Library of Congress Catalog Number 81-20074
International Standard Book Number 0-8089-1417-0
Printed in the United States of America

To my Parents, Isaac and Jamilee Cohen, and to Julie, Adam, and Gideon. And to my patients, who have been willing to share with me their feelings and to trust me with their most precious valuable—their private world. They allowed me to participate in the extraordinary voyage to discover how the human mind works.

Contents

Preface

Recent history has profoundly affected our self-image, our relations to others, and our philosophy of life in general. Two devastating World Wars, national genocides, massive nuclear explosions and stockpiles, runaway poverty in the midst of abundance, and intense ideological polarization of the global order have created a psychology of fatalism, apathy, fear, and futility. "Eat and drink *now,* for tomorrow we shall die" has, for many people, become either a conscious or an unconscious motto for a way of life. At the same time, however, great advances in science and technology, especially in the field of communication, have provided the promise for new vistas to improve the human condition. Unfortunately, much of this progress seems to have increased and reinforced our isolation and alienation.

One can safely assert that no single theory of the mind has proven adequate enough for seriously resolving social or individual deterioration. Even psychoanalysis, perhaps the most exhaustive and encompassing theory of personality that has laid certain foundations to our present understanding of human behavior, has not engendered a unified method that effectively tackles the revolving problems of today's people.

Psychotherapy is often conceptualized as a process that leads to the acquisition of new knowledge about oneself. This means that a change in the cognitive, emotional, and/or physical condition of the self may be expected. In this process the individual becomes aware of choices that were hitherto denied or avoided and, consequently, develops the capacity to integrate these changes.

I have, for a long time, felt that social scientists in general, and psychotherapists in particular, must go beyond the confines of such rigid definitions of the aims of psychotherapy. Solutions to the contemporary human condition must reach further; "peace of mind" does not seem to be enough of a viable goal. Thus, during the past 20 years or more of my professional development, I have gradually become cognizant of a need to reinterpret my role and function as a psychotherapist. I have come to realize that the goals and techniques of traditional psychotherapy are no longer sufficient to rekindle life with meaning in those who are alienated, dejected, and demoralized, and those who are always fighting to keep the status quo of their (painful) condition because they fear partial or total disintegration. This dissatisfaction with existing models of treatment led me to explore additional perspectives of my role and, consequently, to develop new ways of understanding the patient and using myself in the therapeutic encounter. I became convinced that to change one must experience, and, in the treatment situation, this meant that I could not remain aloof or neutral, or just a "wise man" who knew to "hit the nail right on the head" with my "brilliant" interpretations. Increasingly I observed that genuine and continuous interaction could lead to the experience of authenticity by the patient, a rare phenomenon in our time. This often helps to engender an attitude toward life where continuity, self-search, and a sense of personal, historical unfolding provide meaning and substance to the patient's existence, regardless of how psychologically impoverished or impersonalized that history had been.

While these goals may appear utopian, I believe that at least some efforts toward achieving them could not go totally unrewarded. Of course, a certain reorientation is necessary. For example, "healing" as a goal in the traditional sense becomes somewhat obsolete, and in its place "investigation" becomes a primary goal. Understanding of the self through interpersonal exchange between a research team called "the patient and the therapist" surfaces as the centerpiece of the therapeutic work. The process of psychotherapy may be seen as similar to using a geographical map during a trip. Some routes will clearly lead to a defined destination, some will serve as exploration ventures or alternatives, and still others will lead to a dead end. During such a "psychotherapeutic voyage," certain fringe benefits, such as the alleviation of symptoms, may be achieved. The essence of the "trip" in confrontation analysis is the interactive process— the overriding focus of this volume.

In writing this book I attempted to reach advanced and beginning clinicians at various levels of experience and of differing persuasions in psychotherapy. This task, needless to say, created some difficulties, as some sections are oversimplified while others require a more thorough understanding and integration of recent developments in the field. To remedy this problem, I devoted a significant portion of the text to case material to illustrate clinically as many of the positions I have taken as possible. I suspect, however, that a major obstacle in achieving a significant integration between theory and practice is that the theory itself lacks solid scientific grounding, thus providing a fair amount of ambiguity when it comes to its clinical application. These concrete illustrations may, of course, be used as a basis for discussions and critical assessment of the system as a whole. In addition, I hope that their inclusion here will encourage others to, so to speak, open their books.

My clinical experience has led me to conclude that diagnostic labels often used for certain categories in the official psychiatric nomenclature may, at best, substitute for lengthy phenomenological descriptions; however, I believe that most of the time they are used for the purpose of tranquilizing the clinician's mind by creating the illusion of understanding the patient. For this and other reasons, confrontation analysis does not seriously delve into extensive discussions of how it deals with differently diagnosed patients. Rather, the assumption is made that the flexible therapist will be able to adopt strategies and techniques consonant with the patient's unique psychodynamics.

This book does not mean to summarize or critically assess one psychological system or another. At the same time, many of the concepts and techniques are not original and may not have received their proper recognition. I hope I am forgiven this purposeful omission, since my intent was to avoid as much distraction as possible.

Although this volume bears the name of a single author, many individuals, more than I can enumerate, have contributed to what went into its development; in a very real sense, as many as have been involved in my life. It is difficult for me to designate any specific entity as the most influential in my work, although it is pretty clear that psychoanalytic thinking is central to many of my formulations. Along this perspective, I am grateful to my teachers, supervisors, and fellow students at the Postgraduate Center for Mental Health under the guidance of Dr. Lewis R. Wolberg, who gave me so much to think about and who helped me integrate my profession with my person. Especially challenging, supportive, and untiring in their search for meaning were the late Mrs. Asya Kadis and Dr. Emanual K. Schwartz. Dr. Burton B. Pfeffer taught me how honesty and directness can be one's strongest assets and how these need not stand in the way of human kindness and care.

While no one bears the responsibility for the contents of this work except myself, my philosophy of treatment has developed and was presented over the years in the many teaching and supervisory opportunities afforded me at the Postgraduate Center for Mental Health, Columbia University, Hillside Hospital in New Hyde Park, Adelphi University Postdoctoral Institute of Psychological Studies, New York University Medical Center, Albert Einstein College of Medicine, and New York Hospital-Cornell University Medical College. My thanks go to all my students and supervisees in these and other institutions for their challenged responsiveness.

Several friends have read all or parts of the manuscript and offered me their invaluable and helpful comments and advice. I owe special gratitude to Drs. Henry Kellerman and Jerome W. Kosseff, of the Postgraduate Center for Mental Health, and Dr. Ted Saretsky of Adelphi University, for their encouragement, guidance, recommendations, and loving support. Aside from ploughing through the manuscript and sharing their observations, they have indirectly contributed through their openness in our many years of friendship and professional collaboration.

My special thanks go to Mrs. Carol Dowling, whose help and care in the preparation of the entire typescript from its inception was of exceptional quality.

Finally, my wife, Dr. Julie G. Cohen, a most astute and perceptive psychotherapist in her own right, has added not only clarity and wisdom throughout the entire process of writing, but has helped me rethink many issues and steered me away from my natural tendency to engage in narcissistically protecting formulations that did not convey meaning directly and succinctly. This book could not have been finished without her patience, her love, and her help. I am forever thankful to her. My sons, Adam and Gideon, equally deserve my gratitude for their forebearance while I was selfishly preoccupied with my writing. They have always provided me with a source of love and nourishment necessary to be able to bear a certain amount of deprivation while I was engaged in the discipline of writing.

Introduction

Confrontation analysis is a method of investigating, analyzing, and evaluating human behavior in the context of interpersonal interaction. It also contains a theoretical framework within which to understand the evolution, maintenance, and modification of personality dimensions.

The technique of confrontation analysis has evolved from clinical and empirical experience, and its theoretical underpinnings are derived from traditional dynamic psychotherapy and psychoanalysis, object relations theory, existentialism and phenomenology, and communication theory. Through confrontation analysis the therapist helps patients to formulate meaningful life goals consistent with their psychological, social, and biological make-up. The object of confrontation analysis is to guide patients on a voyage of discovering what is significant in life, not only for others, but also for themselves.

Although many elements of the confrontation analysis system have been utilized in the context of other psychotherapeutic approaches, the particular orientation advanced in this book has not previously been developed in a systematic manner. Here an attempt is made to integrate the techniques and strategies of confrontation analysis into a system based on certain theoretical assumptions that are supported by a considerable body of clinical experience and data. In fact, examples of the utilization of some elements of this system are not scarce in the literature;

however, these are usually embedded in theoretical orientations that differ substantially from the central theoretical formulations presented here. For example, one of the most salient elements in this system is that of confrontation itself. The clinical use of confrontation usually generates debate, since it is a highly emotionally charged issue. The fact is, however, that the very definition of confrontation can vary greatly (Adler and Myerson 1973). The term "confrontation analysis," as it is used here, suggests neither confrontation alone nor analysis alone. It refers to the utilization of confrontation in understanding therapeutic transactions and in the analysis of these confrontations within the therapeutic milieu. It is becoming increasingly apparent that many practitioners of psychotherapy and psychoanalysis are already using such an approach, though usually in modified and nonsystematic forms.

The practice of psychotherapy is in the process of an accelerated change. Clinicians seem interested in investigating new and more fruitful ways of dealing with pathology. A great number of scientific papers and books have been written and stimulated by theoreticians such as Kernberg, Kohut, Langs, and Searles. Some of these works have been presented in great detail, including verbatim accounts of the psychotherapeutic process (Goldberg, 1978; Langs, 1973, 1974) and are similar to the accounts often given when presenting new or esoteric approaches (Deutsch, 1955, 1955a). It is clear that the scientific community has been dissatisfied with existing models of personality structure and corresponding procedures and techniques for dealing with pathological developments. In his treatise, *The Life of the Self,* Lifton (1976) stresses this very point:

> We are now in the relatively early phases of a momentous shift in psychological paradigm—a shift from the classical psychoanalytical model of instinct and defense, and even from the approach and perspective in the word 'analysis' itself . . . . Indications are everywhere around us . . . the widely felt though inchoate sense that we are losing rather than gaining ground in our struggles to cope professionally with the increasingly formidable social and psychological forces that confront us.

Thus the trend seems to be gradually shifting from a model of treatment almost exclusively invested in the investigation of *transference* to one that bases its understanding of treatment on *the system as a whole,* specifically *the interactive process.* In such a perspective the core of the therapeutic thrust consists primarily of transactions that deal with the patient–therapist relationship as a whole unit. Consequently, the judicious use of interaction becomes strategically central to the investigation and modification of undesirable behavior patterns. Genetic material, while still occupying a significant role in the therapeutic work, assumes meaning only within the context of the interactive relationship.

This theory of technique emanates from the central theoretical thesis of confrontation analysis regarding personality development. Simply stated, it assumes that the adequacy of the mother's handling of the infant's needs, especially during the first two or three years of life, determines the nature of the personality. Consequently, the structure and vicissitudes of dependency, the earliest and most universal developmental phase in the life of the individual, is hypothesized to be the foundation upon which character and self are formed. Therefore, the interaction between mother and child is perceived as the prototypic process that will serve as a model for the individual throughout life, and will most likely be manifest through the personality's defensive structure.

Confrontation analysis approaches the therapeutic investigation along two parallel tracks that directly result from this central theoretical assumption: (1) the relationship of the patient's symptoms to his overall personality dynamics and life goals, and (2) the meaning that the patient's dynamics and goals assume as the therapeutic process unfolds, especially as the interaction between three ingredients of treatment—the patient, the therapist, and the therapeutic process—affects his perception and attitude toward these goals. In a certain sense, this view of treatment is analogous to Shakespearean or Greek tragedies, which often consist of a play within a play whereby one part cannot be meaningfully understood if it is separated from the other. More specifically, the confrontation analyst attends not only to symptomatology and dynamics, but also to the therapeutic dyadic system that inevitably affects them. The therapeutic situation is thus perceived as a microcosm in which universal issues or conditions, such as dependence, love, separation, territoriality, death, and creativity, are confronted and negotiated in a most personal manner, albeit through the thin or thick armor of symptoms and defenses. This is the essence of confrontation analysis.

Confrontation Analysis is organized with respect to three main considerations: central concepts of the system of confrontation analysis, its theoretical basis, and its treatment goals.

Part I defines the elements of confrontation analysis and deals extensively with the theoretical assumptions upon which it is based. It includes the presentation of detailed clinical case material to illustrate the basic definitions and to provide a cohesive rationale for the systematic use of this approach. It makes explicit its specific understanding of the personality and delves into areas of the personality that are particularly sensitive to developmental influences, as well as into dimensions that this approach regards as central to the adaptive or maladaptive functioning of the self, including dimensions such as dependence, territoriality, competition and cooperation, and anxiety.

Part II focuses attention on the therapeutic goals of confrontation analysis. There are often significant conflicts between the analyst's perception of the treatment goals and those of the patient. For this reason, it seems essential for the analyst to have a clear view of his direction and what the analyst believes to be relevant criteria for the achievement of a healthy functioning of the self. Confrontation analysis considers the following three major areas as most crucial in the life of the individual: communication, emotionality, and identity. Each of these parameters is explored extensively from a clinical and theoretical viewpoint. In fact, the major portion of the book is devoted to this aspect of the therapeutic work.

Finally, *Confrontation Analysis* hopes to contribute to the developing body of knowledge regarding the therapeutic process by considering central personality dynamics and generating both a theory and a technique for dealing with pathological developments of the self.

The Elements
of Confrontation Analysis

1
Definitions

The term *confrontation analysis* describes a psychotherapeutic system that approaches psychopathology through the technique of confrontation and the analysis of confrontations that transpire within the therapeutic setting.

CONFRONTATION

Confrontation is the presentation to the patient of personality attributes that hitherto have been repressed, denied, or in other ways hidden from the patient's awareness. It is an attempt to help the patient stop avoiding or dismissing these realities. The importance of confrontation in the conduct of psychotherapy and psychoanalysis has long been recognized. Thus, Greenson (1967) states, "The term analyzing is a shorthand expression which refers to those insight-furthering techniques. It usually includes four distinct procedures: *confrontation, clarification, interpretation, and working through.* . . . the first step in analyzing a psychic phenomenon is *confrontation.* The phenomenon in question has to be made explicit to the patient's conscious ego."

Along these strictly psychoanalytical lines, Devereux (1951) defines confrontation as the "rewording of the patient's own statements, especially in the form of 'calling a spade a spade.'

Nothing is added to the patient's statement, nor is anything subtracted therefrom, with the exception of the actual wording, which is viewed as an attempt to gloss over the obvious."

According to Devereux, confrontation differs appreciably from interpretation:

> (1) It yields no new insight, and merely focuses the attention of the patient on something which he perceived but failed to register—or refuses to acknowledge openly. In other words, confrontation is a rather superficial manipulation of cathexes, i.e., of attention. (2) It is a starting-point for further productions and for meditation, which in due time, must be dealt with, and brought to fruition, by true interpretations. (3) It is timely if it consolidates transition to new material pertaining to the same configuration, which, in the opinion of the analyst, can eventually be interpreted in terms of the material already produced up to that time (Ripeness).

The same idea is expressed by Dewald (1964): "in essence, confrontation involves directing the patient's attention to elements of experience or behaviour observed in him by the therapist, but without drawing any inferences as to the possible meaning behind them."

The above definitions are rather narrow, however, for they ignore the following important realities:

1. Whenever the therapist intervenes—confrontationally or interpretively—the patient is likely to be affected in some fashion, primarily because of the therapist's role in this special relationship.
2. When the statement is designed to "call a spade a spade," it purposefully intends to alter the patient's level of understanding or awareness of the subject at hand. Can such an intervention be differentiated from a "purely" interpretive one?
3. If such an intervention succeeds in altering the patient's denial, then its use can by no means be considered superficial or less effective in developing the patient's insight. If anything, confrontations are often interpretations with the added dimension of making it difficult for the patient to escape dealing with them. They must, of course, be well timed and appropriately delivered.

Confrontation, as a major technique, is not endorsed wholeheartedly in psychoanalysis or psychoanalytically oriented psychotherapy, and is looked upon as an "inappropriate deviation," one that creates difficulties rather than helping. Myerson (1973), for example, claims that the decision to confront (or not to confront) "is influenced in part by nonrational factors, in effect by our countertransferences." He believes that confrontations are "forceful" interventions used by the therapist as a last resort to resolve an impasse, or when the therapist is unconsciously (and thus countertransferentially) irritated with the patient's "non-progress or non-cooperation." While agreeing with Myerson that confrontations imply the use of force, Murray (1973) notes that *"each interpretation has an element of force"* (emphasis added). The controversy over the use of confrontation obviously stems from this understanding of the concept and its application, namely that "force" must be applied and that this inevitably leads to the manipulation of the patient and the loss of analytic neutrality, and from the assumption that confrontation will contribute further to the patient's resistance and defensiveness.

In confrontation analysis, confrontations are not perceived as primarily or even necessarily imbued with force, or with any kind of a threat or ultimatum. When a physician informs a patient that he has a disease or that he is quite healthy, this can also be viewed as a confrontation, because he was made aware of new information. Of course, once the patient hears the physician's statement, he is free to concern himself with it or discard it. One would expect that both physician and patient would normally be interested in treating the disease as quickly as possible. On the other hand, if the patient is well, they part ways. Similarly, the assumption in psychotherapy is that, at least consciously, both patient and therapist share the same goals, and wish to work together to achieve them as effectively and efficiently as possible. This is usually referred to as "the working alliance" (Greenson, 1965).

There is, nevertheless, an essential ingredient common to all confrontations. By their very definition, confrontations create conditions in which either a conflict will arise or a new awareness will emerge. When these conditions occur, a certain amount of psychic energy becomes available, and this energy must then be dealt with in one way or another. Different individuals have different ways of using such energy. This most important issue is discussed throughout this text. The essential point here is that the confrontation analyst must help the patient recognize the pivotal situation during the interactive process, for without such recognition, treatment cannot progress. Recognition can be accomplished only if at least two conditions are met: (1) the therapist must be genuinely on the patient's side, and not using the patient countertransferentially in the service of his own unconscious gratification; (2) the therapist must have established a reasonably good rapport with the patient. If these two conditions are missing, the confrontations can become useless and even harmful exercises that may (at the least) cause premature termination of treatment. The risks of using confrontations arising from countertransference are, however, no greater than those that may arise when the therapist uses interpretations, or when the patient is allowed to "free associate" indefinitely, or when the therapist attempts to preserve the "neutral" stance when it is totally inappropriate.

The rationale for the use of confrontation as a fundamental technique is based on a number of assumptions, and these are based on clinical experience. This author's experience has been that a confrontation brings out material from the patient's life that is helpful to his growth if analyzed; material that could not be reached through other psychotherapeutic procedures, or could only be reached in an unreasonable amount of time.

However, the eliciting of feelings, thoughts, dreams, past history, and other therapeutic material may, in the long run, be useless if not accompanied by a genuine interest on the part of the therapist. This interest must take the form of helping the patient "own up" to behavior patterns through *negotiations*. Consequently, confrontation can be both a *technique* for eliciting and opening up new material for investigation, as well as an *experience* in learning to interact, relate, integrate, and separate as an independent entity.

One of Alexander's (1961) central concerns about psychoanalysis was its focus on techniques, such as interpretation, which in his opinion, produced changes that were skewed toward intellectual insight rather than significant personality changes: "The intellectual *recognition* of the difference between past and present is secondary to the actual *experiencing* of this difference in interacting with the therapist. In this view the emphasis shifts from insight to experience, although the role of insight as a secondary but often powerful consolidating factor is by no means denied." Of course, one of the rationales for using confrontation as a central technique is to eliminate, as much as possible, the patient's tendency to attempt to unconsciously turn the therapeutic experience into an intellectual exercise—a tendency that interpretations often reinforce. Alexander further comments that, "as long as insight into the origins of the disease were considered as the principle therapeutic factor, the aim of genetic research and psychoanalytic treatment indeed coincided. The stress on emotional experience alters the absolute validity of this contention. . . . Bluntly stated, profound therapeutic results may arise merely from corrective experiences *even if they are not followed by the revival of repressed memories. Cognitive reconstructions alone never have penetrating therapeutic effect.* The appearance of repressed memories is the sign rather than the cause of an emotional change which has already taken place" (emphasis added).

Confrontations have often been perceived as *demands* that the therapist, unreasonably and countertransferentially, makes upon the patient. Perhaps it would be more accurate to view them as signs of a *questioning* attitude on the part of the therapist. When a patient presents material (including accounts of behavior and various other patterns) that does not follow a reasonable logic, unconditional acceptance is hardly therapeutic or helpful. Some experimental evidence supports this view: Truax and Charkuff (1965) found that, "when the therapist offers a condition of empathy and unconditional positive regard, there is a consequent drop in the patient's depth of intrapersonal exploration, and when the therapist's level of conditions rises, there is a consequent rise in the patient's level of self-exploration or process." Confrontations tend to increase the patient's awareness of the therapist's expectation that the patient must deal with the denial system if the troublesome conflicts are to be overcome and resolved.

Another rationale for the use of confrontation derives from observations related to the early development of certain ego functions, such as mastery of the environment. In describing how an infant learns to separate himself from the world, Escalona (1968) clearly suggests that interaction between the infant

and his surroundings must occur where the infant must act upon
the world:

> The combined operation of early ego functions that allow the infant to
> initiate even to that affect desired changes in the environment and to over-
> come obstacles is conveniently referred to as 'mastery activity.' In all mastery
> activities, the infant experiences his own voluntary actions as the causal as-
> pect of changes in the environment (i.e., he shakes a rattle and creates a
> sound, he activates his body in creeping and obtains a previously distant toy).
> In our view, the oft repeated experience of affecting change and of overcoming
> obstacles plays a major role in mediating the awareness of a separation be-
> tween the acting subject and the acted upon object; that is, these experiences
> lay the foundations for the infant's awareness of an objective reality, inde-
> pendent of himself and consisting of permanent objects in space. If this is so,
> mastery activities are significant not only for the development of trust in one's
> own powers (competence) but also for the development of a sense of self as a
> bounded entity.

The active presentation (through confrontation) of an environment (therapist) with which the patient must deal and act
is analogous to the relationship between the infant and the objects surrounding him. Confrontation analysis is thus modelled
after this natural early development in the patient's life, and
makes use, in a systematic manner, of the patient's capacity to
further utilize and develop ego functions.

While the confrontational approach advocated here may be
applied to a variety of diagnostic categories, it is especially effective in dealing with the character disorders, most specifically,
the narcissistic and borderline personality. Kernberg (1974,
1974a) seems to imply his use of this approach in the treatment
of the narcissistic personality, especially in his suggestion that
the analyst ought to systematically interpret the patient's primitive idealization and omnipotent control of the analyst. Kohut
(1979) also uses a certain degree of confrontational work in his
analysis of narcissistic personality syndromes. Confrontation
analysis is exquisitely well-suited for this purpose.

The following examples of confrontations are excerpted
from actual sessions with patients who had been in treatment
for varying lengths of time, and for various reasons. These examples are followed by comments regarding the structure and
content of their confrontational aspect. The "analysis" aspect of
these same examples is introduced and discussed in the next
section.

Penny, a 24-year-old woman, had been in individual therapy for about six months on a twice-a-week basis. Before this, she had seen another therapist for about two years, but left because she had not been helped with her weight problem. She had gained over 30 pounds in her teens, and was unable to lose them on her own. She felt that her previous therapist had accepted her weight unquestionably, even though she was unhappy with it. She felt there was no "challenge" in his approach to her, just as her family had offered "blind" acceptance. She could do no wrong in their eyes, and was always welcomed back home whenever she was self-destructive. The brief exchange that follows is from the middle of a session.

P: I had a lousy weekend. David (*her boyfriend*) and I went to see my parents, and my mother had all the "goodies" lined up, but I was very good and I ate very little.

T: What do you mean by "lousy"?

P: Well, I was so anxious about David's feelings and attitudes about my parents, you know, and I didn't know how it was going to turn out, and he just doesn't mix with them. I guess I might have also put on some weight lately.

T: You said that you ate very little, is that how you gain weight?

P: (*Angry.*) O.K., so maybe not very little, but just less than I would normally eat at my mother's.

T: You mean less than you *should* for your mother's sake?

P: Actually, more than I should to lose weight, but less than I should to please my mother.

T: You mean you were trying to please everybody at the same time—you and your mother?

P: You know, I knew you'd make a big fuss about it and that's why I tried to avoid it.

T: You mean you tried to deny the whole thing by saying you ate very little.

P: Well, I guess it makes it easier. I am very uncomfortable, I feel kind of embarrassed.

T: Oh?

P: I feel I was caught doing something naughty.

T: You obviously wished to reduce the eating problem by getting preoccupied with another legitimate concern—Dave's feelings about your parents.

P: I had both of these things on my mind, but I was trying to hide the eating thing.

T: By getting heavier and bigger?

P: (*Laughs.*) That's absurd! It's so hard for me to be direct and honest.

At this point, Penny felt more relaxed, and an analysis of what had just happened continued for most of the session. (This part of the session will be discussed in the next section.)

The opening statement of the patient allowed for a number of possible interventions: (1) I could have remained silent and waited for additional information; (2) I could have asked the patient to proceed to tell more about the weekend, had she chosen to move on to discuss another topic or had she become silent, as was often the case; (3) I could have elected to focus on the subject of her feelings about her boyfriend or her parents in that context; (4) I could have empathized with her feelings. I made the choice of focusing on one single subject—avoidance and denial of the weight problem. This focus was directed and maintained by the use of the following techniques of confrontation: (1) utilizing and repeating the patient's own words (you "ate very little"); (2) drawing illogical conclusions from the patient's statements, to illustrate for her the denial mechanism used without being theoretical or intellectual about it. A paradoxical statement—"you ate very little, that's how you gained weight"— often makes it necessary for the patient to react in order to relieve the tension that such paradoxes engender because they are, in effect, incomplete gestalten; (3) making a direct interpretation related to the patient's symptom ("you mean less than you should for your mother's sake"); (4) directly turning the patient's attention to the kind of defense mechanism being used to reduce anxiety, which keeps the problem unresolved; (5) utilizing simple and concrete imagery to illustrate the fundamental absurdity of the patient's ways of escape (when the patient became aware of attempting to "hide the eating thing," I presented her with the image of getting bigger and heavier); (6) keeping the patient's primary conflict in the foreground, and utilizing the content of the session to direct therapeutic efforts toward the resolution of this conflict (the patient used a rather popular diversion tact as a defensive measure by introducing the subject of the boyfriend's feelings toward her parents and the subtle rationalization for focusing on him, namely, her anxiety about it: the patient rationalized away her eating by blaming it on the anxiety supposedly emanating from her boyfriend's negative feelings toward her parents).

This kind of defense is frequently used by patients with

unresolved ambivalence toward a significant parent. Unrecognized, unexpressed, and often unconscious hatred toward the parent makes it almost impossible to separate psychologically from that parent, since separation summons up all the anxiety attached to guilt feelings related to the hate. Since food is often identified with such a parental figure, not eating becomes an experience in separating, an unwelcome opening for overwhelming anxiety.

Another illustration in the use of confrontations may now be in order.

Ellen was a 28-year-old woman who had been in treatment for about three months on a twice weekly basis. She began her session by telling me that a former boyfriend with whom she had lost contact for over three years had called her and wanted to see her. Although she felt it was a bad idea to renew the relationship, she agreed to meet him, because he was interested only in a relationship "on a friendly basis." However, when they met in her apartment, "one thing led to another," and she "found" herself in bed with him. She described how disinterested she was in this man and how little feeling she had for him; yet this encounter made her totally confused about her relationship with two other men she had been dating. She described herself as "running like a chicken without a head." Feeling confused and lost, she made plans with a girlfriend to take a two-week vacation in Europe. After a few seconds of silence, she added that she was proud of herself because she had been able to tell all three men that she resented their insensitivity to her. Of course, she continued to see them. I asked why she wanted to see them and torture herself. She went on to describe their other wonderful qualities—after all, nobody is perfect. "I thought you were confused," I said. "But it seems you know exactly what you are doing." I wanted to arouse her curiosity and challenge her to relate in a more meaningful way to her behavior. Her feelings of pain (inflicted by these men) needed to be related directly to her own wishes, rather than to some outside source. However, it appeared that she was too well defended and was not going to give up her defenses so easily. Thus the session continued:

P: I don't know what you mean, I don't understand. Do you really believe I want to torture myself? I keep complaining to you I am in pain and I wish I could feel differently. Both Mike and Lewis (*men she was dating*) have real nice qualities. It's just that they're not too sensitive about my feelings. Or maybe not too perceptive. I mean Mike will jump at any chance to show me how inadequate I am in the office, knowing how I hate my job and my boss. And Lewis completely and totally disregards how I feel physically when he's with me, because no matter what, whether I have a cold or my period or whatever, we must have sex if he wants it. Nothing stands in the way. But I spoke to them about these things. It's like talking to the wall.

T: I guess you have no choice but to talk to the wall, just like you had no choice but to agree to see Norman when he called.

P: No, I didn't have to, but I was curious to know what's happening with him.

T: You were "curious"—interesting word!

P: I was having all kinds of fantasies about him, from time to time, and I wanted to be sure that I really didn't care for him anymore.

T: You have trouble cutting the cord.

P: You said it, boy! (*Long silence.*) You know I just had a thought, it was very comfortable for me to talk about my past, almost like there is no emotional involvement in it here, like talking about things way back then, and I was just thinking I wish I could go back and talk about high school like I did last week, because I just can't sort things out in my mind, a lot of thoughts, but no feelings about anything now, except that I am very tense now and I am thinking that maybe you are right, maybe I do things and pretend that they happen to me, as if I am not involved. (*Silence.*)

T: And when you feel too tense, you run away from it, either by planning a vacation, or becoming silent here, or pretending you are confused.

P: Yeah, but you know if I had to decide what to do about Mike, or Lewis, or even Norman, I would die, because I really don't know what I want, or who I want. I am really lost.

T: I wonder if you're not waiting for me to tell you what to do, just the way you wait for these men to tell you when to have sex, whether you are adequate or not.

P: (*Sarcastically and seductively*) It wouldn't be such a terrible thing if you did tell me what you think, would it, Doctor?

I did not answer this question, but allowed the session to develop further.

This example illustrates the way in which confrontation analysis uses confrontational procedures and strategies to achieve a number of therapeutic goals. Once again I chose to focus on a single theme, and did not allow the patient to ramble when I saw that she was likely to use her versatile life stories about men as a resistance to getting involved in the therapeutic work. The theme was that of separation, and the purpose of the confrontation was to help her become aware, as quickly as possible, of defenses that were keeping her confused, lost, unrelated, and most of all, emotionally "unseparated." She attempted to use a number of diversionary tactics to keep me "off her back," including the statement that I should tell her what to do, which could be translated dynamically into: "Why can't you be my mother and feed me my life patterns over and over?" Her seductive voice and manner were unmistakably immature and childlike, and were designed to appeal to my mothering instinct. However, if I had fallen into the trap, she would have then kept me at a distance the way she did with other men. Any closeness created intense anxiety for her, because that closeness entailed an inevitable separation, something which she could not face at that point. Her repeated complaints that she had no feelings about anything expressed her need to keep distant. Again, the confrontation was designed to alleviate the fear that closeness would annihilate her (or me), and to force her to make some connections between her feelings, her behavior, and her history. Naturally, one session could not do all of that, and yet it could, quite likely, hasten the process of increased awareness and eventual integration of the self.

Both of the above illustrations concentrated on the content of the verbal exchange between patient and therapist. However, nonverbal means of confronting patients are understandably missing from such reporting. These exist in the form of tone of voice and posture, and of body gestures that the therapist uses vis-à-vis each movement of the patient during the session. The nonverbal interplay in a confronting situation is very difficult to describe entirely in words, or even to show through videotaping of the session. Confrontations may take the form of leaning toward the patient's seat, looking away from the patient when he makes certain statements, laughing purposely with the patient and then asking for explanation, throwing the hands up in the air, pointing to the patient's posture during the discussion of certain themes, etcetera. Any communication between patient and therapist is embedded in a total picture composed of both verbal and nonverbal elements, and this theme is explored in the chapters on *communication*.

Categories of Confrontation

Confrontations are statements made by the therapist (and at times the patient) that are designed to enhance consciousness both inside and outside the therapeutic setting. In clinical experience, these statements appear to cluster around three basic areas of concern: (1) the inner life of the patient, (2) destructive behavior patterns, and (3) the relationship between the patient and the therapist.

The Inner Life of the Patient

Most people come into treatment relatively unaware of much of their inner life and the role it plays in their present patterns of behavior. While many enlightened people know that their fantasies, dreams, expectations, and feelings have some meaning, they do not generally tend to give them very much importance as the prime expression of their needs, conflicts, and unconscious strivings. The knowledge and appreciation of these dynamics, and the patient's attitude toward them, makes it possible for the therapist to gauge the patient's potential for self-discovery through his inner life.

The patient is asked to bring dreams and fantasies to the sessions as is done in traditional psychotherapy. Free association is used, and confrontational techniques are employed with dreams and fantasies as well. Both patient and therapist pick out what seem to be the most important themes in a dream or a fantasy, and then the patient is confronted with their significance as they relate to his conflicts and problems, past and present (Stolorow, 1978). In this manner, a number of "subgoals" are achieved: (1) the patient is impressed with the importance of his inner life and the responsibility he has for it and for its understanding; (2) the patient is taught how to recognize and utilize his inner life dynamics in the service of widening consciousness of his self; (3) the therapist gets a "visitor's visa" right to enter the inner life of the patient in order to form a therapeutic alliance by utilizing this most private domain.

A basic difference exists between confrontation analysis and other therapies in their approaches to the "inner life" of the patient. In the former, the therapist's interest goes beyond listening and interpreting and probing. Through the confrontations, the therapist interacts with the patient on various levels, including his most unconscious one, and in this manner helps the patient form necessary connections with various aspects of his personality *in the therapist's presence.* Having shared some of the most primitive aspects of his personality in an interactional manner with the therapist, the patient becomes increasingly less defensive and more comfortable with his inner life. This is illustrated by the following clinical example.

Ellen, whose case was introduced earlier, came to therapy at the age of 28, because of her feelings of depression. Her mother had died from abdominal cancer when Ellen was a junior in college and away from home. Her father, an active political appointee in local government, continued to live in the same house that he had shared with his wife. Ellen moved to New York City, where she graduated from college, and began therapy some nine months before the session presented here.

P: I was sitting in my office yesterday just watching the tape *(Ellen worked as a secretary in a brokerage house on Wall Street)*, and all of a sudden I had a vision of my pocketbook lying in a garbage pail, and it felt like it was me, it was me lying in the garbage pail. I mean I recognize that it's being absolutely ridiculous, but that was the first time I've had that feeling in a long time. And last night I had a dream that I found my pocketbook and it was sitting beside a chair in my living room, in Orlando, but the hat and gloves were gone. But the first thing I went to look for were my credit cards to see if they were all there, but many were missing. That was all there was in the dream.

When I heard Ellen's dream, I remembered the first interview with her, when I asked her to describe her mother, and she mentioned the fact that her mother always wore a hat and gloves, even when she went to the supermarket. This was a clue to her unconscious feelings at that point. She had never denied that she missed her mother a great deal, but she could never get her feelings out in the open, even though she secretly cried over the loss. Her separation from her mother was guilt-ridden, especially since she continued to live away from home during most of her mother's illness. She returned home when the situation became critical, during the last two weeks of her mother's life. She wished to totally repress that experience, and could recall her mother only before the illness—as a vivacious, lively "dynamo." Her associations did not lead to her mother, but were not too far from her either. First she discussed the goings-on in the office, then some women in the office, and eventually she began to refer more to her individual, personal life away from work.

The rest of the session may be seen as emanating from the confrontational techniques used. I knew she had a great deal of resistance to dealing with her feelings about her mother, but I felt that she was ready for the challenge.

P: My mind just goes from one thing to another. A lot of things are going on in the office, as you can imagine, especially with my boss and Joanne, but I'm not really in the mood for all that crap.

T: Is there anything else on your mind?

P: Oh, yeah, my father called me last night. He's been very strange lately.

I don't know what's happening with him. I was in the shower—he knew I was in the shower because I told him—and I asked him if he wanted me to call back, but he said no, he just wanted to say hello and find out how I felt, so I started talking to him, and I asked about the party, and he said it was going to be next weekend, and he asked again whether I would be coming down. This is the fourth time he's asked me. I don't want to go down, I don't want to be there.

T: You sound quite angry, what's this all about?

P: I don't know, I feel down. *(She starts to cry and sob.)* I resent the fact that I should be there, just because I am his daughter. If he wants to give a party, that's his business.

T: What makes you so upset about *his* business?

P: I don't want to be there!

T: You don't want to be there! But you have to, is that it?

P: I don't want to be his hostess, I am not taking my mother's place as hostess, and I don't want to hurt him by not being there. And then he asks me if I am still seeing this guy Alvin to the exclusion of others, and I said no, and he sounded relieved, but I am certainly not going to tell him I am having an affair with Jim; he'll flip. Anyway, after he asked and I answered him, there was dead silence, and I felt very uncomfortable, and the towel kept falling into the tub, and he said that he got my Valentine's card on Tuesday and wished me a Happy Valentine's Day and we hung up. I felt so uncomfortable.

T: What were you thinking about during the silence on the phone?

P: Nothing that I remember, why?

T: Well, you said you didn't want to replace your mother as a hostess, what do you mean?

P: I mean that I didn't want to be with my father as if I were my mother; I am not her and I don't want to be. I mean to cook for him and make the beds, and clean, and so on. But you know I had another dream on Saturday night, which comes to my mind now, but I don't remember anything, except a picture of my mother *(tearful)*. I did wake up because I was quite anxious, and very uncomfortable. Alvin was staying with me that night; we didn't have sex, but it was very nice, and at the same time I was very uncomfortable.

T: What about that picture of your mother? And the gloves and the hat— was she wearing them?

P: *(Tears.)* How do you remember? I know I am still upset about her, and I don't know if I'll ever get over it. *(Cries.)* I keep finding myself doing many things like her, in the way I run around, always doing something or other, and sometimes I don't know who I am, who Ellen is.

T: So when your father wants you to be with him, you lose yourself, who you are.

P: Exactly. (*Silence.*) I suppose that's what my dream is all about; my credit cards must be me, my identity, and much of it was lost when my mother died. I depended on her so much. She even picked out for me the courses I was taking in college, not against my will, but she always considered my feelings, she just helped me out. She wanted to be involved in my life so much, and she was, and I miss that (*continues to cry*). She gave me so much, and yet I feel she left me when I wasn't ready to be on my own. I wonder if I ever will.

T: What about that fantasy you had in the office?

P: What do you mean? Which fantasy?

T: You were lying in the garbage pail!

P: I don't feel that my mother left me in such bad shape. I mean I feel depressed because I miss her, but I don't think that she gave me such a bad image of myself. I think she felt like shit sometimes because my father never appreciated her as a woman, and she used to talk to me about that, and I hated it, but I think that the good things about me come from her, except for the business mind, which comes from my father. I guess the dreams and the fantasy have something to do with my feelings about my parents, and maybe about myself. I know I have a lot of stuff there.

Ellen continued to discuss similarities between herself and her mother, and ended the session in a rather depressed mood. It seemed, however, that she was able to make enough connections between her inner life, her past, and her present feelings about herself, having been confronted with them through the dreams and fantasies. Very little intervention was called for during the following few sessions as she ventilated a great deal of grief and rage toward her mother. At some point she made the connection between the men that she dated and her mother, realizing that she felt the men were a substitute for her mother, although never satisfactory. Hence the compulsive nature of her present relationships.

The confrontation techniques used in this area of the therapeutic process lean heavily on interpretations of early unconscious dynamics, focusing on an affectively loaded theme, discouraging lengthy free association, and introjecting therapist's interventions to enhance sharing of inner life on the part of the patient in a protected atmosphere.

Destructive Behavior Patterns

People come for treatment partially because they have adopted patterns of behavior that inflict pain on them in one form or another, physically and/or emotionally. The symptoms they complain about are usually smokescreens for life problems. From the initial interview, the confrontational analyst must be alert to this human phenomenon, and must let the patient know in a skillful and reasonable manner, by illustration rather than lecture, that his task will be one of helping to uncover rather than cover, to widen consciousness rather than constrict the self, to make rational connections rather than irrational ones. In the area of destructive behavior patterns, the confrontational analyst's objective is to help shift the psychic energy from acting-out behavior to behavior that is creative and helpful in removing the causes of anxiety, and to divert the patient from the pattern of suppressing or repressing, which only creates temporary appeasement and relief. In this area of work, confrontational techniques vary widely. There is practically no prohibition on any technique the therapist may use if the acting-out can be reduced, simply because therapeutic work is very difficult, if not impossible, when the patient is bent on self-destruction. Five techniques that are useful in dealing with this behavior are presented here.

1. Prediction of patient's behavior on the basis of past performance. The acting-out patient is not normally aware of the fantasies that are the motivating force behind self-destructive behavior. Therefore, when the therapist learns what these fantasies are and how they motivate the patient to act out, he might suggest the probability of oncoming behavior to the patient, and make the necessary interpretation related to it. This technique has been especially successful with adolescents (Abt and Weissman, 1965). However, with adults, the prediction that they are likely to repeat their acting-out must be accompanied by a confrontation: "Since you know that you are likely to repeat this behavior, what safeguards or precautions are you making in order not to, and what's the point of discussing this matter with me if your mind is made up to continue doing something you claim you don't want to?" The patient can hardly escape from such confrontations. Although the acting-out may not stop immediately, the issue is forced out into the open, and the patient is forced to deal with it during the therapeutic session, with someone who is willing to help analyze it. Such confrontations also tend to encourage more introspection, which eventually leads to a decrease in acting-out.

2. Detailed discussion of the anatomy of the acting-out behavior. Most patients like to mention self-destructive activites in passing and pretend that they are not significant enough to dwell upon. The confrontational analyst must educate the patient to go over such behavior step by step, "demanding" that a rationale be given for each step. The discussion must involve, also in as much detail as possible, the consequences of such behavior and the degree of control the patient could have exercised at any point in the process. The importance of this technique cannot be overestimated. It brings up many aspects of the patient's life that had hitherto been hidden. Thus the energy invested in every detail that the patient relates becomes a part of the transferential situation, and may be utilized in much the same way as any other transferential object. The analysis of any well-anatomized piece of self-destructive behavior eventually centers around the patient's expectations and assumptions about his world, and how his own projection distorts the reality of this world and his capacity to deal with it. This technique—the anatomy of acting out—is most successful with patients who have a great tendency to deny, avoid, project, repress, rationalize, and displace. Addictive behavior figures significantly in this category.

3. The use of "paradigmatic" model techniques (Nelson, 1968). In this model an appeal is made to the patient to follow his logic to the end, and thereby ultimately and inescapably expose the nature of irrational projections. In this manner, a basis for the patient to act on his own behalf is slowly formed, and the motivation for his behavior is no longer steeped in perceptions that were possibly appropriate in yesteryear. Paradigmatic techniques are best used with chronically depressed patients, whose self-flagellation often arises out of their guilt for feeling angry and rageful toward significant figures in their lives, and with patients having obsessive-compulsive and phobic reactions, whose symptoms arise out of a need to decrease their great anxiety based on a variety of reasons. One must use this technique with a great deal of caution, and must have an excellent rapport with the patient before attempting it. (For a detailed use of this technique, see the case of Eileen, Chapter 10).

4. The use of sarcasm.   Once the therapeutic alliance is formed (which can occur in a very short time with some patients), the use of sarcasm to highlight the patient's irrational behavior may be extremely useful in provoking the patient into *open* combat, so that his unconscious need to keep the status quo comes out of the "underground," and there is a chance to experience open communication without recrimination. Confrontations using sarcasm are effective with passive-aggressive behavior, behavior that is so harmful to the patient, and into which he usually has little insight.

5. Termination of treatment for a short time.   When a patient exhibits the kind of behavior that is self-destructive to the point where the therapeutic sessions are constantly taken up with it, the therapist may confront the patient with this fact and suggest that therapy be terminated by a certain date unless the behavior is stopped. It may be true that the patient had sought treatment for this very behavior (i.e., alcoholism); however, if the patient cannot get into the business of exploring his personality because of the behavior itself, a short period of no treatment may be very effective—if the patient has become attached enough to the therapist through progress made in other areas of his functioning. In this category one finds patients who are quite dependent, with uneven functioning. When such a patient is confronted with the suggestion that therapy be terminated, there is often a panic reaction, followed by a drastic reduction in that specific form of acting-out and a dramatic improvement in overall functioning. This, in patients who have made prior good progress in treatment, is not a passing change, but one that is maintained for a long time. The patient experiences success in the conscious quest to stop the pain from self-destructive patterns, and this becomes an excellent motivating force for further growth.

The following excerpt is from a session with a 28-year-old single woman patient who had been in treatment for about six months.

Carol was seen in individual sessions twice weekly, and for the preceding two-month period had been in a once-a-week group therapy as well. She had been in treatment with another analyst for about three years, and had left him because she felt he was unresponsive to her. She was especially perturbed about his interpretations during the last few months of her treatment: whenever she talked about her wish to leave, he told her that she was resistant and did not want to change. He was not eager to discuss her resentment about his "deafening" silence during most of her relationship with him. Her major complaint, when she first came to see me was the same one with which she had begun treatment previously: she was unable to maintain a successful steady relationship with a man, although she found it easy to meet men. After the second or third date, the men never called back. She was becoming increasingly anxious over the possibility that her behavior might be eliciting negative reactions, although she could not discern exactly what she was doing to provoke these reactions. It seemed that in her previous therapeutic experience she had not discussed how she affected others, but had talked exclusively about how others affected her. This attractive, somewhat large and overbearing woman, was undeniably very bright, professionally efficient and creative, yet she had only a few people she could call her friends, with the exception of one close girl friend. The session excerpted here is rather typical.

P: I was all anxious about coming here today, and I went to work very early this morning, and I go into that train, and suddenly it stops between two stations, and nobody is saying anything to anybody, and the trainman walks up to me and he gave me an explanation of what was wrong with the train. Why? Why? (*Smiles.*) I mean there is something going on with me and people, I don't know what it is. I mean this kind of thing has been happening; I mean I don't know if I am more open to people or what. I think I am open to people, that I don't look hostile, which I think is good. I was told that by a designer who visits our office often, and he said, "You know, you are the easiest person to talk to." And I said, "That's really nice, I want to be that way." (*Carol looks at the tape recorder.*) Is that on?

T: Yes.

P: I am very depressed because it scares me.

T: What scares you?

P: The tape recorder. I mean, to hear myself would probably be depressing.

T: You were just talking about how good you felt about yourself. What happened?

P: I was talking about being open, and I see that tape recorder and I get scared. Maybe I am just kidding myself. The other night I went to dinner with a couple of friends who just got married—and I was the one who introduced them to each other—and I was very depressed when I got back home. I felt very lonely. I was really depressed. And you know, the wife said to me, "When are you going to stop being afraid of getting married?" And I said I stopped. In fact, I had a couple of dreams about having good relationships with people.

T: You sound confused about your feelings. You say you feel good about your relationships with people, and you tell me a story of how depressed you feel when you are with them.

P: Actually, I felt worse when I was home alone. But you're right, when I was with them, I was thinking, why can't I have such a relationship—after all, I introduced them to each other. What's wrong with me (*starts crying*)? I am having a lot of trouble in the office with one woman, this lesbian. I told you about her. Some time ago she made a few passes at me. She is very important for our work, but she is very inefficient, and she is a liar, and my reputation is always on the line, because she never delivers, and I am afraid to say anything because I don't want to be responsible if she is fired. Goddamn it, she takes advantage of the fact that she is a lesbian, and she knows that people are afraid of her.

T: You sound quite angry to me. Angry and upset.

P: I am either angry or upset. I mean I have been in a good mood much of the time, but I am still very angry. As a matter of fact, I had a dream last night which came to my mind now. I was in a group therapy session and there was a woman therapist, and I came down to the session, although I wasn't sure I had a session, and there was a guy who was also a therapist, and he was sitting on the floor, and I said something and I finished, then somebody else went on; he went over to her and sat by her knee, the therapist I mean. She said isn't that amazing that I can get that kind of thing, and I blew up. I just completely exploded that she was talking to him in the middle of what was going on, and I walked to the other side of the room, and I interrupted the other who was talking, and I felt good about doing something, and then I was awakened by my cat who walked across my face. There was another dream, I can't remember the whole thing, but I remember my secretary was in it, and she didn't want to work for me any more, and I couldn't take it or be rational about it and I exploded, and started screaming awful things about her, and I just didn't have control about it. You know, what comes to my mind is my mother and my sister and my brother. Somehow I always felt that my mother favored my brother, and I always felt that if I acted like a boy she would like me, but it never happened (*tears*).

T: I suppose in order to make contact with people, you have to know who you are.

P: For me there is no question that I am a girl, a woman. The fact that my mother favored my brother doesn't mean that I really wanted to be a boy. I just wanted to please her, so I used to act like a boy. I know that a lot of people think I can do many things that men do, like a good job in the office, but I don't think that makes me a man. I am starting to feel really good about myself, about being a woman.

T: What exactly do you mean by "being a woman"?

P: Myself, sometimes, like in terms of the dream, I felt that me, a woman, is like my mother; I mean a woman with a traditional female role that I would imitate. My mother is feminine in some ways, although my brother used to tease her and call her sometimes the "sergeant" or the "general," and in fact my mother is a lot stronger than my father in a lot of ways. For example, in terms of running his business, my father used to depend a lot on her. And my mother is more intelligent than my father in terms of learning and knowing things, and he always says "ask my wife," about a lot of things.

T: In what ways are you like her?

P: Well, if I am around a woman who is very feminine, I don't feel feminine at all. I am like my mother in some ways—I am intelligent, and I think I am a lot more intelligent than the men I meet or the ones in my office, and I am strong, or maybe the word is not strong but stubborn, and I like to order people around; except when it comes to a man, I become like a nothing in the beginning and I try to play the cutesy little girl, but it doesn't take long before my voice starts to get stronger and stronger, and I think I frighten the man, and when I am with a man and another woman, I don't feel I can keep the man. And all my life in school it's the cute little girls, that I wasn't, that were adored. I was always big, fat, tall. I never felt very graceful, but always clumsy and gawky. And since I was big, I felt my voice had to be loud for me to be heard, but I never think of my voice as loud or offensive.

T: What exactly happens when you meet a man? Do you think of all these things about yourself?

P: I always do, and I always know what the end will be; I know I am going to be rejected. I know this is ridiculous, I mean, even men I meet on blind dates, I feel already defeated. I can't trust anybody.

T: So what exactly do you do when you meet a man?

P: Well, before I go on a date I try to pretty myself up, and I put a lot of make-up on. I mean, I was told I look like a doll with it, but I am afraid to show my face. I also wear the sexiest dresses I have, and I know they are not right many times. I mean, maybe I come on too strong, but I don't want to be a mousy little girl.

T: What else do you do on a date?

P: When I went out last time with Lenny, I told you I put on a whole show about my work, and my involvement with it; only now I feel I said all those things to scare him. I knew he was going out also with Mona, and I knew I couldn't compete with her, so I took out all my guns. I know I'm no match for her, because she is so petite and feminine.

T: I still don't know what you think you did wrong to screw up the date.

P: I have been thinking about that just before. I guess I have to say that I was somewhat aggressive and hostile, and as we were finishing up dinner,

I became more and more loud, and I told him about my family and my analysis and there is no question in my mind he thinks I am nuts. I always do that, but now I can see how I start the whole thing from the minute go, with the make-up and all the shit. For crying out loud, everybody tells me I have a beautiful face, why do I have to hide it? Even my fucking mother told me that many times, why do I have to look like a whore when I go out?

T: I suppose, when you go out and you do all these things, it is your intention to prevent the man from rejecting you.

P: Yes.

T: As a matter of fact, it is you who rejects you and think the man is going to, so you try to prevent that.

P: Exactly. I prepare my own bed and I lie in it. I keep feeling I've got to act like my mother—tough and domineering—to be able to get what I want. But I don't usually think I do that.

T: You sometimes act like that here, tough and pushy.

P: I feel *that* sometimes. But I thought I was playing games of assertiveness here. I mean I was told that before, but I thought it was because people just didn't like me, or because my voice was loud. But I do think now that my voice is loud because I am afraid I'll be rejected or not heard the way my mother didn't want to hear me.

T: You mean because your brother came first and his voice was always heard?

P: Actually I feel that my mother always took the spotlight. When I go to Miami to visit them once in a blue moon, my mother won't ever let me finish telling them what I've been doing, even though my father is very proud of me and he is always interested in me, but she doesn't give him a chance, or me a chance.

Although this session may appear rather nonconfrontational, confrontation is not always in opposition to the patient's stream of associations. The therapist stayed with the patient most of the time, but consistently probed and insisted on *continuity, clarity of communication, and accountability.* This is done through focusing purposefully and in detail on the patient's repeated need to act out the complex syndrome of identifying with and attempting to separate from her mother, which ends up in disastrous relationships with men and women. It was important in this particular instance, and as part of a series of sessions on the same theme, to ignore a lot of material that Carol brought in order to focus on one single issue—the kind of thoughts and accompanying behavioral rituals that resulted in self-destructiveness, and eventually in feelings of depression, loneliness, and worthlessness.

Relationship with the Therapist

In traditional psychoanalytic psychotherapy, the relationship between the patient and the analyst is evaluated mostly in terms of transference and countertransference. The object of the analysis is the resolution of the transference neurosis. This relationship is most unusual and unnatural, because the interaction between patient and analyst is mainly concerned with the reactions of the patient, primarily a one-sided form of communication. Although the analyst's interventions are most important, they contribute very little to a *truly dyadic interaction.*

An analogy may be drawn between psychoanalysis and rocket technology, with the patient likened to the rocket and the analyst to the ground controls. As the rocket begins its lonely voyage to another planet, various mechanisms in its structure may have to be readjusted and redirected. Whenever something goes wrong, the ground controls send their signals for adjustment. In the same manner, the patient, in his attempt to reach his goals, may experience difficulties, and thus, now and then, may require the analyst's intervention to redirect or reconstruct his energies. This analogy points up a basic fallacy of psychoanalysis—the assumption that men may be reshaped or guided like machines, through a one-way action between the machine (patient) and the engineer (analyst).

In confrontation analysis, the relationship between patient and therapist is quite different. It involves an interactive process designed to create a two-way relationship where transference is an important aspect of the relationship, but not its totality. While the therapist's reactions are mainly related to the patient's life and problems, the therapist and his personal life experiences are part of the therapeutic situation. The so-called "neutrality" of the analyst is often purposely sacrificed and consciously abandoned in order to help the patient determine, through confrontational working through, what he believes in and what choices must be made.

Many issues that arise in the relationship between the patient and therapist must be dealt with in the therapeutic situation as quickly as possible. The patient must, with appropriate timing, be confronted with each and every issue as part of the therapy, since the interaction with the therapist is of extreme importance. The patient must be continuously challenged by questions: why did the patient choose this particular therapist; what keeps the patient in treatment with the therapist; what makes the patient tell *this* therapist this story rather than another, and in the manner it is told; what feelings, thoughts, dreams, expectations does the patient have of the therapist; what are the patient's and therapist's responsibilities toward each other, as differentiated from those toward others; what initiatives does the patient take to make the therapeutic *relationship* (not the *therapy*) a terminable one (Grinberg, 1980)?

The patient and therapist must negotiate these questions as they move along in the therapeutic process, although at times the therapist will not pursue confrontations that reinforce the patient's defensiveness or anxiety to a degree that is destructive to the pursuit of therapeutic goals. As the patient attempts to deal with these issues, his perception of the therapist shifts a great deal as the world of (important) persons and objects from years past become alive and projected onto the person of the therapist. The therapist must understand these shifts in perception and help the patient experience as many of these objects as possible to enrich his life and deepen his consciousness. Through the discharge of energy attached to these past figures, and the challenge of the here-and-now confrontations with the therapist, the patient learns to separate from past feelings and perceptions he needed to hold onto, and to redirect his attention to the present life. The interactive process between the patient and therapist becomes a model for the patient to live a fuller, more substantial existence in which the past is not encapsulated in unconscious basements, but becomes like a panorama used for greater vision and deeper understanding.

The following excerpt, taken from a session with a 27-year-old single woman, in treatment for about three months, illustrates the interaction described above.

The patient had entered therapy because she was depressed, unhappy with her job, had undergone two abortions within the previous year, and did not know whether she "wanted to get married or become a lesbian." She was an extremely bright and vivacious woman, and her tone during the sessions was continuously angry. Her parents, who lived in another large metropolitan area, were on the brink of separation; while her younger sister had frequently slashed her wrists, sometimes more seriously than others, and at the time of this session was hospitalized as the result of yet another suicide attempt.

P: I had some thoughts of telling you some things, but I forgot what they were. I am sure you'll find what it all means, but I honestly don't remember what it is. Yesterday (*Sunday*), a friend came over to visit me and I wasn't there. I invited him and I forgot all about it. He left town and I didn't see him. I take a responsibility and I don't carry it. I do this with my family too, not only my friends. Last time I was home, Dotty slashed her wrist slightly, but I couldn't really do anything about that, that's really not my responsibility; although I suggested to her to go into treatment. I guess she had been drinking a lot at the time. And she doesn't believe in analysis, too.

T: Too? Who else did you have in mind?

P: (*Laughs.*) Me, of course. I don't know if it can do anything. I don't know if twice a week will be different, as you seemed to imply when you recommended that I do that.

T: Is that what you had forgotten, that you wanted to discuss with me therapy?

P: Yes, and I don't know how I remembered. Anyway, I don't know if you're the right doctor for me.

T: (*sarcastically*) If you don't know if I am the right doctor for you, you certainly wouldn't want to come here twice a week to waste more time.

P: I resent your personality. There's something about you I don't like.

T: For example?

P: You are unsympathetic. I mean you never smile; you are sarcastic; and you are very cold and stand-offish.

T: Is that all you resent about me?

P: Partly it's my problem. I know that I don't trust anybody. Even my best friends. I always have some doubts, that they don't care.

T: And you feel this way about me, that I don't care?

P: Absolutely. You're passive, and my whole life problem is with passive men. I leave here depressed every time. I know I am not as depressed as I was when I came here, but you make me depressed when I am here and when I leave.

T: How so?

P: That's exactly what I mean, "How so?" You always expect me to have an answer, and that's why I am here, because I don't have the answers. You don't give me any guidance. Even a little advice doesn't come from you.

T: Is that what you'd like me to do, give you advice?

P: What's wrong with that?

T: But is that what you want from me?

P: My father was very strict and then very remorseful. He would ask me to do something, and before I started doing it he became terribly angry at himself for having disturbed me. He knew I would get angry if he insisted.

T: And that's what you want from me? To give you advice and then become angry at myself so you can sit back and enjoy it?

P: You really think that I am mean, don't you?

T: I didn't say exactly that.

P: Well, you might as well, because maybe you're right. Do you know that my father used to take showers with me until I was 17? I am embarrassed to tell you this, but that's the truth, and I was quite developed by then. I can't understand my mother, she never said anything about it. I guess it was a habit in our house. There were no restrictions on nudity.

T: And you feel I put restrictions on it here?

P: What do you mean?

T: That you and I don't have the same relationship you had with your father—so you see me as being unsympathetic and not caring.

P: I don't expect you to be like my father, but I also don't think that a little caring on your part would be too much to ask.

T: What do you have in mind?

P: I don't know, but I do know myself, and I know that I had an image in my head—I guess you're right about that—and if the person doesn't fit this image I become bitchy.

T: Or depressed sometimes.

P: Somehow you don't strike me as someone who could care about anyone. If I had to guess, I would say you're not married, you just don't seem to be the type. Are you married?

T: What would that prove?

P: I don't know. My parents have been married for almost 30 years, and when I was a little girl I thought they loved each other, but now they are separating.

T: To you that means they didn't care about each other, or about you.

P: I am really confused. Nothing seems to be stable. My parents are getting divorced, my sister is killing herself, I don't have anybody who cares about me, and I come here every week, and I don't know where I am going.

T: I understand how you're feeling. Everything seems to be falling apart for you. I guess you must feel this way about me too—that if you trust me, I am going to disappear and not care about you.

P: Exactly. I don't trust anybody, not even myself. Why should you care? I wonder what makes for love and the ability to love. Maybe that's what I want. How to be a little more loving and a lot less angry. You didn't answer my question—are you married?

T: Yes, I am.

P: Really? I could swear you are not. Maybe I suspected it, but I didn't believe it. Maybe I didn't want to believe it.

T: How do you feel about me now?

P: I am glad you are, only because it shows me that I make all kinds of assumptions about people, and many times it stands in my way. I think I feel more at ease now that I know you're married. Maybe you're not so bad after all (*laughs*), even though I find you very difficult sometimes. I mean you don't let me get away with anything.

This strenuous exchange, mainly concerned with the relationship between the therapist and the patient, is typical of many sessions for some patients and atypical for others. It is not really unusual, however, and it goes a long way toward defining and redefining the real situation as distinguished from the fantasied one. In this particular case, the subsequent analysis of the meaning of the patient's expression, "You don't let me get away with anything," helped her understand her relationships with men and her own role in attempting to base her identification on sexual confusion. Subsequently, it became clear that she had a tremendous amount of guilt because she felt responsible for watching and wanting her father's genitals, and harbored many fantasies of exchanging her genitalia with his. Yet her conscious thoughts were always directed at his "unscrupulous, immoral, and plain stupid" way of raising children. It also became increasingly clear that her "penis envy" was not related at all to any need for aggressive or masculine attributes, but for a fusion with her mother through the penis that she (in her fantasies) planned to acquire from her father.

The confrontation element is extremely important to the basic philosophy of this system's therapeutic process. Confrontation in psychotherapy is used by many therapists; however, *confrontation analysis* is not used systematically with a unifying theoretical framework as presented here. Confrontation is generally regarded as one of the *techniques,* rather than as an *approach, a system.* This essential distinction is at the core of the present work.

ANALYSIS

The second element of confrontation analysis is the systematic analysis of the individual's patterns of behavior through the use of confrontation technique. Analysis in this type of treatment is carried out on two separate and complementary planes. The first is the analysis of the individual's personality dimensions—more specifically, the etiology and development of the basic conflicts which created the maladaptations for which help is sought. On this level confrontation analysis seeks to help the patient become more conscious of needs, drives, conflicts, and feelings, so that he functions more reasonably and in tune with the requirements of a healthy personality. Perhaps the most comprehensive system that has attempted to achieve these goals is psychoanalysis, which uses mainly the techniques of free association and interpretation. While confrontation analysis often utilizes the interpretive methods of psychoanalysis, it does not allow free association to dominate the therapeutic sessions except in very special situations. Clinical experience has proven that even the most eager, motivated, "decent neurotics" learn after a short time in therapy to use free association as a major means of resistance (Greenson, 1967). They are almost *inevitably* used as such, and therefore the therapist must not only analyze the resistance, as Greenson suggests, but must also understand and deal with the total interactional pattern between the therapist and patient created by the free association technique itself. Confrontation analysis departs from psychoanalysis and other similar systems at the point where the *interaction* between patient and analyst replaces, in a majority of cases, the free association techniques.

The second aspect of confrontation analysis, which distinguishes it from other systems is that great importance is attached to the analysis of the *here and now* of the interaction between therapist and patient and within the confrontational framework. At this level of analysis, the patient makes the connections between past history and present behavior—between his unique dynamics and the unique way that he is impressing and being impressed by the world.

When a patient brings up what appears to be a conflict situation, or a difficulty in life for which he does not seem to have an appropriate solution, the therapist first confronts the patient with it, or attempts to help him become aware of it. The therapist directs the patient's attention to the inconsistencies, irrational conclusions, unwarranted assumptions, and various other ego splits. Once this is done, and barring additional associations related to the same theme, an analysis of the material takes place through the process of interaction between patient and therapist. This process is illustrated with excerpts from sessions with two patients who were introduced earlier, Penny and Ellen.

The reader may recall that I attempted to confront Penny with her need to deny her weight problem and hence to avoid my disapproval. Beyond this, the transferential aspects of her reactions to me were not clear. Therefore, it became necessary to analyze the interaction that emerged between us right there and then, so that the impact of her awareness resulting from the confrontation might become both immediate and lasting. This was done by tying historical material to the present situation as soon as the opportunity presented itself. The excerpt presented here continues from the point where the previous excerpt ended.

P: *(After a long silence)* I really don't know why I do these things. It's so automatic for me to slough things off.

T: How do you feel about my staying on your back?

P: Well, this is why I am here. As a matter of fact, that's why I like to come here. There isn't a day that passes by without my thinking about therapy. It kind of gets into you. You know I didn't have that feeling before when I was with Dr. N *(previous analyst)*. Now I have much less time on my hands, because I am working part-time, which I didn't use to when I was with Dr. N, but I am much more involved with what's going on here. I know that's no good, because of what you said about making this my life, but I do think a lot about it. I was talking to Jenny last night and she wants me to join a woman's group, but I don't even have time to breathe. I have three big papers for my finals, plus statistics assignments, and you know I always had the problem, even in grade school, always last minute cramming, and my parents didn't really mind it. I always managed to pass, but they also never bothered to find out what the hell I was doing, and I wonder if they really cared. I mean did they really care? *(Very angry tone)* I remember once—I think I was five or six—we were all going to visit I think my grandmother, and they were waiting for me to finish my lunch, and I remember so well I dawdled and dawdled, and finally my father got so furious, he snatched the plate and threw it into the sink, and pieces of glass were flying all over the place, and I got so frightened I started to cry so hysterically that both of them were all over me apologizing and telling me what a nice girl I was. You know (*crying*) it makes me feel so terrible, I feel so ashamed of myself for being such a pest, and I made it so hard on them that they were, and still are, so afraid of me.

T: Was dawdling one of the ways you were able to "get" them?

P: I was a dawdler alright. I ate slowly and dressed slowly and walked slowly and didn't do my homework until the last minute.

T: How do you dawdle here?

P: I don't know what you mean. You mean that I do things to slow down my progress?

T: For instance, it took you some time to tell me about your eating earlier in the session and, in a sense, I had to pull it out of you.

P: I never saw it that way.

T: It seems that you dawdle here in the same way that you did with your parents, except of course that I am not your father or mother. Perhaps you expect me to take the plate away from you and scream at you and save you from your own dawdling.

P: I know you can't do it for me, but I guess I do have these thoughts sometimes about how nice it would have been if my father was not such a softy and acted more like you. At least (*crying*) I would know that what I did mattered to him.

The session continued with Penny bringing up a great deal of material related to her feelings about her parents, and the differential care that her younger sibling, a brother, had received from them. After the initial confrontation, she was "allowed" to associate freely (as in the above session) so that dynamic material could emerge.

This strategy also serves to determine if the patient is willing to work on the confrontational material or is resistant to it. Thus, in this case, confrontation strategy helped the patient recognize her transferential reactions as well as understand the historical roots. Had the patient chosen to associate to material that did not directly bear on the theme of the confrontation, the therapist might have waited for an opportunity to bring such resistance to her attention, and if that did not help create a continuity within the session, the patient's behavior would have been a signal that the resistance was too severe for making any additional intervention related to this theme at that time.

The second illustration of the analytic element in confrontation analysis concerns Ellen.

Ellen was confronted with her own decision to follow a pattern of self-destructive behavior—to hold on to men who continually treated her with less than respect. It was important to attempt to analyze what was happening between Ellen and myself during this confrontation in order to arrive at some insight into her behavior outside the therapeutic situation and on a deeper dynamic level. The excerpt presented here occurred after Ellen expressed a wish that I tell her what I thought of what she was doing or, better yet, what she ought to do regarding these men.

T: So you feel lost again and you want me to fish you out of the water?

P: (*Sarcastically*) That's super! I am lost, I feel lost, and I am confused. I don't know who the hell I am, what I am, and what I am supposed to do now. What can I do? (*Short silence, and then uneasy shifting in her chair*) Nothing on my mind. Nothing. I have a total blank!

T: You know Ellen, I am not sure you want to do something. You keep asking *me* to tell you who you are and what to do.

P: I get so frustrated and so tense sometimes; like right now, I just don't know what to do.

T: So you ask me to bail you out and that's supposed to help you, in the same way you lean on your boyfriends to get you out of your feeling of tension and feelings of being lost. I am not sure about your wanting to find out what this tension is all about. You keep trying to avoid it.

P: So I am coming here to waste my time and your time. Why am I coming here? I hurt and, believe me, I don't like this feeling. And I find it difficult to give up old boyfriends and old ways of doing things. Maybe I don't want to give up the old me.

T: The "old" you? You mean the old little girl that's part of you?

P: Yeah, I mean I used to cling when I was a little girl; I always took my beat-up Chinese doll with me any place I went to until I was eight or nine, and I told you about Sandy, my girlfriend—no matter how mean she was with me, I always went back for more. You know (*tears*), I remember I once apologized to her for having cried after she pushed me into the snow. She didn't want to talk to me because I cried. That's sick! I know I still have those fears that I must behave or else I'll lose everyone.

T: Sandy was a very important person in your life!

P: She sure was. You know even my mother didn't like her, but she never told me to get rid of her.

T: I suppose these men are also that important for you now, and no one is telling you to get rid of them.

P: Are you saying that I make them so important, because I know that they can't be that important, but I am still afraid to lose them? I have always been afraid to be alone, as if I won't be able to make it on my own.

T   Perhaps the little girl in you still wins out sometimes, but you feel you
     can't part company with her, she is from the good old times.

P: I do feel like a little girl sometimes, especially around men. Even when
     I come here, I look at myself in the mirror and I fix my hair and makeup.
     I guess I need to please you too. Perhaps that's why I ask you for your
     advice—what to do, what I should do.

This excerpt is typical of the way a confrontation analyst
uses the material brought out in the confrontation to help the
patient gain meaningful insight into undesirable behavior patterns. Interpretations as well as dynamic connections in the
context of interpersonal, dyadic interaction are made during the
flow of the therapeutic session. The interplay between the here-
and-now and the patient's early recollections must be produced
in a very careful and logical manner, and it must always be
related to the therapeutic work that the patient is engaged in
at that time. Otherwise, indoctrination rather than therapy may
take place.

The timing of confrontational techniques and strategies is
difficult and tricky, and requires a thorough understanding of
the patient's dynamics, as well as of the purpose of the confrontation in the context of the total therapeutic effort. However, if the therapist feels that the patient's ego functions are
adequate, confrontational techniques may be used for various
purposes, not only when the therapeutic process is well under
way. Once a good relationship is developed between patient and
therapist, even though the relationship may be new, this
method may be used for purposes of probing into various areas
of the patient's life. Thus areas such as resistance, sensitivity,
taboos, and family and individual secrets may all be approached
through this method. Of course, in any therapeutic encounter
the therapist must have complete respect for the patient's feelings on any subject. Confrontation techniques may also be used
for diagnostic and prognostic purposes, especially with patients
exhibiting characterological defenses in the beginning of treatment. To reiterate, "confrontation" does not mean an attack on
the patient; it is a method of investigating the patient's personality structure. It may be likened to the work of an archaeologist,
who probes the surface, sometimes gently, sometimes firmly,
with professional care and studied purpose, using tools that help
to open and illuminate rather than eliminate (Freud, 1912,
1913, 1914, 1915a).

2

Basic Assumptions and Formulations

The following five formulations are essential to the operation and practice of confrontation analysis:

1. The self
2. Dependence
3. Territoriality
4. Competition and Cooperation
5. Escape from Anxiety

THE SELF

Guntrip (1969) states that "theories that have no practical application can only be of academic interest." When this statement is turned around, it may have a far greater applicability to today's world of mental health and psychotherapy, that is: without a theoretical basis, any psychotherapeutic endeavor is bound to become an empty exercise in ritual and gamesmanship. Confrontation analysis bases its therapeutic techniques and strategy on a certain psychodynamic understanding of human behavior, and it makes central in its therapeutic approach the concept of the self, or the ego. It is the ego that is involved in any encounter with a human being, and everything else, such as the unconscious ego, the superego, or the so-called libidinal or id forces, is only inferential, and does not *directly* pertain to the experience of the therapeutic encounter. Even the most primitive, regressed patients use their ego to deal with the world—however shattered, split, weak, or undefended that ego is. The ego (self) is that part of one's personality that lets one know that one is functioning, in any area and at whatever level. The phenomenological self comprises a number of entities and forces, including its physiological condition, developmental history, and perceptual apparatus.

Freud stressed the importance of focusing on the ego in his later writings, and in "Analysis Terminable and Interminable" (1937) he stated, "We shall achieve our therapeutic purpose only when we can give a greater measure of analytical help to the patient's ego." Lifton (1976) stresses the importance of the self in uncompromising terms: "Central to human experience is the struggle to evoke and preserve the sense of the self as alive, and to avoid the sense of the self as dead." Fromm-Reichman (1950) suggested that the psychoanalytic approach was lacking something important when she stated that "insufficient attention has been given so far to the concept of *self*-realization as a great source, if not the greatest source, of human fulfillment." (emphasis added) Arieti (1967), whose approach is unmistakably interpersonal, attributes to the self the highest significance in personality functioning: "The feelings, the ideas, the choices, the actions of man attain their highest development in the state of social mutuality, but begin and end in the intimacy of the sentient self." After discussing the works of Freud and Sullivan, among others, concerning the aims of psychotherapy, Singer (1965) arrives at the conclusion that the self must be the main focus, as he states that psychotherapy's aim is to "make man comprehensible to him*self*, to help man fearlessly see him*self*, and to help him learn that this process of *self*-recognition, far from producing contempt, implies and brings about the achievement of dignity and *self*-fulfillment." References to the self as a most important aspect of the personality are numerous in most writings on the subject; however, the clinical emphasis has not always followed. Kohut's (1971, 1977) work is a notable exception.

William James (1950), who has a special talent for elucidating psychological concepts, defined the self as follows:

> In its widest possible sense, however, a man's self is the sum total of all that he can call his, not only his body and his psychic powers, but his clothes and his house, his wife, and children, his ancestors and friends, his reputation and works, his lands and horses, and yacht and bank accounts.

While this definition may be too broad for our purposes, it does point to the direction in which confrontation analysis moves; that is, to tackle as many aspects of the patient's life as possible, as long as the patient perceives them as part of life and as important to the investigation of his self or personality. Thus confrontation analysis may be characterized as a therapeutic system that focuses on the analysis of the self through confrontation techniques.

There are two major reasons for selecting the self, or the ego, as the object of therapy or investigation. The first was mentioned in the above paragraph: the self is the only part of the total personality that can deal directly in human transactions. One cannot talk to the unconscious, the superego, or the id. One can, however, directly address a person who is telling a dream (which has unconscious meanings), or someone who is lying (and might have superego lacunae), or a smoker in the elevator (who might be claustrophobic). Whatever the goal with a patient, his self (ego) is the most eloquent expression of what is happening in toto. Hence *the self is the seat of man's existence as a psychological presence.*

The second reason for focusing on the self in therapeutic work relates to our definition of psychotherapy. According to Marmor (1974) psychotherapy is "a method of modifying an individual's symptoms, feelings, thought processes, or behavior by means of communication in an interpersonal relationship." An inference that psychotherapy has indeed taken place may be assumed only if *change is observed,* and change can be observed *directly and indirectly* only through the self, through the modification of behavior, symptoms, or affects. Discernible and recognizable changes brought about by psychotherapy processes in any area of the personality must be mediated through the perceptual apparatus of the self. The inferences made about areas of the personality that are not directly observable, such as unconscious processes, are justifiable only if their expression can be scientifically assessed in some fashion.

Self-perception is central to the operation, maintenance, and modification of the self. (This term is used here interchangeably with self-image, self-concept, ego-identity, and self-esteem.) Self-perception affects every significant area of functioning in daily life, be it emotional-personal, social-interactional, or intrapsychic. Thus, according to Rubin (1967),

> . . . the self-concept is not merely a psychic image, the totality of representations of inner states or of internalized external objects, which have been designated as "self-representations" by Jacobson. It also includes personality traits, attitudes, emotions, behavior patterns, talents, needs, wants, favored capacities and social roles. Some of these may be temperamental, some may be adopted through imitation, identification, trial and error experimentation, and usefulness in satisfying needs or in communication in accordance with the particular growth pattern and familial-cultural environment of the child.

Self-perception is learned through impressions that others "confer" upon one as one grows up; impressions that become organically integrated as part of one's own perceptions of oneself. In other words, self-perception is the outcome of a very rigorous process of learning, and it basically develops in the context of human (or inhuman, as the case may be) interaction. Thus self-perceptions may be thought of as judgments made about one during one's infancy and childhood, which one absorbs, and which, in general, become unconscious. (These impressions are termed *judgments* because an impression is an evaluation of the reality as seen from the evaluator's eyes, and those eyes can see no further than their own capacity allows them to see. Such capacity can never accurately correspond to the reality situation. Therefore it is inevitable that gaps develop between other people's impressions of one—that are eventually incorporated into the self—and what one actually is. Of course, the greater the gap, the greater the distortions in one's self-perceptions. The important point is, however, that self-perceptions are mediated through a learning process that contains judgments that do not necessarily correspond to reality, but are always associated with, or attached to, the individuals—or objects—who initiated this process.)

Escalona (1968) stresses the importance of the development of early ego functions as the basis for social interactions: "Some early ego functions emerge first in passive form during encounters with the mother, but they are actively applied and expanded during transactions with the inanimate environment before they appear as active components of social interactions." Of course, the child or infant may accept or reject impressions "showered" upon him at any time. This quite decidedly influences self-perception, and contributes additional dimensions to self-esteem and ego-identify.

The differential strength with which children accept or reject their parental impressions of them, especially when such impressions do not coincide with their own impressions, is an important factor in the initial development of the self. In addition to physiological factors and temperament, the home atmosphere and the relationship between the parents and with other siblings are obviously extremely important.

Thus psychotherapy has the goal of modifying self-perception so that the self can function *on its own behalf* in a reasonable manner. Why should it be so difficult to reach such an aim when, after all, what has been learned can be unlearned or relearned? The manner in which this development has taken place and its chronology provide clues to the tremendous difficulties involved in effecting changes in the self.

As one grows older, a rather interesting development takes place. On the one hand, early parental impressions become part of one's unconscious life, and one is unaware of them. On the other hand, since they were, so to speak, *given,* one expects, also unconsciously, that they will be *taken,* should one no longer want them—i.e., one acquires the unconscious conviction that one has neither the responsibility nor the control for changing these perceptions. Thus one sees oneself as dependent on the good graces of those who forged one's self-image to change it. Taking the initiative (or responsibility) for modifying certain impressions, feelings, and behavior patterns learned as a result of association and interaction with others means (also unconsciously) that one is separating from those people, and this process creates overwhelming anxiety. Throughout life one seems to be in a continuous struggle, in one form or another, to separate those perceptions that are truly one's own from those that one has been conditioned to adopt. In this struggle one must learn to distinguish what is within oneself and what is outside.

It is this personality dynamic that led various theorists to espouse divergent views with regard to the self and the way in which the self relates to others. Freud (1923), for example, theorized that the individual invests psychic (libido) energy in another person to form a tie (cathexis); while the object relations theorists such as Fairbairn (1952), Winnicott (1958), and Guntrip (1969) suggested that the individual brings external objects into his or her psyche for the purpose of forming and maintaining interpersonal relationships. Both approaches are theoretically useful; however, one must look at the interpersonal context in which the personality develops in order to be able to help the patient "restore the self" (Kohut, 1977), since one cannot truly separate the personal *expression* of psychological phenomena, such as the various functions of the self, from its interpersonal base. The "bell in the desert" has no existence whatsoever without a listening ear!

To summarize briefly, assumptions about the importance of the self as the central target for psychotherapeutic change were made. The self, as seen here, is the organizing entity of personality functioning and at its core lies self-perception. Self-perception is regarded as the totality of impressions learned from others (usually parental figures) during the process of maturation, and it is this part of the self that influences our choices in life as well as our interpersonal relationships. Psychotherapy aims at changes in self-perception, and the difficulties encountered in this process are related to the fear of separation from impressions linked (through learning and conditioning) to important personages in our childhood environment.

DEPENDENCE

There is little in the gamut of personality characteristics or in the conduct of one's life more central than the human condition of *dependence*. Nearly all human behavior (possibly excluding some physical and neurological behavior) is related to some aspect of dependence. This condition exists because one is born without adequate structure for living and growing on one's own—no baby can survive without "mothering." In the formative years, this condition so deeply impresses on one the need for others that one may never feel at any time in life fully independent and without the need for important others or their substitutes. This dependence may take many forms but, however disguised, it is always present. Guntrip (1969) addresses this point when he says that,

> The Oedipus problem, as Freud saw it, was in fact, the gateway opening back into the area of the psychopathology of infancy. Fairbairn's position was essentially simple. Once stated it should be apparent that man's need of a love relationship is the fundamental thing in his life, and the love-hunger and anger set up by frustration of this basic need must constitute the two primary problems of the personality on the emotional level. Freud's guilt over *the incestuous tie to the mother resolves itself ultimately into the primary necessity of overcoming infantile dependence on the parents, and on the mother in particular,* in order to grow up to mature adulthood (emphasis added).

Mahler (1972), discussing the processes of separation-individuation in the first two years of life, underlines the extreme importance of the dependence-independence dimension throughout life:

> For the more or less normal adult, the experience of being both fully "in" and at the same time basically separate from the "world out there" is among the givens of life that are taken for granted. Consciousness of self and absorption without awareness are the two polarities between which we move, with varying ease and with varying degrees of alternation or simultaneity. This, too, is the result of a slowly unfolding process. In particular, this development takes place in relation to (a) one's own body, and (b) the principal representative of the world as the infant experiences it, namely, the primary love object. *As is the case with any intrapsychic process, this one reverberates throughout the life cycle.* It is never finished, it can always become reactivated: new phases of the life cycle witness new derivatives of the earliest process still at work.

In fact, the more disguised the dependency, as in what appears to be an Oedipal problem, the less control one is likely to have over one's life and the less one may experience full and real emancipation.

Dependence is anywhere and everywhere, although it is not always recognized. Dependency needs have such a negative value in this culture that many people feel insulted and indignant when they are confronted with them, as if they are being accused of a sin. For many, such needs are symbolic of immaturity, lack of judgment, impulsivity, and most of all, vulnerability. Because of the negative value attached to dependency needs, people have been quite ingenious in developing ways of hiding these needs from themselves and from others. Examples of such distortions abound.

A popular story of dependence (though unrecognized as such in most cases, and simply seen as a joke) is the case of the man who needed aspirin for his mounting headache. He searched his own house, but could not find any medicine. He decided to ask his neighbor across the hall for some aspirin. However, since it was somewhat late at night, the man thought it might be an imposition on his neighbor. As his headache grew more and more painful, he began to walk toward his neighbor's apartment. He was afraid his neighbor would be extremely angry at being aroused at such a late hour, but his headache made it impossible for him to sleep. As the neighbor's door opened, the man was so beside himself with fear that, not waiting for his neighbor to open his mouth, he blurted out angrily: "I don't need you or your damn aspirin."

A 35-year-old lawyer was referred to me by his friend, who was also in treatment with me. The lawyer related the following as he sat down: "About a year ago, I started to get dizzy spells, and I passed out a couple of times. I went to all these doctors, and finally I ended up with a heart specialist who sent me to a neurologist, and then they told me there was nothing wrong with me physically. They sent me to a psychiatrist. I saw this creep a few times—I don't remember, maybe three or four times—and I didn't like him, so I stopped going to him. During the year I had a lot of headaches, and a couple of days ago I got this dizzy spell again and then I decided to call you. I know you can't do anything about this, being a psychologist, but maybe there is something wrong with me physically. I mean I know I am angry all the time—but I mean *all* the time—and that's because I don't like to take anybody's bullshit—you know what I mean? I like my job, I am the attorney for a bank, and I don't want to depend on these Valiums; I take them four times a day. In fact, I don't want to depend on anybody. These attacks started two years ago, after my mother died; and then the unveiling came and my father came from Montreal and he said he couldn't stay with me—he was going to stay with his girlfriend—and I was quite disappointed, and in the evening I got this headache. Now they are married. Recently, I was talking to my girlfriend and I got very mad at her, and I had this terrible headache and I was paralyzed. I mean I just couldn't talk to her at all."

This patient, a very bright and perceptive individual, could hardly function in a reasonable fashion on a daily basis without continuously relying on tranquillizers. He was always in a state of rage. He considered himself to be an independent person, since he wouldn't "take any shit from anybody." He couldn't see how his anger was related to his deep need for support from the outside world. He mistrusted the world so much that when he received support, he couldn't believe it was genuine. To prove his independence, he "got rid of" three wives before he was 33 years old. To be sure, he had had such poor experiences with his parents that trusting the feelings of others would have been rather irrational for him, if not totally psychotic. However, what is interesting is his complete unconscious denial of the relationship between his early childhood frustrations, related to unfulfilled needs for support and nurturance and his present anger at the slightest signs of rejection. With all the problems that he had encountered throughout his life with women, his expressed goal during that first interview was to be "emotionally tied with a woman who can understand me!" His ambivalence toward his great need for attachment was quite obvious. This patient could, no doubt, be described as having made a schizoid adjustment as a reaction to unresolved dependency needs. As Guntrip (1969) asserts, "The chronic dilemma in which the schizoid individual is placed, namely, that he can neither be in a relationship with another person nor out of it, without in various ways risking the loss of both the object and himself, is due to the fact that he has not yet outgrown the particular kind of dependence on love objects that is characteristic of infancy."

A 40-year-old film producer walked into my office for the first time, shook my hand without looking at me, and, though I showed him to a seat, continued to stand up looking around the office for a couple of minutes, and then, still avoiding my eyes, sat down, nailing his eyes to the floor, and said, "Would you be kind enough to give me an idea of procedure?" I asked him if perhaps he would like to tell me why he had come to see me. The patient replied, "I have a few problems, a few questions—problems I guess. The main question, problem that is, is, you know, has something to do maybe with my turning 40 about three years ago. Well, I guess I have to tell you what the problem actually is. The problem is, well, my inability to obtain an erection and maintain the erection if I have sex with women other than my wife. I had a battery of tests a few months ago and there is nothing wrong with me physically. I have no problems that I know of. By the way, my wife doesn't know anything about all this. When she asked me about the bills, I told her I had pain in my groin and I had to see a specialist, and she accepted this and she doesn't know I am coming to see you. Well, when I go in and out of bed nothing happens, I mean sexually. Why does it happen—is it guilt?"

This very mild-mannered man spoke softly, using many self-demeaning expressions throughout the interview. He was very successful in his profession, both financially and creatively. He had been raised in a rigid Catholic home, and he wanted to provide a good home atmosphere for his two children. He had never considered divorce. He said he had stopped loving his wife 15 years before. He did not believe he would find a wife more attentive to him than his present one, although he also complained that she did not understand him at all: "I've never been ecstatic about my wife's ability in bed, her ability to understand my work or my hobbies, or for that matter her ability to socialize—we never go out anymore, so I stay out a lot and give her the excuse that I am working and she accepts that!" He did not feel that he stayed with her because he was psychologically dependent on her; rather he was "logically" dependent on her—he needed her "for the children" and to keep the "family name" intact. This man's total behavior during the interview expressed his need to avoid his feelings by all means, and any possibility of confrontation was circumvented by all the verbal, intellectual, and nonverbal tricks that he could muster. He was so dependent on the world's approval that he led a double life, and felt unsatisfied in both. It eventually became clear that his avoidance behavior in my office was related to his fear that I would force him to separate either from his wife or his extramarital relationships, both possibilities causing him a great deal of anxiety.

A 25-year-old woman who worked as an editor for a national magazine recognized how dependent she had been on men by the fact that after one date with a man she liked, she would become obsessed with the idea that she would lose him (and she always did). Her actions were not related to her feelings about the man, but rather to the idea of the possible loss of him, and the fear of such loss. Most of her behavior during a date thus became inappropriate, possessive, and exaggerated, and at times desperately submissive and placating. She felt she could not act in any other way, since the only other alternative would have been to act like a "shrew," following in her mother's footsteps. Her mother had divorced her father when the patient was five years old. Her expression was that she wished that she could become a "completely liberated woman who doesn't give a shit about a man!" She also recognized that this attitude would not keep the kind of man she wanted around for very long. This woman's inability to become aware of her dependence on certain images or objects of what a woman "should" be like was the real problem, not her wish to have a man's company. This type of dependence is quite common in men and women who grew up in homes characterized by very rigid expectations of children; homes where the children were unable to develop a positive same-sex identification, either because of poor self-image of the parent or because of the absence of one parent.

Saretsky (1977) discusses this type of behavior with regard to the therapist in a paper on the resolution of impasses in borderline states. He suggests that this defensive structure, manifested by loss of boundaries through submission and surrender on the one hand, and withdrawal and resistance on the other, is designed to "keep a feared reality (loss of the mother bond) from becoming manifest."

These examples illustrate how dependency strivings are denied, and how the defensive patterns that help the individual in the "covering up" operation set in as a result. Such patterns develop in everyone, and they usually exist unrecognized, except in their secondary or tertiary expression through the defensive armor. Although all psychological phenomena cannot be reduced to this single dimension of dependence, the problem of dependence—sometimes called *separation anxiety*—infiltrates self-perception, behavior, and interpersonal relationships. The human mind is extremely ingenious, creative, and devious in its attempt to mask this universal condition, because of its negative valuation in our society. One must not underestimate the pain that society inflicts upon anyone who exhibits dependency needs openly. Klein (1950) writes, "In an adult, dependence on a loved person revives the helplessness of the infant and is felt to be humiliating."

Focusing on dependence does not reduce and constrict the study of personality; it does the opposite: It forces an in-depth study of the person, a search for all the phenomena that unify or disintegrate the self in its rich and multifaceted aspects. However, like the biologist who must isolate the many characteristics of living tissue and reduce them to a primary, basic unit, namely, the cell, in order to understand the working of the total organism, so must the therapist strip the personality, layer by layer, down to that elemental or basic unit, so that he or she can understand it, confront it, and deal with it in an effective manner. Without such an understanding of the "basics" of the human mind, any attempt at changing it would be futile. Therefore, a study of dependence, the "cell" of the self, and knowledge of its effects and manifestations in disguised forms, is essential to work in the field of mental health.

Unfortunately, many psychotherapists abandon the task of uncovering the deepest aspects of dependence—those rooted in the interpersonal contacts between baby and mother. They are aware of the existence of primary dependence, but because their personal analysis and the orientation they have acquired in training have not provided them with a personal confrontation with their deep dependence, they are inclined to avoid the subject. Perhaps alluding to this gap between the analyst's awareness and his application of it in practice, Fenichel (1945) remarks that "practical and theoretical knowledge remain to a certain extent isolated from each other."

Another difficulty inherent in the psychoanalytic approach to change is the great stress that psychoanalysis has placed on the Oedipal situation. Analyst and patient engage in a semi- (or one-way) dyadic interaction that is supposed to explore, define, confront, and resolve the Oedipal situation through resolution of the transference neurosis. While the material that patients produce during analytic sessions may be interpreted on the Oedipal level, it is hard to see how such a limited relationship between patient and analyst could really produce even a simulated Oedipal resurgence, let alone a full-blown transference neurosis with the Oedipal trauma at its core. Rather, in this kind of relationship a transferential development based on a dependency stemming from the oral stage would be most likely to emerge, since the situation itself is so much closer to the original object relations between baby and breast. This may occur even when the patient's fantasies appear, on the surface, to be Oedipal. In her paper on the relationship between "love for the mother and mother love," Balint (1949) recognizes the element of dependency as probably the most significant characteristic in the therapeutic situation:

> The mother is unique and irreplaceable, the child can be replaced by another. We experience the repetition of this conflict in every transference neurosis. Each patient is more or less concerned at some time or another with the relative irreplaceability of the analyst as compared to the real or assumed ease with which the analyst can fill the time vacated by any of his patients.

The usual psychoanalytic technique does not afford the chance for the patient to perceive the analyst as an individual living in the real world and to separate from him or her. Balint stresses that for separation to occur, such a process must take place in childhood (and in this author's opinion, in the therapeutic situation as well): "The detachment from the mother, in the sense of the dissolution of the primitive attachment based on mutuality, means the reconciliation with the fact that the mother is a separate being with her own interests."

Traditional psychoanalytic techniques, such as the analyst's "withholding" during most of the analysis and the offering of interpretations that whet the patient's appetite (since they are so sparsely and "preciously" doled out), have a tendency to increase the patient's need for nurturance and to keep the patient frustrated and thus more dependent. In the continuous deprivation of the analytic hour, the patient does not resolve dependency problems, does not learn to separate, but only pushes such issues deeper into the large store of repressed material. Just as chronically deprived children, whose need for dependence is overwhelming, develop bland, unemotional, detached facades, so may an analysand become a tamed, "understanding," unflappable, and most "objective" being—one who is not genuinely sensitive to his surroundings. Techniques that emanate directly and primarily from a concentration on Oedipal material when, in fact, a pregenital core problem exists, do not lead to self-confrontation, meaningful interaction with others, or a true consideration of alternatives to present life patterns. Confrontation analysis, on the other hand, tackles Oedipal problems as they grow out of the relationship between patient and therapist, *in the context of analyzing the roots of dependency, and within the framework of a true dyadic interaction—"replicating" in some fashion the mother–child relationship.*

TERRITORIALITY

Another issue crucial to the understanding and treatment of the self is what may be called "territoriality" or "territorial privacy." For purposes of clarity, this topic is divided into three sections: The Ego and the I, Psychological Territoriality, and the Relation Between Territoriality, Privacy, and Personality.

The Ego and the I

Recent developments in personality theory place a heavy emphasis on the functions of the ego (Blanck and Blanck 1974). The ego has already been identified with the self. For the purposes of this section, however, *ego* refers to a set of basic and stable patterns of behavior, feelings, and thought processes.

The verbal expression or manifestation of the ego resides in the pronoun *I*. Thus, whenever this pronoun is used, the reference is to the ego *at that given moment.* While the ego is a stable entity, it is possible for the *I,* within a certain range, and under certain conditions, to change and be inconsistent; in conflict with itself, as in ambivalence, or as separate from itself, as in splitting. Thus the statement, "I am depressed," refers to the state of the ego at the time the statement was made, but does not necessarily mean that "my ego," or "my self," or "my personality" is a depressed one. It refers to the transitional condition of the ego. Because the *I* can be variable, one must listen to many of its statements before one understands the ego or the self. On the one hand, the variability of the *I* makes the ego more difficult to know but, on the other hand, it gives the ego its meat, its substance, its depth, and its spread.

The *I* gives the ego uniqueness and identity. In addition, it is specifically and purposefully used to separate the subject from all other objects, and in this manner it asserts the existence of the person. Descartes' statement, *"Je pense donc je suis" (I think therefore I am),* is not sufficient for the operation and maintenance of the personality—there must be awareness of the separateness of the self from the world. Psychological (and quite possibly physical) existence depends to a large measure on the degree of awareness one has of one's distance from other objects, including people. The awareness that it is *I* who is thinking, or feeling, or talking, as distinguished from *you,* or *he,* is what gives one the sure knowledge that one exists and that one exists separately. This separation (and one's awareness of it) expands with general development from infancy. Thus, when a child learns to say *I,* he or she has in fact started (1) to recognize or know some of the ego's substance, and (2) to be aware of separateness from other objects, including mother. The process occurs in normal development roughly between the ages of one and two years (Klein, 1957). During the first year of life, most children ask for a cookie by saying "cookie!" and pointing to the cookie jar, and then progress to the phrase "want cookie," and finally more to the ego-differentiated statement, "I want a cookie."

Some regressed individuals resort to a number of "detours" to avoid using pronouns, especially *I.* For example, a 30-year-old paranoid man used to refer to his mother as "the mother," rather than saying "my mother." This man was extremely dependent on his mother, and this created severe anxiety for him. He was afraid to lose her, and at the same time his attachment to her was so great that he doubted his own separate existence. His avoidance of the use of any term that referred to his ego, such as *I* or *my* was his way of counteracting such fear. He spoke about his wife in the same manner, as "the wife," and he rarely referred to himself, using the third person instead of the first whenever possible. Another example is a woman in her 30s who had made a rather primitive adjustment—she used to address me in the third person, as if I were absent. For instance, whenever she wished to remind me of something I had told her the week before, she would say, "The therapist told me last week . . ." It took me some time to adjust to this phenomenon, since I was not in the habit of being absent and present at the same time! It developed that this mode of address was not primarily related to a castrating or hostile need, but instead to her fear of being swallowed and annihilated. Her only weapon was to erect a symbolic barrier between herself and the therapist in the form of a language perculiarity, one that magically kept her away from the "monster" (the therapist-mother).

The normal development of the ego involves two important processes, those of *individuation* and *separation. Individuation* is the separation of the ego from the drives that are part of the inborn infant and that later remain as part of the unconscious life of the personality. These are often referred to as the unconscious part of the ego or the id, or both. This process of individuation is not enough, however, to establish the boundaries of the self. There is another vital process, mentioned earlier—separation of the ego from its surroundings. Following Mahler's theoretical orientation, Pine (1979) defines separation as "the growth of awareness of separateness, not of actual separation . . . it is an intrapsychic achievement serving reality testing but at the price of emotional pain." His definition of individuation is "the taking of those characteristics that mark the person as a person in his own right . . ." In both examples above, the boundaries between the patient and the world, as well as the awareness of what is inside and what is outside, are blurred, and therefore the expression of the self through the symbolic *I* is lacking.

The ego, functionally invested in the pronoun *I,* is dealt with in psychotherapy by investigating its direct or indirect expressions. Although it is practically impossible to enumerate all its manifestations, some categories of ego "territory" that concern the confrontation analyst are listed in Table 1.

It is often helpful to think of these categories as parts of the ego, and to consider which ones the patient has a preference for, is obsessed with, gives weight to, or occupies most of his or her time with. During the years of maturation, each individual learns to appreciate these categories differentially, and as a result of this learning, energies are invested in one direction or another. Thus, if an individual learns that thoughts are precious and is afraid that they might be "taken" from him, he may become secretive, the company of others may be painful, or he

Table 1
Areas of the Ego Dealt with by Confrontation Analysis

Manifest Behavior	Fantasy Life	Symbolism	Values
Defenses			
Roles and functions	Thoughts and ideas	Language	Social
Expressed feelings and ideas	Fantasies	Art	Moral
Persona	Wishes	Body language	Ethical
Expressed self-perceptions	Dreams	Psychosomatics	Political
Acted-out impulses	Daydreams		Aesthetic
Body language			Religious
Verbal patterns			Familial
Speech peculiarities			

may have a need to "pick everybody's brain" without divulging any of his own ideas to others. Thoughts may become a sacred territory, one not to be invaded. In a real and concrete sense, it is the combinations and permutations of the different areas of the *I* and the attachment of differential values to these areas, that makes people different from each other. Confrontation analysis concerns itself with the exploration and understanding of these different parts of the patient's personality and the way they are arranged in the patient's value system. Of course, not only is the arrangement important, but also the way in which they emerge in the interaction between the therapist and the patient. The ego functions assume a major role in determining the individual's relation to the world, as well as in the overall integration of his personality.

Psychological Territoriality

In the social sciences, the concept of territoriality is primarily used by anthropologists, and it generally refers to

an area of space, whether of water or earth or air, which an animal or group of animals defends as an exclusive preserve. The word is also used to describe the inward compulsion in animate beings to possess and defend such a space. . . . In most but not all territorial species, defense is directed only against fellow members of the species. A squirrel does not regard a mouse as a trespasser (Ardrey 1973).

In attempting to understand a person's relation to his surroundings, this concept is indispensable. Psychologically and psychotherapeutically, the understanding of territoriality is valuable in comprehending the etiology and dynamics of an individual's perception of his inner boundaries and the interactions among various parts of his ego.

In clinical practice, the concept of territoriality may be observed in its behavioral manifestation as soon as a patient walks into a therapist's office for the first time. For instance, if the furniture does not clearly point to a "patient" chair, at first the patient looks around and does not know which seat he "should" take. The patient is generally uncomfortable choosing his own place, primarily because it is not the patient's "territory." The patient may wait for permission to occupy a certain space. This discomfort may continue for some time before he is able to relax in the "new" territory. Some patients, however, seemingly oblivious to the territorial integrity of others, may spontaneously take the clearly designated therapist's chair. This may, at times, be indicative of a confusion in ego boundaries, strong aggressive and hostile feelings, a need for control, or other characteristics. There are also those who quite consciously and purposefully choose a seat at the far corner of the office, quite distant from the therapist. The establishment of territorial distance may be an expresson of their fear of closeness and intimacy, or the threat that authority presents to them within their space. Hall (1959) notes that "The symbolism of the phrase 'to move in on someone' is completely accurate and appropriate. To have a territory is to have one of the essential components of life; to lack one is one of the most precarious of all conditions."

Thus, in the first few moments of the therapeutic relationship, the use of space within the office by the patient may offer important information as to the nature of the immediate concerns of the patient, as well as the kind of interpersonal relationships he is likely to form in initial encounters. It must be noted, however, that the use of space, in most situations, if not all, is in part culturally determined. Space is regarded differentially in all societies. As Hall stresses, "Space (or territoriality) meshes very subtly with the rest of culture in many different ways. Status, for example, is indicated by the distance one sits from the head of the table on formal occasions." People are conditioned to abide by these cultural determinants regarding territoriality, and the conditioning takes place mostly in subtle, nonverbal ways. It is the way in which each individual uses these overt and covert territorial standards that offers important clues to idiosyncratic dynamics related to his self-perception and the perception of others.

A 22-year-old man used the couch during his sessions. In one session, slowly but surely, he managed to slide down far enough for his shoes to reach the wall, which was about two feet away from the couch. With very "creative" circular movements of his feet, he proceeded to draw a nice little mess on the white wall with the help of his black shoes. Being a novice therapist at the time, I did not confront him with this acting-out behavior, but rather felt that a full-blown transference neurosis had to evolve before I could protect my wall! In any case, he reminded me of guerillas who steal into enemy territory during the night, strike, and then retreat. For my patient, this seemed a way of expressing his wish to gain control over me by robbing me of my territorial rights. In his daily life, he maneuvered his behavior to unconsciously, and yet, purposefully, "mess up" other people's space, and remained totally unaware of the consequences of such behavior. While his actions, including this episode of the wall, were a clear expression of his hostility and disdain, this man had very little comprehension of his own psychological boundaries, and thus no appreciation of others' territory. He had been raised in a home where space had no particular meaning of exclusivity or privacy. His mother used to "dump" him to sleep in any bed that was most available and closest to wherever she happened to be. As a result, he would find himself sleeping in his sister's bed or his mother's or his father's, and often with one of them, until the age of 11 or 12 years. His father used to punish him harshly for staying in a room by himself, always accusing him of being a "snot" and a "pervert." He never saw his parents hold each other gently and warmly. There was a custom in the family of not calling out the name of a person whose attention was needed. Instead, people tugged at each other's elbows or backs as a signal that they needed to be heard. These patterns of territorial encroachments became the blueprint for this patient's behavior outside. His inner life was no less confused, with the most salient feature being his paranoid-like distrust of everyone. At the same time, he could not feel comfortable without being in continuous physical proximity to others. Eventually, use of the couch proved helpful in teaching him to be trusting of others, even when he could not see them, touch them, or be "badgered" by them.

The concept of territoriality in interpersonal interaction is often implied by the use of the term *testing the limits*. This generally refers to the attempt to find out "how far" one can go in one's behavior before being stopped or acknowledged by another person. The use of physical, geographical terminology such as *limits, how far,* or *boundaries,* when discussing psychological properties, is not unusual. For example, one often talks about a *bright* (meaning *intelligent*) person, or a *straight* (meaning *honest*) person (Asch, 1952). In the case of territoriality, perhaps the most compelling reason for using "space" terminology is that these psychological dimensions do indeed develop in the context of the territorial aspects of human living, especially within the family relationship. The process of boundary testing, which a baby and its mother must go through to establish where one ends and the other begins, is both exciting and painful. The psychological process that parallels and interacts with the establishment of territoriality in personality development has been called *separation-individuation* (Mahler, 1972).

The process of separation-individuation is a complex one. It is, however, organically bound, if not identical, with the concept of territoriality. This maturation and separation period, which is roughly the first two or two-and-a-half years of life, determines the nature of the personality. There are two important dimensions to such separation: physical and psychological. The physical separation is, of course, easier by far to achieve than the psychological. One can hardly remove an image, or an idea, or a feeling from one's inner personal space, whereas it is possible to separate oneself physically from any space. To be sure, it may be relatively easy for some people to "keep certain things out of their mind," but they cannot ensure their disappearance from the total personality, because of unconscious space. Thus psychological boundaries, emotions, and ideas referring to oneself and to others cannot so easily be established. This is what is meant by psychological territoriality: the space within the personality occupied by various images, ideas, feelings, thoughts, and memories. For some people, the boundaries that separate their own perceptions from those of others may be quite clear, while for others those boundaries constantly change. The resulting personality characteristics thus become quite different. The task of learning to separate psychological boundaries is immense, and the goal of any personality investigation (and restoration) must include a significant investment in the search for present boundary delineations as well as their origin. Confrontation analysis, emphasizing and focusing on the interactional process between patient and analyst, is purposefully geared to meet the goal of relearning and reestablishing the separation-individuation parameters of the personality.

The Relation between Territoriality, Privacy, and Personality

Another fundamental concept related to territoriality, and central to the basic assumptions of confrontation analysis, is that of *privacy*—the belief that human beings must have at least some part of their personality completely and totally their own in order to feel secure, worthwhile, and separate from others. *Privacy* is an individual's knowledge and feeling of certain aspects of life that need not be shared with others and which the individual considers his own property. This concept of privacy must not be confused with *secrecy,* which implies a conscious effort to keep information away from others because of fears of reprisal. The "department of privacy" may include feelings, ideas, and opinions, or patterns of behavior related to oneself or to others, and no guilt feelings are attached to it. Privacy has different meanings to different people, and the value attached to it varies greatly, depending on factors influenced by the developmental history of the individual. The sense of privacy and the need for it grow as the ego matures, and increasingly become part of it.

For example, a young woman in her middle 20s sought treatment because she could not form meaningful relationships with men. She had grown up in a large, poor family with seven siblings. The house she lived in during most of her childhood years was small, and there was nothing she could do, nowhere she could be, without the presence of some family member. Her inner thoughts, fantasies, feelings, and wishes were always experienced in the company of others and, as a consequence, she grew up feeling that anything and everything she experienced could be scrutinized and watched by outsiders. When she finally left her home and lived by herself, she was hardly aware that others were not around "to know" what was on her mind. Her complaints in the beginning of treatment almost always came back to the same theme: men found her attractive and bright, took her out a couple of times, and then never contacted her again. This experience had been painfully repeated from her teens on. When I asked her to tell me in detail what exactly had occurred during these dates, she revealed that she always felt totally "natural" telling these men everything about herself. She assumed, quite unconsciously, that they would find out anyway; but more importantly, she didn't feel there was anything about her which *required* keeping to herself. In addition, she proceeded to relate to them her thoughts about them, voluntarily and in a matter of fact manner. She never dreamed that her behavior could be irritating, although some men had expressed such feelings. She could not grasp the concept that intimacy grows slowly, and that privacy is an essential element for the preservation of one's identity. After a short time in treatment, it was apparent that she attempted unconsciously to recreate with every interpersonal encounter what she felt most comfortable with, namely, the lack of boundaries that she had experienced in her family setting. She had obviously developed a style of interpersonal relationships quite different from what Guntrip (1961) calls "the mature civilized level." His emphasis seems to be on the importance of the separation and mutual respect of the interpersonal privacy, and he suggests that mature relationships are characterized by "mutuality, spontaneity, cooperation, perseveration of individuality, and valuable differences, and by stability."

Treatment of this case presented obvious difficulties. The "normal" resistance, in the form of withholding and inability to free associate, which other patients usually bring into the treatment situation, was clearly missing here. There were practically no inhibitions, no secrets, no embarrassment or hesitation in reporting whatever came to her mind, and almost everything did! The real problem was in balancing the delicate educative process toward privacy without causing the patient to feel that she was being shut off, rejected, or misunderstood, as she had experienced in the outside world. The confrontation here needed to take the form of *"Why are you telling me all this?"* rather than "Why *aren't you* telling me?" The lack of need for a real sense of privacy for herself made it extremely difficult to steer away from questions about my private life without being rude or rejecting in her eyes. At the same time, such questions provided an excellent path to an educative process, in the form of modeling for learning about separation, privacy, and respect for boundaries or territoriality. Such a patient is also likely to evoke powerful countertransferential reactions. The therapist becomes, quite unawares, part of the patient's family, and too soon discovers that he is privy to the most detailed information, normally revealed to a therapist only after a good deal of rapport and trust has developed. The therapist must recognize this trap and learn that the patient's communications are not based on trust but on lack of boundaries and confusion in identity. In the beginning of treatment, the likelihood is that they are not even transferential in nature because, for neurotic transference to occur, a certain sense of the real relationship must exist. Of course, in extreme cases of lack of privacy, a psychotic attachment or transference may occur.

This patient was in a sense fortunate to have developed through childhood and adolescence in a world that was mostly benevolent, positive, and rather nurturing. However, had she experienced an overabundance of negative reactions from her confusing territorial surroundings, it is likely that she would have developed a paranoid-like orientation with consequent withdrawal and extreme lack of motivation for interpersonal communication.

Another example is that of Howard, a handsome 28-year-old school teacher who came for therapy because he had become extremely dejected and depressed after one of his students, with whom he supposedly had a relatively good relationship, had called him one day in anger, and in front of the class, "a fucking faggot." He soon became unreasonably withdrawn from his family and the few friends he had, and was unable to muster enough energy to prepare lesson plans for his classes. He had a rather traumatic history: His father had been killed in a car accident when he was five; his mother, a hysterical, narcissistic woman, remarried soon after the tragedy, and the new husband adopted Howard and his sister, who was two years his senior. Howard described her as a close ally until the age of seven, when she became distant and played only with her girlfriends. The new father was a severe and unapproachable man, verbally and physically abusive toward the children. However, he also used to "spill his guts" to the whole family, discussing and describing everything that occurred to him during his day at work. Howard could conjure up only a few images, passing shadows, of his biological father. His mother used to talk to him about all her troubles, especially with her new husband, and intimated that she had to seek gratification from other men. She had a habit of continuously following Howard around the house, and had him share her bath and that of his sister until the age of 10 or 11. He remembered quite clearly that, until about that period, the family used to gather nude in the living room and play children's games, which always ended up with fights, recriminations, and violent accusations. Howard developed an intense conscious loyalty to his mother and, as a teenager, used to protect her from his stepfather's physical abuse. At the same time, his contempt, shame, and rage toward her festered underneath the surface. In therapy he often called her a "whore," an "uneducated selfish bitch," and "an exploiting slob." He felt somewhat differently about his sister, although he always qualified his feelings about her with the expression "she's got her own problems" or "she would stand up for me whenever she could." As a teenager Howard discovered that he could not trust many people, and he had only a few friends. He could not trust his own mother, but had the habit of calling her daily to recount his troubles to her (especially those with women). He would frequently come away feeling like a fool for having exposed himself. He complained that he could not stop himself from mentioning something or other that would be self-denigrating. He would tell her about his fears of sexual inadequacy and his certainty that women would reject him if he touched them physically. He never made a pass at a woman, and when he would leave a date, he would always tell her that he would call her again, but never did. His mother would always laugh at him, and tell him not to be a baby, but she would also add that "the girls of today are not the same as they used to be."

Howard's description of the environment in which he grew up, where everything was public domain and privacy was not cherished, is quite similar to the previous case, although here there were physical boundaries, and the territorial invasion was psychological in nature. There was another important difference, however—the context in which lack of privacy prevailed. In Howard's case it was experienced in a negative, hostile, and emotionally explosive atmosphere. As a result of this family structure and interactional dynamics, Howard felt that the world always knew what his inner thoughts and feelings were. When his student called him "a fucking faggot," his panic and depression about his own self-perception came to the surface. It was as if someone has broadcast his thoughts to the world. To be sure, he came to realize, much later in therapy, that his attempts to date women were strenuous efforts—defensive maneuvers to ward off homosexual strivings about which he thought everyone knew.

Howard's relationship with me was like a seesaw: he would leap from high praise for me as a sage and the Rock of Gibraltar, to obscene insults when I was critical and judgmental. I could always predict which side of the knife I was likely to receive: when Howard divulged important personal information, the verbal abuse would follow in the next session. He would accuse me of "forcing" him to tell secrets that were not true, but which were beliefs I (or someone else) had thrust upon him. He complained that his privacy could not be maintained in my presence because I was like his stepfather and his devious mother, a "demanding bastard." At other times, he would beg me to tell him whether I approved or disapproved of some self-destructive piece of behavior, and if I remained silent or noncommittal, he likened me to his dead father who "left me when I really needed him." However, when I confronted him with this behavior, then I appeared to be intruding into his life and "purposefully" trying to diminish him in his own eyes. There was no escape from being the "bad mother" as well as the "bad father." I was unable to help Howard break the pattern of these impasses, which occurred on the average of four or five times a year, until, after five years of individual therapy, I asked him to join a group. The group experience was successful in rekindling positive feelings in him,and thus provided an opportunity to split off the transference for the purpose of analyzing the "bad me" aspect of his self and separating it from other, healthier aspects.

These two cases indicate the importance of privacy in the development of personality characteristics related to the individual's orientation toward interpersonal interaction. The knowledge of how a patient acquires a sense of privacy is an invaluable diagnostic cue for the way the therapeutic relationship will develop, and may thus be of great help to the therapist's perspective.

Privacy allows additional dividends: it helps enhance one's feelings of mastery and control, at least over some aspects of the inner self to which no one else has access. In other words, privacy permits one to possess a territory—psychological and physical—that is completely and totally one's own, to put into use in any manner or at any time one sees fit. This territorial privacy does, of course, form the foundation of all free societies. The right to privacy is clearly spelled out in the constitutions of many nations, for it is regarded as organically bound up with the survival needs of the individual. Even our language suggests the survival value of privacy: when reference is made to an individual's reproductive equipment, it is called the "private parts." (One might wonder why the arms or eyes or stomach are not referred to as "private," for after all they do belong solely to that person.) The fact that people have traditionally been ready to fight and even die for the freedom to have privacy, reinforces the view of privacy as one of the most sacred aspects of life.

From a psychological and interpersonal viewpoint, privacy has wide significance. People often feel remorseful if they "spill too much" about themselves to others, even friends or family. In interpersonal relationships a feeling of privacy can affect verbal and nonverbal communications, as well as highly personal attitudes, sentiments, and feelings. Psychotherapy is the profession that must exercise the utmost skill in dealing with privacy, because the most private world of the individual is invaded. In this process, the patient's privacy is private and not private, "secretive" and "open" at the same time. Confrontation analysis, which uses an interpersonal approach to the resolution of personality conflicts, places special emphasis on the familial and social origins of privacy in any given individual because of its psychological ramifications. The process of exploring the private world of an individual through therapeutic transactions, without trespassing on territory unrelated to the patient's need for dependency, is quite difficult. It is not enough to have a patient bare his soul: such "uncovering" must be done in the context of meaningful boundaries between the patient and the outside world, including the therapist.

As concepts, territoriality and privacy have a great deal in common. However, a distinction must be made. Territoriality refers to a defensive position, a position about which one has very little choice. One might almost say that a person is born into it. Despite all the changes in mobility in the last decade or two, most people continue their life within boundaries similar to those with which they grew up. Social, familial, and cultural changes do not come about easily, and in most instances they are accompanied by trauma and, at times, social or psychological disorganization. Generally, one's territory is recognized by others and, to preserve it, one need not do anything unless attacked. However, if a person wishes to change his territory or territorial limits, he must fight aggressively to effect the desired change. Fighting basically involves the same operation as defending, although the strategies may differ.

Privacy, on the other hand, involves making choices without having to defend them. These choices are not always consciously available to the individual, but are nevertheless part of his repertoire of alternatives. Thus, for instance, no other person can force one to choose what one's private world should be. No one has to know what irritates or pleases an individual; what preferences, likes, or dislikes he has. It is up to the individual to convert his privacy into the public domain. Recognizing that unconscious motivation forces one to make certain behavioral moves, it is the judgment of the conscious ego that must be responsible in the final analysis for one's behavior. In therapeutic transactions that deal with issues of privacy, patients often feel that their final choice of what they keep private is unconsciously determined. The fact that any given choice may reflect certain unconscious, self-destructive needs, or that it is based on miscalculations and distortions, does not alter the fact that privacy, its content, scope, and form, is generally a conscious ego function. Because of that, changes in the individual's handling of privacy are easier to obtain than changes one might wish to make in the perception of an individual's territoriality.

While the recognition of unconscious motivation is essential
to the understanding of personality dynamics, confrontation
analysis deals mainly with changes that can be observed
through the here and now self, or the *I* that interacts with the
therapist in the territorial privacy of the office. In a sense a
patient risks his "survival" by "violating" his own privacy
through a commitment to the therapeutic process. For this reason the therapist must strike a balance between the patient's
territoriality, requirements for privacy, and the ultimate goal
of creating an inner psychological atmosphere for greater independence. How can the therapist plow through migraines, job
losses, sexual failure, lack of life goals, depression, compulsive
habits, self-destructive patterns, and the many other symptoms
that patients present in their initial sessions, and focus on the
self so that it can be helped to grow and to occupy an ever-
increasing territory in the patient's personality? A partial answer is that the therapist must focus on the patient's dependency needs, and related anxiety, which are the "organizing"
themes, and on their expression in terms of competition and
cooperation, the basis of the following discussion.

COMPETITION AND COOPERATION

Competition and cooperation are behavioral expressions of
dependency strivings. One learns very early in life that if one
does not satisfy the standards and requirements of those who
surround one—if one does not cooperate—one is likely to suffer
a great deal of pain. In fact, individual survival, and that of
society depends to a large degree on the interplay between competition and cooperation. The support and recognition that one
so badly needs is ultimately tied to how well one learns to play
this game. One must acquire the values of others, mostly of
parental figures, in order to become part of human society. Almost all adult activities reflect the need for recognition and approval, and there is little in daily transactions that does not
require some understanding of the laws of competition and cooperation. The psychological sacrifice involved in such behavior—mostly conditioned in early childhood—is great. The need
to satisfy a value system that promotes adherence to strict rules

of competitiveness and conformity is symbolized by the importance attached to school grades, the type of work one does, the partner one chooses to marry, the size of one's bank account, the number of papers one publishes, the Olympic medals one strives for.

How does the confrontational analyst use these concepts of competition and cooperation in the service of the patient? As a therapist, does one "teach" the patient to beat the system by becoming less or more competitive, or by abandoning this game altogether? Can the therapist teach the patient how to survive without the therapist becoming dehumanized? What does the patient want from the encounter with the therapist? These are questions all therapists must answer, theoretically and clinically.

Some patients who have endured anxiety and misfortune for many years, and who have unsuccessfully explored other avenues for relieving their pain, walk into a therapist's office with a conscious decision to work on their "problem." Yet, in one way or another, these patients find themselves, even as early as the end of the initial interview, repeating the same patterns that brought them into therapy: their inordinate need to compete or to follow instructions. Some let the therapist know that they are more experienced than the therapist in problem solving, while others are only too eager to receive a "prescription for mental health." These patients have difficulty perceiving the therapeutic situation as one of give-and-take. They refuse to let their guard down, and even though they have been repeatedly defeated by their extreme competitiveness, which is an expression of the need for approval, they structure transactions between themselves and the therapist very much in their usual manner, always trying to stay on top. Naturally, this extreme need for approval is another way of expressing how dependent they are on others. It is hard for them to see how much they alienate themselves when they are interacting with others. "Cooperators" have similar motivation: they make pests of themselves "trying to be helpful" and looking desperately for approval. These exaggerated and distorted needs seem to express the individual's progressively degenerating sense of self-respect. Perhaps it is an inability to become totally independent that has necessitated the development of these adaptive (or maladaptive) ego functions. A therapist should always be aware of these two human realities: (1) the individual is inescapably dependent on others, and (2) he is separate from others. Therapists have no less vested interest in gaining approval from their surroundings! If these needs are recognized and accepted, therapists may be able to use their ingenuity to find ways to help patients use these realities in a positive manner.

The therapist must serve as a model for the patient, as one who has learned how to reach goals consonant with his own needs, not the needs of others. The therapist must continuously (and at times, competitively) challenge the patient's (elusive) behavior that is designed to please others and defeat himself.

For example, a 32-year-old school teacher complained in one of her sessions that her school principal constantly exploited her to perform chores that she did not have to do according to her union contract. She had always cooperated because of her fear of this man's anger and disapproval, although she knew that if she had the "guts" to complain to her union representative, the exploitation would cease. This was not her only "cooperative" behavior. Her father, a gambler and a loser as a businessman, came to her every few months for financial help, and promised that he would return the money "as soon as business picked up." He had seriously depleted her substantial savings, yet she could never refuse him. She saw herself as a cooperative person who didn't want to hurt anyone. The competitive aspects of this behavior were not difficult to discern: She had always been afraid that her older sister would become the favored one because she was "prettier" and more "successful" with men. In the previous session, the patient had painfully told of how a repair man had blatantly overcharged her for fixing a television set and she had been unable to confront him with her knowledge. As she was complaining about her principal, my phone rang and I picked it up. It was my landlord, returning a call that I had made to him because he was lax in repairing a leak in my office ceiling. I raised my voice considerably, and told the landlord in no uncertain terms that I would not pay my rent until all repairs were completed. After the conversation, which consisted of just a few exchanges, the patient turned to me and said, "Doctor, you really do what you preach! My God, I cannot believe how you spoke on the phone. I could never do that!" In the following session, she reported that she had gone back to the television repair shop, confronted the owner with her complaint, and received a refund. This was no magical transformation in this patient's personality—the work of confronting and analyzing her submissive and approval-seeking behavior had been going on for a few years; however, I carried on my conversation with the landlord primarily for the patient's benefit. It was important, since the opportunity presented itself, to be a model. One might speculate that her reaction could also have gone the other way; that is, she could have idolized me to such a degree that she would sink further into her feelings of inadequacy and impotence. That was a risk, but I also knew that she had experienced enough confrontational work so that my dealing with the landlord produced a "real" situation with which she was ready to identify, imitate, or compete. Her feelings of competition with me, to which she admitted after my conversation with the landlord, was in the service of achieving her goals and satisfying her needs.

The use of competitiveness as a manipulative tool in the therapeutic work must obviously be done with complete and full awareness of where it may lead. The therapist must always be a step ahead of the patient, not to gain control for the purpose of approval, but rather to help the patient learn how to deal with his own irrational need for control, and ultimately approval.

Another example is that of a 34-year-old, "highly successful" advertising executive who started treatment for marital difficulties, mainly related to his perception of his wife as a competitive, aggressive woman who wouldn't let him be "the master." He complained, for instance, that she kept him in the kitchen mixing drinks when they had company "so she can take over and keep me down." At the end of the first year of treatment, he brought the following dream: "I was somewhere, maybe this national convention of television producers, and I get wind that someone is putting on a show, an amateur kind of performance, and it involved ice-skating. I wanted to participate, but by the time I found out about it they had already decided what the skit was going to be; yet, at the last minute, I got in somehow. The thing took place on stage. I did a few clown-type tricks on the ice, and perhaps some intricate maneuvers, and as I was coming off the ice somebody grabbed me by the waist, and I continued to go around the stage, and the audience liked it very much and I loved it." While this man's story about his wife may or may not be accurate, the important aspect of himself, which this dream revealed (and which he disliked in his wife), was his extreme competitiveness and need for approval—his inchoate recognition that his professional goals were set by others ("they had already decided what the skit was going to be") and his chronic choice of behavior patterns that were dangerously slippery, such as the ice-skating (having extramarital affairs with friends of the family and wives or secretaries of his bosses). Confronted by these self-destructive and energy-draining patterns, he took a deep breath and, with a sigh of despair, looked at me and said, "Now that I got myself into this mess, how do I get out of it?" At this point, while I saw his pain and confusion, I also recognized that the patient derived an inordinate amount of pleasure from this way of life, and that he was not about to give it up so easily. The question then was not "how to get out of it," but whether he indeed did not want the mess. This is where confrontation analysis would depart from traditional psychoanalysis. In psychoanalysis it would be possible to let this man meander for many months, indeed years, until he realized that he was too comfortable in his present life style to be serious about changing it. The future with change would appear too ominous. At this stage of his intellectual understanding of himself, interpretations would be used only in the service of defenses, as often occurs with patients who learn to "conceptualize" about their inner life. Free associations can be quite helpful in getting to the dream and to the intellectual insights related to it, but where does the patient go from there? It is at this point that confrontation analysis challenges the patient's motivation to change. What alternative behaviors, explorations, or goals are available to him? What does he have to give up to get some peace of mind? The same questions that were asked when he first came for treatment are revived: what keeps him in treatment now that he intellectually understands himself? Who are the inner people, the inner images, the persona, the introjects that he must toss out if he is to realize his potential and accomplish what he wants to do? Is he willing to withstand a great deal of anxiety in the transition period—transition from a *relatively* comfortable but unfulfilled self to a possibly more unified and integrated ego that acts and reacts according to his own needs? These questions normally arouse a great deal of anxiety, but at the same time they alert the patient to the work involved and to the potential benefits. It also makes concrete that the relationship between patient and therapist is a real one, not only a "transferential" one, and therefore that the patient must take full responsibility for his behavior. When I put such questions to this patient, he could hardly justify his complaints about his wife's competitiveness, since he recognized how important these "outer-directed" motivational forces were in himself. He was able to understand how his need for approval drove him to be competitive and to need to be in control. Since he felt guilty about his ambitions, he placed himself in the "kitchen" role and let his wife "take over," primarily to atone for his guilt feelings. By confronting him with his dynamics, I became a real person to him and, in this transactional atmosphere, the patient had to renegotiate his priorities and learn to live as a "full partner," not a "junior" one.

For "re-education" and "reconstruction" to occur, the patient must experience the full range of his emotions in the presence of someone (the therapist) who cares enough to take over, transitionally, the parental role, and yet not be a parent. This transitional and real object—the therapist—must help the patient change the many impressions, values, and goals that had been carved out for him as a child, to new ones, consciously and purposefully chosen by him *now as an adult*. The battles, and the responsibilities for the losses as well as the victories, will then be his, not others'. The therapy sessions serve as the experiential battlefield.

While competition and cooperation may be observed among animals as well, it was man's "ingenuity" that enslaved other humans, using these behavioral tendencies to subject them to one another in what appears to be a perfectly "civilized" way for society to survive. Culture has conditioned these patterns of behavior to such a degree that they pervade all aspects of life. For example, we have learned to "enjoy" standing in long lines to buy tickets for some performance or exhibit because others do. In such a competition, we identify with the winners (or losers) as spectators, so we can come out on top and gain that much coveted approval. There are constant incredible, subtle, and blatant pressures on people to be "good" citizens. Because of such realities, the therapist must always be on the alert, and must deal with these issues as soon as they arise, provided, of course, a good rapport with the patient has been established. In most instances, such issues emerge quite readily when a patient starts to feel weighed down by a great need for approval, and the issue of competition and cooperation is especially poignant when a basic relationship is involved. The interplay of these two behavioral manifestations is evident in the following excerpt from the 60th session of a 32-year-old single woman who was in treatment on a three-times-a-week basis because of depression:

P: This has been a hell of a weekend. I was so lonesome and alone. I mean really lonesome. I just walked and walked around, and there was nothing, no one. On top of it all, I got a call from my parents, and my dad gets on the phone and he kept knocking me about my new job and how it's not fitting for me, and that I was much more capable, and he was most concerned about how much money it would be. You see, anyone who makes less than he does is shit. I mean how many people can make that kind of money. I am sure he makes very easily more than just six figures. I know he'll never change, but for God's sake, why can't he accept me, I won't even say love me, for what I am (*crying*). What do I have to do for him to love me? I mean for Christ's sake, they live in Ohio and I live in New York, why can't he give a little, just a little? But I know I can't concentrate on him all the time, and I am trying to be less obsessed with him, so I am doing a lot of things for me, just for me—I think! I am taking French lessons again, and I am seeing some friends,and I am trying to get out of my relationship with Bill, but there's no one else in the meantime. I was on the street on Saturday and everybody was with someone,and I felt so conscious of being alone, and I kept thinking about how Bill was spending the weekend with his wife on the beach. I mean, I know he doesn't want to be with her, but he is. When I spoke to my father, I told him that my boss was leaving or actually being fired, and that I would be in charge in the office, and you know what he said to me? I couldn't believe it! He said you mean you will be the administrator now—and it really floored me, and he went on and on about how administration work is just politics not real work, and I felt so put down. I don't understand—when I get ahead, he criticizes me, and when I don't, when I just work hard on my job, he makes me feel that I am a fool, or that I am failing him and the family because I am not a lawyer, or a doctor. In the last couple of weeks, I was feeling better about myself, and I felt something was happening and then he comes along and everything seems useless (*tears*).

T: I know you have been angry at your father because you feel he is displeased with you, but I also get the impression that you are quite upset with yourself for not living up to his standards. You seem to have the same need to run constantly, to achieve more and more.

P: I guess I do, but I really feel great when I do better, and right now I am happy with my job because I am learning a lot of things and it does have a good future.

T: Then what are you so upset about?

P: My father won't give an inch, he always has to have the last word, and that word, believe you me, is never nice. It's always been like that. I can't be ahead of him in anything. I mean even in tennis. He is 65 and plays better than me.

T: What about you—will you give an inch?

P: What do you mean? I am always trying to be nice to him and to take care of some of his business here, he represents some New York firms you know, and I call them often, and—

T: I know you are a good girl, but that's not what I mean. I mean, do you give up some of the demands you have of yourself and be satisfied without having to be constantly running for approval?

P: When I was about seven or eight I was the only girl of this age on the block, and my father used to be very proud of me when I competed with the boys and won, and I was like a tomboy, and I feel that my father accepted me then. At least when I was ahead of the other boys.

T: So you feel you always have to be out there in front to be bragged about, otherwise you don't count!

P: Yeah! As a matter of fact, I really think that my father would never care if I get married or not. You know, what you said before really hurt, about being a good girl. That's true, I try to be a good girl everywhere, even here!

T: Tell me more about that, about what happens here.

P: I am a good patient, no? I remember when I started coming here, I was so depressed, I didn't want to talk to you or anybody at all. But then I thought to myself that you'll get mad at me and that you'll tell me to leave because you have other patients better than me. I still feel bad when I don't remember my dreams, because I know you told me that dreams are important here.

T: So you want to be the model patient—cooperative with me and competitive with my other patients— all this to be a good girl, to get approval.

P: (*Laughing*) That's what I've been doing all my life. That's me alright!

Emily is only one of many patients who suffer from the same universal "disease," i.e., dependency on approval, and the consuming absorption in finding ways, masked or unmasked, to get it. "Good" patients, like Emily, are often very seductive, and their manipulations may elude even the most experienced analysts, for they give the appearance of working in treatment. With this kind of patient, the therapist must be constantly on the alert for intellectualizing, rationalizing, and "slippery" ego maneuvers, and must untiringly confront, interpret, and probe without letting this ego have enough of a chance to reorganize and defend itself to avoid change (Cohen, 1980).

Emily attempted to cover up her own role in placing herself at the mercy of her father's opinions and approval (as well as those of the therapist), and, as was often the case, she found herself feeling depressed, worthless, alone, and desperate. She had often discussed her relationship with her father, and it seemed that she was ready to handle a confrontation that would force her to start dealing with her responsibility for her own reactions, rather than always waiting for the world (in this case her father) to make things comfortable. May (1969) notes that when "people feel their insignificance as individual persons, they also suffer an undermining of their sense of human responsibility." Eventually, her anger toward her father emerged, transferentially, toward me, with various accusations. In the open exchange, she learned to relate to me in a way she could never have done with her father—on a more equal basis. Her "cooperation" became not an exercise in submission, but part of a joint effort to free herself from the shackles of approval and competitiveness. While some of her motivation was, no doubt, to prove that she was a worthwhile person to her father and to others around her, the end result was salutory because it advanced her movement toward greater independence.

ESCAPE FROM ANXIETY

The Process of Personality Formation and Transformation

It has long been recognized that anxiety is central in man's life. May (1967), one of the most astute existential psychoanalysts, defines anxiety as "the apprehension cued off by a threat to some value which the individual holds essential to his existence as a self. The threat may be to physical life itself, i.e., death; or to psychological life, i.e., loss of freedom." Horney (1939) further makes the distinction between anxiety and fear: "Anxiety is an emotional response to danger, as is fear. What characterizes anxiety in contradistinction to fear is, first, a quality of diffuseness and uncertainty." Horney considers the understanding of an individual's anxiety to be of crucial importance in therapy: "A correct analysis of an anxiety situation is one of the main roads to an understanding of the patient's conflicts." Fromm-Reichmann (1950) suggests that "No one living in this era and culture is expected to be or to remain consistently free from any inklings of anxiety after the termination of treatment."

Anxiety serves two basic functions: it is a signal of danger and a defense against it. Freud (1926) recognized that anxiety is an all-pervasive phenomenon, and that the handling of anxiety is extremely important in the production of neurosis. He concluded that "all symptom formation would be brought about solely in order to avoid anxiety; the symptoms bind the psychic energy which otherwise would be discharged as anxiety, so that anxiety would be the fundamental phenomenon and the central problem of neurosis." Confrontation analysis takes the existence of anxiety for granted and assumes that people always feel anxious in one way or another, although they may not always be aware of it. In other words, when the anxiety is not conscious, it is operating unconsciously through the defensive channels of personality structure. Its most unwelcome and unhealthy manifestations may be observed in the form of neurotic or psychotic defenses. It is primarily these defenses that require the concentrated efforts of the therapist and the patient if they are to be investigated and changed. However, it is also precisely these aspects of human behavior—the constant need to escape the anxiety trap and the idosyncratic ways in which anxiety is transformed into a more tolerable experience (the defensive armor)—that makes each individual's personality unique.

Naturally, within the same "culture," whether this refers to family or community, people are likely to develop some common patterns of behavior as a reaction to anxiety. As one grows up, however, personality differences are shaped not only by hereditary endowment, but by the characteristic patterns of reactions to the basic anxiety condition. Psychological maturation and personality development are, in a sense, molded by the process of anxiety *reduction.* The assumption here is that most people do not learn beneficial ways of escaping or avoiding anxiety but, quite the opposite, they adopt self-destructive modes of operation. Fenichel (1945), Freud's most faithful interpreter, noted that "The problem of anxiety is the essence of any psychology of neurotic conflicts." Anxiety is pervasive in all forms of behavior, not only so-called neurotic behavior. The problem is not only the anxiety itself, but the way in which each individual handles it; for anxiety is a human condition that cannot be totally eliminated.

This assumption turns the study of anxiety into a rather pragmatic one: how can one learn to utilize one's energy to transform self-destructive patterns into more creative, healthy ones; and, at the same time, how can one reduce the level of anxiety to a tolerable level?

Anxiety and Dependence

Dependency needs in human beings are universal and, because they are established very early in life, it is practically impossible to modify them *significantly.* They are a crucial dimension of the *personality* or the *self.* Anxiety is organically bound to every aspect of dependence, since the latter is a consequence of the fact that infants cannot survive without mothers, who in turn cannot be always available to satisfy them, thus necessarily creating an anxiety condition. In this vein, Freud (1926) stated, "Anxiety thus seems to be a reaction to the perception of the absence of the object, and there at once spring to mind the analogies that castration anxiety has also separation from a highly valued object as its content and that the most basic anxiety of all, the primal anxiety of birth, arises in connection with separation from the mother." The fact that almost any anxiety situation may be traced back and connected to classical "separation anxiety" makes the investigation of this phenomenon a very difficult task, even though it does not appear as such on the surface. Two important considerations may account for the difficulty. The first concerns the problem itself: as the infant matures, he develops ways and means of coping with the world outside. Because these "techniques" are often so varied and sophisticated, they appear to be less and less related to the avoidance of anxiety. The web of defenses and symptoms around dependency needs and the anxiety created by separation becomes so impenetrable that the nucleus of the connection between anxiety and dependence eludes investigatory attempts. Consequently, by the time a patient walks into a therapist's office, the defensive armor is too thick for either therapist or patient to penetrate. This is hardly an exaggeration. *In my opinion, therapy never touches the inner core of the self;* although perhaps it can enter the hallways leading to some inner chambers.

The second obstacle to the investigation of the relationship between anxiety and dependence is the investigator. Since even therapists are so bound by their need for protection against any anxiety, the investigation of a phenomenon that points up their own insatiable need for dependency cannot help but create an emotional state of anxiety. The defenses against this anxiety thus render therapists at least partially blind to their subject matter and, of course, they are limited in their capacity to investigate it by the amount of anxiety that they can tolerate. This assumption regarding the ultimate understanding and resolution of the dependence-anxiety dimension of the personality may appear rather fatalistic, but, in my opinion, therapy, regardless of how intensive, extensive, explosive, or implosive it is, only scratches the surface of this need for dependence and approval, and it certainly does not provide any direct or indirect routes to the ultimate breaking of the umbilical tie between anxiety and dependence.

How can energy that is utilized to create self-destructive paths for the purpose of avoiding anxiety be diverted into more rewarding channels? If the childhood conditions that gave rise to the defensive structure of the person entering treatment could be duplicated, perhaps an opportunity for changing undesirable "behavior" would exist. This is obviously impossible. What is perhaps possible is to engender an atmosphere within the therapeutic interactional process that recreates conditions for the emergence of anxiety states that are *somewhat* similar to original childhood experiences in their emotional quality, but different in their critical ego quality. In other words, the therapeutic process must include, in addition to the regressive aspects of the transference, a relationship with the therapist that provides interaction designed to promote separation without anxiety. Neither ritualistic expression of feelings of the kind advocated by the so-called gut or encounter therapists, nor the rather sterile, intellectualized ritual couch talk of traditional psychoanalysis, can serve that goal. The creation of feasible confrontations within the confines of the treatment and the analysis of such confrontations seem to help a great deal toward achieving some measure of independence with decreasing anxiety.

To summarize, confrontation analysis concentrates its therapeutic efforts on the self, often referred to as the ego, because it is perceived as the organizing center of the personality. Its functioning and capacity to change may be observed and directly investigated through a multitude of behavioral and affective reactions. Early learning of self-perception is hypothesized as the basis upon which personal and interpersonal choices are made and, therefore, the target of therapeutic change. In addition, assumptions relative to the development of most significant personality dimensions and their influence on the self's adaptational capacities were discussed in this chapter. These dimensions are: dependence, territoriality, competition and cooperation, and the need to escape from anxiety. The theoretical assumptions and formulations concerning these dimensions were clinically illustrated.

3

The Application of Confrontation Analysis: A Clinical Case History

If confrontation analysis assumes that every behavioral pattern is a result of attempts to escape anxiety related to dependency, what about other developmental stages beyond the first two years of life? Aren't such phases as the anal and phallic basic to the development of the personality's defensive structure? There is no doubt that such stages do indeed exist, and the way in which each child experiences them is of utmost importance. However, confrontation analysis aims its therapeutic efforts at ultimately analyzing *all* behavior on the basis of the most primitive conflict, that of dependence (or separation anxiety), because it shapes the nature of all developmental stages that follow it. Traditional psychoanalysis has concentrated primarily on Oedipal goals and tended to ignore the oral basis for the Oedipal solution, thus failing to resolve fundamental pathology in the course of an analysis. With this perspective in mind, the following case history is presented.

The case of Vinny illustrates how confrontation analysis handles basic problems clinically. Diagnostically, this case would normally be acceptable for treatment by a variety of treatment orientations, such as psychoanalysis, psychoanalytic psychotherapy, and behavior modification. The initial interview revealed a wide range of neurotic personality conflicts with strong obsessive-compulsive features, phobic reactions, pan anxiety, and psychosomatic symptomatology. The transcripts of recorded sessions help to illustrate clearly how the techniques of confrontation analysis are used in a systematic, progressive manner as treatment evolves. Sessions have been chosen that are expressive of this approach, even though at times the content of the patient's productions may seem repetitive.

VINNY: A CASE HISTORY

Vinny, a 27-year-old accountant who had been married for two years, entered therapy because of phobias related to a variety of situations. His most serious fear was attached to underground transportation, especially the New York City subways, on which he depended to commute daily to work. This subway fear was primarily caused, according to Vinny, by the gnawing thought that if the train was stuck between stations, or if the doors were stuck and could not be opened, and he had to move his bowels, he would have to soil his trousers and be exposed to everyone as "a baby who has no control." In the first interview, Vinny asserted that he had ridden the subways for many years without any fear, and that he had even experienced the breaking down of a train between stations a number of times before the onset of the present condition without any problem. The patient dated the onset of the phobia to about six months prior to the initial consultation.

The episode that set off a chain of phobic reactions was a ride with his wife on a deserted road on the way back from a weekend in the country. He apparently took a wrong turn and ended up "driving around in circles," not knowing how to get out. He became extremely panicked, as it was getting somewhat late and the sun was no longer in sight. He needed to move his bowels, but felt he would lose time if he stopped the car, and also the thought came to his mind that the state police might find him and suspect him of being " a weirdo shitting on the roadside," rather than believing that he was lost. However, he could no longer resist the urge to defecate, and, as he stopped the car, he accidentally soiled his pants slightly before reaching a "safe" place. His fear was so intense that he asked his wife to talk to him while he was defecating. If she became silent for a moment, he would panic and scream at her to look out for other cars on the road, just to hear her voice. He was so exhausted by this experience that he begged his wife to drive the rest of the way home, continuously blaming her for this mishap. He was conscious at the time of wanting to divert his attention from the loss of control of his bowels. On the way home he experienced additional anxiety attacks, and his sleep was extremely disturbed that night. He became obsessed with the fear of being "found out" by his wife; if she discovered that he was indeed a baby, she might leave him. He could not look her in the eye the following morning, and he went to work without kissing her, feeling extremely "embarrassed." He called her at home that day at least five times, which was unusual for him. At work, he was quite nervous and avoided everyone's look, but at the same time he had fantasies of crashing into the office of the president of the bank where he worked and screaming "Guess what happened to me yesterday." These fantasies excited him a great deal, and his physical symptoms during these fantasies were similar to the anxiety he had experienced the day before.

A few days after this incident, he noticed that he was starting to become quite anxious in the mornings before he left for work, as well as in the afternoons before he had to take the train back home. He gradually became obsessed with the idea that the train would get stuck and that what happened on the weekend trip would repeat itself. Two weeks after the initial anxiety attack, he would not step out of the house to take the train to work, and he asked his wife to drive him there and pick him up at the end of the day. This did not recur every day, but did recur at least a couple of times a week for about three weeks. This, however, was not the only fear he had. Going any place that required a means of transportation other than his legs, and sometimes his car, became anxiety-provoking. He also began having bouts of diarrhea, and became obsessed with the fear that he would have a recurrence of a previous condition—a pylonidal cyst—for which he had had surgery. He was convinced that he would develop cancer of the rectum.

Vinny developed compulsive habits to a rather extreme degree: he showered at least twice daily; spending at least half an hour in the shower each time. He avoided having sex with his wife, stopped masturbating, and spent at least 15 minutes counting his rosary beads and praying each night before going to bed.

All this was to no avail; his anxieties only increased. People at work began to ask him whether anything was wrong. At this point he finally decided to seek help, and consulted his family physician, who prescribed tranquillizers. He was then able to go to work on his own, although at least once a week he would call his wife or his father and ask them to pick him up at work or from some subway station where he felt that unless he left the train he would faint. He realized that he had to do something beyond taking pills, since they were not helping him suffi- ciently, but he was so suspicious of doctors that he hesitated calling on his physician again. Finally, at the urging of his aunt, who was the "intellectual" in the family, he agreed to see "one of those crazy psychiatrists who only take your money and they don't even give you a prescription." His first encounter with a psychiatrist was a fiasco, because "the psychiatrist told me that my problems all started before that incident with the car, and he tried to convince me that I should see him almost every day. He also told me that it would take at least two to three years to cure my problems. They are all crooks and I know it." The patient was finally referred to me by a friend of his wife's, who told her that I "was not like the other shrinks," even though she warned her that I was "tough." The patient actually liked that description, because he thought that I might have the final an- swer. He also favored psychologists rather than psychiatrists, because he saw them as having lower status, and therefore felt they "will work harder."

Vinny was the only child of an Italian couple, both of whom were born in the United States. He considered himself atypical in that his parents did not have any other children, which was unusual for an Italian family. However, he did not know and was afraid to ask why his parents had never had any other children. He described his father as a hard-working man who knew nothing beyond his work. He was not interested in any- thing, not even his family, and he had peculiar personal habits, such as watching television from the minute he came home from work until he went to bed. He ordered his wife around, and put down his son because of his interest in reading and his interest in his mother. One of the habits that Vinny could not tolerate was his father's chronic "clearing of his throat, which used to drive me up the wall and still does whenever he does that. He has been doing that since I can remember. I don't know why he does it. Sometimes I think he does it on purpose to irritate me or other people around him. I hate him when he does that." Vinny felt that his father was a lonely man who "hated people, especially family, and certainly the neighbors. He never had anything good to say about anybody." Vinny's mother was described in entirely opposite terms. She was "warm, friendly, and wouldn't hurt a fly. Everybody in the neighborhood loves her. She always worries about things, especially about me, and she was always on my back to be careful about this or that. She has always been an anxious person, and I think that a couple of times she was even very depressed, and I think she went to talk to someone—maybe our family doctor—but she never followed through on anything. Her cooking was lousy, and I hated to eat at home. Even in the reserves they gave us better food, but I hated it there too." Vinny felt that his mother was overprotective, although he had a gnawing feeling that she could have been doing that because "she hated my father, just like I did."

In addition to his phobias, Vinny presented other disturbances, mostly in his interpersonal relationships. His basic orientation was paranoid. He trusted no one, believed the world was a place for "aggressive bitches," always anticipated that he would get the axe from someone, and "never had the guts to stand up to any kid when I thought I was right." He described himself further as a "weirdo," who has to have things done his way "otherwise I flip." However, this "flipping" is never expressed outwardly; he sulks, boils inside, and seems dejected and withdrawn from interpersonal contacts. On the surface, he presents a submissive, easy-going façade, but he always feels he can do things better. He never expresses this because of his fear that people might see through his tremendous anger. He feels that people who want to be his friend have only one motive, to find out where his vulnerability is so they can take advantage of him. Vinny was extremely preoccupied with money matters, especially where to hide his cash so that no one would know how much he had and steal it. Every few weeks he would check his safe deposit box to make sure his valuables and cash were still there. At the same time, whenever he had to hire someone to do some work on his home or to repair an appliance, he would never ask what it would cost, and would invariably feel after the work was done that he had been "taken." He claimed he was "embarrassed" about asking because that would amount to a "confrontation," which he would lose anyway.

Vinny may be seen as the typical obsessive-compulsive neurotic with phobias and paranoid trends. He certainly presented this syndrome in a rather typical manner, and one could stop here. However, to understand this so called "anal" character, and to help him overcome the misery and waste he was experiencing daily, one must look beyond this configuration of ambivalence and dig under the competitiveness with which he was struggling and the facade of cooperation and placation. It would not be enough to view this case on the basis of Oedipal fear of castration. To be sure, all these themes and their behavioral manifestations were part of his character and daily life; yet it would be naive to assume that his life style began at the anal phase, for that would orient the therapist toward an approach that would be incomplete and wasteful, although the symptoms would no doubt disappear. The question then remains as to how much "personality reconstruction" can indeed be accomplished by realigning energy in the service of the Oedipal metastructure rather than touching meaningfully on the roots of that energy— the oral-dependent base. There is little doubt that an opening up and analysis of the Oedipal as well as the anal must occur before one gets to the oral. The techniques of psychoanalysis are designed to allow for penetration to the oral stage through the Oedipal and anal in order to achieve the ultimate aim of returning to the Oedipal. However, psychoanalytic techniques and strategy get to that stage very slowly and, once there, the techniques do not contain elements helpful in resolving or dealing effectively with the dependency dimension. With confrontation techniques one has a better chance to tackle dependence and anxiety, and their escape routes.

A number of sessions from Vinny's treatment are presented in the following pages. They illustrate how confrontation analysis techniques are used and when they are used (timing). Much of the material, including the therapeutic interventions, resembles traditional psychoanalytically oriented treatment procedures. Comments precede each session in order to point to the deviations and the rationale for them.

Vinny began his treatment on a twice-weekly basis, and about a year later increased the frequency to thrice-weekly for about two years. In the fourth year, the last year of treatment, he went back to twice a week. From the middle of the second year to the end of the fourth year, he used the couch.

Vinny was a rather psychologically unsophisticated patient who needed a great deal of "education." The first few sessions were devoted almost entirely to a discussion of the relevance of talking to me about his symptoms and other feelings, and how they could possibly be useful to him. The idea that psychological problems could be dealt with by psychological means appeared logical to him; however, he did not wholly understand that he had a psychological problem, and he could not see how, if I did not give him the advice that he asked for, I could be of help to him. Because of his pain he was able to continue the contact, and eventually began to orient his thinking about his feelings in a more psychologically meaningful manner. He was also able to relate a great number of his dreams. In the beginning, this was his way of avoiding dealing with his fear of therapy and his relationship to me. Later, however, the dreams became an important reservoir of material that helped him to make organic connections between his inner life, his conscious behavior, and his history.

The first session presented here is the 23rd session, from about the third month into treatment. The work of confrontation had begun almost from the first session. I felt that Vinny would not last in treatment if he were allowed to complain repetitively about his symptoms, rather than being immediately taught to look somewhat introspectively into them. The problem gradually focused on was that of separation anxiety. The material in this session clearly pointed to this problem and to the fact that he kept avoiding it. It was important that the confrontations in the beginning of the therapeutic relationship be of the mirroring type, rather than interpretive ones. In other words, the patient had to learn to face and become responsible at least for the material he himself brought up in the session. For example, my attempt to confront him with his feelings about the death of his grandmother, who was a central love object for him, took the form of mirroring his need to escape to other topics almost as soon as he mentioned her name. I did not, at this point in the treatment, insist on continuing the probe directly, but used a substitute object that Vinny happened to mention in the dream he brought up—his wife. The confrontation, in other words, was continued, although the patient's need to escape it directly was accomodated. The central conflict of the problem of separation was clearly expressed in his fear of his wife taking a job. When faced with the patient's resistance to looking at his dependency problem, the therapist must help the patient open up as many areas of dependency as possible without "embarrassing" him or raising his anxiety within the session to an intolerable level. To do otherwise would only create increased defensiveness. Thus, in this case, the patient admitted in one way or another to his dependence on his wife, his mother, his grandmother, his father, and the therapist. Only at the end of the session did he become sufficiently anxious to need a supportive statement that helped reduce the anxiety so that work could proceed efficiently in the future and without additional disruption of his daily functioning.

Session 23

P: The past week I've been pretty nervous. I don't know what it is or what. I told you about my wife trying to get another job, and I want her to get it but subconsciously I don't want her. I still feel like the old folks, that a woman's place is at home. I am sure you think that I am nuts for thinking like that, but you know it must really be bothering me, because I had a dream last night and I am sure it was about her. I dreamt that I came home, I was looking in the mailbox—it wasn't my house, it didn't look like it anyway—and a little girl came out and she is the landlord's daughter, and she said "What are you doing home, you're going to be all alone, your wife is working." And you know the things that come to my mind are kind of silly things like the fact that we've gotten a lot of letters this week. I like to get letters, even though most of the time they are just bills. We just got a lot of letters from the insurance company because of the accident that my wife had a couple of weeks ago.

T: What about that little girl?

P: She lives downstairs with her mother and father and they are all nuts. I mean the guy is never there, he works for an ocean liner and we hardly see him. His wife always complains to us about him, and she keeps saying she can't stand him anymore. The little girl reminds me of my little cousin, when she was little and I was little, too—we are the same age— we used to play together, and we always played with dolls, and when I was three or four I wanted a baby carriage for the dolls, and my mother finally bought me one when I was four. My cousin always wanted to play with guns and stuff, and come to think of it, it should have been the opposite, shouldn't it? Anyway, that doesn't seem very important now. I guess it's too late.

T: Too late?

P: Yeah, too late. I couldn't change these things even if I wanted to. Except that as I got older, I used to be teased about it, and when I was seven or eight the fellows used to tease me too, and I got very embarrassed.

T: What fellows were these?

P: Well, they were not my friends, but just older friends of the family, and some people in my family used to tease me, too; but I really don't remember specific instances. A couple of years ago we went to my grandmother's and she showed us some pictures from when I was a little kid, and one of the pictures was me and my cousin—I must've been about three—and I was holding a doll in my hands. That picture used to get me embarrassed, but not anymore.

T: When you say "embarrassed" what exactly do you mean?

P: I knew I wasn't supposed to like dolls, that was for girls. I mean I was shy in general, and I still am, you mentioned it to me yourself, I can't look at you while I am talking to you, I feel you're seeing right through me. Maybe I thought I wasn't what a boy is supposed to be, you know, athletic and daredevil. I was always afraid of something or other, and when I was a little kid I was even more overweight than I am now, kind of flabby and a round face. When the kids teased me I would run to my mother and complain about them, but I would go back to the same friends and pretend that nothing happened. I guess I had no choice, because we all lived in the same neighborhood. Anyway, I stayed home many times, but in the summer I had to go out to play on the street because we had no air-conditioning and it was just terrible inside, so hot that even my mother would sit outside on the stoop and bullshit with some of the Italian ladies that she hated. I was always embarrassed if my friends saw me with her together because she was a slob and fat and a loudmouth. I really hate myself when I talk like this about my parents, but I guess I am supposed to tell you what's on my mind, right? Anyway, my mother never changed. The house is always a mess, and whenever we go to visit them I am always fixing things in the house, even straightening things out. I never brought any friends home because of that, I mean not only that, but I was ashamed of my parents. I am not as ashamed of them now as I used to be, and I don't hate them as much as I do my in-laws. They are exactly the opposite of my parents, I mean their house is spotless, and they are really decent people, but I can't stand them. There is something about them that's very phoney.

T: You sound quite angry at a lot of people; today it has something to do with parents, your parents, your wife's parents. What about your grandmother, the one who had those pictures you were just telling me about?

P: (*silence for a while*) I loved my grandmother very much. I really cared for her a lot. She was very good to me, she lived right next door to us, and I visited her very often. She died last year, about two months before I started coming here. Before she died she got very sick, and she couldn't come to my wedding. Sometimes I guess she wasn't that nice because she wanted me to be very strong like the men in the old country. She came from Sicily, you know, and she would tell me stories which made me feel very weak. Anyway, I always wanted to see her, and my father didn't like the idea that I spent more time in her house than with my friends on the street, which he didn't like either.

T: How did you feel when she died?

P: She died the last Monday in October. Actually, I felt very good when she died; not because she died, but because the Thursday before, my wife and I decided to go see her, just to say hello since she wasn't feeling well and we didn't see her much before, and she mentioned to my mother that she forgot what my wife looked like. So we went to see her, and the following Monday she died, and I was glad I saw her just before she died. When I heard she died I was really shocked. (*Silence for about two minutes*) Do you think that this job with my wife is what is making me anxious? I mean, the fact that I don't really want her to get a job?

T: I was wondering about this myself: you were talking about your grandmother and for some reason or other you started discussing your wife and her job. Have you been thinking about your wife while you were telling me about your grandmother?

P: No, when I stopped talking about her, my wife came to my mind, and the dream which reminded me of her, so I assumed that this is really something important. I don't have anything else to say about my grandmother, may she rest in peace.

T: I had the impression you were not so much resting in peace when she died, but that it is very hard for you to discuss that.

P: I think about my grandmother an awful lot. (*tears*) But this was last year, and I keep saying to myself that, after all, she was pretty old when she died and I was lucky to have seen her just before she died. I know it's kind of stupid, but she really was the only one who really cared about me. I mean, she never teased me or anything, and when she reproached me for some stupid thing or other, she knew what she was talking about. I miss her an awful lot, and even my wife isn't as tolerant as my grandmother was.

T: Your grandmother was very important in your life, and yet this is the first time you have talked about her here. Have you thought about her before while you were here?

P: Oh, yeah, many times, but I was afraid you'd think I was a real baby for hanging on to my grandmother. I didn't think you'd understand what this is all about, and besides, I really want to do something about my nervousness, especially on the subways, and I don't want to waste my time talking about my grandmother. She is gone and nothing will bring her back, but my nerves are really a pain in the ass and I can't shake them off. I am terrified right now thinking about how the hell I am going to take the subway home tonight after work.

T: Your grandmother is gone and you're feeling nervous.

P: Yeah!

T: How about that!

P: How about what? (*In a somewhat panicky tone.*) How about what?

T: I said your grandmother dies and you become nervous.

P: Wait a minute, this thing hadn't happened for months after she died. I don't know what you're driving at.

T: Well, what about your dream? Do you remember what the little girl said?

P: She said—wait a minute—she said—whatever it was, it was about my wife, that she had to work. Oh, now I remember—that I will be all alone because she went to work. What has that job got to do with my grandmother? You know something, my wife is right, you guys make something out of nothing. I can't believe that my wife in the dream is like my grandmother. I am sure that if I sneeze here today you're going to say it's because I miss my grandmother. This is really horseshit. You know, I never use these obscene words outside of here, and I think this is the first time ever here. I guess I must be pretty mad.

T: Are you?

P: I feel like a fool because I think that you led me to this, even though my grandmother was the farthest thing from my mind when I came here today.

T: What do you mean "even though"?

P: I meant to say "because." You know something (*laughing*), there is no winning with you, whatever I say has a meaning. I feel here like I feel about my wife's job, if she gets it it's not good, and if she doesn't get it I'll be unhappy. As you said once, "between the devil and the deep blue sea." I just can't see how my grandmother has anything to do with my "phobias," as you call them.

T: Perhaps your grandmother doesn't have much to do with your anxieties.

Dc you feel your wife does? I mean, what makes it so difficult for you if she works while you're at work too?

P: I don't know what it is, but I am afraid that if I get stuck on the subway, or if I can't get out of my office because I am panicked and she is working, who is going to pick me up and take me home? I know I can call my father like I did a couple of weeks ago, but I don't like to do that because he is grumpy and he keeps telling me I should try again and do it on my own, and if I don't succeed, only then to call him back. I mean I know he doesn't like to be inconvenienced. In any case, I know I can count on Anne if she's not working.

T: You can count on her to rescue you!

P: You can call it that. I don't know what I'd do without her, frankly. She doesn't know that, but I do count on her a lot. If she knew how much I depend on her she'd probably leave me and you know, sometimes that's exactly how I feel—why doesn't she leave, I am a pain in the ass for her, always complaining and frightened, and she never complains, even when she gets sick. I mean, when she has a cold or the flu, she just stays home and never complains—she is really wonderful. She wanted us to go to stay at her parent's home for the weekend—they went to Florida for a couple of months—and it's all private and beautiful, and I was afraid to go there because I was afraid I'll get stuck and I'll feel lonely, even though she'll be with me. I don't know what's with me. Everything we plan falls through because of my crazy shit. And I am so impatient with her and with everything. Everything I have to do or she has to do has to be done right away— everything rush, rush, rush. Even when we have sex, it's rushing. I love it, I mean I love to have sex with Anne, but she doesn't like it—she says I hurt her—and I am still rushing as if I have to get it done and on to the next thing, and I really don't have anything to do at all when I get home. In fact I am bored most of the time. But even when we were traveling to the lake in the summer, I was always driving like a maniac, and once we got there, I couldn't sit still for a minute, let alone lie on the beach and enjoy the sun. It's crazy. I am always afraid that I am missing something. Besides, I hate to sit around and watch all the girls, because they irritate me and I think they do it on purpose. I mean they like to tease, they're all whores.

T: Women on the beach who like to tease are whores. That's quite a statement.

P: You know what I mean.

T: Not really.

P: I mean that they pretend they are interested in you and everything, and as soon as you show them you're interested they use it against you. I don't trust any of them.

T: How about Anne?

P: I trust her up to a certain point, but if an attractive man comes along and was really interested in her, I am not sure what could happen. I never dated in high school just because of that, the good-looking fellows always went out and had a good time, and even in college I could hardly get the courage to ask a girl out, and when I did, it was a one-shot deal, and I always sensed that they didn't want to see me again, and later I always saw these girls with attractive men.

T: So women couldn't be trusted?

P: That's exactly how I feel. I don't think that Anne will ever leave me, but there is always a chance that she'll find someone else more interesting than me . . .

T: You mean someone who doesn't have all these anxieties and fears?

P: Maybe. My mother never even thought of leaving my father, even though he was and still is a pain in the neck. I know she can't stand him, but she'll always be there making his goddamn breakfast.

T: That's what you said about your neighbors—that the wife always complains about her husband, but . . .

P: Yeah.

T: That was related to the dream you had with the little girl who reminded you of your cousin and your grandmother.

P: I don't see my grandmother and this woman or my mother as the same at all. I trusted my grandmother very much but these women I don't trust at all.

T: Because they say one thing and act differently?

P: Exactly. How the hell can they crab about their husbands and continue to live with them. Not only this, but I assume they also go to bed with them. They're hypocrites. Maybe that's why I called the girls on the beach "whores."

T: Is that how you feel about Anne, since you say that she doesn't enjoy sex and yet she does it with you, you feel you can't trust her?

P: That may be. I don't know. I mean I am afraid she might say goodbye one day, but I don't believe it. It's just that—well, I don't know what to say, talking about this gets me so nervous, I am shaking just talking about this, and I don't know why (*visibly shaken, sweating, and constantly looking at me and at the floor in rapid eye movements*).

T: You are frightened whenever the subject of a woman leaving you comes up—whether it's the girlfriends from school or your wife or your grandmother.

P: But nobody is doing this now. I know Anne isn't leaving. Nothing is happening now—why am I so frightened? I don't get it. I just don't get it.

T: We have to stop pretty soon, are you worried about leaving here and being so anxious?

P: I guess I am, because I am thinking about the office now and how I am going to get back and face all the people there, and I am sure they'll notice how tense I am. I don't want to take any Valiums today because I had to take two of them yesterday.

T: Perhaps if you could make sure that I'll be here when you come for the next session on Wednesday, you might feel less nervous. I can tell you from my end that I will be here.

P: (*Manages to force a smile.*) O.K., I know you're always here. I hope *I* can get here.

T: See you Wednesday.

The next session presented followed the above session by two weeks. There are several important aspects of the session that must be explored here because they are in many ways rather typical of the way confrontation analysis is conducted.

Dealing with Resistance

It was obvious from the beginning that Vinny had deep ambivalent feelings about treatment and that he was somewhat reluctant to discuss these feelings. However, as he became more comfortable with me, he allowed his conflicts to come closer to the surface through his dream material, especially his need for my approval and, at the same time, his anger at me. Strategically, the confrontational analyst allows the transference to develop to a certain point at the start of treatment, but confronts the patient with his projections as soon as there is enough material to deal with. This strategy is adapted so that the patient can experience the dependence and separation cycle repeatedly during the session. In this manner, an opportunity for looking into the difficulties, expressed mainly in the form of anxiety and defensiveness, is provided. As a consequence, the patient can learn to deal with the problem of separation-anxiety over and over within the immediacy of the session. The patient may also ignore this need to be dependent, but express it with resistance as may be seen in the beginning statement of the following session: "I was really anxious about coming here today. I was just annoyed that I had to come in this shitty weather. I got all wet and I hate to go outside when it's so dreary; it makes me sad." The patient's resistance may also take the form of a conflict expressed in a dream, somewhat closer to the surface, as may be seen in the following session's dream, where Vinny finds another doctor to whom to escape. Of course, there are many ways in which resistance can be expressed and experienced. Having adopted a strategy that deals with the resistance almost as soon as it comes up, the therapist cannot, then, afford the luxury of waiting for the patient's free associations to take over. The therapist must focus directly on the resistance, as in the following session when I asked Vinny to associate to the doctor in the dream before he became lost in other escape material. Later in the session he drew "a blank" when he was talking about going to the doctor, and there, too, I did not wait for him to remember where he left off because of his resistance to focus in on the treatment issue and his feelings about me, which, if not explored immediately, could only serve as a screen to other material, and thus increase the resistance. This is an important departure from normal psychoanalytic strategy and procedure, and its purpose is to help the patient confront infantile needs and inadequate ways of dealing with the anxiety emanating from them.

Analyzing the Confrontation

Vinny was confronted later in the session with his need to deny his anger at me. The consequences of this kind of behavior were also analyzed—his pain (i.e., anxiety, which is directly related to his keeping his feelings to himself out of a fear of retaliation.) During the interaction between us, I kept the focus on the relationship between his denial and his symptomatology, even though there is a risk in this method—i.e., he might draw back into himself or turn the whole process of understanding his symptoms into an intellectual exercise. Neither of these two possibilities occurred, primarily because he had been educated by the confrontation system to explore and reach further into his unconscious when confronted, rather than to regard the confrontation as an attack on his integrity. Well-timed confrontations are not likely to be perceived as attacks, but rather as a challenge to deal with exciting new ways of looking at oneself. The concentration and focus on his anger toward authority was purposeful, and served as a basis for future exploration of the causative factors of certain personality dimensions, such as his submissiveness and cooperativeness.

There is another important and fundamental aspect of the confrontation analysis method: the confrontation and its analysis create a cycle of an interactional gestalt between patient and therapist that has a beginning, a middle, and an end, with which the patient learns to deal and from which he is able to separate. This microcosmic unit adequately represents a person's relationships with others—others who become part of his or her self when they are encountered. When one must be on one's own, one must be able to let go of these others. This is difficult for many people, and this is what confrontational analysis hopes to resolve. The anxiety emanating from separation is thus dealt with in every session in which such confrontations occur. Of course, the session itself is, in some way, a confrontational unit, for the patient comes in for a short while and then must separate. For such a unit or session to be psychologically meaningful as a learning unit, the therapist must become a participating entity in the interactional process and not just a projection screen reflecting only the patient's distortions. This is required so that the patient deals with his internalized "objects" through a live, "animate" object in a socio-structural environment similar to that in which these objects were initially formed in childhood. Otherwise, if the therapist remains "inanimate," the patient is likely to continue to deal with his objects only in fantasy, and the conflicts related to them would also be dealt with only in fantasy. The work of overcoming dependency strivings, for example, becomes then a "deceptive" exercise in self-reassurance that one is indeed independent. The interaction with the therapist helps the patient integrate within the self what is fantasy and history with what is real and present, rather than continuing to superimpose the former on the latter. In the present case, Vinny demonstrated that this process had begun to take place when he spontaneously discussed his childhood history and his present phobias and feelings about me.

Choice of Material on which to Focus

Most patients have an agenda for each session, although they are not always aware of it. The most blatant expression of this is usually a complaint that the patient presents when he walks into the session, saying: "I don't have anything to talk about today." This statement means "I have not consciously prepared an agenda for today!" The hidden agenda, consciously or unconsciously prepared, invariably refers to the need to fend off anxiety stemming from a variety of reasons, and to struggle to keep things in a status quo as much as possible, since change always means separation from the old, an unwelcome venture. The therapist is therefore constantly bombarded by the patient's "prepared" material, which purports to be an effort on the patient's part to discuss topics currently affecting the functioning self and the wish to change his lot in life. Letting the patient go from one theme to another without helping to focus on the essential reason for his work in therapy in the name of "free association" or some other principle (perhaps a rationalization by the therapist or lack of willingness to take the responsibility invested in the job of therapist-helper) is equivalent to asking a prisoner to be his own guard. Every session brings with it many themes. Choosing which theme to focus on must be governed by the following considerations:

1. Whether the theme is expressive of the central issue for which the patient came for treatment.
2. Whether the patient's defensiveness regarding that theme warrants a confrontation with his acting-out behavior at that time.
3. Whether the relationship between the patient and the therapist—the transference and countertransference dimensions—is directly or indirectly related to the chosen theme. Except in emergency cases, priority is given to the theme affecting these dimensions.

There is an abundant choice of themes in the session that follows. The theme of choice, however, is certainly Vinny's feelings about treatment and, more specifically, about me. Relating this choice to the three points made above, it was clear that the central issue for which Vinny sought treatment was not his symptomatology, but naturally the basic conflict that created those symptoms—his fear of separation. His defensive armor had been penetrated sufficiently by the gradually increasing confrontations from the beginning of treatment, as well as by his extreme pain. Confrontation with his acting out—his indecision about the treatment—had to be dealt with. The evidence for his transference to me as a bad mother-object became substantial enough in that session for me to confront him with it and enable him to start dealing with it. I did not choose to focus on the obvious competitive theme in the dream, or the projective rejection (he rejects me and finds another doctor because he feels I reject him), or the anal sadism associated with his operation, or the sexual overtones of his relationship to his mother, or his counterphobic homosexual reaction to his father. These subjects were ignored for the moment not because they were not related to his central conflicts, but because they would be distracting. Focussing on them would take us away from the immediate resistance that he was putting up through introducing these "juicy" subjects.

Session 27

P: I was really anxious about coming here today. I was just annoyed that I had to come in this shitty weather—I got all wet and I hate to go outside when it's so dreary, it makes me sad. If I stay in the office all day I don't have to see what's happening outside. And just before I came, my boss asked me if we could have lunch together, and I had to find an excuse because I manage to come here every Wednesday on my lunch hour without letting anybody notice it. But I still have to put in an extra hour later in the day no matter what. Anyway, I also had a dream last night, and it was about you. I dreamt that I went to a different doctor and I decided that the other doctor was better, so I decided not to come here anymore. I felt very good, and I remember feeling relieved in the dream that I found a doctor and that I could get better faster with him. I remember that before I went to bed I said to myself, "Oh shit, I have to go to the doctor tomorrow and I will have to get home later because I have to work later." I really don't like coming here because nothing happens. I mean, I still feel nervous.

T: Can you tell me more about the doctor in the dream?

P: Well, it was you, I am sure, but it does remind me of the doctor who did the operation on my pylonidal cyst a couple of years ago. This guy didn't care about anything, not that he was mean or anything like that, but he was completely insensitive. I mean, he disregards the fact that he hurts.

I guess he is not feeling any pain, so what does he care. Whenever I had to go to see him for an examination, I never wanted to go with my bowels because it'll be dirty. This was after the operation. Usually, somebody would drive me because I couldn't sit driving for a long time because it would hurt. I always had to change positions. My father drove me most of the time. I couldn't ask any friend because I was ashamed to tell them what I had. I used to get very embarrassed to say that something was wrong with my ass, especially since I was told that the cause for it was something psychological, and I didn't want anybody to think I am crazy. I mean I don't believe this horseshit myself, but I don't want to be teased about it—I mean it hurts. The wound after the operation had to be dressed for a long time because it didn't heal very fast. The doctor said I was nervous and my bowel movement had something to do with it. When I was in the office I tried to go to the bathroom as little as possible, but sometimes I had to go so bad I couldn't wait. And then when I went to be examined I was so embarrassed because I was afraid it'll be dirty. I mean if I went to the bathroom it'll be dirty, and if I didn't go and held it in it'll be dirty. I used to bleed and ooze, and all kind of shit used to come out. Most of the time my mother dressed it for me, and I felt much better that she did it—I couldn't trust my father to do it. I don't know why. As I talk to you about that I am getting all tense and nervous, and when I came in I wasn't so nervous.

T: You were talking about your mother dressing your ass.

P: I felt ashamed. I mean, he gave her all kinds of stuff to put on it and I had to do it. I guess I was ashamed maybe because of modesty. Not really ashamed—I would say uncomfortable—I just felt funny having my mother see me in the nude. Uncomfortable. Anyway, I was more uncomfortable getting undressed for the examination in front of the doctor than in front of my mother. I don't really know why. Maybe because I didn't like him. I never liked him and I never cared for him. I considered him a big bullshit artist, I felt he just didn't know what he was talking about. He is a very wealthy doctor, my whole family was treated by him.

T: Did you have any thoughts about going to see somebody else since you didn't like him?

P: I know it's crazy. In one minute I thought he was no good, but on the other hand I was afraid of going to another doctor. But I think he is very smart and clever.

T: In some way you felt you had to go to him.

P: Right! I just felt I had no choice. Anybody in the family swears by him. I'd be skeptical of going to anybody else. But after the wound sort of healed I never went to him again. I used to see him before the operation, when I was still in college, and it was about the same condition. For a long time, he kept telling me that there was something wrong with me, and I kept complaining, and finally he told me that I had that cyst, and he said the only thing he could do is to take it out. And the reason I didn't like him was because he used to tell me what's wrong with me before he examined me. I mean, I wasn't a kid at the time—I think I was 21 or 22. He is just like so many other doctors I hear about—they don't want to bother to even look at you, they give the prescription and send you home, and then you have to come back and they charge you an arm and a leg for each visit. Until now I still have pain and it didn't go away completely; it's now the same as it was before the operation, but I don't understand why I still have the pain: I take a bath every morning because I am worried that I have cancer, and I have thoughts of cancer all the time. And a nurse who is a friend of Anne told me it's better not to operate, so I don't really know what's what.

T: I am wondering after having that dream about finding another doctor, and then talking about your operation, whether you are not talking about me.

P: Well, I told you I didn't really like to come here.

T: Yes, you did. But perhaps all these angry feelings about the other doctor are feelings you have also about me.

P: I am not angry at you at all. You can't force me to be here and if I didn't really want to be here I don't think I'd be here. Well, you might say that my nervousness forces me to be here, but that has nothing to do with you. I think you do try to help me, but I can't see how you are, because I am still going bananas in the subway. Now, you see, I get pissed because I had to admit that I need help. I know that's crazy—I mean I am here just for that—but just saying it makes me feel like a jerk, like what's wrong with me, why can't I cut this shit out and not be nervous and have to come here. And I think that you must sit there and look at me like I am crazy to spend my money on doctors for nothing. Yesterday when I was on the train, I remembered—I think I was five or six at the time—my parents were taking me to the doctor. How come I remember this so clearly and I don't remember things that happened later, when I was a teenager? Don't they say that if you don't remember, that means you don't want to? I think I got this in a psychology course in college. I forgot what I wanted to say, that's exactly what happens to me a lot at work—I want to do something, and as I am going to do it, I get distracted, and I can't remember what it was—it drives me nuts. I am completely blank.

T: You were telling me that you were going with your parents to the doctor, when you were five or six.

P: Oh yeah. I was thinking about that in the subway. There was something wrong with my penis. I remember I ran out of the office and they had to bring me back and they forced me on the table, and I was screaming and hollering like a maniac, and he had to put a piece of wire in my penis— long wire. When I went to the bathroom at night it hurt like hell. I don't know what he did, but it was awful. I never liked doctors. I guess most people don't, especially when you're young.

T: This is the second doctor you're telling me about today, and he hurt you too. When I asked if you felt the same way about me—that is, if you were angry with me because I haven't cured your anxieties—you said you weren't angry with me.

P: I am not angry with you. Maybe I resent the fact that I have been coming here for more than three months and I am still sick.

T: You resent the fact?

P: Yeah, I resent the fact.

T: That fact happens to involve you and me.

P: Yeah, it does—so what? Just because I dreamt about another doctor doesn't mean that I am angry with you.

T: Perhaps not. But there is good evidence that you are reluctant to talk to me sometimes about all kinds of things for some reason or another.

P: I get embarrassed to tell you things that are embarrassing, and I resent the fact that you tell me that I have to tell everything that comes to my mind. Sometimes I feel guilty about things I don't tell you, and when I leave here I want to kick myself in the ass for doing this, but I still can't tell you when I am here.

T: So you do have some resentment toward me.

P: I guess so.

T: You guess so?

P: What do you want me to say—that I hate you? Well, I don't. I am angry that you're not helping me enough.

T: Just like the other doctors. But you see, it is very hard for you to tell me directly how you feel. Before, when I mentioned the possibility of your being angry at me, you rejected that immediately.

P: I felt very uncomfortable and trapped. I mean, I felt you knew what was going on, what I was thinking. I swear to God, sometimes I am sure that you see exactly what's going on inside of me, and I get extremely nervous about it. So I guess when you actually tell me something I am afraid of, I have to deny it.

T: You are afraid of being angry at me, so when you are, you prefer to keep it inside.

P: I always do that. I never tell anybody I am angry, except sometimes I explode with Anne, and sometimes with my mother.

T: And today you walk in here being angry for being here, and then you had a dream about replacing me, and you still felt you had to deny your feelings. That must create a lot of pain from keeping all that stuff inside.

P: You said it! I feel I am on the verge of exploding all the time—I shake and I sweat and there isn't one moment I don't feel something bad, even when I am happy. I just can't relax. But I don't like to have enemies. There's this girl at work—she annoys the hell out of me—she's not a girl, a woman, older than me. The other day she really got to me, and I told her off. I shouldn't talk like this to an older woman, but I was in a rage. I was ready to swing at her, but I would never do that. I like the other woman in the office. She's not catty like this one, and she's not always looking for someone to pick on—like my boss, she's always picking on him and talking about him behind his back—it's disgusting. I get so angry about these things. But my boss is a jerk too, because he lets her do that. You think I let people step over me, you should see him—he'll practically do anything for anybody who raises his voice to him. I get along with him—I mean, I don't fight with him at all—but sometimes he's a pain because he doesn't stand up to his boss, and I have to do work that's just busy work and doesn't accomplish anything.

T: And you mean it's hard for you to tell him what you feel, even though he's a pushover?

P: He is not a pushover, but even with him I get all sweaty and anxious when I have to talk to him about some things that are not social—I mean, when it's business and I have to show him something that I did, I am always afraid he won't like it, and I keep saying to myself I shouldn't be frightened of this jerk, but I am, and I get angry at myself for being like that.

T: Keeping all this anger inside is really something isn't it?

P: I don't know what I can do. I mean, I can't go around screaming at everybody.

T: You'd be screaming at everybody if you were allowed?

P: Everybody! I walk around angry all the time, and I mean all the time. Saturday night was the perfect example. There is this couple that we go out with sometimes, and the guy—his name is Frank, we used to be good friends—everytime we go out he mentions his cousin Viola that I used to go out with before I got married. First of all, her family and mine are completely different—I could never get as close to her as my wife, but I keep thinking about her, especially when he brings her up in the conversation. And he keeps telling how Viola was so disappointed that we didn't get married, and the fact that I didn't give her a chance and I got married so fast. She was the type of girl who felt she knew everything and had expensive taste, and I felt like sending her to the moon sometimes. Her grandparents had a lot do with us not getting married; they told my parents that Viola is an expensive girl, and that she is not too reliable, and they didn't want to see me hurt, so my parents talked me out of it. At least part of my decision had to do with that, but frankly I was afraid that she'd leave me after she finds out what I am and who I am. She was a very beautiful girl and she worked as a model for Clairol, so I wasn't so sure I could keep her. But still, if we got married we would be close to the city, probably live in the city, and we'd be close to my family and it would be easy for me to get to the office—that's all I think about.

T: It sounds to me like you're feeling you have lost in this battle too!

P: What do you mean?

T: Your parents prevented you from getting what you wanted—Viola . . .

P: I don't know if I would have married her even if my parents didn't object to it.

T: Well, I sense that you're angry at your parents because of that, and yet you are not quite so sure that you have the right to feel this way.

P: You mean I am doing what I did before? That I can't say I am angry? What good will it do anyway? Besides, my parents were not holding me down by force and ordering me not to marry Viola.

T: Perhaps you do feel that you are imprisoned and you have no choice but submit to the fate—your parents or anybody else's wishes, since you don't feel you can get out, just like when you were little on the doctor's table. I find it interesting that you used the same words, about your parents holding you by force when you had trouble with your penis, and when you were considering marrying Viola. Anybody who feels held down by some outside force must get very frustrated and anxious.

P: That reminds me of the subway—it's like a cage with animals stuck in it, except that in the subway it's people, especially when we go through a tunnel—that's exactly how I feel, anxious and like held down by force, and I want to break out, like I am in jail and someone is choking me. I once had a fleeting image—I don't think I told you about it—while we were having sex, when we had just gotten married, that I was in a cage and Anne is looking from the outside laughing hysterically to herself and saying "now I got you, I trapped you." She is happy because she got me doing whatever she wants to. I think I felt so trapped in bed that I started to pump really hard and I hurt her. This is the first time I've thought about it this way.

T: You mean that you got angry and expressed it sexually?

P: Yeah, but I was enjoying myself then—I wasn't angry at all.

T: You were not aware that you were angry.

P: Not at all, but I guess I was—I don't guess—I was. Now I realize that. What a funny thing, or not so funny. God! This hour seems endless.

T: Are you feeling anxious now that you know that you get angry sometimes and that I know about it, so you want to run away, you want to leave here?

P: I just feel drained. I am not anxious at all now, not nervous, and I feel I just want to get back to work and go home later, and I hope the train doesn't get stuck, especially in the tunnel. I like to have the guarantee that everything is going to turn out O.K., I guess. My father told me when I started getting sick that he used to have these same feelings, that he used to get anxious on the train, but he never thought that he would faint. I am always afraid I'll faint or something. Do you think that can happen because I hold my feelings down?

T: I have no doubt that this way of reacting, not expressing how you feel when you feel it, contributes a lot to the choking feelings you have. Well, we do have to stop here.

P: See you.

The next session presented is from the tenth month of therapy. Vinny had gotten over his symptoms in large measure, although his anxiety attacks did not completely abate. From time to time, he was overwhelmed by his anxiety, and needed to rely on his father or wife to get him to work or from it. On the whole, however, he felt fairly successful in controlling his phobias, although other symptomatology began to emerge— mainly paranoid ideation related to work and therapy, as well as complaints about his wife's discontent with his family and her fears about having children. He also began to think of branching out into business on his own. His feelings about himself as an inadequte, inexperienced, immature, and rigid person began to haunt him during the sessions, and compensatory fantasies and dreams about heroism and masculinity became abundant. His inner life, in general, became richer and deeper. Yet his outlook on the nature of life itself remained somewhat limited by his need to remain enclosed within his impoverished social and familial territory.

Confrontation analysis may imply a continuous barrage of attacks on the patient's defensive system. In this typical session, it is quite clear that the confrontations are presented in the form of probes, interpretations, comments, mirroring, and clarifications. There is neither threat nor any implied threat in the therapist's communications, although the patient may experience them as threats. The important point here is, of course, that the therapist must not feel intimidated by the patient's possible paranoid interpretation of his comments. To do so would be to play into the hands of the patient's resistance, which in such a case would manifest itself in the form of an attack on the therapist's integrity or adequacy. Patients often use this tactic in order to shift the area of responsibility for change from them to the therapist. "Joining the defense," as it were, can be done in relatively few and selected cases—mostly of psychotic symptomatology. Later in this volume, the *join-the-defense* strategy is described and illustrated with clinical case material.

The activity of the therapist depends exclusively on the nature of what transpires during the session, not on the system of confrontation analysis as such. Interventions are made, as evidenced in this session, only when necessary to advance the cause of the treatment goals, not as an exercise in verbal interchange. However, one must stress that while the session belongs to the patient, the treatment process belongs to both patient and therapist, and therefore, the latter must use the right to intervene whenever it is feasible to help the patient move forward, even when that means lengthy verbal output on the part of the therapist.

A case in point is that of a young woman who was referred to me because of her persistent sulkiness and silence both in the college classroom and socially. Her silence during the session was deafening. Even though she expressed a desire to be in therapy, she was unable to talk about her feelings. Her silence was caused by at least two important factors—one present, the other past. The present reason for her silence was her extreme anger and frustration at not being accepted on her terms by her friends—they did not want to be with her most of the time because of her "snobbism." The second reason (which I later gathered from her) was that she had grown up in a home where "talk was unheard of." People didn't communicate verbally with each other, except in unusual circumstances. This pattern existed not because family members disliked one another or were angry at each other, but because this was the accepted style within the family.

At first I did not know what I could do with this patient, and telling her that I could not treat her if she did not talk was not too helpful to her. She told me that she liked to hear my voice and the way I expressed my thoughts, and begged me not to dismiss her, saying that she would eventually learn to talk to me. I agreed to this procedure. I talked most of the time, primarily about her symptoms, her family, the possible problems she might develop, and the possible reasons for her problems. Eventually, I purposefully so exaggerated in my hypothetical assumptions and interpretations about her life that she felt compelled to correct me from time to time, until she felt comfortable enough to tell me her version of things. We arrived at a point where she could get quite angry at me for wasting her time with my discourses on life, and when I protested that at least one of us should be talking, she would say angrily: "Alright already! I know what you're doing. Sometimes you really go too far." I silently agreed with that statement, but did not let up until I was certain she was out of danger of becoming a recluse again. The confrontation in this case, was with her silence. The technique used, although seemingly affrontative, served to mobilize the patient's energy to separate from a family trait, which symbolized her total dependence on the family as an object of support, familiarity, and approval. My activity was thus dictated by the goal of the treatment—separation of the patient from a self-destructive pattern of communication. This meant an "inordinate" amount of talk on my part.

The use of analogies, examples, stories, and sarcasm are important ingredients of the confrontational analyst's armamentarium in dealing with a variety of patients. The more concrete and perceivable the introjected objects are to the patient, the easier it is for the patient to make emotional contact with them on a conscious level, and thus deal with them effectively. Consequently, the use of these techniques is helpful in achieving these goals. The sole use of psychological abstractions such as interpretive, probing, or communicative tools only helps the patient become further removed from his feelings. Analogies that involve concrete objects and real life experiences are preferable because they may be more easily incorporated as jogging the patient's emotionally tinged memories and thus serve as a projective screen for experiencing various feelings in the present, and as associative media for past objects. In the next session, presented from Vinny's case, the cops and robbers analogy was used purposefully to illustrate to the patient the confusion in ego boundaries between himself and his mother (or other dependency objects).

The idea that symptoms are pleasurable in the form of secondary gains, is generally quite difficult for a patient to accept easily. Before presenting this idea to the patient, one must establish the connections between the secondary gains and the symptoms. The connecting tissue is indeed the meat of the therapeutic efforts. In the present case, the patient had to become aware, first of all, of his symptoms—anxiety and phobias. Second, he had to recognize his dependence on others and the behavior that kept him dependent. Third, he had to admit that his behavior was designed to produce attention or approval from others. Fourth, he had to understand how such behavior prevented him from experiencing himself as a free agent, thus producing anxiety. Holding on to the symptom then becomes quite clearly a choice for both pleasure and pain. At the appropriate time, the therapist must confront the patient with this issue, and then work it through over and over in its many expressions and throughout many sessions. In the session that follows, this idea of secondary gains was introduced by a confrontational statement that the patient did not deny ("Someplace inside you would have to be a baby"), and he had to deal with it in the reality of the transferential situation. Once the patient accepts that this is indeed what he does, he then has to be confronted with his responsibility for working it out and not returning to the previous state of waiting for others to do it for him (Wheelis, 1973).

Finally, when the patient's symptoms abate, the confrontational analyst does not need to add reassurance and support at the end of the session in order to sustain the optimal level of anxiety for the patient to conduct daily life, as was necessary in the beginning of treatment in this case of severe phobia. Rather, the patient is sometimes *challenged* toward the end of the session, so that psychological energy can be mobilized to work on problems in a primarily unconscious fashion while the patient is away from the therapist's office. In this session, the patient was challenged about the antagonistic and contrary behavior designed to continue the myth of his independence. His answer, facetious as it may have been, that he "pretends" to be independent, was only the beginning of his awareness that much work needed to be done for him to *be independent* rather than just have the illusion of being independent, in the form of *feeling independent*. There is a great deal of difference between feeling and being, and confrontation analysis sharply makes this distinction. There are many so-called therapies that emphasize the importance of feeling a certain way without insisting that such feelings be based on the realities of the specific person's life situation.

Session 75

P: Last week, when I left here I remembered that I had some questions to ask you; but as the session went on, I forgot them, and then what we talked about was really bothering me the whole day. You said to me that I blamed getting sick on my getting married. I never felt like that, but I know that I was very nervous about leaving home and going to live on my own. I never had that experience, except for a couple of months in the Reserves, and I hated it. I just couldn't stand it. Anyway, I remembered on Friday after the session that the same thing happened to me when I went to that farm. When I was 15 my parents sent me to spend the summer someplace upstate with a farmer and his family. I'll never forget that house—it was so dreary and depressing, especially in the evening. Well, I couldn't take it for more than a week. I called my parents and asked them to bring me back home, and my father pleaded with me to try another week, but I was so anxious that I couldn't, so they had to come all the way up to pick me up and I felt terrible, I really felt lonely there, but I never thought that I got nervous because I was away from home but because the place itself was for the dogs. After what you told me Friday, this came to my mind, and maybe it's true, but I don't think that marrying Anne was the same thing, because I was going to be with someone and not all alone; up there on the farm they hardly talked to me or even to each other. But Friday night I went to bed thinking about the session, and I had a dream—a very long dream, which I remember only part of it: You told me that the problem we are discussing here is going to take a long time to analyze, so you gave me the name of another doctor, and it turned out to be a female doctor. And I went to see her, and I saw her name on a nameplate, and it said Dr. Famely. She told me that if I didn't pay attention to her and didn't talk to her, I wasn't going to get better. But actually she talked all the time, and she gave me a prescription for cocoanut juice to drink whenever I got nervous. I wanted to tell her that I didn't want to get fat, but she folded the prescription and stuck it in my shirt, which for some crazy reason looked like my pajamas. You know, the first thing that came to my mind about this dream was the fact that you sent me to a woman and you didn't even tell me about it. I was so shocked that I was standing there with my mouth open, and I didn't know whether I should sit down on the chair or lie down on the couch, so I just stood there like a little five-year-old. The office looked very small, almost like a bathroom with a big tub in it. But there was something very nice about it, even though I was shocked. I was thinking right now, maybe the dream is telling me something—maybe I should stop coming here because my anxieties and fears about the subways and other things have almost gone completely, or maybe you are really tired of me coming her every time and telling you these crazy dreams and wasting my time, maybe you'll never tell me to leave here because you make money off of me this way. What I don't understand is how come you asked me last week if I wanted to come three times a week now that I feel better, if not for making more money. (*About 4 minutes of silence.*) This is just crazy. I don't say anything because I don't have anything on my mind. What the hell shall I talk about? That silence for a while was driving me nuts. I was looking for something to say but couldn't really think of anything worthwhile.

T: What were you thinking about?

P: I just felt that you were examining me and looking at me, and I got very embarrassed, and it reminded me of when I was in school and the teacher would ask a question, and I never raised my hand because everybody would be looking at me and I hate to be the center of attention—like when Anne and I go to some club and the band starts playing, I never go on the dancing floor unless there were plenty of other people dancing, and Anne thinks I am crazy to be ashamed of being the first on the floor. She doesn't mind kissing me in public, and I am always very shy about that because my mother did that a lot and she still does it, and I hate it; I feel the whole world is looking at me, as if I am some kind of a baby or something like that.

T: I had the impression that you do think of yourself as a baby.

P: I feel that coming here must mean just that, and the fact that I am so shy everywhere and with everybody; it's like I never grew up. It's pathetic. Many times I just want to crawl into someplace and never come out. I get so mad at people who have a lot of money, because they don't have to worry about anything, they don't have to depend on anybody, and I have to be nice to my boss and to my wife and to my friends. You know, the other day on the bus, a big fat lady came up and stood right next to me and stepped on my toe, and it hurt a lot, and what do you think I did? I just moved to the side and said absolutely nothing, nothing whatsoever. I would have liked to punch her right in the nose, but she looked like a bitch, and on top of that she was black—so you can imagine what would have happened if I said anything. She probably had a knife with her. I really think that way many times about black people. I know I am prejudiced, but goddamn it, I was discriminated against too because I am Italian, and some of my Wasp friends, they used to bother the hell out of me just because of my background.

T: Do you think your fear on the bus had something to do with your feeling about being a baby?

P: Definitely. I mean, I am always afraid as if people are going to trample on me and not see me at all, as if I was an invisible little nothing.

T: You feel like a nothing!

P: Most of the time, even when I am not anxious. But this has nothing to do with my fears. I always felt that way. I don't ever remember a moment in my life when I felt really important. Maybe when I was very little and my mother made a big fuss over me—I don't even remember that. My father, forget it! He would die before he'd say anything nice about anybody! I never had a good word from him.

T: In the dream I was sending you to another doctor, so you must have felt that I think of you as nothing too!

P: I don't think you really care about me. You've got your own family to take care of, so why should you worry about me?

T: Should I?

P: I am not saying you should worry about me or think about me all the time, but I bet once I leave this office you are happy because I am not doing as well as you want me to. I don't really know what you want me to do, but I feel that you're dissatisfied with me, and I feel that you disapprove.

T: How do you know that?

P: Just from the questions you ask and the way you ask them—as if I am doing something wrong when I don't know the answer.

T: You mean like your father who is never satisfied with anybody?

P: Exactly! You know, I didn't want to mention this to you, but a couple of months ago, you had a cold and you were coughing a bit, maybe two or three times, but that was just like my father. He used to drive me crazy with his cough, every morning and evening he would be clearing his throat—it drove me up the wall. I was so angry when you did that, but I couldn't tell you. Maybe I can't tell you because on the surface you are really trying to help me and you never said anything against me, so I feel guilty about getting mad at you. But sometimes you say some things to me that irritate the hell out of me, like you throw things from out of left field and I am left with my drawers down.

T: You mean I expose things you don't want to be aware of—like you don't care to know how I feel about you, but you keep telling me what *you think* I feel about you. I guess this is your way of shutting me out!

P: I am afraid to know what you *really* feel about me. I mean, I am sure you wouldn't choose me as one of your friends. I am probably too straight for you. You strike me as one who doesn't care about anything—I don't mean your family, but that you don't have to conform to anything, and I guess I get that from the way you come across. You dress casual and you have a beard like the beatniks, and I wouldn't be surprised if you grew your hair long, down to your shoulders. People like that frighten me—they are too free. I was thinking the other day that maybe it'd be nice to grow a beard or at least a moustache, but I was sure you'd think that I was doing that to imitate you, and that burns me up!

T: What burns you up?

P: Every time I think of doing something, since I started therapy, I have to think of whether you'd approve of it or not—it's just automatic. I mean, the other day I went to buy a turtleneck, and I saw one that I liked, but then I recalled that you had one just like that, or at least the same color.

I didn't buy it. It's really crazy. You tell me I am dependent and that I should become more independent, and I think I am becoming more dependent on you. I heard that this happens a lot, and I figured that you really want me to become more dependent on you and come here forever, and I am afraid sometimes that maybe you're using techniques on me that make me come here like the dope addicts, and when I become so dependent on you, then you'd really take advantage of me. I am ashamed to tell you all this, but I really have these thoughts sometimes. It's just like it was in the dream with that Dr. Famely. She was telling me she wants me to get better, but she wasn't letting me talk and she gave me the cocoanut juice, which to me seemed like giving a drug to be dependent on her.

T: That's a very interesting interpretation of that dream. What comes to your mind about Dr. Famely? Is that a familiar name to you?

P: (*laughing*) Dr. Famely is kind of a funny name. What came to my mind while I was talking before was that Famely had something to do with maybe "family," maybe it had to do with my family, and we have been talking a lot about them here, and now I keep thinking about my relationship to them a whole lot.

T: Dr. Famely was giving a prescription which was going to make you more dependent on her—could that be your "family"?

P: You mean that I am dependent on my family or on my mother?

T: Well you made the doctor in the dream a woman who was interested in herself rather than in you, wasn't that how you described your mother?

P: Yeah, but I'd never think of my mother as a doctor, never. She is such a slob, I had to come from school sometimes and clean up the house or do the laundry. I mean, I don't really think she can be that woman in the dream, although that doctor was fat just like my mother.

T: You don't like to admit that you like your mother to take care of you, and you turn things upside down so you won't feel guilty. I mean, that you say that your mother—or that doctor in the dream—was trying to hold on to you, when in fact you are the one who gets these anxiety attacks and demand that someone—whether it's the doctor in the dream or myself—do something about it. It's like when a cop is running after a robber in a circle—it's hard to know, from a distance, who is running after whom.

P: That whole dream comes back to me now, and it really scares me. I am thinking that if you're right, I mean maybe you're right, maybe I just want to be a baby and I don't want to get better, and I want somebody to take care of me. So maybe that's why I haven't gotten rid of my anxieties and fears completely, and I am still scared to go on the subways even though I go to work on them every day. When I feel good and not nervous, I am afraid to tell you about it because I feel as if I am bragging or boasting, and I felt the same way when I used to come home and brag to my mother about a good grade that I got in school, and I feel that you're not interested in this anyway.

T: So if I am not interested in your changing, your getting over these feelings, why should you do it?

P: That's kind of stupid, but many times I feel like that in the office—if my boss isn't going to see the work I do, I don't do it as well as I can sometimes—but here it's plain stupid. Do you think I do that?

T: Since you felt your mother wasn't interested in what you do, you feel the same way about me, and perhaps since you reacted to her by being such a nice boy, you like to be a "nice" boy here. I mean, you like to keep depending on me as if I am your mother.

P: I know you're being sarcastic, but it's true that I like to please you many times and, I mean, since you never say anything to me that's encouraging, I try harder. Maybe I am less nervous now to please you.

T: You are a good patient!

P: I do feel frightened that if I don't do what I think you want me to do, you'll throw me out of here and I wouldn't know what to do then. When I went to that farm for the summer, I really felt so crummy, I felt so abandoned, I cried every night in my room until my parents came for me. I would feel the same way if you told me to leave, even though I feel that you're a fraud and that you don't really care. I have no other place to go. I have to make a confession now, and that is that almost every time you tell me something I feel like I want to reject what you tell me just to be spiteful, because I hate it when anybody tells me anything—I always want to feel I am better than the guy next to me, or that I am richer, or have a more beautiful wife. I am always jealous, and when you tell me that I am dependent, it bothers me and I want to say "fuck you!" But I am just not that kind of person anyway.

T: What kind of person?

P: The kind of person who says "fuck you" to anybody.

T: But you feel like saying it most of the time when you are angry?

P: Yeah! But I always think that this is something that the street fellows are like. The kind of mouth these guys have—I remember on our block, there were three fellows, all Italian, and they used to curse like nobody's business. They were funny, but they were always in trouble with everybody, including their parents, who beat the shit out of them—but they weren't scared of anyone! I really envied them! My father used to tell me that I'd turn out like them if I didn't behave or something, and when I see people like that I feel embarrassed for them.

T: Expressing how you feel is bad, especially if you are angry.

P: I got that not only at home, but also in school. I mean, in Catholic school they drummed this thing all the time in our heads. No matter what you did you were bad—even if you just thought something bad, you will go to hell. I feel like a traitor telling you even this, it's like I am telling on the priests and the Church. But I know they're all phoney, I know so many stories about them you wouldn't believe it. We had to do everything just right when they were around in Sunday school and in church.

T: So you feel as if you are in jail and you will be punished if you try to do what you want to do. The guards won't let you!

P: That's exactly how I feel. On the subway, when I get good and anxious, I feel like I want to scream so loud "get me out of here!" but I control myself, because if I don't they'll put me in Bellevue.

T: You know, I have the feeling that you're pulling my leg, I mean, that you somehow enjoy all this attention from the people around you, even though you complain about your anxieties bitterly. Someplace inside you would love to be a baby.

P: I am afraid of that. I don't want to be, but I am afraid that inside that's all I am, just a baby.

T: So perhaps when you come here, you expect me to take care of you—to make you feel better.

P: Isn't that why I am here? I mean, isn't that why people go to doctors, so that they take care of them and make them feel better?

T: I am sure that's why a lot of people go to doctors. I thought you were here to try to solve some of the mysteries which make you feel anxious.

P: I wouldn't mind solving my problems, if you say these are my problems.

T: If I say these are your problems?

P: I know that I have problems, that I am dependent on people; but when I am really anxious, all I want is for someone to get me out of it.

T: Perhaps that's how you feel about therapy—that you want to get out of it but you can't!

P: I wish I could get out right now, but I know I can't. I do feel like I am very dependent on coming here, and I am afraid to leave it.

T: Just like your family? That you are so dependent on your parents that you need their approval constantly?

P: I don't think I feel like that always, but many times—yes! Just like here. I am always anxious to please you, even thought I get very angry with you sometimes, because I don't really think that you give a shit! You have your other patients, so if I go you'll get someone else. And, you know, sometimes I say to myself that just because you might want me to leave here, I'll stay longer. That's what I do now with a lot of things—for example, when we go to my in-laws my mother-in-law wants me to eat a lot to prove to Anne that her cooking is great, and I don't eat much on purpose, because I hate her. I hate the both of them, because they are real snobs. They didn't want Anne to marry me for some reason or another. But that's exactly what I mean. Sometimes I feel like doing the opposite of what the other person wants me to do.

T: To feel independent or to be independent!

P: I guess to pretend that I am independent!

The last session in Vinny's case history to be presented here took place when Vinny had been in treatment for about two years. This was the first session after a five-week summer vacation taken by the therapist. Having come back from a "successful" vacation, Vinny appeared quite resistant to going back to therapeutic work. This resistance may be understood on different levels. It is extremely important that such a session become a model for what is to be expected in the future, so that the patient is provided with a continuity from the past—a therapeutic attitude; however, this must be done quite delicately. Vinny wanted to turn this session into a social one; however, without making any interpretive statement, I attempted to help him focus on his feelings, without taking away from his need to share with me something about his vacation. I was also quite purposefully pleased that Vinny had "fun" on his vacation, and I attempted to help him integrate this positive experience in an accepting atmosphere.

The therapist must always remember that all positive feelings that the patient expresses must be accepted, and interpreted or confronted only for purposes of understanding, without predicting that they are only temporary and therefore not valid. In this session, when Vinny asked me again to get away from himself, whether I had ever been in the place he visited, I did not hesitate to answer him immediately without feeling the need to clarify, at that point, his motivation for the question. It was important to find out what his psychological state was, without getting embroiled in his animosity toward me. The transferential aspects of the communications in the beginning of this session were sure to surface later when they could be dealt with more meaningfully, and without removing the human aspects of the interaction.

As the session progressed, the work of the confrontation continued on several levels, and it was related to his feelings and relationship with a number of people, mostly his mother, his wife, and myself. He was "called" on a number of subjects: his ambivalence about the treatment, his secondary gains from his symptoms, his logical and emotional inconsistencies. Since the patient's relationship with me had all the ingredients of what might be called a working alliance, we were able to get involved in the therapeutic confrontations as soon as the occasion afforded it. The patient felt he could not get away with unchallenged resistance, although he tried to put the responsibility on me when he exclaimed "you're back to your true form," meaning that I wouldn't let him escape without a confrontation. The main focus of the session was, however, the transference expressed in his dependence on me as I became a mother figure whom he split into a bad, ungiving object ("How can you sit there and not say anything") and a good nurturing one ("Wouldn't it be nice if one could carry their analyst in their pocket").

Vinny needed to be encouraged to associate to childhood material, because he often could not do it on his own without some hint or word that would give him the starting point. For this reason, I used a word children are quite familiar with, and to whom it has generally a great deal of significance because it represents many things. The word is *lunchbox*. When Vinny heard this word, the conflicts related to dependence on his mother were aroused again, and his difficulty in doing what he perceived as beneficial to himself without his mother's approval surfaced.

Confrontational analysis uses this technique to communicate with the patient's repressed material so that it forces a confrontation between the various ego forces. In this manner, the patient must cooperate with the therapist to find solutions to the struggle instead of continuing to repress it. Thus the therapist's allusion to childhood material is often extremely helpful, and such material does not have to be first brought up by the patient.

Session 210

P: Did you have a nice summer?

T: Yes, I did. Very nice. What about you?

P: Well, we did go to Cape Cod for about five days. Anne drove to Hyannis, and then I drove to Provincetown. You know, I am embarrassed to say this—I guess, because I haven't seen you for at least a month—that I didn't think of you when you were gone. Once you went, it didn't bother me. Before you left I was very worried, as you might remember; but once you left I really didn't think much about you. Not that everything was terrific. The first week was murder—my parents were away every day. They went to the beach, and I couldn't reach them by phone during the day at all, and Anne was at the pool and you were in Europe. And all that happened suddenly, and I really was up shit's creek. I got very nervous, I mean nervous. But after a couple of days, I amazed myself—it was alright. I calmed down, and then the last week, when we went to the Cape, I really amazed myself.

T: How so?

P: Just by going there and not getting as nervous as I thought I would be.

T: Sounds like you had fun, too!

P: Yeah! I really had fun. The place was terrific and the weather was gorgeous, even though it was hot and a bit muggy. But I also did all kinds of things which I would never have dared to do before, even before I got sick with my nerves. We went swimming at night in Narragansstt Bay; it was very nice. Were you ever there?

T: No.

P: I got to reading something that made me anxious a little, but it was also good, because we were able to discuss some things out in the open which we couldn't before. Anne was reading this book—*Boys and Girls Together*—and I read some of it too, and we talked a lot about homosexuality and sex, and I really felt very good about it, even though I am always frightened that I may be a homosexual. Whenever I am on the train, I always look at the boys not the girls, and I always look first at their zippers to see if they have a big prick or not; not that I have a small one, but you know that I come always as soon as I go in, and I always think that other men are better than me, so I try to compare myself with them. And sometimes I think about what it would be like to have something going with a man; not that I would enjoy it, but just curious what it would feel like. When we were at the Cape I wanted to have sex every night and even in the morning sometimes, and we did have a lot of it, and I started to enjoy it, but I still feel I have got some problems with it, because Anne says I am not romantic, even though I like to cuddle a lot. She doesn't go for that. She asked a lot of questions about you when we were on vacation, and I realized that I really didn't know anything about you, and I was even reluctant to describe you to her in a nice way, because she is very attracted to men with beards and with titles, and I was afraid she'd fall in love with you (*laughter*). As a matter of fact, I had many thoughts about something happening to you in Europe or on the way back with the plane, but this was only once or twice. I know what all this means, that

I am jealous of you and that I would like you to die, God forbid—but I really don't feel like that. As a matter of fact, I got better in so many things since I started coming here that sometimes I feel grateful, and I get mad at myself that I can't say this to you. I am afraid you'll get a big head (*laughs*), or should I say an even bigger one!

T: Have you had any other thoughts about me during my absence?

P: No, except when I was coming here today. I was kind of excited about coming back, but I was also thinking, gee, how long is it going to be before I'll be able to go on a train or on a plane, like you, to Europe, without having any twinges of fear and worry that the train might stop and I'd get anxious. It hasn't happened in a long time, but I still worry a little bit.

T: You feel that as soon as your anxiety about travelling goes away completely, you won't have to come here.

P: I know I have other problems. I mean, even today I mentioned at least one other problem, and I know that I won't be through, but that is why I came here, because of my fears about being stuck on the train.

T: That's true. I have the impression, nevertheless, that you've gotten used to coming here, and maybe you're keeping some of the anxiety around so that you can justify to yourself your need to come here.

P: You're back to your true form! Do you really believe that I enjoy this anxiety that comes over me to such a degree that I bring it on myself? That's really absurd! Anyway, I don't have that anxiety anymore, except for very little. I can live with it, and when you were away I didn't miss coming here at all. I can't say I am not glad you're back.

T: You really like to cover yourself from all sides, don't you?

P: What do you mean?

T: First you say you don't miss me, then you're glad I am back.

P: Well, sometimes I really get mad at you because you say things that are hurtful, even though they are true, but this one I can't understand because it is ridiculous. If a million dollars could cure my problems and I had the money, I would give it in no time. I don't want to be here. I mean it's nothing personal, but just to come here is a problem for me. I get disgusted with myself that I am coming here for two years and I still have all kinds of problems. Do you think I can make it? (*Pause.*) I guess you're not going to answer me, like other questions which remain unanswered. I guess that I'll make it because I do feel much better now, and when I was on vacation there were moments when I felt terribly lonely, like there was no one else in the world—I mean, no one I could talk to, no one who can understand me and like me. But I got over this loneliness—not like when I went to the farm and I couldn't take the loneliness, I had to call my parents to get me. In fact I enjoy being by myself sometimes. The last night we were at the Cape I had a dream about you, and it also involved my whole family. We all came to see you, and when I went into your office by myself I noticed that you were loaded, and I said to you, boy, are you drunk! And you said, don't worry about it, and then all my belief in you was sort of crushed. But then I said to myself, he has the right to get drunk, too, and then I left the office and I waved good-bye to you, and I told my parents that I was leaving but that they can wait for you if they wanted to, and then I left. This dream is still very vivid in my head, and it sort of puzzles me. I often think what it would be like to see you drunk, and I am sure that you do some odd things, because you seem to me quite an unconventional type. I certainly don't think that you are a dependent person. I remember when you used the word "shit" the first time—I was shocked. But now I see you as a free person, even though I still don't trust you completely. But I do feel you can help me, because you have. I am just worried that I will become dependent on you, and then who knows what will happen.

T: You don't feel dependent on me now!

P: Well, I do, but not as much as I used to. I mean, when you sit there and not say anything, I don't get as nervous as before. How can you sit there and say nothing for such a long time! But anyway, I was thinking before that I think I can go on a plane now, like you did going to Europe, without panicking. It would help if you could be there, too, just in case I get into some trouble.

T: On the one hand you say you're not as dependent on me; on the other, you'd like me to keep holding your hand forever!

P: That's a slight exaggeration! (*laughs*) But, yeah. I was thinking, wouldn't it be nice if one could kind of carry their analyst in their little pocket and every time they need him he's there, ready to help?

T: You mean like a lunchbox that Mommy prepares for you to have whenever you get hungry?

P: You might say that!

T: Wouldn't it be more pleasant if you could carry around her tits for fresh milk?

P: (*Laughs*) Not a bad idea!

T: So you like to keep around you either your mother or me or both—like in the dream, you brought everybody to my office.

P: I get sometimes confused about that. The other day my mother asked me to drop in after work, and I told her that I couldn't because I had this session with you. And she said, who's more important, your analyst or your mother, and she went on complaining that I didn't go to see them after we came back from the Cape. And I got really upset and confused about what to do—it's like I have to please everybody. I mean, my mother knows why I come here, and she should be glad about it and she should encourage me to do it, but every time I mention it, she says that she hopes I am spending my money wisely, and maybe I should go see an Italian doctor who would know me better because of my background, and all this shit.

T: What is this confusion about your mother and me?

P: I don't know, but I feel like I am torn. I mean, that maybe my mother is right—that you're interested in my money—and maybe I should try it on my own. But I really feel that you helped me even though I believe that you're interested in the money, and not so much me. But, you know, my mother used to pull this kind of shit on me when I was dating. She always thought that the girls were interested in me because I had a profession and I went to college, not because of me. It made me feel like shit, and I still feel that girls wouldn't be interested in me because I really have nothing to offer them.

T: So you brought your mother to my office, in the dream, so I could straighten her out on the subject!

P: I don't know why she was there, but sometimes I have fantasies about them meeting you, and when I think about it, if that really happened, I would be very upset—I am getting nervous just thinking about it.

T: So you wish that we meet and you're afraid of such a meeting!

P: Yeah. I am afraid, because I am kind of ashamed of my parents—they are really old-fashioned people, and you'll think, "No wonder he's such a psycho case," and I would feel very ashamed of them. But also they would think you're crazy, and that I am crazier for coming to see you. They are very prejudiced. But I am also afraid that you'll tell them that I am real sick and that there is no hope for me. I know you wouldn't, but that's what I think sometimes. I think this way more about Anne—I mean, that you probably think to yourself "is he sick!" and that Anne would be better off without me. I thought about that this morning coming to work on the subway. I was watching a guy standing behind a girl and pressing against her, and just watching him do that I was aroused sexually, and I wasn't going to talk about this, but I guess it just came up. If my mother found out about these things she'd flip. She'd put me in the crazy house.

T: Perhaps if I talked to your mother about how normal it is to have sexual feelings and fantasies, she might approve of it and then you'd feel O.K. about having them.

P: I do feel terribly guilty about all this, and I think that it's like cheating on Anne. And I used to talk about this in my confession, and the priest told me it was a sin, so I stopped telling him about them.

T: Getting absolution and forgiveness is very difficult when you depend upon others for it!

P: I have to depend on others to tell me what's right and what's wrong—if everyone decided to do what's right for them, it'd be chaos.

T: What about you—you don't feel capable of telling yourself what's right or wrong for you?

P: I know what's right for me, but I always get frightened that I'll be punished for it. I mean, I felt bad telling you about the priest, because I talked about him in an evil way, or at least not favorably, and you might get the wrong impression. Sometimes I also feel that when I talk about sex, you don't ask me any questions because you don't want me to talk about it. Like before, you didn't ask me about the thing in the subway, aren't you interested in it?

T: I was wondering why you told me about it. I wasn't sure it really bothered you so much.

P: Well, it did stick in my mind, but I thought you might get a kick out of it.

T: You want to entertain me?

P: No, but I thought that you might think that I am a homosexual because I was aroused by looking at a guy, and many times I feel very embarrassed about talking about it or even thinking about it, and I am afraid to discuss this here, and I don't really know why.

T: Perhaps I won't approve of your sexual feelings the way you feel your mother doesn't.

P: I know up here that you don't give a damn, and you don't care one way or another what I do, but I still get a twinge that you might tell me that you can't see me anymore because I am hopeless, because homosexuals never change. Even I know that, from my psych course that I took in college. I used to be terrified in the locker room at the pool, when I had to change, if there were other men around. I still feel uneasy about it, even though my dick is comparatively big. I mean I am not boasting or anything, but I don't feel bad about that. You know, talking about this really gets me nervous. Why? What the hell am I getting so nervous about? You know, I am shaking—why? I am also so afraid that somebody else might find out about it and I would have to go somewhere where nobody knows me. I have a fear that the place is bugged. I mean, I know you have the tape recorder on, but I am afraid that your office might be bugged by someone who can blackmail me. I got used to the tape recorder, and for a long time I couldn't tell you how mad I was at you for having it here, but now I take it for granted. When I was about a teenager, I used to pass by my mother when she got undressed, maybe I was 12 or 13, and it embarrassed the hell out of me. And I used to get mad at her and disgusted that she showed me her breasts and I wasn't supposed to see them, and sometimes I used to hear my parents having sex, and it got me real angry. And once I remember when I heard them I masturbated, and I put it in my underwear and I threw it behind the desk, and my mother found it and she said don't do it anymore, and I didn't know what she meant—don't masturbate or don't throw the underwear like that.

T: You know, just a couple of minutes ago you told me you won't talk about sex with me, and now you seem like you are talking about it. I am not sure what you're talking about. You say you feel guilty about having sexual feelings, and you blame your mother and the Church for this guilt; at the same time you sound like you enjoy these feelings a great deal. What way are you heading? I think you're trying to confuse me

P: I do feel very uncomfortable talking about sex. I don't know why. There are lots of things I can talk about here without getting so upset, but I think that I should talk about sex because I know that I have problems with it. I still come very fast—as soon as I start, almost before I go in, I come and I lose my hard-on—sometimes I can move around inside Anne for about three or four seconds, but I am just disgusted with myself and I don't like to discuss it here.

T: I think you like to have sex, and at the same time you feel it's a real pain—the performance part of it.

P: Yeah, I know I have to perform. I remember in high school, I went with my friend Monte to a peep show, and this guy had a hard-on for about half an hour. Maybe not that long, because the whole thing was about five minutes, but he kept thumping and thumping at this girl during the whole thing, and then my friend said he could do it for an hour, so I feel real shitty that I can't. And I get really scared that Anne will leave me because of that, or that she'll have an affair with someone better and she'll leave me, and I just can't get this off my mind. I mean, I know that if she does that I wouldn't want to have anything to do with her. I mean, she might as well become a whore, but deep down I am afraid of that because I see it all around me—everybody I know is breaking up their marriage, I mean usually the men, because they find a better piece of ass—but I think that's crazy. Even the girls these days are getting to be very loose, and that really scares me. And when I pray before I go to bed, that's one of the things I pray for—for Anne not to turn out to be a whore. Do you think I should talk to a doctor about this?

T: I am a doctor!

P: You know what I mean! I mean, maybe there is something physically wrong with me.

T: You mentioned to me some time ago that once you went to a prostitute and you were not able to have an orgasm when you were inside.

P: Yeah, that was the only time.

T: You feel your apparatus is damaged, but sometimes it works!

P: I don't know anything about these things. I mean, when the guys talk about sex in the office, I pretend I am busy with other things, because I feel they are experienced and sophisticated—they've been to this whore and that whore, and they learned this position and that trick—and I feel like a little boy next to them. I also feel terribly ashamed, because these girls can hear them talk and I don't want to be included.

T: Nice girls don't bother with sex—like Mama said!

P: That's right! I know I feel that way, because sometimes I feel that even Anne is doing this because she is supposed to, not because she feels it's right.

T: So you can't allow yourself to have sexual pleasure with a "decent" woman.

P: You think that's why I come fast?

T: That may be one of the reasons. You feel so many things going in opposite directions—it's a miracle you can keep straight and not get dizzy from swaying back and forth.

P: That sounds very sexual, Doc! (*laughs*) But I don't really understand what you mean by things going in different directions. You mean like I want to have sex but I am afraid, or that I feel sometimes turned onto men, not only women, or what? Is that what you mean—that I am wishy-washy? That I sure am. Even though my friends used to tell me that, I never really grasped its meaning except physically. I always felt like a blob, like nothing—that I am empty—and lately I feel a little more solid—I mean, a bit more sure of myself and a bit more aggressive. When we were on the Cape, I was very aggressive with Anne about sex, and she started to react to me in a more accepting manner. I even made decisions about which restaurant to go to. But then when I come here, I feel like I have nothing to offer.

T: I guess that's how you feel with your mother—a baby without power or control—and since you put me in the same ruling class as your mother, you feel the same way here. I am not your mother, you know!

P: You said this to me a number of times now. I know you're not my mother, but I don't do this on purpose. That's really how I feel. I wish you'd stop telling me that you're not my mother. I know it, I know it.

T: I think you're starting to realize it. That was clear in the dream—you were able to leave me and your family be, and you left to go to your business.

P: I feel more confident in myself sometimes, but it still doesn't last for more than a few days at a time..

T: I am afraid we have to stop here.

P: Bye now.

T: See you Monday.

This session represents a rather important turning point in Vinny's treatment. He acknowledged for the first time that he had the potential to be an independent individual and that there were other factors in his inner self that were unnecessarily limiting his ability to experience life as a creative process. He began to appreciate the pleasurable aspects of sharing innermost feelings with someone he trusted, and his outlook on the investigation of his personality became less ambivalent. He began to recognize that the road ahead needed much work, but not tedious or unworthy work. His phobias and anxieties had practically disappeared, and for the following two years we were able to concentrate a great deal on the structure of Vinny's basic personality traits and the ways he could change them so as to enrich his life and become more productive and contented. Indeed, he terminated treatment after four years, having experienced deep emotions, meeting challenges, that he had learned to face, and evolving a style of dealing with the world that did not leave him feeling like a second-class citizen.

II

The Goals of Treatment

In the minds of many people psychotherapy has become synonymous with psychoanalysis, but these two concepts are not interchangeable. To analyze the psyche does not necessarily mean to treat it; although it may be true that by analyzing it one is also treating it. Psychotherapy is an umbrella term for the many methods advanced to treat the psyche, and psychoanalysis is one of them. Among other known methods one may include chemotherapy, electroshock therapy, behavior therapy, existential therapy, gestalt therapy, dynamic therapy, and group therapy. Each method has its own stated set of assumptions, techniques, and goals, as well as its own theory of the nature of personality, the self, and the development of psychopathological syndromes. Although different in technique and approach, they all share certain overlapping theoretical or technical values. As a cohesive psychotherapeutic system and an approach to the investigation and understanding of human behavior confrontation analysis shares certain basic elements with other systems. Many therapists already incorporate some of its techniques, but this is usually not part of a conscious plan. The goals of confrontation analysis must be explicitly stated in order to clarify its differences and similarities with other approaches.

As in any other therapeutic system, one must first make a diagnostic evaluation of the patient's problems, and then offer a curative course of treatment designed to eliminate or at least alleviate problems. The goal, in other words, seems pretty clear. When dealing with emotional disorders or disturbances of the psyche, however, two issues emerge in one's initial perception of what the goal is: what is the patient's perception of his problems, and what is the therapist's perception of the patient's problems?

Transactions between two or more people always have a purpose, and yet in most instances that purpose is clear neither to the transmitter of the message nor to the receiver. For example, an individual may decide to meet a friend "just to have a drink." However, he may have a *hidden agenda,* an unconscious goal that may have nothing to do with the conscious wish to have a drink. For example, he may wish to use the meeting in the service of escaping an unpleasant situation such as loneliness, morbid thoughts and obsessions, demanding surroundings, anxiety, or tension related to various themes or tasks that require self-discipline. The "healing" professions have long recognized that help-seekers are rarely conscious of their purpose in seeking help, although most of them come to treatment with some conscious and legitimate reason, however vague. It has often been suggested that more than half the visits to physicians have nothing to do with any stated medical symptom, but rather with some unconscious psychological need, which the patient tries to satisfy through such visits. This phenomenon is quite prevalent in the field of psychotherapy. Thus it may not be possible to diagnose a patient's problem solely on the basis of what the patient is conscious of and what he expresses in the first interview. In the same vein, it may not be possible to establish a therapeutic goal either. In most cases, the patient's description of his problems cannot serve as the only basis for establishing goals in the therapist's work with the patient. To be sure, the therapist must have a clear and definite understanding of what brought the patient to seek help, what one claims one's symptoms are, what one believes to be the source of one's difficulties, and what benefits one expects from one's experience in psychotherapy. Only the patient's unfolding dynamics and the interactional process can ultimately help in establishing such goals.

The therapist's perception of the patient's problems can be distorted by a number of factors. One factor is the acceptance, on face value, of the patient's statements and expressions of his problems without learning how they are connected to the patient's self-system as a whole and to treatment goals. This often reflects the therapist's preoccupation with what treatment must achieve to satisfy the therapist's own need for approval from his over-inflated superego standards or ego ideals regarding the therapist's role as a helper. Thus, in the transactions between the patient and the therapist, the latter may also have a hidden agenda; for instance, an unconscious desire to be a father or a mother for patients as a reaction formation to an unresolved need to be a child. This may interfere with helping the patient to become more independent, by dictating the course of treatment rather than allowing it to unfold, thus serving the function of a controlling authority. Another factor, not necessarily related to countertransference problems, is the therapist's confusion in role perception and his lack of recognition of the therapeutic nature of the relationship from the beginning of treatment. Thus the therapist may allow the patient to control the course of treatment, and thus deprive the patient of an analysis of his resistance. The patient may meander from one theme to another, and from one resistance to another, in the name of free association. The therapist may rationalize this strategy in one way or another, but will have contributed very little to the solution of the patient's problems or to the achievement of other therapeutic goals.

The remainder of the book examines the goals that patients have when they seek treatment, and what confrontation analysis can offer them. Since the reasons for seeking help are not always very clear, the goals of treatment elude easy definition. For example, one often hears a patient complain about one symptom or another, and after gaining a certain degree of understanding about it, and after locating alternative ways of alleviating it, one is struck by the persistence with which the patient holds on to patterns designed to maintain that symptom. It soon becomes clear that either the reasons for seeking help are not understood or the stated goals are misleading. It takes time to decipher or decode the patient's messages because every message in interpersonal transactions has a conscious as well as an unconscious origin. Both must be well understood before any meaningful changes can take place. Therefore, the patient's reasons for seeking treatment are categorized as either manifest or latent.

4
The Patient's Goals

MANIFEST GOALS

There are perhaps as many reasons for seeking help as there are people. Common to all is what Sullivan (1954) defines as the reason for conducting a psychiatric interview:

> As I see it, such an interview is a situation of primarily *vocal* communication in a *two-group,* more or less *voluntarily integrated,* on a progressively unfolding *expert–client* basis for the purpose of elucidating *characteristic patterns of living* of the subject person, the patient or client, which patterns he experiences as particularly troublesome or especially valuable, and in the revealing of which he expects to derive benefit.

Of course, in the initial stages of therapy, one does not always easily discern whether what the patient sees as beneficial is indeed so. In any case, the manifest reasons for seeking help are many, and because they often change rather quickly, even after an initial interview, statistics related to them are unreliable and generalizations mostly meaningless.

A case in point is that of a 35-year-old man who was referred for therapy because he was depressed. When the patient entered my office, he indeed seemed rather dejected and sad, and spoke very softly with his head down and his eyes rarely looking up. He seemed embarrassed and awkward. He stated that he had been depressed for over a year now, since he discovered that his wife had been having an affair over a six month period with a mutual acquaintance. He left her and attempted to "erase" his five-year marital experience from his memory by leading a "wild sex life." He also lived for a few months with a woman whom he thought he loved, but his wife's infidelity always haunted him, and he had to leave the last relationship because "I couldn't believe that any woman could love me if my wife, who pretended for years that I was the only one in her life, could do something like that, so how could anyone who knows me for just a couple of months care for me that much?" He cried as he said this, and he also told of a fantasy that had become a daily obsession: to kill his wife's lover in her presence. He recognized that, logically, he "should" be having that fantasy about his wife and not her lover. As he spoke more about his wife, his voice became increasingly louder, until he realized how angry he was and how relieving it was for him to express this anger. Finally, it turned out that he had wanted to leave his wife from the beginning of the marriage for a variety of reasons, but "she always managed to convince me that she was such hot shit that I'd be sorry if I left her, because she'd be like a princess of untold value to men and I'd be lost without her. I was afraid of that, and I always believed that there was something wrong with me, even though I never let her know that because she used every ounce of weakness I had to justify her own crazy shit." Toward the end of this first consultation, he was not feeling depressed as much as confused about his feelings about himself and his judgment about other people, and he stated that he wished to work on these aspects of his personality. Thus we see that the patient's reason for seeking therapy was initially his wish to get rid of his depression, which undeniably gnawed at him. As he was able to further clarify his needs, however, he quickly learned that he wished to express his anger at others. Such cases are not rare. One is hard put to make any definitive statements regarding the reasons for seeking treatment, because such reasons often change and their origins are so elusive. However, one can make a reliable, albeit nonstatistical statement regarding the prevalence of some reasons over others, and perhaps one can formulate some comprehensible categorizations for the purpose of maintaining an overview.

Anxiety, Depression, and Loneliness

Among the most common complaints presented by patients in the first interview are anxiety, depression, and loneliness. These intolerable feelings propel many people to seek help, although many others learn to live with them in one way or another, mostly through the development of self-destructive patterns. Anxiety and depression may be the most devastating psychological killers in that they disrupt the functioning of the self. These two psychological states may affect the functioning of the body to such a degree that dangerous physical and physiological damage ensues, such as skin disease, ulcers, mannerisms, heart attacks, speech impediments, and anorexia. It is hard for many patients with physical symptoms to see how their chronic anxiety or depressive state created or aggravated these symptoms, usually because the symptoms themselves evolved as an unconscious way to avoid anxiety. However, since their anxiety keeps surfacing (because the suppressant—the symptoms—has lost its control power), they seek psychological treatment. Both anxiety and depression, in their extreme manifestations, obviate the need for psychological help; for the subject does not usually find an immediate, rational cause for his state of mind, but becomes driven by the emotional pain.

The same holds true for loneliness—a feeling that has appeared to surface more often in the last decade. One might surmise that tremendous technological advances in the area of communication would help people who feel uninvolved, disinterested, and insensitive. The lack of direct interaction, however, creates an atmosphere of illusion, pretense, impersonality, and constant bombardment of stimuli that purport to be emotionally significant, but only dull the emotions and remove the sense of human contact based on mutual respect and knowledge. Thus feelings of loneliness may be the result of inner emotional conflict, as well as social, industrial, and economic innovations and changes. Feelings of loneliness are rooted in psychological unrelatedness and consequent alienation (Fromm, 1947).

Family or Social Pressure

Patients often seek help when their family or social group pressures them to change personality features that are seen as undesirable or unacceptable. In confrontation analysis such a patient would not be "rejected" because of the element of ambivalence in the patient's very presence in the therapist's office; after all, adults cannot be forced to be in treatment. However, some people seek help in order not to lose wives or husbands or privileges. Among such help seekers, patients with psychopathic tendencies must be watched very carefully. As soon as it becomes clear that the patient is consciously playing games by coming to treatment, and is pretending to be in therapy to please some other person, he or she must be confronted with this psychopathy. The confrontation most likely results in termination of the treatment.

I accepted a young woman for treatment who was "casually" dating another of my patients. Her initial complaints were depression and confusion about careers. It soon became clear that she wanted to prove to me how worthwhile, attractive, intelligent, and generous she was, so that I would influence her friend to commit himself to her. When I called her bluff and told her that I was not a matchmaker, she became angry, cutting, and explosive, but at the same time played nonverbal seductive games with me by dressing provocatively for her sessions. When her attempts failed to produce the desired results with her boyfriend, she became (supposedly) depressed and withdrawn, claimed that I had not helped her, and abruptly terminated treatment. This type of manipulation often occurs—not only when one therapist is treating both parties, but even when both parties are in treatment with different therapists. Patient's fantasies dealing with the wish that their therapist would call their partner's therapist and "straighten things out" are common. Such fantasies are often not necessarily planned psychopathic manipulations, however, but instead relate to dependence on parental magic that will "take care of" the patient.

Other patients in this category include children and adolescents who are forced by their parents or school to be in therapy, as well as criminals ordered to be rehabilitated through therapy. Most of these cases are not "great successes" therapeutically, and are likely to rob the therapist who accepts them of every ounce of energy and peace of mind. When confrontational techniques are used, such candidates do not last long in therapy, mostly because they have very low tolerance for frustration and are not prepared to commit energy to save their lives, let alone share any feelings with a "hostile" intruder!

Repeated Failures

This category is an extensive one, and includes people who have experienced failure over and over and have finally become impressed with the possibility that these failures may have something to do with their own behavior, rather than the people around them. These are individuals who have tried many jobs, or have been involved in a number of intimate relationships and marriages, or have hopped from one school to another. Their mobility is always justified by some rationalization, or what seem to be accidental changes in their surroundings that forced them out of their situation. A close examination of these patterns of failures usually reveals a paranoid orientation toward the world and an extremely low self-esteem, which the individual unconsciously needs to reaffirm through failure. Individuals with this type of adjustment are not likely to seek treatment unless they become aware, through contacts with friends who are more enlightened about therapy, that they can do something to stop this pattern. This category includes some intellectually gifted people who seem to achieve enough to make themselves successful, but who usually undermine their achievement as soon as it becomes clear to them that it is within arm's reach.

Conformity

For a certain segment of society, being in psychotherapy has become an exclusive status symbol. The demand for therapy may be triggered off by a wish to be "in," although the patient is not aware of this need. The manifest reason is a wish to "learn" about oneself, to "understand what makes me tick." Many so-called intellectuals and some over-dependent and affluent individuals seek treatment because it has become "the thing to do." Naturally, if an individual resorts to such devices to prove his worth as a person, one can imagine the feelings of emptiness and inadequacy that are harbored, and how dependent the individual feels on the outside world for validation of his existence.

Another category of people who may fit under this heading are those who recognize the existence of a psychological problem in themselves or in others, and who could, if they tried, resolve it by themselves, but who are not willing to take the initiative or the responsibility. This kind of patient is usually quite motivated to make changes as soon as the alternatives are made apparent, but for some reason or another they have grown to believe that the "experts" are the ones to turn to for any problem. For these patients, short-term treatment, sometimes even one or two sessions, is sufficient to help them make choices.

Physical pain

This category includes patients whose physical or "real" pain has no known physical or physiological cause and who are referred (reluctantly) by their physician for psychotherapy. Many of these patients cannot be easily convinced that their psyche and not their body needs the tuning. The likelihood is that they have searched for relief by frequenting their doctor's office, by switching to various physicians, and by taking medication to relieve the pain, though never getting to its source. However, when the pain becomes intolerable, and when they have exhausted all other possibilities, they walk into the therapist's office, angry, disillusioned, and desperate. They are angry at their doctors for not curing them, and they are angry at their therapist for existing, because the therapist reminds them of what they wish to avoid—their feelings. This category, often referred to as the *psychosomatic syndrome,* is a mixed bag so far as treatment prognosis is concerned. Some patients get "instant" relief as soon as they see the therapist. They are "cured" in a few sessions, leave treatment quite quickly, and are very thankful. They are likely to return for more intensive therapy later, however, usually to another therapist, and usually because of anxiety that has become overwhelming since it no longer has symptoms available to bind it. Others improve and become so enamored with the therapist's "magic powers" that they become extremely dependent. They eventually work through their strong transferential reactions, and leave treatment having benefitted a great deal from it.

A certain number of patients in this category hold tenaciously to their psychosomatic symptoms and are not helped by any amount of psychotherapy. Patients suffering from anorexia nervosa, in many ways a rather strange syndrome, are hardly understood psychologically or physiologically. Anorexia may be the ultimate self-punishment. Such patients may be depressed, obstinate, intelligent, socially and sexually immature, paranoid, and defiantly or rebelliously dependent. They gradually become more and more emotionally impoverished, almost to the point of overlap with their body impoverishment. Their tolerance for ties with others is quite low, and they are not likely to remain in treatment for too long with one therapist. Their manifest reason for seeking help only peripherally touches on their anorexic symptom, and they invariably become furious if the food issue is brought up by the therapist during the session. They are the embodiment of living death, and create an aura of total despair and futility. Perhaps the only hope in the near future for this syndrome is to diagnose it from its earliest signs, so that a "preventive" treatment can be devised.

Panic

Panic is a state of extreme fear or anxiety that disorganizes the individual's ego functions to such a degree that it renders one incapable of controlling one's life. Panic can occur as a result of a stimulus that comes from the outer environment, such as a threat to the individual's life, or from an inner stimulus, such as the belief that an employer is about to fire that individual from an important job. Panicked patients are usually people who have had a history of difficult personality conflicts, but who have never been uncomfortable enough to seek help. This category includes a number of subgroups such as drug abusers, who almost kill themselves before they realize that they must do something about their habits; alcoholics, who find themselves rejected by their family and friends; spouses, who suddenly wake up to the fact that their partners are packing their bags and are ready to leave them; and latent homosexuals, who panic before they recognize where their sexual interests lie. A few, though not too many, wake up one day feeling that their lives have been a waste, and wish to change everything, from their social environment to their professional careers, but find no suitable alternatives.

A young college professor entered therapy just before the academic year was about to start, with the complaint that he had been increasingly anxious about some courses he had to teach. He became panic-stricken when he realized that only a week was left before he had to begin teaching. He could not explain in any rational way why he was so frightened, but wanted to be reassured that he would not panic when he was in front of the class. He thought of having a drink before class, but the thought of drinking liquor at eight o'clock in the morning turned his stomach. As he was able to relate his fantasies about what could happen in the classroom, he realized that the fears were related to his feelings of inadequacy in the intellectual sphere, and the fear that he would be "found out" as soon as he opened his mouth. This manifest reason for seeking help was not new to him, but he claimed that he had never thought of spending his scant salary on "mental masturbation" (of which he did a great deal in the classroom). Eventually, as therapy progressed, this young man made a number of significant connections between his fear of "being found out" as stupid and ingorant and his deep homosexual fears, and his approach to his teaching career was modified appreciably.

Training

Many professionals in the mental health field are required to go through therapy experience as part of their training program. Once they decide to become therapists and thus learn about the nature of personality, many of these students become aware of the need to understand first-hand how therapy works. These students then become aware of their own personality difficulties, and look for help for themselves. Others, however, do not believe they need to be "therapized" in order to become therapists, but they go along with the requirements and try to become patients. However, whether they go for help on their own or feel forced into it, these individuals are generally extremely resistant to the whole process of therapy. They do not consider themselves "sick," and are therefore unwilling to open up. Their resistance may stem from additional unconscious sources, not the least of which is their reason for choosing this field as their career—i.e., by playing therapist they are (so they fantasize) in control rather than out of control. The idea of being placed in the position of the "patient" is thus quite frightening to many, and is often something they did not bargain for when they chose to become therapists.

One such trainee told me that he resented being called "patient," since he was "only in training," and he did not have to say "what's on his mind" just because I asked him to do so. When I then told him that he didn't have to be in therapy if he didn't choose to, he immediately jumped to the conclusion that I resented treating him and wanted to get rid of him because he was paying a reduced fee. He eventually discovered that much of this feeling was a projection of the resentment he had harbored toward an older brother by whom he felt exploited as a child and a teenager. These feelings also interfered a great deal with his relationships with other students at school, and in his work with his own patients. It took a painfully long time for him to realize how his own unconscious conflicts affected his daily living and, more importantly, how therapy was necessary even for a personality as "healthy" as his.

At the other extreme, but equally resistant, is the trainee-therapist who knows all the dynamic answers to his troubles and accepts everything without fighting, without questioning, and without getting truly involved in the process of integrated learning. One of the best therapeutic avenues for such patient-therapists is to place them in a group that has no other "mavins" (people who know) like them, because such a group can often effectively break through their intellectual defenses in a short time, and is extremely helpful in transforming the therapist-patient into a functioning human being without the need to hide behind a professional cloak.

There is, of course, another group of trainees in the field of mental health who are in this field so that they can be in treatment without appearing to be patients. This trainee-patient category is a rather motivated group who need public approval for exploring their personality, and it is a population that is very engaging and rewarding as patients because they are eager to learn, change, and exchange. Eventually, such individuals can become very effective and helpful therapists and very successful human beings, not necessarily without problems, but with a strong basis for creativity and change.

Emptiness

An increasing number of patients, probably representing the population at large, complain of feelings of emptiness, and are driven into therapy after having tried to involve themselves in a multiplicity of projects and after finding themselves unable to overcome these feelings. They do not feel involved in any significant way in their own lives or anyone else's. They complain that they keep looking for goals or direction, but their search ends in disappointment. In part, confrontation analysis evolved when other methods of treatment failed to be responsive to a large segment of the patient population, and particularly to this group. Psychoanalysis was not flexible enough even to accept for treatment the patient who comes with such complaints, because these individuals are likely to be borderline or within the character disorders category, and thus they were not seen as "good" psychoanalytic candidates.

Clinical evaluation of such patients often reveals a personality development in which an immense amount of energy was invested for the sole purpose of reaching "success." This kind of conditioning often succeeds in eliminating important considerations of the individual's psychological makeup in terms of inner needs, or the human needs of those who surround the individual. These individuals grow up operating like machines, producing a "success" devoid of emotional or interpersonal base. Inner life becomes for them an obstacle to achieving the goal of success, rather than the *goal* of the success. Thus inner life is denied any substantial role in their daily affairs. Increasingly, these individual's inner needs become less and less satisfied, and their feelings of emptiness grow deeper. Many of them describe themselves as "shells," which, once cracked, are in danger of collapse, since they are empty inside. Hence the constant preoccupation with ways of strengthening the shell rather than allowing it to open so it can be filled.

Bellak (1974) attributes some of the causes for this type of personality development to the nature of contemporary society, which forces the person to adapt to constant, rapid changes that tax the individual's ego to such a degree that it finds itself in constant crisis. This, according to Bellak, leads to "changes in the nature of object relations." As a result, a personality develops with a character structure that is "shallow" and with "transitory object relations with little subjective feeling."

> ... Dulled by the constant impact of people and events, our senses develop a protective psychologic barrier—a form of adaptation. ... Pleasure in *work for work's sake* (rather than for money, fame or admiration) is rarer in our technologic society. The entire context of rush is not conducive to the development or unfolding of neutralization or sublimation.

These patients may be "fitted" diagnostically into the character disorder category, or the borderline; however, since so many possess this personality structure, one may rightly ask the obvious—i.e., whether this so-called disorder is not a social one, and whether its expression in so many of the patient population is an indication of how pervasive it has become. Many of these "empty" individuals feel uncomfortable enough to seek help, and yet when they come to therapy, the therapist is hardly ready for them, either psychologically or therapeutically. Bellak's assessment of the core problem places a heavy burden on the therapist:

> Deserted by their parents with regard to the superego development, the youth of today strive for group formations to support one another, to find new rules, to create new ideals. Yet the task of creating new constructive ideals has hardly ever been accomplished by youth alone. . . . Although psychoanalysts must keep an open mind, in the area in which we are competent we should throw our weight on the side of reason and adaptiveness, in the service of reality testing and judgment *now.*

This is a bold invitation to the therapist to attack distorted personality structures directly with all of the therapeutic armamentarium, even if he needs to abandon much-cherished, though rigid, procedures.

Many patients with such characterological "defects" or "holes" in their ego have naturally been attracted to the so-called "new" therapies such as encounter or behavior modification remedies that promise "instant" cures or emotional release. Having developed and nourished belief in the importance of the "instant success," these individuals flocked to the halls of the mass confessionals, marked by hysterical self-revelations and emotional explosions, where they encountered leaders devoid of compassion and lacking in judgment and perspective. These so-called leaders do not discriminate between learning through integration and meaningful interaction and mutual trust (that develops only through time and work), and exploitation of a starved, empty soul through their magic solutions. Many who participated in these rituals experienced them with an orgiastic joy they hadn't dared even dream of in the past. However, in the final analysis, these experiences become less and less satisfying, and the feelings of emptiness continue to fill the shells that surrounded them in the first place. The experience for many is often eventually more destructive. Those individuals, or "casualties," who end up in a therapist's office, slowly learn, if their ego has not been deeply shattered, that they must fill their emptiness with substance, not miracle, and that emotional substance evolves from caring, understanding, knowledge, trust, mutuality, exposure, interaction, and intimacy. The manifest and existential feelings of emptiness can be powerful and devastating. In many cases, however, this feeling is only a symptom of hidden and even more painful and unacceptable aspects of the self, such as feelings of inadequacy, loneliness, and infantile terror of abandonment.

Clinical Examples

Of course, most patients present more than one reason and more than one goal (in addition to the wish to be happy). The following statements were taken verbatim from initial interviews, for the purpose of illustrating the above points clinically.

Repeated failures. From a 27-year-old woman referred by another patient-friend:

> I want to be in therapy because I am confused and I don't know what I want. Now I am in publishing and I like it, but I am not crazy about it. I was in advertising, sales, secretarial work, and I don't want any of these things. I also want to lose weight, and I haven't been successful doing it on my own. In the last two weeks I went back to a relationship with a man I used to go out with a year ago, but I don't really know that I want it. Everything I turn to seems to end up uninteresting, or stupid, or plainly below me.
>
> I have been in analysis or therapy, or whatever you want to call it for 20 years, and some ways my life changed tremendously, but in relation to men—zilch! Absolutely nothing. I never had a real long-term meaningful relationship, and I heard that you are different from the other analysts, so here I am!

Depression. From a 58-year-old widow referred by a former patient:

> I am very upset about my job and I would like to change jobs. I have an offer of another job, but every time I think of switching I get nervous. I don't know what I should do. I was in therapy about 23 years ago with Dr. N.—I don't know if you know him—and he was wonderful, but I think I need a different person now. My husband passed away five years ago (*tearful and choking*) and I can't seem to get over it. Every time I think of him I get like this.

Anxiety, psychosomatics. From a 34-year-old woman who lost a revered father two years earlier, and was referred by her friend, a former patient:

In the last few weeks I have been having terrible stomach aches, cramps, and diarrhea, and there is nothing physically wrong with me—at least that's what my doctor says. I have also been getting dizzy sometimes to the point that I am afraid to cross the street by myself. I mean, it's getting so bad I have to stay home sometimes, and I can't do that very often because I work for H. L., and you know he's running for office and it's the middle of his campaign. I don't want to quit, because I love the man and I really want to work for him. I think he is great and he should win.

Loneliness. From a 27-year-old woman who, dissatisfied with her analyst of four years, was referred by a friend:

I was seeing Dr. K. for the last four years, as you know. He is a very nice man, although when I think of it now I shouldn't say that. He never really talked to me. I mean, there was never any exchange. I went to see him at the time because all my relationships with men were pretty bad, and for the last two years I have had none except for some very brief sexual ones—and I mean brief, like a one-night stand. I mean, I never cried in my sessions, and when I told L. *(the referring patient)* that, she thought that was strange. What do you think? I know I must be doing something wrong with men, and I always manage to find men who don't react to me as a person. Even the analyst didn't. I am very active, I do a lot of things, and I am always busy. But lately, with all that, I've been feeling kind of lonely.

Conformity, anxiety, emptiness. From a 27-year-old woman teacher in the New York City school system who presented her problem in this manner:

I have a lot of love, and I want to give it, but I cannot. I feel very insecure about it. People always misunderstand me.

Family pressure, depression. From a 37-year-old English professor, "sent" to me by his wife, who discovered that he had been having an affair with a woman much younger than herself. Even though she did not believe this affair to be a threat to her marriage, she saw it as her husband's way of staving off a devastating depression.

I feel she should be back in therapy, not me, because she doesn't realize that she was the one who drove me into it by telling me constantly that I was such a wonderful person, such a good person, that she could really trust me— as if I were some kind of machine. I mean, eventually I started to believe that I was O.K. and that I could prove that to myself by taking up with a beautiful chick from school. This gal looked up to me as if I was really some kind of god. Once I had a terrible crying spell while I was with her, and she thought that was absolutely "super," as she would put it. My wife would never put up with this. But from my point of view, I really don't want to give up my wife

and my children for an affair that basically gave me only fancy illusions about
how life is greener on the other side of the fence. I realize that my feelings of
inadequacy cannot be solved by getting into a woman's pants, so I am cured
of that fantasy. But I think I can work on this myself. At least that's what I
think.

Panic. From a 28-year-old man who came to me after he
had a very frightening dream:

> I had this dream when I called you: my prick was cut off, and it was lying
> on the floor and I was singing in a high voice—a falsetto—from behind a stage.
> And I think my balls started to disappear, and I started to panic in the dream,
> and that made it even worse, because then even my prick became so small—
> it was just crazy. I stopped singing, and I was just watching and getting more
> and more horrified, and I woke up in a sweat and my heart was pumping like
> a machine gun. I was so upset in the morning, and I couldn't stop thinking
> about a homosexual thing I had with another boy when I was eleven or twelve.
> I mean I started thinking , is that why it's so hard for me to have a good thing
> going with a woman—I mean, is it possible that underneath it all I am really
> a homosexual? That dream really got me, because I knew it must mean some-
> thing!

LATENT GOALS

Latent reasons for seeking treatment are not easy to uncover or to understand, especially in terms of their relationship
to the patient's developmental history. Because there is usually
resistance to the uncovering of unconscious material, the patient's hidden agenda (of which the patient is also unaware)
unfolds with the same pace that other material does. It is often
difficult for a therapist to know why the patient is there; although there is usually the global need to remove emotional
pain. Even this pain is often suspect, however; the therapist
often feels that he is chasing ghosts, for as soon as what seem
to be substantive feelings of the patient and a real wish to get
rid of pain emerge, the patient slips into another defense, another mask. Thus, even with unusually open and "cooperative"
patients, one is allowed only glimpses into their inner world.
Perhaps the best clue to a patient's personality is the material,
verbal and nonverbal, which cannot be controlled completely—
dreams, fantasies, early recollections, speech patterns, body
movement, style and manner of behavior within the therapeutic

session, and the nature of interaction between the patient and the therapist. At the same time, the alertness, spontaneity, perceptivity, and relatedness of the therapist affect the patient's communications, and awareness of this impact is extremely helpful in assessing what is happening from minute to minute, and from one crossroad to another in the therapeutic process. The art of therapeutic work and the key to recognizing latent reasons for entering therapy, as well as the basis for helping the patient become aware of these reasons, lie in understanding what the patient *is* saying and what the patient *is trying* to say, as well as the reasons for his communication at a specific time. Of course, there are more latent reasons for seeking help than there are people.

Resistance to Change

Oddly enough, help-seekers share an underlying unconscious personality force that opposes help in various ways. It is termed *resistance*. This paradox, the conscious wish to recover and the unconscious need to remain the same, has long been recognized by dynamically oriented therapists. Why do patients wish to hold on to their self-destructive patterns? The answer to this question is rather complicated, but one hypothesis seems to me to apply to the majority of cases. Change of any sort requires, on the one hand, the abandonment or loss of the old and, on the other hand, acceptance and integration of the new. As a matter of existential experience, loss can be easily translated into separation. In fact, it is separation, and as such it can cause feelings of anxiety, the intensity of which depends on the individual's degree of resolution of this painful conflict. At the same time, change that involves the acquisition of something new can also present some difficulty, since it implies the acceptance of what seems to be a foreign element into the established structure. Change is often unconsciously perceived, and is often experienced as thought it were an attempt to remove a well-fitting, though rotting pipe from an old plumbing system to replace it with a shiny new pipe, which may not look like part of the system. In the process of making changes in such a system, some flooding, dripping, cutting, and soldering may be inevitable: operations that are liable to cause more or less difficulty, and that all require concentrated, planned effort. The perception of possible pain is so great that the individual is understandably reluctant to let go of old familiar patterns. For example, a 32-year-old woman, who had been married for seven years and who had sought treatment because she was depressed, warned me during the first interview that, "if therapy is going to make me happy only if I separate from my husband, I don't want it. I don't want to break up my marriage." This woman was not aware of her basic conflict regarding change in general. She used her wish to stay married as an excuse to keep her psychological makeup in status quo.

Most help-seekers expect to change "something" about themselves, rather than changing themselves, as if this were possible. There is usually little awareness that change is a two-way street, where the agents of change flow in both directions to effect change: from the total personality to the perceived disturbed area and vice versa. In reality, however, every change in perception, affect, cognition, or behavior is bound to modify in some way or another all other aspects of the self, both psyche and soma.

Nunberg, as reported in Fenichel (1941), recognized that some patients' wishes for change have pathological elements. These consist of the patient's need for "strengthening of his neurotic equilibrium," and the hope to "get infantile wish fulfillments from the analysis." One of the most common pathological reasons for wishing to change is at times expressed openly by some patients when they announce that they don't see anything "wrong" with themselves, but their spouses, or mothers, or friends, or other important personalities in their life want them to change, and therefore they are seeking treatment. They totally submerge their self-value and their right to be what they are, and attempt to please someone else by trying to become "another person." This is a total denial or misunderstanding of what therapy is all about. Such a goal can only increase a person's regression to deeper dependency levels; thus creating a greater schism between one's real, present status as an adult and one's capacity to live realistically.

Parental Love

Another common latent reason for seeking therapy is the need to receive from the therapist the kind of care and love the patient felt was never given when he was growing up. As Nunberg stated above, patients often talk of their expectations that the therapist will be an unending fountain of love and devotion, making up for all the misery, mistreatment, and sometimes hatred they experienced as children or infants. Fantasies and dreams of being held on the therapist's lap or being breast-fed by the therapist, as well as conscious daydreams about living with the therapist or having the therapist take care of them abound, and are expressed in one way or another. A patient who was a rather pampered and extremely dependent child, related some of his feelings in the first interview, and then sat back in his seat and triumphantly said, "That's about it. I don't know if anything can be done, but I heard a lot about you from Lisa (*referring friend*), and I am sure *you* can deal with it." His expectations were that I take care of his problems, or more accurately, of his life.

Many patients are discouraged very quickly after they start therapy. Quite often a review of their frustrations reveals that the love they expected from the therapist, which was to remedy what was lacking in them, was not forthcoming. They may even withdraw from treatment as a result of this disappointment. Such patients often need a therapist who is more active with them in the beginning of treatment as a way of transition to an understanding of what therapy is about and what expectations they must modify so they can work on their conflicts. The degree of the patient's tolerance for frustration often suggests which strategy the therapist must use to educate the client to become a patient, and not simply a mouth in search of a breast.

The wish to be loved by the therapist as a substitute parent is often expressed in various subtle ways. Examples abound:

1. Patients often attempt to change their appointment time solely for the purpose of testing the therapist's love for them; the assumption being that if the therapist is willing to accomodate them, then he or she loves them more than the patient loves himself—the way they fantasize an idealized parent to be.

2. At the end of a session, some patients continue to sit in their chair or lie on the couch, and continue to talk as if nothing had happened. Others will get up, but begin a whole new topic on their way to the door, and unconsciously block the therapist from opening the door. The element of hostility toward the therapist is often transparent, and yet the need to "stick around," to get "more" from the therapist, is also part of the dynamics.

3. Patients sometimes ask to borrow some magazines from the waiting room, even though they can easily and inexpensively buy them. Some patients, ostensibly rather busy, active individuals on the outside, ask if they can sit for a while in the waiting room to read some articles that interest them. The underlying motive is often the need to feel wanted by the therapist beyond the regular session for which they pay.

4. At the end of the first consultation, some patients ask the therapist to lower the fee, even though they knew the fee before requesting the interview. I asked one such patient why she requested this special consideration, and she was unable to explain it, except to say that she would simply feel better if she knew I had given her a break. Later I found out that the patient was quite mischievous as a child, and would always beg for another chance, but never got it. She had never given up this need for testing the limits, so that people could prove to her that she was loved regardless of her behavior. The therapist was no exception.

5. Some patients are anxious to know whether I take notes about their session at the end of the day, and whether I think about them beyond the analytic hour. Again, their wish to be cared about in a way their parents did not is primary, and operates as a motivating factor in their search for help.

6. Certain questions may be viewed as a demand on the part of the patient to be loved in a parental fashion. Such questions require that the analyst answer the patient ("Why don't you answer my questions?"), give constant approval, tell what direction the patient should take in career or family planning, meet a friend or a relative (ostensibly so that the therapist gets to know the patient better), or literally tell the patient what words to use when he talks to various people.

The wish to obtain parental love or to prove (transferentially) that the parents were and continue to be responsible for the patient's pain because they were not loving, is probably the most pervasive and universal latent reason for seeking treatment. It may be the single most powerful need that motivates people to remain with a therapist for long periods of time.

Affirmation of Righteousness

An integral part of the healthy individual's development as a mature, secure, and trusting adult is based upon a consistent affirmation and validation of feelings, perceptions and actions during the early years. Lack of such validation in the individual's environment, especially from parents and siblings, breeds feelings of insecurity, low self-esteem, negative self-image, isolation, and distrust of one's own judgment. As a result of such development, the negative feedback turns into reservoirs of guilt and anxiety, and fear of isolation and destruction. The psychoanalytic concept of the development of the superego may be restated as the process of developing a mechanism that deals with ways of preserving the ego, or the integrity of the self, and saving it from the fear of destruction by guilt, anxiety, and the fear of punishment. Those individuals who grow up under conditions of extreme deprivation in the area of validation of feelings, develop a countermechanism of extreme proportions, and of a defensive character that may be called "the need to be self-righteous." The need to prove one's superiority in the areas of honesty, decency, integrity, and other moral and ethical values, leads many people into therapy because of the defensive nature of such a stance—a defense that creates a host of symptoms that hamper the individual's functioning. The goal of proving one's righteousness emerges quite early in treatment.

Almost from the beginning, and after enumerating the various symptoms for which he ostensibly sought help, the patient launches an assault on anything and everything that has ever crossed his path, always doubting and mistrusting other people's motives with no reality basis for the complaints. This type of personality structure is often the collector of injustices and traumas, and the victim, fantasied and real, of accidents, failures, and in general "bad luck." As analysis progresses, a pattern of such experiences emerges and repeats itself from one session to the next, mainly for the unconscious purpose of proving how rotten the world is, and how, in contrast, the patient has acted in the most noble fashion. The trouble is, of course, that the patient does not feel appreciated for his righteousness but, rather, feels continuously abused for it. Such a patient "knows" what is right, but never follows his instincts, because "somebody" or something prevents it, and thus circumstances turn against the patient.

Crusaders of self-righteousness have a tendency to revere authority as long as it affirms their conviction that they are right and everybody else is wrong, and when they look for help, they hope to find someone who will serve as a substitute parent and give them back their existence. However, as soon as they detect the slightest disagreement or disapproval from the therapist, they are likely to leave and look for one who will give them a free ticket to God's territory. They cannot tolerate lack of support, and since their survival depends on it, the therapeutic relationship is always shaky. In such patients, the ambivalence is so great that their commitment to searching for the source of their need to be always on top is extremely tentative. At the other extreme of this group, however, there are those who are so frightened and reverent of authority that they are likely to stay in therapy for the longest time. In order not to suffer the consequences of not being on top, they become tuned to the therapist's value system, and unconsciously adjust their beliefs and actions to coincide with those of the therapist, so that they gain automatic approval and feel they are "right" because of full identification with the therapist. This, unfortunately, turns them into submissive, oppressed, and blocked individuals, who leave treatment after a long time without having gained or changed much. They do, however, create for themselves, and for others, an illusion of accomplishment and change. The therapist must always be on the alert for such characterological presentations, because they can be elusive. At the same time, the stripping of defenses in a hasty manner from these generally obsessive-compulsive individuals, might throw them into a serious depression, or a paranoid crisis.

Ventilation

Some patients seek help out of a need to find a dumping ground for their emotional state. Such patients often exhibit either of two histories with regard to the expression of feelings. One group includes people who have never found appropriate places and people to share their feelings with, and as the reservoir of feelings can no longer be contained because of changes in the personality equilibrium, they seek a therapist on whom to dump these feelings, without fear of recrimination. Another group includes people who have done the exact opposite, i.e., they have used many of their friends and relatives for this purpose of sharing feelings. However, because their motivation is not really to share, but rather to release and complain, those who are the target objects lose interest and chase these individuals out of their social-psychological territory. This sometimes results in the search for an entity who they believe will accept the role of the garbage can. Such individuals find themselves forever alienating everyone around them by their narcissistic one-way unloading, and they generally have very little insight into their own role in this isolation. A divorced woman in her middle 40s entered therapy because her physician grew tired of prescribing tranquillizers, and finally told her that he could no longer help her. He had been using prescriptions as a way of getting rid of her whenever she wished to see him. He learned she had no one to talk to and that she was using him as her monthly confessional. The first few minutes of the initial consultation confirmed her internist's statement that "this woman wants to tell everybody her troubles, but I don't think she wants to do anything about them." When I asked her why she had come to see me she was direct enough to let me know that she did not believe in psychology, but that her friends would not listen to her anymore, so she had accepted her physician's recommendations to see me as a last resort.

The need to ventilate feelings does not have a negative connotation in therapy. However, when not accompanied by additional goals, it becomes a way of life within the therapeutic situation, and adds to the patient's feelings of impotence. In essence, it deflates the self without supplying other substance. The therapist must always confront these patients regarding the purpose of their continuation in treatment so that their energy does not get consumed in self-pity, self-flagellation, or the projection of anger onto the outside world and at the environment, solely. It must be used in the service of constructive goals—goals designed to help the self grow and conquer new perspectives on life. These perspectives, from the point of view of the confrontation analyst, are the subject of the remainder of this volume.

5

The Confrontation Analyst's Goals

Since it is clear that the patient's goals and reasons for seeking treatment may be in constant inner conflict, the question arises as to why the patient comes for treatment. [After all, confrontation analysis, or any dynamically oriented therapy, can create rather difficult and sometimes painful experiences for the patient as it forces one to confront what one is trying to avoid or deny.] Nunberg (1955) considers a similar dilemma with regard to psychoanalysis:

> The psychoanalyst . . . calls the patient's attention to his inner conflicts, the sources of which are not known to either of them, and asks him to be helpful in discovering the unknown, the repressed. Thus, from the very beginning the aims of the analyst are opposed to those of the patient, to the wishes of his repressing ego.

Every experienced therapist recognizes the ambivalent nature of the patient's call for help, regardless of how eager one is to work on one's "problems." May (1967), discussing this paradoxical situation, notes,

> Or shall we say, here is a person who has a problem and comes to the therapist because he wants to get well? This gets closer to the real situation. But it is, unfortunately, precisely what we don't know; *we cannot be sure that this person wants to get well.* We can indeed be sure getting well is precisely

what he is ambivalent about; *he comes needing to remain ill until other aspects in his existence are changed.* He comes in conflict and his motives are in all probability very much confused (*emphasis added*).

Why, one might ask, does the patient remain in treatment if the self-destructive forces are so deep and strong? There are at least two obvious factors: the first lies with the patient, the second with the therapist. In general, people seek help only when their pain becomes intolerable, and they stay in therapy because the alternative of going back to the level of pain that forced them into treatment is not terribly attractive, even though it has a magnetic pull. At the same time, patients continue in therapy only, as Guntrip (1969) surmises, if they become "steadily convinced that we will stand by them and in the end relieve their misery, and even then, cooperation is opposed by tremendous inner resistances." In a very real sense, when faced with this push-pull situation, the therapist must choose sides. One hopes, of course, that the therapist will choose that side of the healthy ego of the patient that works to remove obstacles to understanding and modification of certain personality dimensions.

Given the patient's need for help, and the wish of the therapist to be the helper, what goals might the therapist set for the patient? Fromm-Reichman (1950) supplies an excellent delineation of treatment goals:

Treatment, of course, is aimed at the solution of the patient's difficulties in living and at the cure of his symptomatology. Ideally these therapeutic goals will be reached by the growth, maturation, and inner independence of the patient. Accomplishment will be further realized by his potential freedom from fear, anxiety, and the entanglements of greed, envy, and jealousy. This goal will also be actualized by the development of his capacity for self-realization, his ability to form durable relationships of intimacy with others, and to give and accept mature love.

This statement of goals in psychotherapy is no doubt acceptable to most analytically oriented therapists, including confrontational analysts, even though, in certain ways, it is rather general.

Here confrontation and analysis of the confrontation are the central therapeutic techniques for effecting personality changes. The techniques are based on the *interaction* between the patient and therapist. Interaction implies a reverberating system in which movement on one side causes movement on the other side. If the goals of the patient are separated from those of the therapist, one creates, theoretically and pragmatically, an artificial wall. It is, nevertheless, essential for the therapist to be clear as to what the therapist, or the therapeutic system, has to offer the patient. The therapist must be there to help, without imposing values on the patient, and at the same time without losing respect for what the patient wishes to accomplish. The therapist's objectives must be defined operationally if possible, and when they are achieved, they must be demonstrably the result of the therapist's procedures and techniques. The latter is essential because of the difficulty in defining elements of behavior as well as cognitive and emotional aspects of the personality to which treatment objectives are aimed. When one speaks of general goals as having something to do with changes in the self, one must refer to those aspects of the person that can be observed and measured. The reference is not to unconscious changes, for by definition these elude observation and direct measurement. Consequently, any changes in the self must be evaluated on the basis of changes in consciousness. As Bonime (1962) suggests, "The evolution of personality is essentially synonymous with evolution of consciousness. Changes of personality are basically changes of consciousness."

The question of goals in psychotherapy has received much attention. Suffice it here to say that the term "psychotherapy" means literally "cure of the mind" or "soul." Certainly, the concept of cure is borrowed from the medical lexicon, and the question is whether it can be legitimately used in connection with the field of personality modification. London (1964) expounds on this subject in *The Modes and Morals of Psychotherapy:*

Insofar as he is concerned with the diagnosis and treatment of illness, the modern psychotherapist has grown up in the tradition of medicine. But the nature of the ailments he deals with and the way he treats them set him apart from the physician and in some ways make him function much like a clergyman. He deals with sickness of the soul, as it were, which cannot be cultured in a laboratory, seen through a microscope, or cured by injection. And his methods have little of the concreteness or obvious empiricism of the physician's—he carries no needle, administers no pill, wraps no bandages. He cures by talking and listening. The infections he seeks to expose and destroy are neither bacterial nor viral—they are ideas, memories of experiences, painful and untoward emotions that debilitate the individual and prevent him from functioning effectively and happily.

Although there is a great deal of possible controversy in this statement, it does describe what the psychotherapist faces in clinical work. Confrontation analysis approaches treatment through a definition of the personality in the broadest sense. *Personality* is a system that includes physiological, intellectual, emotional, and temperamental endowment, as well as the effects of the environment in which an individual operates at a certain time and over time.

EXPANDING THE CONSCIOUSNESS OF THE SELF

The analytically oriented psychotherapies subscribe to a central goal of treatment, one that Freud enunciated—to make the unconscious conscious. Confrontation analysis maintains that without some knowledge of the unconscious very little change can occur in the personality; however, knowledge of one's unconscious may not, in and of itself, prove to be the most valuable factor in effecting change in the self. Marmor (1974) reinforces this point:

> The psychoanalyst is not content to achieve symptomatic improvement— he aims at nothing less than a major characterological overhaul, ending in "genitality" and full emotional maturity. Yet over and over again we have seen a situation occuring that is typified in the well-known ironic riddle which psychoanalysts themselves often bandy about among themselves:
>
> Question: What happens when you analyze a schmoe?
>
> Answer: You get an analyzed schmoe.
>
> The limitations of classical psychoanalytic therapy have not been in intent, but in technique. A method that restricts itself strictly to a dyadic relationship, utilizing free association as its major tool, will indeed uncover a great deal, far more, I am convinced than any nonpsychodynamic technique— but runs the risk of also missing a great deal.

Marmor is not alone in this conviction. The approach of confrontation analysis evolved as a result of this kind of experience and conviction, and the emphasis on interaction as a therapeutic tool was adopted to correct the very possibility that unconscious material that becomes conscious in the course of treatment does not remain unintegrated as part of the functioning ego. Interaction between people, which is posited by confrontation analysis to be the main tool through which learning about oneself occurs, is unfortunately relegated to the lowest priority in the transactions between patient and analyst in the psychoanalytic model of psychotherapy. The rationale for this is that interaction may prevent the development of transference neurosis, which is necessary for analysis. That may be so. However, is the goal of treatment the development of a "good transference," or is it real change in the patient as a result of the therapeutic relationship? Marmor (1974), applying this very point to the field of training as well, poses the same question regarding graduates of psychoanalytic institutes:

> It has long been known in most psychoanalytic institutes that the way to "beat the rap and graduate" is "not to make waves." This has meant learning, in the didactive analysis, to play the "game" of free association well; to "accept" supervision (which means not contradicting the supervising analyst and dutifully following his instructions); to avoid calling too much attention to oneself in seminars; and finally to produce a safe, conservative graduation thesis in which one carefully plays back all the things one has been taught in the preceding four or five or six years. The result is that those candidates who tend to be most conforming and least original in their thinking get through the training system with the fewest difficulties, and eventually become teachers themselves, thus perpetuating the cycle. The original thinker, the non-conformist, is apt to be charged with "resistance" and may have far greater difficulties in completing his training.

The principle of interacting in therapy is, in confrontational analysis, not only used to enhance the relationship, but is also based on the belief that an understanding of behavior cannot take place without the interactional matrix. This is a basic philosophical and psychological deviation from the genetic psychoanalytic approach, and it thus affects not only the techniques of therapy, but also the kinds of goals that are worked on in the encounter between patient and therapist. What goals can be effectively tackled in a system that believes that changes in the self can occur only through an intensive, studied, goal-oriented interactive process? What goals beyond the general one of making the unconscious conscious, can confrontation analysis set? Considering the various reasons why patients seek help, and considering what this system holds to be essential in an individual's growth into an independent, mature person, three major areas of work have been selected as therapeutic goals, with varying degrees of emphasis and energy placed on each, depending, of course, on the patient's needs. These goals are not restricted by procedures and techniques; rather, they can be most effectively dealt with through the confrontation analytic structure and philosophy. These goals were also selected on the basis of what the present system assumes to be people's existential nature and general aspirations, while the procedures and techniques evolved as a result of experiencing what is most helpful in achieving these aspirations. These areas have also been chosen for therapeutic work because they seem to encompass territories of the self in which many patients experience difficulties. The three areas, to be discussed in detail (and with clinical illustrations) are communication, emotionality, and identity.

The Nature of Communication

The role of communication in everyday life can hardly be overestimated. Educational institutions, industrial and governmental agencies, and social and political interest groups are concerned with the field of communication in all its aspects. Hall (1959) views communication as encompassing the totality of culture in general, and as being the essence of any interpersonal activity. From the interpersonal viewpoint, communication may be defined as "the amount of information exchanged between partners and how much of it is understood, ignored, or denied" (Ruesch, 1959). Ruesch also includes another important ingredient in this definition—the extent of information that the transmitter *wishes* the receiver to understand. Communication within the individual, or the *intrapersonal,* may be defined as the degree and depth of openness between conscious and unconscious processes. Spiegel (1959), who argues that "communication deserves to be an essential goal of therapy rather than the incidental achievement it often is," believes that intrapsychic communication must also be part of the therapeutic achievement.

Psychological phenomena may be defined in the language of communication, and symptomatology may be appropriately described in that language (Rycroft, 1958). In clinical practice, the majority of the patients' psychological problems may be perceived as problems in communication between themselves and others, and/or lack of awareness of their own processes of intracommunication; i.e., how unconscious processes transmit messages to the conscious self (resulting in certain experiences) and, vice versa, how conscious perception affects the unconscious world. The flow of messages from various aspects of the self is, therefore, of extreme importance in the conduct of one's life and, obviously, any input during the formation of the self (in infancy and childhood) greatly affects the nature, shape, and degree of the flow of such messages. One of the important goals of confrontation analysis is to help the patient learn to appropriately increase (as in most cases of neurotic repression) or decrease (as in certain cases of impulse flooding) the degree of intrapersonal openness (communication between conscious and unconscious processes), as well as to facilitate the exchange of *desired* (not compulsively motivated) information between oneself and others. The achievement of this goal creates a basis for the patient to assume increased control over his own destiny. Inter- and intrapersonal communication thus form the functional foundation of the dependence-independence dimension of personality organization.

The main purpose here is to explore ways of modifying, through the confrontation system, behavior that is problematic to the patient, and expressed through inadequate communication patterns. According to Singer (1965), "all behavior is communicative—expressive of inner states even when it seems designed to obscure the inner situation." When an individual becomes aware of his communication patterns, he is thus in a position to understand his inner states. Singer asserts that such a position (regarding the role of communication) in psychotherapy "leads to the emphasis upon communicative activity as a hallmark of emotional well-being; to the insistence that human beings are psychologically healthy when their activities are intelligible and validifiable symbols of their inner experiences, and that they are pathological when their pseudo-activities disrupt adequate communicative exchange. This point of view posits that all activity is communicative and is either an adequate or inadequate expression of inner states; that even obscure symbolizations (inevitably associated with inactivity or pseudo-activity) are paradoxically also expressive and thereby communicative." Confrontation analysis is concerned with the modification, or alteration of inadequate communication patterns; however, since these are expressions of inner states, the inner state must be changed first. By the same token, before altering inner states, one needs to learn what these states are, and this is difficult when expression is so distorted in the communicative pattern. This type of thinking may appear to be rather circular, but *communication is not a one-way street*; it does not only proceed from the inner state and out into the communicative-expressive channel. All expression, in turn, affects the inner state of the subject. When an intervening variable, such as the therapist's reaction, enters into expression, the communication may be changed, and this change will have an impact on the inner state. Thus, one needs to understand, through whatever channels of communication the patient makes available, what his or her inner state is. One must react therapeutically to that state, keeping in mind the patient's state of receptivity.

6
Verbal and Nonverbal Communication

Verbal communication has always been regarded as the primary vehicle in therapeutic transactions. Language has thus assumed supreme importance in the understanding of the messages exchanged between patient and therapist. However, Schachtel (1959) expressed a critical perspective on this subject in his book *Metamorphosis*:

> Many people believe that if language could attain the precision of the model of communication in mathematical symbols then all the complex problems of communication would be solved, people would really be in touch with each other, and the source of all misunderstanding would be eliminated. While precision can no doubt do much to reduce the ambiguity of scientific and other language, the belief that human communication in its entirety could be based on the mathematical model rests on a fundamental misconception of the human situation and the nature of experience. There is no concept, no word, and no sign which completely circumscribes and exhausts an experience in the way in which the mathematical symbol completely represents the mathematical concept. Since human experience always concerns man's relation to "being" in its inexhaustible and unfathomable depth and variety, no symbol or word can take its place, and, as it were, limit and fixate that which by its very nature is limitless and always in flux.

The overemphasis on verbal communication in psychotherapy stems from the belief in the "mathematical model," as well as from the (empirical) assumption that so far as language development is concerned, it ought to be considered under the general umbrella of "learned" behavior, thus being governed by principles of conditioning and, therefore, amenable to deconditioning—or at least, to some modification.

Another common assumption, mentioned in the preceding quotation from Singer, is that language is the best tool the individual has to express inner states. Because of these assumptions, psychotherapy depends to a large measure on what transpires *verbally* during the therapeutic session. Nonverbal communication, however, has been assumed to be a random, unintentional expression determined by obscure, biological (genetic) factors, only minimally affected by outside stimuli and, therefore, not considered to follow the principles of "learned" behavior. Consequently, of course, no modification by psychotherapeutic methods was thought possible. This assumption minimized the influence of nonverbal communication in the interactions between children and parents. One can understand the traditional historical lack of interest in nonverbal communication, but these beliefs were based on inaccurate information. To be sure, certain gestures and body movements seem to be constitutional in origin, but even these are influenced by the learning process, mainly through imitation and identification. The latest developments in the field of communication suggest that at least some nonverbal communication ought to be included under the category of learned behavior (Watzlawick et al., 1967). Learning of both verbal and nonverbal (e.g., "silent") communication is inextricably bound with the development of the child's relationship to his parents. The therapeutic process depends upon consideration of these important factors. Verbal and nonverbal communication may be thought of in terms of figure and ground, which are often interchangeable. At times, the verbal aspects of a message are the focus (the figure) of the therapist's concentration, while at other times one must consider the nonverbal communication as the most significant object in the interactive process between patient and therapist.

Nonverbal communication varies in its expression. Gestures, body positions, breathing patterns, focused and nonfocused eye-movements, psychosomatic symptomatology, compulsive tics, stuttering, conversion symptoms, and silence are all manifestations of nonverbal communication—relaying messages with varying degrees of significance at different times during the therapeutic relationship and within the confines of the therapeutic session.

Non-verbal Communication

Silence

For any individual, verbal communication and silence may be regarded as representing the duality of human experience, and their use as the alternating expression of an existential condition at any point in time. *Duality* encompasses the central psychological dimensions in human existence, such as life and death, activity and passivity, attachment and detachment, and unity and fragmentation. The foundation for these dimensions is laid down during infancy and childhood, most importantly during the time when dependency and the interactive patterns that serve it are established. These dimensions grow out of the relationship between (primarily) the mother and the child and, thus, what occurs in that relationship relative to dependency needs assumes major importance for the development of the child's communication structure. Of course, the dependence-independence dimension of the adult self, and its expression in verbal and nonverbal communication patterns depends a great deal on the separation process. Schachtel (1959) perceives this process as expressed very clearly in the feeding interaction between mother and child, and he observes that this activity involves not only the passive flow of milk to the receiving infant, but also active sucking behavior. This activity gradually engenders the perception in the infant that he is, to some degree, separated from the feeding entity, but at the same time dependent on it for the satisfaction of needs. Schachtel uses the terms *embeddedness* and *activity* to emphasize both the phenomenological origin of dependence (*intrauterine embeddedness*) and the behavioral conditions for independence (*activity*), which eventually lead to *relatedness*. He sees this basic condition as a continuing life struggle:

> Man is forever on the road between embeddedness and emergence from embeddedness, where he is on this road at each moment of his life determines and finds expression in, the kind of emotions which he experiences. Thus, the

prevalence of activity—or of embeddedness—affect is both a result and an indication not only of the impact of a particular situation but also of how far man has gone in his development toward emergence from embeddedness and toward relatedness to the world open to him.

Translated into communication language (and a few transitional steps are skipped for purposes of brevity), once the infant's neuro-motor speech apparatus, or "pool of active silence," is physiologically ready for, and capable of, verbal utterances, the infant must either *actively* engage this apparatus to produce verbal utterances or choose to refrain from pulling them out of their embeddedness and remain silent and nonverbal. Such a decision, however conscious or unconscious it may be, is dependent on the present needs of the infant: physiological, emotional, perceptual, or reflexive. Thus any verbal or silent behavior is geared to the satisfaction of needs. Ego communication is always, as in any other behavioral sequence, first need-satisfying and later goal-conditioned. The therapist must therefore question not whether the patient's communications have a purpose, but what that purpose is, what needs the communications serve at that moment. Nonverbal, silent behavior precedes verbal behavior in the development of the total communication network, and this makes its study crucial to the understanding of basic personality dynamics and, more specifically, to the understanding of the therapeutic transactions that often occur in a rather regressive atmosphere. In fact, some scientists believe that language originated from the imitation of gestures made with the arms and head (Miller, 1963).

For a message to be completely understood, one must have enough information about its total context. For example, a verbal message may not be intelligible at all if the nonverbal behavior that accompanies it is ignored, and, vice versa, silent behavior or other nonverbal communication may be totally misinterpreted in the absence of accompanying verbal messages. It is not surprising that the written word has never achieved the impact of the spoken word. Griffin and Patton (1971) believe that "nonverbal communication ultimately defines an interpersonal relationship." According to them, "nonverbal communication can sometimes carry a direct message; at other times, it may function as meta-communication, that is, information indicating how to interpret a verbal message. In either case, nonverbal communication generally is taken to be highly indicative of the true relationship between two people."

Silence, as one aspect of nonverbal communication, has unique properties. It is the basic element out of which verbal communication grows—its bedrock. It represents the initial, existential "presence" of any potential communication process: *in the beginning there was silence*! What follows the silence depends to a large measure on its nature, its structure, and its history with the interactive surroundings. Popular expressions such as "pregnant silence," or "the calm before the storm," suggest that silence is often considered the birthplace of what later develops into an individual's world of communication. In different cultures, silence assumes a variety of meanings. It has both positive and negative values, and it is transmitted from generation to generation as part of the cultural communication heritage. In the smaller unit, the family, silence also assumes idiosyncratic meaning, although even within this unit it tends to vary greatly, usually depending on the interpersonal conditions. Silence may mean approval for one child and disapproval for a sibling under the same "objective" conditions. Remaining silent at the dinner table may connote good manners for one child, fear for another. Traditionally, our civilization has conditioned those it considered less intelligent to be silent, leaving in doubt whether these people are indeed less endowed intellectually or whether they behave in such a manner because of their conditioning. Because of the extreme importance given to the spoken word through approval and disapproval, very few people grow up feeling comfortable and secure about their silence in interpersonal relationships, or able to listen to their own silence when alone. Silence can suggest fear of others, consideration for others, control of others or oneself, punishment, insult, or approval. In the therapeutic realm, the therapist must learn the meaning of each patient's silence, since it is likely to provide important clues to that patient's dynamics, and consequently open up communication pathways in therapy (Khan, 1963; Zeligs, 1961).

In most therapeutic, interpersonal communications, the therapist quite clearly occupies a central place in the life of the patient while investigating his personality. How does the therapist's verbal output *and* silent behavior affect the patient's communications? What messages, silent and verbal, does the therapist send out to the patient to affect his behavior inside and outside of the office? It has traditionally been acceptable to assume that the totally bland and silent therapist is used by the patient as a projection screen, one that is blank and free of any "contamination." In other words, silence is presumed to be noncommunicative (thus "noncontaminatory") when used by the therapist. Psychoanalytic theory does not really consider the way in which the analyst's silence affects the content and structure of the patient's productions, other than assuming that silence "forces" the patient to "confess" secrets that he would not otherwise reveal, and create "clean" transference. Thus Reik (1968) notes that the analyst's silence places pressure on the patient to produce more hitherto hidden material, and Racker (1968) squarely defines silence as "a form of acting," as much as interpretation is, with the difference that the latter is "a health-restoring instrument par excellence, whereas the former may be anti-therapeutic." The double standards and confusion in this area of interpersonal transactions with the analytic situation are quite obvious. Thus, for instance, countertransference is perceived and generally discussed as if it were contained only in the verbal communications of the analyst, and not in the silent ones.

Silence, Resistance, and Transference.

When a patient speaks in individual psychotherapy, the conscious intention is, obviously, to direct communication toward the therapist. Curiously enough, however, when the patient remains silent, more often than not, he does not perceive the silence as directed toward the therapist, often because the silence is not perceived as communication. This belief regarding the nature of communication is not uncommon; as Ruesch (1959) aptly puts it: "Frequently too, verbal communication is identified with intentional expression and nonverbal communication with unintentional expression." Psychoanalysts have always been aware of the fact that *silence is intentional*; however, their understanding of this intention has primarily focused on one aspect—*resistance*. As Greenson (1967) asserts:

This [silence] is the most transparent and frequent form of resistance met with in psychoanalytic practice. Generally, it means that the patient is either consciously or unconsciously unwilling to communicate his thoughts or feelings to the analyst. . . . By and large and for the most practical purposes, silence is a resistance to the analysis and has to be handled as such.

This rather rigid and unilateral approach blatantly ignores the analyst-receiver of the message. Ruesch (1959), however, views this issue differently:

After all, the inner life of another person is accessible only through *verbal and nonverbal exchange* (*emphasis added*), and, in a social situation, what is done or said is determined as much by one participant as by the other. Inferences about personalities, then, depend upon who is looking at them.

When the psychoanalyst assumes that nonverbal communication, such as silence, is mainly used in the service of resistance (thus ignoring the role of the therapist in eliciting it at times), the therapist is clearly making the same type of unwarranted assumption as the patient who does not perceive his own silence as having anything to do with the analyst, or as being part of the communication. As a matter of general theoretical principle, then, psychoanalysis tends to interpret most nonverbal communication that transpires during the analytic hour as "acting out," since the patient is always the subject of the investigation, and since whatever he does that does not follow the rule of free-association is labeled as self-destructive. Interpretations of unconscious conflicts come in very handy to explain this supposed "resistance" when the patient is silent! The silence and other nonverbal activities of the analyst are generally ignored, or interpreted away as techniques or strategy necessary for the process of analysis.

In contrast to this view, confrontation analysis posits that all nonverbal communication must be treated in the same manner as verbal communication, thus refraining from judging the patient's behavior as resistance just because it is nonverbal. This is necessary because of the importance placed on the interactive reality of the dyadic relationship in which the analyst's contributions to the patient's production—directly or indirectly—cannot be denied. This view of the therapeutic relationship raises the issue of how *transference* fits into the communication process.

The psychoanalytic definition of transference refers mainly

to reactions of the patient toward the analyst, although there are some analysts who extend this definition to include people outside the therapeutic situation. Fenichel (1945) defines transference in this manner:

> The patient misunderstands the present in terms of the past, and then instead of remembering the past, he strives, without recognizing the nature of his actions, to relive the past and live it more satisfactorily than he did in childhood. He transfers past attitudes to the present.

Further commenting on the importance and use of transference in psychoanalysis, Fenichel adds,

> The analysand, seeking immediate satisfaction of derivatives instead of facing his original impulses, attempts to use short-circuit substitutes for his repressed drives. On the other hand the transference offers the analyst a unique opportunity to observe directly the past of this patient and thereby to understand the development of his conflicts.

This approach to the analysis of what transpires in the therapeutic hour totally ignores the analyst's contribution to the transference, and requires that the therapist "judge" whether a reaction originates from the patient's past or is a result of the reality of the analytic situation combined with past unresolved conflicts. Fenichel recognizes this important issue, but does not offer any solution:

> The problem is even more complicated when the patient *obviously* misconstrues the real situation and loves or hates the analyst for something which, in the *judgment of the analyst,* is nonexistent. (emphasis added)

The psychoanalyst's interpretation of silence is all too often based on this understanding and definition of transference, without acknowledgment of the analyst's contribution. Thus, the "judgment of the analyst" is colored by the *theory* about what certain behaviors mean in the abstract, rather than what they mean in terms of the immediacy of the interpersonal encounter.

When the analyst views himself as a *tabula rasa*, the interactive element of the therapeutic process is (by force) reduced to a minimum and, quite logically, the procedure that emanates from this theoretical premise must heavily rely on techniques that produce *minimum interaction*, such as free association on the part of the patient, and interpretations on the part of the analyst. Such thinking serves to support the need for the psy-

choanalyst to produce "pure transference" conditions so that
analysis may proceed according to the theoretical model. Indeed,
this can occur only in the mind of the analyst! Goz (1975), however, suggests that the therapist cannot be a *tabula rasa* and
still help in the development of a working alliance. Even if the
analyst could assume a perfectly neutral stance in the analytic
situation, how meaningful would this be for the patient? How
could the patient's "distorted" perception of reality (transference) be modified in such a one-way therapeutic situation, if it
developed *originally* under conditions of interaction and interpersonal exchange? Most people, according to analytic theory,
develop personality characteristics, and especially their attitudes toward themselves and others, *in the presence of and in
relation to others* (significant objects). When the patient "projects"
distortions transferentially, he is likely to experience many associations related to these others. In an attempt to correct these
distortions, the analyst uses the interpretations to drive a wedge
between the transferential distortions and the present reality.
The repetition of these transferential distortions, and the repeated interpretations of the analyst in the "working through"
process are supposed to help the patient react more appropriately to the present. The "concerned," but mostly silent, analyst
is supposed to provide emotional support for the patient while
such changes are occurring.

Basic problems seem to result from this theory of healing.
The first problem, touched upon above, needs further clarification because of its central importance: Psychoanalysis, in its
theory of technique (not its theory of personality dynamics), only
pays lip service to its own assumption that object (person) relations develop in the context of interaction with others, especially significant others. Object relations, the internalized patterns of interactions between introjects and the self and their
expression in interpersonal relationships, are learned and conditioned within such a context and therefore, their modification
through the therapeutic procedure should logically and ideally
contain the element of interaction. Children who grow up in an
environment that is noninteractive, or minimally interactive,
show marked deviations in their personality structure. In fact,
autism is often thought to develop partially because of minimal
interaction or confusing interaction (double-binds and conflict-

ing verbal and nonverbal cues) that infants and children experience in their early development. Interaction certainly includes both patient and therapist and, for this reason, *confrontation analysis regards transferential reactions as units of communication*. As such they can be modified *only* if the receiving end of the message (the therapist) reacts to them in a way that is different from the original experience. The therapist's reactions must ultimately confront the patient with inconsistencies, distortions, inappropriateness, or anything that blocks progress toward his goals. Confrontations take the form of questions, interpretations, suggestions, hypotheses, etc. Through this approach, the patient is alerted to his distorted communication patterns, and can be helped to discover how to communicate more effectively on an inter- and intrapersonal level. Naturally, the therapist must allow the transference to develop optimally so that the confrontation and, later, its analysis, will be meaningful.

This does not necessitate *routine silence* on the part of the therapist. It must be clear to the therapist that any transferential reaction contains not only the patient's distortions, but whatever the therapist presents to the patient from the moment both meet. The therapist's silence affects patients differently at different times, and its timing and use must thus be carefully assessed and monitored as the communication language between patient and therapist unfolds. More specifically, the therapist must be aware of the impact of his presence, his self, and his behavior on a given patient in order for treatment to proceed. The "working alliance" on which therapeutic continuity rests, indeed without which progress may be in jeopardy, depends on the course of such development.

A 25-year-old single woman started therapy because she was depressed and indecisive about a boyfriend who had been maltreating her. However, she also "adored" him because of his great professional successes and "superior brains." She came for therapy three times a week and was not unfamiliar with the process, since she had had two years of therapy as a preadolescent (presumably for enuresis). She was quickly able to divulge a great deal of her history, and in a few weeks I had a fairly good grasp of her family background, her emotional upheavals, and her present feelings concerning her boyfriend. She described her state of mind as generally alternating between depression and anger.

She came to her 15th session a few minutes late, and as she sat down, she scrutinized me rather carefully with what seemed to be contempt, and remained silent for about four minutes—a rather unusual behavior for her. I then asked her what was on her mind. She hesitated, and then said that she missed going to school, even though she perceived college as a waste of time. She said, "I don't know why I have been thinking about it lately, because it's crazy. The more you go to school, the more you lose touch with the real world. I am talking about the social sciences or the humanities. You get involved with stupid details that really have nothing to do with life or anything. It's 'mental masturbation.' That's exactly what school is. I mean the teachers are all supposed to be experts in something or other, but they're so removed from what's happening out there; what exactly do they contribute to the world, or to anybody? It's just depressing." She again fell silent, obviously angry, but visibly trying to calm herself.

Although I was not sure at that point what this was all about, I decided to confront her with a hypothesis—an interpretation—to see where it would take us, risking the possibility that she might become more defensive. At the same time, I felt that letting this precious moment go would have been more of a loss. A lost opportunity is just that—lost—and cannot be recaptured, while defensiveness can be tackled immediately. I thus decided to focus on her lateness and her silence, rather than on her anger about the college professors. I asked whether her lateness and her silence at the beginning of the session were expressions of her anger, her way of communicating such feelings. She denied that her lateness had anything to do with her feeling, because it was due to a malfunction of the elevator in her building, but she admitted that her silence was anger. It later emerged that she was angry at me because of my "digging into details" that she didn't feel had much to do with her present situation, and that at some point in the past, she had made a decision to express her anger in a way that was the exact opposite of her father's way—that is, by remaining silent rather than ranting and hollering as he had. When she came to the session, she said she was not consciously thinking about me, but she was more preoccupied with her need to make a decision to register for a graduate course. As she discussed this more, she became more openly hostile toward me, and launched a surprisingly strong attack on me for "assuming" and "expecting" that she ought to discuss her feelings and her anger my way— verbally. She said, rightfully, "I don't want to be told how to express myself, how to be 'a good patient,' or a 'good student.' I mean I don't have to conform to your style."

While she was talking, I knew that she was right—I had expected her to express her anger verbally, although, consciously, I tried to convince myself that any expression, including the nonverbal one, was all right with me. Of course, I had my own prejudices about the "silent patient" from my analytic training, and she picked that up quite readily. I admitted to her that she was right about my expectation, and accepted her premise that there are many ways of expressing a feeling, and that each person had the right to their own way. I added, however, that I had to know that this was one of her ways of expressing anger, since that would help me understand her feelings when she expressed them in this manner. It became quite clear that her silence, in this instance, was less of a resistance and more an expression of her need to establish her autonomy, her independence from her family, especially her father. To perceive her silence as merely resistance, and to analyze it as such would have been missing the mark. Silence for this patient had many meanings. Subsequent to this encounter with her silence, similar behavior needed to be understood in terms of familial codes of conduct, which were expressed through patterns of communication. The issue was not resistance. In order to work with this patient on changes in her communications network, it was necessary to establish a common understanding of her communication codes, rather than imposing on them a superstructure of meanings, expectations, and interpretations unrelated to this particular individual.

This case illustrates the way in which confrontation analysis attempts to help the patient become aware of communication patterns. I made no comment about the silence until it occurred again within the session and seemed to evolve into a pattern. As the therapeutic work unfolds, the origin of such patterns become increasingly evident, and the interactive model of the confrontational technique then becomes a basis on which the patient can build independent pathways of communication most suited to his personality. From his perspective, the analyst must retain in his mind the patient's *patterns of interaction* with him, and to be ready to use them at appropriate times as part of his interventional strategy.

In the above illustration, the patient was aware of a very strong pull, a need to behave like her father when she was angry, but she also wished to separate from him, and thus needed to mobilize a great deal of energy in order to behave differently (silent rather than explosive when angry). In this manner she attempted to establish her own identity. Obviously, she was not too comfortable with this, simply because there were a number of unresolved inner conflicts related to this issue.

The present approach does not hold that the conflict must be resolved before the behavior changes. Often these two processes must move along parallel lines. Thus the confrontation and the analytic followup contained the following sequence: (1) a challenge to the patient's behavior ("I wonder what's on your mind," and later "I wonder if you were angry in the beginning of the session as you seem to be now with your silence"). (2) Acceptance of the patient's need to behave in her way ("I realize there are many ways of expressing anger, and silence is certainly one of them, sometimes this is your way"). (3) A recognition by the therapist of the validity of the patient's stance regarding the therapist's behavior when it is correct. Novey (1968) recognizes that therapists often misinterpret the patient's communication as transferential (and thus based on distortions), when in fact it may not be so:

> This is not infrequently done at the expense of valid judgments the patient may be making. Especially when the therapist himself is the object of censure is there the tendency to assume that it is a projective defense on the patient's part. This may be used by the therapist as a mode of warding off valid criticisms, and if it is so used, it will interfere with the therapeutic process.

(4) A clarification by the therapist of his own requirements—negotiable and given to change if necessary—for the establishment of a "working alliance," which comes about, partially, by establishing a common communication language as the therapeutic process unfolds ("I must know what the silence means to you at different times so that we can be on the same wavelength.").

The second problem in the psychoanalytic approach, which uses the interpretation as the major tool for effecting changes in personality dynamics, relates to the way patients are liable to use such a tool. While interpretations offer insight about the origin and dynamics of conflicts, patients often accept them, consciously and unconsciously, as if they were the word of God and the truth of all truths. Eventually, they learn to use them as a substitute for real change. This happens even with a most skilled practitioner, mainly because the therapist assumes an inordinate importance in the life of the patient, and whatever happens during the analytic hour becomes holier than thou, despite the resistance, ambivalence, and struggle that the patient experiences during analysis. There is no doubt that, in a sense, interpretations enslave many patients to certain modes of thinking and perceiving that may have little connection with their inner personalities. Their entire analysis may become a superimposed intellectual structure, devoid of any natural or spontaneous character.

Confrontation analysis makes interpretive interventions, too. However, they are all made in the context of interaction; interpretations are not pronounced as part of the Holy Scriptures. Because of this process, the basis on which the self stands—reactions and interactions—is brought back to life in the therapeutic session with past and present interacting and confronting each other, creating an opportunity for examination of what needs to be changed, accepted, or abandoned. The scientist in the laboratory cannot be satisfied solely with announcing observations if he intends to modify certain factors in the environment. But in order to learn what and how changes are to be made, one must go beyond one's observations: one must alter conditions, open up new dimensions through new stimuli, and eventually arrive at conclusions on the basis of a myriad of new conditions, so that the changes and conclusions command meaning and usefulness. The therapist must follow a similar path: he must alter conditions by using a variety of techniques designed to understand the patient from many different angles. Thus, the therapist listens, interprets, confronts, mirrors, empathizes, imitates, irritates, hypothesizes, analyzes, and, above all, investigates. In this context, transferential reactions become therapeutically meaningful, because they emerge from an encounter that is immediate, natural, and spontaneous. Such an encounter has all the ingredients of the scientific laboratory, with the added dimension of emotional involvement, in an appropriate manner, of the experimenter or therapist.

Such an approach has often been criticized as nonanalytic, and as unable to bring forth unconscious material that can be analyzed along the transference neurosis dimension. In fact, the claim is that transference neurosis could not develop with such an approach because the transference is too "contaminated" by the therapist's reactions to "deserve" the name! Of course, confrontation analysis is not psychoanalysis. However, because of the confrontational techniques used with this method of treatment, transferential material not only surfaces and is constantly the object of the therapeutic work, but it becomes more readily available, as the clinical case histories presented in this volume illustrate. Many patients who have gone through long, arduous years of analysis with some very fine and capable psychoanalysts find the challenge of confrontation analysis refreshing, inescapable, demanding of hard work, and helpful in the achievement of their goals. There are, of course, various patients who can more fruitfully use one approach rather than another. However, this is related not to the "missing transference" in the therapeutic relationship, but to inadequate judgment by a therapist who is not flexible enough in assessing a patient's needs.

According to Greenson (1967), the psychoanalyst's silence is mandated to allow for the development of transference. This strategy is advanced as a major cornerstone of psychoanalytic theory and practice. Empirically, it is of course true that most (neurotic) patients, and perhaps most people, tend to project their inner world more when the other side of the communication circle (the receiver-therapist) is more or less mute. Such behavior on the part of the analyst is, however, tantamount to blatant manipulation of one individual by another, with the silent person assuming the role of the authority. Greenson admits to this, although somewhat reticently: "The judicious use of waiting in silence is one of the most important tools for facilitating the development of the transference. Yet, strictly speaking, it is a manipulation." The rationalization that silence promotes the transferential process seems rather contradictory if a manipulation by the analyst is admitted to be a form of acting out, thereby reducing the "transferential purity." In fact, the dogmatic use of silence as part of the strategy has many more disadvantages than advantages. Thus, for instance, silence is, for many patients, a severe punishment, and may be more harmful in the long run. The possibility exists that many psychoanalysts do not use silence "judiciously," as Greenson no doubt meant it to be, for they become engrossed in the technique and conditioned to utilize it rather than listen to the patient's needs. While there are no statistics to substantiate such a belief, there seem to be too many patients who complain that their analyst hardly spoke to them throughout many years of treatment, and they bitterly remember those years as a waste of time. There are, of course, some psychoanalysts who appreciate the positive *and* negative effects of the therapist's silence (Aull and Strean, 1967; Nacht, 1964; Jacobs, 1973).

It is clear that both the communication patterns of those who come for treatment and the strategies devised by the therapist to deal with them are of supreme importance, for this is the "bread and butter" of therapeutic work. Silence as a form of communication holds much meaning for patient and therapist, and serves to emphasize the role of communication in therapy. Perhaps the most devasting effect of a therapist's "nonjudicious" silence is that it may reinforce a dependency pattern from which the patient can hardly extricate himself, even when the patient leaves treatment "improved." Much of the time, silence between partners (and therapy must be thought of as a partnership) breeds inequality, subservience, and a deadening of the interactive contact. It is curious that an entire system, such as psychoanalysis, makes a virtue out of such a clearly destructive "ritual." Ruesch (1959) expressed this notion in a most succinct manner:

> The therapist cannot wait for the results of a test, and he cannot delay for hours or days his responses to the statements of his patients. When a person makes a statement, the reply or lack of reply on the part of the doctor acknowledges, amplifies, contrasts, or contradicts. In tying statement to statement within the mind of the patient and from person to person, reorganization of disturbed communication becomes possible . . . time consuming analytic and reductive methods which break behavior into component parts have proved ineffective and nonsensical.

7

Communication and the Confrontation Analysis Approach

One can hardly conceive of civilization without communication in general, and verbal communication in particular. According to Novey (1968), "psychotherapy and psychoanalysis, despite their interest in and capacity to cope with the emotions, are heavily dependent on verbal process for their investigative and therapeutic applications." Verbal communication is, in fact, more than a vehicle for the transactions that transpire between patient and therapist; it is, in and of itself, the object of therapeutic change. Vaughn and Burgoon (1976) report Goldstein, Heller, and Sechrest's agreement on this conceptualization. They note that, "it should be a surpise to no one that we view the therapeutic and helping relationship as a directed, deliberate application of the psychology of behavior change in which communication as a form of social influence is both the primary object of attention and also the principal vehicle for inducing the desired change." The multidimensional property of communication is part and parcel of every human expression, because it symbolizes the essence of human experience. Indeed, confrontation analysis does not claim monopoly over these areas—they are the basic concern of most *dynamic* theories of psychological healing. However, in certain aspects, the *thera-*

peutic approach of confrontation analysis may differ substantially from the others.

Continuity and Discontinuity in Verbal Communication

If a child's experience of the world lacks cohesive continuity, distorted verbal communication may result. Cohesive continuity refers to the consistency, smoothness, and spontaneity of transition from one psychological condition or state to another as verbally expressed to the child while he interacts with others. Abrupt changes and disruptions cause the child to experience life as discontinuous, as if it consisted of discrete, unrelated events. Such discontinuities may occur as a result of many factors, including physical illnesses and environmental trauma such as a move to unfamiliar surroundings, fires, and loud noises. However, the most impressionistic discontinuities for the child are created by the significant adults whose transactions, either directly with the child or indirectly, through their interaction with each other, are (unconsciously) designed to be noncommunicative, self-centered, and insensitive to the child's immediate needs. When these disruptions are severe and repetitive they are likely to contribute to a self-image that is fragmented, insecure, and lacking in direction, and to an ego that is inadequately defended. In general, the child may develop a self-concept that is not integrated, and a perception of others and a relation to them that may be lacking in objective evaluation and judgment. Ruesch (1957), discussing the etiology of disturbed communication, describes the process:

> Communication belongs to those human functions which are the hardest to master and take the longest to learn. Since each step is built upon the previous one and since decades of continuous practice are required before an individual becomes an effective communicator, any *interference* at an early stage leaves its indelible mark. Stimulation from the environment may be lacking, exaggerated, or ill-timed, and growth therefore may by retarded. Early experiences which constitute the basics for later development may be so inadequate that in spite of proper care in the later years the individual does not reach his full potentiality. The acquisition of skills may be indefinitely postponed if competent teachers are not available or if opportunities for practice are not provided (*emphasis added*).

In the area of verbal communication, discontinuous experiences are of paramount significance, because the spoken language—man's highest achievement—is used to establish fundamental connections with others through the expression of feelings, wishes, ideas, and values. Therefore, when a child is reared in an atmosphere that does not allow one to learn this skill effectively, or worse, if it teaches how to communicate only for negative or destructive purposes, that child's language will constitute one of the greatest hinderances to the achievement of his or her personal goals.

A most potent technique used by parents to create discontinuities in communication, and, thus, in the child's grasp of the situation, is the inappropriate use of silence. For example, refusing to complete a message or to make it comprehensible when it is ambiguous, or utilizing silence as a tool for the expression of discontent or anger. The receiver of the message (the child), having no appropriate information to decode it, gradually develops a system of perceiving and behaving toward the environment on the basis of distorted (autistic) reality and with little consensual validation. Consequently, the child's relationship to the world might be characterized by great distance and by rigid, defensive walls erected for protection. In this vein, Novey (1968) aptly notes that, "all communications have, as one of their characteristics, the capacity to invite greater intimacy or to function as distancing devices."

In psychotherapy, patients manifest disturbances resulting from their developmental history of communication in various forms. Often, the speech pattern is uneven, sometimes it is monotonously even and lacking in appropriate modulation, and at other times it is too "pressured," resulting in threatening unpredictability. The repetitious use of silence by the parents later becomes part of the individual's repertoire of "normal" communication. These silences result from early childhood conditioning, and represent a code of behavior within the family's "normal" verbal communication. In a certain sense, one might think of such silences as a "language" that the child learns within the context of communication. Often, the importance of this language in the therapeutic transactions lies both in its failure to communicate the individual's present state of mind in a comprehensible manner, and in its repetition of the earlier patterns of communication, which were discontinuous and often symptomatic of serious disturbances within the family constellation. Ferreira, Winter, and Poindexter (1966), in investigating certain interactional variables that could differentiate normal from abnormal families, found that silence was a key differentiating factor. Abnormal families used silence in a way that was detrimental to the task set by the experimenters. Their findings were "consistent with clinical impression of lowered efficiency in abnormal families." If the therapeutic situation is conducive to the creation of transference neurosis, then repetition of family patterns of interaction is bound to occur in those situations, both in the patient's psyche and in his behavior. Consequently, if the patient's experience within the family was discontinuous because silence played a significant role, there is no doubt that the patient's silence and that of the analyst will become heavily weighted in the communication network. A pattern similar to the one experienced within the family would become reestablished. Such patterns create difficulties within the therapeutic milieu because they introduce the illusion that life is made up of *unconnected events*. They violate the basic reality that life is an evolving process and must be understood as a continuous process. Clinicians are not unfamiliar with the patient who demands that the symptom be treated apart from the totality of personality. Needless to say, the same phenomenon is also seen nowadays in reverse: some psychotherapies promise symptomatic cures with complete disregard for the whole person (Kubie, 1975).

The main problem to face here is how to deal with discontinuities that seem to be causally related to distorted communication patterns, and to provide a learning framework within which the patient can bridge the gaps in his experiential history so as to become capable of communicating directly and meaningfully. A few central technical, procedural, strategic, and contextual issues clarify the confrontation analysis approach to distorted communication.

The Confrontational Approach to Discontinuity: Content Versus Process Intervention.

Any therapeutic attempts designed to correct the results of unhealthy early childhood experiences, as in discontinuity, must obviously be accomplished through indirect intervention.

This intervention must be aimed at what one might hypothesize to be the specific consequences of these untoward developments. Thus intervention may be directed either at the content of the verbal message or its process. *Content* refers to meaning, or immediate connotation of the message, while *process* refers to its patterning with regard to regularity, manner of delivery, historical (in the personal sense) place and context, and the stimuli that elicit its expressions, especially within the transferential, therapeutic milieu. The therapist must make this distinction in order to map out interventions related to the underlying problems acquired early in the patient's development. This distinction must be handled in a fundamental manner by therapists of all persuasions. The question always arises as to whether the therapist ought to direct interventions on the basis of *what* the patient says (content), or on the basis of *how* the story unfolds (the process the patient uses to communicate inner life). Fenichel (1941) aptly expresses this dilemma: "the infinite multiplicity of situations arising in analysis does not permit the formulation of general rules about how the analyst should act in every situation, because each situation is essentially unique." Of course, this does not mean that some guidelines with regard to content and/or process intervention cannot be advanced. Some analysts implicitly utilize such guidelines. For example, Adatto (1977), describes the sequential—verbal and nonverbal—communications of a patient during an initial interview and interprets them as transferential on the basis of the *process* by which they emerge, as can be seen from the following passage:

> *Sometime during the latter part of the visit he visibly sank into the chair and reported that the mere act of talking to me gave him immediate relief. He felt this was due to his doing something constructive about his problem and also that he sensed that I understood him. After telling me this he straightened up again and said that depending on me for help would be of no use since he would see that as a weakness in himself* (first transference phenomenon).

Adatto's interpretation and manner of relating the patient's messages clearly point to an emphasis on the process that took place in the therapeutic situation. One might surmise that Adatto's process intervention in this particular case afforded the possibility of reaching into the unconscious historical material helpful in clearing the way for analysis of the resistance.

    This example is rather typical of psychoanalysis and other

dynamically oriented psychotherapies, in which the major thrust of the therapeutic efforts centers around the process aspects of the therapeutic transactions. According to this approach, analyzing the content of the messages alone cannot have any lasting effect upon the personality structure, because it only touches superficial defensive aspects of the self. However, the distinction between content and process is not always clear. Therefore, to claim that the therapist must pay more attention to process than to content is easier said than done. Therapeutic transactions often have such an immediacy that they seem to "demand" content-oriented interventions. For example, when a patient is overwhelmingly anxious, it may seem antitherapeutic to make interpretations related to the patient's need to create crisis situations for secondary gains. Yet it is often precisely in these types of therapeutic encounters, when a patient is confronted with a clear pattern of self-destructiveness *during* the crisis, that therapeutic changes begin to take place. Naturally, the timing and skill with which these situations are handled by the therapist are of supreme importance.

Certain nonanalytic approaches, such as client-centered therapy, base their strategy of intervention on a philosophy that views psychotherapy as an evolving process with various, more or less, clear-cut stages. Thus, according to Rogers (1958), the patient's communications indicate where he stands on the continuum of the unfolding therapeutic process, or what stage is involved at that moment. The object of the therapy is, according to this perspective, to move from one stage to the next until the patient becomes capable of responding to new situations on the basis of what is, not on the basis of past experience. The "here and now" orientation of this approach presents certain difficulties when one tries to logically reconcile it with the process (or stages) aspects of the total treatment. However, the theory's principles and the actual practice may not always follow the test of scientific logic. There is no doubt that such is the case with the majority of theories that deal with human dynamics, interaction, and pathology.

Confrontation analysis is especially sensitive to the issue of content and/or process intervention. However, because of its confrontation strategy it may appear that it focuses mainly on content intervention. In order to determine the choice of a specific (content or process) intervention strategy, the therapist must evaluate the patient's status on the dependence–independence dimension as it manifests itself through three major areas of therapeutic concern: communication, emotionality, and identity. The diversity in pathology render's a uniform strategy of intervention useless. In fact, a uniform strategy, even for one patient or one syndrome, cannot be effective throughout the therapeutic work if changes in personality structure and realignment of defenses take place. Nevertheless, there are a number of important issues in verbal communication that provide the therapist with a basis for determining the intervention strategy best suited to serve the central goal of modifying distorted communication patterns.

Differential Intervention Strategy
for Distorted Verbal Communication

A most illuminating exchange between Humpty Dumpty and Alice in *Alice in Wonderland* by Lewis Carroll can be used to understand the kind of problems one encounters in verbal communication:

> "When I use a word," Humpty Dumpty said in a rather scornful tone, "it means just what I choose it to mean—neither more nor less." "The question is," said Alice, "whether you *can* make words mean so many things." "The question is," said Humpty Dumpty, "which is to be master—that's all."

This short exchange exemplifies what occurs in distorted verbal communication. Patients, like other people, have personal meanings attached to their verbal messages, but unlike Humpty Dumpty, they believe these meanings to be universal. This illusion creates many problems in interpersonal communication. Another important problem, one that differentiates people who use distorted communication from those who do not, is expressed in the above exchange, and it is a most crucial aspect in communication: that of mastery, i.e., whether the sender of the message is in control of his own communications. Psychodynamically, this notion may be understood in relation to forces that play a central role in determining what communication patterns dominate the individual's life, both within the therapeutic situation and outside of it. Clearly, the more unconscious forces and motives influence the productions of the ego, the more distortions in one of its primary functions—communication—will result. When such a process takes place, the behavior of the patient tends to appear inconsistent because of the apparent split between conscious wishes and unconscious needs. The therapist, faced with these conflicting messages, must decide to which aspect of the self to respond. This dilemma of therapeutic intervention cannot, however, be resolved instantly. One must first understand the forms these obstacles take and the motivations behind them.

Manifestations of Distorted Communication

Disturbed and pathological communication have many symptomatic manifestations. One of them is silence. To be sure, the silent person, like the verbal one, attempts to convey a message. However, since the nature and content of silences vary, the receiver does not always recognize what the message is. Of course, this is often precisely the intent of the communicator. But when this is not the case, then, more often than not, the intent of the communicator is not achieved. Miller and Steinberg (1975) make a specific assumption:

> . . . all communicative situations require the communicator to make predictions about the effects of his communicative behavior on those with whom he wishes to communicate. Specifically, one chooses from one's available communicative repertoire those specific behaviors, verbal and nonverbal, which seem to have the best chance of being understood and responded to in the way intended.

Silence often achieves the opposite end: it provides the worst opportunity for an individual to be understood. In extreme situations, silence may create more confusion, misinterpretation, and interpersonal distance.

For example, a 48-year-old man sought treatment because he was depressed and unable to "communicate" effectively with his employees. He found himself constantly screaming at whomever happened to be around him. At the end of each day he would leave his office totally dissatisfied with his workers and disgusted with himself because of the way he handled his transactions with them and his clients. An articulate, intelligent, and pleasant man, he demonstrated a rather unusual manner of relating his experiences to me from the first interview. He spoke like a frightened little boy. After every few words, he would stop his verbal activity, stare at me blankly, sometimes scrutinizing me, purse his lips almost defiantly, and resume his talk without always continuing from the point at which he had stopped. His behavior seemed, at the same time, to be a plea to be questioned, even to have me finish his sentences; but most of all, he was asking for permission to proceed. What seemed unusual was his continued use of this style, far beyond the initial interview (when many patients feel hesitant in discussing their intimate life experiences with a stranger). What appeared even more significant than the pattern itself was his complete lack of concern about it. When I would ask him what he had on his mind during his silences, he would always say "Nothing." He did not seem defensive in any way. He even looked puzzled in the beginning, since he was not quite aware of all these discontinuities in his speech pattern. He was not aware of any thoughts, or fantasies, or feelings during these gaps. In his daily life he was involved frequently in hassles with employees over the telephone. They would call him to the phone when a telephone call came in for him, but most of the time he would not acknowledge their call, leaving them in the dark as to whether he had heard them at all. At times he would answer the phone, at others he wouldn't. He could not understand how they could be so "dumb," having worked with him for awhile, and yet not know that this was his way. Of course, he expected new employees to pick up his ways quickly too. This "noncommunicativeness" spilled over into the rest of his business. He expected his employees to understand how the merchandise should be packaged, sent, and billed with little or no guidance from him. At the same time, his tolerance for mistakes (mainly because of his own failure to specify requirements) was very low. He started to become a liability to his own business and was unable to stop the trend. His wife, a "co-sufferer" with others at the plant, finally convinced him that he ought to take care of this problem.

On further explorations into this man's history, I learned that verbal interaction in his childhood had been low on the list of family priorities. He described his father as a harsh, punishing, and "uninvolved" man, with little or no interest in his children's development. He had come to the United States from Europe as a young adult and had no understanding or motivation to learn about the culture around him, and he had made no efforts to learn the language. He was, in general, a sullen, silent man. When he spoke, it was for the purpose of demanding obedience. The patient's mother was apparently terrified of her husband and used to punish the patient in a way that she thought would please her husband. She did not spare the belt, and at times even tied the patient to a bedpost for awhile in order to "keep him in line." Needless to say, he attempted to stay out of the house as much as possible but, even on the street, with his friends, he was shy and withdrawn. When his father would take him to some "pleasurable" activity, he would often cut it short for reasons not totally clear to the patient. He never felt certain what would happen next, and he was always surprised. *Continuity had not been part of his childhood experience.* He was the "smart-bad-boy" at home. The adjective that was used depended on the mood of his parents, and was not related directly to his behavior. Predictably, this created the need for him to guess what his parents wanted from him without their spelling it out and, since he could not do this, their disconnected reactions created an impression of himself as unintegrated and lacking an anchor.

There was no doubt that this man's ego had been severely traumatized by the persistent experience of discontinuity in his early childhood. His relation to the world was characterized by suspicion, distrust, lack of judgment about his impact on others, and in a defensive manner, of others on him. The strange, discontinuous, silence-filled communicative style was no doubt an expression of all these feelings. As his therapist, I at first took his language on face value; did not make any interpretations, nor any comments that alluded to the possibility that there was more behind what the patient told me; merely confronted him with his behavior, of which he was unaware, although he admitted having been told about it innumerable times by his family and his employees. Yet, he was unable to hear it properly, demonstrating his ignorance of the basic quality of communication: *there must be a sender and a receiver.* No communication was taking place between him and others, since one side of the communication network was not tuned in. Perhaps because an authority was diagnosing him and informing him of the diagnosis, he had to listen. After three months in treatment, I asked him why he was treating me in the manner he did, i.e., talking to me with such fear, as if I were going to tie him to a bedpost and beat him. At first he looked shocked, then agitated, and finally, with tears in his eyes, and with a fluency he had not demonstrated prior to this session, he said: "You know, you've said a lot of things to me before, and I must say you really hit the nail on the head each time, and now you did it again: I don't want the rest of my life, whatever is left of it, to be alone, by the bedpost." He then continued to cry for awhile, and when he calmed down, I said to him, "This is the first time you spoke to me in one long sentence without hesitating, and with a lot of feeling. You see, I am still here and you are still here and no one got hurt."

At the following session the patient reported that he was much more relaxed at work and able to hear others and be more informative and patient toward his employees. Even in the sessions, an air of heaviness was less filled with silences. In the beginning of treatment, I had taken the approach of letting him feel comfortable enough by accepting his feelings without any challenge. At the same time, this alone would not have been helpful enough. Therefore, as soon as some rapport was established, I confronted him with his denial of the problem through a *process intervention*. Interpretation was used indirectly by making a concrete statement relating to his experience of being punished (the bedpost) for being a "bad" boy, and the way in which his behavior within the therapeutic situation was associated to it. No direct interpretation was made to connect his rage at his parents and his fear and wish to kill them with his present fear of authority (therapist). However, a statement *alluding* to the transferential situation in a supportive and reassuring manner was made ("you are still here and no one got hurt"). Thus a confrontation of his distorted communication was followed by an interpretation of present behavior with allusion to the past and to unconscious fears, and finally an analysis of the confrontation was made. All these procedural and strategic steps were handled or dispersed in one session. This, in itself, provided an uninterrupted, unambiguous message that, if repeated often enough within the therapeutic relationship, might serve as a model for his own communication processes. Naturally, this alone could not resolve the ingrained conflicts between his inner objects. However, the working-through process proceeds from the outside in, from the interpersonal to the personal, in the same way personality develops. Of course, communication in the therapeutic milieu is, as seen in this case, both the vehicle that takes one into the inner world of the individual, and its very expression. The goal is to help the patient change both *the experience and its expression* when they no longer serve constructive needs for him.

Defensive Communication: The Need to Control and Mask Feelings and Impulses

Verbal communication is one of the primary functions of the ego. It mediates between the inner world of the individual and the environment. It is thus responsible for much of what actually transpires between people; to a large degree it determines the quality and quantity of interpersonal relationships. Most people recognize the power of words and learn to use them for the achievement of their goals. However, some of the forces that govern the behavior of the self are unconscious in origin, and over these the conscious ego has no control. Consequently, some degree of distortion in ego functioning is bound to occur. In the area of verbal communication, one manifestation of such distortion may be the inappropriate use of silence. Other disturbances in this area are mainly defensive in nature. Their expression is designed to mask inner experiences rather than reveal them, to create interpersonal distance rather than intimacy, and to protect the ego from becoming aware of unwelcome feelings, especially those of anxiety, tension, depression, loneliness, and abandonment.

The unconscious fear of expressing certain feelings and unacceptable impulses creates a need in the patient to structure verbal output in a manner that promotes a facade and makes it difficult to get an accurate, realistic reading of inner experience. For example, a patient who wishes to cover up a distaste for the therapist's (painful) interpretations may use placating language. Dependence on the therapist for approval may unconsciously color the quality and quantity of the patient's speech. According to Mehrabian (1972): "People are discouraged, generally from an overt (linguistic) expression of their feelings, so they convey them in less consensual and less easily recognizable forms." The basis for such defensiveness emanates from the type of conditioning in early childhood, conditioning that creates at least two unconnected but parallel forces—the "real" feelings of the child, on the one hand, and those one is permitted to express, on the other. This discontinuity, or splitting, contributes to the formation of conflicts with anxieties and tensions that, in turn, affect the creation of (verbal) communication not consistent with the inner experience of the self. The therapist's task from the confrontation point of view is to help the patient open channels between these conflicting states so that increased awareness of genuine feelings, with a more direct, nondistorted communication, results. Often in such cases, continuity can be reestablished by a strategy of intervention that is based on both content and process, with major emphasis on process.

For example, a 42-year-old man initially sought treatment because of feelings of depression and loneliness. He held a responsible position in a financial firm and had two assistants working for him. His verbal communications were clearly indicative of an individual who lived under pressure created by his own fear of expressing his feelings and wishes in a definite and assertive manner, and eventually resulted in alienating those with whom he worked. When asked about this self-destructive behavior, he rationalized that it was only after he left a situation in which he experienced difficulty because of his fear to communicate that he became aware of his feelings, usually the negative ones, although he also had difficulty with the positive feelings. The session presented here is typical of the confrontation analysis approach in such cases. This patient was in treatment on a twice weekly basis, and the session reported is the 38th.

P: I came home Friday night pretty upset at one of my assistants, George. I spoke about him before, I guess. This is the fellow I've had difficulty dealing with in terms of me wanting him to do things. If he does the errors, I am the one who's stuck with them, and this leaves things unresolved. And there were a couple of other things, during that Friday, I guess, that I was unhappy about and wanted to talk to him about, but he had already gone home, and just before he did it was kind of late, and I didn't have the energy particularly to make a big issue out of it at that point. I just sort of steamed out of that place saying, well, Monday I am going to walk into his office and just sort of have it out with him. And just like the whole car ride home I was just sort of steaming about the thing, and finally I parked the car and turned on the lights, and jotted down, sort of thought about, just what I wanted him to do, I just jotted them down before I got out. And I have described them to Doris *(his wife)*, just what had happened, and I guess I calmed down by the time I was through.

T: Right now you sound as if you have almost forgotten the whole incident. It seems that all your "steaming" feelings have gone up in smoke.

P: I don't think so. Every time I think about it I feel upset and it makes me very depressed. The whole weekend was pretty miserable.

T: Well, you just said you were "sort of" thinking of having it out with George, that doesn't sound very "steaming," perhaps "sort of" steaming. From the way you related your feelings, I couldn't tell whether you were really angry or upset, or felt you should have been angry.

P: *(Smiles)* I was really upset; in fact, I even had a dream about it. It must've been Friday evening.

T: What was the dream?

P: I guess I was back at 17 Roy Avenue in Queens, and George was in the basement, and I don't remember whether I had an argument with him— oh, no, I was having a rehearsal of the confrontation I was going to have with him on Monday, and it was in the basement of our house at 17 Roy Avenue. And I remember I was walking up the stairs to get out of the side of the house, and I passed my other assistant, Desmond, and he had his coat on, maybe to go out to lunch or something. He sort of looked at me and I looked at him, but we didn't; I just sort of, he either sort of walked out without me or I walked out without him, we didn't go together. I was in an uptight mood having just spoken to George in the dream. I remember when I got up it was one of the most vivid dreams I ever had, it was crystal clear.

T: Which part was so clear?

P: Being at 17 Roy Avenue.

T: What was 17 Roy Avenue like?

P: Well, I told you we had lived there practically during most of my life as a child. We moved out after my father died when I was 21. It wasn't much of a neighborhood, but the house itself was very nice, very comfortable furniture, and my father liked to invite people because he was proud of our house, and he was very involved and respected in the community, and I liked that because I got a lot of attention from them. I had my own room and my own radio, and I spent a lot of time home.

T: You have a lot of feelings about that home.

P: *(Looks down on the floor and continues with a tearful voice)* You might say that. As a matter of fact, I took Doris a couple of weeks ago to see my old place, and I couldn't believe what happened to the area. It was like World War II. My house was still there, but the whole neighborhood was like bombed-out. I was very upset. I mean, I left there more than 20 years ago, but it was a terrible sight. I have a lot of nice memories from that house.

T: Were these memories part of your dream—the clear part?

P: As a matter of fact, what came to my mind, it was something about the way it used to be at home with my father there. All kinds of feelings. Mostly very warm and nice feelings. When I look at George, or at least I have a feeling about him as I did with my father, not the warm feelings, but in terms of what used to be the rule: you don't confront—you talk, you discuss, but you don't confront. It's very, very difficult for me to do that, I mean to confront, and certainly to demand something from someone who is a subordinate, because I don't feel I can be or am the authority. I certainly don't confront someone who has a tendency to get upset, like George and like my father. My father used to blow up when he got upset. George does that too.

T: So there was no fighting between you and your father?

P: Just before you asked me this question I was thinking: the basement was a place where I would run away from my father. I remember, a couple of times, I would look up at him—I must've been very little, he was only 5'7"—we had sort of a fight—I mean not really a fight, sort of a verbal fight, it was never a real fight. I remember he was coming after me—he never really hurt me, maybe he came to slap me—I remember running down the stairs, and he never followed me to the basement. My mother would come down and find me in a corner somewhere, and she would ask me to go up and apologize. So I thought that it was kind of interesting that this whole dream happened in the basement of my house, the whole thing with the confrontation with him.

T: What makes it so interesting?

P: Well, I never had a dream happen in the basement. Before I came here I remember that all the other dreams I had with that house, things happened either in the living room or on the top of the stairs, but never in the basement.

T: That basement is really something, isn't it? You like to keep it closed—no one is allowed there!

P: *(Chuckles)* Well, no, it was just a furnished basement and we had a lot of parties there, and all kinds of games. Now that I think about it, for the first time in many, many years, I had a friend from school—he wasn't a particularly good student, he lived a few blocks away, from a very poor family—and he would come over once in awhile, and my mother didn't like it. I guess she thought he was a bad influence on me. We used to have in the basement once in awhile wrestling matches, uh, uh . . . just for fun, not really fighting, and I guess I was bigger than him—I used to get him in a scissor lock between my legs and squeeze him until he said, "OK, I give up"—and we used to make some noise and knock some chairs around, and my mother would come down and yell. And I guess at one time I wanted him to come over because they were going out, but they didn't want him to come—they were afraid or something—so I raised a big fuss and cried and they agreed to have him come. When he came we played in the basement, and I think we had some, well, some sex play—I can't remember what we did exactly, but I know it wasn't what we were supposed to do.

T: You were not supposed to have fun, like other children?

P: Certainly not fooling around with another boy. My father would have killed me.

T: Killed you? For having fun?

P: I don't mean kill me, but he would've been very disappointed in me, and I don't want to hurt him.

T: I had the impression your father died more than 20 years ago.

P: Yes, he did.

T: You just said you "don't" want to hurt him.

P: I meant I didn't at the time. We were a very respected family.

T: You spend a lot of energy trying not to hurt anybody.

P: That's true.

T: Was the basement a place where you could get hurt, like when your mother forced you to apologize for your feelings, even when you didn't feel like it?

P: That's exactly the way I feel when I talk to George: why am I begging him to do the job when it's really his job to do, his responsibility. He is my assistant, he should apologize to me!

T: It's hard for you to know what you feel when you're so busy trying to cover up your feelings, to accomodate everyone so that everyone will like you. How can you have fun that way?

P: Well, we used to have parties in the basement, and that was a lot of fun. I used to be the bartender and my father used to get a kick out of it, for me to serve his friends. That basement, by the way, used to have a lot of big water bugs, and I loved to kill them. I guess I got some vicarious pleasure that way.

T: That basement had a lot of meaning for you, good and bad; bad because you can't talk too much about it—you're afraid you'll be punished for having some fun there—and good because when you have fun, no one has to know and you can keep it a secret—all to yourself. It's like your private world—the holy shrine where no one is allowed except you. And you learned to hide that world by not communicating about it. Do you feel that happens here? I mean, that you talk about things without really expressing the real feelings behind them?

P: Well, sometimes I come here with something in mind to discuss, but as the session goes on I forget it and I get into something else.

T: What about now? Have you felt like you were holding back?

P: No, I don't feel I am holding back anything, but I was not too comfortable discussing something that happened last night, and that is when I got home last night I masturbated for the first time in a long while. There was a cover on a magazine, a seductive picture—I guess I felt uncomfortable telling you about it because I had it on my mind when I came here—but I don't think I would have brought it up myself. I am really too embarrassed about it.

T: Are you embarrassed about it because you feel you shouldn't jerk off, or because you think you ought to be embarrassed about the subject?

P: Well, I do have a wife—I mean, Doris is available most of the time, so why do I need to masturbate? I think this was blocking me from concentrating on the dream.

T: You'd like to avoid this whole subject and go back to the living-room talk rather than the basement? I had the impression you were talking a great deal about the dream—perhaps that made you anxious.

P: A 42-year-old man and still masturbating. I think it's disgusting. I mean, I know intellectually that it's O.K., but I feel ashamed of it. What if my wife finds out?

T: You seem more embarrassed about me finding out. I also have the impression that you're more worried about George and Desmond not thinking of you as a man, the way you think of yourself, because you masturbate! Well, you might have to continue to be nice to them as long as you don't think of yourself as a man, because you're worried they'll find out.

P: I don't think much of myself as a man, that's true. But I can't see how this is connected to my masturbation. Well, I can see how I get frightened whenever there's any sign of possible confrontation with anyone in the office, and I think of myself as a piece of shit—putting on airs of being calm and cool, when I am really shitting in my pants and avoiding other people.

T: I suppose being frightened and trying to cover it up brings out a lot of stuff you don't consciously plan on, and one of the things you're so frightened about is feeling free enough to have any kind of fun without putting yourself down.

P: I always thought of myself as inferior—I mean, inferior to other men. When Bernice wanted a divorce, I was sure it was because I was inferior. I still feel that way. Maybe you're right about this—maybe I am afraid to confront George because I don't think much of myself as a man.

T: Perhaps the dream has something to do with just that. Your feelings of shame for having human needs seem to block you from having business relationships which have nothing to do with your sex drive. They're not your father!

P: I can see how I am mixed up about all this.

This session clearly demonstrates the operation of defensive communication where the verbal messages of the patient are unconsciously aimed at defensive hiding rather than revealing what the patient feels, both in interactions with outside environment and in the therapeutic situation.

The distortions in verbal communication usually manifest themselves in a variety of ways, and in this patient, through certain linguistic patterns and through his attempts to avoid emotional expression through verbal or nonverbal channels. The patient frequently used qualifiers to emotional expressions, such as "sort of," and "I guess." Their usage was no accident, and suggests the operation of the mechanism of denial. This is of crucial importance. When an individual utters a symbolic verbal expression, such as "I am angry," one is not only communicating concrete, existential inner experience, one is at the same time *reinforcing one's commitment to that experience and taking responsibility for it.* In addition, the verbal expression becomes part of the repertoire of communicative devices, and will have a high probability of expression under similar conditions. Thus any therapeutic modification—in this case, of verbal expression—may have a profound effect on the patient's inner experience. Understandably, these changes will have a better chance of occurring, and with more lasting effect, in the context of expanding awareness, first within the security of the therapeutic milieu, and later outside of it.

In their study of the effect of the interpersonal field on semantic patterns, and vice versa, Sluzki and Veron (1973) pose a number of questions that bear on the present discussion. Two of these are especially relevant to intervention strategy: (1) "Whether there are also induced interventions that, instead of reinforcing defense mechanisms, disrupt and redefine the 'spontaneous' semantic field presented by the patient," and (2) "What mechanisms are utilized by the patients in order to 'absorb' eventual disruptions and reorganize their semantic field." They conclude that certain styles of intervention should be avoided, while others should be promoted. Awareness of such "rules" of intervention "would help avoid the danger of a complementariness of styles between patient and therapist that stereotype the treatment through repeating in therapy the interactive milieu that reinforces the patient's behavior." This danger is quite often neglected by the therapist for a variety of reasons, not the least of them being countertransference problems.

In the illustration above, a verbal confrontational technique was specifically aimed at counteracting patterns of nonconfrontation that the patient had learned at an early age through interactions with his father. Among other things, this technique helped to decrease the use of modifiers, at least during the rest of the session, and eventually in the patient's verbal production outside of treatment. On the whole, the patient felt less of a need to use them because of a number of factors: the nonthreatening confrontational interventions; the patient's increasing feelings of comfort and safety with the therapist (during that session perhaps because of the "permission" and support given him to have fun without recrimination); and the inner pressure to ventilate feelings from the past, which surface through associations to unconscious material, such as the dream and the slip of the tongue ("I don't" instead of "I didn't").

A second point relates to the use of content and process intervention. As noted, both are essential to the confrontation analysis system. It is important that the patient becomes aware when his or her verbal messages are not consistent with his behavior. For instance, in the above example, when the patient was discussing how angry he was about the incident with his assistant, his behavior indicated anything but anger, and this was not because he wasn't angry but because he managed to repress his anger almost as soon as it began. Thus, the decision at that point was to use a content-oriented intervention aimed at achieving a number of objectives ("You just said you were 'sort of' thinking of having it out with George, that doesn't sound very 'steaming' "). The first objective is to help the patient become aware of the discrepancy between his words and his conscious experience and behavior. The second objective is to confront the patient with his or her need to deny feelings. (In the session presented, it didn't matter how close to the surface the conflict was, for the intellectual recognition of a defense, such as denial, is an important step toward emotional insight and behavioral change.) The third objective is to accumulate evidence, session after session, of the self-destructive behavior, so that eventually this behavior becomes more ego-alien and, one hopes, abandoned and separated from. The last objective, perhaps the most important, is to establish a common ground with the patient by sharing and understanding his idiosyncratic definitions and experiences, to become familiar with the anatomy of the patient's thoughts and feelings, in order to form a working alliance. Patients quite often express the fear that anyone who *really* finds out who they are will abandon them. Because of this, content intervention by an attentive and interested therapist is similar to sharing a detailed and involving voyage with someone. Many channels of contact are established in this manner, and a common language (shared by both parties) develops. In a certain sense, content intervention precedes process intervention in the same manner that learning how to read a book is preceded by learning what words and sentences mean. Process intervention is this session was exemplified by various probes designed to help the patient look at the present from a perspective that included the past, without undue emphasis on the past (e.g., the question, "So there was no fighting between you and your father?" was not followed immediately by additional probes about the patient's feelings for his father). In addition, certain confrontational interpretations were advanced in order to increase insight and spur further self-search (e.g., "That basement is really something, isn't it? You like to keep it closed—no one is allowed there!").

The interweaving of content and process interventions, whether confrontational or interpretive or both, helps reduce the chances of repetitive verbal distortions, which are usually defensive in nature. The confrontational interventions are used strategically in a way that makes it difficult for the patient to "escape." They are also used as a model in the patient's quest for assertion and independence. In the session presented, no analysis of the confrontations was made. The therapeutic alliance still needed a wider base if transferential interpretations were to be meaningful. The focus was toward opening additional avenues for the patient's feelings to surface, especially at that point, with reference to his father.

This case is, in many ways, typical of many patients who

are dependent on their environment for feelings of security and well-being. The patient's verbal communication is characterized by much "hedging" with regard to his feelings, and he is always protecting himself from possible rejection and abandonment. Transferentially, his behavior was also extremely cautious, like a tightrope walker who must balance his movements on both sides of the rope lest he slip into oblivion. Naturally, the more tense such an acrobat is, the more rigid his body and steps become, putting the acrobat in extreme danger of distorting his movements and upsetting the balance. Similarly, the more tense and fearful the patient is of not being accepted or of being "dropped," the more likely he is to elicit more inappropriate and exaggerated defensive maneuvers, consequently resulting in the eliciting of negative reactions from others. Thus greater dependence on the environment for emotional support also leads to greater distortions in communication. The therapist must always bear this in mind, so that his own communications can be geared toward helping to loosen the patient's rigidity, and the therapist's expressiveness must be used for that purpose.

Diagnosis and Intervention Strategy in Defensive Communication

The discussion of intervention strategy has, so far, been without reference to diagnostic considerations. The purpose was to first isolate a few communication variables and discuss their distortions in the context of the confrontation analysis approach and only then to enter into further exploration of an area as complicated and lacking in defined boundaries as the diagnostic "mess" spectrum. However, without making a "religion" out of the diagnostic categories, the confrontational analyst must take into account the nature of the symptomatology and personality constellation that the patient presents, and that may fit one or another diagnostic entity, in determining the use of intervention strategies designed to modify verbal communication patterns. Such considerations contribute to the decision about the choice of the strategy to be employed.

The raison d'être of language is communication. Yet, when the message of the sender has a meaning different from the spoken words, the receiver is not likely to understand it, unless of course, the meaning had been learned before. Such inconsistencies produce distorted communication, which is expressed differentially by patients with varying symptomatology. In fact, diagnosis itself is largely based on the nature of the patient's communicative patterns, and it is often determined by the therapist's understanding of these patterns.

Confrontation analysis assumes that the individual's need to keep the status quo is basic to all distorted communication. While many patients have a conscious desire to change, the unconscious forces that produced the symptoms are often too overwhelming to overcome through conscious attempts. The therapist's task is thus to join forces with the healthy ego, as expressed through its linguistic functions, in order to tip the scale in its favor. A number of clinical examples from various diagnostic categories and with various manifestations of distorted communication will be presented; however, in general, it is possible to determine early in the therapeutic relationship, often in the first interview, which adjustment, whether neurotic or psychotic, the patient has adopted. No attempt is made to define these categories here; they are used in their broadest sense and with the assumption that diagnoses are best defined on the basis of both symptomatology and dynamics. As Nunberg (1955) advocates,

> . . . the chief difference between the behavior of the neurotic and that of the psychotic is this: the neurotic does not mistake psychic reality for external reality (or if he does, it is only within restricted limits, as for instance, in phobia or fetishism), whereas the psychotic loses this discriminatory capacity and not only mistakes inner reality for the outer, but even replaces the outer reality with the inner. *The neurotic, in his unconscious, retains relations with reality (the objects of the outer world); he represses only the instincts of the id. The psychotic loses also the objects in the unconscious, and consequently has no relationship to them; he represses reality.*

Nevertheless, the lines of demarcation are not always clear or necessarily sensible, and an overlap between the entities is almost inevitable, simply because basic dynamics are universal in nature and describable only in abstract terms that cannot satisfy individual idiosyncracies. Thus, according to Marmor (1974), "neurosis and psychosis should not be regarded as static and fixed entities. *They are dynamic and changeable states of behavior which are potentially reversible, the borders of which are often indistinct.*" Thus the intuition and personality of the therapist are very important factors in this area of concern relative to the therapeutic work.

Pseudo-anal adjustment in a hysterical character: distortions in verbal and nonverbal communication patterns. A 35-year-old woman came for treatment because of marital difficulties, feelings of emptiness, dissatisfaction with her secretarial job, and inability to enjoy physical and sexual relations with her husband. In the initial sessions she felt loving toward her husband, but also extremely fearful of him. She was also in awe of him because of his professional achievements as a lawyer, as well as thankful to him for providing her with a home and a status in society that she had always dreamed of but never believed she could achieve. She came from a very poor family, with parents who provided very little either materially or emotionally. Soon after she introduced her initial concerns, it became clear that her unhappiness stemmed to a large degree from her own self-perception and from the manner in which she conducted her life. She had no goals, no close friends, no family support. She worked part-time as a secretary to escape the routine of taking care of her two-year-old daughter, whom she saw as a burden and as a wedge between herself and her husband. Yet she constantly urged her husband to agree to have more children so that she could feel secure in the marriage. She expressed a wish to work on these negative feelings, and indeed she was able to plunge into an appraisal, past and present, of her assets and liabilities, and began to explore unconscious obstacles that did not allow her to move ahead, to free herself from her feelings about her family and her developmental pains. After a few months in therapy, she was able to gain enough strength to leave a job that was by no means commensurate with her intellectual capacities, and to enroll in school to finish the college education that she had abandoned more than 10 years earlier.

There were many ups and downs, fears and anxieties, especially about her intellectual ability to complete college. Nevertheless, she learned to have more respect for herself (at least consciously) and to demand more from others for herself. As often happens with couples who married for neurotic reasons, her husband, who marginally supported her educational goals at the onset, began to question them and to become irritable about her schooling. The more excited about her studies and interested in them she became, the more verbally abusive he acted toward her, and the more self-destructive he became in his own personal life. His law practice, which was becoming a serious and successful one (to the point that he had to hire a junior lawyer to work for him), began to suffer as he paid less and less attention to it and turned more and more toward alcohol. He also encouraged his wife to participate in this pastime, unconsciously undermining some of the gains she had achieved in therapy. The couple's sexual relationship, which was marginal to begin with, became extremely strained. She began to realize how little they had in common, and how the tension between them existed constantly without extra activities, such as drinking or smoking marijuana. She also felt repulsed sexually by her husband, always thinking "why is he attracted to me, I am such an ugly person, with hair on my legs and a smelly stinking body, and tiny breasts—what does he want from me?" She felt used by him as an outlet for sexual tensions rather than a desired person, a "desired" female. She never complained to him about her sexual feelings, and always agreed to "go through the motions and fake it—and then hate myself and hate him," because she was terrified that he might leave her, an idea she could not allow her conscious mind to consider. She believed she would be totally destroyed if he left her.

After the initial gains and changes, toward the end of the first year in treatment and the beginning of the second year, a significant regression seemed to have been triggered. Self-hatred, suicidal thoughts, headaches, rage and disdain toward herself for her dependence on her husband, and periods of continuous crying dominated many hours of her daily life. Her immature and infantile behavior surfaced once more, and her behavior in the sessions reverted to the dramatic and panicky character that she exhibited in the beginning of treatment. Acting-out during the sessions was quite obvious: Her verbal and nonverbal messages were sexually provocative. She turned and twisted her body suggestively, and came to her sessions dressed in very revealing clothing. As she left home to come to her sessions, she purposefully showed her husband the sexy outfits she planned to wear, pretending to be asking his opinion about a color combination. She also planned her arrival at my office to be at least an hour earlier than her appointment, saying "I couldn't find a more peaceful and comfortable place to spend some free time than here in your office, with you. I have a lot of free time, you know." When all her efforts at seduction failed, she threatened me with additional acting-out, and before any headway could be made toward stopping this acting-out, she began to have an affair with a man who lived in the next building, a friend of her husband's family, and a man who was 30 years her senior, almost the age of her father. She had no understanding of how such acting-out could damage the chances of working on her marriage. She claimed that her encounter with this man was "purely sexual," since he was a "very exciting man," although he did not actually help her to have more sexual feelings or to "fill up" her feelings of emptiness. While she recognized that this man knew the right words to excite her without really caring about her, she was without constructive personality resources. Her preoccupation with this affair was so pervasive that everything else was neglected, although she consciously felt she was handling everything in her life better than before. Denial and dissociation were the order of the day. The only area in which she functioned extremely well was school: she missed no classes, no exams, and no term papers, and she was able to study without any problem. Her relationship to me became more manageable, since she had temporarily decathected me. In fact, she came up with the idea, which she impulsively discussed with her husband before bringing it up in her session, of coming for therapy with her husband. However, as she was telling me about it, she withdrew it immediately. She had suddenly realized that I could not protect her from the consequences of her acting-out; I could not bring her husband back to her. She was also frightened by her husband's possible acceptance of this suggestion, since he wanted to meet her "God shrink," as he called me. It was against this background, and with my summer vacation imminent that the session presented here (the 88th) took place.

P: I've been feeling so much better this year. I don't know what happened. I feel like shit again. I am feeling very sorry for myself *(tears)* uh . . . uh . . . so many little things, I feel so many little things, just all kinds of things, but it all adds up to shit, there is nothing. I am very discouraged, by myself. I don't even know what I am talking about right now. I can't tell you what I am feeling shitty about, but that's how I feel. I've resolved for the millionth time that I'm not gonna drink and I'm not gonna smoke, and I am trying very hard not to give in to Steve's *(husband)* invitations to smoke and drink. I know that when I don't do them I feel sort of self-righteous and excited all over, like I am doing a good thing for myself—but when it comes down to the line, I have to struggle, it's very very hard for me not to do it. *(Leans over very close to my face)* Do you know what I mean, I feel depressed—I know it's ridiculous to think that way—I mean, you're not depriving me, you tell me I can do anything I want to do, but I know I'm doing it for myself—so I decide not to do it and then I do it. So now I've decided to quit the shit and not to do it—I am really not going to do it!

T: What is it that you're not going to do? I am confused about what you're talking about.

P: *(Smiles)* That I'm not gonna smoke and I am not gonna drink, because as shitty as I feel now, I know—well, I was going to say . . . what was I going to say? I forgot what it was. Do you remember what I was saying?

T: I was confused about what you're telling me about the smoking and drinking, and what it is you were thinking when you leaned over before and smiled.

P: I know that you want me to stop all this nonsense, I know it. I was fooling myself into thinking that I feel terrible when I do it, but the fact is that I did it again Sunday night—I just feel I haven't conquered it yet. I am still carrying around that shit. I don't know what happened.

T: You've been carrying around many things, many feelings for a very long time, haven't you? It's very hard to break away from what's familiar!

P: Even Steve was very pleasant in the beginning of the week. He decided, after I told him very calmly what happened in the session last week, that you must be right, and that he should stop all the nonsense, and I had a lot of hope that maybe we won't end up on the Bowery and he won't go bankrupt. But by the end of the week it was all turned around, all the shit came back—he hasn't stopped *at all, at all.* I can't rely on him, I can't do it.

T: So it's hard to break away, you must do what you know.

P: The main thing for me is the self-discipline, to get away from the shit— I must get away from it.

T: You keep talking about the "shit," and what I hear you define as "shit," is what you put in your mouth—the drink and the smoke.

P: *(Laughs hysterically, and I do too, as if it were contagious.)* So shit is food for me, or the other way around, food is shit—which is which, I never thought of it that way. But you're right—that's exactly what I am talking about. Oh, now I know what I wanted to tell you before. I had a fantasy about us—it's really funny—that you were going to suggest to me that we conduct several sessions with us drinking and smoking so you can see me in this condition—I am really very pleasant then, I am fabulous! *(Laughs.)*

T: So you want me to get into it too?

P: Well, it was just a fantasy—but maybe, who knows? I don't know, I feel kind of funny about you lately. I am not too happy about your going away for such a long time. I'll survive, and you're entitled to your vacation—but my God, it's a long, long time. How will you stand it without me?

T: You know, you have a tendency to use very extreme terms. Everything for you is "very" and "my God," and "fabulous," and "shitty." You sound as if you have never learned to use other vocabulary, because if your feelings are the same as your words, you must be constantly exhausted.

P: I don't feel exhausted, but I am always tense, always, always—there I go again. But that's the truth. Specially in the last couple of months, I am really very tense, and I don't know what to do about it. But I felt good in the last session when I admitted my feelings about you and I talked about my parents—it was sort of a relief—and I had a good cry after the session, because I was thinking, my parents really didn't care, they never cared to find out what I needed, what I wanted—always screaming, my father forever disappearing! At least he was never around for me, never, never *(starts crying)*, and when I needed him, when the other kids were torturing me in school, or even my cousin Breena, she shit all over me, and he wouldn't say anything, he thought it was a joke. We never socialized or anything—even during the holidays when everybody looked fabulous, I was always wearing hand-me-downs from my cousins—and I was so ashamed and felt like shit, and I couldn't say anything. And then in the summer—I told you about that—they used to send me to spend the summers with my uncle and cousins on the Jersey Shore, and I was always treated like a second-class citizen—I was the maid and even the cook sometimes. They never asked me if I wanted to go, it was just a fact. My psychology teacher was talking the other day, and he said that if a child doesn't get the right kind of love, then they can't give it, and I was very upset—in fact I had to control myself from crying in class, because I can't believe I can give it, I don't know how to give it, I can't get it out of my mind, that I can't give love, I am closed in, and that I'll never be able to feel love or give it. I don't give Steve any love, or Natalie *(daughter)*, or anybody. Is it true, I mean is it a fact that if one hasn't experienced that love from the parents, that they can never give love to anybody *(sobs)*. It's very upsetting. I feel absolutely stilted and awkward. I feel uncomfortable being loved, I feel uncomfortable when Steve wants to love me, when he shows any kind of affection. I don't like it, I don't like it at all. It's terribly painful to me, just painful. What if what the book says is true, that since I've never experienced it as a child, there's no way I can experience it now. What am I going to do?

T: What exactly do you *want* to do?

P: I want to feel something, all I feel is shit, just shitty and uncomfortable. Even with my daughter, my own daughter I feel uncomfortable, and she is only two years old. What am I going to do? *(In a panicky tone)* I feel like an iceberg. Just like my parents.

T: That's what I meant before about letting go with something familiar, not separating—you want to keep your parents around you.

P: How do I do that? I hardly go to see them, even though they're just minutes from my house.

T: You keep them in the form of feelings. You see them as icebergs and you feel like an iceberg. My impression is that the iceberg feelings you have are your way of hanging on to them. You said they didn't understand you or your needs, and that's how you feel about yourself and your daughter.

P: You're right, I keep blaming Steve for his getting me into the drinking and the smoking, but you're right, through all the reasons and the screens I can see that it doesn't really matter who starts what; the fact is that I feel shitty about myself, the fact is you're right, I am just like my parents.

T: I didn't say you're like your parents. I said you hang on to your parents by keeping feelings similar to theirs. You hear what you like to hear, not what I actually say to you. This is another way of hanging on. You want to keep what you believe so your translation of what I say to you will conform to what you believe.

P: I know, I do this all the time, like with Natty *(daughter's nickname)* when she asks me for something, I feel she wants something else from me—not the milk or the stuffed bear, or the cookie, but something else—like something that I can't give her, and I resent her and I scream at her and I yell at her, and she's only two. I am constantly yelling and screaming at her, but constantly. All the time. You're right, the kid wants something, that's all, and I don't hear her.

T: What do you suppose happens there—what makes it difficult for you to hear her?

P: Maybe I don't really care. I don't really know; I am really exhausted.

T: Perhaps you don't want to know, it's your way of dismissing me by saying you don't know, that you're exhausted. You want me to tell you to take care of her—not like your parents. Perhaps your daughter feels the same way—that she is not heard—the way you felt with your parents.

P: You mean I am doing to her what was done to me? That's horrible, I mean, I said it myself, I said it myself. How can I be so mean? *(Shakes her head in disapproval, then lowers it in what appears to be a very gloomy mood.)*

T: What are you thinking about?

P: Nothing.

T: You were quiet for almost two minutes with your head down.

P: I was just, just . . . I don't know, it's completely blank. I wasn't really thinking about anything. Where was I? *(She appears to have had a short fugue.)* Oh, yeah, Natty. I guess I can't give her because I didn't get.

T: And perhaps you expect me to give you what your parents didn't—that's why you keep leaving it up to me to explain and interpret, and you pretend you don't know. I am not your parents, you know.

P: I know you're not my parents *(annoyed)*. I wish the hell you were *(In a rather childish tone)* Why can't you be? You must have children of your own, do you? One more child wouldn't hurt, would it?

T: You're talking like an orphan, is that how you feel?

P: That's exactly how I feel, that's exactly how I feel all day, all the time. Maybe that's why I go along with Steve and drink and smoke—I don't want to be an orphan, I don't want to be alone all the time. When he comes home early from work, I am glad, even though I hate his guts, I do.

T: Is there anyone else you feel this way about?

P: How do you mean?

T: That you don't like but you can't get rid of?

P: Are you telling me that's how I feel about my parents? I do feel very hateful toward them, and I guess I keep feeling the kind of feelings they gave me about myself, all the shit feelings. So maybe I like to keep them around. Are you saying that Steve is like my parents to me?

T: Well you said you were afraid of your father and that he didn't really care that much about you, and that you wished he was around more when you were growing up. You said the same things about Steve.

P: What about Natalie? I wanted so much to have a baby, and now I treat her like dirt—I should've gone to the opposite end, knowing how rotten it feels to be treated like shit by your parents. I never play with her, or sit with her except to feed her and dress her and bathe her and take her to the doctor. I guess I see where it all came from. I feel like a rock: no feelings, just pretending all the time. Just pretending. I am always programmed, I am never relaxed. When I do something, except thank God for my schoolwork, it's always sudden, it's like it can't wait.

T: A rock doesn't seem to have feelings. That's not the way I experience you here. You do express a lot of feelings here. I must say, when you describe yourself the way you do, there is a shock value to it! You really know how to use your language.

P: But I really feel this way.

T: Like a rock?

P: Yeah.

T: How do you explain your crying—was Moses there to hit the rock?

P: No, but somehow I feel that I have no feelings at all, that I don't care about anything or anybody. Maybe I was really so deprived as a child that there is no love in me whatsoever.

T: If you insist on it, have it your way. I won't buy it because I've seen you express a lot of feelings here. You may have a problem with expressing these feelings outside of here, or even consciously feeling them. I would say that with you 90 percent of your feelings are hidden under the anger that you walk around with.

P: *(Crying and silent for about four minutes.)* It doesn't do me any good if I don't know how to get them out, does it?

T: It is hard to learn new habits. I wonder if you really want to, if you really feel safe enough to express feelings that pop up now and then—I mean, good feelings, positive feelings.

P: Well, last weekend, my sister and her husband came to visit us, and I prepared dinner for them, and I really liked it. And my sister and I never really hit it off, but on Saturday night I felt very nice about her, and I had a very warm, nice feeling for her, but I couldn't say anything; I just couldn't—it was like old times, the same way, I talked to her in the same way and she did the same way. But maybe I am more ready. I know that Sandy *(sister)* would love it. She's waiting for a signal from me. Maybe I'll call her and have a nice chat with her. I feel like a yo-yo. One day nice, another day not so nice.

T: Since you are in such terrible shape, how is it that you are angry about my going away on vacation—after all, things seem to get worse not better when you come to see me.

P: No, I look forward to coming here every session—I always feel that, even when I feel very discouraged—I like to come here. I just feel that even when I am a bad girl and when I feel like shit, that you would still love me, or maybe understand me. I mean, sometimes I talk to Steve about my shit and he listens, but it's not the same. I feel that you're not going to throw me out of here no matter what, and when you're here I don't feel that I am drowning in my own muck. I have a feeling that you know, you kind of predict these things, and whenever I am in trouble you'll give me something—not a prescription—it's like you're like a lighthouse in a storm. But I felt, you'll be away two months, what am I going to do? When I am really feeling shitty, you stop me from feeling like that.

T: I stop you—here we go again, I am responsible for your doing a lot of work on yourself, and I get the credit. Not that I don't like it, but what about you? You're the one who is doing a lot of work. For example, with all the difficult feelings throughout the year, you managed to do extremely well in school, and you managed to dig up some very important stuff about yourself and work on it. I have no doubt that you can manage quite well in the next few weeks.

P: You see what I mean? You just gave me a nice report card.

T: It's what I see happening.

P: I want to believe all this, but then when bad stuff comes along, I start to doubt everything—I start to go back to feelings of aloneness and emptiness. I am still sorry you're going away.

T: I'll see you Thursday.

P: You bet!

The above patient had experienced many discontinuities in her childhood, which led to a neurotic adjustment. From a dynamic point of view she would be diagnosed as hysterical, while symptomatically she fits better into the anal-retentive category. I thus diagnosed her as pseudo-anal adjustment in an hysterical character.

Most of this patient's communications are defensive, although on the surface they may give the impression of being quite direct, expressing genuine feelings without any intention to cover up or "mislead." On many occasions the patient had admitted feeling, and consciously being, "phoney," often expressing impulsively or deliberately feelings that she did not have. She gave many reasons for this behavior. However, by and large, she was not aware of most of her verbal and nonverbal maneuvers. Her communications were defensive, and were consequently distorted because she often had (semi-consciously) different meanings to her words, meanings she kept to herself. For example, her apparent seductiveness, both verbally and nonverbally, was motivated by her need to maintain the status quo of her personality structure and dynamics. She had, in this regard, an additional need to punish her husband (father) by supposedly choosing another man (her therapist), and to show men up so that she could feel justified in destroying them with her anger. The fantasy she has about drinking and smoking with me had precisely this purpose: She wanted to turn me into another failure, like her father, so that she could be with her "father" again. If he acted like her, that might have been a proof, or a sign that he indeed loved her. The change, in other words, had to come from the outside, since she was not ready to make it herself. The externalizing of her object relations was one of her unconscious maneuvers to rid herself of anxiety that was triggered by identification with the rejecting objects.

Another issue with regard to the patient's defensive stance is her habitual and excessive use of acting-out behavior. First, she used language that was dramatic, repetitious, exaggerated, lacking in specificity, often contradictory and confused, and had the earmarks of immaturity, inappropriateness, and pretentiousness. Second, she used drugs and alcohol regularly and compulsively, although she was not an addict. Third, she acted out sexually. Fourth, she persisted for some time with her acting-out (or acting-in) within the therapeutic relationship: in her behavior (such as arriving very early to her sessions and occupying the waiting room for a long time), as well as in her verbal and nonverbal messages, both overt and covert. These aspects of her defensiveness were handled therapeutically in a variety of ways, some of which were utilized in the above session.

As a general principle, the treatment of hysteria requires that the therapist be alert to the following problems:

1. The patient's personality is not as integrated as the diagnosis often implies, and evaluation is thus of paramount importance. In the above example, the patient was able to make a pseudo-adjustment to severe ego defects, and her pathology must be recognized and treated as such. This does not mean that the investigation of underlying dynamics for the removal of destructive defenses should be avoided, rather confrontational interventions must be tempered with support, as is evident in the above session. Even though the patient recognized the maneuvers at times, as long as they are authentically therapeutic in purpose, they can be helpful in advancing the cause of trust in the relationship. However, two parallel procedures must occur at the same time: (1) support, which increases the dependency on the therapist, who will in the proper time analyze it; and (2) confrontation, which gives the patient the chance to explore new avenues as well as the opportunity to learn to stand up for himself without being punished. *Such procedures allow for process intervention as a central strategy, although content intervention is often used to help the patient anchor himself more in reality.*

2.   The hysteric's ego normally has areas of competence that he
     is unable to utilize or be comfortable with. The therapist
     must get to know what these pockets of health are as quickly
     as possible. Encouragement and even insistence on devel-
     oping them is extremely important, because they become
     the foundation on which the process of "peeling off" the de-
     fenses can be based. At the risk of being perceived as, or
     confused with, the real parent, the therapist must, at times,
     reinforce such ego foundations directly, for they will give
     the patient gratification from concrete achievement and the
     constructive use of potentialities. In the above example, I
     encouraged the patient to continue her education by specif-
     ically discussing with her the various alternatives she faced
     when she started treatment. The hysteric often needs such
     support because of feelings of loss, confusion, and disorgan-
     ization; a pattern of behavior has been developed that only
     takes him around in circles. In addition, when the patient
     begins to direct energies into a constructive, purposeful ac-
     tivity, capacity to focus on the therapeutic work increases.
     The hysteric certainly needs such an approach. By making
     interventions that require more and more introspection, the
     therapist helps the patient become increasingly attentive to
     his inner self, rather than looking for solutions from outside
     sources, a most common behavioral and dynamic predispo-
     sition of the hysterical character syndrome.

3.   Because of the hysteric's capacity to dissociate and readily
     deny reality, interpretations as well as interpretive confron-
     tations must be geared toward a combination of past and
     present difficulties. This allows the patient to select that
     part of the interpretation that he is presently most ready to
     tackle. In the above case history the following intervention
     is a good example: "You've been carrying around many
     things, many feelings for a very long time, haven't you? It's
     very hard to break away from what's familiar!" This is an
     interpretive confrontation that is also quite supportive. It
     may refer to any number of things—her parents, her hus-
     band, her drinking, her anger, or anything she may be
     preoccupied with or struggling with. The important point is
     that the intervention refers to the problem of separation—
     a central theme both in that session and during the imme-
     diate past and future. Indeed, she picked up on this inter-

vention (somewhat indirectly) in her response, that she could not rely on her husband—that she had to do it on her own. There was very little or no defensiveness, but a recognition and understanding that separation of herself from the influence of others must take place, and that she must be the one to make it happen.

4. The hysteric is quite capable of suddenly and unexpectedly regressing, slumping into a depression, or getting into a panic. This is not an uncommon pattern, and is one that requires that the therapist exhibit (through interventions and general posture) stability and trust in the patient's capacity to weather the temporary condition. It is during similar times of adversity in childhood that the parents most likely "failed" to understand what was happening with the child and reacted destructively. Thus the therapist must be, in a sense, a "better" parent, one who communicates clearly that he is available and ready to help and intervene in the patient's interest. Even if the patient has a habit of using such sudden changes as a maneuver of some known or unknown reason, such as secondary gains, it is important that the transgression be treated as part of the overall therapeutic picture, not as an accident. The patient must know that everything is negotiable.

5. In confrontation analysis both the communication aspects of the patient's productions and the transferential aspects are scrutinized and worked with for the purpose of change. The hysteric's propensity to play different roles in close succession within the therapeutic hour allows the analyst to see *in vivo* the drama of his object relations. More specifically, the therapist sees it in the quick alterations of transference manifestations. The question that arises is how and under what set of conditions should the patient be confronted with transference projections? Alexander (1963) feels that, in most of these cases, it should be handled as soon as it appears. The fact is, however, that regardless of any strategy used, the patient is surely going to become dependent on the analyst. The possibility exists that interpreting the transference as soon as it is detected may work just in the undesirable direction that Alexander understandably wishes to avoid, by unintentionally endowing the analyst with powers that cause greater and more intense

idealization of the analyst. This is particularly true of the hysteric whose narcissism is in constant search of omnipotent identifications. Thus early transferential interpretations cannot *always* be strategically considered a viable choice when destructive acting out appears likely. Such interventions may often be misinterpreted by the patient as a sign of the analyst's condoning the acting-out. Whenever utilized, such interventions should be accompanied by intensive work on the underlying dynamics of the acting-out behavior. It is unlikely that a well-defended patient would recognize or accept transference interpretations readily, and the analyst must thus wait until he or she observes signs of discomfort in conjunction with the transferential reactions before making direct interpretations. In the above case, transference interpretations were not made directly, they were implied (e.g., "perhaps you expect me to give you what your parents didn't . . . I am not your parents"). There was also indirect interpretation of transference as it related to her husband, *implying* that she reacted to him as if he were her father.

The hysteric's transference to the analyst can sometimes be very difficult to deal with when it is expressed in a direct verbal manner. The patient may directly question the analyst with his feelings about him and makes what appears to be a normal request for feedback. It is not easy at such times to convince the patient that the analyst's "nonparticipation" (in the patient's perception, rejection) in a nontherapeutic (often sexual) activity has nothing to do with the former's personality, behavior, or physical or sexual appeal. The patient's narcissism, which is a major factor in the hysteric's core personality, cannot digest such a "rejection" easily, and cannot understand contractual agreements. Such patients feel, "I want what I want when I want it and all else be damned!" Consequently, the difficulties that such a transference creates, may inadvertently lead the analyst to succumb to the patient's demands in one form or another (not necessarily overt or in any form that is observable to the analyst or the patient). The ability and need of the hysteric to "externalize" his object relations and to shift roles often in the transferential situation has already been noted. Such behavior often acts like a radar signal, scanning the analyst's own unresolved conflicts with certain objects, identifying with them, and thus making it possible (sometimes inevitable) for the analyst to identify unconsciously with the patient. Such countertransferential reactions are more common with hysterical patients. As I listened to the taped session with the above patient, I realized that one of my comments had been triggered off by an unconscious conflict. The comment, in and of itself, was quite appropriate as far as the patient was concerned. When she complained about not having any feelings and compared herself to a rock, I said to her, "How do you explain your crying—was Moses there to hit the rock?" The tone of the comment made it clear that I was irritated with the patient. Two reasons may account for this countertransferential reaction: she didn't readily accept my assertion that she indeed had feelings, thereby hurting my own narcissism, and further, she triggered off associations related to my grandmother, who complained about being unable to eat after having just consumed a hefty amount of food. When she was getting on in age and needed to get attention from the family in some way, she was neither very pleasant about it, nor honest. The family was all quite irritated with her behavior, which occurred when I was a teenager. She died shortly afterward and my resentment toward her produced a great deal of guilt in me. In this instance, the patient became my complaining grandmother. Also, the use of the analogy with Moses was no accident: I was angry with the patient for "demanding" that I perform the impossible, to prove to her what she did not want to know and would rather deny, i.e., that she had feelings for which I expected her to take responsibility.

This is by no means an exhaustive account of the confrontation analysis approach to disturbed verbal communication in the hysterical syndrome. It is, nevertheless, a fairly representative sample of the kind of clinical issues and techniques with which confrontation analysis is concerned. No doubt, the reader may discern some overlap of material with other entities discussed elsewhere in this book, or even with systems of psychotherapy that espouse different theoretical and clinical views. Of course, when goals are not divergent, experienced and compassionate therapists often work in similar ways.

The obsessive-compulsive communication difficulties: clinical and theoretical considerations from the viewpoint of confrontation analysis. While diagnoses are convenient and perhaps necessary for parsimonious interprofessional communication, they often reduce the patient to a "stick figure," devoid of flesh and blood and of unique substance. However, when diagnosis is used as a tool or a hypothesis for further investigation and understanding, rather than as the conclusion of such a process, it can help the therapist look for appropriate ways to work on therapeutic goals. This is especially relevant in the case of the so-called obsessive-compulsive syndrome, because mental health professionals agree on a great many statements that are descriptive of the syndrome, although they may disagree on dynamics and etiology. One of the basic statements that is generally accepted is that the obsessive personality devotes a great deal of psychic energy to the processes of thinking and cognition, and that in such people "intrapsychic communication shows an imbalance between thought, language, and feeling states (Spiegel, 1959)." Spiegel asserts that this "tendency of the obsessive person to construct systems of thought by which he thinks he lives, and which he often tries to enforce on others, is not infrequently associated with distortion of fact. This high premium on the person's own system of thinking and his imposition of it on others, is reminiscent, in miniature, of paranoid thinking and system making." This statement reinforces the previous observation about the overlap of symptomatology and dynamics in the various diagnostic categories. Additional characteristics prominent in the obsessive-compulsive structure may be mentioned here—these are usually seen in aspects of verbal communication, although not always detected in the beginning of treatment.

Central to this syndrome are feelings of inadequacy, inferiority, castration, and most of all dependence. As a result of such feelings, the obsessive is likely to *experience* himself as extremely ineffective and passive, and *equally ambivalent about most important and most insignificant subjects.* He constantly questions relationships with others, sexual identity, career, goals, and belongingness to a social group. Frustrations steadily increase, and result in a reservoir of anger, hostility, and aggression. An enormous amount of energy must be devoted to covering up such feelings, lest they are detected by others or experienced consciously by the patient. The patient's severe and punishing superego demands unswerving loyalty to the highest moral ideals, and tolerates no feelings that have negative value. In attempts to overcome and defend against the anxiety that these feelings engender, the obsessive patient develops a network of compensatory mechanisms—defenses. They help the patient, in some measure, to avoid intolerable anxiety, although he must always be on guard not to lose control of unconscious impulses. Chief among these defenses are denial, reaction-formation, rationalization, intellectualization, emotional isolation, projection, externalization, and in the area of language proper, the patient uses them in the service of keeping his feelings out of the realm of consciousness.

The therapeutic outlook for the obsessive-compulsive personality structure is, on the whole, not too encouraging—in fact, it is often rather bleak. However, when specific, circumscribed areas are the therapeutic target, relative success in one or more of these areas may be achieved. The confrontational approach varies widely from one individual to another, depending on the individual's idiosyncratic defensive structure, familial history, chronicity of the specific symptomatology, and past experience with psychotherapy of any kind. Nevertheless, some guidelines relative to strategy and techniques may be useful.

Since aggression as a defense against dependency strivings is at the core of the obsessive-compulsive personality, it is important for the therapist to explore central areas of frustration in the patient's past and present life. Such an investigation is not easy with this type of person, because of a tendency to overintellectualize, rationalize, or deny emotion. The therapeutic efforts thus become empty intellectual exercises devoid of substance, and little is gained. Because of this therapeutically wasteful pattern, the therapist must summon up all the creativity that can be mustered in order to find ways of "surprising" and "outsmarting" the patient's defeatist attempts. At the same time, the therapist must remember that the majority of these patients are easily hurt because of a deep sensitivity resulting from deprived narcissistic needs in childhood. There is a competitiveness and a general orientation of "kill (in fantasy) or be killed," which produces a "seventh sense" that is always on the lookout for anything or anybody who might "surpass" them.

They must convince themselves that they are "winning" the game, at least outwardly.

For example, a patient who used to be compulsively and punctually late to his sessions always "beat" me to the first sentence with some defensive announcement, such as "I've thought of everything I would have said in the last 20 minutes if I were here, and I decided to summarize it for you, here it is," or, "Don't say it, I know I am resisting therapy and I am angry at you because I am angry at my father. Well, it's time I am angry at him, but I am late because of this habit I've had for years." This need to always win is no doubt an overcompensatory defense for always feeling defeated, regardless of reality. It is not difficult for a therapist to fall into the patient's trap and accomodate the patient by adding more intellectualized, intepretive, and generally useless abstractions to his armamentarium by refuting the statement with impeccable logic or by providing the patient with new interpretations. Because such communications are distorted, *the source of the distortion must be found and addressed rather than working on the verbal communication itself.* For example, from a technical viewpoint, I might not answer such a challenge to spar with the patient, or I might make a self-referent statement, such as: "I would be mad, too, if I felt that I couldn't control my own time and had to be late because of a habit," thus addressing the unconscious anger and alerting the patient to a real lack of control when he believes that he is in control. With some patients where reasonable rapport has been established, I may let them know that I use the time they are late for my own benefit, such as reading, writing, telephoning, listening to music. With certain other patients, I might try to ignore the whole issue of lateness by turning the patient's focus to other issues, using a statement such as, "I am sure you have your reasons for being late, that's O.K. with me, you don't need to apologize. What else is on your mind?" The important thing here is to try not to reinforce the pleasure that the patient derives from the intellectual exercise of setting up a situation where he has to summon up defenses in a "clever" way to account for acting-out. Such exercises normally result in further defensiveness and emotional emptiness. In some instances, however, occasional lateness to a session may indicate a loosening up of the rigid and "uncommutable" schedules the patient has set up, and they may be signs of therapeutic progress.

A strategy based on a cognitive-intellectual approach and rigid adherence to any one intervention theory cannot be viewed as a viable therapeutic alternative for patients falling into the obsessive-compulsive diagnostic category. Often, the use by the patient of placating or consciously or unconsciously accommodating language makes it difficult to penetrate the hidden rage, simply because the patient never allows its signs to be seen or felt. When any "crack" in the defensive armor clearly points to such feelings, the patient is only too ready with "perfect" answers and rationalizations. Furthermore, when an interpretation in the direction of the source of the problems is offered, it is either submissively accepted—prima facia—only to be immediately ignored, discarded, repressed, or used as part of the patient's ammunition for self-flagellation. The masochistic stance is indeed another major aspect of the obsessive-compulsive make-up. The patient cannot enjoy any activity without attaching guilt to it, and when he makes a new self-discovery in treatment, it is turned into another achievement in a long series of achievements that have no bearing on his emotional life—it is another empty conquest.

For example, a patient who had been in therapy for a few months was in the habit of answering almost any interpretation or comment with, "You hit the nail right on the head!" He seemed to derive great joy out of these "insights." However, after some time in therapy it seemed quite obvious that these "orgiastic" proclamations of my wisdom had the conscious purpose of showing me what a great therapist I was and how stupid the patient was for not having thought of the interpretation himself. Unconsciously, it was designed to express his anger at me (transferentially) because the interpretations were bound to fail. The patient continued his compulsive patterns despite these great revelations. The placating, but pretentiously "honest" verbal message was a complete distortion of the patient's inner experience, hence the distorted communication.

The complications of these distortions in the obsessive personality are further illustrated in the case of a 30-year-old married man, Jeff, who sought treatment because of anxiety attacks that disrupted his work and his marital life. These attacks were similar to ones he had experienced during his last year of college. At that time he also sought help and remained in treatment for about a year. The anxiety attacks and other symptoms disappeared, at which point he decided to leave treatment. He also complained in the initial interview that his wife had told him that she had lost respect for him and for his intellectual abilities, and that she was no longer interested in him sexually because he was "too small" and couldn't satisfy her. She wished either to work out some mutually acceptable living arrangement or separate. Jeff complained that his job no longer challenged him, especially since there was no possibility of going higher in that company. Additional symptoms included phobias related to flying, riding a boat, and cancer, an inability to make decisions, and a premonition that he would die without having made it on his own. He had no children, and was fearful of even contemplating having any because "I wouldn't know what to do with them. When a crisis comes up, especially if it involves matters of life or death, I couldn't bear the responsibility."

In the first few months of treatment, Jeff was able to relate his unique developmental history in a fluent manner. He grew up as an only child. His mother "played musical chairs with her husbands." By the age of 13, Jeff had already had three fathers, each one less interested in him than the other. His mother was a nightclub singer and dancer, and used to disappear from the house several nights at a time. His maternal grandmother took care of him most of the time. While Jeff did not remember being physically punished by any of the three "fathers," two of them were verbally abusive and extremely "coarse" people, using language he didn't dare repeat even in his sessions. Jeff was always terrified of these men, as well as ashamed of them. His mother, however, could do no wrong, and he held her in the highest esteem. His descriptions of her approached those of a saint. He once said that "she must've gone through hell with all these men, and then, having to take care of me, to send me to school and to support my wonderful grandmother." He described her as a "beautiful, vivacious, very, very pretty, I mean very pretty and thin woman. She knew how to live and to give generously of herself, to have fun, real fun." As therapy progressed, it became obvious that he had repressed many other feelings about her, especially sexual. She apparently used to walk around the house scantily dressed, discussing sexual matters with her husband or other people quite openly in front of the patient. As a result of this and other feelings he had about himself, he developed an extremely inhibited and embarrassed attitude about his own sexuality. In fact, from the age of 14 until his marriage, he used to wear a jockstrap so that his erections would not be noticed by anyone. In a later session, he remembered that when he was a teenager, he accidently came across some pictures of his mother posed in the nude with a number of sailors. After he told me this story, he quickly added, "I am sure she didn't do anything wrong, like a whore or anything like that." She died when Jeff was attending graduate school studying for a master's degree in mechanical engineering. Two months after her death, he met his present wife and married her after a very short courtship.

As a reaction to his abusive and educationally impoverished home life, Jeff developed escape habits, mostly in the form of intellectual preoccupations. He remembered swearing to himself when he was 12 or 13 that he would never become like his stepfather. He thought, and he thought, and he thought. Action, beyond going to school, became alien to him. In fact, his choice of profession was no doubt related to his fear of human contact, as well as to his need to anchor himself in something that gave him concrete security—security in the form of involvement in minute details that could remove him from the central issues of his existence. Another reaction to his surroundings was the development of a verbal capacity that was linguistically impeccable, articulate, and refined; quite opposite to the speech of his mother and her husbands. He always referred to these men as his mother's "husbands;" even his biological father, who left when Jeff was two years old and who was never heard from again, was referred to in the same manner. In general, Jeff's manners were careful, considerate, and faultless. He always did what was expected. Even therapy was for him a matter of a "should" activity, carried out with as much exactitude as a blueprint drawing of an important machine.

Treatment strategy had to be tailored to these characteristics. The fact that Jeff had already had a previous therapeutic experience, one that helped him symptomatically, complicated the issue of goals in the present treatment. The alleviation of symptoms was still important. A the same time, if the need for the periodic eruptions of symptoms was to be eliminated, a new approach would be required. It was also possible that with time, Jeff's defenses might become less capable of preventing his anxiety attacks, and the repetitive cycles of symptom intensification might erupt in closer and closer succession. However, given his obsessive-compulsive personality structure, there was grave doubt about the reality of achieving meaningful changes. As these considerations were being weighed in the first few months of treatment, Jeff related a dream that indicated more clearly that he had been able to form some positive transference toward me—an encouraging sign for the development of a therapeutic alliance. In a sense, the dream was a turning point—it pointed to his ability to make unconscious connections with a positive object. This is the dream:

> I was sitting in the old apartment on Harvard Drive, and inside there is a mobster with a gun. There is a baby on the couch—I think it's my baby— and the mobster comes from the kitchen—he was a killer. He sits across from me on the chair, and I think he is going to shoot me. I hear a click, and just as I was waking up, before I opened my eyes, I saw my mother's face—she was smiling and saying hello or something like that.

This dream showed that Jeff had introjected, at some point in his development, perhaps as a baby, a good enough mother-object who would come to the rescue when he was in trouble. This object was something that I could use to help him. The dream, which might also have been correctly interpreted at the Oedipal level, had more of an oral-dependent character to it, especially in a transferential sense. It suggested that I might use a variety of techniques to attack the more chronic problems as well as the symptoms.

The importance of forming a working relationship with the patient cannot be overestimated. In the obsessive character, "surprise" is a most important strategy. This helps in the way of giving, or for some, forcing, the patient to make a commitment to treatment. The obsessive patient "pretends" to be in treatment, when in fact he is completely insulated from any contact, and is only doing what he feels one *should* do for the symptoms. Thus, for example, in the beginning phase of treatment with Jeff, the element of surprise came in the form of using the confrontation technique in relation to his need for a commitment to therapy. I questioned and probed his motivation, since after all, he had already been in therapy before and it had not seemed to "cure" him. I also questioned whether treatment had had anything to do with alleviating his symptoms altogether, and assured him that without treatment, he would have survived anyway. "You're coming here for the same symptoms you had six or seven years ago—obviously you were not cured by the psychotherapy, what makes you do this again—why are you here?" Jeff was alarmed and surprised, for he had not expected me to question the efficacy of something in which he had invested a lot of time and money. He said, somewhat impulsively, that if I didn't think that therapy would help him, then he would certainly take my advice and quit. This immediate blind acceptance of something that made some sense on the surface, gave me the opportunity to confront him with his basic problem of dependency. Whatever "authority" decrees must be right! This confrontation, because of its surprising consequences, helped us focus on the real issues rather than on the symptomatology. It also directed Jeff's attention to the fact that in order to change, he must take the initiative and could not expect me to be his "life director," but rather he must use his own judgment. As we intensified our scrutiny of his need for treatment, he became increasingly aware that he only paid lip service to his conscious wish to become more independent.

As a result of this and similar shocking confrontations, his relationship to me began to change, and the above dream was no doubt an expression of such change. I interpreted the dream as an indication of his wish to change, but added that such a change was, in his mind, conditional on someone else's good graces to rescue him. This interpretation put him on notice that I meant business, i.e., I did not plan to accept everything he told me on face value, and that his inner, unconscious feelings would play an important role in shaping his communications during the therapeutic work. Generally, with the obsessive patient such a challenge must be made quite early in the therapeutic relationship, otherwise the routine and ritual of the sessions will defeat the purpose of therapy. The obsessive patient is masterful in spreading around, both in his own mind and in other's, the illusion of change and gain. In fact, the patient is only alluding to a pattern of intellectual exercises that keeps him at the same place, year in and year out.

One of the important factors that distorts the verbal communications of the obsessive patient is the extensive reservoir of aggression. Often, this encapsulated "emotional bomb" manifests itself only in a slightly noticeable form: the patient talks about one or another insignificant subject in such detail that the main problem is camouflaged. These defensive maneuvers are motivated by the need to "drown" the therapist (transferentially) with all the verbiage, "the litter," that the patient can muster in order to prevent himself from becoming aware of deep aggressive feelings. The preoccupation with details and the pouring out of verbiage can often be mistaken for "free association," since the psychotherapeutic process is so intertwined with verbal communication. Of course, there may be other reasons why a therapist might be "fooled" in this manner by a patient. However, these may involve the therapist's unconscious feelings and unresolved conflicts (a subject discussed in a separate section on countertransference). The therapist must very seriously question and *confrontatively* find out from the patient the relevance of the detailed material to his problems in general and to the present condition in particular. Many patients will unhesitatingly defend their style of communication by sarcastically quoting the therapist who had initially instructed them to "say *anything and everything* that comes to your mind . . . ," or they might find other "plausible" rationalizations for their unending barrage of words and more words. When all avenues of investigation with regard to this style of defense result only in additional defensiveness, and they often do, only with different choreography each time, can the therapist then judiciously use a number of other, less conventional techniques. *These techniques ought to be used only by very experienced therapists and only when the therapeutic alliance has struck roots.* Of course, there are some rather intractable cases where the use of unconventional approaches must be considered the treatment of choice, because without them the working alliance itself may not be established.

The first technique is the *paradigmatic technique* advanced by Nelson (1968). This technique may be effectively used within the obsessive-compulsive entity in order to uncover, confront, and analyze. It may be especially beneficial where the following conditions exist: (1) unconscious aggression as it is manifested through "harmless" defensive language; (2) severe superego structure manifested through struggles for self-righteousness; (3) conscious control of emotional expression. This technique must be cautiously used, for it entails making assumptions with regard to the patient's ego strength. Thus, for instance, any assessment that is based only on the manifest content of the communication network is bound to give a distorted impression of the patient's ego capacity for frustration tolerance, a capacity most essential in the use of the paradigmatic technique. A patient who is extremely dependent and in need of constant support, may be a rather poor risk for this technique. On the other hand, a patient who has already gained some insight in therapy, but has regressed during a certain phase, may be an excellent subject for this technique. This technique is also useful with indecisive patients who cannot make a therapeutic commitment stable enough to allow a reasonable amount of work to be accomplished. On the whole, however, one might surmise that if, as a result of the *judicious* use of the paradigmatic technique, the patient is lost to treatment, the probability exists that the patient would not have gained from continued therapy at that time. If not successful, this technique may, in fact, save such patients a great deal of time, money, effort, and agony. They are better off trying other procedures or returning to treatment when they are more ready to change.

The second technique, the *forced projection technique,* is similar to the paradigmatic one in that it uses what might be called "defense saturation," but differs from it in that it requires greater active participation by the therapist. In the classical psychoanalytic technique, the analyst lets the transference (or the patient's projections of significant figures onto the analyst and reactions to them) develop to such a degree that, with the help of interpretations, the patient eventually recognizes the projections as such and thus modifies his behavior. In the forced projection technique, the therapist does not wait endlessly while the patient invokes defenses, but instead forces the projections out in the open, through probing and questioning, or by offering hypotheses and interpretations of the patient's defenses. This technique tends to curtail the patient's defensiveness in a dramatic manner because of the recognition and early anticipation of the defense by the therapist. This approach is especially helpful with patients who are so narcissistically and obsessively engrossed with the insignificant details of their daily routine that they reap pleasure from torturing their listeners, including the therapist, with inconsequential material, and thus "waste" their sessions even though they superficially seem to have discussed everything.

For example, a 29-year-old woman had been in treatment for about two years, initially because of marital difficulties and later because of other problems. She had the habit of recounting every detail of the most minute events in her life, always insisting on the importance of it all. Her emotional expressions were practically nonexistent, except when it came to the subject of her deceased father. It seemed, after awhile, that nothing in the world mattered, except for her words of wisdom, precious pearls that she "generously" showered upon other people. Although her linguistic capacity was indeed phenomenal, the verbal expressions she used to describe her feelings were rarely associated to the actual experience she was relating. There seemed to be little connection between her verbal description of having a feeling and actually having that feeling at that moment. After attempting to use various techniques to penetrate her defenses and failing, I realized she was "cleverly" covering up severe depression. This depression had been triggered off by her divorce a year earlier. For a variety of reasons, she was not willing to "allow" a crack in her armor. I then decided to utilize the forced projection technique in order to help her deal with a depression that seemed to be progressively intensifying. The excerpt presented here is from a session at the point in her treatment where this technique was used.

The patient began the session by asking about a cold I had had a few weeks earlier. When I told her that I had gotten rid of that cold some time ago, she glossed over that fact and said that her cold was still around, and for this reason she couldn't be too productive during the session, although she had a lot of things to talk about. Then, she proceeded on this happy note:

P: I've been feeling, really feeling wonderful, it's a wonderful feeling that things by "happenstance" are almost jigsaw-puzzling, the pieces put together like a jigsaw puzzle. It's just wonderful, when you're working on a big jigsaw puzzle, and it's exciting when you see that everything you're doing is fitting perfectly, just perfect—and I am not talking about silly things fitting in, I am talking about strange things, odd things. It's exciting. These are not ESP things that fit together—I don't believe in ESP anyway, but who knows, maybe there is such a thing. But anyway, today is Bert's (*boyfriend*) birthday: and . . . uh . . . uh . . . and, oh, yeah, I got tickets for a show for us—we're going to see "South Pacific." I heard so many great things about the new cast . . . I'm not sure who is singing the lead, but I love musicals. I don't know anything about music, but I like to go to musicals, they give you such a lift sometimes. But I was going to tell you the crazy stuff that's been happening. One of those things, and it's been happening a lot, I mean things like that, on my way up here, I met an old girlfriend, I haven't seen her for ages and we were talking, and she is going with her husband to "South Pacific" tonight, too—isn't that crazy? I mean that's happenstance! Crazy stuff like that, which makes me feel terrific. Yesterday I was trying to get a cab, and a very attractive man who was looking for a cab, too, asked if he could share one with me since he was in such a hurry. So we shared the cab, and I felt so attractive and glowing, and he turned out to be a very nice guy, and he asked me for my phone number, so I gave it to him. I mean I told him that I am going out with somebody now, but I am not committed to Bert anyway. This guy—his name is Lee—was wearing a very fancy three-piece suit with a very unusual—well, he is a very unusual looking guy.

T: He was wearing unusual clothes?

P: Oh, yeah!

T: Tell me more about it, what made his clothes unusual?

P: Well, he had a striped suit—it looked like it was right out of a fashion magazine—and a beautiful tie . . .

T: What about his shoes, did you notice anything unusual about them?

P: As a matter of fact I did. He was wearing very conservative-type shoes, but they looked quite expensive.

T: What else was unusual about him?

P: Why are you asking me all these questions about this fellow? What's so important about him, anyway?

T: I thought you were interested in talking about him because you were telling me about him and his clothes, so I assumed it was important to you.

P: So you don't like my telling the details about him—or about anything. I know I get involved in this. Well, Bert tells me I do this but he likes to hear me talk, so he says—or he used to say.

T: So what's the problem?

P: I don't know, I feel you're disapproving.

T: Since you're telling me all these important details, I thought I'd try and get into it myself so that I can understand them from your point of view. They must be important to you, I assume, since you spent much of the session discussing all kinds of details.

P: I don't know why I am telling you all this nonsense—I really don't give a damn about any of it. As a matter of fact, I was asking myself this question before you did, but I couldn't stop. I don't know why, I just continued talking and talking. Now I feel lousy. It's not your fault. (*There was a noticeable change in the tone and mood, from elation in the beginning of the session to tension and sadness at this point.*)

T: You seem quite upset. What happened? Suddenly all the wonderful feelings vanished?

P: I really didn't plan on talking about all this crap, but somehow I got into it, and you know me, I can't stop. But I got hurt when you were being sarcastic before. I mean, I know you're right, I know it, but I still got hurt. I was thinking in my office the other day—I do the same thing with Bert, I must bore him to death with boring stories. I mean, he's so sweet he doesn't say anything, and in fact he encourages me to talk, as if I need encouragement. Actually once he told me I should stop all this gossip, he said I sounded like an aunt he despised . . .

The patient continued to use verbiage as a defense, thus preventing her feelings from surfacing. Before this session, she had not responded to other interventional techniques, and her communications had continued to be distorted and irrelevant. However, the forced projection technique seemed to help "move" certain blocks related to her anxiety and feelings of worthlessness. For example, she was not used to revealing (or even being aware of) her feelings of hurt. Although my interventions could be perceived as sarcastic, their purpose was to help her express meaningful aspects of her inner life, and this was a good opportunity, a good exercise, for it. Thus, while the forced projection technique can at times be risky, it may be the intervention of choice at some point in the treatment of "intractable" obsessive-compulsive patterns.

Another technique that can be helpful in overcoming defensiveness, which is expressed through irrelevant, circuitous, detailed, and insignificant information, involves the therapist in a *running personal commentary*. For example, the therapist might tell the patient something from his own personal life that relates in some way to the material with which the patient is concerned. However, such comments by the therapist must be direct, spontaneous, and well-timed. The patient may then identify with the directness of the therapist, and gradually feel less threatened by exposing his own feelings. This technique also helps the patient sift out and recognize, through a kind of matching process, what his own feelings are. The other benefits of this technique—again, when used appropriately—are the establishment of additional avenues for trust between patient and analyst, and the development of conscious and unconscious communication "hooks" or contacts that decrease the patient's feelings of isolation.

There are innumerable techniques that a therapist can use when his goals are clear and the therapist's own communication network is free from distortion. The above techniques may be used separately or together, depending on the nature of the case as well as on the treatment objectives at a certain point in time during the therapeutic process. Needless to say, the therapist must feel comfortable and knowledgeable enough to venture into these or any other innovative techniques. Treatment of the obsessive-compulsive patient may often result in "pseudo" improvements, and, in many cases, both patient and therapist may have the unconscious need to deny the fact that changes are not genuine, or long lasting, or deep enought to be meaningful (Saretsky, 1981). It is not easy for a therapist to accept such a "failure," because of the obvious vested interest in his own competence and his narcissism in working with such patients. It may even be more difficult for the patient to accept the lack of real change, for the patient may perceive it as a "loss" of time, money, effort, and most of all *hope*. The techniques of confrontation analysis make a serious attempt to avoid such an outcome, for its very process of intervention monitors signs of denial closely and opens them up for investigation early in the therapeutic process. Of course, this does not make the techniques foolproof.

8

The Therapist's Communication

At the outset, communication was defined in terms of the sender and the receiver of messages. So far, however, mainly the patient's side of the communication cycle has been examined. There is no doubt that, almost by definition, the therapeutic situation is an unequal one, for one party is the "patient" (or "client"), the other is the "therapist." The latter is expected to provide "therapy": a service for which the patient pays. This service-providing profession is often referred to as the "helping profession" because it is supposed to help the seeker attain something he cannot, or will not, attain alone or through the services of other professions. Without question, the therapist must accept this definition or assumption: he is there to help. Such a commitment is probably the most basic requirement for anyone working in this field. Rosen (1953) spells out this requirement in his discussion of the treatment of psychotic patients:

> Treating a psychotic patient requires more than knowing what the governing principle is or telling the patient, "I am your idealized mother and will love and protect you." This would be as ineffectual as simple reassurance and we all know that it won't work. The way the therapist has to function in order to be the idealized mother is to do certain things consciously and unconsciously in such a way that the patient will understand that he is being loved, protected and provided for.

The same things may be said about the therapist treating any patient, not only the psychotic. Training analysis alone is not sufficient to produce this type of commitment, or the genuine wish to help. Other factors must exist within the basic personality structure of the therapist, factors that create or enhance these feelings of helpfulness (Guntrip, 1969). These factors help create an atmosphere that directly affects the verbal and nonverbal messages of the patient because he is sensitive to them, consciously or unconsciously. Whether the patient welcomes such a wish on the part of the therapist depends to a large degree on his motivation to change and on the density of his defensive armor. On the whole, however, the majority of patients who perceive the therapist in that positive light are more likely to gain from their therapeutic efforts than those, who, often correctly, perceive the therapist as a good technician but a "lousy" parent.

The dual function of the therapist, as "healer" and "significant figure" (transferentially), elicits communications from the therapist that must satisfy both roles: what he says must be authentic and integrated with his role of therapist, and at the same time it must be inviting or open enough to transform him in the patient's mind into a significant figure. Otherwise, transference cannot take place (Cohen, 1974). Thus, when the therapist asks the patient a question such as, "When was your sister born," he must be aware that the question has more impact than it would in other circumstances. First, it is a query expressing an interest in the patient's life with the intention of understanding its significance for his subsequent development and personality structure. Second, it is likely to provoke a transferential reaction in which he is transformed into a certain object in the patient's unconscious and to which the patient reacts on a manifest *and* latent level. Such dual or multiple roles are symbolized and expressed through any communication that the therapist produces. The communication thus becomes not only an expression of the inner life of the therapist (as it is for the patient), but it is also the medium through which the patient can get to know both his own personality and, to a certain degree, that of the therapist.

There are, of course, other influences on the character of the therapist's communications. First among these are the goals of treatment. On the surface, it may appear that, more often than not, when a patient comes for a therapeutic consultation, he has specific, clearcut problems to resolve. However, the manifest and latent reasons for seeking therapy are never clearcut: most patients either do not know what their problems are or they do not know how to communicate them. This state of affairs makes it necessary for the therapist to utilize language that will help the patient become aware of his problems or learn how to communicate their substance. This goal affects not only the kind of interventions to be made, but also their tone and the atmosphere in which they are made. This is a complicated task and requires keen alertness on the part of the therapist.

For example, a young woman came for an interview because she wanted some help with a decision she wished to make about her job. She was very unhappy with what she was doing, but could find no alternatives because, she claimed, she had not been trained to do anything else. She had no skill or professional experience in any other field. She also said that she had been in therapy before, and thus, her goal was not to enter into it again on any "serious long-term basis," but rather, she wished to restrict her discussion to the job situation. Toward the end of the consultation hour, after she had related some of her psychosocial history, she asked if I could help her. I realized that this woman had "encased" herself in a very defensive position and would not easily accept a "yes" or "no" answer. There was no doubt that she was quite miserable on the job. I certainly did not consider myself adequately equipped to render the services of an employment or personnel counselor, and thus I did not see how we could limit our transactions to that topic. Had I presented this thought to her at that moment, I probably would have closed the case, and she was in a great deal of pain. I also understood her wish not to be in treatment again and her motivation for choosing a limited goal. It seemed that whichever path I chose for my intervention would antagonize her ego enough to turn her away from treatment; yet I wanted very much to help her. Her conscious goal for the consultation could not be achieved without working on other aspects of her personality. My goal and hers seemed understandably at odds. Had she been coming for treatment on a regular basis for some time, I might have interpreted her defensiveness as any other resistance, and perhaps with a confrontational technique; but this was an initial interview. The "double binding" situation required an appropriate solution. My communication had to convey at least two messages: an understanding of her problem (the wish to change jobs without having to touch other areas of her personality) and a *motivational assessment* of her goal (without causing her to escape from treatment). The precise language of such a statement is, of course, very important, and it should be based on the therapist's awareness that verbal and nonverbal language must be utilized in a way that satisfies such requirements. In this case, I said the following: "Since you are not a newcomer to therapy, you can perhaps help me learn enough about you in as short a time as possible so that we won't have to spend more time than necessary on things which are not helpful in achieving what you want. I cannot pretend that I am an employment agency or that I can tell you precisely how long it might take us to work on this problem, but certainly whatever you discuss here is your business and I will try to understand what troubles you and help you with it in the way I know best." She understood the message quite readily: she could not "bind" me or restrict my interventions, and she was free to pursue her goals without any restrictions on my part. There was a promise of help—that's what I was there for—but no guarantee of success. She accepted the answer and continued in treatment even though the goals, as expected, turned out to be organically related to other aspects of her life in which she experienced a great deal of difficulty. Had I felt that she was not ready to work on any level, I would have told her quite directly that I could not help her for that reason, and advise her either to return when she felt more open or to seek another therapist's advice.

The analyst's communication in the initial interview often determines the fate of the treatment, i.e., not only whether the patient will continue in treatment, but also how he can expect the therapist to behave in the ensuing relationship—helpful, supportive, and interested, or treating the patient as just "another" case. The therapist must thus consider his communications in the initial interview very carefully. The therapist cannot have a "standard initial interview technique" for all, or even the majority of patients, because the needs, defenses, and personality styles are unique for each one. This does not mean that he should not have certain questions in mind regarding history, etiology, chronicity, and motivation. The point is that the language, approach, and style of communication must be modified to suit the case, not only for the sake of "successful" interviews, but also for future therapeutic interaction between therapist and patient. For example, information related to genetic material from an obsessive-compulsive patient may have to be obtained in quite a different manner than from a borderline, an hysteric, or a schizophrenic patient. Aside from diagnosis, the therapist must quickly assess the patient's social, educational, and linguistic experience so that the therapist's words do not add to the barriers of communication that are bound to exist at the beginning in some form or another.

In an institution for autistic children the policy was that the child's psychiatrist had the responsibility of "delivering" the child to his or her parents. A mother came to pick up her seven-year-old son, Paul, for the weekend. When Dr. M. came into the playroom to bring Paul out to his waiting mother, he found Paul walking around, mouthing the wall, and making his usual autistic sounds. He said, "Paul, your mother is here to take you home for the weekend." Paul continued with his rituals as if nothing had happened. Dr. M. repeated his statement. Nothing changed again. He then said to Paul, "I guess you're ambivalent about your mother!" Of course, nothing earth-shattering occurred! Paul continued with his preoccupation. At that point, Dr. M. took Paul's hand and led him toward his mother. Although this may be an extreme example, it clearly illustrates that some common ground must be established between the patient's way of communication and the therapist's if the therapy is to proceed.

Another important factor that contributes significantly to the communication style of the therapist is the therapist's reasons and motivation for choosing the profession. One may hypothesize from the above example that the psychiatrist's interest at that time, unconscious as it may have been, was to behave the way he envisaged a seasoned psychoanalyst would. What was happening right in front of his eyes didn't seem to affect his verbal message in the direction of the patient. No doubt his conscious goal was to help this confused boy. However, the status of being a psychoanalyst seemed to affect the nature of his communication in a most bizarre manner. His message was as inappropriate as the patient's ritual. Perhaps this psychiatrist's motive for choosing the profession contributed negatively to his functioning in that role. Thus the wish to be helpful is not, and cannot, be enough to guarantee adequate interventions.

Training analysis is designed to explore the therapist's personality, at least to the point of uncovering unconscious motivation for professional choices and hopefully resolving some basic conflicts. The therapist's availability to the patient as a human being is probably the most important ingredient in the therapeutic relationship, rather than the technical mastery, or the therapist's theoretical understanding of human dynamics. Guntrip (1969) puts it succinctly: "The technique of psychoanalysis as *such* does not cure. It is not endowed with any mystic healing power. It is simply a method of psychodynamic science for investigating the unconscious, an instrument of research. It plays an essential part in psychotherapy but is not itself the therapeutic factor."

The following patient's dream and his associations to it seem to reinforce this point—that the therapist must be more than a technician who is interested only in the intricacies of the dream:

> I was coming to see you and I was half an hour early. Actually, I went to the fourth floor first, and I saw a long line, a big line, and it was to Dr. S.'s (*an internist*) office. He was giving out prescriptions to everyone. I got very upset, and I ran upstairs to your office, and then I woke up all sweaty.

The patient associated the fourth floor with his fourth year in therapy, and Dr. S. with his father, who had always told him what to do and demanded order and discipline from him. He said that I was more like his mother, who let him be whatever he wanted to be, "perhaps too much sometimes." His appreciation of me was based on the work we had done together, and on his increased feeling of independence and individuality, not only on the basis of a positive transference. My own history contained themes similar to those of the patient. It had taken me a great deal of therapeutic work to shed my defensiveness regarding my background and my conflicts related to my parents, who had similar characteristics to the patient's parents. No doubt, the patient picked up some of my identification with him through

my communication network, which in turn affected his identification with me. My motivation for choosing the profession had
a great deal to do with my resolution of conflicts related to interpersonal communication, and resulted in my enjoyment of
others and my pleasure in nurturing others. These feelings are
easily communicated to a motivated and struggling patient,
such as the one above. The gains that the patient reaped from
the interaction were not based only on the content of the interventions, but also on my availability to him as a helper.

The psychotherapist's own analysis does not, of course,
guarantee that his communication network will be free from
the influence of unconscious processes. Therefore, some of his
interventions will, no doubt, stem from unresolved unconscious
conflicts and related feelings. This is part of the definition of
countertransference. However, there is a great deal of unconscious material that affects a therapist's communications that
is not only not detrimental, but might have positive effects
and ultimately benefit the patient. Included in this are attributes that make the individual human, especially those responsible for spontaneity and a genuiness. For example, a therapist might choose this profession because of an unconscious need
to care for, and be aligned or identified with, a struggling human
being who is continuously searching for change and growth.
This need may prove very helpful to patients in this condition.
It is interesting that it is perfectly acceptable, even delightful,
for a businessman, a lawyer, or a teacher to be constantly learning and growing—no one expects them to be perfect when they
enter their fields of work. The psychotherapist is, however, expected to meet different requirements—he is not supposed to
"grow" as a result of the interaction with patients, but must be
completely "grown up" when he is treating people. The therapist
cannot have the "luxury" of unconscious identification with patients. Guntrip's (1969) thoughts on this subject are important
to the theory and practice of confrontation analysis: "Real psychotherapy does much for maturing of the therapist as well as
the patient. The patient dominates the situation, but the therapist cannot meet it and remain a stagnant human being. He
cannot pretend or play roles." He adds that the ultimate goal of
therapy is to help the patient feel "real in himself," and the
therapeutic path to this goal must involve "the genuine meeting

of two human beings as persons," not only as patient and therapist.

A session from the ongoing treatment of a young woman illustrates the application of some of these concepts. The patient was a 28-year-old woman, a college graduate, who consulted me after an anxiety attack related to an ultimatum she had received from a boyfriend. He demanded that she make up her mind about marrying him immediately or he would leave her. It is not necessary for the purposes of this illustration to report more details about the patient except to note that, diagnostically, she could very easily fit the obsessive-compulsive category, with various somatizations, such as occasional colitis attacks, skin rashes, and "boils," and "bad temper" resulting in headaches and some "blackouts." She had been in therapy previously for a couple of years in another city, and had terminated treatment when her colitis cleared up. The session presented here took place during her eighth month in therapy with me.

P: Hi, how are you, I am sick (*looks at me rather angrily*). It's so terrible I can't sit in my office for ten minutes without having to run to the bathroom. My guts ache . . . I'm just sick, and I know it's colitis again. I thought I licked it a long time ago. For Christ's sake, what's all this therapy doing for me—I mean to say, to me. . . . That's why I went to see the other shrink in the first place. I am going batty. I mean I know, I read all about my personality in the books, and maybe I am not doing so badly as I should. . . . But for crying out loud, I think I am having a nervous breakdown—I mean, I think I am having a nervous breakdown. I am so nervous about everything! Yesterday I went to a party and I was so nervous, I actually had hives—my body, I broke out all over. I just feel awful.

T: A *nervous* breakdown?

P: I am not doing anything about anything. It's . . . I've been like this before. When I am like this I get sick physically, but now my face knows, and once my face knows it's got me! It's almost like it knows it, but this is the first time that it's happened! Before it was my stomach, like when I got the colitis. My stomach knew it!

T: Your stomach and your face knew—they know you and they act according to what you tell them. And now the colitis is acting on orders from you too?

P: I am sorry it's coming out in an area that I don't know to turn off yet. With the face and the stomach I got used to it, I can deal with it. But the colitis is something else. I am sure it's colitis because my colon has spasms which are caused by nerves, just like ulcers, except that it has to do with the colon. I mean I didn't go for tests, because I've had it before and it went away. It's never been diagnosed officially as colitis, but I know it is. So what's the use of spending more time and money on doctors who can do nothing for you. I mean wouldn't it be stupid to waste money away on doctors? It is a psychological problem, isn't it? But I . . .

T: (*Interrupting her speech*) You gave me the impression that you had taken care of this symptom medically. You sounded pretty definite about it. Now you're saying you haven't. Which one is it?

P: I never went to see a doctor specifically for this, but a friend who was doing his residency in internal medicine told me what it is.

T: This condition, if indeed it is colitis, can be very serious if it becomes aggravated, and since you have some symptoms now, it's important to have it checked out by your internist as soon as possible. I would appreciate a report from him as soon as possible.

P: If you insist. You sound so serious, as if I am dying. Isn't that a psychological problem—I mean, if it turns out that I have colitis?

T: Well, it's both psychological and physical, and needs to be investigated on both fronts.

P: And I am not doing anything, nothing at all.

T: You mean about the colitis?

P: I mean when I am here—I don't know what to talk about, and I waste the whole hour wondering what I am doing here—and when I leave, I have an additional problem, and that's about coming here. I think about how I don't want to come here—I mean, I'm not doing anything and I don't know what to do—what do you think? Should I continue to come here?

T: It's so hard to make decisions, that you want someone else to make them for you, and then they will take the rap for it if these decisions aren't successful. I am not one of these people you line up for the kill—like Gene (*her boyfriend*) or your mother or father. Did you really want me to tell you what to say when you're here? I feel that you're complaining without allowing yourself to say what's on your mind, literally on your mind.

P: I can't get away from the feeling that I don't know what I should do about therapy, whether I should stay or leave. Gene wants me to make the decisions for him. I mean I've been postponing and delaying giving him a final answer. I know I don't want to get married now, but I don't want to lose him either. I don't know what to do. I do want to go to graduate school, but I also want to make a lot of money, and I know there's money to be made in advertising, but I hate it. I hate spending a whole day—a whole day?—sometimes a whole week, on whether we should say the soda is fizzy or effervescent. Who the hell cares? What a waste!

T: Everything in your life seems to have pros and cons at the same time, and you're this way here. I am getting an ulcer myself from all this indecision about therapy—I don't know when I am going to have a couple of free hours! You want corners on a round hat!

P: (*Laughs.*) You know, that's what I like about you, you make light of everything, no matter what I talk about, you always pull out one of your metaphors or analogies, or stories.

T: For a change, you committed yourself to a feeling—or was that with tongue in cheek?

P: What do you mean?

T: You said you like my style of communication, my stories, and so on.

P: No, no, I really meant it, I really like that. I think you have a great sense of humor, which I can't always appreciate. But I wish Gene had the same sense of humor—he's too serious, like my father. Everything, but everything and everybody, he's paranoid about—he doesn't trust anybody around him except me. You come across very free. But maybe that's the way you are here. Are you like that outside of the office? I mean with your wife—you're married aren't you? I seem to remember Joanne telling me you're married, but I am not sure.

T: You want to know how I *really* am! What you see with your own eyes you don't believe—it's not genuine. Sounds a bit like Gene and your father! A bit paranoid!

P: I am like my father—everybody tells me I'm his "true" daughter. That's supposed to be a compliment! I am a real Donovan! I can vomit. But you I trust. I really do trust you.

T: I like that. It's nice to be trusted by a Donovan!

P: For whatever it's worth . . .

T: You're not worth the trust? Are you telling me I shouldn't feel good about your trusting me? You want me to be someone else? Someone who doesn't trust you? Someone who doesn't appreciate your feelings? I suppose you'd like to keep the shades down so that I can't see who you are and you can't look in the mirror because it's dark—so you want to leave. I think you do the same thing with Gene. Just as things move nicely between the two of you, there's some kind of an explosion and you want to run away. The same pattern is happening here. When you discover some feelings about me, you want to leave, either by contemplating leaving therapy or by blanking out.

P: (*Sadly and slowly*) I am very undecided, I don't know what to do. I keep doing things which are not helpful to me, and you're not making it any easier!

T: What am I making so hard?

P: I can't leave because I know you're right. I should work on this nonsense.

T: I never said it was nonsense. On the contrary, you are really fighting and it's not easy. But look, you're treating everything as if it were a matter of life and death. No big tragedies will befall you if you leave therapy. Do you feel you can't make decisions because you can't change them once they're made?

P: No, it's because I *can* change them and probably will that I don't make them—what's the use? You don't know what would happen if you took another route! And I don't want to be like my father, who never made anything of himself because he was always afraid to take the risk. Never in his life! And he's a very intelligent and capable man! He is a Harvard graduate, a very sharp lawyer, but he never takes a stand on anything! There's always the other side of the coin. I don't know what he's doing in law anyway! He does his job for the company, he complains to Mom, and he does nothing about it—absolutely nothing!

T: Perhaps he's waiting for you to help him with his decisions, problems, or maybe for another Messiah!

P: Now you're being sarcastic! Nothing is going to change my father. He's too old even to think about change, let alone actually changing. I don't expect him to change.

T: You're right, I was being sarcastic. I suppose I was irritated with your complaining about your father's psychological paralysis when you're not doing much more than him. It's the same thing when you complain about nothing happening in therapy. My feeling is that what you mean by this is that I am not doing anything for you, and you're waiting for my pearls of wisdom to "open sesame" for you. You know that I am not your father or your mother and you're not two years old, and if you make a mistake by committing yourself one way or another, you have the control to change it or to correct it.

P: First of all you don't know, I mean I don't know when I make a mistake, because how could I predict or know what would have happened if I didn't take that route?

T: I just realized that I made a big mistake by saying what I just said, because I know better than to give speeches. But I also realize now that nothing happened to me or to you as a result of that mistake! What I said was what I believed, but it doesn't really help you. I was barking up the wrong tree. You have to be superwoman before you allow any inner experiences to shine through. And, of course, you never feel like that!

P: I never feel even close to that—I am always feeling shitty and miserable and sick. So how can I make any decisions, especially about important things like marriage or therapy. In this state of mind I am likely to make the worst mistakes, which I'll regret the rest of my life. I'm sorry, but it's not my fault that I can't make up my mind. (*Screaming*) It's not my fault—I am not responsible for that!

T: You sound as if you're certain that any decision you make is going to be a mistake. And certainly you don't want that kind of responsibility!

P: Making up my mind about Gene is like . . . I don't know, it's impossible.

I can't relax. Maybe the whole thing with Gene is an excuse because I don't want to get married. I don't know what to do, and I don't think this therapy is helping me come to a decision. Maybe I am expecting you to decide for me, but I know you won't and you shouldn't. But for Christ's sake, what does he want from me, what's wrong with living together, just like we are now? Why do I have to get married?

T: Who says you have to? Is this a feeling of yours or an obligation to someone else?

P: I never made a decision not to marry Gene, and I never thought I'd never marry him, but I never thought I would. That reminds me of a dream I had last week and I forgot to tell you about it. My family was in that dream. Everybody is in my apartment, it's a very small apartment, the whole apartment is not bigger than your office. My father and my mother and my sister—all of us were reading—and someone was reading in the bathroom, and my father was—I don't know how he got there—but he was taking a shower, and she got into the shower, and somehow I got all wet, and I resented her because my hair was all stringy and wet and because I didn't take the shower. I can't understand this dream at all, but it was very vivid and there was some talk, but I don't remember what was said. I do have this obsession about my body and cleanliness—I mean, I always want to be very clean and I take at least two showers a day. I want to do the right thing, you're right about that. I don't want to make any mistakes. I am always afraid that people won't like me, so I do everything right—no really, I try. But all the people I get involved with, all including Gene, I keep the distance. I was told that I am enigmatic. I know . . .

T: What about the dream—the shower with your father in the bathroom?

P: I thought that was funny because my parents were very strict with us about these things.

T: What things?

P: Well, no one exposed anything, everybody was very proper. The bathroom door was always closed whenever anyone used it. My father is very modest—I mean, he is a handsome man, but very modest. I always had trouble with him when I was in my teens, because I had a crush on him, without knowing it. I discovered that in my last therapy. But somehow he was more like a mother, he was always more kind and giving, much more than my mother. I was always afraid to get close physically because I guess it was too sexual and people might get all kinds of ideas. Even now when I go to visit them, and I am not worried about what others think so much, there isn't more than a peck on the cheek. You know, it's like this with Gene whenever he tries to kiss me in public—even when there are good friends around, I push him away.

T: It's almost like having an affair with your father in public, isn't it? Certainly people won't approve of that! Your life keeps moving through tight narrows and any time you get close to one side, you feel you're too far from the other to be really safe, so you get into a panic.

P: This is exactly how I felt when Gene asked me to marry him. Whichever way I turn, it's going to be a disaster. I think I'd be very happy being married to Gene—he's really a wonderful person, very giving and very understanding, and he loves me. But every time I think this way, I get into a panic. It's like I have no mind of my own, I can't think for myself. I feel like I've had hardening of the arteries at age one. I sit here and I ask you what I should do about the most important thing in my life. You're right, it's ridiculous—what am I here for? My father won't express any opinion, and even if he did, I don't trust his judgment anyway. And my mother, forget it. She is always negative, she always knows what's best for everybody. I don't know why, but I always feel inadequate next to her, and she's really not very intelligent—actually she's stupid. I got nothing from her. I don't think this woman knows what love is. She tells all kinds of stories, and with great pride, about how she used to trick my father into feeding me and cleaning me when I was a baby because she hated doing these chores. I'd rather listen to my girlfriend's opinions about a man than to her. Maybe that's what the dream means . . . everybody was reading, it's like nobody was paying attention to anybody else, that's the way it used to be at home, except for the hollering of mother.

T: So when somebody who's giving and attentive and appreciative like Gene comes along, you panic, because he is more like your father and perhaps also like a mother you never had.

P: Are you saying that I want to have something going with my father? Well, frankly, even though my father is still a very handsome man, he does not appeal to me at all. I used to have all kinds of fantasies about him, but that was a long time ago, and I told you about it anyway. I know all about the Oedipus complex, but I am sure I am past that. I don't even have the kind of feelings you're supposed to have toward your therapist, and I never had them with the other therapist either.

T: So you're not in love with me!

P: I am not, and I don't think you're my type. It's nothing personal, it's just that I don't have these feelings about you. You're more like what you said about my mother, or what I wanted my mother to be. You care and you're open and I like your personality. I mean I don't know much—or any-thing—about you, but I feel that you are a caring person. That makes it difficult for me to justify leaving therapy. Maybe it's the same thing with Gene. I can't leave him because of that, because he is like that. But I don't have very strong sexual or physical feelings about him. Maybe I am too choosy. I know this has been the way my life keeps afloat. I couldn't make any decisions about college until the last minute, and I almost lost a scholarship because of that. I remember when I was a little girl, in the first grade, I always ran from one friend to another and my mother always picked my clothes, practically until I graduated from college. Sometimes

I wish that you'd really tell me what you think about Gene and what you think about me, and if you think I am crazy with this nonsense.

T: I certainly don't think that you're crazy. I do think you have a tendency to depend so much on others for approval that you are paralyzed, and the only action or movement in your life seems to take place within your body and your brain—you think a lot and you have quite a few physical symptoms. What I can tell you is that sometimes I do feel impatient with you because you pretend not to have anything to discuss or to explore, but invariably you bring up very important problems, like you did today.

P: I know that you get impatient, or that you seem impatient sometimes, but I don't always feel free to say everything to you. I feel funny about it. My other analyst was so strict that I was frightened sometimes coming late to the session because he would criticize me, or ask me why I was late—like a school teacher, you know.

T: I wish you'd let me know when you feel like that. I can't always tell. I am not God!

P: Well, too bad. I wish you were for my benefit (*laughs*).

T: I've had these fantasies myself sometimes. But I come down to reality pretty fast. (*Both laugh.*)

P: See you next week.

A science of psychotherapy would comprise not only a theory of treatment, but also a set of techniques and strategies directly related to diagnosis. Such a science is still far from developed, for the knowledge and understanding of the personality under different conditions has not yet reached scientific status. One stumbling block is the lack of separation between the object of investigation and its subject—the person. The existence of unconscious processes makes it quite unlikely that psychotherapy will, in the foreseeable future, become a science similar to such sciences as chemistry or physics. Therefore, when strategies and techniques are discussed, one is naturally referring to those aspects of the transactions that are consciously and deliberately planned by the therapist to achieve desired goals. However, since the influence of unconscious processes on these transactions is quite significant, it is important that its value in the total context of treatment be assessed. But again, such an assessment must be made post hoc, and any conclusions drawn from it must thus be regarded with caution. Remarks about the above session and about techniques in general must be viewed with this understanding in mind.

In general, it is important to seize any relevant opportunity to help the neurotic patient become aware of as many aspects of his inner life as possible in order to achieve a more integrated self. Often such an endeavor is continuously frustrated by a well-defended patient such as as the obsessive-compulsive. In the above session, the patient's continuous defensive escapism took the form of obsessive doubt and indecision, and made it very difficult for her to meaningfully (or even just intellectually) discuss important dynamics in her personality. She repeatedly attempted to focus on subjects (staying or leaving therapy and her boyfriend) that could only make it difficult to resolve her conflicts: she wanted to get to the station without leaving home. Because it was quite clear that she was chasing her own tail, I tried to help her open up as many avenues as possible, notwithstanding the fact that there was one latent theme running throughout the session. It was apparent to me that she was too anxious to be able to focus on one theme. Thus my interventions were directed at alleviating her anxiety and reassuring her of my support. Support was also given through confronting her with certain issues that were close to the surface and with which she could get gradually involved on a feeling level. Her somatization "drained" energy away from dealing with her psychological conflicts, and thus I chose to utilize a strategy that kept her engaged with her inner life throughout the session. This resulted in a somewhat decreased feeling of threat from the transferential situation and a readiness to share more unconscious material, such as the dream. This strategy was consciously followed with an eye to her emotional state at the time.

There were, however, *unconscious components in my communications that also helped build up trust* and a willingness to open up. One of these was concern about her physical condition. This was related to her not only on the basis of "good professional and ethical practice," but also, and to a large degree, on the basis of a spontaneous, unconscious, conditioned habit of feeling sympathetic and helpful to someone who is or may be seriously ill (cf. her colitis). This genuine concern was communicated to her in no uncertain terms, without ambivalence as to its helpfulness in the therapeutic process. This reaction is, in a sense, similar to one a parent might have when a child is perceived to be in some real, immediate danger. There is no indecision at such a moment: the parent takes action to save the child, regardless of circumstances. Such a reaction on the part of a therapist is not countertransferential, for it is not a reaction to the patient's transference nor is it destructive, even though it is often unconsciously motivated. On the whole, such interventions can only be beneficial, for they communicate a genuine concern and caring for the patient as a human being, not only a bundle of problems.

Such beneficial "unconscious" influences on the therapist's communications exist in other areas and under other conditions. In the above session, there were other interventions whose origin was not entirely conscious, yet which were beneficial to the patient. For example, I told her that I might develop an ulcer from her indecisiveness. It's true that such a statement may sound parental or guilt-provoking, however, in the context of the session, it dramatically communicated the effect of her obsessive doubt on other people (an effect that may be related to her unconscious need to punish). More often than not, doubters like her can provoke extremely hostile feelings in others without recognizing their role in it.

From a technical viewpoint, confrontation was utilized in conjunction with a great deal of encouragement and, generally, with the aim of lessening the anxiety, or as an interpretive tool for the purpose of opening up new areas of investigation. Some confrontation was used to legitimize an open discussion of taboo subjects, such as her sexual feelings about me ("so you're not in love with me!"), or for the purpose of exaggerating a feeling so that she would be "forced" to consider it and deal with it, overtly or covertly. The statement I made about her father waiting for her to help him with his decisions was of that nature.

In addition to the confrontations, the projective technique was encouraged (through discussing her father, she recognizes these qualities in herself), sharing some of my feelings with her, and avoiding any subject that could have brought back her obsession (about leaving and staying). For this reason, even the dream was somewhat ignored, because it contained too many explosive elements that might have forced a return of her defensiveness. Themes such as her rivalry with her sister and mother, her guilt about fantasies and some early physical contacts with her father, and sexual frigidity, were carefully avoided. My language was also designed to keep the flow of transactions on a more or less positive tone, because the goal was to overcome the impasse with regard to her commitment to therapy. We had to get off dead center.

It is important to reiterate the initial point made earlier— the value of the therapist's caring for the patient. The expression of such caring must "fit" the patient's personality, and the extent to which he can benefit from it at that point in the treatment. The therapist must view the language of communicating care as an integrated part of a treatment plan, not as an "act of generosity." Techniques can and should be placed in the service of communications, for the latter help shape the nature of the interaction between patient and therapist, and eventually the outcome of therapy.

Countertransference and Communication

The therapist is simultaneously an object of the patient's transferences and an agent of change, and thus is in the difficult role of having to separate what he wishes to communicate for the patient's benefit from what the patient provokes in the therapist unconsciously. Segal (1977) remarks, "At the same time the analyst is opening his mind freely to his impressions, he has to maintain distance from his own feelings and reaction to the patient. He has to observe them, to conclude from them, to use his own state of mind for the understanding of his patient and at no point be swayed by it." Such influence is generally called countertransference, although there is some difference of opinion on the definition of this term. One approach limits the definition to those unconscious reactions of the therapist that are triggered off by the patient's transference (Fenichel, 1945; Greenson, 1967). Another approach defines countertransference in the broadest terms, as any unconsciously provoked reaction of the therapist. However, the majority of authors prefer to limit the definition to include only unconscious reactions to the patient that are detrimental to the therapeutic process. Racker (1968) has labelled such reactions the "countertransference neurosis," and believes that countertransference is an integral part of therapy, a fact of life, so to speak: "The transference is always present and always reveals its presence. Likewise, countertransference is always present and always reveals its presence, although, as in the case of transference, its manifestations are sometimes hard to perceive and interpret." Following Racker, confrontation analysis assumes that unconsciously motivated reactions on the part of the therapist always exist in the treatment situation, and always color the nature of communication. Of course, the use of the term "countertransference" to cover all these unconscious reactions may be overinclusive and, thus, it may lose its discriminatory meaning and clarity. However, all unconscious reactions share at least one element—they are not under the control of the therapist's rational ego, and thus defy scrutiny before they are discharged. Confrontation analysis differs, however, with Racker's thesis regarding the origin of the countertransference neurosis, which is according to him, "centered in the Oedipus complex." Since confrontation analysis views the Oedipal situation as only a "higher order" development of the oral-dependent stage (see Part I), it also hypothesizes that the pathological and destructive reactions of the therapist emanate from the same phase of development, specifically from a faulty mother–child interaction in the first few years of life.

The previous section presented some aspects of unconscious reactions of the therapist that contribute in a positive manner to the treatment. Here, some factors that may influence the therapist's communications in a negative manner are presented. These aspects necessarily overlap because, in one way or another, they are connected to the therapist's basic conflicts—conflicts that affect his personality and its expression through his or her communication network.

The personality of the therapist is the first factor. In this category, countertransference may be considered to arise out of the unresolved unconscious conflicts. The patient becomes the projection screen for the therapist's unacceptable impulses and feelings toward past introjected objects, and therefore, interventions may be based on interpretations of the patient's communications as if they were part of his own world of introjected objects. The roles in such a case become reversed: the patient is unconsciously perceived as the parent who has to fulfill the analyst's early (child) ungratified needs. The inability of the analyst to place enough distance between his neurosis and the patient's results in the formation of language, verbal and nonverbal, that can only serve the neurotic needs of the therapist.

For example, a patient came late to her second session with a therapist-in-training who had reported in supervision that the first session was a "great session," and that the patient was so excited about therapy that she couldn't wait for the following session! When she entered his office late on her second visit, he said rather impatiently, "What made it so difficult for you to come on time?" The patient answered that her boss asked for some information just before she had to leave for her session, and she couldn't refuse to give it to him, which took some time. The therapist then said, "You have to do what your boss needs you to do, I guess." This remark produced a great deal of tension in him, and he later brought the subject up in his own analytic hour. During the supervisory hour, he said he realized that the patient represented his mother, who had a clear preference for his younger sister, and that he felt abandoned by her as soon as the sister was born. The patient's boss became the preferred sister with whom he had always competed for the mother's (patient) affection. After the first session he had secretly and unconsciously hoped that he had pleased his patient (mother) so much that her promise to come back was an indication that he had won her over, but when she failed to arrive on time for the second session, he felt abandoned again. The sharp, hostile questions and comments were no doubt a defensive attack, clearly countertransferential, although he understood the patient's needs dynamically, albeit on an intellectual level.

Such countertransferential reactions are not uncommon among therapists, although not many are willing to admit them. When the therapist's dependency needs are not adequately resolved, or when he is not reasonably aware of them, they may manifest themselves in what seems to be a rational line of investigation, but which is actually only a mask for anger or irritation. There is no doubt that this type of personality problem and its manifestation affect the patient's transference. At times, the therapist's recognition of his own reactions during the session may aggravate subsequent interventions even more when the therapist cannot accept the existence of this operating unconscious process because he would feel so guilty and helpless in front of the patient. The therapist thus attempts to further deny or suppress these reactions. Of course, when such a process takes place, it may parallel the patient's resistance, resulting in a cycle of *resistant interaction*. The therapeutic productivity naturally diminishes, while the frequency of impasses increases. The question is, then, how can such a vicious circle of nonproductive communication be broken? No doubt, additional therapy for the therapist is indicated; but beyond this taken-for-granted step, and beyond exposition and discussion of the case in supervision, the therapist must attempt to become aware of all the symptoms that might predict an "attack" of countertransference (and later perhaps utilize them). Such symptoms are often difficult to discern. In this connection, Racker (1968) aptly points out, "A guide of a certain practical value for knowing whether it is the neurosis that is driving him, is the *compulsiveness* with which he feels the need to give the interpretation. Behind this compulsiveness there clearly lies the invariable sign of neurotic reactions—anxiety." However, anxiety may not always be consciously recognized by the therapist whose omnipotence has gotten the better of him, and countertransference reactions are thus not always easy to detect. Nevertheless, when they are detected, they can be utilized profitably by the therapist in two ways: (1) to better understand the patient, and (2) to learn which themes (in the therapist) are in need of intensified investigation and analysis.

The point has justifiably been made in the literature that countertransference reactions can often be understood as cues of what lies under the patient's resistance, and therefore they can be used to explore the patient's unconscious with more knowledge than overtly communicated information allows (Reik, 1947). Such reactions may thus be understood as the common ground on which object relations of both patient and therapist find a meeting place. Thus certain countertransferential reactions become factors that contribute to the development of a variety of therapeutically advantageous processes—identification, empathy, understanding, and communication. The model for such a development is the earliest relationship between mother and child, which initially grows in a nonverbal manner through the sharing of common territory (the breast) and proceeds through imitation, identification, introjection, and separation. The fact that the therapist unconsciously shares certain feelings (which may or may not be acceptable to him) with some of the patient's unconscious feelings affords an opportunity for language (communication) barriers to be removed. It is important, of course, that the therapist ultimately become aware of this commonality and use it properly.

For example, a candidate in psychoanalytic training who was in treatment first complained in one of his sessions about my "lack of consistency" in my approach to his problems—I was "active" sometimes, "passive" at others. However, after some probing, it turned out that he actually did not care so much about my so-called "inconsistency," because he felt that he was being helped in spite of it. However, he was disturbed because my approach hadn't given him a clear indication of which specific school of thought I espoused, and since he assured himself that asking me directly would be interpreted as resistance, he tried to gather this information indirectly. Thus the complaint about me as a therapist was abandoned in favor of a more "philosophical" and "personal" curiosity about my theoretical orientation, and eventually a pat on the head for doing a "good job."

This was not the first expression of curiosity regarding my credentials. The patient-candidate in fact, knew, a great deal about my training and orientation—these were initially his expressed reasons for choosing me as his therapist. It was thus not clear what he really needed at that time, and what was motivating his "curiosity." One plausible interpretation may be instantly made: he was expressing resistance through the need for immediate gratification in the form of my expected answer. This interpretation would have no doubt been correct for him. He was under a great deal of pressure from the demands of his training, his job, and his family, and he needed some nurturance. However, there was more that he needed at that specific time, something that I understood only later, after I became aware of my countertransference reaction to the patient's request for my credentials at that particular time. I knew that I was irritated, but I was unable to spontaneously associate my displeasure to the patient's "demand" for credentials. In order to buy some time, I phrased a question in the form of a statement as an answer to the patient's question. I wondered aloud, as it were, whether he really didn't know what I stood for, what my credentials were, and that perhaps his question was intended to cover up his wish to get back at the training institute, through me, for giving him so much work to do. Again, this interpretation was no doubt correct, although he said he had not had the institute in mind, but he confirmed that he did sometimes get angry at the whole "training routine." He then recalled a dream that he had had the night before. While he was engaged in recounting it, I realized how I resented the patient's "curiosity," and became aware that my interventions and communications were unconsciously designed to defend against my own anxiety with reference to my credentials.

For a variety of reasons that are not totally pertinent to the present discussion, this patient aroused in me a significant, supposedly resolved, conflict about my professional identity and, on a deeper level, my own personal identity. My father had rather intense objections to my going into the field of psychotherapy, because he didn't consider it an "ethical" profession ("how can you charge for talking to people?"). Without a tangible product for exchange, the profession seemed useless to him. My separation from this part of the introjected object took a great deal of hard work in my own analysis, but obviously more than a slight residue remained. Consequently, when this patient (who was going through a training process similar to what I had experienced) became curious about where I "stood" in the field, he assumed, in my unconscious, the position of my father, and aroused enough anxiety in me to evoke defensiveness. Even though my defensiveness was not too great, it did obscure the real conflict with which the patient was struggling, and my interventions focused on an issue that was not the patient's immediate concern!

At that particular time in the therapeutic work, the real conflict related to the patient's own identity, or the lack of it, and his need to find *in the therapist* an anchor to which he could tie his ship. His parents (both of whom had died before he entered therapy) had continuously "double-bound" him while in college (and before) by impressing on him the financial sacrifice they were making for him. He thus had no significant allies to support him in his arduous road toward professional achievement. His wife, according to him, could not "begin to understand what's involved in becoming an analyst." Underneath his wish to know about my professional orientation was the fantasy of finding a highly educated and committed analyst-parent who could side with him against his rejecting introjects.

After my countertransferential reaction, when I recognized what the patient was trying to tell me in his own distorted communicative manner, it became much easier to see our way through this conflict. The word "our" is used purposefully, because, indeed, I reaped benefit from this experience as much as the patient. In this connection, Gittleson's (1952) remarks are enlightening:

> Countertransferences, like transferences are dynamic and economic phenomena. They exist as facts of any analysis. They are a part of the dynamic and economic problems in every analysis. The analyst must deal with them in himself and, together with his patient, he must deal with them when they intrude into the analytic situation. They are not subject to manipulation and wilfull control. *To the extent to which the analyst is himself open to their analysis and integration, he is in a real sense a vital participant in the analysis with the patient. It is this which constitutes the analyst's real contact with the patient and which lets the patient feel that he is not alone* (Emphasis added).

The similarity of certain past experiences between patient and analyst, as in the above case, is often a mixed blessing: it can be helpful because it may promote the necessary emphatic understanding of the patient's unconscious, but it can also be detrimental if it leads to an unconscious identification that blocks the surfacing of conflicts associated with inner objects related or associated with such an identification.

Other factors in the analyst's personality that can create negative countertransference reactions are too many to enumerate here. However, Gittleson's list of these factors points to the many possibilities for such "traps" that any analyst may fall into, because of the nature of the therapeutic situation, which involves both personalities and in which the analyst brings not only his training and therapeutic know-how, but also his past with all that it includes, such as "vestiges" of unresolved original conflicts.

Another complicating factor that often unconsciously affects the therapist's communications is the patient's personality and the kind of transferential reactions he projects onto the therapist. The patient's "personality" includes (1) the kind of needs that he expects the therapist to fulfill (in the main, expectations that no psychotherapist can possibly gratify), and (2) the manner and style of operation of his personality—the way it is presented in the therapeutic situation. Of special interest is the personality with whom the therapist initially does not find enough common ground to establish sufficiently meaningful communication for a therapeutic relationship to develop.

Now and then every therapist gets a referral of a patient whose intention, sometimes consciously, but more often unconsciously, is not to work on change, but to create (mainly for internal objects' sake) the illusion that he is fulfilling some obligation. Often, patients do not consciously recognize the anxiety that brings them to treatment because they have succeeded in building very intractable defenses around it, thus creating a personality wrapped with a "character armor." The difference between such a patient and the so-called neurotic patient is in the location of the armor: the neurotic "wears it on his sleeve"— the coat is turned inside out where the soft lining (symptoms and anxiety) is on the outside, more accessible to observation and penetration—whereas the so-called "character" defense patient exposes nothing—he wears the coat with the lining inside and affording neither accessibility from the outside nor a perception of his anxiety when he looks in the mirror. It is even difficult to find an open seam! Yet, when an experienced therapist looks at such a person, he is likely to at least observe that the whole coat is distorted, that there is *something* wrong, even though it may not be possible to pinpoint it immediately. Such a perspective is essential for a variety of reasons, not the least of which is the possible countertransferential reactions that might be provoked as a result of an inadequate assessment that overlooks the character problems. At times, overlooking such problems can be accounted for by the overzealous attitude of the therapist. However, someplace within, the therapist knows that he may be dealing with someone who has come for purposes other than treatment—perhaps to appease (unconsciously) the requirements of an authority figure, or because he has been told to do something about deteriorating functioning in work, school, or in family relationships. Some of the problems such patients bring with them are antisocial in character and place a heavy burden on the environment. Thus, when the patient comes for treatment, it is usually either to get these (inner and outer) people off his back, or to revenge his accumulated hurt by defeating the therapist, who may symbolize everything he is fighting—success, dependability, commitment, and human contact, all individual and social attributes that the patient feels he lacks.

The psychotherapist who takes on such a case not infrequently finds himself chasing his own tail, for the patient does not develop a working alliance, and seems to be uninterested in the aims of therapy. The patient is not there to change, rather he expects the therapist to teach him how to get better at what he does best—building a thicker armor. The patient's communications always consist of at least two layers: (1) smooth (or rough, as the case may be) surface messages that are usually extremely misleading, and (2) scheming, manipulating, often paranoid and vindictive, empty, deprived and hungry, and not infrequently, aimless messages. The shifts from one level to another are quick, and leave the therapist wondering about his competence. As soon as the therapist begins to attain some degree of understanding, the patient very skillfully moves into a different gear to prove him wrong. Not only do the props on the stage change, but the stage itself turns around and about so that it is impossible to get a good grip on the substance of the play. While a therapist is supposed to have his own point of reference, his own center column, so to speak, in order not to be distracted by such theatrics, he is still a human being who can slip up now and then and who can struggle unconsciously with such characterological presentations of the patient, and consequently commit "countertransference sins," at the expense of healthier communication.

The experienced therapist, however, quickly becomes aware of the patient's manipulations and of his own unconscious destructive reactions to them. This awareness is usually triggered off by a feeling of discomfort at being with such a patient, a feeling of being in quicksand. Generally, one gets the impression from such patients—if they last beyond the first few interviews—that they are emotionally impoverished, constricted, and lacking in the capacity to form genuine, spontaneous human connections. Because of the nature of their defensive armor, they can mislead the therapist either by their overtly smooth appearance and pretense of being concerned individuals, or by the presentation of what seems on the surface to be perfectly reasonable grievances against their environment. However, the recognition that these are all maneuvers aimed at keeping the status quo forces the therapist to consider not only whether this countertransference is a hindrance to the therapeutic work, but also whether the patient should be seen in a therapeutic setting altogether, or in one that requires a different orientation.

Such patients are not usually welcomed by psychoanalysts of the orthodox school, and perhaps by most psychotherapists who are reluctant to deviate appreciably from traditional techniques. Confrontation analysis, on the other hand, is a system that holds certain basic assumptions about the nature of human development to be different from psychoanalysis, and therefore it views the character disorders in a somewhat different light; specifically, confrontation analysis' notion that central conflicts are the product of inadequate handling of the oral-dependent stage of development, or the first few years of life. Consequently, help must be geared toward the resolution of pregenital fixations. The majority of patients with character disorders who fit the above description, have personalities whose inner self is the most dependent and extremely vulnerable to outside influences, and they feel the need to protect every part of the ego. There is practically no hope that such pathology can be altered in a dyadic treatment if the usual dynamically oriented techniques are utilized. Behavior modification techniques may only reinforce the defenses, and more "exotic" techniques, such as gestalt, are likely to promote their narcissistic etiology. Confrontation analysis, with its flexibility of technique, which begins at the outset to chip away at dependency problems, has at times succeeded in penetrating characterological defenses. In this system, the countertransference is often utilized by the therapist (before the patient misuses it) in a confrontative manner, so that the patient's usual manipulativeness is not denied or avoided. Rather, the patient is confronted with his contribution, his share in the production of countertransferential reactions.

For example, a divorced woman had come for therapy because she was depressed and felt lonely. She admitted that her marriage had suffered because of her own destructive behavior, which included, among other things, badgering her husband about his lack of financial wisdom while at the same time squandering large sums of money. She never felt guilty about this, she said, for she felt "deprived" by her husband, who could not support her "grand" style of living. She grew up in a family of small means, but she was also never given responsibilities as a child because she was "pretty." Neither was she given much love; for her parents, who divorced when she was five, were too involved with their own problems. She felt that her own two children were her "punishment," because they kept her from enjoying herself. She had no interest other than playing cards twice a week with some acquaintances. A few years before her divorce, she had lost interest in sex, and this was followed by a large weight gain, to the point where her husband began to have extramarital affairs, almost in the open. He finally decided to leave her for another woman, a move she never believed he would dare make. Her fantasy was that anyone who had her for a wife had gotten himself the best deal possible, for she regarded herself as most desirable both physically and intellectually. She said, "I let the man think for me. Men like that. I never did anything in our apartment. Jack (*her husband*) did everything, except for cooking. He always knew what the best show in town was, where to go, what was going on in the world. He took care of all that." At the same time, she thought that he would never leave her because he loved the children too much, and he would want to take them with him but he knew he couldn't take care of them alone. "He also knew that if he insisted, I'd let him have them; they are a pain in the neck anyway." Her miscalculation, based on her manipulative, passive-aggressive treatment of those around her, backfired. He left and did not ask to take custody of the children. She had hoped for this, but had not "dared" to initiate it herself.

After a few weeks in therapy, she began to complain about the lack of progress and about my "aloofness and coldness." I was like her mother, she said. She felt I was not interested in her, and that perhaps I didn't know what to do with her. She was still gaining weight and spending money to the point of not having enough to pay her bills. She expressed this in one session: "I'm spending money like crazy. If I had it, alright! I know my budget—I won't be able to pay my bills—I just do everything I shouldn't do. I keep getting in deeper and deeper. I do the same thing with food—eat and eat and eat and then I starve myself. I do the same thing with my daughters—I let them do what they want and then I suddenly yell at them and I want to strangle them. I just don't know where the middle of the road is. I just feel you're not helping me, you're not doing your best . . . I meant to say, I am not doing my best!" That slip of the tongue brought to the surface my feelings about this patient. I realized that indeed I was rather uninterested in her treatment, and that I was not really making serious efforts to establish contact with her. I was not doing my best. At the same time, her slip made it clear what some of my countertransference could be attributed to: she did not want to do any of the work, but attempted to manipulate me into the role of a magician. She had replaced her husband and her parents with me.

After that slip and my realization of the objective truth in it for me as her therapist, I admitted to her that I did feel disconnected from her and that our work must have suffered as a result. I added that perhaps there was something in her attitude that contributed to these feelings of distance in me. I thought, I told her, that other people might have felt similarly—for example, her husband who had left, and the other men she kept meeting and losing. I told her that as a therapist I was not "supposed" to have such feelings, but that for a number of reasons I reacted to her probably the way other people did, and that if she wished, we could try to work this problem out in the therapeutic setting. I wanted to help, but she had to cooperate. Her reaction to this sharing of feelings, which validated hers as well, and to my confronting her with her destructive dependency, was unusually sedate, although later it was accompanied by some crying. She said that I was the first person to tell her that she was an uninteresting and boring person (which I had not said to her at anytime), and that indeed she suspected she was that kind of a person, and this upset her a great deal. But now that other people knew about it, she said she must do something to change the situation immediately, and she came up with a renewed decision to lose weight and to take an evening course at the local college. She thought that these moves would create a more desirable person, for she would then be more appealing and knowledgeable.

Since she had missed my basic point (i.e., that it was hard to make emotional contact with her), I reminded her of it, and interpreted her missing it—almost purposefully—as another indication that she did not want to make an emotional investment in seriously changing, and that she always looked for something outside of herself to change her life. After a brief exchange on the subject, she said, "I wish I was a little girl again—no responsibility. I didn't have to think about anything. Nobody was dependent on me for anything—it just didn't seem difficult then—even though I always felt miserable. There was always the black or white—my parents' way or my way. I never had to decide what's good or bad." Then in a matter of fact manner, she spoke of how oppressive it had been living with her parents, and how she used to tie the venetian-blind cord around her neck, pretending she was going to hang herself. She knew then, she said, she would never kill herself, but her parents always fell for it. As the session progressed, I told her that her pronouncements of wanting to do something for herself when she didn't mean to made me feel uncomfortable, because I recognized not only their manipulative quality, but also their message. I said, "It's like somebody lying in your face, in a sense insulting your intelligence, even though I don't see that you've been lying, but that you feel obligated to make empty statements. No one here will punish you, regardless of how you want to conduct your life." This exchange was typical of others during this patient's treatment, which lasted for about four years, at which time she found another man who lived in another city and with whom she decided to live. No significant changes occurred in her personality; however, she became increasingly aware of her share of the responsibility in interpersonal relationships and of her capacity to become more trusting and confident in herself. She recognized, and eventually followed up, her need for more treatment. I have not heard from her since, but I felt that some of her defenses loosened up and that she was more available for fresh contact with the outside world.

In general, confrontations similar to the one above follow concrete, empty confessions that have become rituals performed for the benefit of an audience. As much as possible, the patient should not be allowed to leave the session having "gotten away with murder," which is precisely what the patient's fantasies are, as they are eventually related when the patient becomes more conscious of them and ready to communicate them. The often successful attempt to put something over on others gives the patient a feeling of omnipotence, and is used in the service of removing anxiety from any conscious area. It is thus important to confront the patient directly and immediately, and to be at least a step ahead—otherwise, the patient is likely to slip away, physically or psychologically, without having found any real comfort.

Other personality dimensions of the patient, such as the patient's style of communication, may activate countertransference reactions. In such cases, more than in others, the therapist must decide, after having discovered what upsets him, whether he can separate such reactions from a clear, objective approach to the patient; for often the style of communication is not connected to psychopathology, but rather to a peculiarity of language conditioning for this particular individual. Such idiosyncrasies, when they do not interfere with the individual's goals, should not be discouraged, and should often be reinforced.

One of the definitions of countertransference is an unconscious reaction to the patient's transference. The therapist is always used by the patient as a lifeline, onto which he can attach any object from the past that continues to float in his unconscious world. These objects often "bump" into other objects, stirring up the water because of the conflicts they engender. Not all lifelines (analysts) are made the same way, even after having passed inspection (analysis), and not all objects have the capacity to stick to all lifelines. The result is, of course, that there are always floating objects in search of lifelines, and vice versa, lifelines in search of objects. Any therapist whose megalomania does not allow acceptance of this premise, that is, that he may not be able to treat every patient who walks through the door, should be looking for a lifeline rather than being one for others! This concept is usually clearer when the patient is involved. For instance, when a patient bemoans his terrible fate upon discovering that not everyone in the world loves him, the immediate question that might occur to the therapist is, "Do you love everyone in the world?" And if the answer is positive, then, of course, that patient should be counted among the saints, and should not be in therapy. It is often the unconscious omnipotence of the therapist that is responsible for the depression he experiences after failing to make therapeutic contact with some patients. Certainly, such feelings require full therapeutic investigation, for they are triggered off by the "savior transference," in which the patient perceives the therapist as his savior—a role the therapist accepts, only to fail in it!

After working with various types of transferences and transference neuroses, the therapist should become familiar with the kinds of object projections and accompanying expectations with which he feels most comfortable. However, some transferences are extremely elusive, and consequently, so are their countertransferences. For this reason, discussion of cases with other colleagues and in supervision can often be an eye-opener.

Additional sources of unconscious reactions on the part of the therapist, reactions that become integrated into his communicative language, include the training of the therapist, the personal identification a therapist develops with a particular form of treatment, and the problems that might naturally occur in the daily realities of the therapist's life (problems for which there are no ready solutions).

There is no doubt that institutes of training in psychotherapy differ, even when they subscribe to the same philosophy of treatment. Institutes have a vested interest (which is pursued consciously and purposefully) in seeing their graduating therapists follow their basic beliefs. Most graduates thus leave not only with the conscious understanding and knowledge, but also with an *unconscious attachment to the institute and its philosophy*. This combination of factors is the basis for what one normally calls "loyalty," or "following in the footsteps." Any deviation from the rules and regulations of how to treat a patient (according to the mother-institute) may bring with it unwelcome feelings of guilt and doubt, as well as the defenses associated with them. Consequently, countertransference reactions may ensue. If, on the other hand, the therapist does not allow himself the "luxury" of perceiving the patient's pathology as requiring modification in his therapeutic approach, he is liable to deny the possibility that he is serving not the patient's needs, but his own. As a result he may feel guilty, and thus increase the chances of more countertransference reactions. The moral is, then, that the less "loyal" the therapist is to his alma mater, the more flexible he will be about alternative interventions. As such, communications will be less distorted by his own defensiveness and can be more patient-centered.

There is, in this light, a rather amusing paragraph in a paper by Winnicott (1965), given at a symposium on countertransference, and in which he was, among other things, reacting to another paper by a Jungian, Dr. Fordham:

> Incidentally, may I remind Dr. Fordham that some of the terms he uses are not of any value to me because they belong to jargon of Jungian conversation. He in turn can tell me which of my words are useless to him. I refer to: transpersonal, transpersonal unconscious, transpersonal analytic ideal, archetypal, the contra-sexual components of the psyche, the animus and the anima, animus-anima conjunction.

Analysts of various schools use other jargon. The point is not only that the use of jargon is in and of itself rather defensive, isolating, and patronizing, but that it is often symptomatic of the kind of rigidity one often encounters in some therapists who hold on to vestiges of their training inappropriately, without being conscious of it or without recognizing its effects on the interpersonal communication in their transactions with the patient.

The next natural source from which countertransference can develop, a source quite similar to the previous one, is the personal identification the therapist develops with his own treatment and therapist. This identification occurs in any dynamically oriented therapy, and after termination, certain aspects may remain unconscious, thus affecting the former-patient-now-therapist in a variety of ways, including his treatment approach, techniques, and verbal and nonverbal communication. Every therapist's emotional investment in his own therapist and treatment process affects his perception of the patients, as well as his strategy of intervention. No one can ever *totally* resolve the central conflicts, some of which become organically bound with transferential feelings toward the analyst. Even *therapists* cannot escape this condition, regardless of how much therapy or analysis they have had. One must thus regard any countertransferential communication as partially dominated by the therapist's inability to fully separate from his own therapist. Although in general, such countertransference reactions do not need to serve the treatment negatively, they do at times affect the interpersonal communications in a way that may introduce distance between the patient and the therapist. These influences may be compared to back-seat drivers (the therapists' therapists), who can either be very helpful in spotting road signs on a foggy day, or very distracting when they assume that they are in control of the wheel, thus giving directions that are not totally consonant with the driver's goals, style of driving, or road conditions.

A final important factor that may affect the therapist's communications in an unconscious manner is the problems that might naturally occur in the daily realities of the therapist's life—problems for which there are no ready solutions (Gittleson, 1952). At least in this respect, the pyschotherapist's job must be thought of as different from that of many others, for the service he delivers is basically himself, unlike, for instance, a businessman, who sells merchandise that is not usually affected by his personality.

As a general rule, however, the more the therapist is conscious of the sources of his own conflicts, the less likely they are to affect him, unless they take on crisis dimensions. It is not uncommon for a beginning therapist to lose more than the usual number of patients if he has just begun his own therapy. This may no doubt be attributed to the therapist's lack of experience. However, another important reason is the therapist's ambivalence about his own therapy, and the unconscious message that he communicates to the patient about treatment. Such countertransference reactions may be expected, especially when one considers the fact that many trainees who have just begun treatment have not dealt with their own conflicts. This is one type of problem. There are, of course, other problems of daily living that produce unconscious reactions, some transitory others more permanent, especially if the therapist has trouble resolving these problems of living. Such difficulties may relate to various repetitive conflicts in the therapist's own family, or financial problems, and so on. The important issue is how the therapist deals with these in the treatment situation, and what safeguards he utilizes to make sure that he doesn't "overload" the system with his own needs.

It goes without saying that in order to correct any condition, one must be aware of it, and since countertransference is by definition unconscious, the whole question of what the therapist can do may seem academic. Of course, one might "decree" that no person who has not fully resolved his unconscious conflicts should be allowed to practice psychotherapy. This would no doubt be absurd, because *no one* will ever be able to achieve this goal. But beyond that, it is not really desirable for a therapist never to experience countertransference reactions, for, as mentioned earlier, it is often these reactions that contribute to two important elements of the therapeutic process: an understanding of the patient's unconscious dynamics and an affirmation (to the patient and the therapist) of the therapist's humanity. Thus the issue becomes not an academic but a very practical one.

One sign of countertransference, already noted, is the therapist's feelings of discomfort with the patient, with a specific problem or theme that is brought up, or with the specific type of transference the patient projects. Sometimes the therapist may feel ill at ease with his own interventions (e.g., "I should have said . . .," or "I was too active or silent . . ."). At times the therapist might realize that his contribution to the process has not been related to the patient's needs at that time, or that his relationship to the patient has gradually and imperceptibly changed its course from a therapeutic one to a more social one, and thus, his interventions were channelled in this direction. It is always good to keep in mind the questions "For what specific purpose am I saying this and what am I about to say?" and "Why am I saying it now?" These ought to become part of any therapist's rehearsed lexicon, because they can serve as safeguards against interventions that are not therapeutically motivated.

In addition to the therapist's discomfort, countertransference reactions may be detected in other areas. One of these is the *therapist's dreams*. They may, for instance, turn to themes that indicate preoccupation or unconscious association with the patient in a destructive manner. At times the patient may be part of the dreams without any disguise, and may reflect the therapist's transference to the patient as a significant object with whom the therapist still has some difficulties. The therapist is thus open to the possibility of defensive reactions toward the patient. Understanding these dreams is, of course, a must for the therapist, for they serve as a red light for countertransference. By the same token, the *patient's dreams* may be an excellent indicator of the therapist's countertransference. Some patients bring up dreams in which the therapist, also undisguised, is the cental figure with whom they are intensely involved. While such dreams may (and usually do) indicate the patient's resistant transferential reactions, they should be considered potential signs of the patient's reaction to certain messages that the therapist is unconsciously communicating to that patient (Gittleson, 1952). If the therapist interprets a patient's dreams as dynamically related only to the patient's past life, he would be doing an injustice to the meaning of the dreams, as well as serving to prevent himself from becoming aware of his own contribution to the patient's unconscious life. This will, of course, make it even more difficult, if not impossible, to prevent future countertransference messages, and, will not enable the therapist to utilize his reactions beneficially when the situation presents itself. For example, there is no reason why the therapist cannot discuss or point to some of his own reactions that may have contributed to the patient's dream. The therapist may at times relate his own dreams to the patient for the purpose of discovering how the interaction dynamically affects the patient's productions (including dreams). Confrontation analysis utilizes these techniques with the aim of promoting more openness and trust, for they validate feelings that the patient has, and in this manner reinforce and strengthen ego functions that are not destructive. Consequently, such techniques gradually help to plant the seeds for the eventual equalization of the therapeutic partnership, a subject that will be discussed in the chapter on termination.

Finally, countertransference reactions may also be recognized indirectly through other reactions of the patient, such as his actual progress or statements about it. Thus lack of change may be partially attributed to the countertransference. At times the patient may respond very minimally to various interventions, or communications may become monotonous or repetitive. At other times, the patient may complain about the treatment, or plunge into a tirade against one or another aspect of his life without any apparent provocation. Or an "impasse" in the treatment suddenly occurs. All these reactions may come under the rubric of resistance, but they may have also been partially provoked by the therapist's countertransference. These situations must be seriously examined to determine what the therapist may have brought to them in the way of unconscious messages. Experience will no doubt confirm the hypothesis that more often than not, when negative countertransference decreases, the patient's motivation and therapeutic productivity is almost certain to increase. In summary, it is important to note that countertransference is an extremely fertile subject for exploration, because it is as important in the conduct of therapy as transference.

Emotionality

Frustrated by the unending, monotonous, and intellectualized discourse of a young university professor in analysis with her for a considerable time, a well known and seasoned Russian, grandmother-type analyst remarked to him in an uncompromising tone, in a thick Russian accent, "Young man, here we talk about things from the neck down!" This anecdote illustrates a goal toward which many psychotherapists work with their patients: the expression of feelings and the integration of affect with cognition and behavior. Hardly any patient comes for treatment who is not in pain. Our civilization has for many years discouraged the expression of feelings and, as a result, the natural emotions of man have increasingly sought outlets in destructive behavior, such as war and violent crime.

In his search for ways to remove psychic pain, Freud came to the early realization that the expression of feelings in and of itself was a major factor in the cure of both psychological and psychosomatic symptoms. The terms catharsis and abreaction became an integral part of therapeutic language. However, Freud soon discovered that abreaction alone was not sufficient to resolve deep-seated conflicts or effect long-lasting personality changes. Nevertheless, he succeeded in focussing attention on a central issue in the treatment of psychological problems—the emotions. Confrontation analysis regards the development and expression of the emotions as organically bound to the organization and maintenance of the independent self.

Emotions are difficult to define, even though the experience of emotion is a universal phenomenon in humans, and possible even in animals. Here, interest in them involves psychotherapeutic goals, and this discussion will not dwell on theoretical aspects of the emotions. A few general remarks for purposes of orientation are, however, in order. An emotion, or a feeling, may be defined as a pyschological reaction anchored in physical sensations, elicited by stimuli emanating from within the individual or outside, and experienced as pleasant or noxious. Certainly, this definition is rather global. Unfortunately, the nature of emotions is so complex that it is hard to find adequate descriptive definitions. Eventually, most theorists in this field get stuck in their search for more scientific explanations, and they end up having to reduce this important subject to the neuroglandular level which, of course, tends to raise more questions than it answers.

Phenomenologists such as Sartre (1948) believe there are no links between stimulus and response, and that the theory of the "black box" is untenable. The experience of an emotion, they claim, is immediate, unconditional, and inevitable when it happens. It is directly and inextricably tied to consciousness, and any link to unconscious motivation is either ignored, denied, or rationalized away. Thus, in his exposition of his theory of emotions, Sartre defines emotion as "a certain way of apprehending the world." For him, the emotions behave according to a "straight line" principle, namely, the absence of intervening variables between stimulus and response: "Emotional consciousness is, at first, unreflective, and on this plane it can be conscious of itself only on the nonpositional mode. Emotional consciousness, is, at first, consciousness of the world." Thus, as Sartre would have it, a stimulus is directly transformed into an emotional state. This theory of the emotions seems rather elegant and parsimonious, but disregards a most important aspect of emotional life—that which gives it its meaning. Psychoanalytic theory, in contrast to the phenomenologists and the gestaltists, places an important emphasis on the role of unconscious processes in the formation of the emotions. While the two points of view may theoretically be at two opposite extremes, confrontation analysis views both as extremely helpful in understanding emotionality and dealing with it.

The phenomenological approach to the understanding of the emotions would justify the use of the interactional strategy in psychotherapy such as confrontation analysis, because it establishes a firm raison d'être for the "I–Thou" model as a basis for the relationship between patient and therapist. It focuses on the immediacy and directness of the interaction. When the patient encounters the therapist, or vice versa, contact between them is established, even if only for a short moment. This moment of contact can produce in the patient a reaction that carries the elements of change. The impact of the immediacy of the interaction upon emotional change can be illuminated by Sartre's exposition of the anatomy of emotions:

> Emotion is a phenomenon of belief. Consciousness does not limit itself to projecting affective signification upon the world around it. It *lives* the new world it has just established. It lives it directly; it is interested in it; it endures the qualities which behavior has set up. This signifies that when, with all paths blocked, consciousness precipitates itself into the magical world of emotion, it does so by degrading itself; it is a new consciousness facing the new world, and it establishes this new world with the deepest and most inward part of itself, with this point of view on the world present to itself without distance. . . . Thus the origin of emotion is a spontaneous and short-lived degradation of consciousness in the face of the world.

The spontaneous reflections and emotional honesty of the analyst can thus deeply affect the emotional consciousness of the patient's "new world."

This orientation is very helpful in the understanding and clinical utilization of the immediacy of the therapeutic encounter. However, for long-term changes in the self, such an approach *alone* is obviously too naive and may, in fact, create undesirable effects, such as the ones mentioned earlier, especially with reference to the ritualization of emotions. The emotional structure of the human being constitutes not only present consciousness, but also unconscious forces that translate the immediacy of the present situation into its total phenomenological significance, which no doubt includes the past as much as the present. It is this very specific psychoanalytic contribution to the understanding of the structure of personality that helps us discriminate and differentiate the dynamics of various patients.

The "here and now," therefore, is irresistibly determined, in large measure, by the "there and then," and thus the use of both dynamics in confrontation analysis is deemed necessary if any lasting change is to occur. The therapist's goal in the emotional sphere is, in a sense, no different than that in the area of communication. One is concerned with eliminating blocks to emotional experience, to expression, and to sharing—dimensions that enhance the development of an independent phenomenological self with a historical perspective and with freedom from pain caused by distorted perception.

This perspective on the emotions directs our attention to two aspects of the personality that the therapist must deal with in order to help the patient do away with painful symptoms, widen horizons, and create an atmosphere for living that restores his existence as a worthy, productive, and reasonably content person. These two broad aspects may be referred to as the existential world of the patient and the motivational life that affects it. Therapists must ascertain what the patient emotionally experiences when he is in the treatment situation, what produces such an experience, and if it is deleterious, how it can be modified.

There are four categories under which emotions are generally discussed in psychotherapy: physical, sexual, personal, and interpersonal. These categories will be treated separately, even though confrontation analysis by necessity touches on all of them during the course of the therapeutic relationship.

9

Physical and Sexual Expression

PHYSICAL EXPRESSION

In his essay on "The Unconscious," Freud (1915) asserted that thought is simply blocked emotion, while the emotions are expressed through body discharge:

Ideas are cathexes—ultimately memory traces—whilst affects and emotions correspond with processes of discharge, the final expression of which is perceived as feeling. In the present state of our knowledge of affects and emotions we cannot express this difference more clearly.

The following case is an example of how the emotional life of some patients is expressed through, and concentrated in, the body.

Joe, a rather unsophisticated 23-year-old high school graduate, was an electronic technician who lived with his parents and 18-year-old sister. He was referred for psychotherapy by his physician because he constantly complained of sore throats, colds, back pain, constipation, and fatigue. All diagnostic, clinical, and laboratory tests proved negative. The patient also complained to his physician that he was constantly "down." In the first interview Joe appeared subdued, somewhat apathetic, and was generally negative about seeing a "shrink," since his symptoms were all physical, except for the "slight unhappy moments I have once in awhile." However, as I reassured him that I was interested in his life in general since he was having so much trouble with his health, he became more open and complained about his lack of interest in his job, although he felt he was being adequately paid. He also "apologetically" complained about his parents, especially his father, who was not too interested in Joe's life. Joe's description of his daily activities gave me the impression that he led a rather empty, impoverished, and lonely existence. Even though he was verbal, he seemed quite constricted and closed into himself. Toward the fourth month of treatment, he increasingly experienced crying and sobbing spells during the twice-a-week sessions, and on several occasions became so distraught that we could not terminate the session on time. The crying was carried on in such an hysterical manner that it simulated somewhat the cries of an infant starved for someone to hold and protect him. A certain sense of panic prevailed at times. These episodes were closely associated with his despair about his physical health and with the expression of extremely low self-image and self-esteem, as manifested in the excerpts presented here.

P: What's wrong with me? Why am I so despicable? I feel like a rat, and when I look in the mirror I see myself as an ugly, dirty rat coming out of the garbage (*sobbing*). I feel crummy (*crying*), my nerves have been bothering me all weekend, and since the last session I have been thinking that I might have a brain tumor or something like that. I heard that people who have a brain tumor cry a lot, and that's exactly what's happening to me (*crying*). I don't want to die. I am always tense at work, and even when I am with Joanne (*recent girl friend*), I feel crummy. I don't have any feelings about her, but I want to have sex with her. I want to have sex with all the girls I see on the street, but I know that they wouldn't want to, and I know I couldn't because my prick is no good. I can hardly manage to get it up when I jerk off. . . .I want to be clean and pure and beautiful, not lustful, I don't really want to have any sexual desire. . . .I might have spoiled myself for marriage—because of all the crazy techniques that I use to be able to masturbate, I might not be able to complete the act (*cries*).

Joe's depression, elation, pleasure, anger, disgust, disappointment, and frustration, were all expressed systematically through feelings about his body, specifically his face, his brains, his penis, his hands, his back, and especially his throat and his rectum. It seemed imperative to me to listen long enough to the repetitious complaints, cries, and negativism so that he could establish some trust, some relatedness to me before I confronted him with this rather unpleasant behavior. At one point I began to feel that Joe was enjoying my "nurturing" attitude, and that he was not willing to give it up without a struggle. As I was contemplating changes in my strategy and techniques, an opportunity to begin the confrontational work presented itself in the 65th session. I knew we could not do much of the analytic work of the confrontation, but I decided instead to mirror to him in a mildly confrontational manner, certain patterns that had begun to surface. I wasn't certain about his reception, although I felt pretty certain that he was so alienated and withdrawn in the outside world that he wouldn't give up his relationship with me easily. Here is what transpired in that session.

Joe started the session rather differently than usual by complaining about his sore throat and his constipation. He said he had had another date with Joanne (whom he began seeing a few weeks earlier), and that he was very happy being with her. He was thinking of marrying her, because she fit his idea of the kind of woman he would like to have for a wife. They agreed on many issues in life, such as no sex before marriage, a house in the country, and a couple of children. Although she was a bit more religious than he was, he believed that when she got older, she would see that going to church on Sundays was just a ritual, empty of real meaning. The important thing was that they would share a house and everything else. And then he continued:

P: I think of the word "house" again—I think of "house" an awful lot, don't I? house . . . house . . . what does "house" mean to me? What does it mean to me?

T: What comes to your mind when you think of a house?

P: House, house, mouse, father, mother, daughter, sister, kill me, kill when, what, but if, house, what house—the fact that the word house comes to my mind bothers me. (*Silence for about three minutes.*)

T: What bothers you about all this?

P: I was thinking about Joanne and love and marriage, and what it's going to be like. It's going to be wonderful, things we are going to share, emotions, feelings, things. Then I was thinking, what about me, what's going to happen to me. I get tired easily, I am no good. We went out for a walk last night, and I got tired so fast. I am still rotten, no good. I am basically undesirable.

T: When did you start feeling undesirable?

P: As far back as I remember. I think it's got something to do with my father. No matter what I did wasn't good enough. (*starts to cry.*)

T: You're crying again, about that?

P: He is a fuckin' bastard, he is a bastard. (*in a loud voice, almost shouting.*) He's made my life so rotten miserable, no matter what I did was no good.

T: What did you do that was no good?

P: I remember in the eighth grade, a man made me jerk him off. I didn't tell my father, I was scared shit of him, why did he have to be such a rotten bastard? Not only me, but he hurt my mother a lot. I am scared shit to talk to him—I always try to avoid him. When I was eleven, he was building the house, and he wanted me around every weekend just to hold the tools for him, and he ordered me around—hold this, don't do this, don't stand there! This shit went on until I was almost 15. He never helped me learn anything. He was just thinking of himself. So fuckin' stupid, so inconsiderate of others. . . . I am having a lot of trouble with my throat and a lot of gas, I don't want to stink up the whole place.

T: When you start getting angry at your father, you suddenly become physically uncomfortable, or you get depressed afterwards, you keep silent here. You are quite mad at your father.

P: (*In a sarcastic tone.*) No kidding! I can kill the fuck! I am so mad at him!

T: This is the first time I've seen you get mad at your father here without crying. It's quite an accomplishment for you!

P: Oh yeah, I forgot to tell you a dream I had over the weekend. It was about Joanne. In the dream she is a virgin, but I was having my first sexual intercourse with her. She said to my mother during the intercourse that she was surprised it didn't hurt, and I wanted to urinate and I did, but at the same time I was worried I wouldn't be able to finish the sexual act. I woke up with my sheet in my mouth, I must've been sucking on it. That happens sometimes when I wake up in the morning. Maybe I had that dream because we did a lot of necking and petting during the weekend.

T: You know, Joe, I have the impression that whenever you get some strong feelings, strong emotions, pleasant or unpleasant, you change these feelings into something physical.

P: What do you mean—I don't understand what you mean.

T: Before you told me the dream, you were angry at your father, and immediately after that your throat started hurting and you were having gas, and in the dream, you were having some sexual feelings, and somehow you changed them into urinating, doing something that would turn off your sexual feelings.

P: I don't know what this is, but obviously I don't recognize my feelings of anger and how I suddenly feel sick. I don't want to have them, and I certainly don't want to feel lousy every day with my throat and all that shit. Do you really think that I get sick because I get angry—I mean, I know when I get angry I don't like it, but I feel angry a lot. I mean, I walk around angry all the time.

This session ended with Joe mulling over the possibility

that psychological, "spiritual" types of feelings could trigger off various physical reactions. Such a possibility had been discussed in the past, and he had certainly heard this type of explanation from the referring physician, but it wasn't until I pointed out to him the sequence of his associations, when he was ready to hear it, that he was able to gain some insight into the workings of his personality. This session was extremely productive for other reasons, too. I did not feel that Joe was ready to tackle the obvious Oedipal and oral material in the dream, nor was he ready to be confronted with his transferential reactions to me. No doubt one could have tapped these aspects of his communications; however, he would have erected such a resistive wall that he would have been lost as a patient. The first order of the therapeutic intervention was *a step-by-step confrontation with his feelings, or a recognition that his physical symptoms were indeed his emotions released in a coded fashion.* These symptoms had to be decoded in an interactional, accepting, and supportive manner. This patient's defensive armor was rather primitive and needed to be handled with unusual sensitivity. Indeed, it took over two years before a full-blown negative transference developed, and only then was he ready to face his deeper negative introjects—the many aspects of his fragmented identifications, mostly with his unloving, self-centered, and competitive father. During the second year of treatment he had also severed his relationship with Joanne.

The expression of emotions through physical channels was a way of life for Joe. He had been sickly for years, and he frequented his internist's office at least once a month. The antidepressant and tranquilizing drugs that he kept taking for many years became as ineffective as sugar pills for him, though he continued to take them for his dependency needs. In the first couple of years of treatment, he refused to even discuss giving them up. At some point, however, soon after the session described above, I told him that it had become very hard to know what was going on with him emotionally, since the drugs were masking his emotions, and that it was important for therapeutic progress that he let go of the drugs. He understood, he said, but he could not give them up so easily. I pointed out to him that lately he had been less preoccupied with his physical symptoms, and that he had begun to be more conscious of his feelings. It would thus not be entirely impossible for him to rely more on himself rather than on external agents. The proof was his ability to give up his destructive relationship with Joanne. I suggested that if giving up Joanne did not kill him, then certainly giving up the drugs would not. Although I did not present him with an ultimatum about the medication, I did press him to give it up. My rationale was that Joe, without being aware of it, in some unconscious, primitive, and irrational manner, connected the medication with his physical symptoms, and giving it up would mean giving up his defensive armor, his symptoms, without having any substitutes for them. While his fear was real, I felt that he had advanced enough in his attachment to me that he could now make the switch. It was not easy to convince him of that. He fought tooth and nail on the drug issue, and he accused me of being a stubborn, hard-headed, old-fashioned doctor who had to have things his way. This rather "mild" criticism continued for a while. I agreed with him that I had strong doubts about the efficacy of the therapeutic relationship if this drug impasse was not resolved, and that he might be wasting his time and money. This "exhortation" seemed to produce a rather dramatic development.

The day following this session, Friday, Joe called me in the evening to tell me that he had had a terrible day with his throat; he was constipated, and he had had to leave work in the afternoon because he felt feverish and dizzy. He wanted to know if he could come to see me on Saturday because he was "feeling very lousy and depressed." I told him that it would be better if he could wait until his regular session on Monday, since there didn't seem to be any undue crisis. He seemed to feel reassured and agreed to wait and see. On Monday, he walked into the office obviously depressed and dejected, and without warning lay on the couch. He normally sat up during his sessions, except for a few sessions when he came from work rather tired and asked if the could use the couch. He was silent for a couple of minutes, and then opened the session with a torrent of verbal abuse, with his voice gaining more and more momentum:

P: Fuck you, fuck you, fuck, go to hell you son of a bitch, you're a goddamn cocksucker, you dirty bum, you bastard you, you rotten fucking bastard, Jew bastard Abe Cohen, fuck you, you and your wife and your kids, and your cunt mother, and your father, you cocksucking scum, you prick, goddamn, goddamn you. (*He paused somewhat breathlessly for a moment and then continued.*) I wanted to say that so many times, you son of a bitch—why is it so hard to tell you this, why? (*deep sigh.*) It was so hard— it is so hard for me to tell somebody "fuck you"—and I kept staying here, and I stayed here, and I stayed here, and I stayed with Joanne, and I wanted to tell her the same thing, and the same thing with Gloria, and I stayed with my first fucking boss for three years—he pretended he liked me and I was the first one he fired. If this happened now I am sure I could tell him to go fuck himself; instead I thanked him and shook his fucking dirty hand. I know I am going to tell Annette tomorrow that I don't want to see her anymore. I don't care, I just don't care. Just like you, like you don't care. You don't give a damn. I don't know why it was so difficult for me to swear at you, you don't give a fuck anyway. You want to shaft me too. I think you want me to give up the medicine so you can see me more often, and all you're interested in is money, and more money. What do you care?

When he became silent at this point, I asked him why he was so angry with me today? He began to cry and said that I didn't care about him, and he just wanted somebody to really care for him—he needed somebody to hold him, to touch him, someone to love him. The hurt and pain he was experiencing seemed very deep, intimate, and touching. My eyes filled with tears; I could not hold back, and instinctively put my hand on his shoulder. While he was still sobbing, I said to him: "Joe, I do care about you. I feel very badly that you have to go through so much pain, and that you had to hide it. I am glad you're telling me how you feel. I know this will help you." Joe continued crying for a short time, got up from the couch, and gave me a bear hug, so hard it felt like he might never let go. Then he sat down, cleared his throat, and in a subdued tone of voice he said: "You know, I feel I can say anything to you, anything I want, even to my father . . . I don't feel like such a dirty person— I mean, I always felt that nobody wanted to come near me." He also talked about how, except for the last few days, he had felt much more relaxed, that his throat was not bothering him as much, and that in general he had been enjoying his discussions with other people much more. He had even met a couple of male friends at work and begun to socialize with them, going dancing and planning to take up skiing. He tempered his progress, however, by his awareness and feeling that he was still quite alienated from others and that his adventures into the human race were forced and somewhat contrived, as he said, "I am doing what I think is good for me." There was no doubt, however, that he was increasingly developing behavioral patterns that he could share with others.

The therapeutic approach with him kept changing. His polarized, ambivalent transference shifted very quickly from one extreme to another. His distrust was deep, and so was his need for constant, intimate nurturance. His borderline adjustment did not work very well for him as he abandoned some of his defenses. During such difficult periods, his need for a semi- or pseudo-symbiotic alliance with me was accepted as a therapeutic strategy. He needed to feel secure with me in those areas, the physical and nonverbal ones, into which he channeled his emotional expression, before he could give them up as inadequate defenses. His dependence on me deepened considerably at one point in the treatment, but his inordinate need for my presence and my availability, physically or through the phone, grated at times. However, it was pretty clear that Joe had to have this type of relationship in order not to decompensate, since he could no longer rely on his physical symptoms to bind his anxiety. Eventually, he met a young woman who was able to relate to him on his level, to accept his gyrations, and yet to leave enough distance between them so that she was not "swallowed" by his almost insatiable need for total succorance. Both his intellectual insights and his learned capacity for emotional release helped keep his functioning reasonably gratifying to him and fairly free from the overwhelming panic and painful depths of depression that he used to experience before the therapeutic work began.

SEXUAL EXPRESSION

There is probably no area in the emotional life of an individual that occupies more energy than the area of sexuality. This subject, which was one of the established taboos for centuries, has become the object of open concern and open investigation and discussion by behavioral scientists, educators, philosophers, politicians, and, most of all, the average "man on the street." In the field of psychology, the subject of sex had not been viewed as theoretically significant until Freud's important contributions at the turn of the century, in which he laid the groundwork for opening up systematic clinical observation and investigation of the role of sex in the development of personality and culture. Indeed, one might quip that Freud's pioneering works gave the field of sexuality its "libido!"

Confrontation analysis assumes that sexuality is biologically based. However, sexual behavior and sexual feelings develop in conjunction with other dimensions of the child's personality not usually perceived as strictly associated with sexuality, such as the emotional and physical relationship with the parents. It is, thus, the nature and quality of the child's interaction with the outside world, not his biological endowment, that eventually defines the meaning of sex for him, and consequently, his sexual behavior and feelings. While this statement may be highly controversial for those who favor the biological orientation, confrontation analysis makes this assumption not on the basis of any convincing statistical data in the field—none are available—but on the basis of clinicial experience, as well as its theoretical convictions regarding the centrality of interpersonal interaction as the basis for personality development. Thus confrontation analysis views sexuality as one of the expressions of emotionality, not the other way around. In other words, the sexual activity and feelings of the individual are not dictated by biological needs, rather, they are emotional needs expressed through channels that are defined as sexual.

The emotions occupy a central position in people's lives, and sex has become one of the primary channels through which the emotions are discharged. Patients do take up a great deal of time during their sessions discussing their sexuality. The range of emotions expressed through sexual life is practically infinite, and there are very few, if any, patients who do not bring up sexual problems, often masked in other areas of concern. The goal of therapy is to help the patient *recognize* how feelings are expressed through sexuality, and then to confront him with patterns of behavior that are detrimental to growth and the achievement of goals.

Case illustration 1: Bertha

Bertha was a very perceptive 25-year-old graduate student who sought treatment because she was depressed and kept getting into "trouble" with men. By the time she arrived to her first consultation, she was keenly aware of the link between her emotions and her sexual behavior. There was no need to translate for her the notion that sexuality was an important means for her to express her mostly negative feelings. Her depression was triggered off after she gave her out-of-wedlock baby up for adoption. While this loss alone provided an understandable basis for her depression, it became clear as therapy progressed that her depression dated way back, no doubt to her infancy. Bertha described her mother as an "insatiably jealous woman," who by favoring her twin brother, made it impossible for Bertha to enjoy her childhood. She was also constantly critical regarding her daughter's personal habits, her choice of friends, and her so-called "passivity." Bertha described her father as a weakling who acted out his own feelings of inadequacy by making unreasonable and impulsive demands bordering on the irrational. For example, he once asked her to pose for a photograph in the middle of a crowded beach while he embraced her in an amorous manner. (She was a well-developed 12-year-old at the time!) Her twin brother was perceived as "a rock around my neck," because "my mother forced me to be responsible for him whenever we were together . . . I had to take care of him all the time. . . . When I was a little girl I always felt he was a part of me, and often I still feel this way. Sometimes I get scared because I get the feeling that maybe I want to be like him or take his place. My mother approved of him, and I used to try to do the kind of things he did, but my father would laugh at me and tell me that girls did different things." The confusion in identity stemming from this relationship alone was severe. Such confusion is often quite severe for different-sex twins. Bertha's feelings were always bottled up, and found expression only indirectly, and most of the time unconsciously, through sexual relationships. She chose sexual partners indiscriminately during her high school years. While in college, she had to interrupt her schooling for over two years because of a bout of depression that negatively affected her excellent intellectual capacity. She could not think or read or absorb what she heard. Instead, she travelled around the country, supporting herself by waiting on tables in restaurants and hotels, and by meeting men who supported her for short periods of time. This "acting out" was rationalized away at the time in a rather naive manner. She later understood that she was taking her "revenge" on these men by "pretending" to be interested in them sexually. This awareness did not come about, however, until her pregnancy and her decision to give her child up for adoption. After only 17 sessions, her need for sexual acting out as an expression of how she felt about herself, her parents, and her brother came to the surface quite clearly. Here are some verbatim statements from several sessions:

—I don't get along with my mother.

—They *(parents)* make you feel so awful, you have to get out of the house.

—I feel I have been rejected by my mother for a long time, so I started to fool around with boys since junior high.

—I don't like how I feel about my mother—I mean, I am still so dependent on her for approval, but I still do everything to spite her—I know that my having the baby was my way of embarrassing her, not because of the baby, but because that proved that I had sex.

—My brother bullies me all the time, so I guess I take it out on other guys *(How?)* By making them believe they're getting something, and they're not because I don't feel anything about them.

—My mother was very jealous about my being close to somebody, even a girlfriend.

—I am not as innocent as people think I am. I can't tell anybody how I really feel.

—Maybe I am searching for something I can't find. *(What would that be?)* I guess ideal love. *(What do you mean?)* Somebody who loves me for me.

—Once you get involved emotionally, you don't have control anymore. . . . I doubt if anybody can love me.

—I feel I can't talk freely with you without knowing you. *(How do you mean that?)* To get to know you more intimately, more personally.

—I want you to like me not just as a patient, or care for me just because I pay you . . . I was just wondering if you care for me as a woman.

—If I didn't start talking, would you say anything to me? I mean would you initiate something on your part without having to be always on top? *(Always on top?)* Well, I feel that if we met socially, you wouldn't come near me, you would want for me to make the first move, wouldn't you?

Bertha stayed in treatment for a very short time, only seventeen sessions. She left treatment without discussing it, but did send me a letter explaining her reasons for terminating. The letter was in essence the expression of her conflicts and the deeply ingrained need to affirm her existence as a person who counts by making sure that other people want her sexually. In this manner she could reaffirm her masochistic need to recreate the image her mother had given her, that is, of a "bad," "manipulative," and "unreliable" person. This, of course, kept her tied to her mother in a negative, dependent way. Even though the signs were glaring (certainly the above statements prove that), I unfortunately did not recognize early enough in the treatment that she needed to be confronted with her acting out immediately, instead of when the transference had become too negative. Perhaps I was overwhelmed by her "insights," as well as what appeared to be her openness. The letter proves that a decisive alliance with the healthy part of her ambivalent ego might have prevented the early termination:

Dear Dr. Cohen,

While I did oversleep for my appointment this morning, the real reason why I missed it was because I hadn't made up my mind about what I wanted to do.

For about two weeks now I have been thinking of quitting therapy. Part of my reason for leaving, or wanting to, has to do with my feelings about you. But I was not able to express these feelings in your presence. On paper I have more courage and I think I'll do better.

In some ways I feel I dislike you because you don't come through the way other men I like do. Some of this feeling is I imagine natural considering our relationship. But part of it may result from your personality, i.e., not *entirely* from *what* you say, but *how* you say it.

I feel constrained with you, and this is maybe just my reaction to therapy. But, I think, it might be lessened if we had established a better rapport, if we talked to each other more, if we got closer. I am trying to be fair, not with you only, but with myself too. I don't mean to place blame on you, but at the same time, does therapy have to be so strictly "professional?"

I hope my abrupt departure won't make me an undesirable patient in the future. When you called me this morning, I felt a lack of warmth on your part, and I felt that you were not willing to change the relationship.

I do appreciate your concern and the help you gave me when I came to you. I am afraid I need something different now.

Sincerely,
Bertha

It seemed that Bertha needed someone who would react to her as her idealized father. Her "carelessness" in getting pregnant and carrying the baby to full-term pregnacy no doubt symbolized that wish: the baby's father was a substitute for her father, and by giving the baby up for adoption she was punishing herself. More significantly, however, giving the baby up symbolized her wish to punish her own mother, as if she were taking herself away from her own mother by identifying with the baby. The final part of the letter was certainly indicative of her great need for support and approval. Her protest that she needed "something different now" was no doubt a confirmation that she depended a great deal on other people for the love and affection of which she felt deprived as she grew up, and that she was not ready to give up the fantasy of regaining her parents' love through acting out—the father by seducing a man, the mother, by identifying with her mother in that seduction. While such dynamics play an important role in most adult relationships, the destructive repetitive pattern is not always present.

Case illustration 2: Mark

The present case concerns a patient for whom sex had played an extremely significant part as the main avenue for the expression of feelings in a multitude of ways, from childhood on. The patient had been in treatment for 11 years. During the first six years he came twice weekly, and in the last five, in combined treatment, once-a-week, in individual and once-a-week in group therapy. The use of various techniques as the treatment progressed seemed not only advisable but mandatory, for Mark presented such a mixed bag of pathological patterns that one approach would have missed the boat.

Mark was a 24-year-old Jewish married man referred by a colleague who was treating his wife for a variety of psychosomatic symptoms. The colleague told me on the phone that Mark was quite resistant to the idea of treatment but that at his wife's request and some threats that she would leave him if he didn't seek help, he was "willing" to see someone to satisfy his curiosity about analysis. He arrived for the initial interview ten minutes late, and apologized by saying he had missed the subway stop. He was quite anxious and tense, and behaved in a rather submissive but verbal and reflective manner. There was also an underlying explosiveness in his speech pattern as he sat at the edge of the chair, apparently ready to obey any command swiftly and accurately. The general impression was that of a flippant, controlled individual who was trying very hard to appear jovial, calm, and mature. At the outset he asked if I had spoken with Dr. S. (his wife's psychiatrist) about him. I said that I had, and he wanted to know whether I had any information about him. I said I knew that he had trouble getting himself to come here. In a somewhat sarcastic manner Mark said, "Oh, no, no, I've got lots of problems, no mistake about that!" and laughed uproariously; but then, with an impish manner, he followed this remark by a list of symptoms that required attention. However, he wasn't sure that psychotherapy was the best way. Uppermost on his mind was the hypertension that he had discovered a few months prior to the interview. His doctor told him that it was not critical, he simply had to take it easy and not get too upset with anything. Mark also noticed that his headaches had increased lately, and he wondered if they were related to the hypertension. He admitted to feeling angry most of the time, and had various fears about getting sick and not having money. He was also temperamental and had "a very bad habit. I have to work things in my mind to the greatest detail; I am always planning." He thought, however, that "this habit might be a good thing; because you don't want to be sloppy—I mean, can you imagine what would happen if an engineer missed a few nuts and bolts on his specs for a bridge?" I commented that for somebody who works that way in his mind, missing the subway stop must have produced quite a feeling of frustration. He agreed immediately, and said that this touched on one of his principle problems, that is, while he works things out in his head to the nth degree, they never come out exactly that way, a matter that annoyed him to no end. Other "inner" problems he cited (in passing) were difficulties in communication with his wife, expressing his real feelings to anyone, and "what you call premature ejaculation."

Mark had been married to Lenore for about a year, after having known her for about six years. She worked as a secretary and he was an assistant producer in an advertising firm. He was quite happy with his work, although he disliked his boss intensely. Mark grew up as the only child in a family that consited of his mother, maternal grandmother, and grandfather. His father left the household when Mark was six months old and was never heard from again. His grandfather spent most of his time at home ordering everyone around. The grandmother also did not work outside the home. Mark's mother, still a young woman, had been working for many years in an administrative capacity in a canning factory and was the main financial support of the family. Mark characterized his relationship to her as "friendly," but he said he could not talk to her ("I avoid her as much as I can"). His relationship to his grandfather was always tense, and when he still lived at home, before he got married, he felt like a slave having to answer to his master-grandfather, who was "mean and selfish." "No matter what was happening around him, he had to have his way, no matter what. He used to beat me up a lot with a strap until I was big enough to stop it." During this initial interview Mark expressed the fantasy of possibly having brothers or sisters, and characterized this fantasy as a "mysterious belief." He also wished he could meet his father sometime in the future. He didn't think he had the "courage" to do that. He expressed some hope that therapy might help him with his schooling, since he was dropped from college because of failing grades and absenteeism. He had finished one year of college, but coult not return both because of his low grades and lack of discipline.

There was a distinct uneveness in Mark's ego functioning. He seemed to have never made any positive, long-lasting relationship with anyone other than his wife. He had done quite well in public school and high school, but not very well in college. Although he was thought of as a good employee, so far as the quality of his work was concerned, he had a great deal of trouble getting along with his boss and some of the other employees in the office. He was able to relate a great deal of information about himself during the initial interview; however, his main interest seemed to be in trying to impress me that he was a "good guy," as he later confessed. He was not about to divulge his real emotional problems and "secrets." He adopted this strategy both consciously and unconsciously. On the conscious level he wanted to let me know that he had problems but that these were the kind of problems that he could handle himself if he only tried. Unconsciously he felt extremely vulnerable, and therefore had erected an impressive defensive system that was very difficult to penetrate. His defenses were characterized by obsessive-compulsive mechanisms, including denial, intellectualization, and excessive sexual acting-out. It would seem that because of his vulnerability and failing defenses, a reasonable psychotherapeutic strategy might dictate a supportive stance in the initial stages of treatment. However, a psychodynamic assessment of his personality indicated that he must be able to withstand more stress than he allowed himself, and that at that time, in the initial formation of the therapeutic relationship, his sensitivity, perceptiveness, and superior intellectual capacity might be "wasted" if he were not confronted with his self-destructive patterns. I wanted to have this initial assessment confirmed, and recommended psychological testing. I was uneasy about Mark's uneven functioning and did not want to lose him as a patient by under- or overestimating his strengths. The results of the psychologicals did indeed point to the possibility of ego disintegration and decompensation should he encounter more emotional stress, yet the report pointed to the fact that this process was already under way and that some drastic measure was needed to keep it from getting worse. I therefore decided to utilize the direct interpretation approach, with analysis of the confrontations early in the process, so that some base could be established from which both could work, rather than the "slippery" basis that Mark favored. I sensed that this man needed a direct, open, and engaging interaction, something he had not experienced with other authority figures, especially his grandfather, whom he could not trust. The road ahead was neither easy nor terribly clear. However, I had taken an immediate liking to Mark, and with all his explosiveness and ambivalence regarding therapy, he seemed to be a promising candidate with a good potential for growth.

During the second session, while still waiting for the psychological report, I kept silent most of the time. Mark recounted some of his life history, but my inactivity seemed to unnerve him. I asked him about that and he admitted that my silence was "puzzling" to him. He felt I was scrutinizing him and perhaps didn't believe what he was telling me. The excerpt presented here followed this comment.

T: There is a Hebrew proverb which says that "a thief's hat always burns on his head," meaning that it's not easy to conceal the truth.

P: So you don't believe me.

T: Should I believe you? I do believe what you say. Of course I can't know what you don't say. Perhaps you feel you've got things to say that you don't want to tell me.

P: Like what? (*I shrug my shoulders and gesture a question mark.*) I think I am telling you everything that's important and without hiding anything, at least not consciously.

T: I see.

P: Lenore told me that her shrink doesn't talk at all. She's been with him for almost a whole year and he hardly said anything to her.

T: I guess you don't want me to be like him.

P: I just can't see how anybody can talk to a wall. What's the point of all this? I mean, I might as well talk to a tape recorder or to myself, which I do sometimes (*laughs*). In fact I was telling Lenore that you said a lot of things last week and I liked that, because I thought you were very sharp and hit the nail right on the head. But there's something I have to talk to you about, and that's money. I don't think I can afford this if my insurance company doesn't cover it, at least part of it. I become very despondent when I talk about money. I don't know what to do about it. When I was a little younger, I used to be dependent on my family for money. I feel very insecure about it. Lenore feels the same way about it, but she wouldn't give up her therapy for anything. Well, I know she's right, but it's also true that we don't have a pot to piss in. Every fucking penny goes—I am not kidding. We're both working, our apartment is not expensive, and we're broke. I mean, sometimes I walk to work to save the car fare. I don't know what will happen if I go back to school and I can't work full time—what'll I do then? I don't know how I started telling you about this, but money is a real problem.

T: The other problems are not real?

P: Yeah, but the landlord has to be paid or else I am out on my ass in the street.

T: The other problems can wait?

P: (*Emphatically:*) I am not saying that!

T: It's hard for you to make up your mind about coming here. You don't know what you'll get out of it. The landlord at least gives shelter and the phone company keeps you in touch with the outside world.

P: Damn right! But if I am not happy, what good is all that?

T: That's a good question.

P: But you know, this is the second time I'm here, and I can't say, I really can't say that I trust you. Before I came here today, I was thinking about that remark you made last week about my being late, I am always late to everything, to work, to meetings with friends, to parties, to school . . . in school I used to be late to every single class. I was going to say even to sex, because lenore was the first girl I ever had sex with. I was almost 21. But maybe that's not abnormal. I don't know. The guys from school talked about sex a lot. But when I was in school, I mean in public school and high school, we used to be ashamed to look at a girl. My friends were all from Yeshiva. I used to "steal a look" now and then and I felt terribly guilty. I guess I still do. I don't think any of my friends even slept with any girl before they got married. We were living in a world of our own, I guess.

Thus, toward the end of the session, Mark began to talk about his sexual experiences. But he kept the discussion quite impersonal, and he coated every statement with platitudes that he seemed to enjoy. Perhaps he felt protected by his pronouncements of universal wisdom. I told him that I knew he had sexual problems from what he mentioned in the initial interview, but that I wasn't clear as to exactly what the problems were. I suggested that we could discuss them in the following session if he wanted to. Mark was somewhat surprised that I remembered what he had told me the week before, but he tried to avoid the subject by saying that he had to look into the insurance policy to see whether he could continue the treatment. Subsequently, he found out he could afford to come for treatment twice a week, as I had recommended

In the following few sessions, unlike many other patients who are anxious to unload their troubling feelings, Mark was extremely guarded. He managed to give me a lot of information about people on the job and their lives and his grandfather's dictatorial ruling of the house when he lived there, but very little about his own involvement. My questions and probings were generally answered by a slippery "I don't know" or "he's a nice guy," or "that was an interesting experience"—never a direct feeling or a commitment of any sort. His control over his feelings was superb, and much of it was no doubt conscious. In the seventh session, while he was telling me about the "waste of time" at New York University where he attended his first year of college, I said to him provocatively, that he seemed to enjoy tearing everything down and that he presented the world as if it were a terrible place in which to live. He immediately denied that he felt that way—facts were facts and the professors at the university didn't really know what they were talking about. I remarked that he sounded like someone on a debating team who had to win the argument, and reminded him that I was neither his professor at the university nor his grandfather. He acknowledged that point:

P: I have to win an argument. I always have to control any discussion. My friends say that when I get into something, it's like arguing with a rabbi, splitting hairs. I know it's a terrible habit, but I get so angry sometimes at people because they are so, . . . so, I don't know what—so irrational or not exact. I get so impatient when they don't get the point right away.

T: You seemed mad at me before, parhaps not for misunderstanding you, but for calling your attention to your own anger.

P: I thought you were telling me or implying that school was okay, and I really don't feel that way, but I wasn't mad at you, I was annoyed that you were drawing conclusions about me without knowing me.

T: You were annoyed but not mad at me. O.K. You win the point!

P: (*Laughs.*) I see what you mean. It's a terrible habit. But it's true, I can't stand it when someone confronts me like that, especially someone in authority. I always had this thing about older people, that they don't understand the younger generation, so I always tear down anyone who's in authority. I was doing that with Lenore about the psychologist who tested me, but when you told me the results, I was really amazed. I was thinking about that. He got a lot out in those two hours I was there. He must be really good, how do they do that?

T: Mark, here we go again—now you want a seminar on psychological tests, anything that'll get you away from you.

P: You don't let anything drift by, do you? You know, somehow I don't get mad about that with you, I really don't. I don't know why, maybe because you are kind and warm. Anyway, I've been thinking about why I am coming here, and what the tests showed. Well, one of the things or maybe problems I didn't tell you about even though it was on my mind every session, was my funny attitude about sex. I think I have a very funny attitude about sex. I don't think I understand it myself. I mean, I've read a lot about this and that. I am not sure how to put it, but it feels strange to talk about it. I guess you know anyway, since you told me about the psychological report—I mean, about the fact that I have sexual problems. I get very nervous, not nervous but tense when I have to talk about this. I remember when I started to masturbate, I think I was about 11 or probably 12 and I used to really get off on it. I started doing it at the Yeshiva. The rabbi was a real mean guy, and I used to hide in the bathroom and do it. I found out other kids were doing it too. One of the kids, a friend of mine, he was a real jerk, but we started to do it together, and I guess we had something going, you might call it something homosexual. We used to jerk each other off. That lasted from almost a year, until we moved to the Bronx for some reason. We were there for almost two years, and I hated it. But I had something like that with a couple of other kids in the Bronx too. But when we moved back into the city we were far away from where this friend lived and all that stuff stopped, even though I continued to masturbate.

T: You mentioned that the rabbi was a mean person, and that you escaped from him and masturbated in the bathroom. Was he mean towards you?

P: Not just me, all the kids. He used to hit, but real hard. I was a fresh kid and he used to throw me out of the classroom many times.

T: So you were angry at him too.

P: I wanted to kill him. I used to get so mad at him; he was a real jerk; I had an uncle just like that. But I kept it all inside, except when I was fresh, I guess.

T: How about when you jerked off—you got some release that way too.

P: Yeah, but this had nothing to do with it, I mean I continued to masturbate long after that. I still do, sometimes.

T: And you still have difficulties expressing how you feel.

P: You mean when I am angry? I can get mad, real mad, but I never tell anybody. I know I feel like putting my hand through the wall sometimes, especially when I get so pissed at Lenore and at Jim (*his boss*). But people can tell, I guess, because my face shows. I was told several times by some friends that they are very careful with me because they're afraid I'll get mad. I feel just the opposite—that I can't say anything because they won't like it, so I appear or try to appear calm and collected, and especially when I talk to girls, I am very nice, like a gentleman.

Mark's awareness of his game-playing in social relationships and his need for control was sharpened by this confrontation. However, the connection I made between his anger and his masturbation was not so readily accepted. I had the feeling that he knew there was something to it, but he could not accept it coming from me—it had to be *his* discovery. In a few weeks he began to see how his sexual activities were motivated by his feelings, primarily his anger. The source of this anger was not clear yet, but that needed a lot more work. I felt that before we tackled this difficult area, it would be necessary for Mark's "confessions" about his sexual activities to be told as he interacted with me, because through this process he was able to express his feelings. The ritualistic, intellectualized confessions that would create only illusionary solutions to the real conflicts thus started to lose their momentum. At that point I told Mark that I knew how difficult it was for him to reveal all these secrets, but that he must know that I didn't get shocked very easily, since I'd heard so many "incredible" stories that nothing shocked me any more. He quickly commented, in his usual sarcastic manner, that my life must be quite dull. I said I got my kicks without having to be shocked. Mark seemed uneasy about the challenge with which I had been presented, i.e., he might have to tell me more "secrets" if he was going to hold my interest, or he might have to give up some of the controls and become more authentic. At that point in the therapeutic process, he was too involved with his need for approval to recognize the "manipulative bait" I had placed before him, and in the following few sessions he revealed much of the "secret" life he had tried to hide, even from himself. He told me of various homosexual experiences, some of which were extremely degrading to him because he actively sought them out, although he was conscious of the struggle and the pain attached to this behavior. These experiences took place during the year he was in college and a few months after that. During the same period, he also dated a few girls, generally much older than himself, but he found himself very awkward in their presence. He felt he was disloyal to Lenore whom he intended to marry, and with whom he never had intercourse before they were married. His dates ended up being "platonic," for he used to masturbate before he met the girls, and during the date he was terrified that it would be found out that he was "inadequate" if he tried to seduce his date.

These sessions were intensely emotional for Mark. He began to recognize more than ever a pattern of appeasement toward men and disdain for women. Since he could not "orgasmatize" (his expression) the woman he "fucked" (his expression), including his wife, he felt like a little boy, not equal to them. He complained that the world was unfair to men because they had to prove themselves, while women had to "just lay down and enjoy it." Hel felt completely and totally dependent on women for his self-esteem as a man and, not being able to obtain this security from them, he expressed deep resentment and loathing toward them. The women with whom he grew up, his mother and grandmother, had very little power, while those he sought out in the last few years held the key to his "manliness." This paradoxical image of women confused him a great deal as he had begun to interact increasingly with them. However, he slowly learned how to manipulate his way around them, and he developed special seductive techniques and character masks. He felt he had the capacity to seduce almost any woman he wanted, and he was quite successful with his techniques. In connection with this he said; "I am constantly on the move, I am always looking for women to fuck. Sometimes I think I am bad." However, he admitted that he had never felt genuinely satisfied, because these women were "too easy to get," and he felt they were "using" him to get something, not because they cared for him. I commented that he was obviously trying to get something he felt he never got from anybody by trying to "steal a woman," and that he was obviously never satisfied because what he was getting had nothing to do with what he had missed as a child, that is, affection. I said, "you couldn't satisfy a thirsty man with a hamburger, could you?" Mark acknowledged it was "stupid" to do that, but then he said his trying to prove himself had become a habit that was difficult to give up, because there was no better substitute. I continued the pressure: "For you, fucking a man or a woman doesn't really matter, because what you do doesn't give you what you need anyway. I think you feel you have to do something to prove to yourself you are a worthy person, that somebody needs you and cares for you." For the first time in therapy he began to cry and, with intermittent sobs, he talked about how he felt that he was a nobody, that no one ever really cared for him. He felt his life was an indication of that, and that his behavior was certainly nothing to write home about.

To prove this point, he sobbingly told me of an incident that had occurred before the first interview. He was in a subway station and had the urge to masturbate after he had seen a very sexy girl parading on the platform while also waiting for the train. He went into the men's room and, while pretending to urinate, he started masturbating, quite consciously exposing himself to the man standing next to him. The man offered to give him a "blow job" if he, Mark, would reciprocate. Mark accepted the offer, and both went into a toilet booth, whereupon this man did what he had promised to do. As they were about to switch positions, Mark felt such a panic that he flung the door open in this man's face and ran out of the station. It was at that point that he called me for an appointment, having had my name for several weeks. His biggest fear, he said, was that he might have bitten this man's penis off, because he became increasingly angry while he was being orally manipulated. He was thinking of the girl on the platform and that she was responsible for this act. Suddenly, he stopped his story, seemed agitated, and fell silent. I said to him, "Mark, you were very courageous to tell me all this. I do appreciate your being open because I feel you have so much bottled up inside." He looked at me with teary eyes and got up to leave, since that was the end of the session. I shook his hand firmly with both of mine, something I do not normally do. I made no interpretation, no further comments about that incident until a few months later, even though Mark mentioned it several times subsequent to that.

Mark was once complaining about how "bitchy" and demanding his wife was becoming. She felt he wasn't working hard enough to resolve the problems between them, and to prove it, she accused him of being callous and insensitive when they made love. She told him that he was not gentle with her, and that instead of caressing her breasts, he bit them. He felt that he was losing himself in the love-making, and that indeed sometimes he didn't even realize there was another person with him. I reminded him of the subway episode and the fantasy about biting the man's penis, and then made the following "direct" interpretation: "Since you feel you never received any love from your mother, you try to take it by force. You said sometime ago that you are a "tit man." So I suppose you are still looking for Mommy to pour the milk of love down your mouth, and to tell you how lovable and worthy you are." He remained silent after this comment. The silence was, for him, one way of assimilating new information. He felt I understood him, and he raised no objections to the interpretation, even though it was still very early in the treatment.

As Mark became more aware of his feelings, he started to disclose more and more how he really felt about his marriage, and without additional confrontations he admitted that he wanted to leave but that he felt tied to Lenore because she was the first woman to put up with all his craziness. He also felt guilty for wanting to abandon her, a subject that brought up his own feelings of abandonment by his father. While discussing these themes, his sexual acting out decreased. Homosexual activity became history, and was the subject of more analysis in later years, but he never went back to it. He kept one relationship with a secretary from the office somewhat alive. Even his sexual relationship with Lenore became part of the background rather than the center of attention. There was much more communication between them, talking to each other rather than at each other. In a very real sense, a complete turnabout in the relationship took place. She became extremely fearful of being abandoned by him, and adopted what seemed to be a hostile, clingy, dependent attitude, while he tried to "wiggle out" of the marriage gracefully. He came to the notion that he did not like his wife, and he realized he had married her to escape his truncated, unloving family.

For a while the sexual acting out was replaced by another kind of acting out—stealing. With this behavior he risked being caught, and as his stealing became rather dangerous (he once walked out of a department store with a leather coat on his back), I decided to "risk" another confrontation, and I told him that it seemed he was trying to sabotage the therapeutic relationship by getting himself slowly but surely into jail, and if he wanted to stop therapy he didn't have to go to jail for it. He noticed I was irritated. I told him we couldn't continue our relationship if he were going to revert to the old ways of expressing his feelings, through stealing something, like an object from a store, or forcing love out of someone. He was shocked by the "ultimatum," and the alarm in my voice. He said he thought treatment was just for that, wasn't it, and what was the purpose of his coming if he didn't have problems. I told him I didn't make jail visits and I couldn't work with someone whose goal was to go to jail. The stealing stopped and brought about a turning point in our relationship. Mark felt I was like a father to him, teaching him right from wrong. I silently accepted the role assigned to me because of Mark's increased insight about the motivation for his activities, and his ability to stop destructive patterns and work on growing and maintaining a functional ego. Mark gradually became more direct. He learned the art of "negotiations," of giving and taking, rather than grabbing, or stealing, or fending off. His original physical symptoms, such as the hypertension, headaches, and lack of ability to concentrate, all disappeared. He eventually went back to school and finished college. He divorced and remarried and, since he always disliked New York winters intensely, moved out to live in a warmer climate on the West Coast. I hear from him from time to time.

The preceding case history is an extremely brief sketch of how confrontation analysis deals with helping the patient *from the beginning of treatment* to better understand the essential links between behavior and feelings—in this case, sexual behavior and anger. Both the techniques and the rationale for them are illustrated. Of course, there were many other aspects to this case. However, the essential point is that notwithstanding the initial assessment of a relatively damaged ego through early deprivation, the choice of the confrontational approach, rather than the supportive one, was made because, as was mentioned earlier, the patient's defensiveness would have made it almost impossible to reach him in this short a time, i.e., less than a year. He would have probably been lost to psychotherapy if the strategy for intervention allowed him to continue this isolation. The interactional-confrontational approach seemed to be the treatment of choice, and while there were obvious risks in using it, the possible advantages outweighed the risks.

10

Personal Expression

The "blessed" zeal to turn the field of psychotherapy into a science has brought with it, in addition to some flourishing and important research programs, the "curse" of at least one danger, that of creating principles and laws of behavior that may, on the whole, be statistically sound, but at the same time misleading and harmful to the patient. They tend to create myths about psychological cure. Society certainly does not need "professionals" who treat people as if they were automated machines ready to be "turned on" to a preprogrammed life that has been decided upon by the "laws and principles of human behavior." As part of the total treatment, the psychotherapist has the obligation to help the patient regain every ounce of personal, idiosyncratic, inner substance that he has lost. Patients who come to a therapist's office have the right to expect to be accepted and respected for what they are, and also to be helped to grow as separate, independent individuals. For this reason, this book avoids discussing psychotherapy in terms of the various nosological categories that disregard the fact that no individual actually fits such categories. One treats individuals, not categories. For purposes of professional communication, a shorthand of diagnostic categories can be helpful, but unfortunately, these categories are often used as though they were real entities. This problem is quite pervasive. This section is devoted to the expression of emotionality through the personal life of the patient. The term *personal* here means the idiosyncratic, unique, particular, individual, and focuses on inner dynamics that pertain to the needs of the self.

Most patients seek treatment for specific symptoms, including anxiety. Those who are not conscious of their anxiety, express some dissatisfaction. Much of this dissatisfaction stems from feelings of alienation or lack of awareness of, and connection with, inner feelings. Many patients fail to see how their lack of communication with their own feelings can cause such alienation or lack of trust or respect for their own emotional needs. Thus many unconsciously abdicate their responsibility to themselves in order to serve others, and they eventually discover that the emotional returns are totally unsatisfying. However, by that time their behavior patterns are set. Even young people, in their late teens or early 20s, come face to face with this sort of emptiness. Some continue to struggle and search for solutions; others abandon hope and become "insignificant" cogs in the wheel.

For example, Marcia was a 22-year-old college graduate who sought therapy because of depression and feelings of inadequacy as a woman. She complained of a variety of psychosomatic symptoms, including rashes, which she interpreted as a "clear sign" of cancer; boils on her face, neck, and chest; occasional vomiting; and dizzy spells. She described herself as a "very social and popular person," but also a very "private" person, meaning that she couldn't confide in anyone or show how she felt. She lived with her parents because, according to her, they needed her psychological support. She felt awkward, however, when she met men, and she had never had any sexual experience beyond "necking" with a boy in the first year of college. She had two sisters at least ten years her senior, both living away from home, and both with a history of serious psychological problems. Marcia felt the family was a very "tight-knit" unit, where separation was considered foreign. The concept of "privacy" also had little meaning while she was growing up. Although the patient's mother was extremely careful not to expose her body to her daughter under any circumstance, she thought it completely natural to walk into the bathroom while Marcia was showering, or bathing, or moving her bowels. Her father was even more forward in that direction: he would often lie down in bed with her to watch television when she was wearing only her underwear and sometimes her brassiere. When she started to protest his behavior at the age of 19 or 20, he would tease her by trying to pinch her breasts or her behind, and if she left the room, which she had started to do occasionally, he would let her know that he felt rejected by her "stupid" behavior, and "childish nonsense." By the time she was 16 or 17, she developed a very rigid habit of covering every exposed part of her body, "out of shame" that it must look "debilitated." She admitted that she recognized that at times she must look like a "freak" to others because of the inappropriateness of her clothing, but she dismissed this concern by setting her priorities according to her fears of invasion of her privacy (through the uncovered skin). She also had the fear that if anyone touched her "diseased" skin, they would "discover" her and never keep her company again.

In therapy, she did not behave differently, at least during the first year or two. She made sure to turn her face in such a way as to hide it from the light, so that I wouldn't get a clear picture and consequently reject her. She loaded her cheeks, eyes, and lips with an incredible amount of make-up, and made sure to run home after work to get dressed up, especially for her sessions. With all these fears of exposure and concern about her physical appearance, I was somewhat puzzled by her "social and popular" personality. As she became somewhat more comfortable with me, the picture became clearer. She managed to develop certain patterns of communication that compensated, almost in a direct fashion, for her feelings of inadequacy and shame, and her fear of "invasion of privacy." Her language was soft, coquettish, whiney, and naive, while her orientation to me (and obviously to others) was that of a perceptive, humorous, gossipy, dependent, and entertaining young lady. She had develped sensitive "tentacles," and was able to spot what pleased others and to behave accordingly. She placated her friends and coworkers by treating them as idols, while openly derogating herself and never daring to express her genuine feelings directly. During the sessions she openly solicited my advice and approval ("Your tone of voice is just like my father's and I used to adore him, you know . . ."), and attempted to become the "model" patient, injecting humorous anecdotes and keeping a running commentary on her associations. Like a hawk, she watched every little muscle twitch in my face and body, for these told her how I was reacting inside, and how she might adjust her own feelings accordingly. In the middle of a sentence she would sometimes stop and say, "O.K., I know what you're thinking, and you're probably right." Most of the time she projected a negative, degrading, and alientating evaluation of her self. She would then express genuine feelings about her low self-esteem. This "drama" continued for some time.

I realized that she was allowing me to observe her pain in the way she particularly liked to express it. The expression of her emotional life, aside from the psychosomatic aspects, was concentrated mainly within her "personal" space, and she did not know how to relate to others or to allow others to participate and give her some feelings back. The system was, in a sense, closed, although not to the extreme of a "catatonic" self-absorption. The sexual and interpersonal channels that are normally used to express emotionality were almost entirely closed to her, although superficially she seemed to function reasonably well so far as others were concerned.

Although the dynamics and developmental history of Marcia's personality were fairly clear, her treatment presented serious difficulties. On the one hand, she acted in a rather inappropriate, extremely dependent, and rigid pattern. On the other hand, she was also quite clever, creative, insightful, and likeable. There was a precarious balance between the self-destructive patterns and the self-saving ones. The therapeutic problem was how to keep her ego functioning and developing as an independent entity without destroying her uniqueness. Forcing a modification of these two extremes into a middle position didn't seem an answer, because her identity would certainly be lost, even though she might become "adjusted" to the world around her, though not to her inner needs.

With slight modifications in tempo and manner, the confrontational techniques discussed in this book were adapted to Marcia's engulfing needs. Through my own, mostly nonverbal, reactions, I let her know that I appreciated her sense of humor, and that I enjoyed her capacity to use her observing and critical ego to look at herself objectively and at times, with great understanding. However, this kind of support stopped there. Whenever the situation presented itself, I was adamant in my pursuit of confronting her with her confusion and inconsistencies, and taught her, step by step, the art of analyzing confrontations. She learned to bring into the sessions episodes from the outside, where she herself did both the confronting work and the analytic work. She became so proficient at it that, while attending a party, she was able to carry on the work of the therapy and encounter other people with decreasing alarm and increasing satisfaction, while making real emotional contact. Her initial resistance to the confrontations was quite stiff. She would often glibly say, "Yeah, yeah, I know. I was joking with you because I wanted you to love me, but how about what I really feel. Maybe I really care about you, and you know I do. So why shouldn't I talk to you the way I talk to my friends?" Such an obvious resistance through counterattack was typical. On most occasions, however, I didn't let her slip away from the work. I would continue the probe in a confronting manner. I challenged her real motivation, the timing of her jokes, and her great appetite for applause. I kept reassuring her that I cared, and when the going was rough and she cried out in pain, I let her know I felt badly for her. But I called her bluffs, her games, her dissociative defensive maneuvers every time they appeared. At times, my tactics called for complete silence on my part for two or three weeks. When she kept looking for clues to her behavior, I would simply say something to this effect: "In the last few sessions I have said nothing, and so far you look perfectly healthy to me. But if you want to prove that you can win by becoming more depressed, or by trying to entertain me more, or by trying to tease me for a reaction, I won't stop you. Go ahead. You have made it on your own so far, you might also consider continuing in the same way. You're doing fine. You know that I don't keep quiet when I have something to say. . . ."

It is extremely important to let the patient know that the therapist is made neither of fragile glass nor or solid steel, and that he too has the right to express himself in a "personal" style. However, the patient must also learn that personal style is useless if it does not achieve the desired goals. Marcia consciously wished to have relationships with people in which she could give and take, not only take. Eventually, she learned that through "serving" her friends and family she was actually taking, not giving, because her basic motivation was to be loved by them. The transference that she developed toward me in the beginning of the therapeutic relationship had to be dealt with in such a way that her dependence would not simply shift from one set of objects (parents) to another (therapist), without Marcia's learning to appreciate personal distance and the separations that can bring about mature closeness. The therapeutic relationship had to be personal but not symbiotic, caring but not seductive, instructive but not authoritarian, emotional but not impulsive, separable but not rejecting. The alternation of support and confrontation, in a consistent and flexible manner, makes the development of such a relationship possible.

Therapists must help patients to differentiate *authentic* emotional expressions from defensive ones. At times this task may be extremely difficult, especially when the patient's central channel of emotional expression is so "personalized" that no one is allowed to share the feelings. Often the patient is not aware that he is expressing any feelings. In such cases, one could apply the "search-expose-analyze" strategy so often used in the therapeutic process. However, if a patient is so overprotective of his privacy that very little can be exposed, let alone analyzed, this strategy will be useless.

At times patients express their feelings in "personal" ways that are often incorrectly interpreted as "resistance" by the therapist. For example, a patient may write a letter to the therapist that expresses feelings, rather than discussing them during the session. Some patients spend hours looking for the "right" New Year's greeting card to send their therapist, and expect this gesture to be a substitute for expressing their feelings about the therapist. In this manner they also avoid their responsibility of exposing what they might consider a vulnerability, that is, their feelings toward the therapist. This type of behavior is often used in the service of resistance. However, there are occasions when such a personal style of emotional expression may be used as the basis for developing and widening the patient's inner self, because it is indicative of the patient's resourcefulness and individuality. The therapist must recognize such special and sometimes "strange" ways of relating as such, and attempt to understand them in the context of the total personality rather than summarily categorize them as resistance, and thus as obstacles to therapeutic progress or to achieving the patient's goals. It is through such "creative resistance" that some patients can be helped to develop emotional independence.

For example, a 28-year-old lawyer complained in one of his sessions that his boss, whom he liked, had begun to be "picky, irrational, and unprofessional." He had reproached the patient several times because he was perennially late to work. The patient reported this complaint in the same monotonous flat tone that he had used to discuss other matters. What surprised me was the content—i.e., that the patient was habitually late to work. He had never been late to any of his sessions. I told him that I understood his resentment about the "professionalism," that as long as he did his work his superior's concern about the time did seem irrational, but he could not understand how he was able to be punctual for his therapy appointments and yet be late to work. He was silent for a minute and seemed most uncomfortable. Then, with a rather unusually expressive tone and change in facial and body posture, he said, "I guess I like you and I couldn't say this to you. That's the way I show it, I guess. It is stupid, isn't it?" As we proceeded, it became quite clear that his way of expressing his feelings was usually indirect, as shown by his behavior on the job and toward me. Previous to this exchange, he was not quite aware of such behavior patterns. In this instance, arriving on time to the sessions symbolized positive feelings toward me. At the same time, however, his behavior on the job was in no way a hostile reaction to his boss, for he liked him and his work in the company. Nor was his lateness an act of rebellion against the establishment or authority. The fact was that this man was operating under these special circumstances in a very rational manner, and was unwilling to yield to his boss' need to control his employees. This patient insisted on expressing his feeling in a very special, personal, private, style. He had never been encouraged to behave in this way by his family. Any expression of individuality was viewed by them as a deviation from the norm, and was not tolerated. My understanding and acceptance of the differential meaning of his punctuality to his sessions and lateness to his job created an atmosphere of trust in which he was able to open up many other facets of his inner life. Had I interpreted his style of operation as resistance, he might have validly perceived this as a repetition of his familial history, thus eliminating the chance for him to accept his idiosyncracies as parts of his self that he did not need to repress, but rather to integrate.

In another case, a research assistant in her early 30s was in treatment because she felt lonely and desperate about finding a husband. A few months after she began treatment, she seemed to have run out of topics to discuss, and she would often remain silent for a long time during her sessions. My probes, interpretations, and confrontations were not too helpful in discovering the source of these silences. These silences did not seem to be the typical silent resistance. Finally, I told her that, so far as I was concerned, if she didn't want to talk about herself or her feelings, I wouldn't mind it if we discussed something neutral, but interesting, such as the movies, rather than staying silent. She didn't believe that I would really do that, since, after all, she was there for therapy, and I wouldn't want to waste our time discussing movies. She said that she had always been interested in the movies, and that she had never felt comfortable talking about it because I might think, like others, that she was a dumb, superficial person. As a matter of fact, not only was she interested in the movies, but she had a fund of information about them equal to that of a scholar of the cinema. She came "alive" in this discussion, and as I encouraged her, in this and subsequent sessions, to tell me more about this area, her entire range of emotional expression broadened, and she became increasingly accepting of her various characteristics and needs. She learned that she did not have to suppress her personal interests, which had been tied to a negative self-image. Rather their expression and expansion helped her deal with her loneliness and feelings of emptiness. The interactive process during the sessions, specifically relating to this aspect of herself, which in a sense, represented her identify, was probably the most single important therapeutic factor leading to a change in her self-image, and evetually to a more satisfying expression of her emotionality.

A third example of how the analyst can deal with certain "personal" expressions of emotionality is the case of Linda, a 34-year-old commercial artist. She had become dejected, depressed, and suicidal after a casual boyfriend jilted her. She couldn't understand why he had done this to her; after all, she cared very much for him. However, it soon turned out that she had never expressed to him what she felt, at least not in a way he could understand or appreciate. During her childhood she was encouraged to express her emotionality by writing about her feelings in a personal diary, rather than through verbal expression or physical interaction. I did not know that she had this pattern of writing until the incident with the boyfriend came up. Afterward, I asked her why she hadn't told him how she felt. She replied, "I've learned long ago, telling someone how you feel takes the real feeling out of it, it destroys it—you just lose it. I could never do that." The therapist agreed that it was important that people express their feelings in their unique way, but then, they might not be understood, and the consequences might not be so desirable. I wondered aloud how she expected me to know how she felt, since she didn't tell me. She said that she always wrote what she felt, that perhaps she could give me some of it to read, though it must be with the stipulation that we would not discuss it. I told her that we could try to do that, but that if it didn't work, we would have to change our interaction. She agreed, and immediately whipped out of her handbag the following poem that she had written several weeks before this session. She apologized, saying that it did not express fully her real feelings, since she had written it under the influence of a favorite poet. Since I had agreed not to discuss it with her, I was not sure who this poem was about, although from subsequent experience it appeared that the subject was myself.

> Ah, you are right.
> I can't be simple any more.
> I can't say anything like
>> I like you
>> I fear you
>> I need you
>> I'm not you
> I can't go directly to anything and use it as I want to.
> I'm always getting in my own way.
> I can't tell you directly anything I want to tell you:
>> I'm happy
>> I'm frightened
>> I'm angry
>> I'm sad
> I don't know how to think of myself.
> I don't know what you think of me:

I'm childish
I'm crazy
I'm stupid
I'm lying
I try always to make someone else speak first
I am always testing everyone, especially you.
I can't trust you
I can't please you
I can't ignore you
I can't forget you
I can't be simple anymore
I want to cry
I want to shout
I want to laugh
I want to say
     I like you.

This approach worked for awhile, but eventually she became increasingly resistant to her own suggestion. She felt uncomfortable about my reading what she had written, but she decided to devote more time to writing on her own without the "help" of a reader. She also felt that therapy was indeed unnecessary for her at that time, since she was quite satisfied with her writing. In a relatively short time, she terminated treatment, with the understanding that she might wish to reestablish contact whenever she felt the need for it.

Thus the individual's uniqueness in emotional expression, a part of the self that is often misunderstood and is difficult to deal with in psychotherapy, may be used by the therapist who is willing to deviate from certain modes of therapeutic intervention to help the patient achieve a fuller emotional experience and integrate it as part of his ego. In this manner, an opportunity for a more positive self-image presents itself, with decreased dependency and increased self-esteem. The illustrations presented were those of relatively "intact" individuals who functioned fairly well in at least one major area in their life, and who were more or less amenable to the normal "talking" therapy.

Some problems in the sphere of emotionality are more difficult for the therapist to tackle because of the lack of a reasonable understanding of the patient's dynamics; the patient's extremely unique, personal (bordering on the bizarre) way of expressing feelings; the lack of techniques for dealing with quickly shifting emotionality *during* the treatment hour; or strong countertransferential reactions that prevent adequate distance between patient and therapist. During the last decade, such problems have often been discussed in professional circles under the label of the "difficult patient" (Saretsky, 1981).

The following is an example of a patient, Mira, who experienced many difficulties in ordinary daily living, primarily because of severely disruptive emotional development during her childhood, and the consequent lack of capacity to derive pleasure from interaction with others. By the age of 40 she had managed to seek the help of many (at least 14) highly qualified analysts and therapists of varied theoretical and clinical approaches. She complained that none of them "cured" her, or even helped her conduct her life in a semi-reasonable way. A salient factor in the development of her distorted self-perception stood out blatantly: she had been persistently rejected by her mother while her father stood idly by, intermittently behaving in a more kindly manner. The mother, a jealous, narcissistic woman, used to severely punish her by silencing her in the company of others, and by constantly attempting to isolate her from her father. At the age of six or seven, the patient was separated from her parents when she had to flee the country with another relative because of the Nazi occupation of Hungary, where she was born. She was reunited with her parents and younger brother after the war, at which time her mother behaved in a still more rejecting manner, and with vehement accusations against the patient's alleged lack of respect for what she, the mother, had gone through during the time of the separation. During the teenage years, mother and daughter were in a constant battle, and when the situation worsened to the point of violent outbursts with physical fighting, the patient's father, who had managed to accumulate considerable wealth through his business acumen, sent his daughter away to boarding school. At the age of 17, in her last year of high school, she met a young man 10 years her senior, with whom she eloped. Her parents were outraged and cut their ties to her, but a few months after her marriage she became pregnant and, when her child was born, a reconciliation took place. When the baby was one year old, the patient decided to leave her husband and child, and moved to another part of the country. Her father continued to support her financially, even though she was continuously unkind to him, and at every opportunity she heaped abuses on him. Eventually she travelled around the world, living for several years in various countries. Despite all the lack of stability, she managed to graduate from college, and she held several inconsequential jobs from which she was fired because, in her words, "nobody could stand me!" She attempted suicide a few times, including two rather serious attempts for which she was hospitalized for a few months. She was referred to me by her last therapist, whom she had seen for three years, longer than any other therapist, and with whom she had formed some attachment, though he too was characterized by her as an "impotent, incompetent, weak shmuck." However, her treatment with him terminated when he became seriously ill and had to give up his practice.

In the initial interview, Mira impressed me as a rather depressed, confused, and lost person. There was no doubt that she was intellectually gifted; she was extremely capable of expressing her feelings verbally, and certainly well-versed in the use of "psychotherapeutic language." From a prognostic viewpoint, her history of wandering from one therapist to another overshadowed her personality gifts, and therefore I was doubtful about what we could achieve. Even her depression seemed to acquire such a syntonicity in her total personality that help in this direction did not seem possible. In addition, during this interview she behaved in such a manner that it was very difficult to focus on any theme. She was extremely dramatic, threatening, obscene, manipulative, indirectly or directly insulting, confronting, and demanding. At the same time she sounded like a little girl who was lost, hurt and whiney, crying, and begging to be looked after. Her behavior was so variable and changeable that she reminded me of those shiny laminated plastic picture postcards whose images change when the card is moved slightly back and forth. In this case, however, Mira didn't need anyone to initiate emotional changes in her, she changed unpredictably much of the time, without even being aware of what was happening. I had the feeling that she was switching her identity automatically in a manner that was rather dissociated and quite disruptive to interpersonal communication. In diagnostic parlance, she would no doubt fit the various descriptions and definitions of the borderline category. The important point, however, is that she expressed her feelings in an extremely personal style that she was herself able to recognize by saying that no analyst could understand her, "escept maybe for the last one . . . and I am not going to be just like anybody else." She said she'd rather die than become a common person—i.e., expressing herself in a manner understandable or acceptable to most people. Indeed, she had not a single friend. She was alone in the full sense of the word.

When I expressed some hesitation about taking her on as a patient, she immediately attacked me as an insensitive person who was probably interested in seeing only those patients who wouldn't give me any trouble. Following this attack she began to cry and whine, but also to demand that I see her because she was so depressed, muttering under her breath that she was suicidal, and that she would probably kill herself regardless of what happened. I then told her that I certainly did not wish to establish any kind of therapeutic relationship if she planned to kill herself, because "my office is not a place for people to die or kill themselves." I also advised her that the subject of her killing herself could not be the object of our discussions, even if she were obsessed with the idea. I told her that I was perfectly aware that she might have been looking for treatment precisely because she was afraid she might kill herself, and added in a half-joking, half-serious manner, that I was very jealous of my reputation as a good therapist and that I didn't want it "stained" by some crazy suicidal patient. She agreed to try to avoid this topic, and we launched into the therapeutic work.

The uniqueness of this woman, the very personal way in which she expressed her feelings, was no doubt her greatest asset and liability. She used her verbal eloquence to express her feelings in the most dramatic, penetrating, and hostile manner. She had conditioned her facial expressions to obey any conscious wish and, once the therapeutic relationship had begun, her dramatic presentations were communicated quite effectively non-verbally. At the same time, she could not hide any unconscious feelings in her facial expression, and it was relatively easy to know what she was feeling by looking at her face. Her inability to hide what she truly felt made it extremely hard for her to keep interpersonal relationships, primarily because she was angry, depressed, and quite narcissistic most of the time. She admitted that she had not an ounce of positive feelings toward anyone.

A few transcribed portions from some sessions illustrate the confrontation analysis approach to this type of "difficult" patient. Again, a major part of the difficulty here is the uniqueness of the patient's expressions of her emotionality and the necessity to deviate from the "traditional" techniques and strategy in order to help the patient "hear" what was transpiring.

The following excerpt is from the beginning of the fourth session. I had let out the patient who had preceded her and asked Mira to come in (about one minure late). As the other patient was leaving, Mira scrutinized him coolly, then walked in, stared at me, showed me a cup of coffee she had brought with her, and, before even sitting down, began to talk.

P: Because you kept me waiting, I spilled half the coffee in your bathroom sink.

T: Kept you waiting?

P: Yeah! (*In a strong uncompromising tone*) I've been waiting for 20 minutes!

T: You came in 20 minutes early waiting to scream at me?

P: (*Laughs*) Don't make fun of this. I had a teacher who hit us with her fist if we were late—even one second—and I'll never forget that.

T: I was one minute late—is that why you're so angry; or are you still yelling at your teacher who is not here?

P: No, not really, but I do resent having to wait, especially for you to finish with that guy (*slight hesitation*). He's cute—I mean, he is not bad-looking.

T: So you are jealous.

P: How come you let him stay extra time, and with me you start looking at your watch five minutes after I get here? (*All this is said in a supposedly joking, slightly seductive manner, but no doubt with a great deal of hostility.*) Why am I talking about this? Do you really think I am jealous? I told you Tuesday that I felt like an old hag and nobody wants to be with me, so why should *you*? (*She stops talking, places her arms out in the air in a desperate gesture, then stands up and walks around the perimeter of the office for a minute, exclaiming:*) Oh, God, good God! Tell me, do you really think I am jealous. I mean does it show? I know I get jealous a lot—anybody I see on the street looks better than me. I pretend I don't care, but I do care—that's crazy, I don't care, I do care, I am crazy, I know it, and you confirmed it as soon as you saw me. But what's the use of knowing that. I am sick of my own company, why should anybody want be with me. That's why I don't go out to meet anybody. It's a bore, a bloody bore. (*She sits down, looks at me*) and you're not helping me. Oh dear. (*In a loud, almost shrieking voice:*) I can't have a decent relationship—one fucking decent relationship. How am I expected to live. This shmucky guy I met on my floor, Stanley, told me yesterday he didn't want to see me anymore, he thinks I am obnoxious. Well, fuck him. Good God! He is so unattractive, this self-pronounced Adonis. Who the hell does he think he is? He rejects me before I reject him. I know I don't give a good damn about him, but it bothers me.

T: That is precisely what you seem to do—isn't it wonderful that you can recognize it at least in somebody else?

P: (*attempting to hide a smile:*) You mean I am obnoxious so that I get rejected? I reject before I get the axe? But honestly, I don't want to be rejected, I've had too much of that! But from that little worm, that idiot! He is a bore! Why should I be nice with him when I don't feel it. I mean I much prefer to stay in any little room than to be with such a big, fat slob. But I have to be with people. I have to be with somebody. I don't go anywhere.

T: Everyone becomes a bore after awhile, don't they? You can ...

P: A very short while. As soon as I meet someone, man or woman, I condemn them. Women even more than men. I know, it's my mother. (*Screams:*) Goddamn you, mother! You have to excuse me, but I've got to get it out (*tears*). I can't trust anybody, especially women. They are all catty, birds of prey perched waiting to attack their next victim. The way women act and think in this country, it makes me vomit.

T: The whole world is kaput for you!

P: People are stupid, most people are. But who knows, maybe I am even more stupid, because they are having a good time and I am not. But I don't want just a good time. I don't want to waste my life. I am forty and I want to do something worthwhile. S-o-m-e-t-h-i-n-g. Oh, God!

T: What makes you suffer for not being with the lowly creatures of the earth, since they are all shit according to you?

P: I can't be honest with people, because as soon as I tell them what I think of them, they run away. I don't even have to tell them. They can see it. I don't know how they know that I am shit, but nobody wants to be around me. Even you didn't want to see me when you found out how sick I was. I think I intimidated you (*she says this with glee*). Tell me the truth, you are afraid of me, aren't you?

T: If by "intimidate" you mean that you make yourself obnoxious, I can see that; eventually, if you keep up the "good works," you will probably succeed with me, too. Look, first I made you lose half of your coffee because I was 60 senconds late; second, other patients get more from me than you get from me; third, I don't want to see you because you are a "sickie;" and fourth, I am intimidated by you. I think you are losing your nuts!

P: (*laughing hysterically:*) Did I say all that? Well, you know I don't mean all that. As a matter of fact, you seem like a nice guy, and maybe you know what you're doing—I get this impression, and I really like you because you have a sense of humor. I hate people without a sense of humor.

T: Thank you for all these compliments. What a nice surprise!

P: It's true I never say anything like that to anybody. But don't get a big head from what I said. *I laugh heartily.*) Am I amusing you?

This short repartee "manipulated" the patient into exposing as much of her emotional projections as possible so as to give me the opportunity to confront her with them without letting them slip away. The assumption I made about her ego strength was that her familiarity with therapy and with these problems of trust could serve as a good basis for interacting with her in a more direct and dramatic manner, something she could identify with and yet challenge. Her inner objects, or most of her introjects, were so badly battered that their exposure could only be beneficial, because she could start to look at them and deal with them, albeit with tremendous resistance. However, such awareness must be associated with positive experiences in the present (while the process of awareness takes place), which Mira could learn to use and enjoy, even if only for the short duration of the session, or part of it. These positive experiences, admittedly somewhat forced and certainly transferential, could become substitutes for the negative introjects that keep feeding her projective mechanism. Mira was obviously locked into her need for nurturance, yet any situation that provided her with such possibilities also symbolized for her the emotional poisoning that her mother had inflicted on her. As a result, her expression of her own emotionality assumed a unique and personal character. These expressions were ego syntonic, and her attachment to them was pathological and mostly unconscious. Most people who tolerated her hostility for awhile eventually had to remove themselves from her company, not only because of the hostility, but primarily because of her bizarre and unpredictable reactions. Notwithstanding her oversensitivity, demandingness, and self-centeredness, I found her surprisingly compassionate, and at times most constructive in the therapeutic work. She drove her need to test out people's loyalty to her to painful confrontations, yet I admired her unrelenting search for truth, even though her motivation was not necessarily altruistic, and was often colored by her obnoxious, almost staged, displays of hysterical outbursts.

My reaction and interventions to Mira were based on the assumption that we must regard each session "as if" it were the last one, primarily because of her impulsivity and past abrupt termination of treatment with other analysts. I felt that each session had to be experienced by her as a whole, and that whatever insight or other benefit she could derive from it should supersede the necessity for the continuity of the therapeutic process that is normally relied upon in psychodynamically oriented types of treatment. Continuity could be achieved only if each session was experienced by Mira as a complete, "well-cooked meal" by itself. The rationale for this approach stems from the observation that many borderline and narcissistic patients like Mira must have a therapist who is firm, flexible, and communicative, and who behaves in a manner that is directly the opposite to their disturbed parents during the patient's maturational years. Otherwise the idea of continuity may be experienced as the vicious cycle out of which they cannot free themselves. Sullivan's (1954) view of the importance of each individual session in the therapeutic process must be stressed twofold when it comes to the treatment of the "difficult" patient who often clearly manifests patterns consistent with the borderline and/or narcissistic character personality organization. Sullivan stresses the interpersonal ingredient, the patient-therapist relationship which confrontation analysis places at the center of its focus. Each session must be as productive, engaging, and challenging as possible:

> The course of the interview situation proceeds on the basic assumption that the interviewee can derive at least some durable benefit from his contact with expert skill, but that this can occur only in the measure that a valid relationship comes into being ... and finally, the interviewer as an expert makes sure that the interviewee "knows himself" the better for the experience (Sullivan, 1954).

Mira had experienced her mother as authoritarian, disruptive, distant, and hypocritical. I attempted to counteract such a history by being firm but not authoritarian, direct, and flexible in my acceptance of her "bizarre" behavior. I believed that she needed a relationship with me that was compassionate yet objective, equal yet instructive, accepting yet confrontational. It was also important to help her bind her anxiety in the completeness of each session, otherwise her daily experiences would disrupt her ego functioning to the point of major disorganization. The trials and tribulations of her treatment continued for a long time; however, she became increasingly more trusting, although she never fully accepted her responsibility in undermining a great number of interpersonal situations. She became more involved in her painting, which she had pursued on and off for many years, sometimes with great success. She even became involved in romance with a man who was patient and loving, but had little to offer her intellectually or socially. Eventually, this relationship ended, of course with electrifying, dramatic maneuvers. She began to sense, however, that her reactions were, for most other people, peculiar, inappropriate, and traumatic. She was, however, unwilling to give them up. She felt these patterns were part of her personality, and it would be impossible for her to let go of them without compromising herself. By objectifying, at least intellectually, her very unique emotionality, she was able to recognize, and *even justify,* other people's rejection of her. The solution was for her to become less anxious about not having everyone approve of her, and she became more involved with selecting a small number of people who satisfied some of her very specific needs.

Her depression never disappeared, but she learned to enjoy certain experiences for the sake of enjoyment, not for "future reference," as she used to say. She also recognized that she needed to be in treatment for a long time, perhaps all her life, and that changing therapists did not help her achieve changes that might do away with the need for professional help. The long-term effects of this understanding could not be ascertained. The excerpt that follows is from a session about six months after she started treatment, and illustrates how she had become more communicative, capable of establishing a relatively "healthy" (for her) transference toward me and learned to place a certain distance between her bizarre behavior and expression of emotionality and her understanding of its origin and inappropriateness. By this time, my interventions were less confrontative and more interpretive, even though from time to time she still needed additional structure and direction.

P: What am I doing here? I don't know what I am doing here. (*Points to my pants:*) Are those navy blue?

T: Yes.

P: Why are you dressed up like a Christmas tree?

T: A Christmas tree?

P: Well, navy blue and brown and beige and black. It's a little too much. I mean you are always a very careful dresser, that's why I am a little surprised (*laughs*). That will be 60 dollars. (*In a loud voice:*) Oh God! God! I really feel bad. (*She walks toward the windows and, while drawing the blinds down, continues:*) I have to close the blinds a bit. This way I have a safer look. Do you mind?

T: Now that you did it, I don't mind (*half sarcastically*).

P: Listen, you've got to help me. I am very bad—very bad.

T: What did you do that's bad?

P: I am in a bad way. (*She drops her voice considerably.*) In a bad way. Honey (*she had never addressed me in this manner*), I have to tell you this. I had this horrible, horrible dream—I mean, I am ashamed to tell you, and don't look at me, you know, like I am some kind of pervert. I think I had it on Thursday night, and I woke up from it and I am ashamed. I'm really ashamed. I'm afraid to tell you these things, because you'd think who does she think she is. This was something like a man's wet dream and, you know, these things don't happen (*laughs and continues to tell me about the dream with what seems to be a great deal of pleasure*). I remember dreaming about some young, very young guy—could've been this chap who delivers the mail once in a while and, you know, we talk sometimes— he's sort of cute, you know, like a mother–child kind of thing. Anyway, but there it was, it wasn't somebody, well somebody I know, this boy has a beard, but in the dream this guy had no beard (*looks at me and at my beard and bursts out laughing*). Oh, no! I just looked at you—no this guy in the dream didn't have a beard, so be quiet! And uh . . . uh . . . so that made me feel awful all Friday and Saturday, just rotten. I had to dream about that! Oh God! I felt miserable, rotten. I had to dream about sex. And then on Saturday I had another dream, not sexual—a strange dream, very strange—with somebody killing someone else, or wants to kill some- body else, and the way to do it was, they tied the person to the front of a car, and this person was inside something, like a living bomb and they ran this car into the car of the person they wanted killed, and I thought, oh, my God, this is a living bomb. It was a woman, I think, but then the last minute she was supposed to get out of it, before this thing exploded, and I remember, I sort of stood by the side and helped undo something that was supposed to let her out. This was a strange contraption. But then I thought to myself, why am I risking my life, why am I doing that, putting my hand there, it could explode any minute. Anyway, it was such a depressed feeling! And with the dream on Thursday, oh, God, what am I going to do, what am I going to do? And just now, on the bus on my way here—this guy, not very young, with a young girl, and he was kissing her hand. Thank God I had to get out, because I couldn't tolerate it. (*She makes a whining, pretentious crying noise that sounds like a little girl.*) I think I am going crazy! I woke up at six in the morning and I started painting early, and this is "bum" time—I look out of my window and you see them, all the bums, coming out of the woodwork, and they start talking. They shout, and they are all angry, and they say "fuck you," "screw you," "goddamn it," "I'll show you," and you know, I am not far away from that, from them. I really mean it.

T: So angry, you mean?

P: Yeah, they wander about screaming at the world, and that's what I do. They are without shelter, without anyone, and they have much more character than I do. Mind you, that's because I have to make believe that I have something or that I am doing something. Oh, yeah . . . I spoke to my father last night. He called me to let me know that he broke his leg falling down a couple of steps, as if I care if he broke his neck. He told me that my mother wanted to come to visit me. Oh, God! Who needs her here! She had to be taken care of like a queen—she puts on this air, this obnoxious tone, this unbelievable way of putting everybody down. Can you imagine her like that! (*I shake my head positively.*) Really? You mean you know such people? (*I keep shaking my head.*) You mean me? (*I keep shaking my head, and she bursts into hysterical laughter.*) Oh, shut up! Not like that—I am not like that. Well, maybe a little. Oh dear, oh dear. And that always put the fear of God in me. I don't know why, is that intended to make me feel guilty. It always did. You haven't said a word, you know! And oh, yes. My father asked about that gallery which was going to show some of my work—he remembered this, and I couldn't tell him that the relationship was broken off, and this is kind of pathetic. I always have to give him a tolerable picture of myself, because if they saw me as I really am, they'd be so full of pity and contempt and, of course, I see myself as they see me, as I really am. And that's awful. Why don't you say something?

T: Mira, tell me more about what you mean by who or what you really are.

P: (*Crying softly:*) I am seen in their eyes as a most dismal person. But then I say to myself, who are they to tell me who I am. But it's really what it is, this is what it is. Nothing. And then I think maybe I should think about the "wonderful" things I've done—I furnished my apartment nicely, I have painted a couple of things, but then I have to tell them that I am still negotiating with the gallery, which is not true. I feel I am a mess. Total chaos. I wonder sometimes, if I don't paint—what's left? Nothing. Absolute zero! I have nothing to offer.

Mira's expression of her emotions always erected a "loud" fence between herself and others because of her uniquely personal, albeit bizarre, style. Her major preoccupation, however, was not her inability to interact decently with others, although this problem was discussed at length. Her pain originated much more from her dissatisfaction with herself as an artist, from her self-imposed isolation, from her narcissistic need to repeatedly reaffirm her worthlessness, from her lack of feeling that she belonged with the human race, from her utter disdain for anything or anyone that came close to being part of the normal social order. From a therapeutic point of view, it was imperative that her idiosyncracies be carefully but quickly assessed and responded to. The therapist's interventions had to be "tailormade" to her very unusual, difficult, challenging, and "trying" personality. In a very real sense, as a patient she was capable of bringing out the best and the worst in a therapist, and she exercised her options. The best was that she was a cooperative and resourceful woman and, therefore, provided an opportunity for the therapist to search for creative and novel solutions. The worst was that she created an aura of depression, explosiveness, and futility that triggered off feelings of inadequacy, impotence, unpleasantness, and pity. In fact, on a number of occasions, I was tempted to ask her to look for another therapist, because I became angry and impatient with the constant barrage of undeserved abuse. However, as I increasingly understood her uniqueness, I felt less threatened by the recognition that I had to change my tactics and techniques quickly, and I consequently overcame these difficulties in dealing with her.

The above illustrations of how confrontation analysis approaches this aspect of emotional expression make it clear how difficult it is for even the most experienced therapist to define treatment goals. The less seasoned therapist can often be caught in a familiar dilemma—i.e., which treatment approach should be pursued. On the one hand, one generally feels bound by some loyalty to the orientation of one's training institute; on the other hand, one also wishes to break out of the mold, since one soon realizes that what one learns in school is not always applicable to daily practice—but one does not *dare* to experiment with techniques that might be more beneficial to one's patients and more suited to one's personality.

For example, Dr. L., a capable young therapist in supervision, told me of a new patient who came to see her because of long-standing problems related mainly to difficulties in interpersonal relationships. Her patient, a young woman in her late 20s, had been in psychoanalysis for over four years with an orthodox analyst, but decided to leave, having reached a plateau. He recommended a female analyst—Dr. L. She saw the patient for a few sessions, and had a good understanding of her dynamics. The recurrent theme in the patient's complaints was her feeling of being empty, apathetic, and incapable of relating to others in any meaningful manner because of her fear that she would alienate everyone by her "stupidity." Defensively, she had developed a style of operation where she would not let anyone around her get into any intimate discussion, by literally interrupting the talker with inappropriate comments and questions (which she quickly answered herself), compulsively bombarding others with her own "blabber." She had developed into an excellent storyteller and a joker, and she learned to use seductive language to mesmerize her audience. Dr. L., trained as a psychoanalyst, reacted very little to her "story-telling." She adopted a similar stand to that of her predecessor. I suggested to her that she might try actively to find out what specifically prompted the patient to leave her first analyst, since it might give her some clue about the kind of transferential situation she was in. Such information can often be helpful in predicting what strategy might be needed as the present transference develops. She agreed that this might be helpful.

A few weeks later, Dr. L. brought up this case for discussion. She had seen the patient for eight sessions by then. As she related the material to me, she seemed most tense and uncomfortable, and I asked her about that. She denied her discomfort, and continued to discuss the patient's dynamics, and eventually, her own thoughts about the difficulties. I noticed that I learned very little about the patient, since Dr. L. was recounting what transpired in the session in a very global manner. I told her that I had difficulties following the case because of that. She said there wasn't much more beyond what she was saying; however, as I probed more into specifics, Dr. L. became increasingly anxious, although she was able to provide more details about her patient. For example, as a child the patient was a stutterer, and her father had insisted that she talk in a nonstop, continuous manner while answering any question or telling a story. He had also forced her to read books aloud, again to "exercise" her talking habit. She learned to master her stuttering through this training, but she also became quite dependent on this communication pattern as a way of warding off possible criticism of her inadequacy, which was consequently generalized to additional areas of ego functions. In her first analytic experience, however, this compulsive talking pattern was unfortunately perceived as a cooperative effort on her part. As the referring analyst put it to Dr. L. on the phone, "the patient is quite verbal and talkative—at least this is not a problem."

Dr. L. recognized how distorted this interpretation was after she had seen the patient a couple of times. Yet she did not know how to help the patient break this ritual. She knew that she had to intervene actively in a way that was antianalytic, although not necessarily antitherapeutic. She felt that the patient was a good "analytic candidate," and she did not want to rob her of the analytic opportunity. She admitted, at the same time, that she could not operate differently from the referring colleague, who had been one of her teachers at the analytic institute, and to whom she felt a sense of loyalty, not only because of the referral, but also because of what he represented for her in her training career. It was for these same reasons that she had blocked out my suggestion that she inquire about the patient's termination with the referring analyst. It was pretty clear that, notwithstanding her excellent grasp of the patient's dynamics, she could not overcome her loyalty and dependence on her training, or her inability to appreciate the very unique manner in which this patient expressed her emotionality (i.e., by actively shutting other people up and thus limiting incoming stimuli). Dr. L. was unable to modify her techniques to accomodate this aspect of the patient's defensive armor. Her discomfort with me, which I discussed toward the end of that supervisory hour, was related to her need to please me by heeding my suggestion to become more interactive with her patient, but not feeling she was "allowed" to do so by her previous conditioning.

This type of conflict often affects the patient's progress and the therapist's sense of well-being in practice. Obviously, the problem of dependency was at the base of both conflicts in the above case, on the part of both patient and therapist, and it was clearly manifest in the supervisory situation.

11

Interpersonal Expression

Emotionality expressed through the physical, sexual, or personal dimension of the self has so far been discussed. Of course, no one expresses feelings exclusively through one aspect of the self, even when the ego is severely limited by various dysfunctions or maladjustments. However, the fact of the matter is that the inexperienced therapist often falls into the same trap as the patient who presents difficulties in living as if they were limited to one part of his or her personality without affecting or being affected by the whole personality. Therefore it is imperative to examine every sign and symptom with this perspective in mind, regardless of how "trivial" or "inconsequential" it may initially appear. Emotionality expressed in the interpersonal sphere is the most complex and encompassing of all the other areas of emotional expression. In psychotherapy, an important and complicating factor is the therapist's involvement in the interpersonal transactions, and his very significant contribution to the patient's range and depth of emotional expression.

Interpersonal expression is the release or communication of feelings by an individual in the presence of one or more people. This definition excludes those instances in which people emote without the actual physical presence of others, even though these emotions may be in response to fantasies that include other individuals. The style, extent, and manner in which people express themselves emotionally in interpersonal relationships may often be used as informative indices of central personality characteristics and behavior patterns, and are thus helpful in any assessment for diagnostic and prognostic purposes in psychotherapy. One must, however, understand the nature and origin of interpersonal communication in general to fully appreciate the meaning of the transactions that transpire during the treatment process. The central question of how bonds are established between people give important clues in the search into the elements of emotional expression interpersonally, and the role it plays in the larger frame of human behavior. What makes people "relate" to each other? How do they form "connections" between them, often lasting a lifetime?

The answers given by social scientists in the past relate to concepts of gregariousness and need for survival. These explanations are no longer sufficient to satisfy the present understanding of the nature of interpersonal communication. Greater import is attached to the mother–child relationship as the basis for most future interactions, and to the developmental nature of this relationship during infancy and chilhood. To quote Escalona (1968), "Some early ego functions emerge first in passive form during encounters with the mother, but they are actively applied and expanded during transactions with the inanimate environment before they appear as active components of social interactions."

The nature of emotionality in any individual is organically connected with the nature of conditioning, modeling, and *interactive* patterns that mothering provides for the baby in its first two or three years of life. This understanding, however, does not reduce the diffculty in clearly discerning direct connecting lines between what *exactly* the mothering figure does to produce emotional reactions in the child that eventually become the "bond" or "link" that connects, or inter-relates, the child to her, and later to other people. Of course, several concrete physical activities of mothering are essential in the maintenance of a healthy development: feeding, holding and (physical) comforting. Interference with any of these functions may eventually lead to disturbed development. To be sure, by performing certain very specific need-satisfying activities for the child, the mother does in fact convey the feeling that she is responding to the child's needs; thus completing the interactive cycle that starts with the child's needs and ends with the mother's reactions to them. The continuous repetition of this complete cycle defines a condition in human behavior that is termed *interpersonal.* The assumption is made that, through the mechanism of introjection, and, later, projective identification, the child develops an emotional tendency that allows him to "relate" to others. This feeling is sometimes called "empathy," i.e., "feeling with" another person what the latter might be feeling, thus making it possible to interact in a manner that is *responsive* to this other person. Sullivan (1954), referring to this process of understanding another person as "empathy," agrees that it is quite difficult to assign a scientific definition to it. When the empathic process suffers as the child matures, the expression of feelings in the interpersonal sphere also suffers, and consequently, interpersonal communication, in general, becomes disturbed. Thus, when individuals meet for some purpose, what transpires between them can be directly related to their capacity for empathy. All in all, it may be assumed that the adult's style of interpersonal emotionality represents a model of the inner structure of childhood "molds of empathy" learned through the mother–child relationship.

From a therapeutic viewpoint, this orientation is very crucial. It implicitly defines the basic understanding of any therapeutic relationship in terms of empathic emotional interaction between patient and therapist, and further, it makes it absolutely important for the therapist to know as much as possible about the patient's childhood relationships, especially with the mothering figure. Naturally, this is the basis for central transferential (and countertransferential) reactions. The majority of patients do not initially recognize this transferential truism and, when confronted with it, they will say, "I am so different outside, I can't understand why I act like this here." The difficulty in separating reality from fantasy in this realm is great. For example, patients often insist that their emotional reactions to the therapist are based on the reality of existential transactions, regardless of how inappropriate they may seem. The fact that their emotional reactions are childhood-related is vehemently denied, and sometimes ridiculed in the best tradition of psychotherapy stereotyping.

For example, I asked a patient why he was so indignant when I would not give him information about my family. The patient said that he could not understand why I was so "secretive and obsequious." After all, he had revealed so much to me about his own life. I replied that I didn't see how the patient's knowledge of my family could enhance the therapeutic progress, adding the interpretive note that the patient had told me that as a child his mother tried to keep him away from his father's family because she considered them below her social status, and that perhaps his interest in my family was related to some feelings about that part of his history. The patient blew up, saying, "You know, it really pisses me off when you do that. I ask you a simple question, whether you have children or not, and you give me this horseshit about my fucking mother and all this psychology crap. For crying out loud, why can't you be direct with me like you ask me to be with you or with anybody else?"

Patients often come for treatment because they are unable to maintain adequate interpersonal relationships that allow them to express their emotionality; or even when they do express their feelings, they bring them out in the most inappropriate manner. Many patients complain that they cannot *control* their emotional expression, let alone its content. The net result is usually inappropriate behavior with disastrous consequences: instead of getting closer to someone whose company they crave, they manage to alienate themselves. Instead of dealing with an employer in a manner that increases chances for advancement, they find themselves looking for another job. Instead of developing social relationships, they create obstacles to meeting others. It soon becomes clear that the need to control what one feels, when to feel it, or with whom, creates serious difficulties. Openness and spontaneity are needed for the genuine experiencing of any feeling, such as empathy, sadness, hurt, joy, longingness and sharing—and they are prerequisites for authentic interpersonal communication. Any attempt at controlling these feelings, mostly for fear of rejection and ultimate threat of separation, arouses ego defensive operations that stand in the way of meaningful and satisfying expression of emotionality. Distortions in the expression of emotionality thus become unconsciously patterned in the service of defending a frightened and insecure self.

The above example is a case in point. The patient's reactions to me were typical of the way such patterns operate. For instance, although he consciously knew from past experience that I would not answer such a request, he insisted on asking the question. There was no doubt that he had an unconscious agenda, to prove over and over that his mother had rejected him (repeated here in the transferential situation), and that there must have been something detestable about his father's family (also represented in the transferential situation—his need to know about my family), as his mother so often taught him. His emotional ties to his mother, who had utter contempt for her husband and had always openly communicated it to the patient, reinforced in him an indentification with his father that was mostly negative (lacking in self-worth). His father's passivity highlighted his mother's disdain, which further added to his reservoir of self-negation. Had I answered this particular question directly and immediately, I would have undoubtedly lost an invaluable opportunity to help the patient learn to separate fantasy from reality, i.e., his transferential reactions from his "real" ones.

As it happened, the strategy worked well. As the session proceeded, the patient acknowledged my "right" not to give him any information related to my family because the patient was there for himself. Yet he could not understand why he blew up. I asked him about his father's family, whatever little he knew. "I wish I could tell you," he said with a big sigh. "When my father died (about 10 years earlier, when the patient was about 24), I wanted to visit his cousin, because he lived with my father when they were growing up. I knew he could tell me a lot about him, but my mother convinced me that he was too sick for a visit—he was suffering from emphysema. So I didn't." (Here the patient remained silent for a minute, looked down at the floor, and started to cry quietly.) "My father wanted to talk to me so many times, but I was always running with my friends, and I never had time for him. I know that he wanted to open up to me, but I was always afraid, I don't know why. I wish I knew more about his childhood. We don't even have any pictures. I took the kids to camp on Sunday, and on the way back I was crying so much I couldn't see ahead of me. And I know it wasn't my kids. I remembered how my father once took me fishing, and he told me about his father—my grandfather. I never met him—he died in the old country—and he was so sad, I knew that he felt sad about his father, and I wanted to put my arms around him but I couldn't, I just couldn't. Oh, God, I miss him (*sobs for awhile*). Maybe you're right. Maybe I am angry at myself for not getting closer to my father and I was taking it out on you. . . ."

The original interpretation about his wish to know more about his own family was, in a sense, also a confrontation, which prompted him to express genuine feelings of sadness and loss in the presence of another person (myself), without being punished. He also began to learn to separate fantasy from reality, in this case his own defensive anger, related to past objects (especially his mother), from the present reality of his relationship with me as his therapist. In the relatively short time he had been in treatment, the patient had learned enough to analyze the confrontations himself with very little help.

This case history is rather typical of what one encounters in therapeutic settings, with the typical transferential reactions and the techniques used to deal with them. The usual confrontational, interpretive, and/or supportive procedures are generally helpful in expanding the patient's awareness regarding the expression of his emotionality, as well as pointing the way to modifying distortions that interfere with satisfactory interpersonal relationships. Often, however, certain neurotic patients display such extreme expressions of emotionality in a consistent manner that they require therapeutic techniques and strategies that deviate from the typical ones. The "wait and see" attitude that some therapists adopt in such situations is often extremely costly to the patient, both emotionally and financially, and does not bring about the desired changes. And since the patient does not show any significant change, the therapist then attributes the responsibility of the failure to the patient, by labelling him as having a "character disorder," which by definition is hard to change. However, assuming that the patient does have a character disorder, and is therefore not amenable to quick change, the therapist must take the responsibility for being the flexible one and modify his procedures to suit the patient's needs.

In the following few sections distortions in the experience

and expression of emotionality in interpersonal situations that require significant changes of approach on the part of the therapist will be discussed. While the cases illustrating these issues may seem typical, they occur frequently enough to cause, at times, some feelings of futility, if not despair, on the therapist's part. Psychotherapy has failed to help patients whose emotionality is inappropriately utilized by the self more than any other group, even though this category seems to be a major one in the population at large.

This group is arbitrarily divided into three subgroups for purposes of investigation and clarification. Those who (1) exhibit extreme feelings of hostility, detachment, aggressivity, and self-righteousness; (2) exhibit extreme feelings of "love," deference, and submission; or (3) alternate their behavior ambivalently, between the above two categories.

Extreme Negative Emotionality in Interpersonal Communication

Negative feelings are motivated by a multitude of factors, and their expression takes on a variety of forms in different people. Indeed, even one person often manifests angry or hostile feelings in many ways. However, most people are likely to develop consistent patterns of expressing such feelings. A great number of patients come for treatment because they feel continuously negative, and thus wish to change. Others do not seek help until, at some point just before they call for an appointment, they react explosively to an innocuous incident, and consequently recognize their reaction as unreasonable, irrational, or even dangerous, thus requiring the immediate attention of an expert. Yet, notwithstanding such a revelation, these patients tend to continue the same behavior patterns, which can be easily discernible in the therapeutic situation. The goals of treatment for these problems are to reduce the irrational reaction of anger to a minimum, to channel the energy invested in the "hate factory" to other, more constructive enterprises, and to help the patient develop a wider range of emotional reactivity.

Additional issues related to the dynamics and treatment of the angry self are discussed in conjunction with the case history of Marlene, a 39-year-old woman who came for treatment because, according to her, she felt she had to. "Frankly I don't know why I am here. I am at the end of my rope. Monte (*another patient, who referred her to me*) must have told you what happened last week. I had to talk to somebody and he happened to be there. I could no longer take it. I was like a raving maniac. I threw a pot of stew on the dining room wall. I never do things like that. I mean, violence was never part of my vocabulary. My husband thought I was fit to be tied and put in a strait jacket. He has never seen me like that. I do shout and scream sometimes, but that's all. Luckily nothing happened to me. My hand got a little scratched, but nothing that my dog won't do to me once in awhile." These were Marlene's first words in the initial consultation. They were expressed in a very firm and terse manner. There could have been no doubt about what she felt. It was rage, even during the recount of the story, more than a week after the incident. At the same time, she seemed quite disturbed and in disbelief at what she had done. Following this introduction, she launched a head-on attack against her husband and 13-year-old daughter. Her attack was interspersed with two statements; the first about her husband, the second relating to her daughter: "But I don't want you to get the wrong idea, because Bob is a sweetheart," and "Jackie can be a wonderful girl." She told me that Bob was "deader than a door knob" when it came to the subject of interpersonal communication. He would not initiate a conversation, and often would not respond at all to her questions or statements. Needless to say, this was a source of untold frustration to her. She also complained that her daughter "behaves as if I wasn't there most of the time. She just doesn't hear me, or should I say she hears but doesn't listen?" As the initial interview progressed, and in consequent sessions, it became increasingly clear that Marlene believed that her problems were really her husband, her daughter, and her mother. She did realize somewhat that her anger, at times, assumed unreasonable proportions and needed change. But she also felt that she had done everything in her power to make the family life as "cogent and loving" as possible, only to meet with lack of cooperation from the concerned individuals. When I asked her what she felt she had done specifically to improve the interpersonal atmosphere at home, she replied that she had sent her daughter to a psychiatrist for help, and she had worked for her husband's firm for more than two years before her daughter was born. She expressed angry feelings about that period, some 14 years before, because her husband rejected many of her suggestions concerning improvement of his business.

Marlene was the only child of a middle-class, Protestant family, who grew up in a California suburb with all the luxuries that such surroundings can provide. Her father, a successful businessman, died about 10 years after the family moved to New York, when she was about 32 years old. He left his wife substantial financial support. Marlene had very strong positive feelings about him, even though he used to travel at least six months a year for his business. He was, according to her, "an old fashioned man," meaning that he wanted her to always behave like "a lady." In turn, she tried in every possible way to satisfy him by being "the best little girl in town." And that, indeed, she was. She was the first to get up in the morning, the first to prepare breakfast, the first to arrive at school, and the first in her class. She took up extra studies and excelled in them, was able to secure college scholarships on the basis of achievement, not need, and she followed her father's advice and married the man he openly approved.

When she described her mother, Marlene used only negative terms. She thought of her as a nonentity while her husband was alive. She was "pampered, spoiled, and satisfied in every possible way by my father." She was not very demanding, had very little understanding of her husband's business or the social world around her, and had no interest in her daughter's social or academic life. Marlene felt more identified with her father and his interests, although he tried to discourage her from entering the world of business, because he believed that a woman's place was at home, with her family.

During her first few months in treatment, Marlene unloaded a great deal, and almost all her feelings were negative. She rambled and intellectualized and demanded immediate solutions. She was impatient, although she tried to control her dismay during the sessions. She said she felt inadequate intellectually, yet she knew she was a very bright woman; she felt completely and totally undesirable to men, yet she knew she was attractive; she felt sexually frigid and disinterested, yet she longed for physical and sexual attention—at least from her husband; she strove to be a helpful mother, yet she refused to recognize her daughter's needs. Professionally, she felt she was being held back by her inability to decide what goals she wanted to pursue as well as by her bosses, who would not allow her to advance appreciably because she was a woman. But most of all, her emotions were constantly drained by her unhappy dealings with her mother who, after her husband's death, became a demanding, nagging, complaining, unhappy, and hard-to-please woman. She became, according to Marlene, selfish, self-centered, and so jealous of her comforts that she manipulated everyone to cater to her. Marlene became increasingly furious with her, and she occupied much of Marlene's ideational and emotional life. As a result, there was hardly any session during the first few months in which the subject of Marlene's rage at her mother did not surface. She expressed, unhaltingly, bitter hatred toward her mother, and she could not wait for her to die. She said in one session, "The sooner she dies, the better for everyone concerned. I know this sounds terribly cold, but I really don't like her, I can't stand her, and if there wasn't a lot of money involved (*inheritance*) I would have dropped her a long time ago."

In the beginning of treatment, I adopted a general wait-and-see strategy, although at the same time I gave her significant support. Because of her driving hostility toward most of the people around her, and particularly her mother, I decided to wait for a strong positive transference to develop. For one thing, I didn't feel that she'd last too long in treatment if I gave her ammunition with which to lash out at me. I also did not cherish the idea of her turning on me with her incredibly capable tongue, especially if my confrontations were too reminiscent of her mother's demands, and if some of her anger toward her father started to move closer to consciousness. Unlike other cases, where I tended to confront the patient with inconsistencies and distortions fairly early in the therapeutic relationship, Marlene was allowed to carry the ball wherever she wanted, knowing that at some point I had to stop her before things went too far. An example of this strategy is the session transcribed

verbatim below. It took place some three months after Marlene
started therapy on a twice-a-week basis.

P: Did you change your desk over there? Don't tell me it was always that
way? I didn't even notice it. Hey! Just first off, it would appear that I
would have to be in Miami next week, and probably the following week
too. I may also find out tomorrow morning that this thing is all but can-
celled. The Ram's coach keeps changing signals, but at the moment it
would appear those days are out. Fortunately, this is not a big problem
for me. I don't like to be away from home too much, and especially out in
Miami. I don't like Miami. The pressure, uh, oh, my mother's fine. There
was really never anything wrong with mother. As a matter of fact, although she does not believe it, or does not remember it, or does not choose
to remember it, the doctor appeared in her room Friday morning when
she came back from surgery and said to her everything was fine, including
every last little problem that she had had. She thought she had polyps on
her throat, she was sure she had a heart condition—there is nothing
wrong, really nothing wrong. So whatever numbers she chooses to pull
from here on in, healthwise, although she "really" doesn't remember that
he said any of those things, I am fully informed, so in some way that helps
me tremendously. As a matter of fact, by Saturday afternoon, she was
sitting on her bed chirping and talking about other people on the floor,
and ate a lunch that I would have been happy to put away under any other
circumstance, with chocolate cake and all of that, so I figured that's it. So
I figured I did what I thought was right. O.K., by week's end, with all the
pressure from the office and other pressures, by Saturday I become a
screaming banshee, throwing temper tantrums that I hadn't thrown in a
long time. Yelling at everybody—not everybody, Bob and Jackie—and no
way of stopping, and not getting any answer back from them. Up until
that time I was sort of deluding myself, saying that things are sort of
working out, and that the problems in the office, well, that they will work
themselves out if I get enough wisdom to handle them, really surfacing
in all sorts of situations. I began to take a longer range view on things,
and uh, where I am vis-à-vis six months ago, and where I am heading,
because I truly felt that I am no further along now than I was six months
ago in my work, but also emotionally, with my family situation, certainly
has not improved. Jackie, if anything, has stonewalled me totally. Bob,
if anything, he's certainly not responded to my numerous requests for
help in areas that cause friction between us. Certainly if I go back over
the money situation, just helping me by providing information to me on
where exactly we stood so that I could, at least, understand what the
limitations were, how much income he thinks he is going to be producing,
so I can begin to see between this, that, and the other, the fixed expenses,
how much more leeway we have on spending for other things. And it's six
months since I had nagged him about this. And suddenly it dawned on
me, Bob had spoken to me at the office, and he was upset about something
that happened in the office. I couldn't believe that Bob had let himself
become upset by this, that he concentrated on what had happened rather

than making sure that it never happened again, which of course, it is as much criticism of my own approach to things as it is his. And all of a sudden it seemed to me that I shouldn't have been giving Bob advice for things, saying, "but darling whose error was it—it wasn't your error, it's another person's error—and maybe this person shouldn't be working for you." And I am sitting and thinking, I can't do that, I shouldn't do that.

T: You shouldn't do what? What do you mean you *shouldn't*? You mean that you would have liked to have control over Bob's behavior, but you feel you can't and you shouldn't?

P: If Bob *does not want* to do it, Bob *will not* do it, and if I ask Bob to help me rearrange the furniture and Bob doesn't help me, no matter how many times I ask him, Bob is telling me by his not doing it that he does not want to do it. But I am aggravated that it is not done, I feel let down that it's not done, instead of saying to myself that if it's important to me to have it done, I'll have to find a way to do it. Same thing with Jackie. I've tried very consciously—I've sat down with the family and I said, "Listen, our biggest problem, or complaint all year, has been that weekends, we want to spend weekends together. But then when the weekend is over, everyone is very depressed because nothing has happened. Nothing has happened because nobody has planned for the weekend. Instead, what happens is that the three of us become trapped with each other." And if I would like to do this, that, or the other thing, I get shot down because Jackie doesn't want to go to this movie, or Bob has to work in the office, and I have enough work in my briefcase to do to take me until four weeks from now, and I have the marketing to do. Part of this is because I have to get up at quarter to seven on Saturday morning to stand in line in the freezing cold for tickets for the King Tut exhibit, because nobody else would stand in line with you—but *I* want to go to King Tut, so *I* did, I want to go! "What would you like to do with your day, Jackie, when I come back?" Silence. "Jackie, on the way home I passed by a dress store, and they had some pretty dresses, and I had them put a couple on the side for you, would you like to go to try them on?" Well, she doesn't know what they look like. My immediate reaction was: screw it! I mean if I am going to get that kind of an answer from you, why should I go with you, but instead, I said, "They're pretty dresses, dear!" Well I tell you, we went, she tried them on, she got the dresses, never showed them to her father when we got home, and at 10 o'clock, when I finished yelling at everybody, I went into her room and they were still in the bag. Now if *I* had brought home new dresses, I would hang them up right away—but with her! And this is how the afternoon went, even if I made a tactical error, that was her automatic reaction. Everything was doing me a major favor, it lasted the full day. I am very worried about her. She has friends in school, but nobody at home. There is no relief.

The above monologue went on for awhile. Every word was clearly enunciated, even though it came out with the force and speed of machinegun bullets. Marlene was obviously quite distressed, and her anger, triggered off by her frustration in the interaction between herself and her husband and daughter, seemed to have no bounds. Her conflict seemed insurmountable: she kept asking, not in so many words, for support from her family, yet she also kept approaching them in a hostile, demanding, and manipulative manner that only caused more distance, thus denying her the very support she said she needed. This vicious cycle, which created an unsavory, tense atmosphere at home, was constantly fed by two sources: her need for control and her dependence upon others for emotional support. She felt stalemated, and she expressed it during the session, saying, "I try to brighten her (*Jackie's*) day, I try to dance around Bob, and in the long run I am so exhausted from everything, and so worried about how I am going to achieve other things, and taking a look at my longer range career situation, which is right back where it was before. I am still doing the same kind of work. It's crazy, *nothing is happening with me,* and the frustration is really stifling." She was obviously still waiting for changes in others to affect changes in her.

With all this, I was weighing the pros and cons of intervention and silence. However, since my "trial balloon" of asking her about her need to control her husband had failed, I decided to wait longer, because she was still pouting and engulfed by her violent anger. I felt that any intervention at that point would be lost, and would endanger my effectiveness later. In a way I wished that my silence would be felt not in the manner she perceived other people's—i.e., as a rejection—but rather as a support for her right to be heard, something she kept emphasizing constantly. As the volume of her voice rose, I became visibly more curious about her plight in a *nonverbal* communicative technique ranging from simple shaking of the head up and down, in recognition and understanding, to leaning over in the chair to be physically closer to the patient for concretized support when she was most defensive. As the session continued, I had the impression that Marlene was shedding her resistance slightly by admitting, at least intellectually, that she was losing control and that she was ready to hear what I had to say.

T: I can fully appreciate how difficult all this is to you. It seems to me that your life is so full of activities, inside and outside—I mean inside your head—that there is no enjoyment and no time for pleasure.

P: That's exactly it. There is no time for anything. Having a private life with Bob, with her going to bed pretty late every nite, 11 or 12 o'clock, doesn't leave us any time.

T: Any time for what?

P: Well, any time for intimacy. No time for making love or anything else. The net result of this is that before Jackie came back from camp, until this weekend, Bob didn't even touch me. That leaves me feeling, um, um, so alarmed at my feelings—at my anger, at my frustration. And my mother—well forget it, her manipulations, as you know, the fact that I am not with her day and night—she makes clear that she is "so understanding," but that I am such a crumb, that I finally said to Bob, "I am just trying not to be such a frigid bitch." And that's the end of the whole thing (*starts crying with a great deal of control*). I don't know what I am talking about, I am so confused! I tell you, when I get angry (*stops crying and regains her composure*), when I get angry (*clasps hands explosively*) within two minutes I have forgotten my words. They are gone! I find it frightening, and I don't want to live that way. I ended Saturday night at 11 o'clock yelling, "I hate it here! I can't live like this!"

Marlene went on describing how after such an upheaval, everyone concerned "behaved" themselves the next day, especially how lovely Jackie was, and how attentive Bob was. I was interested in finding out how she felt about all this, and especially in finding out how she communicated her displeasure to her husband for not spending enough time with her, since she complained to me about his spending Saturdays in the office.

T: Have you told him what you're telling me?

P: I tell him all this, the other day . . .

T: What did you tell him?

P: He didn't deny it. He ignores all this, he doesn't fire it back, none of this comes back.

T: Did you put it in the form of a passing statement, or did you ask him directly?

P: It was not a direct question, it was a statement. Well he said that some of this, that I am over-exaggerating some of this. Sometimes I make outlandish statements, I mean if they are outlandish I would like him to say, "woops—cut!" Bob does not get angry back at me. Now I can tell you that he kept being around me Sunday night—can I bring you some brandy, and this and that and the other thing. But I don't want that, damn it! I don't want *good behavior!* I feel awful that I behave like a bitch and I get good behavior. I don't want to conduct my life this way. I don't realize the depth of my anger! A few weeks ago I told you I was blocked in my creativity. I haven't made much progress. I am blocked in other areas too.

I feel very proud of myself—I think I finally heard your message that I can't conduct Bob's life, but I would like to have some honesty from Bob.

T: Honesty?

P: Well, I needed a figure from Bob, and if he doesn't want to give it to me, he should tell me. He just doesn't say anything.

T: It sounds to me like you want something from him, and you keep asking for the wrong thing.

P: What do you mean? Well, yes, something, what do you mean?

T: I have the impression that you want to ask him for emotional support.

P: (*Teary, almost choking:*) I guess that does wrap it up!

T: Can you try to open it up, open the wrappings?

P: Well, my thought Saturday night was, what the hell do I need this for? I mean, if it comes down to purely income, if this is a definition of love, this is surely not a marriage. I am using him as a service company. "Darling, I am going to be with my boss all day, can you please arrange to get some flowers up to the hospital for my mother?" "My service corporation dear, it's Friday, can you go to the bank and get some money for the weekend?" "On the way home, dear, can you pick up five bananas?" I don't know what's there. You know, I hate to look at it, really there is no excitement in the marriage. I find myself saying, I don't like being a wife to this, or a mother to that, and I don't like living in that apartment, what am I coming down to—only to be within myself? When I went to that conference in Chicago—I told you about it—last month, a couple of very handsome and successful men made very obvious passes at me, but with all my craziness and confusion, I didn't want to have anything to do with it—I know it's not a solution, not even temporary. Well, the only way I seem to express love these days is to say, "I love you, but, goddamn it, I seem to be yelling at you lately. So please understand that I love you?" If somebody behaved in such an angry way all the time and yelled at me that they loved me, I wouldn't quite believe that they do! But Bob sometimes behaves like he did Sunday, like a sweetheart, and maybe he loves me, but he is not giving me his emotional support!

T: What about your feelings? Aside from your anger, are there any other feelings about Bob?

P: I guess so. But you know, other than washing the dishes once in a while, there is no sharing of experience. I try to do that, but nothing comes back.

T: What kind of an effort do *you* make to share experiences?

P: I try to have time available for the two of us to spend together, with my rigid schedule.

T: What specifically do you do to be available?

P: Well, I think what it boils down to is to find something outside of the home to participate in, going to a restaurant. . . . So Friday night, ten minutes before we have to leave to go to the restaurant, Jackie's still in jeans, and I say to her we're going to a fancy restaurant, wear a skirt, and she's angry.

T: It's hard for you to stay away from complaining. (*She shakes her head in agreement.*) What about the sharing of experiences, of feelings, without going out?

P: At home? Not very much. I don't know, Jackie would rather watch television, and during meals at home there are strictly 20 minutes shared time. I am sure I am giving very negative feelings at home.

T: What are these feelings?

P: Tired, preoccupied, end-of-the day feelings. Bob might wash the dishes, and then I go to my desk and work there, and if I say "so long" to the briefcase—sure, I've never done that! You know, now that you're asking, I've never done that! And on the theory. . . . Well, I am just wondering how much I am blaming everybody else. I guess I am doing just that much of the time. Maybe if I showed Bob that I am interested in making love, maybe things would change. But I always wait for him to approach me, and I guess since I am so angry most of the time, he doesn't do that.

T: It's not really clear to me—do you want to be with Bob?

P: Truthfully? I wouldn't know what it's like to be with him. I never really gave it a chance. I am constantly fighting something or other, and it always comes out with him.

T: Tell me more about what does happen when you are together.

P: I can't recall when we really sat and talked about things, and it's, it does not happen. I mean he wanted to discuss some things a couple of times— I remember very clearly I kind of brushed him aside. We just seem to have office talk. And I find myself sometimes trying to listen to his suggestions, because I know he has a lot of experience, and he has a very sound and clear mind especially about things you might call experience in life in general, and my resentment builds up and I start to argue with him, from the minute go. He doesn't like to tell me things about himself anymore because he is afraid I'll start arguing with him, so he is silent most of the time. I am afraid I killed what could have been, or could have developed into a sound relationship, by my being so concentrated on my needs and interests, which I could never satisfy by being turned off to Bob (*cries*). I want to change that. I want to change it. I feel I hurt him enough—I mean, I know he's got his own problems, but I know I have been living within my own world, even though I blame everybody else.

T: It looks to me as though you were trying to communicate to him and he to you, but both of you are standing on two sides of one-way mirrors waving to each other without seeing each other, and as a result not getting the right feedback. I suppose your anger makes it difficult for you to reach out honestly to him, since you get no reinforcement from him.

P: I don't know if I can really be honest with him now. I hurt him so much with my ever-pouring anger that I can't see how he can stand me. I used to be able to justify my feelings to myself, and I still try, but I know, at least in my head, that Bob has very little to do with my anger. I wish I could erase all the horrible stuff I did. I don't know how to do it.

T: Not being honest certainly doesn't seem to have helped in the past.

P: I know, but it's still so hard for me to just not be so angry.

Marlene's case illustrates rather clearly a certain category of patients whose emotionality is expressed mainly through the interpersonal channel. She demonstrated to me and to herself that every single feeling she had, be it sexual, intellectual, creative, or physical, was tied to her relationships with immediate others. It was also obvious that her angry orientation, which was so intertwined with her ego, her physiognomy, indeed her whole style of conduct, was the result of a great deal of hurt after being (feeling) "obliterated" as a separate individual by her parents, especially her father, who insisted on molding her into a "perfect specimen of a lady." She developed an "armor" to protect herself from additional hurt, and insisted on keeping every ounce of control to ward off anything that looked like, or smelled like what her parents wanted her to be—a nice little girl. Yet, in many ways, because of her great need for dependence, she had to be that nice little girl, at least in her unconscious strivings. Her phobic reaction to the world around her was chronic, and began to emerge in her late teens. However, she was able to keep her "disposition" under control for a very long time, even though she was often viewed by others as a "strict" person. The incident that brought her into treatment was only the smoke that signalled the inner turmoil.

This type of patient raises crucial issues for the therapist, mainly issues related to strategy and technique. This is not the "average" patient, where one can safely say that the best strategy would be to follow the "terrain," and every now and then, when the opportunity presents itself, to dig deeper. The terrain, the top layer of the patient's personality, is too sharp, with too many pitfalls, to be treated with ordinary techniques. However, technique must be suited to the specific goals of a patient, and in the case of Marlene, the goals were to get rid of the irrational anger, to learn to share feelings with her immediate family, and to become more creative as a professional. While these goals seemed quite reasonable, Marlene's "character armor" was so thick that any therapist would have doubts about the possibility of reaching them. What, then, should the therapist aim for? The patient's anger cannot be entirely or even significantly removed from her personality structure. It has become too organically tied to her self-concept. Nevertheless, the chances of diverting some of the energy invested in this mode of emotionality into other channels, such as creativity in her professional life, existed to a certain degree. Learning to share a wider range of feelings and experiences with the family could be attained as soon as her angry stance changed somewhat and she learned to accept some responsibility for her contribution to the disturbed family interaction. The preceding illustration proved that the patient reached such an insight, albeit an intellectual rather than an emotional one. However, since it occurred in conjunction with the expression of her need for emotional support, there was hope that some deeper understanding and realignment of energy could follow. Developing flexible, creative ways of growing professionally could not be therapeutically assessed at the time, simply because it was dependent on other developments, and was also relatively little discussed. This goal was not very clear either to the patient or to me, although it was discussed in general terms.

Strategies and techniques must take into account the important factors related to both chronicity of the character traits and the symptomatology emanating from them, as well as the availability of ego strengths that might be enlisted in the service of therapeutic work. The type of patient discussed in this section is generally very sensitive to any comment of the therapist, especially when such comments relate directly to the patient. The therapist must therefore wait until the patient becomes comfortable enough to hear what he might perceive as negative criticism without having to escape from treatment. The pressure that necessarily results from any confrontation is likely to be too threatening for the chronically hostile patient, and therefore all confrontations in the beginning of the therapeutic relationship must be presented in the form of clarifying probes, rather than inescapable juxtapositions of conflicts.

This strategy also affords the therapist the opportunity to study the patient who gives very little emotionally—except for the anger—in the beginning, because of his vulnerability. At the same time, the therapist must be firm and consistent, because the patient's need for control is so great that he may attempt to take charge of the sessions, and, if successful, is likely to leave treatment. This stance should not exclude flexibility by the therapist, but too much flexibility may be interpreted as weakness and incompetence. As therapy progresses, flexibility must become the order of the day, at times even at the therapist's "expense" or "sacrifice." The nature of confrontations that follow the beginning, probing ones must change to include insistence on specificity and accountability, forcing more introspection and an honest search for the motives that propel the hostile orientation. Many patients, like Marlene, are highly intelligent, and speak so fluently and convincingly about their perceptions that they might create an illusion of imparting new information or of providing information that is totally objective and related to fact. Often a gentle request for specificity helps such patients become more aware of their own participation in producing whatever affects they complain about, thus recognizing how their own feelings are (ego-syntonically) attached to their behavior. These are the first steps toward converting some of these ego-syntonic patterns into ego-alien ones. Eventually, the patient becomes more open to the origins of his feelings— namely, that they come from within rather than from the outside world—at which time the therapist can confront the patient with his inconsistencies and conflicts. This three-step confrontation strategy is essential if some crack is to be made in the very difficult characterological distortions expressed through such interpersonal emotionality.

Considering the need for detachment and self-righteousness in these patients, who are, no doubt, "superego casualties," the therapist must be extra-sensitive to their emotional needs, because they do not exhibit such needs overtly and readily. Language must be geared to helping the patient let down his guard toward becoming less self-critical and self-punishing. A concrete example of how the therapist might handle such situations involves a young man in his early 20's from an orthodox Jewish background, who was in treatment because of moderate depression, difficulties in social relationships, especially devastating passivity with regard to women, and a Machiavellian control of his parents (with whom he was living) so far as religion was concerned. On one session he went on and on complaining about the girls in college, whom he constantly referred to as "whores" and "dumcopfs" (thick, stupid), and maintained that he was so nauseated by them that he could no longer even look at them. He described in detail what he thought they did to seduce men, students and professors alike, and how the world of academia, the places of higher learning, were becoming nothing more than legitimatized institutions of ill-repute. When I felt that he had gone far enough with this barrage, I leaned over, looked the patient directly in the eyes, and said, "You'd like to fuck each and every one of them, wouldn't you?" The patient first went into what looked like an emotional shock, then became visibly disturbed, blushed, and, finally, looking down on the floor with a sheepish smile, replied with a big "yeah" and a sigh of relief. With this direct interpretive confrontation, the pretense and utter indignation, and the need to be socially detached because of an immense flooding of emotionally charged sexual fantasies almost evaporated. His approach toward women became almost abruptly aggressive, although often quite inappropriate. However, he needed this very shock to move into a position opposite to his traditional one, if only to experience something new, which he could eventually modify to suit his real needs.

The use of strong emotional language can be extremely beneficial when the patient's conflict is between severe superego and blocked impulses. This is an important technical tool that the therapist can use *judiciously* with similar cases. As a matter of fact, if the patient's parental introjects are extremely rigid, ungiving, detached, inordinately serious, and generally uncommunicative, then the therapist's strategy and behavior during the treatment must be exactly the opposite, naturally with appropriate timing. The one-sided, rigid, often unpleasant interpersonal expression of emotionality in this category of patients requires extreme flexibility, and the use of a variety of techniques and strategies on the part of the therapist, because the therapist must, in many ways, represent an alternative, a second chance, someone for the patient to consider as a model. For the patient, the therapist becomes the new parent, the new source from whom new identities, new directions, and new channels of expression emerge.

Another important problem that such patients often bring with them is their need for achievement. They are ready to practically demolish anything and anyone who stands in the way of their achievement. They have an insatiable need to accumulate medals. This need for achievement and their negative emotionality usually puts them in an extremely precarious position with friends, because trust, intimacy, loyalty—the ingredients, indeed the musts, for close friendships—are all secondary to the achievement motive. Their emotional life becomes consumed with competitiveness and the accumulation of "piles of approval." However, since these are never-ending, never perfect, never enough, they become extremely frustrated and emotionally impoverished. The therapist must help the patient become more benevolent toward his own self, and more reasonable with his irrational need to conquer the world with achievements. The techniques used for this purpose vary, and range from the analytic-interpretive ones used with the patient who needs to please his parents by producing a lot, to the extremely confrontational ones that force the patient to emotionally recognize the irrational component and let go of it. It goes without saying that any technique must be designed to ultimately lead to the crucial awareness of the roots of this defensive need for achievement, namely, the patient's dependency, as well as the roots of the aggressive and hostile emotionality, most probably, the patient's deep narcissistic injury.

Extreme Positive Emotionality in Interpersonal Communication

Many patients enter psychotherapy with positive feelings and hopes of change. Such an attitude often contributes a great deal to the success of the therapeutic work, especially in the beginning. Not all such patients, however, find their therapist likeable or acceptable. Some continue with the same therapist and never resolve these feelings; others leave. There are those, however, who enter treatment and quickly become enamored of their therapist, with extremely strong positive feelings and without any reservations about his or her "powers." The therapist can do no wrong—this inappropriate, consuming positive transference soon becomes a rather difficult situation between patient and therapist. This is not what is sometimes called "psychotic transference;" these are neurotic patients who manifest positive emotionality interpersonally, and specifically toward the therapist, in ways that create a type of resistance requiring special, sometimes "devious" techniques and strategy.

This category normally contains fewer patients. Notwithstanding the popular belief that all patients "fall in love" with their analyst, there are very few who do; although many, perhaps most, develop certain positive, even loving feelings toward him. This category illustrates how confrontation analysis understands and deals with the interpersonal manifestations of extreme positive emotionality. The dynamics and accompanying symptomatology of this group of patients varies a great deal, although there seem to be a number of common dimensions that they all share. The most prominent is, of course, the one they share with all other people, namely, dependency. Needless to say, in this category the dependency is quite extreme. The depth, tenacity, and intensity of the dependency is at times overwhelming, both within the therapeutic situation and outside of it. These patients always find themselves looking for someone to approve of their choices in every aspect of life, rarely trusting their own judgments or preferences. Priority lists do not exist for them—these are determined by what is acceptable to others—hence they keep changing their mind about what they want, like, or hate according to who happens to be their favorite mother or father figure at a particular time. While these patients share this dimension, and can be helped to become aware of it and its ramifications for their life, overcoming *extreme* dependency is one of the most frustrating problems in this field, and its success varies markedly from patient to patient.

Another characteristic shared by patients in this category is the tendency to infantilize their interpersonal relationships. The quality of their communications, the actual overt messages, are often clearly infantile in content and structure, and are recognized as such by the subject. Nevertheless, there is a tendency to deny the symbolic importance of these messages in the functioning of the total self, and these patients do not see that their communications are inappropriate. Rather, they often treat them as cherished idiosyncracies, which they feel contribute to their uniqueness. A typical example is that of a young man in treatment who revealed, readily and boastingly, that he often played children's games with his girlfriend. They would talk baby talk for an entire evening, and would pretend that she was his sister, and that she was two years old and he was eight. The severe disturbance in this area is in the need to be treated as a child and the use of various maneuvers that the patient learns to ensure being so treated. An intelligent and "worldly" man used to always telephone his father for advice on what to say to a woman on a date, what to wear, where to go. He would get into a panic whenever the father's plan failed to work, and yet he would not let go of this habit. His transferential reactions to me manifested themselves through incessant questioning as to whether he was doing the right thing in treatment, saying the right words, having the correct attitude, etc.

A peculiar characteristic of this group is a certain amount of what might be perceived as snobbism. It may seem incongruent for a submissive, dependent, infantile patient to be a snob. However, many of these patients have a need to express, and to feel consciously, a degree of superiority over other people. This is expressed through disapproval of others, and through overtly comparing themselves favorably with them, while at the same time denigrating them. Of course, from a dynamic point of view this may be seen as a reaction formation, but this defense is least expected in these patients because of the general meekness and feelings of submission that characterize them. One rather homely looking young woman refused to socialize with her colleagues because they were, according to her, "the ugliest bunch of people you ever saw," and "I would be ashamed to be seen with them at a party." At the same time, she felt she was the "ugliest girl" she knew, splitting and completely dissociating these two feelings from each other. She could not explain the discrepancy, although intellectually she believed that her feelings were incongruous.

Another frequent phenomenon among this patient group, where extreme positive emotionality is focused within interpersonal relationships, is the inordinately sexualized transference toward the therapist—for both men and women. In women, the most obvious manifestation is their direct expression of a wish to have a sexual relationship with the male therapist, while the least obvious one is the lack of discussion of sexuality altogether during the sessions. Some female patients openly invite the therapist to have an affair, and continue incessantly in their efforts to seduce him for the purpose of changing the relationship from a therapeutic to a romantic one. The more adamant the therapist is about keeping the initial contract, the more clinging, dependent, "loving," and inappropriately demonstrative they become. A 35-year-old married woman told me in one of her sessions that she could not stand the thought of not having me as her lover. Every time she faced me during the session she felt blocked and could not think about anything else but her love for me. After some discussion, I decided to ask her to use the couch so that she wouldn't face me. She agreed to try it, and indeed for a couple of weeks she was able to discuss feelings and problems not directly related to her dependence on me. However, soon she began to act out nonverbally and perhaps semiconsciously, in that she appeared for her sessions with lowcut dresses and slit skirts, thus exposing much of her breasts and thighs. Her insistence on seducing me was detrimental to the therapeutic situation, but it did, at the same time, concretize her basic conflicts in the therapeutic setting. It was not until she was absolutely convinced that her inappropriateness would not achieve what she was striving for that she let go of it—very slowly, and with occasional reenactments.

There are also patients whose sexual submission can only be detected from the lack of sexual references in sessions. These patients behave like little boys and girls who have something on their minds but are determined to keep it a secret until it is pulled out of them, placing them in a position of humility and deference. In these cases the therapist's insistence on bringing up the subject of sexuality in its various manifestations is usually the strategy of choice, for otherwise whatever transpires during the sessions is only a smokescreen for their genuine emotionality, which hides behind the strong "clandestine" sexual-dependent transference.

The male patients' sexual transference toward the male therapist is often manifested in a way that is similar to a female patient who does not discuss sexuality during the sessions. While the dynamics in both cases are similar—namely the fear of disapproval for having powerful, inappropriate feelings toward the taboo figure (the therapist-parent)—the male patient also worries about sexual competition with the male therapist on a purely sexual level and therefore attempts to avoid the whole issue. Many such patients have had extremely domineering fathers who did not allow them to exercise their own judgment as they were maturing, and nagging, demanding mothers, whose love never significantly touched the patient. There are also patients in this category who grew up with powerful fathers who gave some attention to their children but only out of guilt rather than as an expression of genuine affection. In the therapeutic situation, the patient perceives the therapist as both parents, whom he tries to satisfy, and not knowing which way to turn first, he keeps his feelings of sexuality to himself, attempting to avoid the wrath of either parent. Thus the therapist is, on the one hand, feared and admired, loved and submitted to, and on the other hand, he is perceived as untrustworthy and selfish. Most of these feelings are deeply unconscious.

Another category of male patients who readily express their emotionality through sexual dependency on the therapist are the homosexuals. These patients often become very explicit yet quite detached about their sexual activities, and they directly challenge the therapist to join them through these exhibitionist-seductive journeys. The placating, inappropriate submissiveness of the homosexual patient is only one symptom of his difficulties in expressing positive emotionality in a genuine manner, through an interpersonal relationship. The female therapist encounters similar issues with male and female patients.

These are only some of the characteristics of such patients. However, these are important dimensions, and ones that psychotherapy finds technically challenging.

For example, Lynn was a 32-year-old single woman who came to therapy because she was depressed and suffered from a number of psychosomatic symptoms, such as frequent rashes on her neck and chest, occasional eruptions of psoriasis covering many areas of her body, fairly frequent headaches, and occasional vaginal irritations unrelated to any known physical cause, and eluding medical treatment. Turning to psychotherapy for help was not an easy decision for her, since her family, to whom she was emotionally still very attached, looked down upon it. This included, significantly, her older brother, who was a physician, and supposedly more liberal minded than her parents.

Lynn's childhood and adolescent years were described by her as a waste because they were spent in the service of her family. Females were not valued in that family, and were relegated to the role of "maids." This, indeed, was her self-image, an image acquired very early, and reinforced by parents who always praised Lynn's two older brothers, who were apparently highly gifted intellectually. Lynn was occasionally admired for her striking beauty as a child. However, she developed various physical problems that only aggravated and negated any positive feedback. She was a very skinny young girl, partially because of a lack of appetite, which seemed to have developed as a reaction to an irrational fear that she would be accused of impoverishing the family by eating too much. She was always seen as a burden to the family—a belief reinforced by her mother, who never bought new clothes for her but always managed to obtain used clothes from others in the family. Lynn chronically perceived herself as "stupid, ugly, and disgusting," and she decided, with her family's full encouragement, to leave school at the age of 16 to go to work to help the family financially. Actually, her father's business was doing well, and the family was additionally helped by her brother who, by that time, was contributing significantly from his budding medical practice. Lynn had no illusions about going to college: she felt she would never be admitted, let alone make the grade.

Lynn obtained a job as a receptionist for a large company, and within a couple of years became a versatile and competent secretary. Her boss liked her work, and helped her advance through learning secretarial skills. Her life centered around pleasing him. Aside from her fear of displeasing him, she developed a crush on him, and soon after her promotion to the level of secretary (a position her family was "proud of" because they had never believed she could learn to do anything beyond washing dishes), she began to have an affair with him, a married man with a number of children. This affair lasted for almost 6 years. Lynn remembered these years as the most painful in her life, for she felt completely bound to this man, who would lose interest in her for many weeks at a time when he would be engaged in other extramarital affairs. She felt totally powerless and out of control. On the few occasions when she confronted him, he managed to soothe her with loving words and promises of future dreams together. However, this man's wife discovered the affair and left him, and very shortly after his split with his wife, he terminated the relationship with Lynn, both personally and professionally. Having saved enough money during this affair, she was able to move to New York City, where she felt she could start a new life, and where she would be, at least geographically, separated from her family.

However, once settled in the big city, Lynn's life experiences assumed an amazingly repetitive pattern, similar to the one she thought she had left behind. This pattern consisted of easily finding jobs, becoming sexually involved either with her boss or another man in the company, and then having to leave because of intolerable anxiety and tension created by the situation. After several years of this merry-go-round, she began to experience increasingly longer bouts of depression with parallel psychosomatic symptoms. Her decision to seek help was, in a sense, prescribed by her physician, although she had entertained the idea before his recommendation.

Lynn walked into the office for her first visit with typical symptoms of depression. She kept on her heavy coat, her handbag clenched in her hand, her head down while talking, her speech slow and interspersed by many silences and tears. She related the story of her life with a great deal of pain and resignation, and she looked at me from time to time for signs of approval, or at least, attentiveness. Her soft voice, occasional smile, and attractive features made it perfectly clear how she could easily win the hearts of men. Her passive-aggressive orientation, often whining and phlegmatic in character, could be detected only much later, primarily because of her ability to mask it so well with her pain, resignation, and constant self-deprecation. In a few weeks, however, and interesting transferential pattern began to emerge. She made several comments about the office furniture, my clothing, my personality, my looks, and finally how well I fitted the ideal image of a man she admired, revered, and even "could" love. My words to her were always received as if they were pearls of wisdom. Parallel to this manifestation of great "adoration," her complaints about her life, especially about her family and the men she chose to involve herself with, increased. It seemed pretty clear that her self-destructive behavior was being acted out within the therapeutic situation. During the 13th session she told me that a man she had been dating was treating her very poorly. I wondered aloud, at some point in the beginning of the session, whether she had done something to encourage this behavior on his part. As usual, she immediately agreed, and added that she must have hurt him in some way, and that he was probably reacting to the hurt she had inflicted on him. Here is part of the exchange that followed:

P: If I knew how he was going to take it, I would have never said anything to Dina about joining us. I never believed that our relationship meant so much to him that he would be so hurt if we went out with my girlfriend on Saturday night. I just don't know what I mean to him and what he means to me, how I hurt him and how he hurts me.

T: What exactly happened?

P: Why does he treat me so badly? I just don't understand. Everything was so nice in the beginning, he was so considerate. There is nothing I do now that he doesn't criticize. Saturday night we were going to eat out, and he suggested that we go to a local restaurant down the street so that we could have more time to be together. I thought it was a good idea, but as we were leaving, the phone rang and it was Dina. When I told her we were going to have dinner at the restaurant, she asked if she could join us with her husband Bert. I said yes without even thinking about it because I haven't seen her and Bert for awhile. I can't tell you how that enraged Alan. He was so furious, he just didn't have enough sarcastic words to throw my way, and he said he was fed up with my lack of interest in him, and that he was sure we'd end up spending the whole evening with them. I can't understand how being with other people, especially good friends, takes anything away from him. I don't complain when we go to his tennis parties and we waste, at least I waste, a whole evening talking to people I don't want to look at. I just think he is jealous of my friendship with Dina and Bert, especially with Bert. Bert is just a good friend—I don't have anything romantic with him. Every time I want to be with other people, he doesn't like it.

T: What about his "hurt" business—who's hurting who?

P: He told me I hurt him, and I believe I did—I know I did—otherwise I can't see why he would be so angry at me. You know, you're right, I did something to hurt him, but I am not aware of it. So far as Saturday night, I was just being sociable. It's no skin off his hide if some friends eat with us at a restaurant!

T: I am not sure you're convinced you hurt him. But it looks like you felt you had to agree with me when I mentioned the possibility you might have contributed something to his reaction.

P: But you *were* right—when you mentioned that, it dawned on me that I probably hurt him by not asking his consent about my friends joining us. But again, he was right there, he could have said no. He just got mad. . . . But now that I think about it, maybe I didn't really want to be with him alone, because he always wants to be alone, he never wants to go out, he never wants to do anything outside of the house. My father was just like that. Always in the house and watching the matches or football, and I couldn't do a thing that might disturb him. I certainly couldn't bring any girlfriends home during the weekend (*starts to cry*). I don't know why I do these things. I really feel I am rotten. I get the feeling inside of me that I am to blame for everything. I wish I knew why I keep hurting people. So my father was rotten, why should I take it out on Alan?

T: You know you keep saying that you're always hurting people, and yet you always seem to be hurt yourself. It seems that the same thing went on in your family. They hurt you and you hurt them back!

P: You know, while I was lying in bed with Alan on Saturday I was thinking how it would feel freed of all this. I was just thinking about how much you helped me to start looking and digging and understanding. I lived in a fog all my life. I am trying to educate myself in this area. I know I still have a long way to go. I remember when I was living at home, it was just miserable, when I came back from work, I went up to my room, and everything was just miserable, everything was in disarray. My brother had been there, and he went through all my correspondence. I was just livid, but when I started to scream and carry on, my mother said that I had no right to speak about my brother that way, or to make such a big fuss because, after all, there was nothing so important about my life that needed such secrecy. Maybe she was right, but I can't accept the fact that I am such a little person! Or even worse, a nobody!

T: Whatever your family says, goes. You accept whatever they say as the truth, and the only truth—just like here, whatever I say to you becomes like the word of God.

P: Not exactly. I don't think I am such a goodie-goodie. But maybe your're right, because I was also thinking this weekend why I have this obsession to be so good. Ever since I remember I always turned the other cheek, I never fought back. I used to believe in God, and I always prayed to Him and said I'll be good. I don't know how I can get rid of this curse? I am always afraid to stop being wishy-washy. It's not so easy. Really, I am still in a fog, and whenever I try to be strong, I get discouraged by all the physical things I get, like this itch I have in my vagina. It started on Friday, and it's driving me crazy. It's acting up right now. And the treatment for it is so expensive, they inject some powder and jelly. I get it usually before my period, but this time it's after my period. Do you think it's psychosomatic or whatever?

T: I thought that's what your gynecologist told you, and maybe it's also related to the treatment here in some way.

P: I know I get all kinds of feelings here, but do you really think this (*points to pubic area*) itch is also related to my coming here? I mean I had it before I started therapy. In fact, that's what got me here.

T: What I meant was that your need to be so good and nice keeps your other feelings from coming out into the open, and perhaps they come out in the form of your vaginal itch, just like the redness you get on your neck when you feel frustrated or angry. I suppose that when you have the itch you don't have sex?

P: (*Looking at me seductively:*) That depends on who's lying next to me. If it's Alan, then I can't have it, but if it's somebody else, who knows (*laughs*). Talking to you right now I can't tell you how strong this itch has just gotten. I could scream. It's very frustrating. I am confused about how long it'll take to find a solution. I guess I have to talk about it. But I don't really feel I am stupid anymore, even though I still don't know what to talk about or where and how to begin. I know already that in the short time I am in therapy, even though I cry a lot here, when I leave I think about it, and I understand, and you have helped me so much. All of a sudden I am becoming aware of things I never thought about before. I never used to think, period!

Lynn's seductive transference continued to emerge, and her need to placate me and play the shy little girl who is in love with me assumed increased proportions during subsequent sessions. She sat sulking for a number of sessions because I wouldn't respond positively to her request for an affair with me. Gentle as well as direct confronting interpretations were sideswept by a variety of infantile or angry, sulky reactions, or more ingratiating "sweet" remarks, such as the above one: "you have helped me so much. . . ." It was true that her awareness of certain acting out patterns was increasing, but her very strong emotional-sexual tie to me was increasing as well. Eventually, because of her emotional attachment, Lynn began to avoid discussing her sexual relationships with other men. She characterized the men she dated as not worth the trouble, only "to kill lonely time." During that period she obsessed a great deal about not having anything to talk about, although she kept reassuring herself that she got a lot out of the sessions.

An impasse was no doubt solidifying. I interpreted this impasse to her as a need on her part to hold back so that I wouldn't reject her as a sexual partner by throwing her out of therapy. She was willing to admit that the idea had crossed her mind, and in the following session she brought in a dream that indicated that her transference had assumed another infantile character rather than what appeared on the surface (through her verbalized fantasies and wishes) as an Oedipal one: "You and I were walking along the aisles at the A&P and you were walking ahead of me, and then you turned and picked me up and you put me in the cart, the way they put little children, and I got very excited because you gave me a marshmallow to eat, and then you disappeared. I got out of the cart, I don't know how. I think I fell out, and I looked for you. I finally found you, and you had funny shoes on—they looked like ladies' shoes—and you said something to me in Yiddish, but I didn't get it."

This dream and her strong statements of loyalty and love toward me made it quite clear that she perceived me as the wished for, *ideal* "good mother" who fed her and was available to her, although I disappeared for awhile in the dream. I was, for her, what her mother was not, at least so far as the introject image of her mother. However, because she had to leave me at the end of each session, she also perceived me as a rejecting father whom she needed to placate regardless of the cost to her. Her relationships with men were primarily motivated by her perception of them as holding the key to her survival, since women, like her mother and herself, were perceived as weak, unreliable, stupid, and undesirable. Thus the search for men was always a search for the good mother, since a woman could not satisfy her infantile needs. Of course, neither did men, except that they held the controls in her programmed life. Her father and brothers had ruled the family. The dream and her associations to it left little doubt about her personality dynamics. However, the transferential situations posed interesting theoretical and technical questions.

Lynn's depression, her major complaint, can be understood as a reaction to an overwhelmingly punitive superego development, which evolved as a result of her interaction with a self-righteous, depriving, moralizing, and alienating father, on the one hand, and a self-effacing, guilt-ridden, passive, and demoralized mother, on the other. This combination of factors helped create feelings of guilt and self-reproachment for any impulses and unconscious wishes that were, by necessity, contrary to her parents' perception of her place and value in the family. In addition, the accumulation of a reservoir of resentment and rage for the obliteration of her identity by the entire family (directly by her parents and indirectly by her brothers, who stole "center stage"), was turned inward and became manifest in the chronic state of dejection and depression.

No doubt all this can be dynamically understood through "straight-line" analytic reasoning. Moreover, her sexual acting-out may be understood as a defensive reaction to her depression, or as a revenge or rebellion against the prohibitions placed on her with regard to her worth as a woman, and, indeed, as a separate person. However, such an interpretation would only be a partial one, for looking at her history of isolation by the family and the consequent development of psychosomatic symptoms such as the psoriasis, one might have reasonably expected a developmental orientation toward social withdrawal rather than sexual acting-out. Lynn's ego was too shattered to muster enough energy to fight back through rebellion or to strike at her "masters" by sexually defying the codes she had been taught. There is, however, another way of looking at her behavior.

I examined her personality dynamics, especially those related to the sexual acting-out and the psychosomatic symptoms, in terms of Winnicott's (1958) concept of the "transitional object." From this viewpoint, the men in her life may be perceived as "interchangeable anchors," used to temporarily feel secure, loved, and wanted, as well as objects of negative relatedness that reaffirmed her identity as a tool of convenience for others and unconsciously made her feel she was part of a "family." Thus she could skip from one father-figure (or mother-figure as the case may be) to another, without having to be alone. In other words, she brought the men and the psychosomatic symptoms into her world of experience as objects of comfort, regardless of how destructive and painful this comfort turned out to be in the long run. These experiences were often repeated, always with dire consequences, and without insight or understanding. These "security blankets" kept her from separating from her negative self-image (identity with mother), her depression (her omnipotent, punitive, "strong" father), and her fear of being abandoned (cut off from the family as a whole). In the dream related above, she risks falling out of a high cart to avoid the separation. Both her sexual acting-out and her psychosomatic symptoms neatly bound her fear of separation and anxiety, and carried her from day to day, like transitional objects carried by little children from room to room. In this manner, she did not have to give up anything, at least not in fantasy. In effect she has been developmentally arrested at the stage when she began to separate, but never learned to do so successfully. This interpretation of Lynn's personality dynamics opens the therapeutic efforts to various alternative strategies, and requires that a number of questions related to treatment goals be clarified.

The first issue relates to the material that the patient brings to the session and the need for the therapist to make a determination as to what to focus on, what themes to give priority. Naturally, such decisions must be based on the patient's actual concerns and productions. However, the therapist always has a choice of focus, because opportunities invariably arise where connections between whatever transpires in the session and the therapeutic goals can be made, even when the patient is anxious to avoid the subject. With Lynn, the main goal was to help her move beyond the transitional object stage and into the ego relatedness stage (Winnicott, 1958), with the accompanying development of ego boundaries and ego strength. Keeping this goal in mind, and in light of the alternating depression-acting-out behavior pattern, it seemed safe to assume that focusing on her early family relationships would only serve to promote additional breast-beating because of guilt emanating from her rage at them. It would also provide a base for justification of her acting-out. At the same time, discussing her present acting-out could be used to avoid looking into the initial problems that had produced it. A third possibility, namely, focussing on transferential aspects of the treatment, might feed into her attempted ploy to do just that—to centralize her psychic energies around her feelings toward me as she had done with other authority figures, other men. Combining all these alternatives seems most effective. There is no doubt that meaningful changes occur in therapy as a result of the interweaving of genetic and transferential material. This case is, in general, no different. However, there is a special problem here—namely, the patient's great need to block or resist the therapeutic efforts through overlibidinizing the therapist for the purpose of turning him into another transitional object. A number of possible techniques and strategies must be considered.

The first major question considered was whether the patient could benefit from the use of traditional psychoanalytic techniques—free association, interpretation, and some "well-timed" confrontations. However, since Lynn had become very quickly enamored of me, and dependent on my reactions, I felt that these techniques would further intensify her overeroticized cathexis, and create an intolerable therapeutic relationship. The signs that such a development could easily occur were manifested in her early pronouncements of my "savior" qualities, as well as in her dreams, in which I always appeared as her "Prince Charming," endowed with all the qualities of a "saint," and one she had always fantasized as an ideal husband (father). But more than that, through the psychoanalytic posture, I would also no doubt satisfy her need to relive her family relationships, with me playing, in her transferential strivings, whatever roles she wished to fantasize. The fact that I would keep frustrating her fantasies by the mere reality and analysis that I was not what she wished me to be, would do little to change these fantasies because of the very strong denial mechanism she had developed, a mechanism that was obvious in her daily social-sexual relationships with other men. Thus neither the time element—an important psychoanalytic strategy—nor the interpretive techniques seemed to offer a viable strategy to help her eliminate the need for "security blankets."

It is interesting to note that in one of her sessions she declared that "women have a natural hostility, natural resentment toward men." Yet, in the same session, when I confronted her with her choice of a male analyst she said, "I felt that a male analyst can help me more—not that men are superior, but they know what women are all about." This ambivalent sentiment is no doubt a key to understanding her deep unconscious need to attach herself to men for "security" reasons, provided she could keep herself in the little girl role and the man in the dominant, controlling position. As such, she did not need to *feel* separated or independent, which to her meant abandoned.

To help her move from this position I felt that I had to offer her alternatives, which must be less frightening than the lonely detachment of the couch, a detachment only too familiar to her from her childhood. At the same time, I was not convinced that a more confronting strategy, with less frequent weekly visits, would be a more viable alternative for a number of reasons: (1) Her depression required more frequent visits to help her form a meaningful cathexis to me with less confrontation because that might be interpreted as accusatory, and therefore used as additional fuel to her reservoir of guilt and lowered self-esteem, resulting in further depression. (2) Her acting-out required a continuity in the therapeutic relationship that could help "drain off" excess destructive energy, and redirect the energy into the transferential communication, where it could be analyzed and worked through. More frequent sessions could increase the dependency and attachment, however, which might not be analyzable because of its intense sexualized character, and the confrontations in and of themselves might be too traumatizing for her to remain in treatment, thus defeating the purpose of the whole process.

Because of these and other conflicting considerations, it was difficult to decide on a coherent approach to this case. I felt the need to have a more thorough understanding of the patient's personality dynamics, or at least some confirmation of what seemed to be a rather fragile personality structure. I thus asked her to take some psychological tests, mainly projective tests that tap deeper unconscious layers. The psychological report confirmed my suspicion that she was indeed "action-oriented," and that "her ability to control her behavior is decreasing, and her judgment is inadequate." Rorschach percepts showed her to be "ambivalent in all aspects of her functioning." Two successive responses to one card indicated this ambivalence in an interesting manner: "Geyser spurting from the ground with the earth opening up," and "down-pour of rain with the earth opening up." These two reactions may have been related to her depression, resulting from "repressive" as well as "oppressive" factors, and suggest that her acting-out was a result of impulsive breakthroughs leading to guilt and a compulsive attempt to deny her depression. Other percepts indicated that she was psychosexually "inadequate, childish, and demanding, and may be characterized as anticipating rejection, and demonstrating a great need for nurturance." The psychologist hypothesized from the testing material that her "typical mode of behavior is likely to involve manipulation of the male, in a passive and obstructive way, and to be exceedingly dependent." In addition, her projective drawings showed "gross and significant transparencies . . . and suggest profound denial and distortion with regard to her body . . . These indicate greater pathology than what she presents on the surface, and the possibility of a borderline personality cannot be ruled out."

This description of the patient's personality dynamics suggested that one single therapeutic approach might not serve the goals outlined earlier. For one thing, the transference had to be "diluted" in some fashion, but at the same time, I had to be careful not to let her lose the feeling of contact and communication that she seemed to have established with me notwithstanding its over-eroticized nature. In order to prevent too strong an attachment from developing, I felt that a *modified* confrontational strategy could be followed. This meant that the confrontations should be regular and frequent in order to increase awareness and introspection and slowly help her arrive at a sense of responsibility without guilt for her behavior. The confrontational techniques designed to help her discriminate between transferential and nontransferential reactions would comprise a number of elements not normally used with other patient categories, such as manipulation of the frequency of sessions (Alexander, 1963), sharing certain personal experiences, purposefully using language indicative of my existence as a human being not a god, and *underutilizing* her passive-receptive nature normally used to increase the transferential ties (Guntrip, 1969). I also envisaged certain sessions where total silence would be the confrontational strategy, helping to encourage the development of a separation-individuation-relatedness pattern, learned through this therapeutic prototype.

The Course of Treatment

Six months after Lynn started therapy, she confessed that she had been witholding a great deal of information, fearing I might think she was too disturbed. It turned out that while she was professing her great love for me she was embroiled in an extremely destructive relationship with a man who didn't want to marry her, supposedly because he was embarrassed to be seen with her in public since she was too short. She said he treated her "like a rag," reaffirming her negative self-image, especially her body-image. In addition, during her weekly call to her family, her father would reproach her for not compensating for her "shortness" in some way so that she wouldn't lose this wonderful "catch." Then he would remind her how he always knew that she would never amount to anything by herself, apparently in an attempt to spur her to prove him wrong. Of course, such tactics only renewed her self-admonitions to act more like a second-class citizen with her boyfriend, behavior that led to more disaster for her. Following this disclosure, she also told me that she had been finding it hard to come to her sessions because the pain was too great, and because "you would formulate something in your mind about me that's horrible, and you'd be right, but I don't want to lose you." I decided to "test" her sincerity about her fear of losing me by confronting her with her own pronouncements that she really wanted to separate herself emotionally from her family and her continuing to phone so often, thus further incurring the pain inflicted upon her by her family. I then suggested that instead of her calls, she write me a letter in which she could express whatever she wished to communicate to her family on the phone. I offered myself as a temporary substitute. She accepted the invitation to this (one-way) correspondence somewhat hesitantly, perceiving the suggestion as a "prescription," since this would eliminate her own responsibility in separating from her parents. She also agreed to it because in this manner she could tell me what she felt about me without having to be confronted with it spontaneously. She thought that the letters might reveal more about her identity, fearing that "the more I find out about myself, the less you'll like me."

Lynn was able to pursue the "agreement" about the letters for about two months. She called her parents only two or three times, and she wrote a total of four letters. These contained poignant themes: her worries about her future as a single woman and her need to have a man to add to her significance; her rage at her parents for not "allowing" her to have a chance to get an education; her strange feelings that she is probably a "freak," and therefore her disgust with men who find her desirable in bed; her loneliness at all times, except when she was writing the letters to me; her fantasies about my returning love for hers; and, finally, some vague memories about a close girl-friend from a very early age, perhaps four or five, who had moved away and was never heard from again. After the fourth letter, she came to her session quite agitated, since I had not made any comments about the letters except to say that I had received them. Here is some of what transpired during that session, after she said she wished to discontinue the correspondence:

P: I felt I wasn't equal to you. It suddenly dawned on me, it hit me that I am so neurotic, so sick—I mean, I felt quite good about it, but then I realized it was a one-sided affair. I write, I pour my guts out, and you don't respond. I mean even here you don't say anything. I don't know anything about you—that's what I mean by not feeling equal to you—like you're a complete mystery to me. I just know your name. My girlfriend tells me that *she* decides what she wants to talk about to her analyst, but with me it's different. It's like you have me in the palm of your hand.

T: You sound like you've been quite angry with me for some time now.

P: I know why I am angry with you. You have this power, it's uncanny—it's not just when I come here, but it's 24 hours a day.

T: I have power over you all the time—I control your life?

P: It certainly feels like that. Sometimes I feel it's true, that you have control over me. I know it's crazy, but still, whatever you say I jump to it. You told me not to phone my folks every week, and I did it. You told me to write letters, and I did it. I feel like a little toy in your hands. I mean, I want you to like me very much—I'll do anything for you to like me. It's just a very new experience with me to like you and to be angry with you.

T: I am glad you are telling me how you feel. Certainly keeping all these feelings to yourself doesn't make them go away—the pain stays. But what about this control business—I had the impression you agreed to write the letters on your own volition—I didn't exactly twist your arm, did I?

P: Well, in the beginning it was kind of fun—I felt like I was indulging myself writing all these things and you reading them. But I got angry that I had to do this. I don't have to write you letters not to call my parents. I mean I can see now something I knew before, that I feel much better when I don't speak to my father every week, and they never call, so it's up to me. I just don't want to cut off all my relationship with them completely. I feel guilty about not phoning them, and I think about what they might be thinking. But really, if they're interested in me they can afford to pick up the phone once in awhile.

T: So you feel it's a one-way street with them too.

P: Absolutely! Sometimes I think that they don't call because they are from the old country and they're not used to spending the money on a telephone call to find out how their daughter is doing. But the fact is that they don't call and I never said anything to them.

T: What about the letters—you started to resent writing them, but you kept doing it to please me, I suppose, just like the phone calls. You didn't want it to be a one-sided affair, but you kept calling them and expected them to call you back, and then you say they're controlling your life, just like you said I control you. I don't see how—I am not your parents, and you're not five years old. If you don't want to write the letters, it's okay with me.

P: I thought about this all weekend. I was thinking, I hope I don't make him angry because I don't want to write anymore. I couldn't even write this in the letter. But you're right, I was making a mountain out of a molehill. I don't have to write if I don't want to, and I don't have to call my parents if I don't want to either. I am just wondering what you thought about the letters. I really would like to know.

T: I am glad gou're asking me directly about it now. I learned a great deal more about you, and I found out what a wealth of life experience you have accumulated without being able to utilize it. That's bad.

P: (*crying:*) I don't know what it is, I guess somewhere I believe what you said. I believe that I have something to give but I don't get the opportunity. It's never accepted. I just remembered a dream I had last night, again about a party. I don't know why I dream so much about parties. (*Sobbing.*) I guess I never felt happy, so at least I can dream about it. When I walked in, there was a man standing there, and I was very glad to see him, and I went over and I embraced him, and as I was embracing him I looked over his shoulder and I saw an old boyfriend, from many years ago, and he called me and he said he wanted me to take his shirts to the cleaners, and I started crying because I knew I couldn't get out of it, and I was very upset, and I woke up crying. The first man was someone I've never seen before, but there was something familiar about him.

T: That dream sounds familiar, doesn't it!

P: Well, you know, I had a few dreams of going to a party, like the one I had last week, and when . . .

T: I meant the feeling in the dream that you were trapped, that you had to please this man and go to the cleaners. You always feel controlled because you have to please. You have to take care of other people's dirty laundry.

P: Yeah! (*a big sigh*). I don't know if I told you this—I don't think so because I don't remember having thought about this for many years—but when I was five, maybe six, I lived in dirt, I mean real dirt, and I picked up all kinds of diseases, and my head was full of bugs, and my mother soaked my head in kerosene. Kerosene—can you believe this! And she cut my hair very short—I mean, very, very short, shorter than a boy's—and it was terrible, because we lived in a gentile neighborhood, and the kids would hit me, and I'd tell my mother and my father, and they always sent me back (*crying*). I felt so ashamed. I still feel this way.

There were more childhood memories and explorations into her past, something she hadn't been able to do for many weeks before the letters, partially because of her extreme concentration on her relationship to me. The combination of the letter writing, the lessening of concrete contact with family, especially her father, my expression of feeling touched by her pain, and the confrontation with her self-inflicted submissiveness, all helped move the therapeutic situation from a difficult impasse to a new level of efforts to meaningfully analyze some of her conflicts. The task was not as simple as it might appear on the surface, mostly because of her entrenchment in the sexual acting out, and because of her fear of losing me if she didn't *force* (unconsciously) feelings of deep love for me. A few more months of work on her separation from her family continued to be focal in the work, but when the summer months, with my impending vacation, drew near, she again became less productive and more depressed, and a few psychosomatic symptoms suddenly erupted, after they had abated for the longest time in her memory. She also began to complain of feeling empty, lonely, and incapable of enjoying sex with the men she dated now and then. She said that her life seemed "like an Ingmar Bergman movie with no beginning, no end, full of meaning, yet totally empty, depressed and depressing, completely blah!"

A week before I was about to leave for my vacation, she brought in a dream in which I was going on vacation never to come back. As I was informing her about my going away I was laughing at her because she hadn't realized that I was a woman not a man, and I said to her, "You were fooled again." She felt panicked, and tried to hide inside a grotesquely huge rag doll, but she couldn't because she was too skinny. She said the dream was almost like a nightmare, even though she was pretty sure, *even in the dream,* that I would come back, that is, if I didn't drive in Europe and get hit by a crazy European driver. This anxiety dream was expressive of her concern over the separation, but also more symbolically of certain material that I could not bring to her attention at that time, precisely because of my five-week vacation. However, I asked her to remember the dream if she could, so that we might discuss it when I returned, and reassured her, that her letters, if she wished to write me, would be read carefully, and that I would not see them as a burden. She appreciated the offer, and thought she might take me up on it.

I had suspected for sometime that Lynn's anger toward men, and her submission to them, could not fully be understood as a reaction to the wrongs done by her family, especially her father, or as a fixation of transitional objects that kept her tied to her family. There was at least one other component that began to emerge toward the end of the first year of treatment, symbolized in the above "dream-gift" she gave me before I embarked on my vacation. There was a disguised homosexual concern, never before floating so close to the surface. I was somewhat worried about taking my vacation at that time, because of possible serious regression. I communicated my concern to her, indirectly, by saying that perhaps she ought to write to me anyway, even if she thought it was a silly idea, simply to keep in touch. She recognized my concern, and in the last session before I left, she reassured me in a subdued but surprisingly patronizing manner, that she would do nothing "foolish," as she jokingly added, "if you promise to behave yourself!" I promised her to do everything in my power to be back in time for our sessions in one piece. She laughed, and asked if she could give me a hug before she left my office.

The letters that I received from her only confirmed my suspicion that she was in a controlled state of panic and that she needed all the support I could extend to her, including the hug. She wrote three letters, mostly expressing how much she missed our sessions. She said she had "seriously" entertained the thought of coming to Europe to meet me, and she didn't very much care that I would probably be with "a wife," and then she added, with a playful sarcasm, "after all, your work comes first, right?" This outpouring of dependency needs was rather disappointing after her show of progressive emancipation from her parents. I couldn't make head or tail out of it, although I knew that as long as I was getting the letters, she was not likely to act out in a very dangerous manner. But I sent her a postcard telling her that I had received her letters and was glad to hear from her, and that I was having a nice vacation, learning a great deal about the peoples and cultures I visited, and that I was looking forward to returning soon.

When the sessions resumed, I found out that she had had a serious anxiety attack after I had left, and was unable to go to work for a couple of days. As she began to realize how dependent she had been on me, her fury at me assumed new proportions, and she began to wonder whether I was the right therapist for her, even though she was "in love" with me. She kept all this information to herself, and wrote only about normal, everyday complaints and some positive feelings. A girlfriend who also was in therapy advised her to seek a female therapist, since "men don't understand women." This friend also told Lynn that if I were a good therapist, she wouldn't have had such a hard time when I went away because I would have prepared her. She added that when her therapist went on vacation or got sick she was only too happy because of the money she saved. While this might have been said in a tongue-in-cheek fashion, Lynn took it seriously. She appeared quite distant during the first session, and she informed me that, during my absence, she learned that she hadn't really changed much. She had called an old boyfriend who had been very destructive to her and had a mini-affair that lasted a few days, after which she "hated" herself and felt very guilty. But toward the end of the session she said that she had had a dream a week before I came back that "horrified" her. She wasn't sure she wanted to tell it. However, she decided to mention it "anyway" in the following session: "I was in bed with a man—I don't know who it was—and he was manipulating me. Slowly my clitoris grew and became like such a tremendous organ, the largest I've ever seen, and he wanted me to touch it. I don't remember if I did or not, but then a woman's face appeared, a very attractive woman. She had black hair combed just like mine, and she said, 'Don't let him bother you (*meaning the man in the dream*), you can do it yourself,' and I continued to masturbate, and I came in her face and I was very excited."

Lynn identified herself with the beautiful woman, and the men in her life as the ones with the "large organ." She completely ignored, with this interpretive association, the fact that in the dream it was she who grew the penis. I confronted her with this denial, and asked her if she could relate to that aspect of the dream. She immediately produced another interpretation saying that, of course, she had always fantasized about what it would be like to be a man, and many times wished she could change her sex because it's easier for men in this world. She then added that if she were a man she would fall in love with the beautiful woman in the dream "in no time."

The more she associated and interpreted and tried to hide the ultimate meaning of the dream material, the more her narcissism and her homosexual feelings rose to the surface. As she discussed her feelings about men, it became increasingly clear that her preoccupation with this subject was only a facade to protect herself from facing her unacceptable, and largely insatiable, unconscious need for continuous feeding, continuous approval, and continuous adoration. The nucleus of her self was very much deprived, wanting, and hungry, and her *overt* behavioral orientation toward the world was juxtaposed to her needs. Thus, she always appeared on the manifest level as giving, nurturing, and sacrificing, because this was the only acceptable way she could satisfy her immediate environment. But, unconsciously, all her giving was, in a distorted manner, really taking. Her contact with the world thus never satisfied her. It was indeed a one-way street, with the supplies moving toward her. Such functioning could only mean, in the long run, feelings of alienation, for in effect, she did not reciprocate, and thus was left feeling cut off. This sense of separateness and aloneness was not produced by others, as she tended to believe, but by herself. It may be noted that the transitional object theory could very well explain this structure, in that the object held by the child is so important, that *giving it up*, separating from it, means *giving it to* someone else, and, of course, that is inconceivable. However, only when such an object is given up, and the child moves to another attachment, does the object become recognized, ex post facto, as a transitional one. The familiar "eternal student" syndrome, the student who attends one university after another, and one course after another until he or she is old and gray, without actually *leaving* the structure for outside world experiences, can be included in the category of persons whose life is filled with transitional objects—(such as the university). These individuals may be diagnosed as *transitional subjects* because their selves lack anchoring (Winnicott, 1953). Lynn was no doubt a member of this class.

This additional understanding of Lynn, which resulted from her willingness to share information that became available to her consciously after her new experiences in treatment, shed a new light on her therapy. I felt that, even though she was given to regressions, she was probably ready to be confronted with her "reverse" narcissistic behavior. I utilized head-on confrontational techniques without anticipating unbearable vulnerability. Whenever she complained that I was too harsh on her I reminded her that she was the producer of whatever transpired in treatment, and that my input was only an interpretive-mirroring-probing one. And when she complained about that fact, i.e., that I didn't give her advice and didn't involve myself, I threatened to take up a lot of time in the session talking about myself—and I had a lot to say. She rejected that idea pretty quickly.

From this point on, we moved fairly quickly into discussions of her sexuality, her feelings about her body, her envy of other women's bodies and minds, and the emptiness of her obsessions regarding men as long as she felt worthless, disfigured, and empty. She went through a long period of craving for a mother who would take care of her and fill her with "real substance—mom's milk." I became that figure for her, and was willing to supply her more as she required more. I offered her additional sessions, sometimes without fee, since I felt she could use some *concrete* mothering. This phase lasted more than a year, during which she was depressed and happy, giving and taking and developing more ties to women friends rather than constantly having men orbiting around her. She also constantly tested my caring for her, and part of this testing was manifested by her making attempts to "experience homosexual relationships." She had a couple of contacts, but did not enjoy them. She was trying to make me jealous, but this jealousy was more oral than Oedipal, as she wished for the mother's possessiveness.

This narcissistic element in her attachment to me was characterized also by her need to have me completely and totally, without necessarily sexual connotation. She hated the patients who came before her and after her. Every phone call I received was seen as taking away from her, even when I did not answer it. Once in a while I let her have the floor for the entire session to let her know that I was present but not taking. And at the end of such sessions I would say to her, to concretize the reality for her (Bernd, 1972), "You see Lynn, I didn't say a single word today, and you survived it all. You have a lot to offer to yourself and to others."

A dream that seemed to indicate the passing of this phase helped a great deal in revealing to her what her next step had to be, that is, to start taking care of herself in a constructive way, not by wasting her energy on acting out, on oversexualizing her relationships, or on psychosomatic symptoms, but by making efforts to utilize her resources to gain something real for herself. The dream and some of what transpired consequent to it are presented from the transcript of the session:

P: My whole family and myself were going to a wedding, and on the tables there were big heavy drapes instead of tablecloths. My mother said to me. "Let's take this drape home, I can make two dresses—one for me and one for you." I told her I had my own drapes at home. She started yelling at me, but I got up and I drew the drapes between the kitchen and the wedding hall, and then I walked to the band. I started to conduct it. I was reading the music, even though I can't read one single note. . . . I was very surprised when I woke up and I felt really good, like I could conquer the world, and I said to myself "Wait till Abie (*referring to me*) hears that one (*laughs, and starts, for no apparent reason, to cry and then sob*).

T: What are you so upset about? You seemed like you were having such a nice time in that dream.

P: (*Still crying:*) I am so happy I can't tell you. I am crying because something happened—I can't exactly describe what it is, I just can't—maybe I just feel free from my family. I know I'll never go back to them. I mean, I'll never allow them to make me feel so rotten and dependent on them again. I just know that my mother always wanted me to be tied to her—maybe to save her loneliness. I don't know. Now I understand what you told me a long time ago, that she had her own problems. I feel that I can make it on my own, and it's a great feeling. (*She saw me wipe some tears from the corners of my eyes.*) You're not crying are you?

T: Something like that. I think you're right about your interpretation of your dream. It's nice to see you cry out of happiness rather than pain. I am happy too.

P: (*With tears:*) I never believed my stories did anything for anybody. I just feel that you really care, not that I didn't believe it before, but it's really something.

T: What about that dream—you were conducting the band without knowing how to read music, that's kind of interesting and puzzling.

P: Well, I don't know about that, but I know that I have to do something for me, and this morning I came to the realization that I've been "futzing" (*loafing*) around enough. I want to go back to school, I want to go to college, not just to get a diploma, but I don't want to be a secretary forever.

T: You want to learn to read the music, and maybe write it yourself!

P: You're really something. You know there's one thing I never told you, I love the way you put things—the words—especially when you use these analogies. You remind me a lot of my Uncle Leo. I really loved him and I know he loved me, he was so different from the rest of the family.

There was obviously a more mature, more decisive development. Of course, this was not characteristic of every session from there on. Lynn's therapy continued for five additional years, a total of seven. During the last three years she was in group therapy as well, at my recommendation. There were many difficulties along the way. She re-entered the dating arena, but she was much more discriminating in her choice of men and her sexual behavior. She became orgasmic again, although not as fully as she used to be when she started therapy. By the end of treatment she still had not found a "suitable" husband. Her contention that there weren't enough available men in New York City was partially true. She did not, however, retreat to a life of celibacy—she continued to be socially active. She also started college, and by the time of termination of treatment had only one year left to graduate, and was already making plans to enter graduate school. Her relationship with the family changed drastically: she became the focus of their attention, and she was treated with respect, although always with certain elements of disdain, suspiciousness, and disbelief about her achievements. In the group, Lynn had a very difficult time in the first year, primarily because of her narcissistic orientation. There wasn't a story, a feeling, an opinion that some member expressed to which she didn't immediately hook on, and in this manner divert the group's attention to her. However, she was soon confronted with this largely insensitive, self-centered, focus on herself, and she struggled very hard with it. Eventually, she learned the rules of the game and became an important *contributing* member of the group. Termination of treatment did not signify a total resolution of her conflicts, of course. Rather, she had developed an awareness and a capability for dealing with them constructively. Much of her depression, feelings of emptiness, and worthlessness disappeared. She remained generally narcissistic, although more socially oriented in her interpersonal interaction and less inappropriately angry. Her functioning improved considerably as she learned to deal with her daily routine directly rather than through suppression and defensive maneuvers. These were significant changes, which justified termination at that time.

Greenson (1967), discussing patients who suffer from eroticized transference, claims that they are "prone to very destructive acting out. All these patients have transference resistances that stem from underlying impulses of hatred. They seek only to discharge these feelings and oppose the analytic work." This observation may be easily related to the above clinical illustration. It is remarkably difficult to chart a course of treatment that can be followed in any systematic manner, because the patient's development in the treatment is highly unpredictable. The therapist must be extremely flexible in the entire approach, and very alert to the patient's subtle changes in energy equilibrium. The "standard psychoanalytic techniques," as it were, cannot be espoused without chasing the patient quickly out of treatment, or reinforcing his real narcissistic stance without any real changes in ego-relatedness. This type of case, where the patient's major emotional discharge is lodged in sexual expression or physical (psychosomatic) symptoms, may give a deceptive appearance as to the motivation for therapeutic work, because of the tendency to an instant, emotional attachment to the therapist. Striking a balance between the patient's transference resistance and the need for nurturance requires a willingness to utilize a variety of techniques, some of which are analytic, some nonanalytic, and also a readiness on the part of the therapist to become, de facto at times, a transitional object. Of course, the above illustration is only a sampling of the therapeutic strategy and techniques that such cases of extreme positive emotionality may need. The confrontational analytic aspects of confrontation analysis can often prove helpful in dealing, somewhat successfully, although not ideally, with such cases.

Extreme Ambivalence with Expression of Emotionality: The Borderline Personality

This category of patients is probably one of the most challenging to the psychotherapist because of the difficulties it presents from a diagnostic and therapeutic point of view. It includes those individuals who express their emotionality interpersonally in an extreme fashion, unpredictably vacillating between negative and positive feelings. Although unpredictable, and often elusive and incomprehensible, their behavior patterns are stable and have a definite character. Lately, this category of patients has been given a great deal of attention in the writings of prominent writers in this field—the so-called "borderline personality organization" (Schmideberg, 1955, Kernberg, 1967), "schizoid" personality (Guntrip, 1969), or "stormy personality" (Arieti, 1955). Descriptions of this category vary from author to author, and treatment approaches often contradict each other (Gunderson and Singer, 1975). The presentation here will be limited to a number of issues pertinent to the treatment of the borderline by the confrontation analysis approach. Since not all borderline personalities are the same, the purpose of the following illustration is only to present some ideas and ways of approaching a difficult problem rather than to be all encompassing. It is especially important to note that treatment of the borderline personality requires sensitive therapeutic flexibility and creativity, which can be unusually taxing for the therapist.

Eileen was a 25-year-old single woman who started therapy because she was depressed, frightened, and feeling generally disorganized and chaotic. When asked why she sought treatment, she said, "For the last four months I have had suicidal thoughts everyday. I am very frightened of life and the future." She said she would have done away with her life if she hadn't thought her parents would suffer, and if her church sanctioned it. Other complaints in the initial interview were an inability to concentrate on her job as a telephone operator, a compulsive need to talk and to be socially active, overeating and overdrinking, and pan-anxiety when alone. While there was some loosening of associations and grandiose delusional material, on the whole she was coherent and had a fairly good sense of reality.

Eileen's parents were of Irish Catholic origin, poor and uneducated, and gave little attention to their children's development. There was a great deal of neglect because of their drinking. However, Eileen's mother insisted on taking her to church on Sundays, only to embarrass her in front of the congregation by her (the mother's) unkempt appearance and inappropriate behavior. The father was described as a "passive slob," "poor soul," "the weak force in the family dominated by the mother." Eileen recalls her childhood as having been spent mostly on the street rather than in school. She quit school at age 16, and started working at various jobs, primarily low paying, unskilled factory and office jobs. When she came for treatment, she had been working as a telephone operator for a city institution for several years.

From the initial contacts it appeared quite clearly that Eileen's pathology was fairly serious and prognostically rather uninviting. However, she seemed to have a certain vitality, sense of humor, uncanny perceptiveness, and intellectual capacity that made her a potentially challenging, interesting, and perhaps more hopeful candidate for change than appeared on the surface. There was little doubt that her symptoms and their chronicity would make the course of treatment anything but smooth. She was overweight, alcoholic, educationally impoverished, suicidal, emotionally labile, rather naive about psychological processes, unusually impulsive, and not infrequently delusional.

The immediate treatment objectives were pretty clear: to help her through and out of the agitated depression, and to lay the foundation for a therapeutic alliance, if at all possible. Both of these objectives were frustrated almost as soon as she entered treatment. Knowing that she was quite depressed, she attempted to overcome this depression by totally denying it. She developed a pattern of "living it up" every moment she could by drinking at the bars after work, eating constantly, acting out sexually with men who reinforced her grandiose delusions by promising to make her a Hollywood star and by showering her with material objects. About three weeks after she began therapy, she attempted suicide in the presence of a man who had been promising her open entry into Hollywood. He obviously could not deliver. She managed to find a physician who did not report her suicide attempt and kept her out of the hospital. However, from that time on, she became progressively demoralized at work, increasingly manic, and finally unable to function reasonably on her job. She had to be hospitalized, since treatment on an outpatient basis was not possible and she had no environment that could attend to her needs for safety from impulsive suicidal behavior. She allowed me to hospitalize her even though both of us knew that she was not, basically, "hospital material." Drugs that she had tried before were not effective in reducing her anxiety and keeping her from extremely destructive acting out. In the hospital, she was not able to drink or act out sexually, and she received heavy dosages of tranquillizers, which stabilized her behavior somewhat. She was, however, more of an observer there than an involved patient.

I continued my contacts with her while she was in the hospital, and assured her that when she got out we would get to working on some of her problems. My continued interest and support were extremely important subsequent to her hospitalization. She believed that I was interested in her welfare, and my influence on her behavior increased a great deal. I used this influence to obtain a certain contract from her. I told her that I could not help her with other problems if she did not stop the drinking; she would have to join Alcoholics Anonymous if she wished to be in therapy with me. My insistence on this agreement was not very easy for her. However, she knew that my "prescription" had to be followed. This "confrontation" with her had a number of meanings to her, not all of which were appreciated at that time: (1) I was interested enough in her welfare to insist on a course of action that was therapeutic, not placating, even if it meant "losing her "business." (2) I, representing an interested authority, had enough confidence in her ability to overcome her drinking problem through a rational, albeit unpleasant, method. (3) A *man* had seriously intervened on her behalf, not against her as she had been used to. (4) I was the first person to present her with a challenge commensurate more with her strength than her weakness.

After a couple of weeks of hesitation she joined AA and treatment resumed. However, simply joining this organization was not enough to keep her off alcohol. I utilized every trick I could devise to help her with this difficult goal, and, except for two or three relatively insignificant slips in the eight years of treatment, she remained dry and without developing destructive substitutes. She always knew that going back to alcohol would definitely mean severing the relationship with me.

Having accomplished the difficult goal of sobriety, the sessions increasingly concentrated on her inner life rather than on the uses and abuses of alcohol. She became more introspective and self-searching, and began to recognize that she had brains that could be used productively and creatively. However, her lack of discipline and inability to focus on any one direction in her life also created intolerable frustrations for her. It was as if she were brought to the water but was not capable of drinking it. Her deep doubts about her capabilities and her impoverished and negative self-image very often surfaced during the sessions, only to increase her frustrations and render any attempt to help her gain feelings of confidence almost ludicrous. Reading, going to school, planning a career were all alien to her system, indeed to her entire personal culture. At the same time, understandably, her grandiose fantasies persisted, and she develped a delusion that she could quickly turn out the greatest novel or play ever written, without having to know the basics of writing or learning the discipline necessary for any serious writer.

While this development was taking place, I began to have my own doubts about what therapy could contribute to her. I wondered whether I was not pursuing a course of treatment that might be self-defeating, almost delusional. Yet, there were some clues that she was interested in changing, especially since her sexual acting-out had decreased considerably. She continued to weigh her future plans, but was never able to come to any decisions. She knew that she could not continue with the dull job she had, nor could she see herself going to school to be able, eventually, to work at something that used her potential.

Her ambivalence brought about an impasse. I felt that she needed to learn the art of self-discipline before she could resolve her ambivalence, which was, in the final analysis, related to her self-image. Learning to reverse another self-destructive habit related to her body-image, namely, her excessive eating, held the promise of moving away from the impasse. Obesity is generally a stubborn symptom, and taking a new approach to it at that time seemed like a reasonable plan. Since the confrontation about her drinking had produced positive results, another similar attempt was contemplated. However, presenting her with an ultimatum in which she had to choose between eating and therapy did not seem viable, simply because dieting is a process that takes time and cannot be achieved by one single decision. Therefore, I chose a different technique to achieve that purpose—a variation of the paradigmatic technique (Nelson, 1968).

A basic goal of the paradigmatic method is to produce a psychological atmosphere in which retention of certain self-destructive conditions (such as depression, obsessive thoughts, certain habits, etc.) no longer achieves worthwhile secondary gains for the patient, and only keeps him from functioning adequately in daily activities, including treatment. This is accomplished by using techniques that attempt to motivate the patient's healthy ego to reject the destructive behavior. The therapist uses a technique that mirrors to the patient the pathological part of his or her ego to such an extreme degree that the patient can no longer tolerate its existence because of its overwhelming impact. For example, a patient who is depressed, and thus unable to function adequately on his job, may be told by the therapist that the depression is not deep enough to warrant such poor performance, and therefore the patient is expected to become more depressed. The patient then acquiesces, but as the demand for more depression from the therapist increases, the patient begins to fight back, and the depression eventually lifts. This is a grossly simplified description of this technique. When used appropriately and skillfully, however, it can be very helpful. It is not used to resolve any problem, but rather to help remove certain behavioral and defensive operations that prevent the problem from surfacing. In the case of Eileen, a modified paradigmatic method and some desensitization techniques relative to her weight were utilized to achieve this goal.

Like most addicts, Eileen's denial mechanism was her primary defense, and like the majority of overeaters, she denied that her overweight was due to overeating. It was, in her mind, a matter of hormonal-genetic imbalance. Nevertheless, I decided to pursue the subject, and after a number of sessions in which we delved in detail into her eating habits, it seemed that her regular diet was relatively reasonable. However, when I insisted on tracing her daily activities practically *minute by minuete,* we both discovered where all the weight came from—a fact that she had unconsciously denied and thus forgotten. As part of her daily routine on her way to work and when she left work, she would buy about a dozen cupcakes and proceed to consume them before arrival. Her awareness of this behavior was almost nil—it was as automated for her as chewing gum. She continued to deny the possibility that those cakes were contributing to her weight, and the discussion that ensued turned into an intellectual exercise. She rationalized that the cakes only compensated for food she didn't eat with her regular meals, and if she stopped eating them, she would probably add more food to her daily diet because of her "natural" needs. She confirmed the general notion that reasoning with an addict yields little results, since the unconscious motivation is not likely to be touched—the habits become too autonomous and are no longer associated with the original cause, and are too important as defenses. Such an individual either rationalizes his habits away, or refuses to consider them a problem, or if considered a problem, does not feel responsible for them, and thus is without any control over them.

Since Eileen was addicted to cupcakes, the rational approach would obviously be the removal of this specific addiction in the hope that she would not replace it by another as destructive. To help her achieve this difficult task, I used another drastic method—I made an agreement with her that I would be willing to exchange the fee for the following session for 15 cupcakes and one poundcake that she would buy and bring with her. She agreed to this exchange, and when she brought the cakes I asked her to eat as many cakes as possible while she talked about her feelings. After the initial shock, she expressed the feeling that I must have left part of my brains at home, but that nevertheless she was willing to go along because I must know what I was doing. As she ate and talked, I made a number of remarks regarding her food habits, her mannerisms, how enjoyable she must find it to stuff herself at someone's request, and how eating and talking had become her devices for stopping being aware of her feelings. Other remarks referred to the sloppiness and mess that such a situation often creates, and how her relationships to other people must be affected by this habit. After finishing some 10 or 11 cupcakes, she said she was not able to eat anymore. I implored her to have some of the poundcake as a "dessert." She continued the feast, but after eating about a quarter of it, announced that she could no longer eat, since she was ready to vomit. I "accepted" her inability to continue, because "I didn't want my carpet dirtied by an overeater."

As the session was drawing to its end, she asked me for an explanation of my behavior. She did not offer any explanation of hers, except that she was complying with a request that had come from an authority. I told her that I was trying to learn as much as I could about her food habits, and that eating in front of me might give me some clues, because the cupcakes were not simply means to satisfy her hunger, but something that satisfied other needs. Since this was learning for me, I would not charge her for the sessions to which I asked her to bring food. I asked that we repeat the same procedure for the following session. She again showed up with a shopping bag full of cupcakes. I asked her to start eating them, and basically continued with the same procedure as in the previous session. However, while eating the fourth cupcake, what I had hoped for began to happen. She showed very clear signs of irritability, and later open resentment, and said that she did not wish to be a "disgusting pig," especially in front of me, and it was not fair for me to *make* her go through this "torture."

I reminded her that whatever she was doing was the result of an "accord" we had reached, and that I could not "make" her do anything she did not wish to do. It was her mouth, not mine, that was chewing the cakes, and since she was the one who had control over it, she could have stopped at any moment, before getting nauseous, or before starting altogether. She recognized, then, that the "torture" was the awareness of her role as a participating partner in self-destructive behavior, over which she could exercise total control. As a result of this awareness, she became angry for "degrading" herself in front of me. She felt the full impact of what it meant to be submissive, when in fact there was a real opportunity for her to take control. It was her conscious goal to lose weight, not mine, but she always felt that she had no control over the achievement of her goal. When she stopped eating the cakes, she recognized semiconsciously that she did not have to do what she did not want to do, whether the "push" for eating came from an outside authority or an unconscious need to win approval from an inner object demanding that she eat. After that session, which was fairly stormy in its multilevel confrontations and their consequent analysis, she refused to continue to bring food to the sessions, and the loss of weight, her goal, became primarily a matter of time, not a daily struggle. She achieved her weight goal in a few months, and maintained it continuously. Ten years after these sessions, she was still exercising full control over her weight.

Controlling the weight also had a beneficial effect on maintaining the sobriety. Naturally, her sense of mastery over her own destiny gradually deepened, but another process was also in the making at the same time. Her dependence on me as the performer of miracles developed serious dimensions. Two important factors accounted for this development. The first was the help I gave her in overcoming the alcoholism and overeating. She felt that, while she was the one who achieved these goals, I was the one who put her on the correct course. The second reason for her great dependence was the achievement of a slowing-down or near elimination of her "maniacal" overactivity socially and sexually. She no longer felt that she had much in common with many former friends. Simultaneously, however, her feelings of lack of self-worth returned, and she believed she had nothing to offer anyone who she considered educated, socially enlightened, sophisticated, and financially successful. As a result, since her sessions could not fill up all of her time, life outside of the therapeutic hours became frightening and depressing. The depression, however, was a dimension of her existence that could at least be recognized and dealt with, now that no outside agent, such as food or alcohol, interfered. A therapeutic continuity could be established that was reasonable enough to allow a search for the discontinuous elements in the structure of her ego in order to achieve continuity and integration. It was possible to become meaningfully involved in discussing her dynamics and the links between past and present. Two years after she began treatment, she was able to quit her job (which was obviously much below her potential), and enroll in a full-time college program. She managed to support herself through various odd jobs, as well as through financial aid from the state government. She slowly developed an intense interest in writing, however, a subject that could not have been chosen without some unconscious need to undermine whatever she had achieved by then.

To say the least, I was rather skeptical about the choice of writing for a variety of reasons; nevertheless, I did not totally discourage her from pursuing it. She was extremely adamant about this choice. It was pretty clear, of course, that if she could learn the behavioral and cognitive discipline required of a person seriously interested in developing as a writer, she could then feel secure enough to eventually choose whatever other career or training she wished if the writing turned out unsuited to her personality or her talents. As a writer she had to endure loneliness, despair, depression, feelings of isolation, emptiness, lack of reinforcement, and a continuous dependence on outside sources for financial support.

Her writing was so incoherent in the beginning phases that she was often ready to give up. During these difficult times, it appeared that whatever therapeutic progress she had made seemed only a superficial learning of the rules of therapy, and any pinprick was liable to expose that progress as a myth in which both participants wanted to believe. However, although the course of treatment continued to be extremely rocky and often tenuous, her disengagement from her destructive, addictive habits, led me to believe that Eileen's dynamics were amenable to understanding and treatment. Indeed, her personality structure clearly surfaced as a "borderline personality," although initially the narcissistic component was of central significance. I continued her treatment on that basis, and used any techniques that were necessary to help her resolve some of the basic problems she had brought to treatment.

As mentioned earlier, Eileen's dependence intensified—something she resented and learned to express openly by continuously questioning my competence in helping her arrive at a more balanced life. As evidence she brought up the fact that "therapy" had turned her into a hermit—her social life was nonexistent. Only once in a while would she be invited for dinners with an old friend, but by and large, most of her so-called friends abandoned her. She justified their attitude toward her because she was able to recognize that her behavior had been quite immature, destructive, and incoherent. But now that she felt more integrated, she lamented her lack of friends, and complained of her inability, or rather lack of knowledge, of how to establish relationships with "desirable" people. Her taste in people changed, so she claimed, because she had gotten to know me and she wished to have friends of my "calibre." Her loneliness was so intense at times that I couldn't help but empathize with her, and sometimes cry with her when she cried. However, her suffering did not prevent her from functioning at school and eventually learning to discipline herself and work very hard on her writing, at times sitting more than ten hours a day at the typewriter. Slowly her diligence began to pay off, especially because she started to enjoy her writing and occupy her mind with creating her characters rather than with schemes of a grandiose nature. Her instructors recognized her talent and encouraged her writing, and when she finished college and went on to graduate school, she had already written a number of high quality essays and begun an ambitious new novel.

The sessions were quite stormy at times, simply because she still could not accept herself as a full-fledged member of society, primarily because of her low self-esteem. Yet, paradoxically, she was engaged in productive and creative work, and she took excellent care of her body through her diet, sobriety, and physical exercise. It seemed as though she was still holding on to her past without giving enough credit to her present achievement. There was no doubt that the time had come for me to confront her with what I felt was the crux of the problem at that time—her deep dependent transference to me. She readily recognized this problem, but also managed to rationalize away her lack of separation from me by her contention that she was too involved with her work to pay attention to "social" relationships. Underneath this facade, however, there was a semiconscious fantasy that when she became a full-fledged famous writer, I would abandon my family and take off with her into the sunset, and then I could take care of her for the rest of her life. This fantasy was by no means Oedipal; it was completely and surely of an oral dependency type. The battle for separation continued for over two years, during which she wrote me letters when I was on vacation. Finally, she began to accept the painful reality of my unavailability for her as a mate, and began to be more outgoing, to enjoy reasonably social encounters, and to widen her horizons in general. Termination of treatment after eight years seemed both natural and inevitable.

Further Comments on the Treatment of the Borderline Personality.

While writers often disagree as to which symptomatology and dynamics to include under the wide umbrella of the borderline category, there is a general consensus that the treatment approach employed for these patients must be different from the one used for other categories. Schmideberg (1955), for example, writes, "The borderline patient poses a serious therapeutic problem, as the accepted method with which we approach both the psychoses and the neuroses are inadequate." According to her, the therapist must be much more actively involved when treating a borderline: "We cannot, as in classical analysis, remain detached onlookers, allowing the therapeutic process to unfold." The therapist is required to vary his techniques and strategy, as illustrated in the case of Eileen. The question, however, always remains as to what goals one can develop for the borderline, or even whether it is altogether reasonable to contemplate any kind of planning. Schmideberg feels that one should "distinguish between long- and short-term aims. . . . The short-term aim is to establish contact, bring some relief, make the situation tolerable for the patient and others, and, in particular, limit his acting out or withdrawal. Then we can gradually proceed to socialize him. Without initial improvement, treatment is likely to be broken off." The achievement of short-term goals is certainly no easy task in most cases, primarily because of the ever-shifting, inconsistent, labile patterns that the borderlines manifest. The nature of the patient's pathology and dynamics inevitably places the therapist in the difficult position of being perceived by the patient as siding with one extreme part of his ego or the other, regardless of how the therapist intervenes, because both parts can be simultaneously available to the patient and utilized in the service of camouflaging the sources of his anger. These constant changes do not help the patient recognize and resolve the problems that produce the anxiety, nor do they allow the therapist to plan ahead for a reasonable interventional strategy. Arieti (1955), describing one type of borderline personality writes, "The changes in mood and attitudes do not relieve these patients. They often resort to excessive use of drugs and alcohol. The crises they go through weaken them progressively."

Yet, it is essential that such a patient be looked at as a lost child looking for a direction from a consistent, strong, and benevolent source, who can guide the patient to reach secure shores. Although work with borderline patients often necessitates the adoption of strategies quite different from the ones used with the neurotic or psychotic patient, the central confrontation analysis goal may also be pursued—i.e., the resolution of basic dependency conflicts through the satisfactory expression of interpersonal emotionality and communication, and through the evolution of a unique identity. Arieti also sees dependency as the root or motivating factor in the borderline (stormy) personality's pathological adjustment:

> In their attempt to gain approval and love, and to avoid disapproval, they try all types of attitudes, and all of them to an extreme degree. They have to try all possible means of defense and reactions, because none of them seems actually able to remove the existing anxiety. This uncertainty about the way of reacting is enhanced by the inconsistency of the parents. Thus, the early environmental situation promotes in them a capacity to change their attitudes toward life repeatedly. The changes may be slow or abrupt, oftener, they are sudden, violent, and drastic.

It is clear then, that in the treatment situation with the borderline personality there exists an immediate block to establishing a therapeutic contact, precisely because of such characteristics as the unpredictable alterability of the patient's reactions through the use of an outside agent, such as alcohol, which blocks a direct contact or communication. What, then, can the therapist do to get to first base in the face of such an active, overt characterological resistance? A strategy of confrontation should not be ruled out. Of course, confrontations are defined on a variety of levels and have many aspects, and they carry differential meanings to different types of borderline patients. The borderline patient is already constantly dealing with a variety of confrontations within his inner self because of very dynamic fluctuations from one stance to another, or "splitting." The borderline carries these inner confrontations up to a point, however, not long enough to experience a continuity of feeling, precisely because such feelings might be too threatening. Dynamically this process could be interpreted as the repetition, as Arieti suggests, of the inconsistencies that the patient experienced as a child in interactions with inconsistent parents. As he grew up, these patterns of inconsistent reactions were internalized, and now, as an adult, any insistence (by a therapist) on a consistent set of reactions becomes too overwhelming for the patient to handle and, thus, a flooding of anxiety might bring about the tendency to flee. If the pain is too great, decompensation becomes a real possibility. Yet without *some* constancy there can be no possibility of any real engagement of the patient therapeutically. The choice seems clear. To confront the patient, *not* with his pathology or inconsistency, and demand that the patient "lose" the syndrome on the way to the therapeutic hour would accomplish very little. The patient may be confronted, however, with the therapist's understanding of how the therapist can work with him to help. The patient is not told that the symptoms (e.g. alcoholism) are bad for him, because such statements are likely to be interpreted as a reproach by the therapist (Kibel, 1978), but the patient can be told that his symptoms stand in the way of understanding what his or her problems might be, which makes it impossible to chart a course of treatment. Thus, from the beginning, the therapist lets the patient in on how he works, and in a gentle yet firm manner, establishes a foundation for a workable therapeutic contract.

Acceptance of such a contract by the patient will probably affect the course of treatment, as was the case with Eileen. In fact, such a contract is almost a sine qua non to working effectively with borderline addictive personalities. No therapist can help an individual make basic personality changes if there is no continuity to the sessions, with the treatment conducted only on an irregular basis, depending on the anxiety level of that individual. Such treatment cannot be called therapy, which is a systematic approach to the amelioration of psychological problems, although it may be therapeutic, meaning that it could be helpful in relieving immediate or transient difficulties. The therapist must admittedly and openly take the responsibility for "prescribing" to the patient (at least) the immediate course of treatment, which will inevitably result in the intensification of the patient's dependency. Without the creation of therapeutic dependency, however, there is very little chance for any transferential relationship to develop, and, hence, a therapeutic one.

The borderline patient lacks the basic "tools" needed to live free of overwhelming anxiety or depression and, therefore, the therapist must create the psychological atmosphere in which he can acquire such tools. These "tools" are the behavior patterns normally developed during the individual's greatest dependency period, in the first and second years of life. This dependency on the parents *forces* the child to imitate, and, consequently, incorporate some of what transpires in this matrix of interaction. Thus the characteristic patterns of inconsistency of the borderline syndrome stem from this early conditioning occurring in the context of dependency. When the therapist purposefully fosters, by his strategy, dependence on himself, it is intended to simulate the relational matrix of early childhood, thus enabling the therapist and the patient to work through, in the here and now, the present distortions and pathological adjustment that had not been resolved during maturation.

A multitude of techniques are used in treatment of the borderline. These techniques are not unique to confrontation analysis, except, of course, in one aspect: the confrontation analysis sequence must be closely adhered to—i.e., analysis of the confrontations must be carried through within the same session. (In the treatment of neurotic patients, analysis of the confrontations can wait for later sessions because the ego is not as fragmented as it is with the borderline patient.) Needless to say, confrontations and their analysis occur quite frequently, and they are always geared toward strengthening the patient's ability to integrate new material.

The Projective Technique

The borderline patient is often reluctant to discuss his feelings directly because of overwhelming distress and distrust of the listener. The therapist might then encourage such a patient to talk more about other people, perhaps close friends, relatives, neighbors, etc. In this manner the patient is likely to project his own feelings unconsciously onto others; but eventually, when the projections become increasingly removed from objective reality, the patient might, with little interpretive or confrontational statements, recognize himself in these projections. This technique, appropriately called "projective," is very useful with a variety of patients where denial mechanisms are major defenses, as well as with children. In fact, play therapy techniques are based on this technique and its theoretical ratioanle. In the case of Eileen, this technique was used quite often, as she was only too eager to delve into her fantasies about other people, especially parents, and wished-for identification figures, such as famous actors and writers. It was interesting, however, that although she often recognized her own projections as such, she did not feel inhibited about continuing to use others for the expression of her own feelings. The borderline patient often has an unusually rich fantasy life, with a capacity to bring out deep unconscious material veiled in these projections. There are, of course, some borderline patients whose mental activity has become so curtailed that their communications and general expression of emotionality are painfully monotonous, colorless, and most superficial. The projective technique is less likely to be helpful in these cases.

Another aspect of this technique is the use of drawings in conjunction with story-telling or letter-writing. The patient is asked to draw a picture, whatever he wishes to draw—an object, a feeling, a person, a family, a tree, and then to tell a story about it. This technique is an extension of the projective tests often used by psychologists in psychological evaluations. In this use, however, the patient is encouraged to associate freely to the material produced, as well as to specific, past or present, life situations, including therapeutic goals. An addition to this technique is the inclusion, with certain patients, of letter-writing: the patient writes letters from one object of the drawing to another. At times, when the patient feels too inhibited or stumped, and cannot think of using the drawing as a springboard for writing, he may be asked to compose a statement to send to the object of the drawing, or to write a letter from that person or object to the therapist, and then perhaps to imagine what answer he is likely to receive. The material stimulated by this technique is at times fascinating, and is used to enhance the communicative interaction between the patient and the therapist. This technique and its variations are practically limitless in the kind of projections one can help the patient produce, and the more the better, since projections are extremely useful in understanding the inner life of any individual, and they may be used as grist for the mill, just like any other material. Of course, all transference manifestations are, in fact, projections too, and must be analyzed and interpreted.

Projections are helpful in the treatment of borderline patients for additional reasons. As the patient projects his inner life onto objects in the outside without punishment or recrimination, he comes to feel increasingly more secure relating to those objects in a conscious manner and with lowered anxiety. This process may be likened to a situation where a child is able to confront an unpleasant or threatening situation while holding on to his mother. Thus, projections under these conditions become transitional (communication) objects that eventually lead to more direct communications. The therapist's role in these transactions is to help the patient become aware of the possibility of various alternative communications and emotional reactions to the projected objects, so that a set of interpersonal interactions are learned that are most suitable for the patient emotionally. The repetitiveness of this process under different emotional states during the therapeutic sessions provides opportunities for re-education in the area of socialization, realignment of object relations, and, indeed redefinition of the nature of the patient's identification with these objects. Regression in the service of therapeutic changes naturally occurs in all projections in the treatment situation, but the presence of the dependable personality of the therapist enables the patient to work through conflicts and to emerge with a less defective ego rather than decompensating, as some authors seem to suggest (Frosch, 1964; Gunderson and Singer, 1975; Wolberg, 1973; Kibel, 1978). Schmideberg (1955) agrees that the personality of the therapist is of crucial importance, since the patient's "ego develops largely through identification, and, hence, identification with a therapist who has a strong personality is desirable."

It has often been mentioned that the borderline symptomatology emerges as a defensive maneuver against extreme unacceptable rage and, therefore, confrontation with the symptomatology might be too threatening because the rage might then flood the ego and result in decompensation (Kibel, 1978). However, precisely because of this possibility, the patient who is confronted with his projections through this technique, in the presence of the protective atmosphere of the therapeutic alliance, has the chance to become desensitized to fears of world and self-destruction, as well as to the megalomanic delusional tendencies that his fantasies keep promoting as long as they are kept brewing without *some* expression. Since the patient is not consciously talking about himself in this technique, he eventually begins to recognize the difference between reality and fantasy, between what happens internally and outside. Of course, this does not apply to those patients whose ego is so brittle that any direct or indirect threat might cause ego disintegration and lead to psychotic manifestations. These patients should not be included in the borderline category, because their characterological organization does not maintain the kind of stability that the borderline possesses. In fact, resiliency in the face of crises is often greater in the borderline than even in the neurotic, largely because of the borderline's ability to identify with the catastrophic elements of the crisis while at the same time shifting the focus of attention, through detachment and splitting, to another area of concern, thus avoiding crippling anxiety. While this is *not typical* of all borderline patients, it is at times surprising how many of them are capable of weathering difficult situtions.

Involvement of Therapist

Unlike the "average" neurotic patient, the borderline patient requires a willingness on the part of the therapist to become much more personally involved—of course, without jeopardizing the therapeutic relationship. At times, the therapist must be willing to give the patient direct suggestions and to help the patient comprehend the relationship between the suggestions and his goals. An example of this technique would be the presentation of concrete alternatives from which the patient might choose in areas of education, business, jobs, and interpersonal relationships, and where he might be experiencing the kind of indecision that cripples movement in one direction or another. The therapist's involvement is also helpful where a pattern of rigid, compulsive, or impulsive behavior has developed that affects the patient's life to a degree that is dangerous. Naturally, all possible advantages and disadvantages must be weighed before the therapist makes a recommendation. The time spent in helping a patient cope with decisions about daily functioning is often more productive than analysis of a gnawing chronic conflict, simply because the patient may have never had an opportunity to learn how to begin to search for alternatives, or cannot integrate any intellectual insights when anxiety is too overwhelming. Some patients never acquire these basic "skills" during their development, and when faced with certain requirements from their environment, their behavior seems so inappropiate to others that it creates a great deal of distance and, consequently, isolation, awkwardness, and suspicion and fear of the outside world.

Personal involvement of the therapist involves a type of interaction that is similar to that encountered between friends, such as accepting invitations to certain (circumscribed) important functions in which the patient is an active participant, such as the patient's own wedding, or his participation as an artist in a concert or as an exhibitor of art work at a gallery, or the launching of a new business, or a graduation ceremony. Schmideberg (1955), discussing her own approach, warns that,

> the therapist must avoid a mirror-like, objective attitude and must not be afraid to be himself, take responsibility, voice opinions and values, and show initiative. This is yet another reason why a self-effacement of the classical analyst is ill-advised for borderline patients. Much of this detachment is defensive on the part of the therapist and is unnecessary if we are capable of coping with the patient.

Schmideberg thus advocates a more personal approach:

> I talk spontaneously, and often make a point of appearing nonprofessional. If a patient finds it diffcult to talk, I ask questions or talk myself, attempting to put him at ease. Sometimes, I may start talking about myself or my interests, with controlled spontaneity, or I discuss subjects in which he might be interested. I occasionally offer a cigarette, have coffee with the patient, lend him a book, etc.

This sensible approach is accompanied in confrontation analysis by a continuous examination, within the session, of the interaction between the patient and the therapist, with the aim of reinforcing (and reeducating) an open interpersonal communication. The patient will gradually discover that the therapist is neither parent, nor adversary.

For example, during the fifth year of Eileen's treatment, she walked in to her session and inquired whether she could ask me a personal question. She had asked personal questions before, so I was somewhat surprised that she asked for permission. She then said, "Every time I come here, you open the door in the same way, and you're always smiling. Are you really always happy to see me, or are you trying to cover up something?" I laughed spontaneously in appreciation of her perceptiveness, and what appeared to be her sarcasm, but before I answered, she continued, "And don't give me one of your smart alecky answers. I mean, Dr. Cohen, you can't be feeling happy all the time, because, well, I imagine you must feel something. I mean I know you are the therapist, but sometimes I see somebody coming out of here crying their eyes out, and you open the door, and you smile at me." I was truly embarrassed by this observation about my inappropriate behavior, and said to her, "You know, you're absolutely right. I am embarrassed. I don't think I have ever thought about my expression when I greet you, but I am sure that I don't always feel that happy, so I must be doing something to hide my feelings. I appreciate your bringing this to my attention. Perhaps I am trying too hard to be nice. Do you have any idea why I do that?" She didn't have any interpretation, but seemed quite pleased by the impact she had made. I was interested in this phenomenon in myself, and after awhile, I came up with a certain understanding of my behavior, although this was obviously not the whole picture. It had something to do with my past history, which I related to her, "It occurred to me that my inappropriate smile when I open the door had something to do with the way I was trained. As a little boy, I was told to welcome relatives and other guests nicely, regardless of how I felt about them, or how I felt at the time. My parents insisted on hiding from the world whatever was happening inside our house, and their best approach was to pretend that everything was in tip-top shape. I guess I have developed a habit like that. You know you are the only one who was courageous enough to tell me this." She then said that it had been on her mind for quite a while, but she had been afraid to confront me. It was this fear of confronting other people, especially men, with the obvious lack of congruence between their feelings and their behavior toward her, that perpetuated her resentment toward them. Later in the session, we were able to begin a dialogue relating to her feelings of discomfort with the inconsistencies of her own behavior and her need to deny real feelings because of the fear of abandonment. My opening up to her on this level and sharing with her some of my of own dynamics and history made it possible for her to become less defensive, thus enabling her to look at discontinuities in her own functioning. This type of personal input on the part of the therapist, when well-timed, is no doubt a technique that can be extremely helpful to the patient, but obviously does not suit every therapist's philosophy of treatment or personal style. The therapist must be comfortable with this style of operation, otherwise he might appear to be patronizing, pretentious, and self-serving.

Physical Activity

One of the outstanding characteristics of the borderline patient is a negative, and often distorted, self-image, based in the parents' impressions of, and reactions to, the child's physical self. This self is thus the "container" for all incoming reactions that are eventually absorbed and integrated as part of the total personality. As part of the total image of the self, the body image occupies an important amount of psychological space. One of the striking psychological factors that is greatly distorted in the borderline patient is body image, and confrontation analysis attempts to help such a patient reassess this image, and actively works on this aspect of the self. The rationale is quite simple: an enlightened body image can significantly contribute to a healthier perception of the self. At times, a program of physical exercises should be added to the routine activities of the patient. Such a program often helps the borderline in a variety of areas: development of mastery over body movement, the planning and execution of activities on a routine basis, development of concrete (physical) ego boundaries, and disposal of a great deal of energy encapsulating the reservoir of rage. Patients may be encouraged to seek physical fitness programs, and helped to plan specific time schedules, places for exercise, types of exercise, and a host of other related subjects that promote knowledge of their body and their physical capabilities. This will often result in dramatic changes in self-image in patients who have begun to treat themselves in a more respectful, kindly, and pleasurable manner.

A 32-year-old borderline high school teacher who had been overprotected by his mother, was extremely overweight, and had thought he was incapable of running more than ten feet without collapsing, was finally convinced to leave his "scholarly" detachment one weekend and join a teachers' ski tour that had been organized by one of his colleagues. The joy and excitement that he experienced sliding down the little slope generated an incredible amount of enthusiasm, which eventually turned him into an avid skier. His interpersonal relationships improved dramatically, and in a relatively short time, he became courageous enough to chance social encounters that he had never dared previously. Of course, skiing was not the only factor, but it was, for this man, a determining one, for it restored a certain amount of pride and confidence in his body image, and helped reinforce many of the psychological insights that he had already acquired about his self-image, thus encouraging behavior more commensurate with his insights. Getting in touch with positive feelings about his body helped him get in touch with his self-imposed isolation and fear of separation from his protective family, and changed his course of existence in the direction of emotional interaction with the outside world. As a high school mathematics teacher, he had always felt intimidated by the physical prowess of his students, and for years had assumed a scapegoat stance, which he studiously denied through his detachment and isolation. His confrontation with his own body, which he was able to achieve through his participation in the skiing activities, eventually helped him to see himself as part of the social order, rather than as a "reject." Finally, his participation, first physically and then socially, also helped deflate and drain a great deal of his rage at his mother, which was bound to burst out self-destructively had he not taken those initial steps to follow up on the direct therapeutic recommendations.

The techniques described here are by no means exhaustive. They are only illustrations of the variety of available possibilities that the therapist can, and sometimes must, use with the borderline patient to achieve therapeutic aims. While these techniques must be considered just that, and not as the totality of treatment, they are nevertheless a challenge to both patient and therapist, because they must be used with extreme sensitivity, knowledge of the patient's dynamics, and the willingness to deviate from rigidly conditioned patterns of treatment. Needless to say, not all therapists can or should use such techniques, because some of these techniques may be ill-suited to their personality style or their treatment philosophy.

Identity

THE SEARCH FOR A DEFINITION

Two central goals of confrontation analysis have so far been discussed: modification of distorted communication and achievement of a balanced emotional life. Both goals are necessary for the building of a personality in which dependency needs do not play an inordinate role. There is another vitally important treatment objective, also organically intertwined with the problem of dependence, namely, the establishment of a unique identity. The relationship between identity, at times referred to as *self* and/or *ego* (Guntrip, 1969), and dependence has been clearly implied by Erikson (1962), in his analytical study of Martin Luther:

> The timespan of man's dependence on the personal and cultural style of the person or persons who first take care of him is very long: and the firmness of his early ego development depends on the consistency of the style of that person.

Identity is perhaps the essence of psychotherapeutic goals in general. Freud spelled out this aim in his later writings, and in his 1937 essay, "Analysis Terminable and Interminable," he wrote,

Our aim will not be to rub off every peculiarity of human character for the sake of a schematic "normality" nor yet to demand that the person who had been "thoroughly analyzed" shall feel no passion and develop no internal conflicts. The business of analysis is to secure the best possible psychological conditions for the functions of the ego; with that it has discharged its task.

In a similar vein, Guntrip (1969) states that, "psychoanalysis has become the search for the ego as the core of reality in the person."

Identity is a most complex concept, one that defies a parsimonious, operational definition. According to Erikson (1968), identity should not be confused with identification, although "linguistically as well as psychologically, identity and identification have common roots." Thus he does not favor a definition of identity as "the mere sum of earlier identifications," or "an additional set of identifications," because he considers the mechanism of identification to have a "limited usefulness." He states that,

Identity formulation, finally begins where the usefulness of identification ends. It arises from the selective repudiation and mutual assimilation of childhood identifications and their absorption in a new configuration, which, in turn, is dependent on the process by which a society (often through subsocieties) identifies the young individual, recognizing him as somebody who had to become the way he is and who, often not without some initial mistrust, gives such recognition with a display of surprise and pleasure in making the acquaintance of a newly emerging individual.

The fact that this concept eludes a simple or a unified definition can be appreciated from Erikson's (1968) own struggle with it, and his usage of it in a multiplicity of meanings in a variety of contextual frameworks. Thus he states,

So far I have tried out the term identity almost deliberately—I like to think—in many different connotations. At one time it seemed to refer to a conscious sense of individual uniqueness, at another to an unconscious striving for a continuity of experience, and at a third, as a solidarity with a group's ideals.

Yet, at one place in his exposition of the subject, he does make use of the concept of identification in a very basic manner in order to arrive at a reasonable understanding of identity:

the final identity, then, as fixed at the end of adolescence, is superordinated to any single identification with individuals of the past: *it includes all significant identifications* but it also alters them in order to make a unique and reasonably coherent whole of them (*emphasis added*).

Erikson's approach to the question of identity is very helpful, because he utilizes developmental, structural, and dynamic elements to define it, thus making it comprehensive and specific at the same time. It allows for an understanding of identity as a flexible, changing, and modifiable entity, and it points to a direction for investigating its phenomenology and history, although not without certain difficulties. In an earlier essay concerning the subject of identity, Erikson (1959) widened the scope of the term by including as part of the definition the inner experience of the person, not only his "persona." Thus he writes, "It (identity) connotes both a persistent sameness within one's self (self-sameness) and a persistent sharing of some kind of essential character with others." The general idea one gets from Erikson's view of identity is that he perceived it to be multifaceted, consisting of numerous elements, and yet unified through an integrational process that makes one person unique and different from another. Such a conception is daily validated through every clinician's experience with most patients' unmistakeable quest for knowledge of their identity. The statement, often made by those who enter treatment, "I want to find out who I am," is no simple cliché, but an honest expression of their search for an identity that is not someone else's but uniquely theirs. Their lack of knowledge of their identity pertains to both the confused inner experience of their selfhood and the image they project to others around them and for them. The term is here used interchangeably with such concepts as ego, self, and personality. The reason for this is that identity encompasses, at different times, in different contexts, and on various levels of abstraction, all of these aspects of the person, thus making it at least impractical, if not imposible, to separate them in any meaningfully *operational* manner. The purpose here is not to provide theoretical or semantic models, but rather to deal with these concepts in their accepted use in the literature, in order to show how the confrontation analysis system differs, or is in agreement, with other therapeutic systems in clinical practice. Naturally, on occasions where certain concepts must be clarified or redefined in order to have consistency and cohesion of the presentation, an attempt is made in that direction. To achieve this goal, the issue of identity will be approached from several therapeutically central parameters—parameters that have repeatedly been dealt with in previous sections, but obviously, in their relation to other themes.

The modus vivendi and modus operandi of identity depend on the nature of the individual's earliest relationship with mothering and other supporting environments. It grows in and out of the universal condition of dependency, a condition that leaves an indelible mark on the structure of the personality and its behavior patterns. As the individual grows, personality gradually and increasingly assumes a uniqueness of its own, both as he experiences it and as others perceive it. The baby starts to recognize differences between himself and others quite early, perhaps by the third or fourth month, and with increased awareness also develops a sense of separateness and a beginning knowledge of where he ends and others start. These early months in the life of the child, and the following year or two when the child becomes more mobile and physically exploratory of his surroundings, are of supreme significance, for they determine how he will develop that sense of self as a separate entity with needs and pathways to satisfy them. An ideal environment in which to develop a personality with a relatively distinct identity is supportive, nurturing, with adequate structuring and boundary setting, and where the child is experienced as a welcome part of it. In reality, however, since optimum conditions are not easy to obtain, the development of various degrees of distortion in an individual's sense of identity is inevitable. These distortions necessarily manifest themselves in every aspect of the individual's life, including the therapeutic situation.

The assumptions, hypotheses, and conclusions that are presented are based on clinical material, and generalizations from it may thus be risky, although not unreasonable if one accepts the premise that the therapeutic setting, to some measure, unconsciously represents the outside environment for the patient.

12
Identity and Dependence

Part I of this book offered an approach to the resolution of human conflicts based on the dependency hypothesis. This hypothesis makes the explicit assumption that dependency is a universal condition encountered by every human being from the moment of birth onward, and that its nature and development is dictated, to a considerable degree, by the nature of the interaction between the infant and its mother. This means that, eventually, such interaction also affects the kind of personality that the individual will develop and the kind of distortions in its various dimensions and traits. These dimensions are part of the individual's identity, and therefore, distortions in their development are, in one way or another, synonymous with distortions in identity. It may therefore seem redundant to discuss identity as a goal and how confrontation analysis approaches it in the therapeutic setting, since these dimensions have already been dealt with earlier in the book. Yet, as Erikson (1968) noted, the concept of identity refers to something more than the sum of its parts, and the course of its development is organically bound to the individual's struggle with dependency strivings. Thus there are a number of aspects of the structure of identity in which the level of dependency plays a crucial role.

378

Personal and Familial History

The extent and nature of an individual's sense of his own personal history, as it relates to family origins, is often an excellent indicator of that individual's own sense of identity. The less aware and appreciative a person is of the continuity of his life history and how it emanates from his original group—the family—the more likely he is to experience problems in identity, in the sense of self. The extreme opposite of such an awareness leads to similar results: if an individual is too obsessed with his history and "family tree," that individual is likely to manifest (and no doubt experience) problems in self-identity. While this statement seems self-evident, its relationship to the problem of dependence is not apparent. In fact it is not often discussed in the pertinent literature, possibly because the concept of identity is generally thought of as a social-psychological one rather than "purely" psychological or belonging to the psychodynamics of personality development. Identity as such is very rarely discussed in psychoanalytic or dynamically oriented psychotherapy texts in any extensive manner, except, usually, as it pertains to adolescence. Perhaps this is because, as mentioned earlier, other terms are employed to represent it, such as ego, self, personality, character, or ego-identity.

The case of Alice presents a clinical example of distortions in the sense of identity as related to problems of dependence emanating from *familial discontinuities*. Alice was a 29-year-old single woman who sought treatment because of depression and feelings of isolation. She was a highly intelligent, capable, and attractive woman who worked as an editor in a publishing company. Although her speech was pressured and quite angry during the first consultation, she was generally coherent and unusually fluent verbally. Her general manner was, however, that of someone who was trying very hard to please. For example, many of her statements were accompanied by a forced smile, seemingly related to "normal," initial-session anxiety. Yet, her depression, which she attributed mostly to the absence of a satisfying relationship with a man and lack of advancement on the job, clearly seemed to relate more to her nonverbal rather than verbal communication.

Treatment was not new to Alice—she had been in and out of it for the preceding ten years, with three different analysts.

She said she had always left treatment dissatisfied because she was getting nowhere with it; it had not helped her "find" herself or given her any guidance and direction for the future. While she did not directly blame her therapists for this state of affairs, she characterized them as being "very passive" and perhaps afraid of her. I found this assessment of her therapists rather likely in view of her behavior in the initial stages of treatment: she was rather belligerent, verbally very active and quite capable of shutting out others, psychologically fairly sophisticated, and, in a seductive way, very adept at playing the "patient role." Thus, I could imagine a back-seat attitude on the part of some therapists for a long time, at which point it becomes too late to "change seats." Alice knew how to talk about all the "relevant" material—from dreams to childhood memories, from parents to teachers and supervisors, from anger and depression to sexual fantasies and acting-out. Her versatility was so superior that it was hard at times to keep in mind that she was a patient rather than a lecturer on the philosophical aspects of life and its vicissitudes!

On the surface one would hardly associate this patient's basic conflicts with a lack of well-defined identity or strong ego boundaries. She might, in fact, have been characterized by the casual observer as having a rather distinct identity because of her forceful and aggressive style. Indeed, she reported that on a number of occasions, her friends and some colleagues at work marvelled at her strength of character and "unique" personality. Yet these very people attempted to keep their distance from her. Only after some time in therapy was it possible to delineate more clearly this seeming contradiction, and understand its roots within her personality dynamics rather than attribute it simply to these people's fear and feelings of threat because of her aggressive style, a theory she liked to hold onto for dear life.

In the initial interview Alice was quite verbal, but clearly with an underlying depressive tone. She said she was concerned about the possibility of losing her job, in which she had been "stuck" for over five years. She believed that she was intensely disliked by two other women in her department who probably "have it *in for* me and *in with* my boss, if you understand what I mean." It later developed that these two women were, according to her, jealous of her capacity to attract men, especially her seductiveness toward the men at work, and they were also "envious" of her capacity to express herself "openly" in social situations.

This story about her job situation was followed by a discussion in a very methodical, historical fashion, of the various affairs she had had with men, some lasting for over a year, others for much shorter periods (perhaps one or two weeks), all of which were terminated by her, usually in an explosive manner. She characterized all the men she had been involved with as very passive, immature, unreliable, sexually unsatisfying, and most of all lacking in "substance." The last man, who she had left just about a week before she came to see me, was a "dope pusher," a man who had been "hiding from himself for as long as I knew him." Her attachment to him was rationalized by her feeling that he was a "good lover," which meant that he was able to help her reach an orgasm by the use of mechanical objects during their so-called lovemaking. Although this was the only way she could gain sexual satisfaction, she considered herself lucky (at least on a conscious level) because she believed that "90 percent of my friends never reach an orgasm no matter what they do, and they always pretend, like I did with every man I slept."

From this subject Alice proceeded to discuss her family history with an increasingly depressed tone, although she never lost her verbal fluency. She was the oldest of four children— three sisters and a brother, the youngest. She characterized her parents as "two children who made children to feel grown up," and she had no respect for either one, considering both of them to be failures on every item down the list, "lost in the world of make believe," and never capable of "giving me a clear and meaningful way of life. Especially my dad." Later she added that her father was "very strict, but then he would become remorseful and change his mind." Her father wished that Alice were in an occupation or profession different from the one in which she was engaged because he considered her to be "the commercial, bright, not very deep type." She bemoaned, "He always tore me down, always told me I had no backbone, that I wasn't a real part of the lineage," disdainfully adding "as if he were somebody with a backbone. Oh God!" She did accept his evaluation of her, however; for after all she was "only an extension of him." Alice's mother came through as much more vague. She was, according to Alice, "an overwhelmingly hostile, nagging mother, just like the secretaries in my office: whenever I' turn around they start talking about me." She complained that her mother always told her sisters whatever confidences she, Alice, entrusted in her, and that, in the final analysis, both parents punished her "for everything." Again, she felt she deserved the punishments because she was "a bully, a bossy-bully." She said that she liked her sisters but that the younger one was the real favorite with the parents, even though she was quite a nuisance to them because of her great need for attention, which was expressed, according to Alice, by her attempt to kill herself several times, requiring hospitalization. This younger sister was always "allowed to crawl up to my father's lap anytime. I was never able to do that, I mean never! And I was always jealous." Alice felt closest to her brother, although he was quite the opposite from her, and liked to keep to himself much of time.

Finally, toward the end of the session, she related a dream from the night before the interview that involved, among others, her last therapist, Dr. S.: "Dr. S. was doing a TV show about a homosexual detective, and he wanted me to be with him in the show because he needed a partner. He was pursuing me, I guess, and I felt embarrassed, like a bad person. He kept looking and looking at my breasts as if he never saw anything like that, or maybe there was something wrong with me. Then we went to a strange place with a lot of people, and there was a very pretty French girl, and I was speaking to her in French, and I was interested in her, I mean sexually. She asked me to go home with her, but I was afraid that I might lose my way back so I got very upset, and I told Dr. S. not to tell my mother about it, and he started laughing and laughing hysterically. I was really very upset when I woke up." This is more or less where the initial interview ended.

One of the most fascinating aspects of this initial interview was its excellent representation of the patient's personality and character. Alice was, without a doubt, "sophisticated" about the therapeutic marketplace. But more than that, she was also extremely adept at making herself seem totally understandable, when in reality she remained inaccessible and not as transparent as one might be led to believe. Although she appeared to have been telling a great deal about herself through her stories, her ingenuity at hiding her true feelings was expressed through a rather subtle technique: every person, every character, and every situation seemed to fit quite "naturally" the plan she devised, leaving no room for surprises, no place for unaccountable consequences. Thus, for instance, her parents' behavior and her office mates, even her analyst in the dream, all possessed masterfully orchestrated roles that led to a perception of herself that could easily "justify" her life style without excess anxiety. This unconscious deception was designed primarily to fend off her unconscious fear that she had a "ghost identity"—an identity without shape, form, or content, that had no history except one of constant denial. This could be seen, for example, through her complicated network of identifications, which were discernible only through their projective mirror images. For this reason she could not *see* herself as a hostile, aggressive woman like her mother, but could easily *talk about* her parents (introjected objects) as unacceptable identification objects because of the negative, bitchy, hostile traits she perceived in them. In this manner she consciously separated herself from them, in fact, from the family constellation as a whole.

This was a defensive, self-centered, basically narcissistic maneuver: First the patient severed, through a denial mechanism, the connection from the family by denouncing all the (perceived) negative attributes she could find in them, and then, supposedly floating in a cloud of total isolation as a result of this emotional severance, she pursued the unconscious fantasy that she had been robbed of the vital substance necessary to fill and shape her identity. Consequently, she felt justified in *demanding* to have her identity filled—or refilled—so that she could be complete as a person. Alice was capable, for instance, of claiming that she was totally different from her parents who, in her eyes, lacked any "backbone," demanding that she be given an identity, an ego, at least by the therapists, as one gathers from her verbalized complaints about them. Thus Alice's early need to emotionally remove or disconnect herself from her family created a psychological vacuum that did not allow her the development of a sense of identity. It may be hypothesized that such a defensive, narcissistic cocoon generally develops as a result of a failure in emotional continuity between mother and child that, through a process of interpersonal interaction during the child's growth in the first few years, normally provides the tools and materials that are the building blocks of identity.

The initial interview provided a great deal of material that demonstrated that the patient's manifest problems had their roots in her lack of identity or the sense of identity. These dynamics are often encountered in clinical practice; however, much of the time they are not recognized as problems in identity.

Perhaps the most striking features of the initial consultation were its well-organized delivery, its planning, and the specific and "rational" ordering of its themes. Normally, depressed or distraught patients present a different picture; they are often more emotionally charged, with little or no organization. They are likely to ask for direction, rarely volunteer a straighforward autobiographical history, and concern themselves mainly with the immediate issues that prompted them to seek help. Even if one allows, in this case, for the patient's experience of having been in treatment before, this session was clearly indicative of rather intense defensiveness, comparable to the resistance that some patients manifest when they come to their session with a prepared or written agenda. In this manner, they avoid the risks that unstructured situations may entail. Defenses serve the need of the ego to prevent the flooding of unmanageable anxiety, and, in this instance, the patient's behavior was a reaction to this feeling of threat. The question is, however, what the source of this particular anxiety was for the patient to have to be so well "prepared." As a general rule, overpreparation often stems from fears of failing in the task at hand and, of course, the ensuing danger of being left at the mercy of those who are in a (fantasized or real) position to evaluate the results.

The patient "prepared" a description of herself in what seemed a most logical manner: she started with a summary of her present most compelling problems, and without any probing or guidance, continued to discuss her family background, and finally ended the session with material (the dream) normally considered "appropriate" for therapeutic work. Since the patient had not *consciously* prepared the session in advance (this was learned in subsequent sessions), it seems reasonable to assume that the unconscious preparation was designed to guard against any awareness of her lack of sense of identity or of the content of her identity. Thus she had adopted a (fairly hardened) facade—a persona—that diminished the possibility of confrontation with her feelings of emptiness.

This unconscious defensiveness was so well entrenched that the social environment perceived her abrasiveness, aggression, and "organized self" as the expression of a "strong character." The feelings of inadequacy, emptiness, lack of uniqueness and inability to experience herself as a "real" person who stood for values she could call her own, did not begin to surface or be recognized before she was confronted with my insistence on knowing what was happening behind that thick armor. Of course, the therapeutic strategy had to take into account her ego strength—the resources that could be counted on if she had to give up some of her defenses. Fortunately, despite her indirect insistence on a "blackout" with regard to her identity, significant data were obtained, even from the first consultation alone, that allowed some understanding of the nature of her ego.

For one thing, Alice was quite ambivalent about most subjects she discussed during the initial interview. For example, while she claimed that she wished to have a satisfying relationship with a man, she also managed to paint a very negative image of men. By the same token, she was worried about losing a job that she did not care for and felt "stuck" with. Another subject of ambivalence was therapy: she concluded that she had not gained much from it, yet she continued to seek it and stay in it, at least for some time with each therapist. What can be made of this? There was a great deal of indecision—she was and was not involved in whatever she did. The meaning of indecision, often associated with ambivalence, can be traced to basic unresolved conflicts concerning the need for dependence and the fear of it. Alice maneuvered her life between these two polarities because, to her, an anchor in one place, a decision to follow one direction or another, meant giving up or separating from the opposite side, and her early childhood experiences had taught her that venturing out on her own would cause her a great deal of grief, a removal of support, or even worse, punishment. Her unsuccessful, repeated attempts to separate from such conditioning in her childhood robbed her of the capacity to function independently in a smooth manner, and at the same time to have a relationship with her parents without a rebelliousness characterized by a denial of her need for emotional support. The attachment to her parents was a negative one, and so was her identity. She unconsciously denied to herself the right and the capacity to have a positive identity. The result was, of course, an impoverished sense of self, a rather frightening prospect with which to face the world. Her solution was, inappropriate as it may be, the building of an armor that covered up this emptiness. It was a "struggle against identity" (Greenson, 1954). The very clear reason for the development of an aggressive and abrasive facade was no doubt to insure having some semblance of an identity for the sake of psychological survival, self-preservation. Dynamically, she was certainly unconsciously acting in line with her parental models—there was a significant identification with the "aggressor," behavior in which secondary gains are clearly related to approval from her parents by being, so to speak, like them.

Alice's lack of a sense of identity was also expressed through her negative perception of the generational bonds within the family. She reported that her parents' inability to convey a unified, consistent image of themselves in their everyday transactions was accompanied by a negative relationship toward their own parents, Alice's grandparents. When she was a child, her mother's parents lived with them, and Alice was constantly exposed to daily harsh arguments and "incredibly open" and direct instructions by her mother to "forget" her grandparents because "they're not worth it." In fact, Alice was not certain who her grandfather really was because her mother used to tell her "in a joking way" that Jack (the man living in the house and considered officially as the grandfather) "was not my real grandfather," but that Benny (a close friend of the family) was. In one of her sessions, she said, "I used to resent Jack tremendously." Her mother also always addressed her own father (Jack) by his first name, as if he were a stranger. These experiential confusions and discontinuities weakened Alice's chances to integrate her identity. Certainly, the combination of the parental rejection and lack of positive ties with other members of the family created a sense of emotional deprivation with a very real need to compensate for it. This compensation was often manifested by angry, controlling, and self-centered behavior. Some statements from the first interview clearly point to this problem:

"I never understood who belonged to whom."

"My (*maternal*) grandmother can't stand my mother."

"My father has a false confidence in himself and in me."

"I really feel that my father has always had contempt for me, as if I were some kind of an enemy or a freak."

"I make appointments with family and friends, and I don't keep them." (*Why not?*) "I know I am not going to be missed."

"Men are interested in me sexually, but they have no appreciation whatsoever of me as a person. I am just a hole to them, I am nothing."

"It's so hard to admit to yourself that you are promiscuous because that means that you are a nobody—nobody really cares for you as a special person and you don't care for anybody."

This brief clinical sketch clearly demonstrates how the lack of positive generational continuity within the family adversely affects the development of a sense of identity in the individual, as well as the organic link between pathological dependence and the absence of a healthy identity. Therefore, in a very real sense, one might conclude that commitment in a positive, nonpathological fashion to one's family history can indeed be a fairly accurate indication of a well-established identity.

Discussion of additional aspects of problems in identity and dependence follow, using clinical material from Alice's case for illustrative purposes.

Effects of Group Membership

Many patients seek treatment because they feel isolated and alienated from their surroundings and, as a result, they gradually lose their sense of well-being and become depressed or detached. The antecedents to such a development are numerous, not the least of which is the absence of the feeling of belongingness to a group—social, cultural, religious, political, educational, or familial. In the healthy individual, a feeling of belongingness need not be attached to an existent or actual group, but could be associated with a fantasied group with whom the individual shares something in common. The importance of such belonging cannot be overestimated because it is the source from which the individual receives feedback for his existence as a social animal. Such feedback is essential because it serves as a guide to behavior within the context of a specific human environment. When such feedback is missing, the individual cannot appreciate the relative appropriateness of his reactions to others and to himself, a situation that is conductive to inadequate interpersonal communication. Isolation (i.e., the consistent lack of feedback over prolonged periods of time) frequently produces most bizarre behavior patterns, and can also create an affective state that causes a great deal of pain. It is the interpersonal, as well as the physical, feedback that helps the child build a sense of individuality and a repertoire of discriminatory behavior. During infancy and early childhood, the individual receives his first and most solid foundation for identity, feelings of belongingness, and capacity for relatedness as a separate entity from his parents, especially the nurturing, mothering parent. When this parental web of communication, which provides feedback through structure and content, lacks essential elements of communicative interaction, the child grows up with an ego that is incapable of adequately defining its own boundaries.

These boundaries are the sine qua non for the establishment of feelings of belongingness to a group without the loss of identity. When such a process is absent because of faulty early object relationships, feelings of isolation are practically inevitable. Toward the end of the first year of life and the beginning of the second, the development of a sense of identity and separateness is established. During this time the child's struggle toward independence is most difficult because of the intrapsychic conflict between "regressive longings for refusion" with the mother, and the "developmental thrust towards individuation and self-reliance" (Burland, 1975). Burland adds that, according to Mahler's Rapprochement Subphase, the conflict "shows itself in the distress and contradictory push—pull behavior which characterizes the mother–child interaction during this subphase. Related to it there is also the elaboration of a double mental image of the mother, the . . . bad . . . *mother of separation* who is seen as excluding her child from sharing in her fantasied omnipotence and the . . . good . . . mother to whom the child turns when threatened or overwhelmed." This description parallels what happens in the relationship between the individual's identity and his belongingness to a group. If during the process of separation–individuation, boundaries are not clearly set, then either parasitic dependence or distancing and isolation can develop. In healthy development, the solution to this subphase conflict is, according to Burland, "the development of a new kind of relationship with mother, one that is loving but predicated on separateness and independence, and one in which therefore the good-mother–bad-mother split is healed." In the context of group membership, the healthy individual feels the sense of belonging without the need to give up his uniqueness, even though some idiosyncratic needs may have to be somewhat "compromised." On the other hand, when this process leads to isolation and lack of relatedness, many ego functions are distorted, and manifest themselves not only in the individual's behavior but also in the unconscious symbolic world obtained during regressed states such as dreaming and fantasizing, and in the context of transference.

With regard to identity, group membership, isolation, and ego distortions expressed in unconscious symbolism, Alice's dream from the initial interview has many implications; only a few will be explored here. The dream may be characterized as having manifest themes (Stolorow, 1978) of attachment–separation difficulties, sexual confusion and embarrassment, fear of mother, and fear of derision.

Attachment–separation. The patient dreamt about her previous therapist. While this is quite understandable, at least from the point of view of the time element, since she had only recently left him, the dream also indicated that her termination with him was by no means worked through, and that leaving at the time she did was a reaction to her fear of extreme dependence and vulnerability. However, since she could not bear the idea and the feeling of separation, she managed to produce a fantasied situation that would keep her tied to him—her projection that *he* needed a partner, not that *she* needed one. A projective defense in a dream such as this one is not an uncommon phenomenon in the highly intellectualized, obsessive personality. The lack of separation can also be inferred from *her* embarrassment about *his* pursuit. Another indication of her fear of separation was later related with reference to the strong pull, in the dream, not to pursue the interest in the French girl because she was afraid of losing her way back home. Although all of these were definite signs of dependency strivings, the overwhelming impression of the dream is also that of a person who is unable to function as a separate entity with an identity of her own.

Sexual confusion and embarrassment.   In the dream Alice was embarrassed about a man pursuing her, and simultaneously frightened by sexual feelings of a woman toward her, as well as her own feelings toward this woman. She often defined herself in sexual terms (e.g., the number of men she could attract as a sexual object) and yet, for a long time she did not feel free to discuss her sexual fantasies and feelings in any clear and specific manner in therapy. Her sexual interests were often directed toward women, although she was fearful of acting upon them, as is expressed in the dream. She behaved in a rather teasing and provocative way when the opportunity presented itself in the presence of otherwise likely female candidates, but she always withdrew in a childlike, immature manner. After a couple of years in therapy, however, her questions concerning her identity, especially her sexual identity, intensified, and with this pressure, reinforced by the pervasive influence of the Women's Liberation Movement, she felt compelled to act upon her feelings and to experience a homosexual relationship. Failing to experience any physical or sexual pleasure after the first homosexual encounter, she attempted a few more similar relationships, all of which were similarly experienced, with negative results, and proved not too different from her sexual experiences with men. In her fantasies, she always imagined the breasts as very attractive; however, when the actual physical contact became available, there was no excitement or enjoyment. Analysis of her behavior relative to these encounters revealed that she had a strong need to have a substitute mother, and a drive to "blend" into another woman because she felt her own self to be insignificant, unwanted by anybody, "bad," and "totally ungiving." Any attachment she made to another woman would be broken almost as fast as it was made, because she felt that her mother was part of any woman, and she was frightened of the prospect of living under the thumb of this "evil." She was also panic-stricken whenever she stayed with one woman more than a few days, because this signified that she could never have "a real family," meaning a man. Thus here again she felt that she had no home, no place for herself, and therefore, no identity. In the dream, she appears to have mixed the identities rather cleverly: in the beginning her analyst was playing a skit that included a homosexual character, but then he was also interested in her. Later, perhaps as she regresses further in the dream, her own sexual confusion surfaces with the interest in the French girl. She also projected her own feelings of inadequacy as a woman onto her doctor, as well as her sexual ambivalence, by assuming that he might have been looking at her breast because "there was something wrong with me."

Fear of mother.   On the manifest level, Alice's dream clearly indicated that she was fearful that her mother would find out that she was interested in another woman, a relationship strongly condemned. However, the underlying dynamics pointed to far more serious consequences. Alice's mother regarded her daughter as an undesirable child for many reasons that had nothing to do with Alice's behavior. For one, Alice was not born a boy, thus frustrating her mother's "integrity"—she had promised her husband a male child for the first-born. Alice was also unwelcome because her mother had felt unwelcome herself by her own mother (Alice's grandmother). Thus Alice's mother could not demonstrate, in a modeling fashion, a feeling that she did not possess about herself, let alone another person, and especially a female child. When Alice was a baby, her mother expected her to be all the things she felt she was not herself but wanted to be, naturally creating a self-fulfilling prophecy that she was worthless and whatever she produced was the same. Thus, feeling worthless and wanting, she deprived Alice—in a certain sense, her alter-self—of any positive feedback. This attitude created the basis for her daughter to perpetuate the "generational tradition" of isolation, lack of feeling of belonging, interpersonal distance, and, finally, impoverished identity. Any movement on Alice's part toward closeness with a man *or* a woman was thus understandably experienced as *treason* against the family tradition—something to be avoided for emotional survival.

Thus the basic dependence on the approval of the family, however unconscious and deeply ingrained it may be, floats to the surface whenever regressive forces take control of the patient's inner life. This basic dependence, when reinforced through emotional deprivation and constant negative input in the communication network between mother and child, eventually results in the establishment of a vicious cycle comprised of poor identity leading to emotional isolation, interpersonal withdrawal, absence of feedback, activation of poor self-image, which leads to a poor sense of identity, and so on.

Psychoanalytic theory posits that identity is primarily influenced and results from the successful resolution of the Oedipal situation, involving mainly superego structures. In my opinion this theory discards the unavoidable, observable fact that identity develops as a result of the infant's successful learning to separate and individuate much earlier than the Oedipal phase, during the oral phase, primarily involving id and ego structures as well as the reality principle, especially as it relates to the mothering figure. This does not necessarily minimize the role of the father in the formation of a healthy identity; however, the father's role during that phase is not inevitably the voice of the superego; although it can be, and often is, the voice of the ego whose task is, among other things, to help the child divert some of his energy away from the mother so that separation can be carried out less traumatically. In addition, the father offers the child alternatives for identifications that may be more suitable to the child's basic temperament than the mother's. The psychoanalytic literature is prone to discuss the father as the authority figure more than the mother, although basically the process of separation from the mother may be experienced by the child as carrying a much more severe threat of punishment than the father's cloak of authority. Therefore, it is confusing to discuss authority on the basis of traditional notions of parental roles rather than on the basis of what authority means to the child, how he experiences it and with whom this experience is associated, existentially.

Feelings of derision. Alice reported that her analyst appeared laughing at her in the dream, although it was not clear why he was laughing. Consonant with the dream, she felt, in general, that she was the laughing stock of her colleagues at work, and that she had always been the target of other's jokes when she was a schoolgirl. It also became quite clear later that she was worried about my impression of her, and whether I was going to join everyone else in mocking her. The possibility that her dream was, at least partially, dreamt for my benefit is not a far-fetched hypothesis, since she had a very strong tendency to try to control other people's reactions to her by unconsciously manipulating her own feelings and attitudes. In any case, derision is, in general, a source of constant concern for many people with low self-esteem and an inadequate, perforated identity. These people are aften judged as being "too sensitive" or "too straight" to understand a joke, especially when it relates to them. Such people often have a great deal of fear of others and feel constantly persecuted. They are often so narcissistic that their contact with others, especially their empathic reactions to them (a basic requirement for a sense of humor) is superficial and extremely dependent. Consequently, they are always watching for any signs of disapproval, and cannot bear the thought that a joke may be associated with them. Because laughter requires the loosening of ego controls, those who feel their identity to be constantly threatened are rarely capable of extending their emotionality to new experiences of verbal and nonverbal communication with others. Rather, they often compensate for this ego weakness by becoming socially overcontrolling, rigidly task-oriented and, not infrequently, constantly complaining and angry about most people and situations they encounter in their daily life. Naturally, such dynamics and behavior only reinforce further distance from others, and produce additional feelings of isolation, confusion, loss of creative inner life, and finally, further impoverishment of ego identity. This description accurately fits Alice's personality and style, although she was rather untiring in her zeal to establish contact with others, regardless of the innumerable frustrations. The problem was, of course, that her rigidity prevented her from developing more appropriate channels for her communication so that she could feel less isolated.

The Clinical Application of Confrontation Analysis

Initially, Alice had wanted to start treatment on a once-weekly basis because she could not afford more financially. Realizing after the initial interview that she was too emotionally isolated and intellectualized, I told her that my preference would be for her to come three times a week, but that I would be willing to try it on a twice-weekly basis, but certainly not less than that, and that since financially she could not afford it, I offered to recommend a good clinic to her. She balked at my suggestion, but called a few days later to ask if I had changed my mind about the frequency of the sessions; she did not ask for a reduction in fees so that she could afford to come twice-a-week. When my answer was again negative, she said that she would like to start treatment, and that she was going to begin to live on an "austerity budget" so that she could do it. Once she started her therapy, however, her financial condition never became an issue again.

In the session preceding the one presented below, Alice discussed her relationshp to a man she had met a few days before, and the immediate intense bond she had formed with him by dating him daily over a ten-day period. This was a typical pattern in her relationships to men. Since she obviously did not wish to reveal too many details about this relationship, she brought the subject up only toward the end of that session.

Session No. 43

P: I was with Mike again last night, it was really nice. I like him better than anything else. I still see other people—I mean, I would like to see other people, but I've been going out with Mike practically every evening. He reminds me a little of Dave Adams because he is also very good-looking, but Dave was a very tense guy. He always had to assert his masculinity, but he also made me realize that I am incapable of giving anything. I had a revulsion about having sex with him, I don't know why. I just couldn't do it more than twice or maybe three times with him. It was a complete failure. It wasn't his fault, because I did find him very attractive. Maybe because he was so tense and so controlling, I don't know.

T: What's different about Mike?

P: Mike is more relaxed. He doesn't push in any direction. Whatever we do is fine. Maybe because he smokes a lot, he's always high.

T: When you say whatever you do is fine, what do you mean—who makes the decisions about what you do?

P: It sort of works out. I guess I am the one who suggests things, and he goes along. I don't mean to say that I control what happens, but I am the one who usually makes the first move. Even going to bed with him the first time, I kind of seduced him by wearing a very suggestive blouse. I didn't want to appear like a stuck-up JAP (*Jewish American Princess*) and pretend that I was a virgin-hard-to-get. I remember in my freshman year, the first guy I slept with, Alex—I gave him such a hard time, and I was dying to go to bed with somebody because everybody else on campus was doing it. Not only this—I started menstruating only when I was 16, and when I went to college at 17, I was very anxious to make up for all my feelings of doubt about my sexual and physical adequacy. I wasn't sure that I was really a female. The net result was that I had a terrible time, it was very unpleasant, and Alex started to be disgusted with me, and finally, when I did it, I didn't feel anything at all, except maybe some physical discomfort. It wasn't exciting or anything like that. I made up my mind then that I was frigid. I wasn't ready for it, physically or psychologically. Then I met this salesman, and we went to his hotel room. It was supposed to be romantic, but even with him I didn't feel anything at all. I was like an iceberg all through college.

T: Alice, you have told me most of this before. I wonder why you're repeating it to me now.

P: Yeah, I remember telling you some of these things even in my first session—I don't know. I wasn't sure you'd remember. I guess maybe I was also going off to show you how I've changed. I don't like to go through any bullshit now, if the guys are allowed to be aggressive and tell the girls what they want as soon as they meet them, why can't I do the same thing?

T: What about what you were telling me about Mike?

P: Well, I was just saying that they are different. Dave was a real womanizer—he knew how to talk to a woman sometimes in a very romantic way, even though he really didn't care very much about how I felt. I never felt sexually more with him than what I feel with Mike, who is by no means what you might call a stud. Dave used to last forever, but it never did anything for me anyway—I mean, it was like masturbating—he had no real feelings. Maybe this is why I got nauseated. I knew that I stayed with him for a while because it gave me the illusion of romance, but I knew I was fooling myself. Somehow I didn't feel I had real control over my life at the time, and I was very depressed, so I was running away from it all. That affair with Dave only made me more depressed and more bitchy. Actually, I never feel that I know who I really am, even with Mike who is very nice and very gentle, I just lose myself. But with Mike, I feel he isn't going to give me a hard time. In fact, I feel that maybe something can work out with him.

T: What do you have in mind?

P: I was just thinking—look at my parents. They have had a terrible marriage, but they are together and they haven't left each other even though my father used to threaten my mother that he was leaving quite often. I know that if he left I would have been devastated. Even now, when I think of my parents splitting . . . But my mother took pride in being the pillar of integrity in the family; personally, I don't think she was or is the pillar of anything. But it was reassuring that there was someone in the family who at least considered themselves stable. I wouldn't want to be like her at all, but I know I have many of her characteristics, so maybe I can be the stabilizing force in a family of my own. I know it sounds kind of ridiculous for me to say that because, so far, I am 30 and I haven't had one single good relationship. I am always walking out.

T: It does seem somewhat baffling—your parents, according to you, had a bad marriage; you keep running away from men, and you have a fantasy of having a stable family. You feel that you have your mother's personality in terms of being hostile to men, but you act out your father's wish to leave by giving up your own relationships. It's certainly not very clear where you stand.

P: Well, I told you I am confused, and I know I am confused because my parents are. Everytime I speak to them I realize more and more how crazy they are and how they drive me nuts. This weekend was a perfect example. I owe my father some money from my college years, and I also borrowed from him a few hundred dollars about three years ago to buy some furniture when I moved. So this weekend I called to say hello, and my father made some comments about my not paying back—and I got really furious, because when he lent me the money he told me very clearly that I could return it whenever it was convenient, no matter how long it takes. He always says things without thinking much about them. This happened all the time when I lived at home. So then he calls back and says he's sorry. And on top of all that my mother tried to turn us against my father, so how can I have any good feelings about men? I understand this whole thing very well—I talked about it endlessly with my other analysts. Because of that, I think that with Mike it's different because I do have nice feelings about him and he has about me, and this kind of thing is completely foreign to me. I can't guarantee how long this is going to last, but I know that Mike is a nice guy. I don't think my mother would approve of him, because he doesn't come from a wealthy family like Dave, and he is also too feminine. I don't mean feminine—but he doesn't have the macho attitude like Dave—but I think that once she got to know him better, it'll be alright. After all, I am the one who's going to live with him not she. And yeah, that reminds me—the most ridiculous thing—she told me that she's going to sue my father for adultery—it's absolutely crazy—they live together, they're not separated, she doesn't mean to leave him, and she's going to sue him! This stuff goes on all the time—I mean all the time—since I can remember.

T: So how are you going to get out of this mess?

P: I am not in this mess, only when I speak with them or I go to visit I get into it. They involve me in their affairs constantly, and they accuse me of not being sympathetic just because they really don't want to know the truth.

T: What kind of truth?

P: What I think about them.

T: I thought you always told them what you thought of them.

P: And they don't like it.

T: And you want them to like it—you're still looking for their approval.

P: There was no approval from them at all, at any time, for any reason. So why should I expect it now?

T: Something must happen in you that you keep expecting it.

P: I don't think I expect it. I don't understand why you're saying that when you know that I am always fighting with them.

T: You may be right about your not expecting them to like what you say to them, but I think you do want their approval, and maybe in some way you get it by doing with them what's familiar—fighting. Being like your mother with her anger, and like your father with his indecision, perhaps pleases them in some unconscious way as much as it pleases you someplace. It's a family tradition that you are part of.

P: You might have something there. Perhaps this is why I could never bring any friend to our house. I knew things were going to be unpleasant. In fact, I was not welcome in other kids' homes because I was always considered a bad influence, even though I was one of the brightest kids in school. Actually, I picked a small college hoping to become part of the campus life, but I stood out as pushy and ambitious. I just felt the student body was bristling against me—that's why I transferred to a larger school after my freshman year. I went to Boston University, which happened to have been my father's college, too.

T: You've been having a lot of trouble becoming a member of other groups, it seems—perhaps because you are still a member of your family in the negative sense—always in the fighting position.

P: (*Looks visibly upset but remains quite controlled.*) I've tried so many times to act differently, but I just can't. It's so difficult for me to keep my mouth shut when I know I should, and it doesn't do me any good.

T: It's like talking to your parents? Always feeling you have to fight for some unknown reason?

P: I have this same urge with Mike, but I can control myself. Sometimes I feel like I want to argue with you, too, but I know you're right most of the time. It's not easy for me to go along with other people. Sometimes I think that you laugh at me because it's so stupid. Maybe that's what gets me depressed more than anything else. I just feel that I am not the same as everybody else. I was going to call you yesterday but I didn't, I decided to wait. I had a very depressing day at work. It looks like I have antagonized a lot of people. It's my abruptness—I don't suggest things, I tell people what to do. They recognize it in my tone of voice, no matter how sweet I try to make it sound. I must appear very aggressive. I mean I *am* very aggressive. I speak without thinking, and it really bothers me. I have such an urge to be liked by people and I go around antagonizing everybody. And it happens with men and women, although I am more pushy with men. Maybe I have more problems with men because my father never gave me an idea of what a man should be like. He was so changeable, and still is, and my mother showed me how lousy men are by constantly pointing a finger at my father. She was always suspicious of dad, and she made no bones about it. Everybody knew what she was talking about. You keep telling me that I have more problems with women, and I keep having problems with men. I don't know.

T: So you don't know how to be or what to be, and your parents seem to be responsible for this state of affairs—they didn't give you the blueprint for your identity, for who you should be. Now we can wait for them to send you your identity printout and everything will be fine.

P: That's exactly what I mean by people laughing at me. I think your sarcasm isn't very helpful, even though I know you are trying to illustrate something. I don't know, maybe it does. I don't know anything.

T: We'll ask your parents—they know!

P: What are you telling me, that I am not taking responsibility for myself and blaming my parents for creating a blob? Yeah, a blob—that's me!

T: Well, your father is a wishy-washy fellow, according to you; your mother is a bitch—so why should you be different? After all, you are an extension of them, no?

P: Well it's true that I act like this many times, but I feel exactly the opposite from what you said—I don't feel I am an extension, I feel I have absolutely no ties with anybody—I don't want to be associated with them by any means. That's why I came to New York.

T: It's very hard to know who you are without them, isn't it?

P: I don't really know who I am, period. With them or without them. My father doesn't see his children as another generation, but an extension of himself. In fact, we all look like him except for Jimmy (*younger brother*). He looks more like my mother. Every picture I have as a child I am either crying or looking very sad. I was so morose, just like my father. But when I was nine or ten I became very aggressive. My father thought of me as the pretty one, and my sister as the bright one. I can't really understand this at all. My parents are very bright people—how can they do this to us?

T: Your parents are really something else, aren't they?

P: Maybe you're right, maybe I do blame them and I don't know it—so what can I do? I mean all this is fine—it's easy for you to laugh at me and make all kinds of comments about my not taking responsibility for myself—but I am not aware of all that, what can I do about it?

T: You're really angry at me, aren't you?

P: Yeah, I am angry because you sound exactly like my mother. She keeps nagging and nagging and she doesn't let up. You're doing the same thing. Alright, so what do you want me to do, confess? I think this is your way of controlling me by keeping silent, almost without a word, for hours on end. It's like you force your opinions on people. This is like when my mother used to hide the pants from me when I went to junior high because she didn't want me to become a tomboy. She wanted me to wear skirts all the time, and she didn't care what the other girls used to wear. So I was always different, and she always got her way.

T: What has your mother got to do with all this—I am not your mother!

P: I didn't say you were, but it feels like it because you have some ideas and you don't let go—I mean, I don't think that you care about how I feel.

T: What makes you say that?

P: Well, I have been feeling very uncomfortable in the last 10 to 15 minutes, and I don't think that it bothers you. I have never felt so uncomfortable here before.

T: I think that when you are confronted with your wishy-washiness and your unwillingness to take responsibility for the way you are, you become annoyed and angry—this is your way of running away from examining your need to be like your parents underneath your so-called aggressiveness, which is not getting you anywhere.

P: (*Tears, crying.*) I had this terrible dream a few days ago, and I think that I didn't bring it up here because I was afraid of what it meant. My mother died in it—I don't know if she got hit by a car—and I ran to the hospital, and she was dead and I was worried—I was afraid I'll have to take care of my little brother because my father cannot take the responsibility. I was afraid that the dream would mean that I really wanted to kill my mother, and I didn't want to tell you about it, but I guess what you said to me before really makes sense—I do want to live my own life and not my parents', but I am really frightened—I get panicky when I think about all this. I think this is the first time I cried in here. It's not that I don't cry, I just don't let anybody know how I am feeling (*crying and sobbing*). My mother looks older—she is aging, she looks like an embittered 63, she smokes like crazy. I never really thought of her dying before, except for some fantasies I had when I was a little girl. But not in reality. I don't know why I would have this dream now—I can't imagine. Right now, except for that telephone call, my parents are not on my mind at all.

T: Maybe they are not consciously on your mind, but when you have a relationship like the one with Mike, they must be there someplace giving you all kinds of orders on how to behave, how to be, and you are obviously putting up a real struggle.

P: I know the time is up, but I really wanted to talk about Mike, too.

Confrontation analysis attempts, in general, to help the patient focus on central dynamic issues as early in the treatment as possible, preferably as soon as a working relationship has been established. In the case of Alice, however, because of her previous experience in treatment and her pattern of acting out by leaving therapy before serious work is done, I decided to utilize confrontational techniques shortly after the beginning of treatment. There was, of course, the danger of premature termination because of this strategy. However, not utilizing it presented a greater danger—namely, that of reinforcing the illusion that all she needed to do to change was just to drift from one analyst to another until she found her savior. Her defenses were not accessible to scrutiny without giving her the chance to experience them and struggle with them openly within the therapeutic situation, a task that could not be achieved without the use of techniques to which she was not accustomed, and which at the same time, tapped significant sources of anxiety.

The utilization of confrontation analysis techniques in any single session requires that confrontations and their analyses take place in a developmental, sequential order, regardless of the issue or conflict involved at any point during the treatment. The progression must proceed from "simple" questions or statements for clarifications, which in and of themselves may prove to be slightly confrontative, to more direct interpretive statements that are designed to produce reactions that strip away a certain amount of defensiveness and, one hopes, pave the way to freer access to unconscious material and insight.

This sequence is fairly clear in the session presented. At first, the patient was asked to clarify, and, in the process, indirectly consider more carefully, behavior that had always resulted in an undesirable outcome. Specifically, this related to her choice of men. It is sometimes surprising how people infinitely repeat the same "mistakes" without appraising their own contributions to the results. Alice was too fearful of letting feelings of emptiness and lack of self-definition surface to awareness, and she thus always covered them up by keeping company with men who were willing to accept her defensive need to control and structure their life. For this reason, the question (confrontative to a degree) about the difference between her present boyfriend and the previous one was designed to sharpen the focus on the factors that unconsciously contributed to her choice of men. Although it may have been inadvertent at the time, it certainly succeeded in bringing out her need to control. The question was also intended to continue her education toward more introspection, since she was habituated to acting-out. In effect, the question "What's different about Mike?" could actually be restated as "What's different about your need to select a man according to neurotic motives?" Thus there is a refocusing, indirectly as it may appear, on the patient and her inner life and dynamics rather than on the environment, although on the surface the question may seem to be doing exactly the opposite. Her description of the difference is primarily a projection of her own inner needs. Such an "innocuous," simple question also reinforces the notion that the therapist is very interested in the details of the patient's life as they relate to her concerns and feelings. Such a notion provides additional grounds for trust, and consequently, a greater willingness to share more information with the therapist. Naturally, this is likely to happen more readily when the therapist is genuinely interested in the patient rather than superficially probing to "perform his duty."

As the session progressed, an additional, slightly more demanding confrontation was utilized ("You have told me most of this before, I wonder why you're repeating it to me now?"). This probe had a number of purposes. The first was to give the patient support by letting her know that I remembered what she had told me, which meant that she did make some imprint on her environment important enough to remember. Her answer clearly indicated that she might have been testing me ("I wasn't sure you'd remember. . . "). At the same time it was also indicative of her lack of feeling that she counted. It was imperative for me to provide her with an experience that could, in some measure, counteract these feelings whenever the opportunity presented itself. Another purpose for this confrontation was to redirect her attention, to help her focus on her feelings rather than her intellectually regurgitated sexual history, which had no meaning to her in the present except as a tactic of escape. Yet another aim for this somewhat intensified confrontation was to enhance the chances for transferential *reactions* to develop, since Alice had very carefully avoided them. Obviously, without transference, few therapeutic transactions of any value are likely to transpire in any dynamically oriented psychotherapy (Cohen, 1974).

As the patient became more expressive of her central problems of identity in terms of her need to belong, the lack of independent self-expression, the generational continuity–discontinuity conflicts, and the fears of destruction through derision, the confrontations became increasingly interpretive, thus encouraging further investigation and lending support to her attempts at separation and individuation. The roots of her identity conflicts were located in the fragmented identifications with earlier objects, and they could be discerned only through the defensive projections in which she was constantly engaged, especially her self-perception of emptiness and lack of significance as a person. As a result of these feelings, her transference to me as a mother could only frustrate her, thus repeating, or replaying, the structure of her inner object relationships. There was therefore, a compelling and most therapeutically appropriate strategy to follow, a strategy that could help her separate the outside world from her mother or, more precisely, her need for mothering from her mother projections. For this reason, I reaffirmed to her that I indeed was not her mother, a statement that helped her, at least temporarily, and as a link in a chain of such statements, helped to bring out into the open her very strong need to have a caring mother, however uncomfortable the concept of mother was to her.

These confrontative interpretations (progressively and systematically utilized in intra- and inter-session strategy) brought about a rather intense emotional release, not very common for this patient. It also helped transpose the transferential relationship to deeper levels, thus creating more possibilities for working through some of the confused and destructive introjections and identifications.

It may be argued that this approach is not drastically different from most dynamic psychotherapies with a psychoanalytic or other, similar orientation. It must be noted, however, that the two most outstanding assumptions that differentiate confrontation analysis from other psychoanalytic psychotherapies, and may be observed in the above transcript of the session are (1) related to the assumption that the major conflicts in all spheres of personality functioning are rooted in the oral-dependence stage and, therefore, the strategy and the techniques are specifically geared to funnel the focus of the therapeutic work into this developmental stage, and (2) the interactional model on which this therapeutic interventional philosophy and strategy rests.

Fairbairn's (1952) theoretical approach is similar to the first assumption, in that he, too, insists on the importance of dependence in ego ("identity") development:

> The process of ego-development may thus be regarded as having three stages, (a) a stage of infantile dependence (corresponding to Abraham's "oral phases"); (b) a transitional stage; and (c) a stage of adult or mature dependence (corresponding to Abraham's "genital phase").

The various interventions throughout the above session intentionally directed the patient's attention to her need for dependence upon approval, especially by her internalized objects, and attempted to clarify the implication that such dependence had for her sense of identity, as expressed in the lack of feelings of having substance and direction.

The second assumption is also amply illustrated in the same session. There was no hesitation to interact, verbally and nonverbally, with the patient, and to systematically analyze these interactions. In fact, the lack of rigidity about "formalities" of language behavior in the therapeutic setting is exemplified by the utilization of "sarcasm" as a technique for facilitating the expression of certain reactions that could be analyzed within the transference framework without "contaminating" or "diluting" it. Such techniques are often very helpful, when appropriately used, in the working through of problems of separation and individuation.

Additional clarification of the use of confrontation analysis with problems of identity as treatment reaches critical stages of working through is provided through excerpts from a session from the middle stage of Alice's treatment. This session is from the fourth year of treatment. To put it mildly, the process and the course of treatment with Alice had been rather rocky. She constantly attempted to sabotage any progress by threatening to quit, sexually acting out, leaving two jobs without seriously discussing her decision in therapy, and not infrequently, slumping into a depressed, withdrawn, and angry stance. Transferentially, it was not easy to discern her object of reference as it shifted, like quicksand, swiftly and with subtlety. Countertransference reactions were more evident than usual. Notwithstanding all these difficulties, the sessions continued to chip away at the inner emptiness and to gradually refill the space with emotionally laden transactions within the sessions, increasing the opportunity for openness to positive feedback from the outside world, and supporting the drive to separate from the many negative part-object identifications.

About a year before the present session, Alice met a young man from the same town in which she had grown up, and discovered that they shared many friends. There was an instant attraction, but of course, with predictable regularity, she began to push him away. She was, however, also able to consciously feel and verbally express her concern over this self-destructive pattern, and she spontaneously asked to increase the frequency of her sessions to three times a week, which was done. This greatly helped to cut down on her acting-out, and six months after she had started living with this man, they decided to marry. This decision was accompanied by a serious depressive episode, however, which lasted for three or four weeks, and was characterized by a great deal of suicidal fantasies and obsessive fears that her fiance would, soon after the marriage, find out that she was indeed only "a shell," or that he would get tired of her anger and depression and abandon her.

There was no doubt that Alice had, by that time, traveled a long way in her treatment. Two areas of concern had improved significantly: she became more emotionally reactive, and she learned to communicate in a more direct and genuine manner in her interpersonal transactions. Yet, her quest for identity was only partially satisfied. She continued to feel empty and alienated to a large degree. She lacked membership in a natural group, and her awareness that her family, especially her parents, were not going to provide her with an identity increased. She felt robbed of an identity, robbed of a place to be unique. There was, however, one exception: she did, in relation to this subject, develop different feelings toward me. She became more trusting, and in fantasy, began to incorporate me as part of her family. This was an important change, since otherwise she could not acquire new, more positive and caring introjections and identifications. But again, making a few forward steps in this direction always elicited, for her own sense of survival, temporary retreats, or regressions to the old "empty self" that needed to be defensive and self-destructive. *Her "non-identity" was synonymous with identity,* and therefore, any new "clothes" (identifications) felt too heavy on her brittle, thin skin (existing ago). This familiar pattern required increased vigilance from me, and demanded, therapeutically, interventions that concentrated and focused on ego-relatedness. I had to navigate between therapeutically optimal interaction, and unpredictable projections of her unconscious object relationships that could easily, and often did, clash with my interventions. Thus, as soon as we seemed to establish some modicum of therapeutic stability, the "blinds" would come down and the defensive armor would pop right up, as if it had come out of nowhere. Nevertheless, she slowly became less "moody," more communicative, and less self-critical.

In the excerpt presented here, Alice again attempts to rationalize her destructive patterns and her compulsion to prove that, in the final analysis, she is alone and must remain alone because she is not wanted and does not deserve to be wanted. There is, however, also the growing feeling that she does have something valuable to offer, that her self is not altogether empty, that she can find a source of nourishment to revitalize herself and grow. Confrontation analysis is, here too, designed to clear out as many bastions of entrenched dependence as possible, while examining the resources from which an independent ego can be reconstructed.

In the beginning of the session, Alice discussed that she had gone back to writing some poetry in her spare time, and that she had found it extraordinarily more difficult to concentrate and discipline herself than was the case when she wrote during her college and post-college years. She was not too pleased about that, but that was not her major concern, which was her uneasiness about her relationship with her husband and the state of the marriage. At the time of the session, she had been married about three months.

P: I am anxious about the fact that Paul (*husband*) is depressed. Getting married—I don't know if getting married, but for sure after we got married—things became more difficult. I don't know why. Usually when I am in good spirits things go well between us, but sometimes things got out of hand, and I just can't take it, that's all. I just can't take everything.

T: What specifically are you referring to?

P: Well, Paul is kind of boorish and disgusting. His table manners are horrible. He is always belching, farting as if he is sitting on the toilet in the bathroom by himself. He apologizes, but he doesn't consider this to be bad manners or in poor taste. But he is extremely sensitive, too. Well, things are not particularly looking up. I am afraid my marriage is not going to work. I always had this feeling that it won't work, but I felt that I had to do it because I had to try, and I knew that you warned me about problems. I just feel that I am being leaned on, just like before, with other boyfriends. Paul is very unhappy about his job situation but he won't do anything about it. I told him he should go to school or come here to talk to you, or do something to get out of this depression.

T: You said you always had the feeling your marriage won't work, and yet you went ahead with it—how do you explain this beyond your curiosity to try it, so to speak.

P: I am not saying that I am getting out of it, but it is becoming a problem. Not only this, I am attracted to other men, especially to this guy I told you about, Tony. He is in the marketing department. He is not particularly handsome or anything but, anyway, I had lunch with him yesterday, and then we went to his place and we had sex. I was really turned on to him. I mean, I am aware of his tremendous hostility toward women. He is known to screw anything in a skirt, but I didn't care about that. I don't even know what attracted me to him. He is just a pleasant guy. I don't really know why I went to bed with him.

T: Is it perhaps your familiar way of dealing with your own depression?

P: Well, it did give me a lift, but I know that I was back where I started last night when I left work. Naturally, Paul also wanted to fuck and I wasn't in the mood, but I didn't say anything, so we did it. And I can't even say that I felt like a whore, although the thought of having two men inside me in one day does make me wonder. In fact, sex with Paul wasn't as bad as I thought it would be.

T: What was good about it?

P: Well, I was thinking a lot about Tony and how he is in bed and all that, and I was getting some kick out of it, I guess? Paul was working so hard to please me and to please himself because he couldn't come. Finally I had to do it for him, which was alright.

T: You had fun with the idea of having two cocks in you.

P: Once I had almost done just that but the men chickened out. I tried to arrange once to have sex with two men at the same time, and I worked it all out with each one alone—this was many years ago, maybe six or seven years ago. I think I was really flipped out then. But the last minute they couldn't go through it, so I dropped the whole idea.

T: I see.

P: I know this sounds bizarre, but I even had this fantasy about you. I don't mean with another man, but just what it would be like to have you—I don't mean to have you, but I mean to have sex or an affair with you. And last night I had a dream about you. Well, not just you, but you were in it. I was like in a dining room, in a hospital bed, or it seemed like a hospital, and I was wearing a nightgown with black lace (*laughs and giggles*), very nice, and you were at another table, like one of the doctors. I was jumping up and down in my bed, and then you came over and I turned around in a kind of, kind of a startle. Yeah, I was startled. Then I saw you handing over to another doctor something that looked like one of those giant electric bulbs, like the ones photographers use when they shoot movies. This other doctor then put this bulb in my bed for a second and removed it. I didn't even have a chance to see it very clearly. There was something else, but I can't remember. I was going to tell Paul about this dream this morning, but he was in no mood to listen to my nonsense. Even though I feel somewhat hopeless about our marriage, for some reason the dream makes me feel pretty good. When I was jumping up and down in my bed, I was really very happy, and I was also very happy to see you there.

T: This dream has many interesting things, what else comes to your mind?

P: Nothing much really.

T: What about this jumping?

P: It just reminds me that when I was six or seven, maybe a little older—but not more than seven because it was still in our old house—I once went to my parents' drawers and I found some rubbers, and I know I had a lot of fun with them, because I filled them with water, and they looked like balloons that you can bounce. This also reminds me of my own oversized breasts, which I hated when I was in college because that's what the guys always looked at. My mother has big breasts too and I don't think they're very attractive. When my mother found out about the rubbers, she took a belt to me. I remember that very, very clearly.

T: It occurred to me that you enjoy the fantasy of having two penises in you, perhaps because they are like breasts which feed you when they are inside; but of course the breasts you were accustomed to weren't too kind to you, so that your mother's breasts, like yours, don't seem too palatable to you, so you keep trying to deny that you have them by making them ugly in your eyes, having no value for you.

P: (*With a smiling face:*) Wait a minute, that's, that's heavy stuff! I don't really understand—how could the penises be breasts? I mean, well, when you have oral sex maybe it's like sucking—you mean that when I am having sex I am really sucking on the breast because I want to be fed?

T: I mean just that—you keep trying to fill your sense of emptiness with the wrong hose—instead of fucking you're sucking—so you get frustrated on both counts: you don't enjoy sex because you really want to take, and the men you choose need to take for themselves, just like you, and at the same time you don't feel fulfilled because sex can't substitute for the love you felt deprived of as a child.

P: I certainly feel like that with Paul. He always wants me to support him and to be patient with him and his depression. Nobody cares about how I feel (*crying*).

T: Nobody?

P: Nobody. I don't know anyone who really cares (*cries for a couple of minutes while I stay silent*).

T: What about your dream—you put me in it and you were happy to see me there, and you see me here, for a few years now.

P: I think you care, I mean I am sure you care. As a matter of fact, I think my marriage is holding because I think you care and you want me to work on it and to succeed in it.

T: And perhaps I am also in the way of your trying to undermine it, so you are angry at me for that. You don't like it when I confront you with what we are talking about.

P: That's not true. I am glad that you are forcing me to look at things, but I just don't think about therapy when I am not here, like when I was with Tony. I know it's bad for me and I know you don't approve, but when . . .

T: Wait a minute. I am not your mother to approve or disapprove, but I am concerned about your need to throw a monkey wrench in the works by this acting-out, by not giving yourself a chance to find out how you really feel about Paul—he can't be wonderful before the marriage and hopeless after it. Maybe what you feel doesn't really have much to do with him, at least at this point.

P: I don't know what to do. I am afraid to let him know how I really feel about the stuff that's going down. I don't want him to leave. I think—I don't think—I know he's a good man, and I know I am screwed up.

Alice was somewhat confused in her relationship to me since I didn't behave, according to her, like other men—or women, for that matter. She was not hesitant to compare me to a "good" mother at times, to see me as standing by her side (as in the dream), and to let me know, often indirectly, how she was being nurtured through our interaction. At the same time, it was extremely difficult for her to transfer such feelings of trust to another person. However, her marriage to Paul, a depressed, though quite patient and accepting man, gave her the opportunity to "practice" some of the changes in her feelings toward men, and through his reactions, to receive some feedback regarding her own projections as a woman and as a competent person, in general. Her confusion with me stemmed not only from her own ambivalence and uncertainty about her basic unconscious identifications and her "struggle" against such identification (Greenson, 1954), but also from what seemed like a duality of my own behavior—namely, being both nurturing (like a "good mother") and confronting (like a reproaching authority). However, she found an anchor for her empty, floating self in me and in the therapeutic process. She was able to relinquish her defensive avoidance of investigating her identity with an increased recognition of a variety of identifications, which was achieved through a process of approach–avoidance responses to the outside world, and to me. Thus progressive and regressive steps were inevitable. My flexibility in my approach to her, with an emphasis on sharing with her interpretations that were not always perfectly accurate, and therefore requiring retractions on my part, helped in decreasing her feelings of worthlessness and in the development of some feelings of belonging to the human society.

Her relationships to her family continued to present certain basic problems; however, her unconscious expectations of being "remade" by them with loving and tender care diminished considerably. She was also eventually able to recognize how these expectations affected her relationships with others in her immediate surroundings. As a result, her interpersonal relationships became satisfying enough for her to establish a rather stable circle of friends who shared common interests. Her husband entered treatment with another analyst, and both of them made serious attempts to bridge some communicative gaps between them. Alice's own depressive episodes became infrequent, and when she terminated treatment eight years after she had started, the structure of her ego took on a rather defined frame with an exciting content.

13
Independence and Termination

The gamut of psychological elements that comprise the concept of identity are obviously too intricate to spell out, regardless of how comprehensive an attempt is made. Therefore, when one speaks of the achievement of identity as a therapeutic goal, one can obtain only a partial understanding of such an achievement, and only as it manifests itself through a variety of personality characteristics and behavior patterns. The exposition of the effects of dependence on the growth and maturation of personal identity leads to the conclusion that unresolved dependency needs stunt the development of a healthy identity, and emotional independence affords a chance for the various elements of identity to find their "right" place in the mosaic of the self. Therefore, in evaluating the results of any therapeutic efforts in connection with the status of identity, it is important to assess the behavioral and emotional criteria that may serve as "signs" or indicators of the individual's location on the dependence—independence dimension at any time. Such an assessment is inevitable and most necessary during the termination phase of therapy.

Criteria for Psychological Independence

Acceptance of One's Uniqueness

There seems to be a popular belief that psychotherapy aims at helping those who seek it to find a modicum of "adjustment." A number of textbooks and chapters on the subject of abnormal behavior or psychotherapy are titled with misleading labels such as "the psychology of adjustment." The term *adjustment* frequently implies that the goal is to effect change in the individual's behavior to conform with that of the majority of people or to a statistical norm. In the last decade or two, there has been significant change in this notion, however; that is, adjustment in dynamic psychotherapy refers to the understanding of an individual's psychological make-up in terms of needs, feelings, and behavior, and the pursuit of goals that are in tune with them. Such a view of psychotherapy, which is also the foundation of confrontation analysis, fosters an attitude that promotes the investigation and analysis of the patient's uniqueness, and the exploration of how he may be helped to accept and enhance it. Not infrequently, the patient's long-standing conflicts and symptoms stem from, and are an expression of, the inability to accept his individuality because of a dependence on others, and, dynamically, because of the need to satisfy his demanding superego introjects. A variety of complaints accompanied by very intense feelings in this area are commonly obtained from patients who are beginning psychotherapy, with a resurgence of similar feelings during the termination phases. Naturally, uniqueness or individuality results from a special combination and integration of many aspects of the self, although it may often be manifest only in certain aspects of its behavior. For example, one person's kindness, generosity, or approach to a certain situation may always be perceptible through his interaction with colleagues, while similar characteristics in another person may be known only through his non verbal, and "behind the scenes" actions. Some individuals may find these traits and the behavior patterns that accompany them desirable and acceptable, while others may view the ownership of such characteristics as detrimental and unacceptable, for a variety of reasons.

For example, a 22-year-old art student sought treatment because he felt he was wasting his time "doing sculpture I don't really dig," and because "I am behaving in a very strange way in general to the point that I don't have any really good relationship with anybody." He felt lonely and alienated, and wished he could become more socially active. However, as therapy proceeded, it was obvious that this young man had an unusually keen sense of humor and an uncommon sensitivity to human subtleties. It further became apparent that he was conditioned to view these rare characteristics as harmful and unbecoming to a "gentleman" in his social class, as his mother used to advise him. Nevertheless, he felt compelled to express these talents in the company of others; however, he turned his humor on himself in a self-destructive manner, as well as using it socially in an inappropriate and inordinate way, thus overwhelming others with his "magnificent" perceptiveness. In other words, he reacted to the rejection of his uniqueness, especially by his mother, by developing a defensive, spiteful stance that was unconsciously designed to punish his mother, and at the same time elicit approval from his surroundings. However, he also unconsciously reacted to the outside world as if it were his mother, expressing his anger toward her through this reaction. The consequence was feelings of alienation and distance from others, who shunned him; for in essence, he was not in touch with his feelings. Therapeutic efforts concentrated on loosening his emotional dependency on his family so that he could recognize his uniqueness without attaching a negative value to it. The goal was to help him accept it and appropriately express it in his interpersonal interaction. In addition, his work as a sculptor could benefit from this uniqueness, and his satisfaction from it could become a solid source of expanding the territorial boundaries of his identity.

Another young man of 25 was convinced that he was "weird" because he did not have many friends, he was not a rock-and-roll fan, he did not know "the right way" to kiss a girl, and he twice flunked out of college. He did not dare separate himself enough from the influence of his environment to accept the possiblity that his disinterest in school, dance, and music did not necessarily prove that he was strange, but that perhaps it provided a good ground for the development of a separate self, an identity, and a life style appropriate to his unique needs and his unique manner of expressing them. Indeed, after a relatively short time in confrontative–interpretive treatment, it became obvious to him that his interests in philosophy and psychology in late adolescence were perfectly legitimate and needed to be developed rather than squelched, as his parents wished. Thus his search for an identity for himself led him into a rather deep interest in his religion, and he eventually made the study, and later teaching, of religion and philosophy his life goal and occupation. His initial interview statement—"I never felt attached to anything or anybody"—turned to "I never felt *more* attached to anything," as he later wrote to the therapist from his university teaching post. He added in his letter, "I now feel truly amongst my peoole, my family, my work, my students, and my feelings. My roots seem to strike deeper anchors into the ground. While in the past I had felt that I belonged to nothing, I now feel I belong. I make decisions, and I don't very often feel shy as I used to. It is hard to believe how, when I started therapy, I told you about identifying with Professor Rodd in *The Blue Angel* (with Marlene Dietrich). The naivete and humiliation which he suffered, and I suffered, seem rather far from me now, although every now and then I immerse myself in feelings of depression and loneliness." This patient had been in treatment for about three years, and then continued with another therapist on the campus of the university he attended. A very bright and indeed very unique young man, he was able to remove the obstacles to his identity by emotionally (and geographically) removing himself from the powerful influence of his mother and his (rejecting) stepfather.

An attractive, divorced 25-year-old woman came for treatment because of a mixture of psychosomatic symptoms such as spastic colon, stomach aches, headaches, increased tension and anxiety , and depression. The patient had previously had therapy for several years and found it helpful at the time. She felt, however, that she could not resolve one of her important problems: after having a sexual relationship with a man, she could not let go of him, and tended to keep him as a "friend." As a result, her social relationships became increasingly difficult to handle, and she was "like an open book to everybody. Everyone knows my business—practically every man in my group of friends, I went to bed with him." She felt she was "spread all over the place," to the point of not having any "substance and existence of my own . . . I depend on so many people to keep me company that I don't exist by myself. I just can't be alone, I have to have somebody around, not just somebody—a man." From the outset it seemed that therapy with this patient was going to be very uneven, perhaps very difficult, primarily because of the extent and chronicity of the history of acting out, the primitivization of symptomatology, and the undefined, although, on the surface, quite verbal and manipulative ego structure. Her parents were divorced when she was very young, and she did not see her father after the divorce until a few days before his death, some three years before she came to see me.

Limit-setting in the area of acting-out in the first year of treatment was absolutely necessary and clearly spelled out, at times with an implied threat that she might lose me as her therapist if she did not live up to our contract. As therapy progressed, my interaction with her assumed an increasingly confrontative, yet openly and directly supportive character, and concentrated primarily on the definition of her self in every possible situation, often comparing her thoughts on the subject with mine. For example, when she brought up her conversations with her superiors and other colleagues on the job, we worked on those aspects of the messages that, in addition to their significance in impressing them with her uniqueness, were unconsciously designed to portray her as a "swinger" who did not care about anybody's opinion of her. As she would tell a story, I would repeat it to her with some commentaries and interpretations, and then confront her with her intentions. At times I would even offer a number of alternatives that could have taken place without necessarily losing her unique, vivacious, and entertaining style and individual integrity. Her cooperation and motivation to change was, curiously enough, always deep and available. Thus, after about five years of hard work, termination was being considered. She had lost all her psychosomatic symptoms by then, and had grown to appreciate her uniqueness without the (previously) attached negative self-deprecation and self-mutilation that she had needed. While a major aspect of the treatment process involved the dual dimensions of modeling (on my part) and identification (on her part), her dependence on a father or father substitute to save her from "nothingness" was relinquished by a set of convictions and beliefs about her own worth that became the basis for a healthier and more independent identity.

The acceptance (or nonacceptance) of one's uniqueness may often be discerned from unconscious material such as dreams. Thus a 30-year-old psychologist in psychotherapy for about six years began to discuss termination, although, he said, he did not wish to sever *all* contacts with me. He was thinking of asking me to supervise his private patients because I knew him so well and would therefore understand his treatment style better than anyone else. He brought in a dream that pointed out certain significant changes in his self-perception and acceptance of some aspects of his personality that did not change, aspects that typified his uniqueness: "I was having dinner at my parents. I particularly remember my father being there and a friend of his from his old law firm. I was introduced to this guy's son, whom I recognized from before, even though he was clean shaven, without the beard which he used to have. He had a certain way of talking which had irritated me the first time I met him. This time I wasn't upset at all. I was about to start dinner and my father smiled at me and winked, something he never does in real life. Then I remember having a conversation with this fellow—I don't really remember what we talked about, but it wasn't bad at all—kind of pleasant, almost familiar. The house itself—I mean, my parents' house—looked like the lobby of a big hotel, decorated in early Americana and all kinds of antiques, with a big lantern." In his associations to the dream, the patient recognized his "old self" with a variety of behavioral and emotional patterns that were not acceptable to him in the beginning of treatment, and his present self, which had not given up some of these patterns, but which he had managed to learn to accept and integrate as part of it. During the discussions about termination, he realized that he still felt somewhat dependent on me, and had difficulties cutting the cord—an element represented in the dream by his going to his parents' house with furniture similar to my office. At the same time, he also felt he was part of the family and accepted by it, especially his father, despite his uniqueness. In reality his parents had not changed their disapproving stance toward him, for many reasons, but primarily because he did not look or behave as they did. However, the patient learned to separate from them emotionally and enjoy his own identity, part of which was belonging to a family that did not endorse his style of life. Thus he developed his sense of belongingness without capitulating or losing his sense of independence.

Continuous Search into the Self

According to Singer (1965), formal therapy can terminate when the patient is prepared for "persistent self-investigation and self-awareness," which can be achieved when the obstacles to the patient's becoming his own therapist are removed. Such an outcome of psychotherapeutic efforts results from the reduction in the patient's dependence on others for self-evaluation. Thus, when the patient's behavior becomes unburdened by what seems "appropriate" or "right" for others, or by the fear or anxiety that emanates from the lack of self-propelled authority to act on the self's behalf, the patient and the therapist may conclude that the external coach-therapist is no longer needed for the patient to live out satisfactorily whatever potentials are in store. When enough confidence in the self exists to handle daily events and problems without the tacit support and affirmation of a therapist, termination must be considered without delay. The question is then what criteria or signals can be used to make sure that neither resistance nor countertransference are motivating the process of termination.

The unconscious is too "tricky" not to invent a variety of defensive maneuvers to keep the status quo and avoid changes Perhaps the best place to look for such signs is, to start with, the transference situation and concurrently the patient's interpersonal life outside of treatment.

Transferential signals. A number of "signals" indicating the progressive adoption of a self-investigating attitude and associated either with timely or premature termination must be considered. Such signals, manifested either in the formal-structural aspects of the session or in its contents, are organically bound with the transferential dimensions of the dyadic interaction. The first of these to be considered is the tone in which the patient carries the session. Normally, there would be an increased feeling of calm and comfort, which is communicated within the session even when the patient termporarily goes through some emotional upheaval. The voice is then expressive of the trust invested in the analyst, as well as the security the patient feels in his independent investigation of personality. When the patient does become more independent, his tone takes on a quality of curiosity, interest, and excitement, searching for more clues and insights into self, or identity. In some way, one can detect "the voice of authority" in these deliberations, a voice less dependent on the analyst, perhaps more equal. The patient increasingly communicates in a tone of voice more natural and less strained from the transferential projections of the past. This is not to say that termination inevitably spells such peace; however, the gist and the atmosphere of the ordinary session during this phase can be expected to adhere to this kind of development fairly regularly with many of the patients.

Another sign, in the structural sense, is the *fluency* of the patient's associations. With decreased obstructions from ambivalence toward inner objects, the transferential reactions become less encumbered by tension or anxiety; in other words, the more separation and individuation takes place, the less distortion can be discerned from the reactions to the analyst, because of decreased dependence in the associative capacity. Repressive hesitation with regard to various themes and feelings, or to past experiences and memories, is reduced, and therefore, the self-searching patient fluently talks with less direction from the therapist. This does not mean that interaction between patient and therapist decreases. As a matter of fact, because of the changes in the patient's self-concept with regard to equality with the therapist, more interaction may indeed occur; however, the nature of this interaction is different, and approximates more closely the interaction that transpires between two equals.

Yet another indicator showing that the patient has acquired the self-search attitude, and is therefore ready for termination, is the way he utilizes the *nonverbal* communication that transpires in the session between patient and therapist, or within. There is an honest search for the meaning of any nonverbal message that he might be sending, without the probing of the therapist. This does not mean that the patient interprets every twitch of the eyebrow, but rather that he has the notion and the awareness that there is a meaning to any and all communications, and that he is not attempting, consciously or unconsciously, to deny messages because of their noxious effects. Such an understanding is another indication that the patient has integrated the analytic investigatory attitude as part of self, part of identity. Nonverbal communication is often more revealing and meaningful than verbal communication, and therefore, when a patient learns to read such behavior, he is likely to have added to the armamentarium of self-analysis a very significant tool for self-understanding and for the fight against defensive operations of the unconscious. Transference, in general, thus assumes a significantly decreased intensity.

From the *content* aspect of what transpires during the termination phase, one can learn a great deal about priorities and concerns that the patient is planning once treatment has been completed. Patients often report having complete conversations with themselves outside the analytic hour, indicating at times, the patient's self-sufficiency and capacity to understand feelings as well as act upon them in a constructive way. They might also be indicative of how well the introspective and integrative efforts of the therapeutic process have been internalized and become, so to speak, second nature. Often these one-way conversations relate to the existence of an awareness about conflicts and problems and their working through within the self. Of course, while the reporting of such experiences to the the therapist may seem like an intellectual exercise or a defensive obsessive maneuver, (it is often so in the early phases of treatment), it is not likely during termination. At this stage the patient is likely to be more open to receive the analyst's feedback than to engage in a power struggle to prove his superior capacity to work things out without any help. Transferentially, the patient perceives the analyst more as a partner interested in sharing the planning without competitiveness and without retaliation. Thus this aspect of the self-search and its discussion in the analytic hour is more analogous to the situation where an individual asks a colleague or an expert to critique his work for the purpose of learning from the feedback, not for getting a grade. Of course, there will always be an element of the need for approval, regardless of how independent that individual is.

Nevertheless, the patient's wish to explore his inner self without turning this search into an intellectual exercise is no easy task to achieve in a psychodynamically oriented therapy. The fact remains that many so-called "well-analyzed" individuals are people whose analysis taught them to use analytic jargon, often quite accurately, only to label and intellectualize their perceptions without adequately integrating their understanding into their emotional life. Thus, after a few years in therapy or analysis, some patients start to feel that they *should* be ready to leave treatment, since they "understand" their problems so well, and since they have been in it long enough. They have "served their sentence," and now they're cleansed and ready to independently tackle their daily problems. Such resistant patients often convince the analyst of their readiness to terminate, and thus leave prematurely. Of course, the question that immediately arises in such instances must pertain to the efficacy of the whole treatment, let alone termination. In many of these cases, the patient's personality structure, especially as it relates to characterological deficiencies, could not allow the process to penetrate deeper than the mere surface of the self. In many others, the problem often lies with countertransference difficulties. In the majority of cases, of course, both characterological difficulties of the patient and unresolved unconscious conflicts of the therapist are responsible for premature terminations.

Since the concern here is with the concept of self-investigation and its manifestation in the transferential situation, one must remember at this point that transference refers to the perception of, and reaction to, the analyst as if he were a significant figure from the patient's early childhood. This also implies that the child's capacity to encounter these figures in a meaningful interaction at those early stages was inadequate, perhaps because he was not allowed to express or to develop reactions in a way that could be integrated as part of his identity, his self. This would result, in the therapeutic situation, in the patient's reaction to the analyst as if he were being treated in the same "autocratic" manner experienced in infancy and childhood. Therefore a process that aims at achieving freedom from the unconscious wish to have somebody (parents) understand (approve) one's needs and satisfy them can be attained only as a result of the acceptance of one's separateness, i.e., the reality of one's real capacity, as an adult, of satisfying one's needs. Thus, when termination is being considered, two *seemingly* contradictory processes must be simultaneously at work. On the one hand, the patient must be able to confront the analyst without the fear of losing his love (approval). At the same time, such confrontations are direct communications that lead to a clearer definition of one's independence and identity, and inevitably to separation from the therapist. The transferential dimension is particularly sensitive to this aspect of the therapeutic interaction, and requires that the analyst detect who the references (unconscious objects) of any confrontation are.

For example, a patient may feel resentful if his therapist does not provide a make-up session to substitute for one missed for "legitimate," not resistant reasons. If, before the patient inquires about the analyst's reasons for this refusal, he perceives it as a rejection or as a "calculated" or "typical" deprivation (hence, the resentment), one can then assume that the reaction was the result of the patient's transference stemming from the need to re-experience early deprivation. If, however, the patient attempts to logically and reasonably clarify the situation, i.e., find out whether the refusal was due to a "contract" that the analyst had in mind but did not make explicit, or to the analyst's lack of time, or to a distorted (assumed) perception of the reasons for missing the session, it is pretty clear that such inquiry (confrontation) should not be considered transferential in essence, but rather a "technique" that the patient has learned to use in order to get what he wants, a technique that is not defensive in nature. Reactions such as this ought to lessen concern about premature termination, for they are not rooted in unconscious distortions, and they are really more attuned to the reality of the interaction between patient and therapist. The patient would then appear to be open and ready for interpersonal transactions that are designed to help his self-search, and to widen the horizons and the territory of his identity. The patient will likely utilize these self-actualizing processes in the future without the structure of the formal treatment.

Premature termination resulting from transferential problems is not, however, uncommon, especially in the character neuroses and the borderline categories. These cases afford an excellent opportunity to learn about indicators that lead *away* from the achievement of independence and a healthy identity.

While many of these cases may be diagnosed and detected fairly early in the treatment, sometimes as early as the initital interview, they nevertheless pose a serious challenge with regard to the strategy and techniques best suited for them.

For example, a 25-year-old high school carpentry teacher sought treatment after several years of prompting from his friends, who saw him "going down and down to the ground, depressed, like a dying tree." The patient stated that he was ready to see a therapist only after he had closed himself in his apartment during the previous three weekends without answering the phone or communicating in any other way with the outside world. The pain was too great. He expressed specific doubts about consulting with me after being confronted with the possibility that his objections might be connected with his fear of self-knowledge, as his history of avoiding treatment. His reasons for doubting whether I could help were:(1) I was Jewish and he did not wish to be reminded of his own Jewishness, and (2) he wanted to see an analyst "much older, a man in his 60s or even 70s." After recognizing that it was not my fault that he was referred to me even though I did not fulfill his requirements—facts he knew before he made his call—he related a rather painful history in a very sad, almost "pitiful" tone.

His father had been killed in the war when the patient was two years old, and his mother remarried when he was ten. The man she married had custody of his own son from a previous marriage. The patient also had a sister two years his senior. The stepfather apparently treated him and his sister in a very harsh and hostile manner. His mother was herself always disgruntled, and seemed to have perceived her own children as a burden and as the cause of her marrying a cruel man—the reasoning being that they needed a father and that she was tired of providing for them. The patient's last name was automatically changed to the stepfather's name without adoptive procedures, and without consent. The resentment toward the stepfather was quite deep, but was not overtly expressed until the patient was about 24 when in an argument he told his stepfather in no uncertain terms that he would strike him if he continued to abuse and insult him. The patient had a history of poor performance in school, although he was able to correct his scholastic achievement in college. His social life consisted of dating once in a while, and this, only if his sister was able to find him a girl. Although he was a handsome man, he believed there was something fundamentally wrong with his looks, and a few months after he began treatment, he insisted on having the direction of his ears corrected by plastic surgery. His intense, almost agitated manner, his anger, and his underlying depression were quite evident from the first few minutes of the inital interview. He also manifested a rather marked "effeminate" body posture and hand gestures.

My suggestion that he see another therapist, since he had doubts about me was immediately dismissed because he found me to be, toward the end of the session, kinder than he expected according to my "reputation," and he also believed that I would understand his problems more than "a lot of other people, including and specifically, an older man." Later it became clearer what he meant in this context by his "problems"—namely, his homosexual "tendencies," which he also did not want a gentile doctor to know about.

As therapy unfolded, it seemed clear that this unhappy young man was looking for an ideal father who would not abandon him or reject him, and a mother who would take care of him before she attended to herself. There was no question that his narcissism was deep and his self-centeredness an obstacle to any meaningful interpersonal communication. Thus any therapeutic move that could help him gain some perspective had to be very carefully planned; otherwise his defensive, narcissistic preoccupation would easily crumble, and a serious regressive trend would take place. Moreover, the fragility of his ego was also manifested by the many defensive maneuvers with which he had surrounded himself, such as his overintellectualized pseudo-interest in cultural affairs, activities he felt compelled to pursue to prove his (fantasied) belonging to the educated elite, and the need to date only beautiful women to convince himself he was a desirable man. He complained that women were willing to go out with him only because they were stupid, because they were fooled by his good looks or his nonexistent intelligence. He confessed that actually he could never "perform" sexually. He blamed his sexual failure or impotence (he had attempted sex no more than three or four times) on the women's "demandingness," a stereotype he needed to retain. He could not consciously admit that he had a rather strong homosexual drive, although his dreams often pointed to this dynamic factor. He insisted that even if he were to discover that he was a homosexual, he would never practice it because that would mean to him a total loss of self-respect, and it would prove his stepfather's persistent taunting accusations that he was a "weakling," "a failure," "a loser," and "a fag."

Transferentially, there were very clear, abrupt shifts from positive to negative objects, although much of the time his anger and constant feelings of distrust prevailed. There were occasional positive reactions. Interestingly enough, however, he developed an intense dependence on me. He continuously asked for, or rather demanded, advice about any and all aspects of his life, completely disregarding my verbal and nonverbal commitment to let him make the decisions for himself by himself. When I fell into the trap every now and then, my answers were always thrown back at me at some future time, as if I had purposefully caused him the greatest pain. He always tried to guess what I would like him to be or do, and would come to the session having carried out orders, like a soldier, only to find either "a silent listener who doesn't give a damn," or "an interrogator." He wanted very desperately to shape himself after someone—anyone who was willing to slice some ego out of his own personality and hand it to him. He was so lonely, dependent, and vulnerable that most of his interactions with others were felt as dangerous and existentially phoney. Thus, in the transferential situation, he could not for any reasonable time really latch onto any internalized object and project it onto me. His reactions were quite unpredictable, except for his polymorphous anger and rage, which remained constant. My presence as a constant object did not help much to anchor or bind his anxiety long enough to work through his conflicts.

Thus, after three years, when we were still struggling with the attempt to establish a trusting relationship, the patient wished to terminate, claiming that he was no longer getting the "deep" depressions he used to get, that he had learned a "great deal" anyway, and that it was time to stop. He also concluded that I was not going to "make" him potent, and therefore could not help him with a woman. He said he knew he had to do this on his own and wished to try it. It was pretty evident that he was unable to learn in this process to introspect or open-mindedly investigate his feelings and perceptions, which were rather disturbing, distorted, and inappropriate. He was by no means ready to terminate.

When I confronted him with his need to return to the isolation he had imposed on himself before coming for treatment, he acknowledged the veracity of the hypothesis, but also confessed that he was not willing to go further from fear that he would become more dependent on me, and then I would abandon him, just like his father. He said he did not want therapy to confirm what he already believed of himself, that he was a "superficial kid from nowhere, just a face without a name."

This illustration of the role of transference in premature termination clearly indicates that, in a certain sense, no strategy or technique is likely to be helpful when the patient's history is so chaotic, and when the basic orientation that has been acquired in childhood is that of the passive recipient of negative feedback, which causes a narcissistic, self-preservative shell to form around the self, and indeed become a core part of it. Intransigent transference, where the analyst does not become just the object of projection of an introjected whole or part-image, but where his actions and reactions become directly (not representationally) perceived and interpreted as if they were the reactions of an actual parent, cannot be understood merely in terms of resistance. Such transferential reactions may be termed *self-transferences*—the projection of the patient's total self onto the analyst, rather than only objects that had been introjected in early childhood and had formed the basis for the evolving self. In such a transference, the self, or the ego, does not have a reasonable perspective between subject and object, (patient and therapist), and between past (parent) and present (therapist), thus paving the way for a blurred, symbiotic (not quite psychotic) transference. Intense reactions on an undifferentiated level with definite fusion processes with the analyst may occur. This self-transference is similar (in its unconscious cathected projections) to the undifferentiated ego in the first few months of the infant's life, where the ego's inner experiences are not separated from the mothering object and are dependent on it for its very existence.

In the self-transference of the borderline or character (especially narcissistic) disorder, the primitive self of the patient is "overcoated" by the many layers of life experiences, chronological know-how, and developmental defensiveness, which gives it the appearance of being differentiated and integrated. A similar development may also be observed in the psychopathic category, where the individual often appears well-integrated, but a slight stress may produce serious disorganization. The intense transferential situation in confrontation analysis does at times bring up this type of self-transference in narcissistic constellations, whereas under other conditions such behavior may not be too noticeable. Patients often refer to this situation with an exclamation: "This happens to me only here! I don't behave this way outside." This type of total self-transference is not the same as "regression in the service of the ego," but is a transgression in the service of narcissistic needs, or a movement toward the renunciation of identity and interdependence. The dynamics of the self-transference phenomenon may be understood in terms of the ego-splitting operations to which Freud (1938) made reference. Later this concept was further refined and investigated by Kernberg (1976).

The dream life of a patient can be diagnostically helpful in locating conflicts that impede the patient's capacity to launch into a self-investigation. During the termination phase, dreams are a particularly sensitive barometer for unresolved conflicts centering around early object relationships that are loaded with intense feelings of hatred (Greenson, 1967). The idea of separation from the therapist recreates and revives a great deal of turmoil in the patient's unconscious , which often brings to the surface feelings that may have been defended against throughout the analysis, indeed not infrequently throughout life. Therefore, when dreams indicate that such feelings are not altogether available to the conscious self, special efforts must be made to fully investigate them and to determine whether they are transient or constitute territory that has not heretofore been covered. Confrontation analysis techniques are especially useful in this process of unearthing.

For example, a 36-year-old depressed woman who had been in therapy on a three-times-a-week basis for about three years had been reporting steady improvement in her relationship with her two daughters and an increased involvement in her work.

She began to complain that the sessions became boring, and that she could use the money she was spending on therapy on other, more necessary items. She declared that she planned to terminate treatment and wished to set a definite date. As we began exploring her termination plans, she reported a fragment of a dream that puzzled me a great deal. She said that most of the people in the dream were clients and office personnel, but the only clear part that she was able to remember was, "I was going to be fired. They were going to let me go," alluding to her employers. Her associations led to her boss, who had quit the job a couple of weeks earlier, and had been replaced by another man with whom the patient formed an instant alliance. She had disliked the former boss rather intensely. She was, however, quite upset about his leaving, although she had been aware for some time of her wish that he leave. She could not relate her dream to her present status on the job, because she didn't believe she was about to lose it.

I reminded her of her plans to leave treatment and, somewhat confrontatively, said something to the effect that she was planning to fire me from therapy, perhaps before I fired her. I related this to her experience of the sudden death of her father, an experience she had discussed very little and always shunned whenever the subject came up. She then started to relate to this confrontative interpretation indirectly by talking about the night before the session, when she could not sleep or even watch her favorite television show because she was too preoccupied with "thinking about the past." She was so upset that she had to cry herself to sleep. Soon after this revelation she began to discuss her guilt over her anger toward her father, who had died before she could tell him how angry she had been at him. She believed there was a great deal of unfinished business with her father, especially her inability to let him know how fearful she had been of him, how oppressed she had felt, and how she had found him to be a most ungiving and unrelenting father. She felt that he could never have understood her life style, and certainly never approve of it, and that he would have severely criticized her for not being able to cope with her daily problems on her own. When he had died some nine years earlier, suddenly and at a relatively young age, she could not seriously mourn his death because her anger from early childhood on would, in her words, make it an "absurdity and a travesty" if she pretended that his loss had meant anything to her. She was, she said, glad to know that perhaps his death would help unchain her feelings of imprisonment. However, in her dealings with the oustide world, especially with men, she continued to behave similarly to the way she had acted with her father: submissive, obsequious, controlled, and rather placating. Consequently, in her transferential reactions to me she always seemed positive and appreciative for what I had done for her, while her anger festered underground rather unobtrusively. In a very real sense, her wish to terminate had triggered off unconscious material that she had never dared to approach, and I had never been able to get to in order to help her. The dream and the associations to it were a genuine breakthrough that had to be swiftly and confrontatively seized, so that a premature termination could be avoided and the impasse overcome.

From that point on she felt free enough to discuss long "buried" feelings, and her transferential projections included a variety of positive and very negative introjects. Her terror that I would kick her out of treatment because she wasn't a "good person" subsided, and she was able to eloquently pour out a heavily encapsulated history of hate toward men—and women—without the nagging fear of reprisal (her father's domain with her). Her false feelings of independence gradually surfaced, and she was able to continue her investigation of her self in the treatment situation for a long time.

Changes in interpersonal conditions outside of treatment. Changes in the psychic reality of the patient within the therapeutic situation and manifest through the transference must be accompanied by external changes if they are to be of appreciable value for the patient. The patient cannot live on improved transference alone, nor can the therapist be satisfied only with changes in the therapeutic milieu. There must be demonstrable progress in the external environment to ascertain that the patient's independence is not simply an illusion created through learning how to play the psychotherapy "game," but is an everyday bread-and-butter routine. Since the therapist is not with the patient outside the confines of his office, he must rely on the latter's accounts about external changes, and on the patient's own judgment as to their relevance and extent vis-à-vis the therapeutic goals. It is not enough to observe the patient's communication patterns, expression of emotions, and the demonstration of a sturdy identity change satisfactorily within the office limits. These changes must be progressively and concretely applied in the patient's life in general. The "external" changes that represent progress toward the achievement of a self-investigatory attitude and, consequently, psychological independence, can be assessed along basic variables.

Patients come for treatment because they feel stuck and incapable of dealing with problems on their own. They believe that they must effect changes either in their daily behavior or in their perception of themselves and those around them. Many also believe that they must learn how to change others so that they can feel comfortable. The history that they provide in the early sessions is often indicative of how strikingly few real changes they have made throughout their life, although on the surface their activities may appear to be a history of constant change: *tout ça change, tout c'est la même chose.* An important ingredient that can affect significant change, and seems to be frequently missing from these accounts, is an honest self-search attitude, which could serve to prevent futile repetitious illusory change. External changes are often the barometer for inner psychic changes, because how an individual utilizes his time often defines chosen roles and functions on the one hand, and on the other, points to the structure of internalized objects. Thus the clue to the inability to resolve difficulties must lie within these parameters: what the individual does, how he does it, and how it relates to personality needs. The relationship between these parameters, implicitly or explicitly, has, at times, been used in defining the concept of "normality" (Offer and Sabshin, 1966). Confrontation analysis questions the usefulness of the concept of normality in general, although it may be somewhat fruitful for a global and a beginning investigation of comparative studies of human behavior. However, concepts such as "adaptation and productivity" (Buhler, 1959), "flexibility" in making changes, "assimilation" of new experiences (Rogers, 1959), and ability to learn from experience (Maslow and Mittleman, 1951) are especially helpful.

External changes may also be evaluated by comparing the

patterns and contents of the patient's work, emotional history, interpersonal relationships, educational growth, recreational habits, and physical condition before treatment with their status during the termination phase. Since dynamically oriented psychotherapy, such as confrontation analysis, deals with the patient as one unit rather than as a disjointed self, changes that occur in one area are taken for granted to affect the rest of the self in varying degrees. When, for instance, as a result of resolving authority conflicts, a patient changes career, chances are that the patient will reexamine his interpersonal world and make some changes in it, overtly or covertly. Psychotherapy, especially confrontation analysis, does not necessarily aim at helping the patient change his feelings of perception of himself by encouraging him to change careers; however, it would seem rather incomprehensible if, after serious efforts in therapy, the patient's relation to his work remained unchanged. "External change" does not necessarily mean changes in one's actual career or interpersonal relationships, but when it does occur in treatment, it is usually preceded by changes in one's perception and approach to what one does or to whom one relates. Therefore, as the patient's self-evaluation depends less and less on others, decisions about how he is to spend his time and with whom assume a quality of independence based on his own needs. The patient becomes increasingly less driven by the compulsion to fulfill the commands of a life-script inherited from childhood object relations. The ego is freer to move about spontaneously, in labor and in love, and this freedom is communicated in the therapeutic hour by deliberately taking charge of the "message center," and by carefully planning and gradually executing plans.

The patient invariably and inevitably places roadblocks in the way of transferring changes in the therapeutic milieu to the outside, "real" world, and the therapist must be instrumental in challenging, confronting, and analyzing the patient's subterfuge. Perhaps more important than the changes themselves is whether the patient is aware that changes are part of an everlasting, unending process in the search for continued growth, and whether the patient is ready to continue this process after formally leaving therapy. The extent and depth of such awareness may be excellent criteria for judging the patient's readiness for termination, and such awareness may in turn be evaluated on the basis of the actual adaptation of this self-search orientation before termination. It must become part of the patient's identity before he leaves treatment, rather than remain an illusory promise to be fulfilled after termination. Patients may say after a couple of years of treatment, "I want to try it on my own now because I have a feeling I can make it without therapy." This resistance is not easily dismissed, because sometimes narcissistic pride is easily injured if the patient is confronted with the simple, but provocative question, "If you can do it on your own, how do I, or coming here for therapy, stand in the way of achieving your goals?" This type of resistance points up the patient's denial of extreme dependence (to wit: therapy prevents the patient from acting upon his own wishes) and, also, fear of it—consequently, the need to escape it. It is extremely important, therefore, that the therapist seize such "resistance" as an opportunity to examine the patient's motivation for termination, and real or fantasized need to remain dependent rather than become independent by leaving the arena of self-investigation. It is also crucial to confront the patient with the great amount of energy utilized to stay in the same place rather than to work on conscious goals to achieve psychological independence.

While changes in one's external environment can legitimately create conditions for a more fulfilling life, the quality of these changes must be evaluated on the basis of the patient's intellectual and emotional potentials and needs. Perhaps one of the most disasterous consequences of the rapid development of communication in the 20th century has been the increased ease of vocational and social mobility. These social and technological changes have created tremendous problems for individuals who were forced to "catch up," even though such changes were totally inappropriate for their needs, and in fact aggravated their psychological stress. Thus an excellent technician in the computer field bitterly complained about being practically forced to move into a managerial position that involved more responsibility, control, and money. He was not interested in the "glamor" of being an administrator, and wished to remain, as he put it, "a soldier, not a general." Yet, because of his great dependency needs, he could not reject this "wonderful" opportunity to climb up the corporate hierarchy. In the majority of cases, however, people vie for such opportunities only because of their compulsion to please and receive recognition and approval rather than because of genuine interest in the new position. Eventually, such individuals feel demoralized and unproductive without being aware of the source of the pain. In therapy, such patients must be very carefully diagnosed and monitored, because too often they appear to have been progressing on the road to happiness, when in reality, they are enslaving their ego to a life of compulsive (though perhaps socially acceptable) acting-out. Thus the initiation of external changes must be made only after careful examination of the self's healthy and pathological needs, and an incessant confrontation with the discrepancies between the patient's wish for change and the relevance of change for an independent self.

In summary, the existence of criteria for the acquisition of a self-investigatory attitude, which is a significant element in psychological independence and identity, and thus an important consideration for termination, may be inferred from at least two sources in the therapeutic situation: changes in the quality and depth of the transference and in the external life of the patient as reported during the sessions. External changes must be ego appropriate, and it is the therapist's responsibility to confront the patient with any discrepancies between therapeutic progress and its representation and execution in the patient's life outside the treatment relationship.

Mutuality of Interpersonal Interaction

One of the essential elements of psychological independence is the adequacy of the individual's interpersonal relationships. It may seem rather paradoxical to place such importance on an aspect of ego functions that must, by definition, involve the concept of dependence as a major ingredient for its operation. Yet it is almost an axiom that no interpersonal interaction can exist without dependence: each side of the equation in any interpersonal transaction depends on the other, and certainly, for the continuity of such transactions to survive, a certain degree of feedback (interdependence) between the two parties must exist. This interdependency phenomenon in the life of the self provides fertile grounds for the evolution of a variety of behavioral and emotional patterns that characterize the individual's functioning in interpersonal interaction, and place one at a certain time on a specific coordinate of the dependence–independence map.

Sullivan's (1953) definition of what constitutes mental health clearly subscribes to this viewpoint: "One achieves mental health to the extent to which one becomes aware of one's interpersonal relations."

The Relationship between the Patient and the Therapist

The relationship between the patient and the therapist is continually available for examination during treatment, and maintains its significance by representing relationships outside of therapy. As treatment progresses, the patient's relationship to the therapist changes, and when termination is around the corner, the interaction assumes a quality substantially different from the one experienced in the beginning of treatment. Perhaps the single most important dimension in this regard is the patient's realistic acceptance of his role and that of the therapist. It would seem obvious that in this relationship the patient is the patient and the analyst is the analyst and everybody knows that; yet, when transferential and countertransferential reactions are superimposed on this relationship, as they must be, the interaction between patient and analyst depends, to a greater or lesser degree, on the structure of their introjects and the relationships among them. Of course, the less dependent each of them is on these unconscious configurations, the more reality-oriented will be their reactions to each other. This means that the patient begins to perceive the analyst as such, i.e., as someone who is there to help him understand the distortions and change behavior that blocks the achievement of goals—not any other figure on whom he depends for satisfying needs that were inadequately or never satisfied in the past. So far as the analyst is concerned, this means that the patient does not provoke interventions that reinforce dependency strivings or reactions that can only produce more resistance. Such a development will help the patient recognize that he must be the initiator and producer of change, and is responsible for his own resistance. In psychoanalysis such a therapeutic condition is called the "working alliance" (Greenson, 1967), and it must develop as the basis for any successful working-through process. In addition to this assumption or understanding, confrontation analysis presumes that when the working alliance is established, it can be perceived as the beginning of the termination phase of treatment. In other words, once you have brought the horse to the water, he should be able to drink by himself, and hopefully, know how to look for water on his own in the future.

The resultant reality-oriented interaction in this dyadic relationship is marked by additional qualities. One of these is the feeling that the sessions can be a source of pleasure, and thus enjoyed without any consequent punishment. The patient enjoys the interaction with the analyst, and does not have the authority-serving, submissive-dependence that intense transference often produces. The interests of the patient in the analyst are no longer as self-referent (projective) as they are at the beginning of treatment, but they indicate increased curiosity about the analyst, not for resistance, placating, unconscious dependency reasons, but because the patient's independence allows him to relate to the person of the analyst as a friend.

The patient does not blur boundaries nor lose identity when this process takes place. It is the recognition that the analyst is an entity with whom contact can be made on an equal basis. The freedom and feeling of security that mark the condition of his ego are manifest in the comfort, ease, and pleasure with which he is able to discuss innermost feelings and fantasies. This is not to say that the patient becomes the analyst's friend, although friendship feelings are not altogether inappropriate in the termination phase. After all, independence requires that friends are selected not forced, and in the treatment situation, neither the patient nor the analyst had contracted for this relationship to be that of friendship. It is a professional relationship, and as such it is by definition skewed toward inequality in the quantity and quality of the transactions, thereby producing interactions that are not entirely balanced. The analyst cannot reveal himself in a nontherapeutic manner until the treatment is over, and when that happens, the patient's interest in the analyst as a friend is not based on data (and feelings) obtained in an otherwise normal encounter of friends. At the same time, much of the analyst's privileged information about the patient from the treatment may be the kind of knowledge that does not necessarily enter the sphere of interaction between friends, intimate as they may be. Consequently, the so-called "principle of mutuality in interpersonal relationships" may be violated and, therefore, such a relationship may not contain the seeds of equality—a dimension that is necessary as the basis for a natural friendship.

There are two additional reasons for negative consideration of the establishment of friendship relations between patient and analyst *after* termination. The first relates to the possibility that the analyst may not have been able to detect the patient's maneuvers, which may have produced material that falsely warranted serious considerations of termination. In fact, such a production may have been only a masked, defensive operation characterized by reaction formation in which the patient succeeded in turning his unconscious need for dependence into conscious signs of independence. If, indeed, such a process takes place, it would be extremely difficult, if not impossible, to analyze this resistance after friendship relations develop, for obvious reasons. It is thus important to discourage such a process from taking place, through the analysis of the patient's expectations and fantasies and a serious search into countertransference needs. This may help in preventing blind spots on the part of the analyst, and eventually allow for the confrontation and analysis of this type of resistance.

The second reason for frowning upon such relations concerns the possibility that in the future the patient may encounter certain difficulties in life that he or she may wish to discuss with the analyst, but then would not be able to do so because the analyst would no longer be professionally available. This occurrence is not uncommon in the practice of psychotherapy, a profession that deals with life problems that can and do recur or develop into new forms, and whose victims include not only people who were never analyzed, but also those who were quite adequately analyzed. Therapy is, after all, not surgery that cuts away a part of the body forever; rather, it is a process of change that does not stop with formal termination. Therapeutic growth does not imply absence of conflict, and, even after termination, conflicts may become severe enough to warrant a return to therapy. For this reason, the relationship between the patient and the analyst at termination must remain professional, albeit friendly and affectionate.

Unfortunately, termination may be hampered or deferred at times by the analyst's countertransference needs relating to the analyst's own unresolved conflicts in the area of interpersonal relationships. Thus, when a patient expresses readiness to leave treatment, the analyst may erroneously interpret this as resistance, and attempt to analyze it as such. This may create conflicts with the patient that may in turn be regarded by the therapist as proof of the patient's resistance stemming from unfinished working-through. Countertransference reactions that tend to keep the patient unnecessarily longer in treatment, expressed in the interpersonal interaction at the termination phase, stem from a number of sources: (1) the therapist may unconsciously select some patients to keep around because they provide emotional stimulation not received on the outside; (2) the therapist may have difficulties expressing his own feelings, and thus use certain patients vicariously for this purpose; (3) the therapist may feel competitive with some patients, so that termination could mean that the therapist is not as successful as they are (they are perceived as moving forward while he is staying in the same place); (4) the therapist may unconsciously identify these patients with a significant parent to whom there is still a neurotic attachment. Needless to say, all these needs of the analyst touch directly upon his own position on the dependence–independence dimension, and his own degree of resolution of conflicts related to identity and the interpersonal world outside professional work.

Countertransferential reactions that are manifested in the area of interpersonal interaction often result in premature termination of treatment. Of course, it would be inaccurate to perceive one side of the interacting team, in this instance, the therapist, as responsible for the fate of the whole interaction, since, by definition, both sides are mutually affected by what transpires between them. Nevertheless, in order to clarify the issues at hand, this presentation will follow tradition and explore it as if it were indeed possible to separate one side from the other.

The most obvious and easily detected countertransference reaction that can contribute to the premature ending of therapy is the therapist's unconscious anger at the patient, expressed verbally or nonverbally. Such reactions are often masked by subtle defenses, and do not allow optimal understanding of the patient's needs during the working-through phases, thus stunting his capacity to grow in the therapeutic milieu. Not infrequently, this anger is connected with the therapist's frustrated expectations of the patient, especially in terms of performance within the therapeutic setting. Such frustrations may lead to an impasse because the therapist reacts negatively to the patient's resistance, which is actually aimed at the transferential object. The therapist may, in other words, react to the patient like the parent who is being resented and resisted, even when the therapist is trying to do his best to help the child-patient. The therapist's interaction with the patient may then assume all the characteristics of a power struggle between child and parent in which neither wins, and only a stalemate results. In such instances, the therapist's internalized objects, with whom he obviously still has a great deal of conflict, need to be carefully examined.

When the patient's ego is still too brittle and incapable of confronting the therapist's anger, the patient is likely to look for, and find conscious or unconscious ways of escaping the threat, one of which may be withdrawal from treatment. The patient may often read the therapist correctly, in that the latter may, in fact, be feeling too uncomfortable with or resentful of the patient, but may not be aware of such feelings. If both patient and therapist deny the negative undercurrents in the interaction, then the termination is likely to be perceived both as sensible and timely, only to be discovered later—much later at times—that it was triggered off by resistance and countertransference, perhaps mostly by countertransference. The patient is not likely to return to the therapist for continued investigation of his personality. Of course, when the therapist recognizes his share in such premature termination, he would do well to investigate the feelings and unresolved conflicts in such interpersonal interaction more closely, perhaps with the help of a colleague, supervisor, or analyst, lest he be blinded by the same spot with other patients.

Confrontation analysis attempts to prevent such occurrences by insisting that the patient be educated from the beginning of treatment to utilize any perception he has of the analyst as important data to be released and analyzed. Thus, when termination thoughts and fantasies begin to surface, the patient is ready to look at them within the interactional context of the therapy, and if there is anything disturbing to the patient, he would be "conditioned" to confront the therapist in the same manner that the therapist had confronted him. Such confrontations initiated by the patient help him learn further how to separate and become independent, and at the same time continue to pursue the relationship with reasonable communication and interaction. Adequately integrated processes such as this help both patient and therapist recognize openly that they have been acting as a parent–child unit rather than as two adults. Corrections can then be attempted. Naturally, such an interactive quality requires a well-developed sense of identity on the therapist's side, as well as an interpersonal atmosphere that promotes flexibility, humility, willingness to learn from the patient without losing self-esteem, and accepting of responsibility for interventions that cannot be justified as therapeutic. This is not a question of magnanimity, but rather of ethical and professional conduct and sound therapeutic value.

A second potential source for countertransference that can set off premature termination is a condition in which the patient appears to merge psychologically with the therapist, thus losing his boundaries. This situation occurs mostly with patients whose identity is so undefined, and whose need for dependence and support so overwhelming, that they maneuver themselves into a transferential position that simulates intimacy and closeness to the therapist, but in reality does not contain the appropriate qualities for such a relationship. The therapist may then become too anxious and frightened because of his own unresolved unconscious symbiotic yearnings. This type of countertransferential reaction will tend to be triggered off when the patient's symptoms for which he had sought treatment, rather than the pathology behind them, become the focus of treatment. The reasons for failing to analyze the patient's real pathology early enough are too many to enumerate at this point, but such developments are not infrequent. Once the symtpoms have been overcome or substituted, treatment ends prematurely, not infrequently because of the therapist's unconscious fears. Perhaps the best examples may be seen in the treatment of homosexuals who come for therapy for a variety of symptoms, and when these disappear and the sexual identity then becomes next on the agenda, the therapist's anxiety about his own homosexual feelings may needlessly prolong the treatment, as Chessick (1971) observed, or bring about its premature termination.

The goal of mutuality in interpersonal interactions as a criterion for independence is difficult to achieve because of the dangers involved if not handled properly. It involves basic dimensions of living with others, and requires constant judgments by the individual about the reasonable distance and closeness that he needs to maintain for an adequate functioning of his self. The treatment strategy and techniques related to this dimension must be carefully balanced by the therapist, who must, at all times, keep in perspective his own needs for interpersonal nourishment on the one hand, and, on the other hand, the patient's attempts to utilize the therapeutic interaction for nurturing rather than gaining insight from it. The allure of intimacy or closeness that some patients offer can be extremely tempting at times for the therapist who is constantly separating from one patient after another in the course of daily practice, and who may not have a satisfying world of interpersonal relationships. A so-called completed analysis of the therapist is not always a perfect guarantee against such occurrences. The important thing is, however, that the therapist recognize these potential hazards and continuously search for them.

Finally, there is an additional source of problematic countertransferential interventions that can affect interactions with the patient, and also tend to cause premature termination. When the therapist is over-concerned with his self-esteem, many reactions of the patient can become potential blows to his narcissism, thus producing defensive operations. Consequently, the therapist may discharge the patient in an impulsive manner, or intervene in such a negative and hostile way that the patient breaks off treatment. These blows to the therapist's self-esteem arise at times from the patient's need to challenge the authority and the competence of the therapist by comparing him to other therapists whose therapeutic results are idealized and glorified, or by doubting the correctness of his interpretations. The patient's self-destructive, regressive behavior is often defensively used in this manner, and if the therapist is not alert to these maneuvers because of unresolved narcissistic needs, he may cause the patient to flee.

Interpersonal Interaction Outside Treatment

The data that the patient provides (or, in some instances, withholds) can be an excellent barometer for changes resulting from the therapeutic experience. Some patients (and therapists) have a tendency to focus their attention during the therapeutic hour more on the inner life than on what actually happens outside in daily encounters. Of course, such a direction is quite important; however, at times, it tends to avoid examination of significant aspects of the self as it functions in real-life situations. In fact, some patients may withhold much of their outside life from the therapist, even when changes do develop. This may occur for a variety of reasons, not the least of which is their need to cling to the relationship with the analyst in the therapeutic dependency framework. Such clinging is often motivated by masochism.

Masochism is often used as a defensive posture against anxiety stemming from the ego's vulnerability to forces that threaten it with expansion of awareness of its inadequacy and insecurity. The masochistic stance probably exists in an unconscious state in the majority of people, perhaps in all people. However, precisely because of its universality, it is taken for granted and not normally perceived as masochism. Masochism can be seen as a way of avoiding punishment by others through self-flagellation, a way of presenting the self to others by masking the anxiety that normally accompanies feelings of inadequacy, impotence, and resulting dependency needs. It is thus a defense against interpersonal closeness, because closeness might reveal the individual's faulty or lacking identity, and it is a subtle maneuver designed to place others in the position of responsibility for one's crippled capacity to deal with them in a sensible, meaningful way. Masochistic behavior may be an important aspect of ego identity, as Saretsky (1976) suggests for the borderline constellation. His conception may be expanded to include the majority of pathological interpersonal interactions. According to Saretsky, ". . . borderline patients set up unbearable situations where they are bound to fail, get hurt, or become very disappointed in order to feel their feelings and own them." One of the rationales for expanding this thesis to include other

categories is the assumption of confrontation analysis that no
one ever achieves a completely solid sense of self or identity
and, thus, during certain interpersonal encounters the masochistic defense can often surface. Of course, this masochistic
maneuver, or the infliction of pain on oneself, does not always
manifest itself in the same fashion even in the same individual,
although certain patterns may often be discerned. Close examination of distorted interpersonal relationships invariably reveals self-destructive, pain-producing aspects of the self. From
this view of the role of masochism in interpersonal interaction,
it is clear that the development of mutuality in interpersonal
relationships depends to an appreciable extent on the decreased
need or presence of masochism or masochistic behavior in the
patient. There are a number of behavioral indicators for such a
healthy development.

Parental perspectives.   An important indicator during the
termination phase is the patient's reports that signal that his
interpersonal interactions have been modified with old and new
friends. The therapist must be convinced that these changes are
based more on equality and mutuality than on the parent–child
model. Not infrequently, the patient reports that friends and
family notice new patterns of behavior in his approach to them,
as the patient generally becomes more expressive of needs and
wishes, and communications become increasingly clearer and
attuned to his goals. There is less fear of punishment or disapproval, even when it is anticipated or actually forthcoming. The
patient learns to *negotiate* with friends and family, rather than
categorically or impulsively accept or reject what transpires. In
the past this had happened because of an unconscious need to
defend against reliving the abmiguity of parental demands that
might have been experienced during the patient's maturation.
The patient no longer needs to cater to figures who, in his or her
mind, represent a punishing authority or a depriving mother,
no does he have to defensively control, again in his mind, others'
behavior or state of being and feeling, especially in relation to
him. Interactions with others that simulate early childhood
models of interaction where intrusiveness and lack of privacy
had been experienced, and had (prior to treatment) to be unconsciously and compulsively relived because of their familiarity

as part of the patient's identity, are no longer acceptable. In the termination phase, the therapist is often reminded by the patient that his interpersonal world has been extensively overhauled, if not entirely changed. This is welcome progress, because it attests that the patient is moving about in an environment that is neither coercive nor amorphous, and that "support systems" are orchestrated by the patient's ego to play his own tune, for his own enjoyment.

Heterogeneity of interpersonal relations. From the above exposition it might erroneously be assumed that the best interpersonal environment is one characterized as a "mutual admiration society," but this is precisely the kind of environment that the masochistic orientation tends to create. The masochist thrives on finding people who reinforce his pathology or share his pathological suffering because, in this manner, pain can be increased by additionally identifying with other sorrow-bearers. For this reason, the patient who is genuinely close to termination is more likely to have widened the horizons of his social and familial circles, and thus, the choice of relationships would, in many ways, represent a capacity for understanding and tolerating many aspects of the self mirrored by others, and of which the patient was never heretofore conscious or accepting. These dimensions of his self often represent past introject objects that make up the basic identity and become more integrated as part of the personality.

A man in his thirties who grew up in a fairly religious Jewish home and who rejected his religion substantially from his teens on, developed a close relationship with an orthodox Jew with whom he would not have been "caught dead" just a few years before his last year in treatment. He recognized that the "expulsion" of this type of person from his interpersonal territory was a rejection of an important part of his identification and ego structure, which had caused him a great deal of self-inflicted pain. However, his "non-identity" image of himself was his "proud and stubborn me-ness," a distorted type of identity that he had needed to defensively ward off panic stemming from feelings of emptiness and worthlessness. He had once characterized himself in the initial stages of treatment as "Noah's ark filled with *empty* animal cages, floating helplessly at the mercy of a scornful God!"

14
Termination and the Quest for Meaning

The nature of the therapeutic process requires constant movement, from present to past, from conscious to unconscious, from reality to fantasy, from transference–countertransference interaction to direct, defense-free interaction. Strategically and technically, the process must be imbued with flexibility as it unfolds and as changes take place. Thus, for example, one must alternately focus on interpretation and confrontation, on the analysis of dreams and the analysis of behavior, and on the communication of messages through verbal channels and non-verbal ones. The therapist is always in the "forced" position of making interventional decisions; whether he *overtly* does or does not intervene, everything that happens from the therapist's end of the dyadic relationship must be considered as an intervention. For all intents and purposes, interventions are aimed at either short-term goals, such as the alleviation of symptoms, or at long-term goals, such as the achievement of a healthy identity.

Most patients seek treatment for specific or nonspecific symptomatology. The majority seem, however, to be in search of something beyond the solution to symptoms, although this search may not be recognized as such on a conscious level—a search for *meaning* in one's life, as well as a search for *meaningfulness*. Guntrip (1969) was probably alluding to this very dimension when he wrote that,

> psychoanalytic theory had for a long time the appearance of the exploration of a circle which had no obvious center until ego-psychology got underway. Exploration had to begin with peripheral phenomena—behavior, moods, symptoms, conflicts. . . . All this is naturally important and must find its place in the total theory, but actually it is all secondary to some absolutely fundamental factor which is the "core" of the "person" as such.

Meaning refers to the individual's feeling that he or she has substance, a valuable core, frequently referred to as "self-worth" and based on the intrinsic value any individual has without any "strings attached," such as achievement or status. *Meaningfulness* refers to the individual's feeling that he is important to others and desired or needed by them. This quest can also be described as the search for a life with meaning and a place among other people. This goal is organically linked to the development and maintenance of a viable self with a capacity to preserve its integrity, independence, and identity. Thus, when termination is being considered, the status of these important dimensions of the self must be carefully assessed. For purposes of clarity, this area of investigation has been arbitrarily subdivided into (1) territoriality, loneliness, and aloneness; and (2) death and suicide.

Territoriality, Loneliness and Aloneness

Territoriality

The concept of territoriality is assumed to be an organic dimension of the functioning self. It becomes increasingly necessary to understand this aspect of the self during the termination phase because of its relationship to identity and other criteria of readiness for termination. Hall (1959) regarded the possession of "territory" as a crucial aspect of life: "To have a territory is to have one of the essential components of life; to lack one is one of the most precarious of all conditions." Thus, if the concept of identity is to be further clarified, it seems clear that territoriality must be part of its definition. Of course, territoriality encompasses the notion of boundaries. In individual psychodynamics it may actually define the nature and substance of the individual's identity. This is similar to a political entity, where territoriality refers to geographical boundaries that define not only location but also, by implication, important characteristics. Historically, nations whose people are unified and whose goals and direction are clearly perceived can more successfully defend their territories against outside intrusion.

Keeping this analogy in mind, the individual, too, must have a clear perception of his goals, and must chart his own direction through life. Obviously, no nation can be so integrated and clearly defined territorially that it will be without problems or vulnerabilities, as world history has proved. The individual is, of course, in much the same condition. In fact, even the individual's physical territory, the limits of his skin, may, at times, be in question. For example, under overcrowded conditions, individuals often adopt behavior patterns that seem to deny the existence of boundaries, such as pushing, trampling, or otherwise blurring one's perception of others. Psychological territoriality is even more difficult to define, and disturbances related to ego boundaries are numerous. Thus, for instance, there is, at times, no clear-cut separation between conscious wishes and unconscious motivation, and, as a result, the self may receive and transmit mixed signals that compel it to act incomprehensibly. When this happens, the person's identity may be subjectively experienced, as well as perceived by others, as having "permeable" boundaries and as being unpredictable and lacking in clear direction.

During the termination phase, the patient's territoriality, that is, the clarity of his self-image as well as his awareness of his needs and the means to satisfy them, becomes the object of transactions within the therapeutic sessions in a very focused manner. For example, the patient may increasingly feel that the therapist's office, while more comfortable and pleasurable than before, is also "foreign" territory, in that he must ultimately leave it. This is analogous to the *separation* process in the mother–child relationship, although not exactly the same. The patient perceives himself more realistically, sees the capability of surviving satisfactorily without depending on the therapist, and at the same time, he becomes more cognizant and accepting of his own substance, of the various dimensions of his self that are his own and make him different from, and similar to, others, including the therapist (mother). Mahler's (1972) concept of the individuation process is at the base of this phase. In a certain sense, *individuation is fundamentally the establishment of identity,* although in the adult, this process includes additional dimensions, such as the acquisition of a sense of purpose and meaning. The lack of these important ingredients—the emptiness in one's inner territory and the massive defensiveness against the fear of its collapse—often, if not always, brings a patient into the treatment situation. *The recovery of one's core and the regaining of meaningful territoriality are thus at the heart of the termination phase.*

The recognition of one's territory and the optimal use of it without undue waste of psychic energy are frequently manifested during the termination phase in the form of acceptance of one's potentials and limitations. Thus the patient begins to act upon this knowledge without being hampered by excessive competitiveness or the need for approval, and mobilizes his energies to reach his goals with flexibility and ease. Within the sessions, his delivery is both free and directed: free in that he spontaneously allows the various aspects of his ego to interact without having to compartmentalize them, and directed in that his investigation into himself assumes a definite character and focuses on what is relevant without being rigid. The patient needs less interventions from the therapist, and resistance to them is minimal, since he no longer experiences them as an invasion of territory. The dialogue that the patient has learned to open between acceptable and unacceptable aspects of his personality becomes the model for his interaction with others. Relationships become relatively tension-free as he does not need to keep pseudo-control over others through a persona, since the perception of his territory is clearer and he is less confused as to where his own needs end and those of others begin. He becomes a negotiator, not a guard or a defender of a vulnerable and empty ego.

The amalgamation of the territoriality of the self is, then, a salutory consequence of the separation–individuation process, and may be thought of as the dynamic representation of the self's identity. As such, its manifestations within the treatment situation are, transferentially and interpersonally, important sign posts in the termination phase. A number of clinical and behavioral conditions are closely identified with distortions in the territorial integrity of the individual, and require additional therapeutic efforts. Two of these—*loneliness* and aloneness seem to present a problem for many patients, and indeed, possibly, for many people who do not suffer from other, clearly definable symptoms.

Loneliness

Guntrip (1969) refers to *loneliness* as

> an inescapable result of schizoid introversion and abolition of external relationships. It reveals itself in the intense longing for friendships and love which repeatedly break through. Loneliness in the midst of a crowd is the experience of the schizoid cut off from affective rapport.

This description probably comes closest to the experience that many patients describe, especially when they enter treatment. From this vantage point, loneliness emerges as the inability to make vital emotional contact with others, either in fantasy or in reality, and it results in the feeling of being "cut off," disconnected from them. On the surface, this phenomen may appear to be only a problem in interpersonal communication, and is thus treated as such. However, treatment centering only on this aspect of the loneliness syndrome may lead to the development of compulsive interpersonal patterns of interaction as a substitution for genuine emotional contact. In the long run, this will tend to increase, rather than decrease, the lonely experience, and probably further mask its underlying causes. It is likely that these causes are primarily connected to the patient's lack of ego identity and to distortions in his perception of the adequacy and integration of his self-system. Thus recurrent feelings of loneliness must be regarded, especially if they persist in the termination phase, as pathonomonic signals that important aspects of the ego have not surfaced or been sufficiently worked through to warrant termination.

The linkage between territoriality and loneliness resides in the hypothesis that a lonely person is one who has not been able to accept his uniqueness and separateness enough to experience himself as part of a relationship—not apart from it (Singer, 1965). And, as noted earlier, the development and establishment of feelings of uniqueness and independence are central to the concept of identity—an important criterion for termination. The clinical picture of loneliness is, however, frequently misleading because, considering the intense pain it generates, the individual attempts to avoid or deny it, often using a variety of defenses that camouflage it. It is not unusual for a patient to utilize what appears to be genuine feelings of boredom, sadness, depression, or emptiness as front-line defenses against "the lonely experience." At times, loneliness resulting from the inability to form genuine attachments is masked by overcompensatory behavior—patterns of gregariousness, multiple (superficially) intimate relationships accompanied by fantasies of narcissistic gratification through popular acclaim and desirability. In the therapeutic transactions, such defensive maneuvers are not always easy to recognize as such, let alone to analyze and resolve. Reich (1949) called attention to this difficulty when he discussed what he called "psychic contactlessness," which seems to refer to the essence of loneliness. Illustrating the problem through the dynamics of a patient in treatment with him, Reich noted that analysis of this patient revealed

> a marked lack of contact with the world. . . . The patient himself had not immediate awareness of this; on the contrary, his passive-feminine tendency to lean on others deceived him about it and gave him the feeling that he had especially intensive relations with the outer world. This seemed a difficult contradiction; on the one hand, there was the libidinal stickiness, his readiness to be of help and service, that is, seemingly intensive object relationships, and on the other hand there was doubtless a contactlessness.

Experiencing the same problem of loneliness at the other extreme of the defensive continuum, a patient, himself a therapist who had been in treatment for a few years and was contemplating termination after making substantial progress in some areas of his life, came one day to his session very agitated, and complained that he had been in deep pain, depressed from the moment his wife left for a week's visit to her mother in another town. This was the first time in the marriage that he had been separated from her for more than 24 hours. He was unable to concentrate on his work, and he did not feel comfortable enough to visit friends in her absence. While he had, in the past, mentioned feeling lonely on a number of occasions, he had always dismissed the experience as something "everybody feels now and then." The present experience was, however, more traumatic than any other he could remember. Further investigation and opening up of the whole subject revealed how lonely he had always felt while attending any family or professional meetings, but at the same time, how he could also not be with himself for any length of time without starting to panic about the *possibility* of feeling lonely. He always made sure to be with others, although this did not quite resolve his lonely feelings, but did help him pretend he was not. It was easier for him to conjure up his denial system in this manner. He was convinced that his contributions in social and professional circumstances were always perceived as "stupid" or "commonplace." Thus, when his wife left, his panic about being unwanted and abandoned, feelings he had unconsciously and semiconsciously kept from me and from himself, surfaced. He was worried that I would think of him as an incompetent therapist. (For a comparison of similar problems in candidates who are undergoing "training analysis," see Benedek, 1955.) This patient's development as a child was marred by inconsistent and discontinuous mothering between the ages of six months and four years, caused by his mother's intermittent hospitalizations for serious physical illnesses. His "contactlessness" was successfully covered over as far as other people were concerned. His own awareness of it was skin deep, for he constructed his life style, both professionally and personally, in such an insulated manner that no one was able to trespass his territory and confront him with his lack of relatedness. He was not perceived as lonely or lacking in essential ingredients for a healthy identity. He impressed others as a bright, capable, hard-working psychotherapist who simply cherished his privacy and was perhaps somewhat on the depressed side. His defensive armor was, in effect, the expression of a fragile ego whose boundaries contained serious discontinuities and loose links.

Treatment for this patient proceeded for quite a long time before certain elements, crucial in his history and present dynamics, emerged. While he was no doubt partially responsible for his slow development, I believed that I was no less responsible for not having recognized this "resistance" earlier, attributing this failure to a number of factors, mostly countertransferential in nature: I had certain knowledge of the patient from outside sources, specifically from the referring colleague who was on the faculty of the training institute in which my patient was a candidate. This colleague told me that my patient was "an exceptional, highly intelligent, knowledgeable young man, with very little pathology and a great deal going for him." Indeed, when I first met the patient, and in the subsequent therapeutic relationship, my colleague's impression seemed accurate. As a result, I developed an unconscious attitude toward the patient that discounted much of his pathology by rationalizing it away as due to immediate stresses of real-life situations, expecially the tremendous demands placed on him by the training institute.

There was no doubt that I had, to a certain degree, unconsciously identified with him on this level, since I had gone through similar training not too many years before. This, however, was not the only countertransferential obstacle. Two additional factors were also operating: Because the patient was in analytic training, I refrained from utilizing a strategy and technique that could not be considered strictly analytical by this institute and might possibly not be acceptable, although there were neither implicit nor explicit guidelines for the training analysts. I rationalized that it would be confusing to the patient if I used my own personal understanding of the analytic process. Eventually, however, I became aware of the restriction I had placed on myself, and that it made me rather uncomfortable. I then convinced myself that it would be untenable to change course in midstream, because it would violate the principle of object constancy. While I was able to live with this rationale for awhile, my interaction with the patient became somewhat artificial and strained, since my normal therapeutic approach was not utilized.

Parallel to this, the patient's perception of me as a revered figure who clearly fit his ego ideal reinforced my unconscious narcissistic needs, and added to an unconscious pleasure I was not willing to give up. I had already "arrived," so to speak, as far as the patient was concerned, and I was obviously not ready to give up such an idealized image by utilizing techniques that could knock the pedestal out from under my feet. This position made it difficult for me to recognize the unconscious conspiracy in this exchange of mutual narcissistic gratification between the patient and myself. Here is the-perfect-patient-with-the-perfect-therapist syndrome!

Another source of countertransference lay in the problem of loneliness itself. It can bring about powerful emotions and, at times, trigger off a strong need on the part of the therapist to rush to the patient's rescue like a "good mother." Defensively, and obviously because of unresolved dependency needs on my part, I failed to recognize this underlying problem in the patient. Thus I successfully avoided a confrontation with my own fear of loneliness, at least for quite awhile. Needless to say, when the patient could no longer hide his intense feelings of desolation (triggered off by the short absence of his wife) I became readily aware of the dynamics of this destructive "transference-countertransference set-up" and attempted to remedy the situation. I apprised the patient of my understanding of the history of our relationship, how we used each other to avoid the issue and to avoid making the real contact that is at the base of the problem of loneliness, and how I went along with it because of my own blind spots. This was indeed a turning point in the treatment, not toward termination, but rather toward further and deeper re-examination of the patient's multiple aspects of his self.

The territorial confusion of ego boundaries in this dyadic interaction was greatest in those spheres of the ego in which the me-not-me aspects were not clearly differentiated, both *inter*personally and *intra*personally. However, from that point on, the confrontational analysis strategy and techiques were fully utilized with very encouraging results (not in terms of structural changes in the patient's personality, but rather in the development of a capacity to mobilize knowledge about what had triggered off his loneliness and to deal constructively with it). Although we were unable to find a way to completely eliminate these feelings from his repertoire, his capacity to deal with them decreased his sense of impotence and worthlessness. He learned to interact with others more genuinely, and his feelings of loneliness were no longer as frequent as before. His life assumed more meaning as he became more of an initiator of steps to satisfy his needs, rather than waiting for others to save him, and his interpersonal relationships were less frequently characterized by a defensive, panic-stricken avoidance.

Aloneness

The concept of *aloneness* is often confused with that of *loneliness*. It is possible to be alone without being lonely and, vice versa, to be lonely without being alone. *Aloneness* is the capacity of the individual to be contented with himself *in the presence or absence* of others, and without the (compulsive) need to seek to relate to others for the purpose of support or communication. The "capacity to be alone," as Winnicott (1958) calls it, is an important sign of an individual's independence and maturity, and eventually, his sense of separate identity. Therefore, the achievement of this capacity is an integral part of the termination process.

Winnicott (1958) notes that the idea of aloneness has been treated in negative terms in the literature and, not infrequently, similarly in clinical practice, in that it was regarded as a defensive operation, a withdrawal mechanism, possibly designed to escape anticipated attack or hurt. In "The Capacity to Be Alone," Winnicott remarked that, "in the psycho-analytical literature more has been written on the *fear* of being alone or the *wish* to be alone than the *ability* to be alone; also a considerable amount of work has been done on the withdrawn state, a defensive organization implying an expectation of persecution." Since this article, not too much has been added in this area. To be alone is still largely viewed as a negative experience. Clinically, the capacity to be alone may be represented in the silence of the patient during the session, according to Winnicott. In fact, a whole silent session or a "silent phase" during the analysis may be indicative of this capacity. Winnicott regards this capacity as clearly signaling "emotional maturity." It is also the hallmark of the patient's recognition and acceptance of his capacity to lead a meaningful life, an independence in which relatedness to others is not an obstacle or a threat. Thus the capacity to be alone as a significant criterion for termination must be manifested through a variety of the patient's activities within the sessions and outside of them.

Within the therapeutic relationship, the patient becomes more self-sufficient, yet does not negate or deny the therapist's contributions. The patient is less reliant on the therapist for his judgment and decision-making mechanism, increasingly expressing feelings of security and pleasure in discovering and relating whatever enters his mind and, at the same time, not feeling guilty for withholding what seems irrelevant to divulge. Transferentially, this condition may, as Winnicott believes, have its origins in the early mother–child relationship where the child learns to feel sufficiently secure alone *in the presence of the mother.* The one-year-old who can enjoy playing alone for awhile as his mother is nearby attending to another matter is analogous to the patient who has the capacity to explore his own world verbally or silently in the presence of the therapist. The transference at that point might very well be presumed to implicate the ever-present mother who is neither intrusive (hovering, overprotective) nor expulsive (rejecting, punishing) for the (child) patient.

Another indication within the therapeutic milieu that the patient has developed an emotional maturity to a level where he derives *pleasure from the capacity to be alone* can be assessed from the nature and content of his plans for post-termination. Some patients expect a heavy weight to be lifted from them upon termination. Such expectations are not infrequently evidence of the patient's lack of genuine involvement in the treatment process, and its perception as merely a necessary tool for the alleviation of symptoms. There may be, in such circumstances, the possibility that meaningful contact had never taken place between patient and therapist, something the latter may have totally neglected. Therefore, a thorough search by the therapist of his own understanding of the patient and commitment to him must be undertaken, and renewed efforts at clarifying and perhaps redefining the goals of treatment must take place. This process may prove beneficial in and of itself, even if the patient does not continue with the treatment. Only when the patient's plans for termination are discussed in the context of *separation from the therapist rather than from therapy itself* can he be considered as dealing with his capacity to be alone in a genuine attempt at separation rather than an escape from it. The rationale for this assumption is based on the notion or definition that in a true separation the patient does not reject those aspects of the relationship that had been helpful, but rather incorporates them. Therefore one does not need to separate from a process that proves essential to one's growth, but may separate from the person who had been instrumental in introducing the process. For this reason, the *therapist* becomes "obsolete" once the patient has mastered the self-search techniques, but when he wishes to leave *therapy*—the process by which growth occurs—rather than the therapist, it is clear that termination is a maneuver to escape—a defensive retreat.

The patient's plans for future termination ought to contain the intent to continue the search, even though he will be outside of the formal therapeutic relationship. His capacity for aloneness should incorporate those aspects of the therapeutic process that were beneficial—similar in many ways to the incorporation of the mother's supportive and educative qualities as part of the child's self. The therapist must assess, during termination, the patient's capacity for solitude after termination, and whether the separation itself will not stand in the way of deepening and enriching the pleasure that can be derived from this capacity. On the surface, this statement may seem to be contradictory, for after all, solitude or aloneness in effect mean separation. However, the roots of the capacity to be alone are in a time when the mother was present, and in the therapeutic situation, this may be interpreted as if the statement proposes that the therapist be present if this capacity is to grow. To some extent this is true up to a point, where the therapist's presence only fosters dependence rather than helping the patient to do the job independently. Thus the genuine capacity for aloneness encompasses the feeling of security in one's self *and* having others' reasonable support and reliable availability.

Outside the therapeutic relationship, specifically in the realm of interpersonal interaction, the patient's capacity to be alone is gradually fashioned after what he has learned from the model relationship of the therapeutic dyad. Thus he becomes increasingly attentive to his needs and pursuant of goals without losing emotional relatedness to others and sensitivity toward his surroundings. The capacity to be alone is, in fact, the opposite extreme of the feeling of loneliness, where "contactlessness" is at the base of the emotional experience. During the termination phase the patient becomes increasingly aware of how his real relationships reflect introjected object relationships. Such an awareness results in the availability to the self of healthier alternatives in interpersonal interactions. He can then more easily exercise his prerogatives in the choice of friends and in the manner and style he wishes to relate to them without being self-destructive, or subservient to early object relationships.

This newly found source of energy, which helps the patient determine more rationally his interpersonal world, results from, among other things, the development of the capacity to be alone. It is often negatively perceived and misinterpreted by some of the patient's friends and relatives as rejection, abandonment, or narcissistic greed, as if the patient had no right to reorganize his options. However, such negative motivation, if it indeed exists, ought not be associated with the capacity to be alone. Rather, it can usually be traced to unresolved persecutory conflicts and feelings of oral omnipotence, probably dating back from the first two years of the patient's relationship with his parents, especially the mother. If this is the patient's motivation to be alone, then it obviates the need for further work on the therapeutic relationship between the patient and the therapist. Confrontation analysis sees this as an important area that needs concentrated effort during the termination phase.

The work of confrontation analysis attends to goals primarily designed to achieve greater independence of the self. This is done through an examination of three major subgoals— the achievement of adequate emotionality, identity, and inter- and intrapersonal communication. In addition to interpretation and free association, the techniques utilize a confrontation strategy that relies on the principle of interpersonal interaction within the therapeutic relationship. This approach may appear contraindicated for the goal of developing the capacity to be alone, for it may seem to provide an interactional model that does not allow for the experience of aloneness within the therapeutic sessions. However, this does not take into account the theoretical underpinnings of the capacity to be alone: the role of interaction between mother and child that serves as its original basis. In addition, the mother's presence, initially her physical proximity and later her image in the child's unconscious, define the developmentally appropriate boundaries of this capacity—i.e., to be alone with the presence of another person in the background. By definition, then, the origin of the concept of a healthy aloneness makes the *interaction* between patient (child) and therapist (mother) a necessary element in the attempt to analyze and resolve pathological developments in this area of the patient's personality.

Death and Suicide

Dependency is a universal condition that deeply affects the nature and development of the self, indeed of the basic structure of the total personality (Gaylin, 1968). Its vicissitudes, in combination with constitutional and other temperamental factors, provide the basis for the establishment of the individual's uniqueness—his very special identity—including its pathological distortions. Another universal condition that the human being must learn to deal with is his own demise. Psychologically, there exists an important, almost organic relationship between these two conditions, death and dependence, especially as they affect the formation of a unique identity. This relationship is of crucial concern in the therapeutic work, especially during the termination phase. It is also one of the foundations upon which the quest for meaning is built.

The Relationship Between Death and Dependence

The relationship between death and dependence is often best observed in the preoccupations and concerns of older people and people struck by a fatal illness. One often witnesses a great increase in the feelings and expressions of dependency in the older person, much beyond what their physical or intellectual decline warrants. At the same time, there also develops an increase in preoccupation about death, not altogether unreasonable, since the inevitable end is, in reality, closer than ever before. This parallel development is of special interest because it substantially illuminates the psychological understanding of individual differences, including the manifestations of undesirable symptomatology.

The most pertinent dimension in the relationship between death and dependence is the concept of separation, with death being a complete and final one. The symbolic meaning of death as separation is deeply affected by the magnitude of the individual's need for dependence. This is because dependency is, in fact, operationally defined in terms of the difficulty or ease of separating, mostly from a significant object or one who comes to represent such an object, in reality or in fantasy (Becker, 1973). Thus one might surmise that undue preoccupation with death is, by necessity, based upon problems in separation, not only the existential fear of the inevitable. Parenthetically, one might add here that there is little doubt that "true believers" in life after death are likely to be less preoccupied with death, or fearful of it (Seigel, 1980). This is not because they have fewer problems in the sphere of separation, but because the nature of the belief in life after death denies the essence of death, that it is indeed a complete and final separation (Feifel, 1977). Such a belief asserts that death is a "transitional" condition that takes the individual from one phase of existence to another. Psychodynamically, this *belief* may be seen as a *transitional object* that helps the believer devalue the importance of the significant object because of the inevitability of its loss, and hence, shifts dependency onto the new object, the belief in the afterlife. This type of denial may bring about ritualistic behavior into which the energy, previously invested in the object of dependency (mother), may be redirected. These compulsive acts are often observed both in "true believers" (e.g., the religious rituals), and in children who insist on certain perseverative behavior when they feel threatened with an impending separation (e.g., a baby may insist on hugging his mother endlessly before letting her go).

Another most crucial point is, of course, the fact that the inevitability of death renders the individual totally impotent and helpless in its face, and arouses most intense fears regarding one's lack of control over one's own life. This condition can easily be compared to the infant's helplessness at birth, where control is also lacking, and where only involuntary mechanisms are at work. Such helplessness creates a variety of reactions. A most common one is that of denial. The fact that our culture as a whole has developed taboos related to death proves how ill-equipped it is to deal with it. These taboos, which are still persistent in an otherwise "enlightened" generation, may perhaps be more understood when the meaning of death is examined in terms of its symbolism along the dependence–separation dimension. In other words, the pain related to separation is transformed into defensive maneuvers to avoid not only the thought of death, but also the fear, anger, and feelings of vulnerability that accompany it.

An additional central issue dynamically (through the projective identification mechanism) associated with death and dependence is that separation from an object of dependency often forces the individual to assess his sense of self-worth relative to others, a process that may consequently arouse powerful feelings about adequacy, desirability, and importance. When separation anxiety is too great and problems of dependency are still unresolved, the concept of death may indeed trigger off renewed (from infancy) feelings of inadequacy and questions about one's role in life as a significant and contributing member of society. Thus, if one's emotional capacity to function without inordinate need for emotional support from others is meager, death fantasies would represent final separation, thus signaling the annihilation of the self. A deep narcissistic injury because of one's dispensability might then be experienced. If one dies and the world continues to function just as smoothly, then how significant can one's existence be?

From a psychodynamic viewpoint, the fear of death and its relationship to dependency are intricately bound with the individual's development of self or identity through the process of identification with significant adults. Two separate but parallel levels or paths may contribute to the painful perception of death, and may be understood in terms of the mechanisms of projection and projective identification.

The first path may be called the narcissistic pain of death fantasies, which refers to hurt feelings associated with the death of oneself. In reality, death itself, not illness that might precede it, cannot cause one to feel pain, since death is by definition the absence of all sensation—thus no pain can be rationally expected. The pain associated with thoughts about self-death must then be attributed to another, different set of cognitive and emotional factors. It may be reasonable to posit the following sequence of psychological processes: When the self is invested with an *over-identification* with the significant object, the fantasied separation (death) from this self (i.e., the significant object) is likely to result in feeings of depletion, since it was not successful during its maturation in replacing the significant object with its own needs. The unbearable fear of death by the narcissistic personality is, thus, directly proportional to the amount of grandiosity and omnipotence that the self has developed as a result of overidentification with the idealized significant object (Kohut, 1971). This is a projective identification process, partially based on the overinvestment of libidinal energy in early childhood identification.

For example, a 32-year-old man who came for treatment because he felt isolated from the many friends he insisted he had, related a recurring fantasy over a period of five years while in treatment. This fantasy has always frightened and depressed him: "I am driving on a country road all by myself and a cow comes out of the bushes and starts to cross the road. I can't stop, and I crash. I see the cow dead, and then I die. Then my mother finds out about the accident and she asks the hospital people to freeze my body immediately because she can't stand to see my face and fingers get all wrinkled up. They don't listen to her, and she ages so much in a matter of hours to the point that I almost don't recognize her. Her sorrow transforms her into a withering leaf."

This narcissistic patient often complained about the inconvenience that the death of relatives or friends' parents caused him when he had to attend funerals; and he had never expressed any genuine empathy or feeling of loss beyond some passing comments. However, he became quite agitated by any thoughts of his own death, not infrequently crying over such prospects. He was totally dependent on his widowed mother's not too extravagant income to support him, something she was "only too happy" to do, according to him. This symbiotic, controlling, and very dependent relationship seemed to be clearly responsible for the lack of ego boundaries, poor identity, and frequent death fantasies with their depressing effect. The cow in the fantasy represented the patient's mother (he often referred to her as the "Golden Cow" because of her unconditional and unlimited willingness to support him), and when she dies (in the fantasy), he dies too. When his body wastes, she must undergo the same torture. Thus there was very little differentiation between himself and his mother, as his fantasy, and certainly his life pattern, clearly indicated. It was interesting that, even though he had developed an impressive entourage of friends, his feelings of isolation never disappeared. Apparently, he had "bought" these so-called friends with bribes in the form of expensive gifts, in the same manner that his mother had successfully sought to seduce him into the symbiotic relationship through her "unconditional" financial support. The overidentification of this patient with his mother, and his dependency on her, clearly triggered off feelings of insecurity and lack of anchoring whenever fantasies about her death cropped up; her death meant his too, and vice versa, his death meant hers.

The second path in which death may be experienced as a frightening and unacceptable conscious thought, with consequent defensive overreactions, refers to the death of other people. The process here is somewhat easier to comprehend when it involves a direct dependency relationship (as in the above case illustration), where the patient unconsciously feels that he would be totally lost by a permanent separation (unlike the above case where the patient was not *consciously* worried about his mother's death; in fact, he often verbally expressed his *wish* for her death). While initially understandable, some patients cannot easily deal with this fear, and only after a thorough search for its dynamics can one understand its structure. Frequently the patient unconsciously perceives, through a projective defense, the fantasied death object as his own self, which if lost, would mean the loss of the self. Consequently, any perceived threat to the object of the self-projection is naturally experienced as a threat to the self and its integrity. As a result, the patient's behavior might assume a placating stance, easily observed in the diligent, "good boy" individual who attends very properly to this object of dependence, when in effect, he unconsciously means to be taking care of himself. A great deal of resentment, even rage, is often associated with this behavior, and it can be frequently detected in subtle complaints of the patient about a variety of items indirectly bearing on the subject.

An example of this behavior is that of a patient who moved to a house less than an hour away from his parents and experienced *constant fear of their death*, often complaining about the "horrible" neighborhood in which they lived. It was "painful" for him to see them live under conditions of deterioration of the streets around them. In reality, the neighborhood had changed very little from the time he had lived there and, in fact, whenever his memories of his childhood took him there, he experienced a surge of nostalgic, positive, warm feelings about it, as long as he was not discussing his *obligation* to visit his parents. The patient's identity was quite fuzzy, and he continued to feel a lack of self-worth without the protection of his "highly esteemed parents within their community." When he left that community, he was unable to establish his own individual significance among new acquaintances and within himself—the subject of a great deal of pain that almost "forced" his return to his parents' house, a condition that initially brought him to treatment.

These aspects of the "death complex" are, then, tied quite understandably with the problems of separation and conflicts related to identity and dependency. When termination is being considered, this theme can become the top one on the agenda, because the termination itself is a separation—a most important one to be sure—and, in many cases, a final one. The importance of such a separation cannot be overestimated, because the therapist becomes the alter or surrogate parent for the patient, and in a very real sense, the object of tremendous emotional investment. At times, therapists deny this importance by dissociating themselves from the responsibility of thoroughly investigating and resolving the separation aspects of the termination. To be sure, the relationship between patient and therapist is not the same as the one between patient and parent, because it is largely transferential. Yet the bonds that are created must be considered as real, too, because regardless of how detached, inactive, orthodox, objective, or professional the therapist is throughout the treatment, it is not humanly possible for the patient to totally ignore or avoid the *real* person of the therapist and not react to him as such. Especially during the termination phase, the therapist must also acknowledge the gradual bridging of the distance between himself and the patient, a result mainly attributable to the patient's evolution as a mature person with a distinct identity and at least equal understanding and acceptance of himself. Termination can be the last opportunity for both patient and therapist to deal with issues of identity, death, and separation, which are eternal issues for all people because of the nature of the human condition, and because they are changeable as a result of the therapeutic work. At the termination phase these issues may be dealt with from yet additional perspectives.

Meaning in Life Through Analysis of Death for Patient and Therapist

Consideration of the relationship between death and dependence only as a problem representing difficulties in separation may be justified only insofar as it is an attempt to understand where the overwhelming anxiety about death originates; however, the analysis of death issues may often lead to areas of investigation far broader than that of separation, issues that may be thought of as the essence, the raison d'être, of the therapy. After all, *psychotherapy does not offer cures like medicine, but an attitude about life,* a way of thinking about important aspects of life—its very meaning. This does not imply, of course, that psychotherapy should engage in abstract philosophical polemics about *meaning* in the life of the individual in treatment. However, the therapist cannot be so naive or (professionally) overprotected as to dismiss certain questions that surface in the mind of the patient, as well as in his own mind, especially during the termination phase.

One of the questions that the patient brings up is his *readiness* for termination. How does the patient know when to terminate, since his original symptoms are no longer problematic and he *feels* much better. Almost simultaneously, the patient may also question whether he should not continue, because, after all, it can't hurt to bounce things off an objective person. Would staying in therapy mean the perpetuation of dependence or an honest drive to better understand oneself? Such questions are no doubt *partially* stimulated by the imminent therapeutic separation; but quite often, during termination, patients discuss their future plans, and the subject of death is certain to come up—*they* are getting older, their *parents* are certainly getting closer to death, and the *analyst* becomes also part of this category of those who are going to die, either through the separation or because he is indeed also getting older. Discussions about this taboo subject of death (and separation) stimulate an inner search for how therapy has helped. While not all patients who have had a positive experience in therapy have been successful in eliminating all their problems and terminate conflict-free, many leave with the feeling that they learned to look at life, at themselves, and at others with a perspective somewhat different than the one they came in with, and they express the view that treatment has added a new dimension to their lives. It is true, of course, that patients have a vested interest in defending their venture into psychotherapy, a defense often manifested in its idealization. In the majority of cases, however, therapy is probably the single most significant step they have taken for their growth since childhood. This is so because, as noted earlier, it does not only offer relief from symptoms, but it helps them redefine their self, and recompose or reconstruct their identity. When a patient can sincerely satisfy himself with the answer, "I now have meaning in my life," he is ready for termination. This is not a philosophical cliche, but a summary statement of the achievement of a number of recognizable goals that the patient has worked on in his treatment, and which culminate in a healthy identity that includes the acceptance of the self and of life as finite and as everchangeable in substance and direction. A healthy identity cannot be satisfied with fixed and rigid boundaries—it is flexible enough to be able to integrate and synthesize new experiences without losing its own core. For this reason, in the context of the termination phase, consideration of separation and death fantasies often brings with it the necessity to investigate the meaning of life for the patient from a new perspective.

Parallel to the patient's questions, the therapist must ask similar questions, especially with reference to his work and goals. When a patient terminates, obviously it is also a termination for the therapist. Bonds are formed between the two, since the therapist had cared for the patient and guided him through the thick and thin of his inner life and outside adventures. The therapist has shared much of the patient's experiences over the years and, thus the iminent separation triggers off a host of feelings in him too. If both partners in this dyad seriously worked at their tasks, the patient is not the only beneficiary. The therapist also grows—growth that is attached to the specific patient. This "reverse mothering" must thus have its separation pains and cannot go unnoticed—consciously or unconsciously—by the therapist. In this therapeutic equation, the patient has the therapist to discuss separation problems with. From a certain vantage point, however, the therapist generally has no one to consult about his fantasies, associations, and feelings about the separation. This may result in certain dangers, one of which may be the arousal of strong counter-transferential feelings that are aimed at fostering the patient's dependency, making termination quite problematic for the patient. The therapist's dependency needs are then satisfied, while the patient continues to pay for them. This kind of danger, however, is not likely to occur frequently if the therapist's experience with termination from his own treatment had been successful and if the patient's ego is healthy enough not to allow it. When the patient is ready to leave, he is not likely to submit to the therapist's irrational reasoning for too long. It is entirely possible, of course, that the termination wishes of the patient may be the result of his need to flee from a fantasy of an ultimate rejection by the therapist. This type of resistance in the form of a wish for termination is not likely to trigger the therapist's separation anxiety, because it is defensive in nature, and the patient must be immediately confronted with it.

Analysis of the fear of death and its relationship to meaning in the patient's life and its dependency origins are clinically utilized in the confrontation analysis approach to promote an ever-increased awareness of boundaries between patient and therapist, without losing distance or emotional contact between them. To achieve this goal, certain *changes* in interactive patterns and treatment strategy may be necessary during discussions of separation-termination. For example, the therapist might share with the patient some of his own experiences with separation or death. Or he might utilize other techniques that require more involvement on his part, such as the techniques of "guided fantasy." The therapist might ask the patient to imagine a separation, discuss his reactions to it, and the plan of action he might take. This interaction gives the patient an object relations model to take when he leaves treatment; it intensifies the significance of the human contact without any vested interest on the therapist's part in continuing a dependency relationship.

Suicide

Suicide is a rather curious phenomenon because of its paradoxical nature. On the one hand, it is an *active* termination of life, i.e., the individual must do something to achieve this goal. On the other hand, in most cases, this behavior is controlled by unconscious motives that render its real character *passive*. In some instances of heroism or euthanasia, suicide may be considered as an active type of behavior, because the decision to die has, normally, a worked-out "rational" plan, with more or less social sanction. Yet, even in these conditions, it would be naive to believe that only the "good of the country" or the futility of continued treatment of terminal illness are the only reasons for the decision to suicide. There are always additional unconscious needs for martyrdom in cases of heroism, usually associated with the ultimate need for "purification" and acceptance and, in cases of euthanasia, the need for approval in the act of being "rational," courageous, level-headed, and at times, "sacrificial" for the benefit of the suffering family. Thus, suicide in general must be considered, at least partially, as an irrational act that is carried out in the service of unconscious needs.

Suicide, separation, and dependence. While, psychologically, suicide may reasonably be considered under the rubric of separation, it does not need to be rigidly associated with it. On the whole, there seems to be a general agreement among writers that the suicidal act often symbolizes a kind of punishment that the individual forces upon those whom he hates. The explanation of this curious type of punishment, where the punisher is actually the one punished, often emanates from the theory that when separation from the incorporated loved object is not successful enough, extreme or accumulated anger or hatred toward it results in suicide. This theory is plausible for those who have at some point in time considered suicide as an alternative course of action that they either ultimately rejected or half-heartedly attempted. There are, of course, people who seriously attempt it but are somehow rescued by unexpected events. Yet even these people may clearly belong to the above category, namely, to those who have separation problems. However, some of the people in this category may attempt suicide again with a more "successful" scheme, and their basic problem may therefore not be that of separation, but rather that of *separateness*.

The distinction between those who *attempt* suicide and those who actually *kill* themselves is important because of the difference in motivation and in the basic personality dynamics between these two categories. "Real" or "successful" suicides occur mostly with people whose major problem is not that of separation but that of *separateness from the world and confusion about their role and function it it.* This type of personality is generally either profusely labile, or is steeped in a pattern of reactive or chronic depressions. The basic interaction with others is not one of genuine attachment, but rather one of deliberate, "forced" character, and may, at times, have the quality of a frantic search for a connection, a bridge to the world, not because of dependency needs but mainly because of a lack of identity and meaningful anchor in the environment. These are people who have never acquired psychological tools for making genuine human contacts, and therefore, they do not know what it means to have them, although they constantly feel a lack of "something" they are unable to identify. Their reasoning and the reality-testing components of their egos tell them that they are missing something, and thus, they continuously reach but never obtain anything more than, at best, superficially "adequate" interpersonal goals. Eventually, when they become convinced that they cannot reach their goals, they conclude that their function in this world is totally inconsequential, and they decide to sever their "nothingness" through the suicidal act. This relieves them of the pain of their separateness and the futile search for objects that will affirm their existence as worthwhile, objects they never found in their childhood. Put another way, these are extremely dependent individuals who never tasted the real flavor of nurturance. Suicide for them becomes the only "logical" alternative: they regard themselves, in their final accounting to themselves, as "obsolete" entities deserving destruction or abandonment.

On the other hand, individuals who make various gestures to kill themselves and are constantly in the throes of inner turmoil are often those whose main conflicts reflect an inability to become emotionally independent, because separation from others or from destructive aspects of their selves means a total abandonment or severance from their lifeline. These are people whose early development had been clearly marred by intense emotional ambivalence of their parents toward them, having received confusing positive *and* negative messages with regard to their self-worth and self-esteem. Any separation (suicide), then, may become a symbolic representation of their negative self-worth and their parents' (conscious or unconscious) wish that they disappear. Suicide can thus be a maneuver of the obedient, "good child," in search of parental approval. At the same time, the fact that it is only an "attempt," may also represent the individual's incorporation of some positive self-image and the basis for building increased ego strength and maturity. In other words, like any symptom that represents the fear and the wish in the separation conflict, and thus binds the anxiety, the attempt to suicide represents the wish to please both sides of the ambivalent introjects. From this point of view, then, suicide as a violent statement of anger can be understood as the result of frustration from an impasse with regard to the ambivalent objects, an impulsive resolution of the conflict. Along this line of reasoning, the suicidal attempt can thus be taken as an expression of revenge against those who were instrumental in the incorporation of the individual's confused self-image, namely, the parents or those parts of them with which he identified and had become incongruent with the total self at a certain time. The "attempt" to escape from this image often occurs when the defensive structure, mostly denial and dissociation, is no longer effective in repressing the anxiety stemming from increased pressure that requires the resolution of the inconsistencies in the self. Such pressure can tip the balance toward one side of the ambivalence, resulting in the suicidal attempt.

Differential Factors in Real and Attempted Suicide.

It is not easy to make the differential diagnosis between the potential for a successful ending of one's life and an attempted suicide, but a few significant factors may be helpful in understanding this complex issue, both during an initial interview, as well as during therapy, and certainly during (premature) termination. These are not exclusive issues, nor are they always easily discernible.

Emotionality factors in early childhood. The patient must be assessed with regard to the nature of the emotional bonds among the various members of his family during childhood. If these were lacking, especially if there was little or no emotional interaction between the parents, the probability or potential for a real or successful suicide is quite great in the depressed, psychotic, or borderline constellation *after* an unusually stressful period. Because there was no emotional glue, as it were, between family members, whatever emotions were displayed were likely to be defensive in nature, nonspontaneous, and a subtle mask to keep real distance from others.

Interaction The quality of the patient's communicative system must also be assessed on the basis of two factors. The first concerns interactions with others, especially his model of early communication with parents and other significant objects. If no flow of understandable messages between the parents took place, especially when these messages were self-centered and lacking in sensitivity and empathy, the core of the self is experienced as being cut off, alienated, and most importantly, not equipped with the knowledge and capacity normally required for the creation of genuine connection with others. Thus the interaction that is carried out with others is, for such an individual, only a mask that hides a basic inadequacy and separateness, and will, given a certain opportune time, result in a real suicidal act. On the other hand, when the individual has an overwhelming feeling that there was a fairly good understanding within the family, notwithstanding certain inconsistencies and discontinuities, he is likely, in times of great stress, to attempt some escape through a suicidal gesture without being seriously or deeply committed to this behavior. The second factor that the therapist must be alert to is the quality of the interaction within the therapeutic situation itself. When there is a genuine investment of feelings in the therapist and in the process of change, the probability of a successful attempt is greatly diminished.

Narcissism. In general, narcissism and real suicide are inversely related, i.e., the more narcissistic the patient, the smaller the risk of suicide. Narcissism is not infrequently a reaction either to an inordinate amount of frustration during early development or an overwhelming amount of overstimulation and lack of opportunity for reality-testing because of overpro-

tection on the part of the mothering figure. This emotional abandonment or overevaluation of the child as an object of the parents' gratification can create a serious narcissistic character
founded on crippling dependency. Consequently, separations become so unbearable and injurious to the self as the object of
love, that a real suicide is unlikely. At the same time, however,
such a narcissistic personality make-up often results in poor
judgment, which may end up as an "unplanned," but successful
suicide. In narcissism that also has a significant symbiotic factor, successful suicide during a depressive episode is quite possible.

Impulsivity.   Impulsive individuals are extremely dependent people who keep trying to escape their feelings of imprisonment and submission through acts that are supposed to lib-
erate them from the tyranny of those upon whom they depend.
Their judgment is also impaired and, while they don't normally
fancy real suicide as an alternative to life, their involvement
with magical solutions to their conflicts may lead to such an
alternative—a grand suicidal gesture. For example, a 30-year-
old narcissistic woman was in treatment for depression after
having impulsively quit an excellent job because of a minor tiff
with her boss, who "unjustly" called her "selfish." She related
that a few years earlier she had had a violent argument with
a man with whom she was living concerning the amount of time
he wished to spend with his children from a previous marriage.
In the midst of the argument, she ran to the bathroom screaming that she was going to kill herself. She locked the bathroom
door and proceeded to swallow a mouthful of aspirins, and then
returned to the livingroom with a handful of other assorted pills
and swallowed them in front of her boyfriend with the help of
half a glass of whiskey. She was comatose for more than 48
hours after her stomach was pumped, and when she woke up
from this unsuccessful attempted separation, she confessed that
her intention was clearly to force him to give up seeing his
children more than once a month so that he could devote more
time to her. This had not been the first time she had used this
type of manipulative behavior, although this was the first episode that could have killed her.

Recognition and acceptance of assets. When a patient recognizes that he has positive assets capable of contributing something of value to the continuity of his own life and perhaps that of others or to society in general, the probability of real suicide is decreased. Such a person has a potential for accepting such assets as a real part of himself that does not need to be destroyed for the achievement of other goals, such as expressing anger at others or frustration, or manipulating family or social relationships. However, if such assets cannot be recognized as unique and specific to that individual, the capacity to form genuine empathic relationships is then curtailed, and the feelings of alienation, nonbelonging, and lack of self-worth might seriously provide fertile grounds for a suicidal act, which terminates a life thought to be redundant anyway.

Incomplete as they obviously are, the above factors can help the therapist identify areas of the ego that need concentration, especially when the patient's goals are interrupted because of obsessive suicidal thoughts. They can serve as indicators, signals to focus either on reinforcing and nurturing dependency within the therapeutic situation when the suicidal risk is real, or to tackle directly the problem of separation when the patient is going through a stressful period. All in all, the relationship between suicide, dependence, and separation is extremely important to understand because it is central to major psychodynamic issues.

Integration

15
The Capacity for Love

An individual's capacity for love involves communication, emotionality, and identity. These are the three goals considered most significant in confrontation analysis. The range and depth of this capacity hinges, to a large measure, upon the progressive development of a healthy identity, and this is linked to the criteria for psychological independence. In the final analysis, termination is most appropriately considered in the context of the patient's capacity to fulfill his own needs—needs that are inevitably (and most significantly) gratified through interpersonal relationships (Sullivan, 1953) and through adequate utilization of potentials and talents.

A variety of behavioral and affective concepts have been used to describe and understand the nature and meaning of love. These include empathy, concern, compassion, identification, idealization, genital satisfaction, tenderness, integration of internalized object relations, guilt, care, and dependency (Kernberg, 1976). All these concepts may be directly or indirectly associated with the experience of loving, although it seems likely that, at different times, some are more operational than others.

Loving is a complex phenomenon that depends on the achievement of the capacity to integrate the self's emotional life, the capacity to communicate effectively one's feelings and needs, and the knowledge of one's identity. The nature of love is further complicated because, in addition to the above descriptive terms used by Kernberg and others, it involves in the deepest sense, the individual's feelings of security, trust, vulnerability, generosity, confidence, and history of interpersonal interaction. Consequently the manifest behavior of any individual in relation to the dimension of love must be assessed from a variety of perspectives, including the therapeutic relationship. It is important to note, however, that distinction must be made between the existential experience of loving and its behavioral expression, verbal and nonverbal. Individuals who have the capacity to experience feelings of love are not always equipped with either the capacity to express it or if they know how to express it, with judgment to do so at the appropriate time and with the appropriate person.

Kernberg (1976) believes that the capacity for mature love emanates from the successful resolution of Oedipal conflicts. Such a resolution leads to the development of a positive self-concept because the child is able to integrate his object relations, and thus diminish the prohibitions against sexual relations with another person.

Utilization of the Oedipal construct to account for the capacity for love relationships seems cumbersome and unnecessary, however, since the relationship between mother and child in the first few years of life contains the natural seeds for mature love. Of course, Oedipal strivings may further illuminate the individual's interpersonal functioning, where sexual or social-intimate prohibitions are triangularly structured. In the beginning of the child's life, prohibition (basically synonymous with castration because it eliminates, or intends to eliminate, action) is exercised first and foremost by the mother's inevitable frustration of some of the child's needs. Thus prohibitions that become introjected, and later, projected as persecutory (as in the paranoid position), are primarily associated with one object, namely, the mother (Klein, 1957). Therefore castration anxiety need not orginate from the so-called Oedipal triangle, i.e., from the parent of the opposite sex. In fact, it comes with the mother's frustrating the infant's needs, and later, it is transferentially projected onto a third party—usually the father—because of the fear of loss of the loved object, the mother. The capacity for involvement in a full love relationship evolves through the process of identifying with the mother as a part object and then synthesizing the many part objects into an identification with a whole object. Interference in this process of identification leads to difficulties in the formation of stable, loving relationships with others (Kernberg, 1976). A number of parameters considered by confrontation analysis to be central to the understanding of the self must be investigated in connection with such interferences during the termination phase.

DIFFICULTIES IN FORMING LOVE RELATIONSHIPS

Dependence and Love

The basic assumptions of confrontation analysis include a number of "universal" conditions hypothesized to contribute significantly to the structure and development of the self. Dependence, the most fundamental, is the core around which a variety of interpersonal and intrapersonal interactions cluster. These interactions constitute the character of the personality as expressed through the functioning self or ego. Thus, for instance, dependence on the mother for survival creates the necessity for the infant to imitate her, and later, through the process of introjection, to identify with her along given dimensions. In a general sense, one learns to be human by observing and repeating what other humans do. However, where mothering is disturbed to the extent that it threatens the infant's integrity for psychological survival, the latter may choose not to identify with the former, but rather to defend against such an identification (Greenson, 1954).

The capacity of the individual to develop and maintain love relationships depends on the content of his identifications, as well as on the mechanisms to expressing them that have been acquired during the formative years. The mother's care, tenderness, sensitivity to the child's needs (*and* to hers), and the continuity of a supportive environment can eventually, through the process of identification, be translated into the capacity to own such deep feelings toward another person, including sexual attachments. Failure to develop the capacity to maintain such relationships may be attributed in part to problems in early identifications because of inadequate handling of the dependency needs of the infant.

A most extreme cause for a total lack of the capacity for love is the mother's inability to give her child any concrete expression of positive care. The relationship with the child may be arbitrary, neglectful, apathetic. Such an attitude toward children is not infrequently observed in orphanages, or foster homes, and in mothers whose narcissism is too deep to enable them to adequately attend to the child. The result—although not always as simply or directly discernible—is the child's, and later the adult's, self-perception as empty and worthless, a person who has nothing to give and nothing to gain from getting. When such an individual is offered love and support, it is experienced as an invasion of his unlovable self, or as a misguided, unwarranted behavior (since he is not worth the "sacrifice"). The individual may also interpret any emotional offering in a paranoid manner—that its aim is to force the exposure of his empty shell. The probability of developing even the most primitive loving relationships is negligible in this type of personality structure. In a real sense, dependence plays an insignificant role in the life of such individuals, because as children they were left to fend for themselves, and their basic survival needs were satisfied without the accompaniment of positive emotional or physical support. Dependency strivings become so repressed that they are almost extinguished, to the extent that no motivational energy is available to search for dependency objects to replace the deprivation (what was never experienced is never missed). This often leads to the development of a chronic depressive posture, as in the so-called social isolate or "hermit" in the schizoid personality organization.

A 54-year-old mechanical engineer came for treatment because he was depressed and was increasingly experiencing feelings of estrangement from his wife and alienation from his business associates. He had also been having difficulties on the job with his boss, because he was habitually late in delivering blueprints for his assigned projects, and was not following the required specifications for the design of such projects. It was clear that he had a compulsive need to be called on the carpet because of his "unintentional" incompetence. He felt he was not completing assignments on time because his work was superior to that of other employees. In addition, while he overtly agreed with his employer's position regarding handling of specific projects, he secretly felt that his employer was only interested in controlling him, rather than in designing more efficient machines. He complained that his blueprints were always returned to him with trivial corrections. He was unable to tell his boss how insulted he felt, and instead walked around the factory feeling dejected and isolated from everyone.

The patient's relationship to his wife was really a "nonrelationship," since there was no communication beyond necessary routine transactions. He had been sexually impotent for many years, and had no interest in physical contact with anyone. He claimed he had married his wife after graduating from college only because she was a most independent woman who made no demands on him that he could not handle. In the beginning of the marriage, sex was engaged in as "a necessary evil" for the relationship to continue. He derived no pleasure from sexual encounters with his wife, and had no extramarital sexual experience.

The patient was the younger of two children with an unusual family history. His father had died in a train accident a few weeks after the patient's birth. His mother attempted suicide when the patient was six months old, and was hospitalized on and off thereafter for much of her life. The patient and his sister (who was six years his senior) were then cared for by an aunt for a few months, and then both were placed in two different orphanages. The patient remained there until the first grade, when he was transferred to another orphanage, where he remained until he graduated from high school. His visits with his mother were infrequent and very unpleasant, since she would hardly speak to him. He was, in fact, somewhat more attached to his aunt, who would occasionally take him to her house to see the family on holidays. However, during most weekends when other children had visitors, he had none. He remembered that after awhile he became immune to the terrible feelings of shame and abandonment.

Because of his superior intellectual ability, the patient was able to win some scholarships for college and to obtain a job that supported him throughout the school years. He studied engineering. He was never able to develop close friendships beyond school acquaintances. His sense of isolation prompted him to seek some social outlets, and he found ballroom dancing lounges most responsive to his needs. He learned to be a good dancer, and enjoyed this activity more than anything else in his life. He derived pleasure from his capacity for synchronizing his steps to the music, rather than from transient interactions with dancing partners. These encounters never resulted in close relationships. He met his wife in a college class during his senior year. Soon after the marriage, his feelings of alienation and detachment caused some conflicts with his wife. He sought treatment at that time, and remained in individual therapy for over ten years, then returning to it after several years for another three years of individual and group therapy. Although he felt that he had learned a great deal about himself, he was unable to translate his understanding into emotional change. He continued to feel separate, socially awkward, and inadequate. He compensated somewhat for these feelings by becoming active in his local political club. The other club members may have viewed his detachment as level-headedness and objectivity, for he was repeatedly elected treasurer of the club. In this way he was able to serve the community, but he never felt he was truly a part of it.

The patient's treatment objectives centered around his feelings of alienation and nonbelonging, his wife's "control" of him, and his boss' treatment of him as a nonprofessional. His resentment had never been expressed openly and directly. Even in treatment, he tended to deny such feelings.

The patient's history did not offer a hopeful prognosis, especially given the early traumas of continuous emotional deprivation and lack of attachment to one constant mothering object. In addition, his attempts to change the structure and content of his inner self through treatment had in the past been futile. He did not appear to have serious resistance to therapy, and was willing to do anything to change. However, the most important ingredient that is necessary for any hope of therapeutic change—i.e., the capacity to form some emotional attachment to the therapist—seemed to be lacking. The establishment of a workable transference seemed almost hopeless, and he was well aware of this problem, as he noted in the first consultation with the present therapist that he found it *peculiar,* but *not disturbing,* that he had not developed any feelings towards his first therapist even though he had been in treatment with him for many years.

Treatment initially focused on the pressing immediate concerns: his fear that his wife would leave him and that he would be fired from his job, only six months after he had begun. This was not an unfamiliar pattern, although this time it seemed especially disconcerting because the job market was disasterous for his profession, and because his wife had decided to quit her job a few months earlier. He was, to put it mildly, in a state of panic. After a few months of supportive, explorative, and somewhat interventive strategy, he was able to feel more secure about his job because he became more alert to the self-destructive elements in his dawdling on assigned projects and his obsequious relationship with his boss. We worked together on ways to prevent him from positioning himself on the "firing line," even though that meant that, at times, he had to operate on the job according to my "suggestions." Slowly his talents began to be more enthusiastically recognized, yet he did not feel that he was being praised for his "professionalism," but rather for what he could do for the company—something he regarded as secondary and superficial. Instead of feeling unique, he felt like a cog in the wheel. Nevertheless, his performance improved to such a degree that one of the partners hinted to him that he was close to being asked to become a junior partner. When he heard this news he was thrilled and frightened, primarily because of the implication for social interaction. As a partner, his interpersonal contacts would involve greater intimacy, something he did not feel he could handle. He could not understand why anyone would want to associate with him on that level.

In this general vein, treatment continued for two more years. His wife was pleased with his progress on the professional front, but she became increasingly impatient with his inability to translate his business success into their interpersonal interaction. He continued to be uninvolved and distant from her emotionally, yet quite in need of her presence in his life (Winnicott, 1958). His dependence on her was as amorphous as it was pervasive, and he could never express his need for her in specific positive emotional terms.

Throughout his life, he had always worried that without any warning he would be mercilessly pushed out on to the street, and then he would be destroyed. The lack of objects onto which to anchor his self for purposes of integrating the various identifications, and creating an entity capable of enduring the vulnerability of a close relationship, made it very difficult for him to feel secure enough in the therapeutic setting to let down his guard. He did not expect the therapeutic experience to mean much in the long run, and each session was thus experienced as a separate, discrete, transient, "lesson." In a certain sense, therapy was another orphanage home for him, the difference being the absence of the cruelty that had been so frequent in the orphanage, and the presence of intellectual stimulation in his transactions with me.

To no one's surprise, the subject of termination soon came up, since he admittedly felt that there was no hope for him to change his emotional make-up. I agreed with him that if he perceived treatment as a vehicle for changing his life, termination was the order of the day. At the same time I confronted him with the issue of genuine communication, which he had claimed he wanted to attain. If indeed this goal was important to him, then he had to abandon the grandiose illusion that he would change the structure of his personality, and concentrate instead on obtaining gratification from brief human encounters such as the therapeutic relationship. He had to start thinking "small," I told him, because he could not replace the deprivations of childhood at his age, but he could focus on the "here and now," and not dream about making up for the "there and then."

This confrontation, totally unorthodox, and perhaps painful in its directness and bluntness, stunned him. For the first time in his life he sat in disbelief that someone was not treating him like a "poor orphan," and instead was leveling with him. At the same time, he also experienced my suggestion that he use the psychotherapeutic relationship as a genuine (not just task-oriented) interaction—something he had never been invited to participate in, not even with his wife. His extremely low self-image and lack of self-worth made it difficult for him to understand why anyone would care to waste any time on him. So far as he was concerned, being an orphan was synonymous with having a contagious disease. Because of his sensitivity and paranoid orientation, he initially balked at this confrontation. However, fortunately, he quickly recovered from the shock and accepted the challenge. He said that he was moved by my "direct and nontherapeutic" approach to him, and felt that I was talking to him as if he were my son, rather than my patient. He said he would try to be as genuine with me as possible, and indicated that he had always been aware of a certain discomfort whenever he came for sessions with me and with previous therapists. He then asked me if he could address me by my first name, and without any hesitation or exploration I spontaneously answered with an enthusiastic yes. From this point on in the treatment, there was visible relaxation in his body posture, and his verbal communications became increasingly less formal.

The work did not terminate for another year, during which his relationship to his wife became more expressive and less strained, and he became eager to open up more of his inner life to her. It is hard to say that a "love" relationship developed, but enough positive interaction transpired to save the marriage from strangulation through apathy and lack of communication. Because deeper changes were not expected, it seemed most reasonable to terminate treatment at that point. Occasional supportive and "energizing" sessions were contemplated at the time of termination, and eventually used infrequently.

In this fairly extreme case, the difficulties in the patient's capacity to love were established by traumatic and violent events in his first year of life and continued for many years thereafter. The therapeutic approach was both supportive and confrontative. It did not deny the patient's unconscious conviction that he was psychologically damaged in a serious manner, and it utilized a strategy that attacked the patient's unrealistc expectations from therapy and from life, when it was quite clear that nothing could be lost by such an approach. Timing for this strategy and the therapist's genuine feelings for the patient were combined to help the patient make a risky, yet "anchoring," commitment to expand and open up the gates of his emotionality, regardless of how meager or empty it seemed to him. The expectations of the therapist were clearly spelled out and worked on, and the therapeutic alliance became rooted more in the present contract than in some illusory or foggy object from the past. Although a "love" relationship did not result, a more communicative and dependent relationship did grow, notwith-standing the patient's "crusty" personality, in which tenderness, passion, and intimacy had no real chance to survive.

Dependence can easily be regarded as the foundation, so to speak, of all identifications. These may or may not contain the elements for the capacity to love. When the mother's reactions to the infant and child are those of rejection, frustration, anger, and insensitivity, a number of identification pathways may de-velop in the growing child that may be manifested in his choice of object relationships as an adolescent or an adult.

The first pathway involves the search for objects whose basic attributes correspond, in one way or another, to those of the mother, because of the child's dependence on her. Thus the individual, as an adult, may find a rejecting, hostile person as an ideal choice, simply because, unconsciously, he has not been able to separate rejection from survival (which mothering may represent for him). Such an individual may perceive positive reactions as a threat to survival. Thus loving, sensitive, and supportive people will be feared, suspected, distrusted, and avoided. Certainly, feelings of love and compassion that may, for a variety of reasons, surface within, are perceived as em-barrassing or as a sign of weakness, and they will be either unconsciously denied or consciously dismissed or controlled. Many relationships that are characterized by negative interac-tion may be maintained for a long time because they are rooted in childhood identifications with negative part or whole objects, primarily the mother, or the mothering entity. The interlocking unresolved dependency needs of both partners makes changes in such relationships quite difficult, if not impossible, especially if such a system has had a long history of its own. The chronicity and systematization of the couple's interactions over the years does not allow a foreign agency to easily penetrate the system for fear of annihilation.

A 55-year-old married woman came to therapy because she was distraught over her husband's lack of sexual interest in her. The interaction between them had so deteriorated that she was ready to leave the marriage and start a new life, in which love and affection could be part of life, not "something you only see on TV." She was not sure whether treatment for her would be of any value, but since her husband had benefitted from it in the past, she thought she might give it a chance. She then launched into a lengthy tirade against her husband, who had been depressed for many years, and had begun drinking heavily in the preceding year. She also complained about his total disorganization at home, leaving heaps of work-related papers and correspondence all over the house, to the point that she no longer had enough closet space for her clothes.

The patient's delivery was succinct and coherent. She left no doubt that her husband had serious difficulties, and when I asked her why she had come to see me, rather than sending her husband, she managed to admit that her only problem was her fear of leaving him. Her speech was aggressive and controlling throughout the initial interview, with strategically interspersed compliments about my work and the enormous help I had given to the friend who had referred her to me. The obvious inconsistencies in her posture, including her feelings about treatment, were not confronted at that time because I sensed she was not a patient yet, and her resistance might only grow worse, thus creating additional barriers to forming a therapeutic alliance. She agreed to return for further exploration of what could be done to improve the home atmosphere and to discover what her needs were in that situation.

This patient was the middle of three sisters with about eight years' difference in age from the other two. The mother, who was still living, was described as a highly controlling, screaming, impulsive woman who was never satisfied with the patient's life style, and doted exclusively on her oldest daughter. As soon as the patient was capable of taking care of household chores, she was placed in charge of these responsibilities (the older sister was never required to perform any of the household routines). The patient heard her mother repeatedly justify this discriminatory behavior by alluding to her belief that it was a disgrace to have a second female child. The patient was continuously exposed to implicit and explicit devaluation of the female by her mother. She had, therefore, a very negative image with which to identify. At the same time, she also heard her mother glorify and idealize the idea of a male baby, while expressing utter disdain for her husband, whom she accused of wanting to have the girls all for himself. She implied that he was deliberately responsible for their not having had a male child.

Treatment during the first three months centered around her perception of her husband as a passive, unloving, and self-centered person. The only area of communication they shared was the theater. Both of them loved to see plays and discuss them, although they would almost invariably end their discussions with a fight. She usually heaped abuse upon him, and he withdrew into drinking, while threatening her with making love to other women. In the session I experienced her as controlling, aggressive, or overwhelming, but she did not see herself that way. There were no positive feelings left for her husband, except in her memories of the early years of their relationship. When I confronted her with my own experiences with her, she responded with silent anger, which manifested itself defensively through reaction formation in her attempts to ingratiate herself. Very little could be accomplished in view of her lack of motivation for working on her own conflicts, and, after a few months, I suggested that we ought to take a break. She was quite relieved, and immediately offered her husband to replace her. I agreed to see him, as I felt that getting to know him would allow me to better understand their relationship.

The husband eagerly came to see me. He behaved in a very submissive and "shrinking" manner, precisely as she had described him. His perception of the relationship was similar to hers, except that he attributed the responsibility for the negative interaction to her. Because of her controlling manner, he was indeed turned off to her sexually, and he had learned to deal with her by withdrawing from the scene as much as possible. This was also his excuse for his drinking and for a number of secret affairs that he had carried on during the preceding five years. He was not willing to leave the marriage unless she agreed to leave the house, something she swore she would never do. The message from both seemed to be clear: neither of them was ready to make any changes in the marital status, but perhaps in some of their interactions.

After a few interviews with the husband, I asked to see them together for a joint session. In that session, which proved to be quite stormy in the beginning because of the wife's attacks upon her husband, I expressed my doubts about the feasibility of changing the situation in any significant or genuine manner, except to help them learn to react less violently to each other.

I impressed on them the fact that both of them brought a lot of personal difficulties to the relationship, and that both must work on these problems, which stemmed from early childhood. The wife was willing to admit that she must contribute something to the discord, but she was adamant about waiting for her husband to stop his drinking before she got involved in treatment. He expressed genuine concern about his drinking and his own behavior, and he was willing to begin treatment for himself. We decided to proceed with this plan, although the wife asked to see me every now and then, primarily to complain about her husband, whose childhood was no less traumatic than hers. His mother was a psychotic woman who had been hospitalized a number of times, and her behavior was quite unpredictable, not too dissimilar to his wife's personality structure. While he was quite aware of this fact, and he persistently claimed that he wished to separate from this "crazy woman," he could not leave what he himself considered a substitute mother. However, it was quite clear that this man's capacity to have positive and even loving feelings were far greater than his wife's, and he occasionally expressed those feelings to her and in the sessions. Treatment for him (and for his wife through him), including the few interspersed sessions with her, proved successful in a specific area, namely, the sexual. The husband stopped his uncontrollable drinking and approached his wife sexually on occasion, something she did not expect. Her violent verbal abuse decreased considerably, although her communications could by no means be characterized as strictly positive. There was some acceptance of responsibility on her part for the constant tension and altercations. Termination of treatment for both was initiated when the sessions became repetitious and no new material could be elicited to justify the financial expense, time, and effort. However, when things started to get out of hand, both would come in for a joint session in which they perceived me as an arbitrator, and both accepted my evaluation of what needed to be done.

In general, in cases where there seems to be little positive prognosis for major personality changes, confrontation analysis utilizes all possible resources to enable the patient to reduce the self-destructiveness and waste of energy that are the hallmark of hostile interpersonal interactions. Thus flexibility in strategy and techniques is a must; this may involve inclusion of other family members in the treatment of outside helpful agents (of course, with the patient's permission), and the utilization of a variety of techniques on the confrontative–interpretive continuum. In the above illustration, while the results appear rather meager on the surface, they were justified in that other approaches that the couple had attempted had not benefitted them at all.

Another serious impediment to the capacity to love stems from dependency needs characterized by a symbiotic attachment to the parents, especially the mother, during infancy and childhood. When unresolved, such attachments perpetuate the individual's inability to establish an identity that he can call his own. Interpersonal relationships for such an individual can evolve only on the basis of emotional interaction that confirms the continuous *exclusive* presence of the other person. This requirement from a relationship has basically nothing to do with the uniqueness of the other person, but is instead an expression of the individual's feeling that he cannot survive without the other. This absence of a capacity to feel secure within one's own boundaries, without having to merge with another person, often makes it difficult in an initial consultation to recognize that the so-called love feelings for another person are nothing but a manifestation of severe dependency needs parading in a more acceptable guise to the self. Of course, it is far more difficult to differentially diagnose such a condition when the individual is totally unaware of its possible existence.

This pathological condition of early symbiotic attachment negatively affects the capacity to establish love relationships, most significantly because, as mentioned earlier, identity boundaries are blurred. Interestingly, such individuals often succeed in forming rather stable relationships; however, these are characterized by immaturity, intense possessiveness, envy, jealousy, and not infrequently, a repeated pattern of explosive anger. Close analysis of the feelings of patients who develop such relationships reveals that they are obsessed with the other person in order to affirm their own existence—their selfhood. Their behavior is often clearly indicative of unrelenting unconscious signals that they keep receiving, signals that warn them of imminent abandonment. Thus they must hold on to their partners (mother), and they cling, they slobber, they won't let their eyes off their partners, they are constantly worried that their life-line (the partner-breast) is going to be snatched away. Their behavior is characterized either by openly and aggressively guarding the other person like a prized possession, or by constantly playing the role of the poor victim about to be sacrificed. Needless to say, the partner who participates in such interaction can certainly be considered to be dependent, frightened of hurt and abandonement, and lacking in clear identity boundaries.

An individual involved in such a symbiotic relationship does not normally seek treatment until the balance of the psychological field of interaction shifts significantly to create extreme anxiety or depression. In such interactional matrices, problems are likely to remain suppressed for many years because of the fear that any attempt at their amelioration might affect the relationship in such a way as to threaten its existence. Therefore, when a patient in this personality category finally arrives in the therapist's office, he is likely to present an extremely resistant, "sticky" challenge, notwithstanding his immediate agitation. While the therapist must explore the patient's history and the etiology of his difficulties very carefully, the patient's need to establish an unusually dependent transference must also be recognized if he stays in treatment, and therefore, the therapist must plan his strategy cautiously. It is not altogether ego-inflating nor very comforting for the therapist when the patient relates to him as if he were the only source of energy for living. Such a transference may create serious difficulties in the treatment, both from a technical viewpoint and from the strong countertransferential reactions that are likely to occur.

Confrontation analysis utilizes techniques that are designed to minimize the intensity of the transference, although at times this may prolong the process. The rationale is that without a reasonable therapeutic relationship, in this case aiming at helping the patient keep some distance from the therapist, interventions will have no impact whatsoever; they will be merged (swallowed) without any chance of becoming part of a self that is differentiated rather than one that is submerged. Technically, reality statements with reference to the therapist, the therapeutic approach, and the therapist's relationship to the patient need to be emphasized and expressed more often than probes that further reinforce the patient's symbiotic fantasies.

Anxiety and Love

More prevalent than any other difficulty in the capacity to establish and maintain love relationships is anxiety orginating in ambivalence toward the mothering figure. Irreconcilable feelings of love and hate coexist toward the mother, and are either alternately experienced and expressed, depending on certain psychological conditions at the time, or are associated with such deep feelings of guilt that they are defensively denied and consciously experienced as apathy, lack of emotional interest, and diminished sexual desire. Anxiety caused by ambivalence also affects regressive trends that block the resolution of dependency strivings, and disrupt the process of synthesizing the multitude of identifications into a cohesive identity. Depending on the severity of the ambivalence, the individual's capacity for intimacy may be in a more or less constant danger of being undermined by the anxiety, resulting in unrelenting struggles to maintain meaningful interpersonal relationships.

Ambivalence is dynamically and etiologically related to a number of factors in the child's development. The first factor that adversely affects the establishment of identity in the child is the mother's own lack of a sufficiently integrated ego, which may project itself in an uneven handling of the infant's needs. This will tend to confuse the child's introjections, and may result in a self-perception consiting of incongruent identifications. This lack of cohesion in the formation of identity will, in turn, prevent the individual from being aware of his needs as they keep shifting ground from one part object to another. Thus stable direction, or the establishment of clear cut priorities for the self, may be seriously hampered. The mother who does not send clear signals to the infant arouses extreme anxiety, for her reactions do not have a reasonable predictable pattern on which the infant can anchor his own expectations and reactions. Thus ambivalence toward the mother, as well as toward his own reactions, inevitably develops. Love and hate, passivity and agression, intimacy and distance become routine experiences, neither one ever comfortable enough to sustain. Whenever the individual moves in one direction, his anxiety level mounts because he is, psychologically and emotionally, separating from the other direction, which symbolizes the same object. The capacity for love requires a consistent, although not necessarily permanent, movement in one direction—that of intimacy—without the burden of defensive anxiety that interferes with the feelings of love and passion.

Another factor closely associated with ambivalence is the mother's projection of a negative sexual identity onto the infant and child. Two important deleterious developments may result in connection with such behavior. The first is the mother's disappointment in the child's gender, the second is the actual devaluation of her own gender. In the first instance, ambivalence must result in the infant because of the reality of its own gender, which is in conflict with the wishes of the love object, the mother. In the second instance, ambivalence develops through the process of identification with the love object who is negatively valued by itself and yet, in some sense, positively valued by the infant because of its mothering function. Additionally, when the child grows up, mothering is perceived as a negative attribute and denied or repressed in the person's own identity, thus leaving out an essential dimension in the capacity to establish and maintain a reciprocal love relationship.

In well-defended individuals, the defensive structure that results from anxiety is not easily discerned or recognized even after many years in treatment. For example, competitive and cooperative behavior, defensive territorial maneuvers, and conflict in sexual identity, are often perceived and taken for granted as "natural" human dilemmas. While they may be universal phenomena in human development, they are not "natural" from a constitutional perspective, rather, they are reactions to anxiety, often emanating from interpersonal interaction. In adults, such interaction, which is designed to "open" communication and allow for emotional interchange, is one of the most powerful agents for anxiety development. As a reaction to such painful anxiety, competitive or cooperative behavior may ensue, and it may stand in the way of experiencing and expressing intimate emotionality. The fear of loss of territoriality in the form of panic reactions to the *perceived* threat to one's identity is another frequent reaction to anxiety stemming from interpersonal interaction designed to promote closeness.

For example, a 32-year-old man, who initially entered treatment because of a depressive episode immediately following his father's death, persisted in experiencing serious difficulties in forming meaningful sexual attachments to women. After an infatuation and some dating during his senior year in high school, he ended the relationship because the girl, with whom he was in love, was "too interested in other guys." In college he had no girl friends, nor did he develop any intimate sexual relationships with anyone up to entering treatment. His social relationships with women were limited to one or two whom he had known from his grammar school years. He was, however, sexually involved with prostitutes, whom he visited regularly. He also often masturbated with fantasies that mostly involved his high school "girlfriend" or women he met in his building.

The first two years in treatment focused on his feelings of loss because of his father's death, and his father slowly emerged as the parent who had cared for him during most of his childhood years, since his mother was an "emotional cripple." The patient idealized his father, and spent many sessions expressing his sense of deep loss. His mother was the subject of very little discussion, and he always dismissed her as "pitiful" or "incompetent," or "too detached" to really understand him, while he perceived his father as the only significant person who had ever paid any attention to him.

As the patient's depression lifted considerably, he felt more comfortable discussing his concerns about his inability to communicate with women on an intimate basis. Whenever he met a woman who was psychologically available for a relationship, his attitude toward her invariably assumed an avoidance pattern, because he perceived her either as aggressive, demanding, or threatening, or as a weakling who would become a burden to anyone associated with her. The only women he was able to be somewhat comfortable with socially, but never sexually, were those whose physical appearance resembled a sickly, underdeveloped adolescent, lacking clear sexual differentiation. The more he discussed the issue in treatment and expressed his anxiety, the less he socialized, the more he withdrew into his apartment, and the more he acted-out with the prostitutes, every week masochistically berating himself for his behavior. His addiction to the prostitutes started to become a barrier even to his functioning on his job, because he constantly felt embarrassed, guilty, shameful, and envious of the relationships that his colleagues at work had with their wives or girlfriends. Therapy became only a confessional booth, without any relief from the compulsive behavior or anxiety attached to it.

As treatment headed toward an impasse, it was necessary to strategically shift gears and focus on a phenomenon that was primarily related to the therapeutic relationship and, of course, to the nature of the transference. While the patient was ostensibly comfortable with his interaction, I detected on occasion what seemed to be an embarrassed as well as a resentful note in his delivery. The embarrassment was manifest in his nonverbal behavior, in that as he entered the office and sat down, he would not look at me, but focused his eyes on the floor. The resentment was manifest from his expressions of disappointment that the intellectual understanding was not sufficient to help him with his anxiety or with his approach to women. The resentment was, however, masked by his demeanor of appreciation of what I did for a living. For a very long time, I did not want to confront him with this attitude because of both his very strong denial system and my doubts about the strength of our therapeutic relationship.

In one session, as he began to talk, the same type of embarrassed, avoidant behavior emerged. I decided to confront him with it. I told him that I needed some clarification of his behavior within the confines of the office, since I was getting double messages from him. He was coming for treatment to me, yet he seemed to be directing his comments to someone else, and I pointed out his nonverbal avoidance. He denied that his avoidance had anything to do with me, but admitted that he was embarrassed because of the content of the material he had been discussing. I then confronted him with what he had just been talking about—something (moving to another apartment) that did not seem embarrassing to me, yet his behavior had not changed. The evidence was overwhelming that something was happening in relation to me that he could not directly or easily deny. So he said that he was probably "acting" in the same way he does outside of treatment. I agreed that this was a possibility, yet I wondered, confrontationally, what his feelings about me were. He seemed embarrassed again, resentful, and silent for awhile. Then he said he had thought about me often, but he was not aware of any real bad feelings, although he thought that perhaps I seemed uninterested in his deep feelings about his father after the initial contact. The session ended about here with my commenting that we needed to explore these feelings further.

In the sessions that followed, such confrontations and their analyses were consistently utilized, resulting in an extremely fruitful understanding of the dynamics of this man's difficulties in establishing intimate relationships. The techniques yielded many memories that the patient had hitherto unconsciously kept out of the therapeutic arena, and those were quite helpful in establishing, through the sharing process, a therapeutic relationship that led to a genuine working alliance.

The patient's suspicion that I was not interested in feelings about his father was primarily a projection, that is to say, his own conscious feelings about him were not the main problem. He felt (unconsciously) guilty relative to his lack of deep positive feelings and to the existence of a great deal of resentment and anger that he had harbored toward his father for many years. This projection gave me some clues about his relationship to me, i.e., that it was similar to the one he had with his father, which was later discovered to have been a pleasant, superficial one, and mutually obligatory within the confines of the social guidelines of what a father–son relationship ought to be.

The patient superficially perceived his father to be a nurturing object; however, he felt deprived of real mothering, and he was eventually able to become conscious of, and to express, his very deep anger toward his father, whom he accused of alienating him from his mother. The patient had always craved intimacy with his mother, but he was always prevented from satisfying such a need by his disapproving father, who openly rationalized his stance by bringing up the mother's "craziness" and his wish to protect his son from learning to be like his mother.

When the patient was six or seven years old, he learned from his father that his mother was quite capable of caring for him during the first two or three years of his life, but that her care became increasingly disrupted by depressive episodes. It was during these times that the father begrudgingly began to take care of the patient.

When the patient was about 11 years old, his mother became physically sick one day, vomitted a great deal, and nearly fainted in his arms. She asked her son to change her clothing and wash her face, and while he was in the midst of helping her, his father unexpectedly came home. Without attempting to find out what was happening, he screamed ragefully at his wife and showered her with many obscenities. In his rage, he also let his son know that he had not slept with his wife for many years because she was a "whore—like all women."

As the patient explored his relationship to his father after these revelations, his ambivalence toward him assumed central focus. It was not, however, until additional painful confrontations were analyzed, that the patient started to interact with me in a more communicative and genuine manner. At that point, his transferential reactions became dynamically clearer.

Analysis of the patient's object relations revealed that the father was used as a substitute mother, who had to be pacified and upon whom dependency needs had to be projected; yet a genuine deep feeling or tie to him was never developed. The patient could never allow himself to become aware of this because of his fear of abandonment. Such fear of abandonment was clearly discerned from the patient's later description of his anger toward his father because of his abandonment of the patient's mother (with whom the patient identified a great deal).

The patient's aloofness in the transferential situation was eventually analyzed in terms of his ambivalence. On the one hand, he had been conditioned to feel superficially grateful to his "caring" father, and this translated in the treatment situation into his behaving like a "good patient." On the other hand, a more intimate relationship to the therapist would be unconsciously perceived as movement toward his mother, who at one time had taken good care of him, and thus, consequently, aroused guilt feelings over his supposed abandonment or disloyalty to his father.

The interaction between the inner objects and their manifest expression in the patient's external interpersonal relationships explains not only the transferential situation, but also the patient's difficulties in his capacity to feel deeply and positively about a woman without experiencing paralyzing anxiety. The patient's compulsive interaction with prostitutes was, in one sense, an ideal unconscious solution; one that satisfied the demands of most of his inner objects. First, it affirmed his father's perception that all women are whores, thus allowing him to identify with his father on this issue. (After all, he was married to one.) Second, he reenacted an unconscious identification with his mother by being (in fantasy aided by the reality) with her. Third, it satisfied his partial identification with his father as a male by proving it through repetitious sexual performance. Fourth, it prevented him from experiencing the overwhelming anxiety he would have felt had he attempted to relate to a woman on a deeper emotional level. Fifth, the patient's identity was not liable to be tested, since the relationship with the prostitutes was perceived as a business deal and did not require his functioning as a whole person.

The interactional–confrontational strategy in which the therapist takes great pains not to be judgmental or prescriptive was the single most important factor in helping the patient to slowly risk expression of genuine positive feelings. To be sure, the patient learned that I was not in favor of his acting out with prostitutes, but my attitudes was based not on moralistic grounds, but rather stemmed from the belief that such compulsions could only keep him away from his expressed goal of developing a satisfying heterosexual relationship, instead of a fragment of such a relationship. At times, this strategy created major conflicts in the treatment, since the patient was not easily persuaded that I was not his father, and did not have a vested interest in perpetuating my own ideas of what people are and what they should do. Needless to say, a compulsive defense such as this is not easily relinquished, because it gives the constant illusion that one is not alone, or that one has some relationship to other people. (This is certainly true when one thinks of those patients who completely withdraw from human interaction.)

Nevertheless, the patient had obviously incorporated a positive mothering image sufficiently so that his transference eventually assumed this character. He came to perceive me as a caring and even loving object who was indeed interested in his welfare, at times with a clinging dependency characteristic of the discontinuous mothering experience in infancy. Consequently, he began to relate more positively to women, and became part of a social group that included several women. Yet he was not able to readily give up his prostitutes, and used to visit them even when he began to date a number of women more seriously. Stressful crises like breaking up with a girlfriend or an argument brought about a strong urge to run to the prostitute. All this was now analyzed and permitted to be discussed openly. After several years, he fell in love with a woman and lived with her for over six months. At that point he completely gave up his acting-out with prostitutes. After breaking up the relationship because of this woman's demands that they marry, he continued to search for more suitable love partners, and he terminated treatment when it was clear that his capacity for love had acquired a reasonable scope

In summarizing this case, it is safe to conclude that the patient's basic anxiety, which had developed as a result of inadequate resolution of his dependency needs, in part because of discontinuities in mothering, as well as inability to integrate his early identifications into a coherent self-system, prevented him from developing the capacity to experience deeply felt emotions, and thus from forming meaningful heterosexual relationships. Confrontation techniques were utilized to allow the emergence of transferential reactions through which the patient's capacity for positive interpersonal interaction could be enhanced and expressed. The focus here has been mainly on this aspect of the treatment, although there were, of course, many other aspects related directly or indirectly to the issues of identity and love, and their relationship to the termination process. Thus, for instance, important dimensions of this patient's emotionality, such as his jealousy, his difficulties in extending himself, his struggles with sexual identity, his homosexual conflicts, and a host of others were not presented here. It seems to me that the richness and depth of incursions into other aspects of the patient's personality could not have been possible without utilization of the confrontational approach. It is also clear that, while anxiety can be crippling, the investigation of its sources can produce exciting possibilities for the expansion of the self's horizons. This was no doubt the case here.

THE DEVELOPMENT OF THE CAPACITY
FOR LOVE IN THERAPY: BEYOND
TRANSFERENCE

The capacity for love is a fundamental dimension of the individual's identity, and, therefore, its place in the total functioning of the self cannot be overestimated. The question is how therapy can help the patient utilize and develop as much of this capacity as possible.

In his analysis of Freud's personality and influence, Erich Fromm (1959) underlines the importance of the mother in shaping the child's personality: "The understanding of the factors (aside from constitutional ones) which determine the development of any man's character must begin with his relatedness to his mother." This thesis is, of course, the basis for the philosophy of human development that confrontation analysis espouses in a theoretical and clinical sense. Its significance in treatment is related to the fact that the psychotherapist is often perceived, by himself as well as by the patient, as an entity fulfilling a role similar to the mother's in many ways, especially through helping, nurturing, and caring. The therapist is thus in a position to help create an atmosphere within the therapeutic milieu that is conducive to expansion of the patient's capacity for intimate interpersonal relations. a number of factors in the therapist's personality and in the essence of his role can either promote or inhibit the evolution of the capacity for love in the patient. These factors are themselves expressions of love, not withstanding the contractual nature of the relationship.

The first element in the therapist's personality and role might be called "formal" caring. The therapeutic condition requires the therapist to be *reliable, trustworthy,* and *dependable.* This means that he must be in his office at the exact appointed hour, give the patient complete and undivided *attention* while there, and be *available* in emergencies and crises. The therapist must also *interact with the patient directly,* in one way or another, regardless of his theory or techniques. In addition, he must adhere to the *regularity* of the sessions without being swayed by his own needs to abandon the patient unnecessarily: the patient's needs must be given primary consideration. Therefore, changes or deviations from the contract by the therapist (not only by the patient) must always be examined in light of their effects on the treatment process, in which *continuity* is supremely essential. While all these dimensions can be considered the "formal" aspects of the therapeutic contract, and can be taken for granted, they do represent *at least* a "formal" commitment to the patient. This type of caring is normally part of the mother's functions when the infant is still very dependent on her. It is not characteristic of other relationships, not even of very close friendships. The therapist's adherence to these so-called procedural formalities will help expand the patient's capacity for intimacy and love through the process of identification, primarily because they are also expression of caring.

The therapist's caring is, of course, manifest in dimensions that reach beyond the formal requirements of the contract between therapist and patient. A most important one is his investigatory attitude which, because of its scientific orientation, accords the patient the right to explore his personality in the manner and direction *he* chooses, without losing the therapist's support, respect, and empathy. Identification with the therapist's honest search for knowledge opens up the capacity in the patient's mind to look into a variety of alternative behavioral and emotional patterns without fear or threat. This means that the patient can choose to allow the flow of positive feelings about himself and others, and others' positive feelings toward him, and to accept these alternatives as part of the reaction repertoire of self. Empathy and genuine sensitivity basically consist of the capacity to contain a multiplicity of emotional and perceptual reactions, often contradictory, that can become available at the appropriate time and in the presence of the appropriate object. This capacity, which is an expression of caring and love by the therapist, is directly connected with his scientific attitude.

Psychotherapy is extremely time-consuming, infinitely discouraging and disillusioning at times for patient and therapist, and frequently demanding of a painful emotional involvement for the therapist, as well as the patient. In addition, so-called "results" are neither concrete in the usual sense, nor immediate. The therapist is, thus, required to be unusually *patient*, and must have a fair degree of conviction in the therapeutic process, as well as a commitment and loyalty to the patient. This is not easily achieved without a serious emotional investment on the therapist's part. When conveyed to the patient (without triggering off parental guilt and feelings of obligation), this patience and commitment can become integrated as part of the patient's ego, especially in helping him develop the capacity for intimate interaction with others.

The business of the therapist is for the most part a lonely one. Patients come and go, spill their feelings, complain, get angry, cry and laugh, question and analyze, while the therapist listens and feeds (even if he does not intervene, his listening can be, and often is, a feeding reaction). His inner life remains inside during working hours. The focus is the patient, not the therapist. In addition, while the patient separates from the therapist every time the session ends, he does this *once* a day. The therapist, on the other hand, must separate from *every* patient throughtout the day. In fact, he does not only separate, but more correctly, is "abandoned" by every patient who leaves, and even though this becomes routine, it must nevertheless affect the therapist. It adds to his loneliness, because these "abandonments" must register somewhere in his ego. This loneliness can become associated with caring in the mind of the patient, for it must be transcended if the therapist is to attend to the patient's needs.

There are additional dimensions in the therapist's personality that contribute to the development of the patient's capacity for love. These include the therapist's sense of responsibility and risk-taking, the courage to confront the patient with his findings, and the willingness to work without external rewards. Naturally, all this can be useful to the patient only if he is able to identify with the therapist and accept those dimensions that are consonant with the healthy needs of the ego.

In summary, the capacity for love has been discussed in the context of the achievement of a healthy identity, and its reasonable development as another reference point for a successful termination of treatment. Since communicative and emotionally satisfying interpersonal interaction is considered a central goal in confrontation analysis, the capacity for love assumes, of course, a decisive place throughout the therapeutic work. Many issues related to this capacity, such as narcissism, psychotic or borderline attachments, sexual dysfunctions, countertransference, and others, have been either discussed in previous sections in the book or do not seem to pose special strategic or technical difficulties that need to be handled significantly differently from other problems. Needless to say, one can hardly cover all or most aspects of such a vast subject in one book on psychotherapy.

16
Psychotherapy and Confrontation Analysis: A Perspective

Psychotherapy is neither a science nor an art. Perhaps it may be "characterized" (rather than defined) as an odyssey, as one might characerize the writing of a book, especially a systems work. The common element in both is that one never knows what one is getting into! This should not discourage any psychotherapist or author from attempting to define operationally whatever they are doing, if at all possible.

At the present stage of our knowledge of personality, it is doubtful that there exists a scientifically tested theory of personality, or a set of rules and principles about the "nature of the beast" that can withstand the rigors of logical consistency. Any rigid set of procedures based on a particular personality theory will probably ignore that side of the equation for whom this entire process was (allegedly) invented—the patient. Patients are unique individuals who are searching for meaning in life. Logical theory cannot generate meaning, if only because life is itself contradictory, enigmatic, and inconsistent. In this connection it must be mentioned that both psychoanalysis and its "antithesis," behavior modification, have so far failed to generate meaningful, scientifically consistent theory, perhaps because in both the subject, the person, is treated as if he were any object in the inanimate world.

The theory that is presented in this volume cannot be seriously considered a scientific theory, since many of its assumptions could not withstand the test of cross-validation, or, if they did, their internal consistency would leave much to be desired. From this perspective, the presentation here is not too dissimilar from other works in the field—although many of these works insist on their scientific status. On the other hand, it seems reasonable and profitable to engage in theorizing from the clinical presentations—a reversal of usual hypothetico-deductive scientific thinking and procedure.

Now that the reader has labored through this exposition, he may question how confrontation analysis fits with other psychotherapeutic approaches or systems. Although this book has not followed "traditional" lines of inquiry, it has perhaps followed a natural line of development from an historical point of view: from the orthodox Freudians to the neo-Freudians to the object relations theorists to the interactional school of thought. It has, in a sense, developed from genetics to communication, from a focus on the patient to one on the dyadic relationship. Confrontation analysis, as presented here, attempts to extend the subject of therapeutic investigation, in clinical terms, from one-sided transference interpretations to a systems overview of the totality of the therapeutic encounter. The most viable way to understand the clinical material that the patient produces is to examine the total context, the inner life of the patient, and the therapist's impact on this life, in which such material is produced.

Another consideration that must be central to any psychotherapeutic system is the scope of the investigation. To begin with, there is the issue of which entity to explore—the total personality or part of it. The self, considered by many clinicians and theoreticians to be the true representation of the person, is the focus of the interactive relationship in confrontation analysis. Second, the core from which the self's character (including its defensive armor) evolves must be chosen and analyzed. Confrontation analysis singles out a universal condition—dependence—as the most productive element for analysis in order to achieve the major goal of helping the patient find meaning in life. (While "meaning in life" is a reasonable goal for anyone, it seems too vague to be clinically accessible.) A third consideration is thus the reduction of the "meaning in life" goal to workable and meaningful elements. These elements are (1) acquisition of authentic communication, (2) spontaneous emotionality, and (3) integrated identity. An attempt has been made here to show what a confrontation analyst actually does, and at the same time to provide clinical illustrations of the theoretical assumptions of confrontation analysis.

Ultimately, both clinicians and theoreticians must decide whether particular procedures and techniques actually work in practice and whether particular theories can be directly and practically applied. After all, psychotherapy and pure science are not necessarily "blood brothers." Confrontation analysis has advanced a number of suggestions concerning the efficacy of certain procedures, strategies, and techniques in the conduct of therapy. The rationale for their use was also spelled out whenever possible, even though the rationale did not always precede the clinical judgment. Among the most important aspects of the therapeutic activities described here is the interaction between patient and analyst. This is considered most likely to produce change, as is the therapist's confrontation of the patient's defenses, the analysis of the patient's reactions to these confrontations, and the continuous and progressive evolution of the therapeutic relationship from a relatively unequal one to a more or less equal one toward the termination phase of the treatment. The human aspects of the relationship in this interactive process assume important dimensions. This means that transference and countertransference reactions are confronted as soon as they become known and are seen to be important in the process of developing maturity and independence.

Finally, psychotherapy works when it touches the individual emotionally as well as cognitively. It works when that individual learns to experience and experiences to learn, for the best learning comes through the senses. The approach that any therapist chooses will have an impact, not only on the patient but on the therapist as well, as he evolves into a growing, learning, and helping individual. If the therapeutic approach becomes "holy," everyone loses, for then the interaction becomes ritualized and devoid of meaning. On the other hand, when the therapist is aware of his chief function, that is, to help the patient remove the shackles of dependence on ritualized reactions, and concentrates on this rather then on "selling" the system to the patient, the approach or system becomes less and less important, and the experience is likely to be liberating for both patient and therapist.

REFERENCES

Abt LE, Weissman SL (1965). *Acting Out: Theoretical and Clinical Aspects.* New York: Grune & Stratton.

Adatto CP (1977). Transference phenomena in initial interviews. *International Journal of Psychoanalytic Psychotherapy* 6: 3–13.

Adler G, Myerson PG (1973). *Confrontation in Psychotherapy.* New York: Science House.

Alexander F (1961). *The Scope of Psychoanalysis,* 1921–1961, New York: Basic Books.

Alexander F (1963). *Fundamentals of Psychoanalysis.* New York: W.W. Norton.

Ardrey R (1973). *The Territorial Imperative.* New York: Dell Publishing.

Arieti S (1955). *Interpretation of Schizophrenia.* New York: Brunner.

Arieti S (1967). *The Intrapsychic Self.* New York: Basic Books.

Asch SE (1952). *Social Psychology.* New York: Prentice-Hall.

Aull G, Strean H (1967). The analyst's silence. *The Psychoanalytic Forum* 2: 72–80.

Balint A (1949). Love for mother and mother love. *International Journal of Psychoanalysis* 30: 251–259.

Becker E (1973). *The Denial of Death.* New York: The Free Press.

Bellak L (1974). Contemporary character as crisis adaption. *American Journal of Psychotherapy* 28: 46–58.

Benedek T (1955). A contribution to the problem of termination of training analysis. *Journal of the American Psychoanalytical Association* 3: 615–629.

Bernd SM (1972). Clinical notes on narcissism. *Journal of Clinical Issues in Psychology* 3: 25–35.

Blanck G, Blanck R (1974). *Ego Psychology Theory and Practice.* New York: Columbia University Press.

Bonime W (1962). *The Clinical Use of Dreams.* New York: Basic Books.

Buhler CB (1959). Theoretical observations about life's basic tendencies. *American Journal of Psychotherapy* 13: 561–581.

Burland JA (1975). Separation-individuation and reconstruction in psycho-analysis. *International Journal of Psychoanalytic Psychotherapy* 4: 303–335.

Chessik RD (1971). *Why Psychotherapists Fail*. New York: Science House.

Cohen AI (1974). Treating the black patient: transference questions. *American Journal of Psychotherapy* 28: 137–143.

Cohen AI (1980). The double session: modifications in psychoanalysis. *The Psychoanalytic Review* 67: 69–81.

Deutsch F (1955). *The Clinical Interview, Vol. I.*, New York: International Universities Press.

Deutsch F (1955a). *The Clinical Interview, Volume II*. New York: International Universities Press.

Devereux G (1951). Some criteria for the timing of confrontations and inter-pretations. *International Journal of Psychoanalysis* 32: 19–24.

Dewald PA (1964). *Psychotherapy, A Dynamic Approach*. New York: Basic Books.

Erikson EH (1959). Identity and the life cycle. *Psychological Issues* 1: 5–164.

Erikson EH (1962. *Young Martin Luther*. New York: W.W. Norton & Co.

Erikson EH (1968). *Identity Youth and Crises*. New York: W.W. Norton & Co.

Escalona SK (1968). *The Roots of Individuality*. Chicago: Aldrine Publishing Co.

Fairbairn WD (1952). *An Object Relations Theory of Personality*. New York: Basic Books.

Feifel H (ed.) (1977). *The Meaning of Death*. New York: McGraw-Hill.

Fenichel O (1941). *Problems of Psychoanalytic Techniques*. New York: The Psychoanalytic Quarterly.

Fenichel O (1945). *The Psychoanalytic Theory of Neuroses*. New York: W.W. Norton.

Ferreira AJ, Winter WD, Poindexter EJ (1966). Some interactional variables in normal and abnormal families, *Family Process* 5: 60–75.

Freud S (1912). Recommendations to physicians practicing psychoanalysis. *Standard Edition* 12: 111–120.

Freud S (1913). On beginning the treatment (further recommendations on the technique of psychoanalysis, I). *Standard Edition* 12: 121–144.

Freud S (1914). Remembering, repeating, and working through (further rec-ommendations on the technique of psycho-analysis, II). *Standard Editions* 12: 145–156.

Freud S (1915). Observations on transference-love (further recommendations on the technique of psycho-analysis, III). *Standard Edition* 12: 157–171.

Freud S (1915a). The Unconscious. *Standard Edition* 14: 109–140.

Freud S (1923). The ego and the id. *Standard Edition* 14: 3–66.

Freud S (1926). *The Problem of Anxiety*. New York: W.W. Norton.

Freud S (1937). Analysis terminable and interminable. *Standard Edition* 23: 209–253.

Freud S (1938). Splitting of the ego in the process of defense. *Standard Edition* 23: 273–272.

Fromm E (1947). *Man for Himself*. New York: Rinehart & Co.

Fromm E (1959). *Sigmund Freud's Mission*. New York: Harpers & Brothers.

Fromm-Reichman F (1950). *Principles of Intensive Psychotherapy*. Chicago: University of Chicago Press.

Frosch J (1964). The psychotic character: clinical psychiatric considerations. *Psychiatric Quarterly* 38: 81–96.

Gaylin W (Ed.) (1968). *The Meaning of Despair*. New York: Science House.

Gittleson M (1952). The emotional position of the analyst in the psychoanalytic situation. *International Journal of Psychoanalysis* 33: 1–10.

Goldberg A (Ed.) (1978). *The Psychology of the Self—A Casebook*. New York: International Universities Press.

Goz R (1975). On knowing the therapist "as a person." *International Journal of Psychoanalytic Psychotherapy* 4: 437–458.

Greenson RR (1954). The struggle against identification. *Journal of the American Psychoanalytic Association* 2: 200–217.

Greenson RR (1965). The working alliance and the transference neurosis. *Psychoanalytic Quarterly* 34: 155–181.

Greenson RR (1967). *The Technique and Practice of Psychanalysis*. New York: International Universities Press.

Griffin K, Patton BR (1971). *Fundamentals of Interpersonal Communication*. New York: Harper & Row.

Grinberg L (1980). The closing phase of the psychoanalysis—the search for truth about oneself. *International Journal of Psychoanalysis* 61: 25–37.

Gunderson JG, Singer MY (1975). Defining borderline patients: an overview. *American Journal of Psychiatry* 132: 1–10.

Guntrip H (1961). *Personality Structure and Human Interaction*. New York: International Universities Press.

Guntrip H (1969). *Schizoid Phenomena, Object Relations, and the Self*. New York: International Universities Press.

Hall ET (1959). *The Silent Language*. Connecticut: Fawcett Publication.

Horney K (1939). *New Ways in Psychoanalysis*. New York: W.W. Norton.

Jacobs TJ (1973). Posture, gesture, the movement in the analyst: cues to interpretation and countertransference. *Journal of the American Psychoanalytic Association* 21: 77–92.

James W (1950). *Principles of Psychology*. U.S.A. Dover Publications.

Kernberg O (1967). Borderline personality organization. *Journal of the American Psychoanalytic Association* 15: 641–685.

Kernberg OF (1974). Contrasting viewpoints regarding the nature and psychoanalytic treatment of narcissistic personalities: a preliminary communication. *Journal of the American Psychoanalytic Association* 22: 255–267.

Kernberg OF (1974a). Further contributions to the treatment of narcissistic personalities. *International Journal of Psycho-Analysis* 55: 215–239.

Kernberg O (1976). *Object Relations Theory and Clinical Psychoanalysis*. New York: Jason Aronson.

Khan MMR (1963). Silence as a communication. *Bulletin of the Menninger Clinic* 27: 300–313.

Kibel H (1978). Group psychotherapy for borderline patients. *International Journal of Group Psychotherapy* 28: 339–358.

Klein M (1950). *Contributions to Psychoanalysis, 1921–1945.* London: The Hogarth Press.

Klein M (1957). *Envy and Gratitude.* London: Tavistock Publications Ltd.

Koch S (1971). The image of man implicit in encounter group therapy. *Journal of Humanistic Psychology* 11: 109–127.

Kohut H (1971). *The Analysis of the Self.* New York: International Universities Press.

Kohut H (1977). *The Restoration of the Self.* New York: International Universities Press.

Kohut H (1979). The two analyses of Mr. Z. *International Journal of Psycho-Analysis* 60: 3–27.

Kubie LS (1975). *Practical and Theoretical Aspects of Psychoanalysis.* New York: International Universities Press.

Langs R (1973). *The Technique of Psychoananlytic Psychotherapy, Vol. I.* New York: Jason Aronson.

Langs R (1974). *The Technique of Psychoanalytic Psychotherapy, Vol. II.* New York: Jason Aroson.

Lifton RJ (1976). *The Life of the Self.* New York: Simon and Schuster.

London P (1964). *The Modes and Morals of Psychotherapy.* New York: Holt, Rinehart and Winston.

Mahler M (1972). The rapprochement subphase of the separation–individuation process. *Psychoanalytic Quarterly* 41: 487–506.

Marmor J (1974). *Psychiatry in Transition.* New York: Brunner-Mazel.

Maslow AH, Mittleman B (1951). *Principles of Abnormal Psychology.* New York: Harper and Brothers.

May R (1967). *Psychology and the Human Dilemma.* New York: Van Nostrand.

Mehrabian A (1972). *Nonverbal Communication.* Chicago-New York: Aldine-Atherton.

Miller GA (1963). *Language and Communication.* New York: McGraw Hill Book Co.

Miller GR, and Steinberg M (1975). *Between People: A New Analysis of Interpersonal Communication.* Palo Alto, California: Science Research Associates.

Murray J (1973). The purpose of confrontation, in Adler G, Myerson, PG, (Ed.) *Confrontation in Psychotherapy.* New York: Science House.

Myerson PG (1973). The meanings of confrontation, in Adler G, Meyerson PG (Eds.): *Confrontation in Psychotherapy,* New York: Science House.

Nacht S (1964). Silence as an integrative factor. *International Journal of Psychoanalysis* 45: 299–303.

Nelson MC (1968). *Roles and Paradigms in Psychotherapy.* New York: Grune and Stratton.

Novey S (1968). *The Second Look.* Baltimore: The Johns Hopkins Press.

Nunberg H (1955). *Principles of Psychoanalysis.* New York: International Universities Press.

Offer D, Sabshin M (1966). *Normality.* New York: Basic Books.

Pine F (1979). On the pathology of the separation–individuation process as manifested in later clinical work: an attempt at delineation. *International Journal of Psychoanalysis* 60: 225–242.

Racker H (1968). Transference and Countertransference. New York: International Universities Press.

Reich W (1949). *Character Analysis*. New York: The Noonday Press.

Reik T (1947). *Listening With the Third Ear*. New York: Farrar, Straus and Company.

Reik T (1968). The Psychological meaning of silence. *The Psychoanalytic Review* 55: 172–186.

Rogers CA (1958). A process conception of psychotherapy. *The American Psychologist* 13: 142–149.

Rogers C R (1959). A theory of therapy, personality and interpersonal relationships, as developed in client-centered framework, in Koch S (Ed.): *Psychology as a Study of Science, Vol. 3*. New York: McGraw-Hill.

Rosen J (1953). *Direct Analysis*. New York: Grune and Stratton.

Rubin JL (1968). Self-awareness and body image, self-concept and identity. In J.H. Masserman JH (Ed.): *The Ego*. New York: Grune & Stratton.

Ruesch J (1957). *Disturbed Communication*. New York: W.W. Norton.

Ruesch J (1959). General theory of communication in psychiatry, in Arieti S (Ed.): *American Handbook of Psychiatry, Vol. 1*. New York: Basic Books.

Rycroft C (1958). An inquiry into the function of words in the psychoanalytic situation. *International Journal of Psychoanalysis* 39: 408–415.

Saretsky T (1976) Masochism and ego identity in borderline states. *Contemporary Psychoanalysis* 12: 433–447.

Saretsky T (1977). The resolution of impasses in borderline states. *Contemporary Psychoanalysis* 13: 519–532.

Saretsky T (1981). *Resolving Treatment Impasses*. New York: Human Sciences House.

Sartre JP (1948). *The Emotions, Outline of a Theory*. New York: Philosophy Library.

Schachtel E (1959). *Metamorphosis*. Basic Books, New York.

Schmideberg M (1955). The borderline patient, in Arieti A (Ed.): *American Handbook of Psychiatry*. New York: Basic Books.

Seigel RK (1980). The Psychology of life after death. *The American Psychologist* 35: 911–931.

Segal H (1977). Countertranference. *International Journal of Psychoanalytic Psychotherapy* 6: 31–38.

Singer E (1965). *Key Concepts in Psychotherapy*. New York: Random House.

Sluzki CE, Veron E (1973). Interpersonal effects of semantic patterns, in Arieti S (Ed.): *The World Biennial of Psychiatry and Psychotherapy, Vol. 1*. New York: Basic Books.

Spiegel R (1959). Specific problems of communication psychiatric conditions, in Arieti S (Ed.): *American Handbook of Psychiatry, Vol. 1*. New York: Basic Books.

Stolorow RD (1978). Themes in dreams: A brief contribution to therapeutic technique. *International Journal of Psycho-Analysis* 59: 473–475.

Sullivan HS (1953). *Conceptions of Modern Psychiatry*. New York: W.W. Norton.

Sullivan HS (1954). *The Psychiatric Interview*. New York: W.W. Norton.

Truax CB, Charkuff RR (1965). Experimental manipulation of therapeutic conditions. *Journal of Consulting Psychology* 29: 119–124.

Vaughn DR, Burgoon M (1976). Interpersonal communication in the therapeutic setting: pariah or messiah?, in Miller GA (Ed.): *Explorations in Interpersonal Communication*. Beverly Hills: Sage Publications.

Watzlawick P, Beavin J, Jackson D (1967). *Pragmatics of Human Communication: A Study of Interactional Patterns, Pathologies, and Paradoxes*. New York: W.W. Norton.

Wheelis A (1973). *How People Change*. New York: Harper & Row.

Winnicott DW (1953). Transitional objects and transitional phenomena, in *Maturational Processes and the Facilitating Environment*. New York: International Universities Press.

Winnicott DW (1958). The capacity to be alone, in *Collected Papers*. New York: Basic Books.

Winnicott DW (1965). *The Maturational Processes and the Faciliating Environment*. New York: International Universities Press.

Wolberg A (1973). *The Borderline Patient*. New York: Stratton Intercontinental Medical Book Corporation.

Zeligs MA (1961). The psychology of silence: its role in transference, countertransference, and the psychoanalytic process. *Journal of the American Psychoanalytic Association* 9: 7–43.

Author Index

Subject Index